W9-AGY-595

PRINCIPLES of INFORMATION SECURITY

Second Edition

Dr. Michael E. Whitman, CISSP
Herbert J. Mattord, CISSP

THOMSON
━━━━━━━✴━━━━━━━ ™
COURSE TECHNOLOGY

Australia • Canada • Mexico • Singapore • Spain • United Kingdom • United States

THOMSON

COURSE TECHNOLOGY
™

Principles of Information Security, Second Edition

by Michael E. Whitman, Ph.D., CISSP, and Herbert J. Mattord, M.B.A., CISSP

Executive Editor:
Maureen Martin

Product Manager:
Beth Paquin

Developmental Editors:
Saher Alam and Lynne Raughley

Production Editor:
Pamela Elizian

Associate Product Manager:
Mirella Misiaszek

Editorial Assistant:
Jennifer Smith

Marketing Manager:
Karen Seitz

Photo Researcher:
Abigail Reip

Text Designer:
Books By Design

Cover Designer:
Laura Rickenbach

Manufacturing Coordinator:
Laura Burns

Compositor:
GEX Publishing Services

To Rhonda, Rachel, Alex, and Meghan, thank you for your loving support.

—MEW

Thanks to my family for your support and understanding.

—HJM

Table of Contents

Preface xv

Chapter 1
Introduction to Information Security 1

Introduction 3
The History of Information Security 3
The 1960s 4
The 1970s and 80s 5
The 1990s 7
The Present 8
What Is Security? 8
Critical Characteristics of Information 9
Availability 10
Accuracy 10
Authenticity 10
Confidentiality 10
Integrity 12
Utility 12
Possession 12
NSTISSC Security Model 13
Components of an Information System 14
Software 14
Hardware 14
Data 15
People 15
Procedures 16
Networks 16
Securing Components 16
Balancing Information Security and Access 17
Approaches to Information Security Implementation 18

The Systems Development Life Cycle 20
   Methodology 20
   Phases 20
   Investigation 21
   Analysis 21
   Logical Design 21
   Physical Design 22
   Implementation 22
   Maintenance and Change 22
The Security Systems Development Life Cycle 23
   Investigation 23
   Analysis 23
   Logical Design 23
   Physical Design 24
   Implementation 24
   Maintenance and Change 24
Security Professionals and the Organization 26
   Senior Management 26
   Information Security Project Team 26
   Data Ownership 27
Communities of Interest 27
   Information Security Management and Professionals 28
   Information Technology Management and Professionals 28
   Organizational Management and Professionals 28
Information Security: Is it an Art or a Science? 28
   Security as Art 29
   Security as Science 29
   Security as a Social Science 29
Information Security Terminology 30
Chapter Summary 32
Review Questions 32
Exercises 33
Case Exercises 33

Chapter 2

The Need for Security 35
Introduction 36
Business Needs First 37
   Protecting the Functionality of an Organization 37
   Enabling the Safe Operation of Applications 37
   Protecting Data that Organizations Collect and Use 38
   Safeguarding Technology Assets in Organizations 38

Threats 38
   Acts of Human Error or Failure 40
   Compromises to Intellectual Property 41
   Deliberate Acts of Espionage or Trespass 43
   Deliberate Acts of Information Extortion 48
   Deliberate Acts of Sabotage or Vandalism 49
   Deliberate Acts of Theft 51
   Deliberate Software Attacks 51
   Forces of Nature 56
   Deviations in Quality of Service 57
   Technical Hardware Failures or Errors 59
   Technical Software Failures or Errors 60
   Technological Obsolescence 60
Attacks 60
   Malicious Code 60
   Hoaxes 61
   Back Doors 61
   Password Crack 62
   Brute Force 62
   Dictionary 62
   Denial-of-Service (DoS) and Distributed Denial-of-Service (DDoS) 62
   Spoofing 63
   Man-in-the-Middle 64
   Spam 65
   Mail Bombing 65
   Sniffers 66
   Social Engineering 66
   Buffer Overflow 67
   Timing Attack 68
Chapter Summary 68
Review Questions 70
Exercises 71
Case Exercises 71

Chapter 3
Legal, Ethical, and Professional Issues in Information Security 75
Introduction 76
Law and Ethics in Information Security 76
Types of Law 77
Relevant U.S. Laws 77
   General Computer Crime Laws 77
   Privacy 78

Export and Espionage Laws 82
U.S. Copyright Law 83
Financial Reporting 84
Freedom of Information Act of 1966 (FOIA) 85
State and Local Regulations 85
International Laws and Legal Bodies 85
European Council Cyber-Crime Convention 86
Digital Millennium Copyright Act (DMCA) 87
United Nations Charter 88
Policy versus Law 89
Ethics and Information Security 89
Ethical Differences Across Cultures 90
Software License Infringement 90
Illicit Use 91
Misuse of Corporate Resources 91
Ethics and Education 94
Deterrence to Unethical and Illegal Behavior 95
Codes of Ethics and Professional Organizations 96
Major Professional Organizations for IT 97
Other Security Organizations 99
Key U.S. Federal Agencies 99
Organizational Liability and the Need for Counsel 103
Chapter Summary 104
Review Questions 105
Exercises 105
Case Exercises 106

Chapter 4
Risk Management 109

Introduction 110
An Overview of Risk Management 112
Know Yourself 112
Know the Enemy 113
The Roles of the Communities of Interest 113
Risk Identification 114
Asset Identification and Valuation 115
Automated Risk Management Tools 118
Information Asset Classification 118
Information Asset Valuation 119
Listing Assets in Order of Importance 121
Data Classification and Management 122
Security Clearances 124
Management of Classified Data 124
Threat Identification 126

Identify and Prioritize Threats and Threat Agents 126
Vulnerability Identification 130
Risk Assessment 132
Introduction to Risk Assessment 132
Likelihood 133
Valuation of Information Assets 133
Risk Determination 134
Identify Possible Controls 134
Access Controls 135
Documenting the Results of Risk Assessment 137
Risk Control Strategies 138
Avoidance 138
Implementing Avoidance 139
Transference 141
Mitigation 142
Disaster Recovery Plan 143
Acceptance 144
Selecting a Risk Control Strategy 145
Evaluation, Assessment, and Maintenance of Risk Controls 146
Categories of Controls 147
Feasibility Studies 149
Other Feasibility Studies 159
Risk Management Discussion Points 161
Risk Appetite 161
Residual Risk 162
Documenting Results 163
Recommended Practices in Controlling Risk 164
Qualitative Measures 164
Delphi Technique 165
Chapter Summary 165
Review Questions 166
Exercises 167
Case Exercises 168

Chapter 5
Planning for Security 171
Introduction 172
Information Security Policy, Standards, and Practices 172
Definitions 174
Enterprise Information Security Policy (EISP) 175
Issue-Specific Security Policy (ISSP) 176
Systems-Specific Policy (SysSP) 179
Policy Management 183
Information Classification 185

The Information Security Blueprint 186
    ISO 17799/BS7799 187
    NIST Security Models 189
    IETF Security Architecture 194
    VISA International Security Model 195
    Baselining and Best Business Practices 195
    Hybrid Framework for a Blueprint of an Information Security System 196
    Design of Security Architecture 199
Security Education, Training, and Awareness Program 203
    Security Education 204
    Security Training 205
    Security Awareness 205
Continuity Strategies 206
    Business Impact Analysis 209
    Incident Response Planning 212
    Disaster Recovery Planning 226
    Business Continuity Planning 228
    Model for a Consolidated Contingency Plan 230
    Law Enforcement Involvement 232
Chapter Summary 234
Review Questions 235
Exercises 236
Case Exercises 237

Chapter 6
Security Technology: Firewalls and VPNs 239

Introduction 240
Physical Design 241
Firewalls 241
    Firewall Categorization Methods 241
    Firewall Architectures 256
    Selecting the Right Firewall 260
    Configuring and Managing Firewalls 260
    Content Filters 268
Protecting Remote Connections 269
    Dial-Up 270
    Virtual Private Networks (VPNs) 274
Chapter Summary 277
Review Questions 278
Exercises 279
Case Exercises 279

Chapter 7
Security Technology: Intrusion Detection, Access Control, and Other Security Tools

. . . . 281
Introduction 283
Intrusion Detection Systems (IDSs) 284
   IDS Terminology 284
   Why Use an IDS? 286
   Types of IDSs and Detection Methods 288
   IDS Response Behavior 297
   Selecting IDS Approaches and Products 300
   Strengths and Limitations of IDSs 304
   Deployment and Implementation of an IDS 305
   Measuring the Effectiveness of IDSs 312
Honey Pots, Honey Nets, and Padded Cell Systems 314
   Trap and Trace Systems 316
   Active Intrusion Prevention 317
Scanning and Analysis Tools 317
   Port Scanners 320
   Firewall Analysis Tools 321
   Operating System Detection Tools 322
   Vulnerability Scanners 323
   Packet Sniffers 329
   Wireless Security Tools 330
Access Control Devices 332
   Authentication 332
   Effectiveness of Biometrics 335
   Acceptability of Biometrics 336
Chapter Summary 337
Review Questions 337
Exercises 338
Case Exercises 338

Chapter 8
Cryptography

. . . . 341
Introduction 342
A Short History of Cryptology 343
Principles of Cryptography 346
   Basic Encryption Definitions 346
   Cipher Methods 347
   Elements of Cryptosystems 347
   Encryption Key Size 366
   Conclusions Regarding the Principles of Cryptography 368

Cryptography Tools 368
   Public Key Infrastructure (PKI) 368
   Digital Signatures 370
   Digital Certificates 371
   Hybrid Cryptography Systems 373
   Steganography 374
Protocols for Secure Communications 375
   Securing Internet Communication with S-HTTP and SSL 376
   Securing E-mail with S/MIME, PEM, and PGP 377
   Securing Web Transactions with SET, SSL, and S-HTTP 378
   Securing TCP/IP with IPSec and PGP 378
Attacks on Cryptosystems 382
   Man-in-the-Middle Attack 383
   Correlation Attacks 383
   Dictionary Attacks 383
   Timing Attacks 384
   Defending From Attacks 384
Chapter Summary 385
Review Questions 386
Exercises 387
Case Exercises 387

Chapter 9

Physical Security 389
Introduction 391
Physical Access Controls 392
   Controls for Protecting the Secure Facility 393
Fire Security and Safety 401
   Fire Detection and Response 401
Failure of Supporting Utilities and Structural Collapse 408
   Heating, Ventilation, and Air Conditioning 408
   Power Management and Conditioning 410
   Water Problems 414
   Structural Collapse 415
   Maintenance of Facility Systems 415
Interception of Data 415
Mobile and Portable Systems 417
   Remote Computing Security 418
Special Considerations for Physical Security Threats 420
   Inventory Management 421
Chapter Summary 421
Review Questions 422
Exercises 423
Case Exercises 424

Chapter 10
Implementing Information Security 427

Introduction 429

Project Management for Information Security 430

Developing the Project Plan 430

Project Planning Considerations 436

Scope Considerations 438

The Need for Project Management 439

Technical Topics of Implementation 441

Conversion Strategies 441

The Bull's-Eye Model for Information Security Project Planning 442

To Outsource or Not 444

Technology Governance and Change Control 444

Nontechnical Aspects of Implementation 445

The Culture of Change Management 445

Considerations for Organizational Change 446

Chapter Summary 447

Review Questions 448

Exercises 449

Case Exercises 449

Chapter 11
Security and Personnel 451

Introduction 453

Positioning and Staffing the Security Function 453

Staffing the Information Security Function 455

Credentials of Information Security Professionals 462

Certified Information Systems Security Professional (CISSP) and Systems
Security Certified Practitioner (SSCP) 463

Certified Information Systems Auditor (CISA) and Certified Information
Security Manager (CISM) 465

Global Information Assurance Certification (GIAC) 466

Security Certified Professional (SCP) 467

TruSecure ICSA Certified Security Associate (TICSA) 467

Security+ 468

Certified Information Forensics Investigator 469

Related Certifications 469

Cost of Being Certified 470

Advice for Information Security Professionals 471

Employment Policies and Practices 472

Job Descriptions 473

Interviews 473

Background Checks 473

Employment Contracts 474

New Hire Orientation 475

On-the-Job Security Training 475

Performance Evaluation 476

Termination 476

Security Considerations for Nonemployees 478

Temporary Employees 478

Contract Employees 479

Consultants 479

Business Partners 480

Separation of Duties and Collusion 480

Privacy and the Security of Personnel Data 482

Chapter Summary 482

Review Questions 484

Exercises 485

Case Exercises 485

Chapter 12

IInformation Security Maintenance 489

Introduction 490

Security Management Models 492

The ISO Network Management Model 492

The Maintenance Model 500

Monitoring the External Environment 501

Monitoring the Internal Environment 507

Planning and Risk Assessment 511

Vulnerability Assessment and Remediation 517

Readiness and Review 525

Chapter Summary 527

Review Questions 528

Exercises 529

Case Exercises 529

Glossary 531

Index 553

Preface

AS GLOBAL NETWORKS EXPAND the interconnection of the world's information systems, the smooth operation of communication and computing solutions becomes vital. However, recurring events such as virus and worm attacks and the success of criminal attackers illustrate the weaknesses in current information technologies and the need to provide heightened security for these systems.

The immediate need for organizations to protect critical information assets continues to increase. In an attempt to secure their existing systems and networks, organizations must draw on the current pool of information security practitioners. But to develop more secure computing environments in the future, these same organizations are counting on the next generation of professionals to have the correct mix of skills and experience necessary to anticipate and manage the complex information security issues that are sure to arise. Thus, improved texts with supporting materials, along with the efforts of college and university faculty, are needed to prepare students of technology to recognize the threats and vulnerabilities present in existing systems and to learn to design and develop the secure systems needed in the near future.

The purpose of *Principles of Information Security*, Second Edition, is to fill the need for a quality academic textbook that surveys the discipline of information security. Although there are dozens of quality publications on information security and assurance that are oriented to the practitioner, there is a dramatic lack of textbooks that provide the student with a balanced introduction to both security management and the technical components of security. By creating a book specifically designed for information systems students, we hope to close this gap. This book also addresses another aspect of how information security as a discipline must be taught. As the field of information security has developed, it has been found that there is a clear need to include practitioners and students of other disciplines such as information systems, criminal justice, political science, and accounting information systems in the audience for this curriculum. It is necessary that future practitioners in these fields gain an understanding of the principles of information security because security issues are likely to affect their own industries and careers. As a result, the essential tenet of this textbook is that information security in the modern organization is a problem for management to solve—not a problem that technology can address alone. In other words, the information security of an organization has important economic consequences, for which management will be held accountable.

Approach

Principles of Information Security, Second Edition, provides a broad review of the entire field of information security, background on many related elements, and enough detail to facilitate an understanding of the topic as a whole. The book covers the terminology of the field, the history of the discipline, and an overview of how to manage an information security program.

Here are some features of the book's approach to the topic of information security:

Certified Information Systems Security Professionals Common Body of Knowledge—Because the authors each hold the Certified Information Systems Security Professional (CISSP) credential, the CISSP knowledge domains have had an influence in the design of the text. Although care was taken to avoid producing another CISSP study guide, the authors' backgrounds have ensured that the book's treatment of information security integrates, to some degree, much of the CISSP Common Body of Knowledge (CBK).

Chapter Scenarios—Each chapter opens with a short story that features the same fictional company as it encounters information security issues commonly found in real-life organizations. At the end of each chapter, there is a brief follow-up to the opening story and a set of discussion questions that gives the student and the instructor an opportunity to discuss the issues that underlie the story's content.

Offline and Technical Details Boxes—Interspersed throughout the textbook, these sections highlight interesting topics and detailed technical issues, giving the student the option of delving into various information security topics in greater detail.

Hands-On Learning—At the end of each chapter, students find a Chapter Summary and Review Questions as well as Exercises, which give them the opportunity to examine the information security arena outside the classroom. In the Exercises, the students are asked to research, analyze, and write responses to questions that are intended to reinforce learning objectives and deepen the students' understanding of the text.

Changes in the Second Edition—The second edition of *Principles of Information Security* includes a much more streamlined approach to the Security Systems Development Life Cycle, and substantially enhanced chapters on security technologies. Also, the following changes were integrated into the second edition:

- Coverage of technical controls was expanded to three complete chapters that encompass content such as firewalls, VPNs, intrusion detection systems, cryptography, vulnerability detection tools, and more.

- Risk management has been consolidated into a single chapter, providing a more succinct approach to this topic, which is central to the field of information security.

- Planning, which includes security program blueprinting, general planning, as well as incident response, disaster recovery, and business continuity planning, has been combined into a single chapter to integrate the coverage of these complex and interrelated topics.

In general, the changes to the second edition have brought the content of the book into better alignment with the general-purpose needs of courses that offer a survey of the information security discipline. These changes have also updated the currency of various topics to ensure that the book provides a cutting-edge treatment of the many varied elements of information security.

Author Team

Michael Whitman and Herbert Mattord have jointly developed this text to merge knowledge from the world of academic study with practical experience from the business world.

Michael Whitman, Ph.D., CISSP is a Professor of Information Systems in the Computer Science and Information Systems Department at Kennesaw State University, Kennesaw, Georgia, where he is also the Director of the Masters of Science in Information Systems and the Director of the KSU Center for Information Security Education (*infosec.kennesaw.edu*). Dr. Whitman is an active researcher in Information Security, Fair and Responsible Use Policies, Ethical Computing, and Information Systems Research Methods. He currently teaches graduate and undergraduate courses in Information Security, Local Area Networking, and Data Communications. He has published articles in the top journals in his field, including *Information Systems Research, Communications of the ACM, Information and Management, Journal of International Business Studies,* and *Journal of Computer Information Systems.* He is a member of the Information Systems Security Association, the Computer Security Institute, the Human Firewall Council, the Association for Computing Machinery, and the Association for Information Systems. Dr. Whitman is also the co-author of *Management of Information Security, Readings and Cases in the Management of Information Security,* and *The Hands-On Information Security Lab Manual,* all published by Course Technology. Prior to his career in academia, Dr. Whitman was an armored cavalry officer in the United States Army.

Herbert Mattord, M.B.A., CISSP completed 24 years of IT industry experience as an application developer, database administrator, project manager, and information security practitioner before joining the faculty at Kennesaw State University in 2002. Professor Mattord is the Operations Manager of the KSU Center for Information Security Education and Awareness (*infosec.kennesaw.edu*), as well as the coordinator for the KSU department of Computer Science and Information Systems Certificate in Information Security and Assurance. During his career as an IT practitioner, he has been an adjunct professor at Kennesaw State University, Southern Polytechnic State University in Marietta, Georgia; Austin Community College in Austin, Texas; and Texas State University: San Marcos. He currently teaches undergraduate courses in Information Security, Data Communications, Local Area Networks, Database Technology, Project Management, Systems Analysis & Design, and Information Resources Management and Policy. He was formerly the Manager of Corporate Information Technology Security at Georgia-Pacific Corporation, where much of the practical knowledge found in this textbook was acquired. Professor Mattord is also the co-author of *Management of Information Security, Readings and Cases in the Management of Information Security,* and *The Hands-On Information Security Lab Manual,* all published by Course Technology.

Structure

Principles of Information Security, Second Edition, is structured to follow a model called the Security Systems Development Life Cycle (or SecSDLC). This structured methodology can be used to implement information security in an organization that has little or no formal information security in place. SecSDLC can also serve as a method for improving established information security programs. The SecSDLC provides a solid framework very similar to that used in application development, software engineering, traditional systems analysis and design, and networking. This textbook's use of a structured methodology is intended to provide a supportive but not overriding theme that will guide instructors and students through an examination of the various components of the information domains of information security. To serve this end, the book is organized into seven sections and twelve chapters.

Section I—Introduction

Chapter 1—Introduction to Information Security

The opening chapter establishes the foundation for understanding the broader field of information security. This is accomplished by defining key terms, explaining essential concepts, and providing a review of the origins of the field.

Section II—Security Investigation Phase

Chapter 2—The Need for Security

Chapter 2 examines the business drivers that are propelling the increased interest in information security. It examines what modern organizations need in the area of information security, emphasizing and building on the concepts presented in Chapter 1. One principle concept presented here is that information security is primarily a management-related issue, rather than a technological one. To put it another way, the best practices within the field of information security involve applying technology only after considering the business needs.

The chapter also examines the various threats facing organizations and presents the process of ranking these threats (in order to assign them relative priority) that organizations can use when they begin their security planning process. The chapter continues with a detailed examination of the types of attacks that could result from these threats, and how these attacks could impact the organization's information systems. The chapter concludes with a further discussion of the key principles of information security, some of which were introduced in Chapter 1: confidentiality, integrity, availability, authentication and identification, authorization, accountability, and privacy.

Chapter 3—Legal, Ethical, and Professional Issues in Information Security

In addition to being a fundamental part of the SecSDLC investigation process, a careful examination of current legislation, regulation, and common ethical expectations of both national and international entities provides key insights into the regulatory constraints that govern business. This chapter examines several key laws that shape the field of information security and presents a detailed examination of the computer ethics that those who implement security must adhere to. Although ignorance of a law is no excuse, it's considered better than negligence (that is, knowing the law but doing nothing to comply with it). This chapter also presents several legal and ethical issues that are commonly found in today's organizations, as well as formal and professional organizations that promote ethics and legal responsibility.

Section III—Security Analysis

Chapter 4—Risk Management

Before the design of a new information security solution can begin, the information security analysts must first understand the current state of the organization and its relationship to information security. Does the organization have any formal information security mechanisms in place? How effective are they? What policies and procedures have been published and distributed to the security managers and end users? This chapter discusses how to conduct a fundamental information security assessment by describing the procedures for identifying and prioritizing threats and assets, and the procedures for identifying what controls are in place to protect these assets from threats. The chapter also provides a discussion of the various types of control mechanisms available and identifies the steps involved in performing the initial risk assessment. The chapter continues by defining risk management as the process of identifying, assessing, and reducing risk to an acceptable level and implementing effective control measures to maintain that level of risk. The chapter concludes with a discussion of risk analysis and the various types of feasibility analyses.

Section IV—Logical Design

Chapter 5—Planning for Security

Chapter 5 presents a number of widely accepted security models and frameworks. It examines best business practices and standards of due care and due diligence, and offers an overview of the development of security policy. This chapter details the major components, scope, and target audience for each of the levels of security policy. This chapter also explains data classification schemes, both military and private, as well as the security education training and awareness (SETA) program. The chapter examines the planning process that supports business continuity, disaster recovery, and incident response; it also describes the organization's role during incidents and when the organization should involve outside law enforcement agencies.

Section V—Physical Design

Author's Note: The material in this section is sequenced to introduce students of information systems to technical controls used within the field of information security. If you are not familiar with networking technology and the TCP/IP protocol, the material in Chapters 6, 7, and 8 may prove difficult. It is recommended that students who do not have a grounding in network protocols prepare for their study of the chapters in this section by reading a chapter or two from a networking textbook on the TCP/IP protocol.

Chapter 6—Security Technology: Firewalls and VPNs

Chapter 6 provides a detailed perspective on the configuration and use of technologies designed to segregate the organization from the insecure Internet. This chapter examines the various definitions and categorizations of firewall technologies and the architectures under which firewalls may be deployed. The chapter continues with a discussion of the rules and guidelines associated with the proper configuration and use of firewalls. Chapter 6 also discusses Remote Dial-Up Services, and the security precautions necessary to secure this access point for organizations with this older technology still deployed. The chapter continues with a presentation of content-filtering capabilities and considerations. The chapter concludes with an examination of technologies designed to provide remote access to authorized users through Virtual Private Networks.

Chapter 7—Security Technology: Intrusion Detection, Access Control, and Other Security Tools

Chapter 7 continues the discussion of security technologies by examining the concept of the intrusion and the technologies necessary to prevent, detect, react, and recover from intrusions. Specific types of Intrusion Detection Systems (IDSs)—the Host IDS, Network IDS, and Application IDS—and their respective configurations and uses are also presented and discussed. The chapter continues with an examination of the specialized detection technologies that are designed to entice attackers into decoy systems (and thus away from critical systems) or simply to identify the attackers' entry into these decoy areas, which are known as honey pots, honey nets, and padded cell systems. Also examined are trace-back systems, which are designed to track down the true address of attackers who were lured into decoy systems. The chapter continues with a detailed examination of some of the key security tools an information security professional can use to examine the current state of his or her organization's systems, and to identify any potential vulnerabilities or weaknesses that may exist in the systems or in the organization's overall security posture. The chapter concludes with a discussion of access control devices commonly deployed through modern operating systems, and new technologies in the area of biometrics that can provide strong authentication to existing implementations.

Chapter 8—Cryptography

Chapter 8 presents the underlying foundations of modern cryptosystems, as well as a discussion of the architectures and implementations of those cryptosystems. The chapter begins with an overview of the history of modern cryptography, and a discussion of the various types of ciphers that played key roles in that history. The chapter also examines some of the mathematical techniques that comprise cryptosystems, including hash functions. The chapter extends this discussion by comparing traditional symmetric encryption systems with more modern asymmetric encryption systems. The chapter also examines the role of asymmetric systems as the foundation of Public Key Encryption systems. Also covered in this chapter are the cryptography-based protocols used in secure communications; these include protocols such as SHTTP, SMIME, SET, SSH, and several others. The chapter then provides a discussion of steganography, and its emerging role as an effective means of hiding information. The chapter concludes by revisiting those attacks on information security that are specifically targeted at cryptosystems.

Chapter 9—Physical Security

As a vital part of any information security process, physical security is concerned with the management of the physical facilities, the implementation of physical access control, and the oversight of environmental controls. From designing a secure data center to assessing the relative value of guards and watchdogs to resolving the technical issues involved in fire suppression and power conditioning, physical security involves a wide range of special considerations. Chapter 9 examines these considerations by factoring in the various physical security threats that modern organizations face.

Section VI—Implementation

Chapter 10—Implementing Security

The preceding chapters provided guidelines for how an organization might design an information security program for itself. Chapter 10 examines the elements critical to *implementing* this design. Key areas in this chapter include the bull's-eye model for implementing information security and a discussion of whether an organization should outsource the various components of an information security program. Change management, program improvement, and additional planning for the business continuity efforts are also discussed.

Chapter 11—Personnel Security

The next area in the implementation stage addresses people issues. Chapter 11 examines both sides of the personnel coin: security personnel and security of personnel. It examines staffing issues, professional security credentials, and the implementation of employment policies and practices. The chapter also discusses how information security policy affects, and is affected by, consultants, temporary workers, and outside business partners.

Section VII—Maintenance and Change

Chapter 12—Information Security Maintenance

Last and most important is the discussion on maintenance and change. Chapter 12 presents the ongoing technical and administrative evaluation of the information security program that an organization must perform to maintain the security of its information systems. This chapter explores ongoing risk analysis, risk evaluation, and measurement, all of which maintain the effectiveness of a risk management program. The chapter includes coverage of the practices used to establish and manage vulnerability analysis and penetration testing.

Instructor Resources

A variety of teaching tools have been prepared to support this textbook and offer many options to enhance the classroom learning experience:

Electronic Instructor's Manual—The Instructor's Manual includes suggestions and strategies for using this text, and even suggestions for lecture topics. The Instructor's Manual also includes answers to the Review Questions and suggested solutions to the Exercises at the end of each chapter.

Figure Files—Figure files allow instructors to create their own presentations using figures taken from the text.

PowerPoint Presentations—This book comes with Microsoft PowerPoint slides for each chapter. These are included as a teaching aid to be used for classroom presentation, to be made available to students on the network for chapter review, or to be printed for classroom distribution. Instructors can add their own slides for additional topics they introduce to the class.

Lab Manual—Course Technology has developed a lab manual to accompany this and other books: *The Hands-On Information Security Lab Manual* (ISBN 0-619-21631-X). The lab manual provides hands-on security exercises on footprinting, enumeration, and firewall configuration, as well as a number of detailed exercises and cases that can serve to supplement the book as laboratory components or as in-class projects. Contact your Course Technology sales representative for more information.

ExamView—ExamView®, the ultimate tool for objective-based testing needs. Exam-View® is a powerful objective-based test generator that enables instructors to create paper, LAN- or Web-based tests from testbanks designed specifically for their Course Technology text. Instructors can utilize the ultra-efficient QuickTest Wizard to create tests in less than five minutes by taking advantage of Course Technology's question banks, or customize their own exams from scratch.

Acknowledgments

The authors would like to thank their families for their support and understanding for the many hours dedicated to this project, hours taken away, in many cases, from family activities. Special thanks to Carola Mattord, doctoral student of English at Georgia State University. Her reviews of early drafts and suggestions for keeping the writing focused on the students resulted in a more readable manuscript.

Contributors

Several people and organizations have also contributed materials that were used in the preparation of this textbook, and we thank them for their contributions:

- Anthony J. Nichols—Contributed to early drafts of the materials on cryptography
- John W. Lampe—Contributed draft content on several topics in the area of technical security controls
- The National Institute of Standards and Technology is the source of many references, tables, figures, and other content used in many places in the textbook

Reviewers

We are indebted to the following individuals for their respective contributions of perceptive feedback on the initial proposal, the project outline, and the chapter-by-chapter reviews of the text:

- Snehamay Banerjee, Rutgers University
- Michael L. Casper, Central Piedmont Community College
- Lawrence R. Knupp, DeVry University
- Robert Lipton, Pennsylvania State University
- Patrick Massaro, Long Island University
- David Ozag, Gettysburg College
- Denise Padavano, Peirce College
- Sara Robben, DeVry University
- JoAnna Burley Shore, Frostburg State University
- Robert Statica, New Jersey Institute of Technology
- Eileen M. Vidrine, Northern Virginia Community College

Special Thanks

The authors wish to thank the Editorial and Production teams at Course Technology. Their diligent and professional efforts greatly enhanced the final product:

- Beth Paquin, Product Manager
- Saher Alam and Lynne Raughley, Developmental Editors
- Maureen Martin, Executive Editor
- Pamela Elizian, Associate Production Manager
- Mirella Misiaszek, Associate Product Manager
- Abigail Reip, Photo Researcher

In addition, several professional and commercial organizations and individuals have aided the development of the textbook by providing information and inspiration, and the authors wish to acknowledge their contribution:

- Tenable Network Security, Inc.
- The Human Firewall Council
- NetIQ, Inc.
- Charles Cresson Wood
- Georgia-Pacific Corporation
- Our colleagues in the Department of Computer Science and Information Systems, Kennesaw State University
- Professor Merle King, Chair of the Department of Computer Science and Information Systems, Kennesaw State University
- Dr. Larry Petersen, Dean of the College of Science and Mathematics, Kennesaw State University

Our Commitment

The authors are committed to serving the needs of the adopters and readers of this book. We would be pleased and honored to receive feedback on the textbook and its supporting materials. You can contact us through Course Technology, via e-mail at mis@course.com.

Introduction to Information Security

> Do not figure on opponents not attacking;
> worry about your own lack of preparation.
> **BOOK OF THE FIVE RINGS**

IT STARTED OUT LIKE ANY OTHER DAY for Amy at the Sequential Label and Supply Company (SLS). She liked her technical support job at the help desk. Taking calls and helping the office workers with PC problems was not glamorous, but it was challenging and paid pretty well. Some of her friends worked at bigger companies, some at higher-tech companies, but everyone kept up with each other, and they all agreed that technology jobs were a good way to pay the bills.

The phone rang. This was not a big deal for Amy. She answered her phone about 35 times an hour, 315 times a day, nine days every two weeks. The first call of the day started out the same as usual, with a worried user hoping Amy could help him out of a jam. The call display on her screen gave her all the facts: the user's name, his phone number, the department in which he worked, where his office was on the company campus, and a list of all the calls he'd made in the past.

"Hi, Bob," she said. "Did you get that document formatting problem squared away after our last call?"

"Sure did, Amy. Hope we can figure out what's going on today."

"We'll try, Bob. Tell me about it."

"Well, my PC is acting weird," Bob said. "When I go to the screen that has my e-mail program running, it doesn't respond to the mouse or the keyboard."

"Did you try a reboot yet, Bob?"

"Sure did. But the window wouldn't close, and I had to turn it off. Once it finished the reboot and I opened the e-mail program, it's just like it was before—no response at all. The other stuff is working OK, but really, really slowly. Even my Internet browser is sluggish."

"OK, Bob. We've tried the usual stuff we can do over the phone. Let me open a case, and I'll dispatch a tech over as soon as possible."

Amy looked up at the LED tally board on the wall at the end of the room. She saw that there were only two technicians dispatched to deskside support at the moment, and since it was the day shift, there were four available.

"Shouldn't be long at all, Bob."

She clicked off the line from Bob and typed her notes into ISIS, the company's Information Status and Issues System. She assigned the newly generated case to the deskside dispatch queue, knowing the roving deskside team would be paged with the details and would attend to Bob's problem in just a few minutes.

A moment later, Amy looked up to see Charles Moody walking briskly down the hall. Charlie was the senior manager of the server administration team. He was being trailed by three of his senior technicians as he made a beeline from his office to the door of the server room where the company servers were kept in a controlled environment. They all looked worried.

Just then, Amy's screen beeped to alert her of a new e-mail. She glanced down. It beeped again—and again. It started beeping constantly. She clicked on the envelope icon and, after a short delay, the mail window opened. She had 47 new e-mails in her inbox. She opened one from Davey Martinez, an acquaintance from the Accounting Department. The subject line said, "Wait till you see this." The message body read, "Look what this has to say about our managers' salaries…" There was an icon for a file attachment that Amy did not recognize. But, she knew Davey often sent her interesting and funny e-mails. She clicked on the icon.

Her PC showed the hourglass pointer icon for a second and then resumed showing its normal pointer. Nothing happened. She clicked on the icon for the next e-mail message. Nothing happened. Her phone rang again. She clicked on the ISIS icon on her computer desktop to activate the call management software and activated her headset. "Hello, Tech Support, how can I help you?" She couldn't greet the caller by name because ISIS had not yet opened the screen on her PC.

"Hello, this is Erin Williams in Receiving."

Amy glanced down at her screen. Still no ISIS. She glanced up to the tally board and was surprised to see the inbound call counter tallying up waiting calls like digits on a stopwatch. Amy had never seen so many calls come in at one time.

"Hi, Erin," Amy said. "What's up?"

"Nothing," Erin answered. "That's the problem." The rest of the call was an exact replay of Bob's earlier call, except Amy couldn't type the notes into ISIS and had to jot them down on a legal pad. She also couldn't dispatch the deskside support team either. She looked at the tally board. It had gone dark. No numbers at all.

Then she saw Charlie running down the hall from the server room. He didn't look worried anymore. He looked frantic.

Amy picked up the phone. She wanted to check with her supervisor about what to do now. There was no dial tone.

LEARNING OBJECTIVES:

Upon completion of this material, you should be able to:

- Understand the definition of information security
- Comprehend the history of computer security and how it evolved into information security
- Understand the key terms and critical concepts of information security as presented in the chapter
- Outline the phases of the security systems development life cycle
- Understand the roles of professionals involved in information security within an organization

Introduction

James Anderson, Vice President of Information Security at Inovant, the world's largest commercial processor of financial payment transactions, believes information security in today's enterprise is a "well-informed sense of assurance that the information risks and controls are in balance."

The opening scenario of this chapter illustrates that the information risks and controls are not in balance at Sequential Label and Supply. Though Amy works in a technical support role and her duties are to solve technical problems, she does not even consider that a virus or worm might be the agent of the company's current ills. Management also shows signs of confusion and is at a loss about how to contain this kind of situation. If you were in Amy's place and were faced with a similar situation, what would you do? How would you react? Would it occur to you that something far more insidious than a simple technical malfunction was happening at your company? As you study the following chapters and learn more about information security, you will become better able to answer these questions. But before you can begin analyzing the details of the discipline of information security, you must first review the history and evolution of the field.

The History of Information Security

The history of information security begins with the history of **computer security**. The need for computer security—that is, the need to secure physical locations, hardware, and software from outside threats—began during World War II when the first mainframes, developed to aid computations for code breaking (see Figure 1-1), were put to use.

Multiple levels of security were implemented to protect these mainframes and secure data integrity. Access to sensitive military locations, for example, was controlled through the use of badges, keys, and the facial recognition of authorized personnel by security guards. The growing need to maintain national security, however, eventually expanded the procedures of computer security to embrace more complex and more technologically sophisticated safeguards.

Earlier versions of the German code machine Enigma were first broken by the Poles in the 1930s. The British and Americans managed to break later, more complex versions during World War II. The increasingly complex versions of the Enigma, especially the submarine or *Unterseeboot* version of the Enigma, caused considerable anguish to allied forces before finally being cracked. The information gained from decrypted transmissions was used to anticipate the actions of German armed forces. "Some ask why, if we were reading the Enigma, we did not win the war earlier. One might ask, instead, when, if ever, we would have won the war if we hadn't read it."

Courtesy of National Security Agency

FIGURE 1-1 The Enigma[1]

During these early years, **information security** was rudimentary and mainly composed of simple document classification schemes. There were no application classification projects for computers or operating systems at that time, because the primary threats to security were physical theft of equipment, espionage against the products of the systems, and sabotage. One of the first documented security problems that was not physical in nature occurred in the early 1960s, when a systems administrator was working on an MOTD (message of the day) file, and another administrator was editing the password file. A software glitch mixed the two files, and the entire password file was printed on every output file.[2]

The 1960s

During the Cold War, many more mainframes were brought online to accomplish more complex and sophisticated tasks. It became necessary to find a way to enable these mainframes to communicate with each other using a less cumbersome process than mailing magnetic tapes between computer centers. In response to this need, the Department of Defense's Advanced Research Project Agency (ARPA) began examining the feasibility of a redundant, networked communications system to support the military's exchange of information. Larry Roberts, known as the founder of the Internet, developed the project from its inception. This project, called ARPANET, is the origin of today's Internet (see Figure 1-2 for an excerpt from the ARPANET Program Plan).

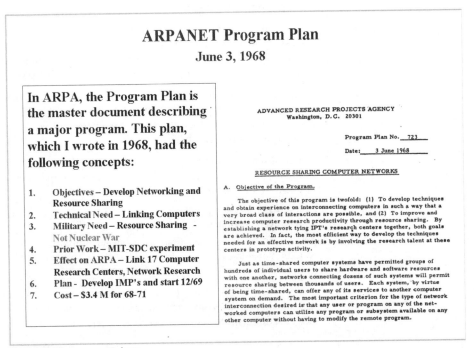

ARPANET Program Plan

June 3, 1968

In ARPA, the Program Plan is the master document describing a major program. This plan, which I wrote in 1968, had the following concepts:

1. **Objectives – Develop Networking and Resource Sharing**
2. **Technical Need – Linking Computers**
3. **Military Need – Resource Sharing** - Not Nuclear War
4. **Prior Work – MIT-SDC experiment**
5. **Effect on ARPA – Link 17 Computer Research Centers, Network Research**
6. **Plan - Develop IMP's and start 12/69**
7. **Cost – $3.4 M for 68-71**

ADVANCED RESEARCH PROJECTS AGENCY
Washington, D.C. 20301

Program Plan No. _723_

Date: _3 June 1968_

RESOURCE SHARING COMPUTER NETWORKS

A. Objective of the Program.

The objective of this program is twofold: (1) To develop techniques and obtain experience on interconnecting computers in such a way that a very broad class of interactions are possible, and (2) To improve and increase computer research productivity through resource sharing. By establishing a network tying IPT's research centers together, both goals are achieved. In fact, the most efficient way to develop the techniques needed for an effective network is by involving the research talent at these centers in prototype activity.

Just as time-shared computer systems have permitted groups of hundreds of individual users to share hardware and software resources with one another, networks connecting dozens of such systems will permit resource sharing between thousands of users. Each system, by virtue of being time-shared, can offer any of its services to another computer system on demand. The most important criterion for the type of network interconnection desired is that any user or program on any of the networked computers can utilize any program or subsystem available on any other computer without having to modify the remote program.

Courtesy of Dr. Lawrence Roberts

FIGURE 1-2 Development of the ARPANET Program Plan[3]

The 1970s and 80s

During the next decade, the ARPANET grew in popularity and use, and so did the potential for its misuse. In December of 1973, Robert M. "Bob" Metcalfe, who is credited with the development of the Ethernet, one of the most popular protocols for networking, identified fundamental problems with ARPANET security. Individual remote users' sites did not have sufficient controls and safeguards to protect data against unauthorized remote users. Other problems abounded: the vulnerability of password structure and formats; lack of safety procedures for dial-up connections; nonexistent user identification and authorization to the system. Phone numbers were widely distributed and openly publicized on the walls of phone booths, giving hackers easy access to the ARPANET. Because of the range and frequency of computer security violations and the explosion in numbers of hosts and users on the ARPANET, network security was referred to as network insecurity.[4] In 1978, a famous study entitled "Protection Analysis: Final Report" was published. It focused on a project undertaken by ARPA to discover the vulnerabilities of operating system security. For a timeline that includes this and other seminal studies of computer security, see Table 1-1.

TABLE 1-1	Key Dates for Seminal Works in Early Computer Security
Date	**Documents**
1968	Maurice Wilkes discusses password security in *Time-Sharing Computer Systems*.
1973	Schell, Downey, and Popek examine the need for additional security in military systems in "Preliminary Notes on the Design of Secure Military Computer Systems."[5]
1975	The Federal Information Processing Standards (FIPS) examines DES (Digital Encryption Standard) in the *Federal Register*.
1978	Bisbey and Hollingworth publish their study "Protection Analysis: Final Report," discussing the Protection Analysis project created by ARPA to understand better the vulnerabilities of operating system security and examine the possibility of automated vulnerability detection techniques in existing system software.[6]
1979	Morris and Thompson author "Password Security: A Case History," published in the *Communications of the Association for Computing Machinery* (ACM). The paper examines the history of a design for a password security scheme on a remotely accessed, time-sharing system.
1979	Dennis Ritchie publishes "On the Security of UNIX" and "Protection of Data File Contents," discussing secure user IDs and secure group IDs, and the problems inherent in the systems.
1984	Grampp and Morris write "UNIX Operating System Security." In this report, the authors examine four "important handles to computer security": physical control of premises and computer facilities, management commitment to security objectives, education of employees, and administrative procedures aimed at increased security.[7]
1984	Reeds and Weinberger publish "File Security and the UNIX System Crypt Command." Their premise was: "No technique can be secure against wiretapping or its equivalent on the computer. Therefore no technique can be secure against the systems administrator or other privileged users... the naive user has no chance."[8]

The movement toward security that went beyond protecting physical locations began with a single paper sponsored by the Department of Defense, the Rand Report R-609, which attempted to define the multiple controls and mechanisms necessary for the protection of a multilevel computer system. The document was classified for almost ten years, and is now referred to as "the paper that started the study of computer security."

The security of the systems sharing resources within the Department of Defense was brought to the attention of researchers in the spring and summer of 1967. At that time, systems were being acquired at a rapid rate and the problem of securing them was a pressing concern for both the military and defense contractors.

In June of 1967, the Advanced Research Projects Agency formed a task force to study the process of securing classified information systems. The Task Force was assembled in October of 1967 and met regularly to formulate recommendations, which ultimately became the contents of the Rand Report R-609.[9]

The Rand Report R-609 was the first widely recognized published document to identify the role of management and policy issues in computer security. It noted that the wide utilization of networking components in information systems in the military introduced complexities that went beyond the routine practices then used to secure these systems.[10]

This paper signaled a pivotal moment in computer security history—when the scope of computer security expanded significantly. The scope grew from the safety of physical locations and hardware to include:

- Safety of the data
- Limiting random and unauthorized access to that data
- Involvement of personnel from multiple levels of the organization

MULTICS

Much of the focus for research on computer security centered on a system called MULTICS (Multiplexed Information and Computing Service). Although this operating system is now obsolete, MULTICS is noteworthy because it was the first and *only* operating system created with security as its primary goal. It was a mainframe, time-sharing operating system developed in the mid-1960s by a consortium from General Electric (GE), Bell Labs, and the Massachusetts Institute of Technology (MIT).

In mid-1969, not long after the restructuring of the MULTICS project, several of its key players (Ken Thompson, Dennis Ritchie, Rudd Canaday, and Doug McIlro) created a new operating system called UNIX. While the MULTICS system implemented multiple security levels and passwords, the UNIX system did not. Its primary purpose, text processing, did not require the same level of security as that of its predecessor. In fact, it was not until the early 1970s that even the simplest component of security, the password function, was implemented as a component of the operating system.

In the late 1970s, the microprocessor brought in a new age of computing. The personal computer, built with this microprocessor technology, became the workhorse of modern computing, thereby decentralizing the exclusive domain of the data center. With this decentralization of data, the need for resource sharing increased during the 1980s, driving owners of personal computers to interconnect their machines. These networking abilities worked for both mainframe and microcomputers, and gave the entire computing community the opportunity to make all their computing resources work together.

The 1990s

At the close of the twentieth century, networks of computers became more common, as did the need to connect these networks to each other. This gave rise to the Internet, the first manifestation of a global network of networks. This networking resource was made more available to the general public in the 1990s, having previously been the domain of government, academia, and dedicated industry professionals. The Internet brought connectivity to virtually all computers that could reach a phone line or an Internet-connected Local Area Network (LAN). After the Internet was commercialized, the technology became pervasive, reaching almost every corner of the globe with an expanding universe of uses.

Since its inception as a tool for sharing defense information, the Internet has grown steadily with the interconnection of millions of networks. At first, these connections were based on *de facto* standards, because industry standards for interconnection of networks did not exist at that time. These *de facto* standards did not consider the security of information to be a critical factor, but as these precursor technologies were more widely adopted and became industry standards, some degree of security was introduced. However, early Internet deployment treated security as a low priority. For example, many of the problems that plague e-mail on the Internet today are the result of this early lack of security. Early computing approaches relied on security that was built into the physical environment of the data center that housed the computers. As networked computers became the dominant style of computing, the ability to physically secure a networked computer was lost, and the stored information became more exposed to security threats.

The Present

Today, the Internet has brought millions of unsecured computer networks into communication with each other. The security of each computer's stored information is now contingent on the level of security of every other computer to which it is connected.

What Is Security?

In general, **security** is "the quality or state of being secure—to be free from danger."[11] In other words, building protection against adversaries—from those who would do harm, intentionally or otherwise—is the objective. National security, for example, is a multilayered system that protects the sovereignty of a state, its assets, its resources, and its people. Achieving the appropriate level of security for an organization also depends on a multifaceted system.

A successful organization should have the following multiple layers of security in place to protect its operations:

- **Physical security** addresses the issues necessary to protect the physical items, objects, or areas of an organization from unauthorized access and misuse.
- **Personal security** involves the protection of the individual or group of individuals who are authorized to access the organization and its operations.
- **Operations security** focuses on the protection of the details of a particular operation or series of activities.
- **Communications security** encompasses the protection of an organization's communications media, technology, and content.
- **Network security** is the protection of networking components, connections, and contents.
- **Information security** is discussed in more detail in the following section.

Information security (InfoSec), as defined by the standards published by the Committee on National Security Systems (CNSS), formerly the National Security Telecommunications and Information Systems Security Committee (NSTISSC)[12], is the protection of information and its critical elements, including the systems and hardware that use, store, and transmit that information. Figure 1-3 shows that information security includes the broad areas of information security management (the topic of this book), computer and data security, and network security. To protect information and its related systems, organizations must implement such tools as policy, awareness, training and education, and technology. The NSTISSC model of information security evolved from a concept developed by the computer security industry known as the C.I.A. triangle. The **C.I.A. triangle** has been the industry standard for computer security since the development of the mainframe. It is based on the three characteristics of information that give it value for its use in organizations: confidentiality, integrity, and availability. The security of these three characteristics of information is as important today as it has always been, but the C.I.A. triangle model no longer adequately addresses the constantly changing environment of the computer industry. The threats to information confidentiality, integrity, and availability have evolved into a vast collection of events, including accidental or intentional damage, destruction, theft, unintended or unauthorized modification, or other misuses from human or nonhuman threats. This new environment of many constantly evolving threats has prompted the development of a more robust intellectual model that addresses the complexities of the current information security environment. This expanded C.I.A. triangle consists of a list of critical characteristics of information, which are described in the next section. C.I.A. triangle terminology is used in this chapter because of the breadth of material that is based on it.

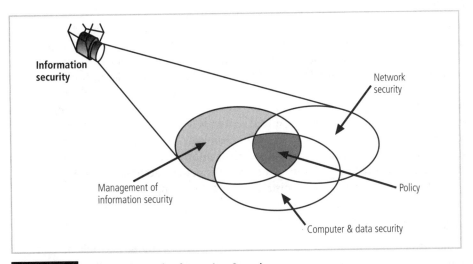

FIGURE 1-3 Components of Information Security

Critical Characteristics of Information

The value of information comes from the characteristics it possesses. When a characteristic of information changes, the value of that information either increases or, more commonly, decreases. Some characteristics affect information's value to users more than others do. The timeliness of information can be a critical factor, because information often loses all value when it is delivered too late. Though information security professionals and end users share the same understanding of the characteristics of information, tensions can arise when the need to secure the integrity of information from threats conflicts with the end users' need for unhindered access to the information. For example, end users may perceive a tenth-of-a-second delay in the computation of data to be an unnecessary annoyance. Information security professionals, however, may perceive that tenth-of-a-second as a minor delay that was necessary for the accomplishment of an important task, like the encryption of data. Each critical characteristic of information of the expanded C.I.A. triangle is defined in the sections below.

Availability

Availability enables authorized users—persons or computer systems—to access information without interference or obstruction, and to receive it in the required format. Consider, for example, research libraries that require identification before entrance. Librarians protect the contents of the library so that they are available only to authorized patrons. This means that the librarian must see and accept a patron's proof of identification before that patron has free and easy access to the contents available in the bookroom. Once authorized patrons have access to the contents of the bookroom, they expect to find the information they need available in a useable format and familiar language, which in this case means bound in a book and written in English.

Accuracy

Information has **accuracy** when it is free from mistakes or errors and it has the value that the end user expects. If information contains a value different from the user's expectations, due to the intentional or unintentional modification of its content, it is no longer accurate. Consider, for example, a checking account. You assume that the information contained in your checking account is an accurate representation of your finances. Inaccuracy of the information in your checking account can be caused by external or internal means. If a bank teller, for instance, mistakenly adds or subtracts too much from your account, the value of the information will be changed. Also, as the user of your bank account, you may accidentally enter an incorrect amount into your account register. This also changes the value of the information. Either way, the inaccuracy of your bank account could cause you to make mistakes, such as bouncing a check.

Authenticity

Authenticity of information is the quality or state of being genuine or original, rather than a reproduction or fabrication. Information is authentic when it is the information that was originally created, placed, stored, or transferred. Consider for a moment some of the assumptions made about e-mail. When you receive e-mail, you assume that a specific individual or group of individuals created and transmitted the e-mail—you assume you know the origin of the e-mail. This is not always the case. **E-mail spoofing**, the process of sending an e-mail message with a modified field, is a problem for many individuals today, because many times the field modified is the address of the originator. Spoofing the address of origin can fool the e-mail recipient into thinking that the message is legitimate traffic. In this way, the spoofer can induce e-mail readers into opening e-mail they otherwise might not have opened. The attack known as spoofing can also be applied to the transmission of data across a network, as in the case of user data protocol (UDP) packet spoofing, which can enable the attacker to get unauthorized access to data stored on computing systems.

Confidentiality

Information has **confidentiality** when disclosure or exposure to unauthorized individuals or systems is prevented. Confidentiality ensures that *only* those with the rights and privileges to access information are able to do so. When unauthorized individuals or systems can view information, confidentiality is breached. To protect the confidentiality of information, you can use a number of measures:

- Information classification
- Secure document storage
- Application of general security policies
- Education of information custodians and end users

Confidentiality, like most of the characteristics of information, is interdependent with other characteristics, and is most closely related to the characteristic known as privacy. The relationship between these two characteristics is covered in more detail in Chapter 3, "Legal and Ethical Issues in Security."

In an organization, the value of confidentiality of information is especially high when it involves personal information about employees, customers, or patients. Individuals who deal with an organization expect that their personal information will remain confidential, whether the organization is a federal agency, such as the Internal Revenue Service, or a business. Problems arise when companies disclose sensitive information that was deemed confidential. Sometimes this disclosure is intentional, but there are times when disclosure of confidential information happens by mistake—for example, when confidential information is mistakenly e-mailed to someone *outside* the organization rather than to someone *inside* the organization. The famous case of privacy violation by Eli Lilly and Co. from July, 2001 is outlined in Offline: Unintentional Disclosures.

OFFLINE

Unintentional Disclosures

The giant pharmaceutical organization Eli Lilly and Co. released the e-mail addresses of 600 patients to one another in 2001. The American Civil Liberties Union (ACLU) denounced this breach of privacy, and information technology industry analysts noted that it was likely to influence the public debate on privacy legislation.

The company claimed that the mishap was caused by a programming error that occurred when patients who used a specific drug produced by the company signed up for an e-mail service to access support materials provided by the company. About 600 patient addresses were exposed in the mass e-mail.[13]

In another incident, the intellectual property of Jerome Stevens Pharmaceuticals, a small prescription drug manufacturer from New York, was compromised when the FDA released documents the company had filed with the agency. It remains unclear whether this was a purposeful act by the FDA or a simple error; but either way, the company secrets were posted to a public Web site for several months before being removed.[14]

Other examples of a breach of confidentiality are an employee throwing away a document containing critical information without shredding it, or a hacker who successfully breaks into an internal database of a Web-based organization and steals sensitive information about the clients, such as names, addresses, and credit card numbers.

As a consumer, you give up pieces of your confidential information in exchange for convenience or value almost daily. By using a "members only card" at a grocery store, you disclose some of your spending habits. When you fill out an online survey, you exchange pieces of your personal history for access to online privileges. The bits and pieces of your information that you disclose are copied, sold, replicated, distributed and eventually coalesced into profiles and even complete dossiers of yourself and your life. A similar technique is used in a criminal enterprise called **salami theft**. A deli worker knows he or she cannot steal the entire salami, but a few slices here or there can be taken home without notice. Eventually the deli worker has stolen the whole salami. In information security, salami theft occurs when an employee steals a few pieces of information at a time, knowing that taking more would be noticed—but eventually the employee gets the whole thing.

Integrity

Information has **integrity** when it is whole, complete, and uncorrupted. The integrity of information is threatened when the information is exposed to corruption, damage, destruction, or other disruption of its authentic state. The threat of corruption can occur while information is being stored or transmitted. Many computer viruses and worms are designed with the explicit purpose of corrupting data. For this reason, a key method for detecting a virus or worm is to look for changes in file integrity as shown by the size of the file. Another key methodology for assuring information integrity is through **file hashing**, in which a file is read by a special algorithm that uses the value of the bits in the file to compute a single large number called a **hash value**. The hash value for any combination of bits will provide a unique value. If the computer system performs the same hashing algorithm before trusting the contents of the file and returns a different number than the posted hash value for that file, the file has been compromised and the integrity of the information is lost. Information integrity is the cornerstone of information systems, because information is of no value or use if users cannot verify its integrity.

The corruption of a file does not always come from external forces, such as hackers. Noise in the transmission media, for instance, can also cause data to lose its integrity. Transmitting data on a circuit with a low voltage level can cause the receiving system to receive the data with inaccurate values. Redundancy bits and check bits can compensate for internal and external threats to the integrity of information. During each transmission, algorithms, hash values, and the error-correcting codes ensure the integrity of the information. Data whose integrity has been compromised is retransmitted.

Utility

The **utility** of information is the quality or state of having value for some purpose or end. Information has value when it serves a particular purpose. This means that if information is available, but not in a format meaningful to the end user, it is not useful. Thus, the value of the information depends on its utility. For example, to a private citizen U.S. Census data can quickly become overwhelming and difficult to interpret; however, for a politician, the results of the U.S. Census reveals information about the voters in a district, to what political party these voters belong, their race, gender, age, and so on. This information can help form a politician's next campaign strategy.

Possession

The **possession** of information is the quality or state of having ownership or control of some object or item. Information is said to be in one's possession if one obtains it, independent of format or other characteristics. While a breach of confidentiality always results in a breach of possession, a breach of possession does not always result in a breach of confidentiality. For example, assume a company stores its critical customer data using an encrypted file system. An employee who has quit decides to take a copy of the tape backups to sell the customer records to the competition. The removal of the tapes from their secure environment is a breach of possession. But, because the data is encrypted, neither the employee nor anyone else can read it without the proper decryption methods; therefore, there is no breach of confidentiality. Today, individuals caught selling company secrets face increasingly stiff fines with the likelihood of jail time. Also, companies are growing more and more reluctant to hire individuals who have demonstrated untrustworthiness in their past.

NSTISSC Security Model

The definition for information security presented earlier is based in part on the National Security Telecommunications and Information Systems Security Committee document that is now called the National Training Standard for Information Security Professionals NSTISSI No. 4011 (see *www.nstissc.gov/html/library.html*). This document presents a comprehensive model for information security and is becoming the evaluation standard for the security of information systems. The security model, as represented in Figure 1-4, shows three dimensions. If extrapolated, the three dimensions of each axis become a 3 x 3 x 3 cube with 27 cells representing areas that must be addressed to secure today's information systems. To ensure system security, each of the 27 cells must be properly addressed during the security process. For example, the intersection between the technology, integrity, and storage areas requires a control or safeguard that addresses the need to use *technology* to protect the *integrity* of information while in *storage*. One such control would be a system for detecting host intrusion that protects the integrity of information by alerting the security administrators to the potential modification of a critical file. What is commonly left out of such a model is the need for guidelines and policies that provide direction for the practices and implementations of technologies. The need for policy is discussed in later chapters.

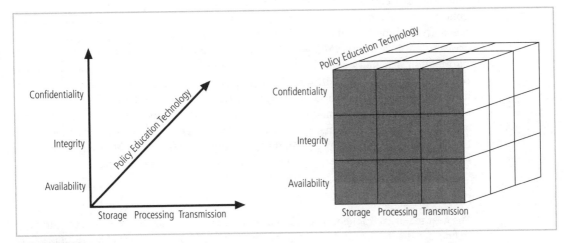

FIGURE 1-4 NSTISSC Security Model

Components of an Information System

As shown in Figure 1-5, an **Information System (IS)** is much more than computer hardware; it is the entire set of software, hardware, data, people, procedures, and networks necessary to use information as a resource in the organization. These are the six critical components that enable information to be input, processed, output, and stored. Each of these components of the IS has its own strengths and weaknesses—its own characteristics and uses. More important to remember, each component of the information system has its own security requirements.

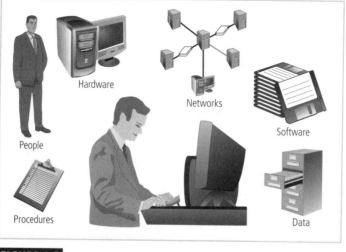

FIGURE 1-5   Components of an Information System

Software

The first major component of an IS to be discussed here is software. The software component of the IS comprises applications, operating systems, and assorted command utilities. Software is perhaps the most difficult IS component to secure. The exploitation of errors in software programming accounts for a substantial portion of the attacks on information. The news is filled with reports warning of holes, bugs, weaknesses, or other fundamental problems in software. Software programs are the vessels that carry the lifeblood of information through an organization. Unfortunately, software programs are often created under the demanding constraints of project management, which limit time, cost, and manpower. Information security is all too often implemented as an afterthought rather than developed as an integral component from the beginning. In this way, software programs become an easy target of accidental or intentional attacks.

Hardware

The next major component of an IS to be discussed is hardware. Hardware is the physical technology that houses and executes the software, stores and carries the data, and provides interfaces for the entry and removal of information from the system. Physical security policies deal with hardware as a physical asset and with the protection of these physical assets from harm or theft. Applying the traditional tools of physical security, such as locks and keys, restricts access to and interaction with the hardware components of an information system. Securing the physical location of computers and the computers themselves is important because a breach of physical security can result in a loss of information. Unfortunately, most information systems are built on hardware platforms that cannot guarantee any level of information security if unrestricted access to the hardware is possible.

Before September 11, 2001, laptop thefts in airports were common. A two-person team worked to steal a computer as its owner passed it through the conveyor scanning devices. The first perpetrator entered the security area ahead of an unsuspecting target and quickly went through. Then, the second perpetrator followed the intended victim, waiting behind the target until the target placed his/her computer on the baggage scanner. As the computer was whisked through, the second agent slipped ahead of the victim and entered the metal detector with a substantial collection of keys, coins, and the like, thereby slowing the detection process, and allowing the first perpetrator to grab the computer and disappear in a crowded walkway.

While the tragic events of September 11, 2001 did change the security measures at airports, hardware can still be stolen in these kinds of public places. Although laptops or notebook computers are worth a few thousand dollars, the information contained in them can be worth a great deal more to an organization.

Data

Data stored, processed, and transmitted through a computer system must be protected. Data is often the most valuable asset possessed by an organization and it is the main target of intentional attacks. Systems developed in recent years are likely to have been created to make use of database management systems. When done properly, this should improve the security of the data and the application. Unfortunately, many system development projects are not done in ways that make use of the database management system's security capabilities, and in some cases, the database is implemented in ways that are less secure than traditional file systems.

People

Though often overlooked in computer security considerations, people have always been a threat to information security. Legend has it that around 200 B.C. a great army threatened the security and stability of the Chinese empire. So ferocious were the invaders that the Chinese emperor commanded the construction of a great wall that would defend against the Hun invaders. Around 1275 A.D., Kublai Khan finally achieved what the Huns had been trying for thousands of years. Initially, Khan's army tried to climb over, dig under, and break through the wall. In the end, Khan simply bribed the gatekeeper to open the gates—and the rest is history. Whether this event actually occurred or not, the moral of the story is that people can be the weakest link in an organization's information security program. And unless policy, education and training, awareness, and technology are properly employed to prevent people from accidentally or intentionally damaging or losing information, they will remain the weakest link. Social engineering can prey on the tendency to cut corners and the commonplace nature of human error. It can be used to manipulate the actions of people to obtain access information about a system. This topic is discussed in more detail in Chapter 2, "The Need for Security."

Procedures

Another frequently overlooked component of an IS is procedures. Procedures are written instructions for accomplishing a specific task. When an unauthorized user obtains an organization's procedures, this poses a threat to the integrity of the information. For example, a consultant to a bank learned how to wire funds by using the computer center's procedures, which were readily available. By taking advantage of a security weakness (lack of authentication), this bank consultant ordered millions of dollars to be transferred by wire to an unauthorized account. Lax security procedures caused the loss of over ten million dollars before the situation was corrected. Most organizations distribute procedures to their legitimate employees so they can access the information system, but many of these companies often fail to provide proper education on the protection of the procedures. Educating employees about safeguarding the procedures is as important as securing the information system. After all, procedures are information in their own right. Therefore, knowledge of procedures, as with all critical information, should be disseminated among members of the organization only on a need-to-know basis.

Networks

The IS component that created much of the need for increased computer and information security is networking. When information systems are connected to each other to form Local Area Networks (LANs), and these LANs are connected to other networks such as the Internet, new security challenges rapidly emerge. The physical technology that enables network functions is becoming more and more accessible to organizations of every size. Applying the traditional tools of physical security, such as locks and keys, to restrict access to and interaction with the hardware components of an information system are still important; but when computer systems are networked, this approach is no longer enough. Steps to provide network security are essential, as is the implementation of alarm and intrusion systems to make system owners aware of ongoing compromises.

Securing Components

The security of information and its systems entails securing all components and protecting them from potential misuse and abuse by unauthorized users. When considering the security of information systems components, it is important to understand the concept of the computer as the subject of an attack as opposed to the computer as the object of an attack. When a computer is the **subject of an attack**, it is used as an active tool to conduct the attack. When a computer is the **object of an attack**, it is the entity being attacked. Figure 1-6 illustrates computers as subject and object. There are also two types of attacks: **direct attacks** and **indirect attacks**. A direct attack is when a hacker uses his personal computer to break into a system. An indirect attack is when a system is compromised and used to attack other systems, such as in a distributed denial of service attack. Direct attacks originate from the threat itself. Indirect attacks originate from a system or resource that itself has been attacked, and is malfunctioning or working under the control of a threat. A computer can, therefore, be both the subject and object of an attack when, for example, it is first the object of an attack and then compromised and used to attack other systems, at which point it becomes the subject of an attack.

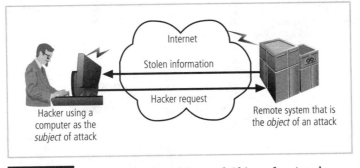

FIGURE 1-6   Computer as the Subject and Object of an Attack

Balancing Information Security and Access

Even with the best planning and implementation, it is impossible to obtain perfect information security. Recall James Anderson's statement at the beginning of this chapter. Information security cannot be an absolute: it is a process, not a goal. Information security should balance protection and availability. It is possible to allow a system to have unrestricted access, so that it is available to anyone, anywhere, anytime, through any means. However, this kind of access poses a danger to the integrity of the information. On the other hand, complete information security of an information system would not allow anyone access. For instance, to achieve the desired security certification, TCSEC C-2, for its Windows operating system, Microsoft had to remove all networking components and operate the computer solely in a secured room.[15]

To achieve balance—that is, to operate an information system to the satisfaction of the user and the security professional—the level of security must allow reasonable access, yet protect against threats. Figure 1-7 shows some of the competing voices that must be reconciled in the information security versus access balancing act.

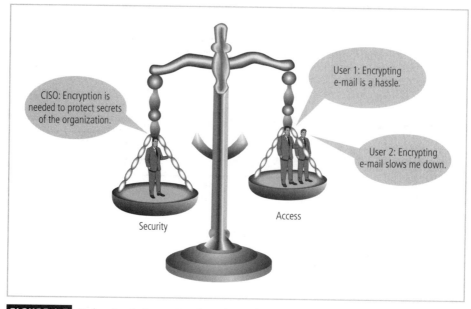

FIGURE 1-7   Balancing Information Security and Access

Because of today's security concerns and issues, an information system or data-processing department can get too entrenched in its responsibility to manage and protect systems. An imbalance can occur when the needs of the end user are undermined by too heavy a focus on protecting and administering the information systems. Both the information security technologists and end users must exercise patience and cooperation when interacting with each other, as both groups share the same overall goals of the organization—to ensure the data is available when, where, and how it is needed, with minimal delays or obstacles. In an ideal world, this level of availability is met even after concerns about loss, damage, interception, or destruction have been addressed.

Approaches to Information Security Implementation

The implementation of information security in an organization must begin somewhere. After all, the security of all systems does not magically appear overnight. Securing information assets is in fact an incremental process that requires coordination, time, and patience. Information security can begin as a grassroots effort in which systems administrators attempt to improve the security of their systems. This is often referred to as a **bottom-up approach**. The key advantage of the bottom-up approach is the technical expertise of the individual administrators. Working with information systems on a day-to-day basis, these administrators possess in-depth knowledge that can greatly enhance the development of an information security system. They know and understand the threats to their systems and the mechanisms needed to protect them successfully. Unfortunately, this approach seldom works, as it lacks a number of critical features, such as participant support and organizational staying power.

The approach that has a higher probability of success is called the **top-down approach**. In this approach, the project is initiated by upper-level managers who issue policy, procedures, and processes, dictate the goals and expected outcomes of the project, and determine who is accountable for each of the required actions. The top-down approach has strong upper-management support, a dedicated champion, usually dedicated funding, a clear planning and implementation process, and the means of influencing organizational culture. The most successful kind of top-down approach also involves a formal development strategy referred to as a systems development life cycle.

For any organization-wide effort to succeed, however, management must buy into and totally support it. The role played in this effort by the champion cannot be overstated. Typically, this champion is an executive, such as a chief information officer (CIO), or the vice president of information technology (VP-IT), who moves the project forward, ensures that it is properly managed, and pushes for acceptance throughout the organization. Without this high-level support, many of the mid-level administrators fail to make time for the project or dismiss it as a low priority. Also critical to the success of this type of project is the involvement and support of the end users. These individuals are most directly affected by the process and outcome of the project and must be included in the information security process. Key end users should be assigned to a developmental team, known as the joint application development team, or JAD. To succeed, the JAD must have staying power. It must be able to survive employee turnover and should not be vulnerable to changes in the personnel team that is developing the information security system. This means the processes and procedures must be documented and integrated into the organizational culture. They must be adopted *and promoted* by the organization's management.

The organizational hierarchy and the bottom-up and top-down approaches are illustrated in Figure 1-8.

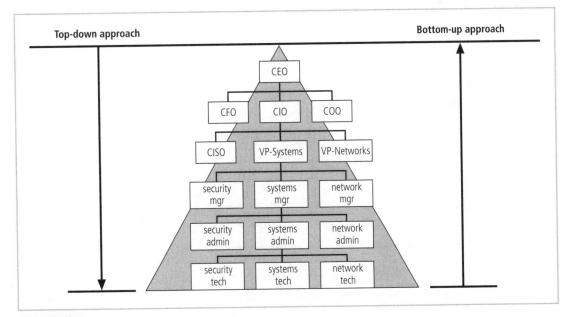

FIGURE 1-8 Approaches to Information Security Implementation

The Systems Development Life Cycle

Information security must be managed in a manner similar to any other major system implemented in an organization. One approach for implementing an information security system in an organization with little or no formal security in place is to use a variation of the systems development life cycle (SDLC): the security systems development life cycle (SecSDLC). To understand a *security* systems development life cycle, you must first review the basics of the method upon which it is based: the systems development life cycle.

Methodology

The **systems development life cycle (SDLC)** is a methodology for the design and implementation of an information system in an organization. A **methodology** is a formal approach to solving a problem based on a structured sequence of procedures. Using a methodology ensures a rigorous process and avoids missing those steps that can lead to compromising the end goal. The goal in this case is creating a comprehensive information security posture. A methodology also increases the probability of success. Once a methodology has been adopted, the key milestones are established and a team of individuals is selected and made accountable for accomplishing the project goals.

Phases

The traditional SDLC consists of six general phases. If you have taken a system analysis and design course, you may have been exposed to a model consisting of a different number of phases. The different variations of SDLC range from having three to twelve phases, all of which have been mapped into the six presented here. The **waterfall model** pictured in Figure 1-9 illustrates that each phase begins with the results and information gained from the previous phase.

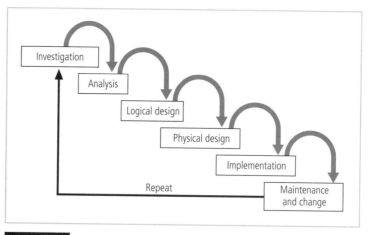

FIGURE 1-9   SDLC Waterfall Methodology

The process may be initiated in response to specific conditions or combinations of conditions. The impetus to begin any project may be event-driven—that is, started in response to some occurrence in the business community, inside the organization, or within the ranks of employees, customers, or other stakeholders. It may be plan-driven, or a result of a carefully developed implementation strategy. Either way, once the need for information security is recognized, the SDLC methodology ensures that development proceeds in an orderly, comprehensive fashion. At the end of each phase comes a structured review or reality check, during which the team determines if the project should be continued, discontinued, outsourced, or postponed, depending on the need for additional expertise, organizational knowledge, or resources.

The process begins with an investigation of the problem facing the organization, continues with an analysis of current organizational practices considered in the context of the investigation, and then proceeds to the logical and physical design phases. During the design phases, potential solutions are identified and are associated with evaluation criteria. In the implementation phase, solutions are evaluated, selected, and acquired through a make-or-buy process. These solutions, whether made or bought, are tested, installed, and tested again. Users of systems are trained and documentation developed. Finally, the system becomes mature and is maintained (and modified) over the remainder of its operational life. Any information systems implementation may have multiple iterations, as the cycle is repeated over time. Only through constant examination and renewal can any system, especially an information security program, perform up to expectations in the constantly changing environment in which it is placed. The following sections describe the activities of each phase of the traditional SDLC.[16]

Investigation

The first phase, investigation, is the most important. What problem is the system being developed to solve? The investigation phase begins with an examination of the event or plan that initiates the process. During the investigation phase, the objectives, constraints, and scope of the project are specified. A preliminary cost-benefit analysis is developed to evaluate the perceived benefits and the appropriate levels of cost for those benefits. At the conclusion of this phase, and at every phase following, a feasibility analysis is performed, which assesses the economic, technical, and behavioral feasibilities of the process and ensures that implementation is worth the organization's time and effort.

Analysis

The analysis phase begins with the information gained during the investigation phase. This phase consists primarily of assessments of the organization, the status of current systems, and the capability to support the proposed systems. Analysts begin by determining what the new system is expected to do, and how it will interact with existing systems. This phase ends with the documentation of the findings and an update of the feasibility analysis.

Logical Design

In the logical design phase, the information gained from the analysis phase is used to begin creating a systems solution for a business problem. In any systems solution, it is imperative that the first and driving factor is the business need. Then, based on the business need, applications are selected that are capable of providing needed services. Based on the applications needed, data support and structures capable of providing the needed inputs are then chosen. Finally, based on all of the above, specific technologies to implement the physical solution are delineated. The logical design is, therefore, the blueprint for the desired solution. This is discussed in greater detail in Chapter 5. The logical design is implementation independent, meaning that it contains no reference to specific technologies, vendors, or products. It addresses, instead, how the proposed system will solve the problem at hand. In this stage, analysts generate a number of alternative solutions, each with corresponding strengths and weaknesses, and costs and benefits, allowing for a general comparison of available options. At the end of this phase, another feasibility analysis is performed.

Physical Design

During the physical design phase, specific technologies are selected to support the alternatives identified and evaluated in the logical design. The selected components are evaluated based on a make-or-buy decision (develop the components in-house or purchase them from a vendor). Final designs integrate various components and technologies. After yet another feasibility analysis, the entire solution is presented to the organizational management for approval.

Implementation

In the implementation phase, any needed software is created. Components are ordered, received, and tested. Afterwards, users are trained and supporting documentation created. Once all components are tested individually, they are installed and tested as a system. Again a feasibility analysis is prepared, and the sponsors are then presented with the system for a performance review and acceptance test.

Maintenance and Change

The maintenance and change phase is the longest and most expensive phase of the process. This phase consists of the tasks necessary to support and modify the system for the remainder of its useful life cycle. Even though formal development may conclude during this phase, the life cycle of the project continues until it is determined that the process should begin again from the investigation phase. At periodic points, the system is tested for compliance, and the feasibility of continuance versus discontinuance is evaluated. Upgrades, updates, and patches are managed. As the needs of the organization change, the systems that support the organization must also change. It is imperative that those who manage the systems, as well as those who support them, continually monitor the effectiveness of the systems in relation to the organization's environment. When a current system can no longer support the evolving mission of the organization, the project is terminated and a new project is implemented.

The Security Systems Development Life Cycle

The same phases used in the traditional SDLC can be adapted to support the implementation of an information security project. While the two processes may differ in intent and specific activities, the overall methodology is the same. At its heart, implementing information security involves identifying specific threats and creating specific controls to counter those threats. The SecSDLC unifies this process and makes it a coherent program rather than a series of random, seemingly unconnected actions. (Other organizations use a risk management approach to implement information security systems. This approach is discussed in later chapters.)

Investigation

The investigation phase of the SecSDLC begins with a directive from upper management, dictating the process, outcomes, and goals of the project, as well as its budget and other constraints. Frequently, this phase begins with an **enterprise information security policy**, which outlines the implementation of a security program within the organization. Teams of responsible managers, employees, and contractors are organized; problems are analyzed; and the scope of the project, as well as specific goals and objectives, and any additional constraints not covered in the program policy, are defined. Finally, an organizational feasibility analysis is performed to determine whether the organization has the resources and commitment necessary to conduct a successful security analysis and design.

Analysis

In the analysis phase, the documents from the investigation phase are studied. The development team conducts a preliminary analysis of existing security policies or programs, along with that of documented current threats and associated controls. This phase also includes an analysis of relevant legal issues that could affect the design of the security solution. Increasingly, privacy laws have become a major consideration when making decisions about information systems that manage personal information. Recently, many states have implemented legislation making certain computer-related activities illegal. A detailed understanding of these issues is vital. The risk management task also begins in this stage. **Risk management** is the process of identifying, assessing, and evaluating the levels of risk facing the organization, specifically the threats to the organization's security and to the information stored and processed by the organization.

Logical Design

The logical design phase creates and develops the blueprints for information security, and examines and implements key policies that influence later decisions. Also at this stage, the team plans the incident response actions to be taken in the event of partial or catastrophic loss. The planning answers the following questions:

- Continuity planning: How will business continue in the event of a loss?
- Incident response: What steps are taken when an attack occurs?
- Disaster recovery: What must be done to recover information and vital systems immediately after a disastrous event?

Next, a feasibility analysis determines whether or not the project should be continued or be outsourced.

Physical Design

In the physical design phase, the information security technology needed to support the blueprint outlined in the logical design is evaluated, alternative solutions generated, and a final design agreed upon. The information security blueprint may be revisited to keep it in line with the changes needed when the physical design is completed. Criteria for determining the definition of successful solutions are also prepared during this phase. Included at this time are the designs for physical security measures to support the proposed technological solutions. At the end of this phase, a feasibility study should determine the readiness of the organization for the proposed project, and then the champion and sponsors are presented with the design. At this time, all parties involved have a chance to approve the project before implementation begins.

Implementation

The implementation phase in of SecSDLC is also similar to that of the traditional SDLC. The security solutions are acquired (made or bought), tested, implemented, and tested again. Personnel issues are evaluated, and specific training and education programs conducted. Finally, the entire tested package is presented to upper management for final approval.

Maintenance and Change

The maintenance and change phase, though last, is perhaps most important, given the current ever-changing threat environment. Today's information security systems need constant monitoring, testing, modification, updating, and repairing. Traditional applications systems developed within the framework of the traditional SDLC are not designed to anticipate a vicious attack that would require some degree of application reconstruction. In information security, the battle for stable, reliable systems is a defensive one. Often, repairing damage and restoring information is a constant effort against an unseen adversary. As new threats emerge and old threats evolve, the information security profile of an organization requires constant adaptation to prevent threats from successfully penetrating sensitive data. This constant vigilance and security can be compared to that of a fortress where threats from outside as well as from within must be constantly monitored and checked with continuously new and more innovative technologies.

Table 1-2 summarizes the steps performed in both the systems development life cycle and the security systems development life cycle. Since the security systems development life cycle is based on the systems development life cycle, the steps in the cycles are similar, and thus those common to both cycles are outlined in column 2. Column 3 shows the steps unique to the security systems development life cycle that are performed in each phase.

TABLE 1-2 SDLC and SecSDLC Phase Summary

Phases	Steps common to both the systems development life cycle and the security systems development life cycle	Steps unique to the security systems development life cycle
Phase 1: Investigation	<ul><li>Outline project scope and goals</li><li>Estimate costs</li><li>Evaluate existing resources</li><li>Analyze feasibility</li></ul>	<ul><li>Management defines project processes and goals and documents these in the program security policy</li></ul>
Phase 2: Analysis	<ul><li>Assess current system against plan developed in Phase 1</li><li>Develop preliminary system requirements</li><li>Study integration of new system with existing system</li><li>Document findings and update feasibility analysis</li></ul>	<ul><li>Analyze existing security policies and programs</li><li>Analyze current threats and controls</li><li>Examine legal issues</li><li>Perform risk analysis</li></ul>
Phase 3: Logical Design	<ul><li>Assess current business needs against plan developed in Phase 2</li><li>Select applications, data support, and structures</li><li>Generate multiple solutions for consideration</li><li>Document findings and update feasibility analysis</li></ul>	<ul><li>Develop security blueprint</li><li>Plan incident response actions</li><li>Plan business response to disaster</li><li>Determine feasibility of continuing and/or outsourcing the project</li></ul>
Phase 4: Physical Design	<ul><li>Select technologies to support solutions developed in Phase 3</li><li>Select the best solution</li><li>Decide to make or buy components</li><li>Document findings and update feasibility analysis</li></ul>	<ul><li>Select technologies needed to support security blueprint</li><li>Develop definition of successful solution</li><li>Design physical security measures to support technological solutions</li><li>Review and approve project</li></ul>
Phase 5: Implementation	<ul><li>Develop or buy software</li><li>Order components</li><li>Document the system</li><li>Train users</li><li>Update feasibility analysis</li><li>Present system to users</li><li>Test system and review performance</li></ul>	<ul><li>Buy or develop security solutions</li><li>At end of phase, present tested package to management for approval</li></ul>
Phase 6: Maintenance	<ul><li>Support and modify system during its useful life</li><li>Test periodically for compliance with business needs</li><li>Upgrade and patch as necessary</li></ul>	<ul><li>Constantly monitor, test, modify, update, and repair to meet changing threats</li></ul>

Security Professionals and the Organization

It takes a wide range of professionals to support a diverse information security program. As noted earlier in this chapter, information security must be initiated from the top down. Senior management is the key component and the vital force for a successful implementation of an information security program. But administrative support is also needed to develop and execute specific security policies and procedures, and technical expertise is necessary of course, to implement the details of the information security program. The following sections describe the information security roles of various professionals in a typical organization.

Senior Management

Chief information officer: The senior technology officer is typically the **chief information officer (CIO)**, although other titles such as vice president of information, VP of information technology, and VP of systems may be used. The CIO is primarily responsible for advising the chief executive officer, president, or company owner on the strategic planning that affects the management of information in the organization. The CIO translates the strategic plans of the organization as a whole into strategic information plans for the Information Systems or Data Processing Division of the organization. Once this is accomplished, CIOs work with subordinate managers to develop tactical and operational plans for the division and to enable planning and management of the systems that support the organization.

Chief information security officer: The **chief information security officer (CISO)** is the individual primarily responsible for the assessment, management, and implementation of information security in the organization. The CISO may also be referred to as the manager for IT security, the security administrator, or a similar title. The CISO usually reports directly to the CIO, although in larger organizations it is not uncommon for one or more layers of management to exist between the two. However, the recommendations of the CISO to the CIO should not be subordinated to less important issues. The CISO's recommendations are as important as, if not more important than, other technology and information-related decisions. The placement of the CISO and supporting security staff in organizational hierarchies is the subject of current debate across the industry.[17]

Information Security Project Team

Information security is a field with a vast array of technical and nontechnical requirements. The **project team** should consist of a number of individuals who are experienced in one or multiple facets of the technical and nontechnical areas. Many of the same skills needed to manage and implement security are also needed to design it. Members of the security project team fill the following roles:

- **Champion:** A senior executive who, as indicated earlier, promotes the project and ensures its support, both financially and administratively, at the highest levels of the organization.
- **Team leader:** A project manager, who may be a departmental line manager or staff unit manager, who understands project management, personnel management, and information security technical requirements.

- **Security policy developers:** Individuals who understand the organizational culture, existing policies, and requirements for developing and implementing successful policies.
- **Risk assessment specialists:** Individuals who understand financial risk assessment techniques, the value of organizational assets, and the security methods to be used.
- **Security professionals:** Dedicated, trained, and well-educated specialists in all aspects of information security from both a technical and nontechnical standpoint.
- **Systems administrators:** Individuals with the primary responsibility for administering the systems that house the information used by the organization.
- **End users:** Those whom the new system will most directly affect. Ideally, a selection of users from various departments, levels, and degrees of technical knowledge assist the team in focusing on the application of realistic controls applied in ways that do not disrupt the essential business activities they seek to safeguard.

Data Ownership

Three types of data ownership and their respective responsibilities are outlined below:

- **Data owners:** Those responsible for the security and use of a particular set of information. They are usually members of senior management and could be CIOs. The data owners usually determine the level of data classification (discussed later) associated with the data, as well as the changes to that classification required by organizational change. The data owners work with subordinate managers to oversee the day-to-day administration of the data.
- **Data custodians:** Working directly with data owners, data custodians are responsible for the storage, maintenance, and protection of the information. Depending on the size of the organization, this may be a dedicated position, such as the CISO, or it may be an additional responsibility of a systems administrator or other technology manager. The duties of a data custodian often include overseeing data storage and backups, implementing the specific procedures and policies laid out in the security policies and plans, and reporting to the data owner.
- **Data users:** End users who work with the information to perform their daily jobs supporting the mission of the organization. Everyone in the organization is responsible for the security of data, so data users are included here as individuals with an information security role.

Communities of Interest

Each organization develops and maintains its own unique culture and values. Within that **organizational culture**, there are communities of interest. As defined here, a **community of interest** is a group of individuals who are united by similar interests or values within an organization and who share a common goal of making the organization function to meet its objectives. This book identifies three communities of interest that have roles and responsibilities in information security. In theory each role must complement the other; in practice, this is often not the case.

Information Security Management and Professionals

The roles of the information security professionals as described above are aligned with the goals and mission of the information security community of interest. These job functions and organizational roles focus on protecting the organization's information systems and stored information from attacks.

Information Technology Management and Professionals

Others in the organization are oriented to deliver value to the organization by designing, building, or operating information systems. This community of interest is made up of IT managers and various groups of skilled professionals in systems design, programming, networks, and other related disciplines usually categorized as IT, or information technology. This community has many of the same objectives as the information security community. Its members focus, however, more on costs of system creation and operation, ease of use for system users, timeliness of system creation, as well as transaction response time. The goals of the IT community and the information security community are not always in complete alignment, and depending on the organizational structure, this may cause conflict.

Organizational Management and Professionals

The organization's general management team and the rest of the resources in the organization make up the other major community of interest. This large group is almost always made up of subsets of other interests as well, including executive management, production management, human resources, accounting, and legal, to name just a few. The IT community often categorizes these groups as users of information technology systems, while the information security community categorizes them as security subjects. In fact, this community serves as the greatest reminder that all IT systems and information security objectives are created to implement the objectives of the broader organizational community and safeguard their effective use and operation. The most efficient IT systems operated in the most secure fashion ever devised are of no significance if they do not bring value to the broad objectives of the organization as a whole.

Information Security: Is it an Art or a Science?

Given the level of complexity in today's information systems, the implementation of information security has often been described as a combination of art and science. It is not difficult to see how this perspective has evolved along with the concept of the information security community of interest. The concept of the *security artesan*[18] is based on the way individuals have perceived systems technologists since computers became commonplace. Those with the gift for managing and operating computers and computer-based systems have long been suspected of using more than a little magic to keep the systems running and functioning as expected. Everyone who has studied computer systems can appreciate the anxiety most people feel when faced with complex technology. Consider the inner workings of the computer: with the mind-boggling functions of the transistors in a CPU, the interaction of various capacitors, and the memory storage units on the circuit boards, it's a miracle these things work at all.

Security as Art

The security administrators and technicians who implement security can be compared with a painter applying oils to canvas. A touch of color here, a brush stroke there, just enough to represent the image the artist wants to convey without overwhelming the viewer, or in security terms, without overly restricting user access. There are no hard and fast rules regulating the installation of various security mechanisms, nor are there many universally accepted complete solutions. While there are many manuals to support individual systems, once these systems are interconnected, there is no manual for implementing security throughout the entire system. This is especially true with the complex levels of interaction between users, policy, and technology controls.

Security as Science

Technology developed by computer scientists and engineers—technology designed to perform at rigorous levels of performance—makes information security a science as well as an art. With the complexity of the technology, most scientists agree that specific scientific conditions cause virtually all actions in computer systems. Almost every fault, security hole, and systems malfunction is a result of the interaction of specific hardware and software. If the developers had sufficient time, they could resolve and eliminate these faults.

The faults that remain are usually the result of technology malfunctioning for any one of a thousand possible reasons. There are many sources of recognized and approved security methods and techniques that provide sound technical security advise. Best practices, standards of due care, and other tried-and-true methods can minimize the level of guesswork necessary to secure an organization's information and systems.

Security as a Social Science

There is a third view to consider when examining information security: security as social science. This view integrates some of the components of art and science, and adds another dimension to the discussion. Social science examines the behavior of individuals as they interact with systems, whether these are societal systems or, as in this context, information systems. Information security begins and ends with the people inside the organization and the people that interact with the system, intentionally or otherwise. End users who need the very information the security personnel are trying to protect may be the weakest link in the security chain. By understanding some of the behavioral aspects of organizational science and change management, security administrators can greatly reduce the levels of risk caused by end users, and create more acceptable and supportable security profiles. These measures, coupled with appropriate policy and training issues, can substantially improve the performance of end users and result in a more secure information system.

Information Security Terminology

Throughout this chapter and the rest of the textbook, a number of key terms are used that require careful attention.

- Access: A subject or object's ability to use, manipulate, modify, or affect another subject or object is referred to as **access**. Authorized users have legal access to a system, whereas hackers have illegal access to a system.

- Asset: An **asset** is the organizational resource that is being protected. An asset can be logical, such as a Web site, information, or data; or an asset can be physical, such as a person, computer system, or other tangible object. Assets, and particularly information assets, are the focus of security efforts and are what is being protected.

- Attack: An **attack** is an intentional or unintentional attempt to cause damage to or otherwise compromise the information and/or the systems that support it. If someone casually reads sensitive information not intended for his or her use, this is considered a passive attack. If a hacker attempts to break into an information system, the attack is considered active. If a lightning strike causes a fire in a building, the attack is unintentional.

- Control, safeguard, or countermeasure: These terms, all synonymous with **control,** represent security mechanisms, policies, or procedures that can successfully counter attacks, reduce risk, resolve vulnerabilities, and otherwise improve the security within an organization. The various levels and types of controls are discussed more fully in the following chapters.

- Exploit: There are two common uses of this term in security. First, hackers may attempt to exploit a system or information by using it illegally for their personal gains. Second, an **exploit** can be a targeted solution to misuse a specific hole or vulnerability, usually in software, that a hacker creates to formulate an attack. In this regard, an exploit is either the attempt to take advantage of a known vulnerability or weakness, or it is a method for taking advantage of a known vulnerability or weakness. In security, the latter is the more common usage.

- Exposure: The **exposure** of an information system is a single instance when the system is open to damage. Vulnerabilities can cause an exposure to potential damage or attack from a threat. Total exposure is the degree to which an organization's assets are at risk of attack from a threat. Total exposure is sometimes quantified in dollars by applying a formula based on the value of the asset, the likelihood of the loss (the risk), and the number of exposures. This term is sometimes used as a summation measure of risk across various areas of security in an organization.

- Hacking: **Hacking** can be defined positively and negatively: "1) to write computer programs for enjoyment, 2) to gain access to a computer illegally."[19] In the early days of computing, computer enthusiasts were called hacks, or hackers, because they could tear apart the computer instruction code, or even the computer itself, to manipulate its output. The term hacker at one time expressed respect for another's ability to make computing technology work as desired in the face of adversity. In recent years, the association with an illegal activity has negatively tinged the term.

- Object: An **object** is a *passive* entity in the information system that receives or contains information. Objects are assigned specific controls that restrict or prevent access by unauthorized subjects. Examples include printers, servers, databases, or any other shared resource.

- Risk: **Risk** is the probability that something can happen. In information security, it could be the probability of a threat to a system, the probability of a vulnerability being discovered, or the probability of equipment or software malfunctioning. Risk can be measured in quantitative terms, as in "a 25% chance of attack," or in qualitative terms, as in "a low probability of malfunction."

- Security blueprint: The **security blueprint** is the plan for the implementation of new security measures in the organization. Sometimes called a framework, the blueprint presents an organized approach to the security planning process. The security blueprint is the most significant work produced during the design phases of the SecS-DLC. See Chapter 5, "Planning for Security," for further information on the security blueprint.

- Security model: A **security model** is a collection of specific security rules that represents the implementation of a security policy. Some recognized security models are examined in later chapters.

- Security posture or security profile: The **security posture** or **profile** refers to the implementation of security in organization. It is a general label for the combination of all policy, procedures, technology, and programs that make up the total security effort currently in place and is sometimes called the information security program.

- Subject: A **subject** is an *active* entity that interacts with an information system and causes information to move through the system for a specific purpose. A subject can be an individual, technical component, or computer process. Users, servers, and threads are examples of subjects.

- Threats: A **threat** is a category of objects, persons, or other entities that pose a potential danger to an asset. Threats are always present. Some threats manifest themselves in accidental occurrences, while others are purposeful. For example, all hackers represent a potential danger or threat to an unprotected information system. Severe storms are also a threat to buildings and their contents.

- Threat agent: A **threat agent** is the specific instance or component of a threat. For example, you can think of all hackers in the world as a collective threat, and Kevin Mitnick, who was convicted for hacking into phone systems, as a specific threat agent. Likewise, a specific lightning strike, hailstorm, or tornado is a threat agent that is part of the threat of severe storms.

- Vulnerability: Weaknesses or faults in a system or protection mechanism that expose information to attack or damage are known as **vulnerabilities**. They can range from a flaw in a software package, to an unprotected system port or an unlocked door. Vulnerabilities that have been examined, documented, and published are referred to as **well-known vulnerabilities**.

Chapter Summary

- Information security evolved from the early field of computer security.

- Security is the protection from danger. There are a number of types of security: physical security, personal security, operations security, communications security, national security, and network security, to name a few.

- Information security is the protection of information assets that use, store, or transmit that information from the risk of loss through the application of policy, education, and technology.

- The confidentiality, integrity, and availability of information, also known as the C.I.A. triangle, must be protected at all times; this protection is implemented by multiple measures (policies, education training and awareness, and technology).

- Information systems are made up of six major components: hardware, software, data, people, procedures, and networks.

- Upper management drives the top-down approach to security implementation, in contrast with the bottom-up approach or grassroots effort, whereby each individual chooses security implementation strategies.

- The traditional systems development life cycle (SDLC) is an approach to implementing a system in an organization and has been adapted to provide the outline of a security systems development life cycle (SecSDLC).

- Information security has been described as both an art and a science, and also comprises many aspects of social science.

Review Questions

1. What is the difference between a threat agent and a threat?
2. What is the difference between vulnerability and exposure?
3. How has the definition of "hack" evolved over the last 30 years?
4. What type of security was dominant in the early years of computing?
5. What are the three components of the C.I.A. triangle? What are they used for?
6. If the C.I.A. triangle is incomplete, why is it so commonly used in security?
7. Describe the critical characteristics of information. How are they used in the study of computer security?
8. Identify the five components of an information system. Which are most directly impacted by the study of computer security? Which are most commonly associated with its study?
9. In the history of the study of computer security, what system is the father of almost all modern multiuser systems?
10. What paper is the foundation of all subsequent studies of computer security?
11. How is the top-down approach to information security superior to the bottom-up approach?
12. Why is a methodology important in the implementation of information security? How does a methodology improve the process?
13. Who is involved in the security development life cycle? Who leads the process?

14. How does the practice of information security qualify as both an art and a science? How does security as a social science influence its practice?

15. Who is ultimately responsible for the security of information in the organization?

16. What is the relationship between the MULTICS project and early development of computer security?

17. How has computer security evolved into modern information security?

18. What was important about Rand Report R-609?

19. What does it mean to discover an exploit? How does an exploit differ from a vulnerability?

20. Who should lead a security team? Should the approach to security be more managerial or technical?

Exercises

1. Look up "the paper that started the study of computer security." Prepare a summary of the key points. What in this paper specifically addresses security in areas previously unexamined?

2. Assume that a security model is needed for the protection of information in your class. Using the NSTISSC model, examine each of the cells and write a brief statement on how you would address the three components represented in that cell.

3. Consider the information stored on your personal computer. For each of the terms listed, find an example and document it: threat, threat agent, vulnerability, exposure, risk, attack, and exploit.

4. Using the Web, identify the chief information officer, chief information security officer, and systems administrator for your school. Which of these individuals represents the data owner? Data custodian?

5. Using the Web, find out who Kevin Mitnick was. What did he do? Who caught him? Write a short summary of his activities and why he is infamous.

Case Exercises

The next day at SLS found everyone in technical support busy restoring computer systems to their former state and installing new virus and worm control software. Amy found herself learning how to install desktop computer operating systems and applications as SLS made a heroic effort to recover from the attack of the previous day.

Questions:

1. Do you think this event was caused by an insider or outsider? Why do you think this?

2. Other than installing virus and worm control software, what can SLS do to be ready for the next incident?

3. Do you think this attack was the result of a virus, or a worm? Why do you think this?

Endnotes

1. NSA. "The Enigma" [Cited 8 Feb, 2004]. Available from the World Wide Web *<http://www.nsa.gov/museum/enigma.html>*.

2. Peter Salus. "Net Insecurity: Then and Now (1969-1998)." *Sane '98 Online.* 19 November 1998. [Cited 8 February 2004]. Available from the World Wide Web *<http://www.nluug.nl/events/sane98/aftermath/salus.html>*.

3. Roberts, Larry. "Program Plan for the ARPANET" [Cited 8 Feb 2004]. Available from the World Wide Web *<http://www.ziplink.net/%7Elroberts/SIGCOMM99_files/frame.htm>*.

4. Roberts, Larry. "Program Plan for the ARPANET" [Cited 8 Feb 2004]. Available from the World Wide Web. *<http://www.ziplink.net/%7Elroberts/SIGCOMM99_files/frame.htm>*.

5. *Preliminary Notes on the Design of Secure Military Computer Systems*, (Jan. 1973), by Roger R. Schell, Peter J. Downey, and Gerald J. Popek, file, MCI-73-1, ESD/AFSC, Hanscom AFB, Bedford, MA 01731.

6. *Protection Analysis: Final Report*, (May 1978), by Richard Bisbey II and Dennis Hollingworth, final report, ISI/SR-78-13, USC/Information Sciences Institute, Marina Del Rey, CA 90291.

7. F. T. Grampp and R. H. Morris, "UNIX Operating System Security," *AT&T Bell Laboratories Technical Journal* 63, no. 8 (1984): 1649-1672.

8. *Net Insecurity: Then and Now (1969-1998)*.

9. Willis Ware. "Security Controls for Computer Systems: Report of Defense Science Board Task Force on Computer Security." *Rand Online.* 10 October 1979. [Cited 8 February 2004]. Available from the World Wide Web *<http://www.rand.org/publications/R/R609.1/R609.1.html>*.

10. Willis Ware. "Security Controls for Computer Systems: Report of Defense Science Board Task Force on Computer Security." *Rand Online.* 10 October 1979. [Cited 8 February 2004]. Available from the World Wide Web *<http://www.rand.org/publications/R/R609.1/R609.1.html>*.

11. Merriam-Webster. "security." *Merriam-Webster Online.* [Cited 8 February 2004]. Available from the World Wide Web *<http://www.m-w.com>*.

12. National Security Telecommunications and Information Systems Security, *National Training Standard for Information Systems Security (Infosec) Professionals*, 20 June 1994, file, 4011, [Cited 8 Feb 2004]. Available from the World Wide Web *<http://www.nstissc.gov/Assets/pdf/4011.pdf>*.

13. Julekha Dash, "ACLU Knocks Eli Lilly for Divulging E-Mail Addresses," *Computerworld* 35, no. 28 (9 July 2001): 6.

14. CyberCrime Staff, "FDA Flub." TechTV. [Cited 8 February 2004]. Available from the World Wide Web *<http://www.techtv.com/cybercrime/features/story/0,23008,3398433,00.html>*.

15. Microsoft. "C2 Evaluation and Certification for Windows NT (Q93662)." *Microsoft Online.* 26 November 2001. [Cited 8 February 2004]. Available from the World Wide Web *< http://support.microsoft.com/default.aspx?scid=kb;en-us;93362 >*.

16. Adapted from Sandra D. Dewitz, *Systems Analysis and Design and the Transition to Objects* (New York: McGraw Hill Publishers, 1996), 94.

17. Mary Hayes, "Where The Chief Security Officer Belongs," *InformationWeek*, no. 877 (Feb 25, 2002): 38.

18. D. B. Parker, *Fighting Computer Crime* (New York: Wiley Publishing, 1998), 189.

19. Merriam-Webster. "hack." *Merriam-Webster Online.* [Cited 8 February 2004]. Available from the World Wide Web *<http://www.m-w.com/>*.

The Need for Security

> Our bad neighbor makes us early stirrers,
> Which is both healthful and good husbandry.
>
> **WILLIAM SHAKESPEARE (1564–1616),**
> **KING HENRY, IN HENRY V, ACT 4, SC. 1, L. 6-7.**

FRED CHIN, CEO OF SEQUENTIAL LABEL AND SUPPLY, LEANED BACK in his leather chair. He propped his feet up on the long mahogany table in the conference room where the SLS Board of Directors had just adjourned their quarterly meeting.

"What do you think about our computer security problem?" he asked Gladys Williams, the company's chief information officer, or CIO. He was referring to last month's outbreak of a malicious worm on the company's computer network.

Gladys replied, "I think we have a real problem this time, and we need to put together a real solution, not just a quick patch like the last time." Eighteen months ago someone had brought an infected floppy disk in from home and infected the network. To prevent this from happening again, all the floppy drives were removed from the company computers.

Fred wasn't convinced. "Let's just add another thousand dollars in the next training budget to fix it up."

Gladys shook her head. "You've known for some time now that this business runs on technology. That's why you hired me as CIO. I've been researching information security, and my staff and I have some ideas to discuss with you. I've asked Charlie Moody to come in today to talk about it. He's waiting to speak with us."

Charlie joined the meeting. Fred said, "Hello, Charlie. As you know the Board of Directors met today. They received a report on the expenses and lost production from the virus outbreak last month, and they directed us to improve the security of our technology. Gladys says you can help me understand what we need to do about it."

"To start with," Charlie said, "instead of setting up a computer security solution, we need to develop an information security program. We need a thorough review of our policies and practices, and we need to establish an ongoing risk management program. There are some other things that are part of the process as well, but these would be a good start."

"Sounds expensive," said Fred.

Charlie looked at Gladys, then answered, "Well, there will be some extra expenses for specific controls and software tools, and we may have to slow down our product development projects a bit, but the program will be more of a change in our attitude about security than a spending spree. I don't have accurate estimates yet, but you can be sure we will put cost-benefit worksheets in front of you before we spend any money."

Fred thought about this for a few seconds. "OK. What is our next step?"

Gladys answered, "To start with, we need to initiate a project plan to develop our new information security program. We'll use our usual systems development and project management approach. There are a few differences, but we can adapt our current models easily. We will need to appoint or hire a person to be responsible for information security."

"Information security? What about computer security?" asked Fred.

Charlie responded, "Information security includes all the things we use to do business: software, procedures, data, networks, our staff, and computers."

"I see," Fred said. "Bring me the draft project plan and budget in two weeks. The audit committee of the board meets in four weeks, and we'll need to report our progress."

LEARNING OBJECTIVES:

Upon completion of this material, you should be able to:

- Understand the business need for information security
- Understand that a successful information security program is the responsibility of both an organization's general management and IT management
- Identify the threats posed to information security and the more common attacks associated with those threats
- Differentiate *threats* to the information within systems from *attacks* against the information within systems

Introduction

Unlike any other aspect of information technology, information security's primary mission is to ensure that systems and their contents remain the same. Organizations spend hundreds of thousands of dollars and expend thousands of man-hours to maintain their information systems. If threats to information and systems didn't exist, this energy could be channeled towards improving the systems that support the information. However, attacks on information systems are a daily occurrence, and the need for information security increases as the sophistication of such attacks increase.

Organizations must, therefore, understand the environment in which information security operates and the problems it must address. This chapter examines this environment and identifies the threats it poses to organizations and their information.

Business Needs First

Information security performs four important functions for an organization:

1. Protects the organization's ability to function
2. Enables the safe operation of applications implemented on the organization's IT systems
3. Protects the data the organization collects and uses
4. Safeguards the technology assets in use at the organization

Protecting the Functionality of an Organization

Both general management and IT management are responsible for implementing information security that protects the organization's ability to function. Decision makers in organizations must set policy and operate their organizations in compliance with the complex, shifting legislation that controls the use of technology. Although many business and government managers shy away from addressing information security because they perceive it to be a technically complex task, in fact implementing information security has more to do with *management* than with *technology*. Just as managing payroll has more to do with management than with mathematical wage computations, managing information security has more to do with policy and its enforcement than with the technology of its implementation. As the noted information security author Charles Cresson Wood has stated,

> "In fact, a lot of [information security] is good management for information technology. Many people think that a solution to a technology problem is more technology. Well, not necessarily… So a lot of my work, out of necessity, has been trying to get my clients to pay more attention to information security as a management issue in addition to a technical issue, information security as a people issue in addition to the technical issue."[1]

To address information security needs, each of the organization's communities of interest must address information security in terms of business impact and the cost of business interruption, rather than focusing on security as a technical problem.

Enabling the Safe Operation of Applications

Today's organizations are under immense pressure to acquire and operate integrated, efficient, and capable applications. The modern organization needs to create an environment that safeguards applications using the organization's IT systems, particularly those applications that serve as important elements of the infrastructure of the organization—operating system platforms, electronic mail (e-mail), and instant messaging (IM) applications. Organizations acquire these elements either by outsourcing from a service provider or by building their own. Once an organization's infrastructure is in place, management must continue to oversee it, and not abdicate the responsibility for the entire infrastructure to the IT department.

Protecting Data that Organizations Collect and Use

Without data, an organization loses its record of transactions and/or its ability to deliver value to its customers. Any business, educational institution, or government agency that functions within the modern context of connected and responsive services relies on information systems to support these transactions. Even if the transaction is not online, information systems and the data they process enable the creation and movement of goods and services. Therefore, protecting *data in motion* and *data at rest* are both critical aspects of information security. The value of data motivates attackers to steal, sabotage, or corrupt it. An effective information security program implemented by management is essential to the protection of the integrity and value of the organization's data.

Safeguarding Technology Assets in Organizations

To perform effectively, organizations must add secure infrastructure services based on the size and scope of the enterprise. For instance, a small business may get by with using an e-mail service provided by an ISP and augmented with a personal encryption tool. When an organization grows, it must develop additional security services. For example, organizational growth could lead to the need for Public Key Infrastructure (PKI), an integrated system of software, encryption methodologies, and legal agreements that can be used to support the entire information infrastructure of an organization.

Chapter 8 describes PKI in more detail, but for now know that PKI involves the use of digital certificates to ensure the confidentiality of Internet communications and transactions. Into each of these digital certificates, a certificate authority embeds an individual's or an organization's public encryption key, along with other identifying information, and then cryptographically signs the certificate with a tamper-proof seal, thus verifying the integrity of the data within the certificate and validating its use.

In general, as the organization's network grows to accommodate changing needs, more robust technology solutions may be needed to replace security programs the organization has outgrown. An example of a robust solution is a firewall, a device that keeps certain kinds of network traffic out of a private network. Another example is caching network appliances, which are devices that store local copies of Internet content, such as Web pages that are frequently referred to by employees. The appliance displays the cached pages to users, rather than accessing the pages from the server each time.

Threats

Around 500 B.C., the Chinese general Sun Tzu Wu wrote *Art of War*, a war treatise that emphasizes the importance of knowing yourself as well as the threats you face[2]. To protect an organization's information, you must, 1) know yourself; that is, be familiar with the information to be protected, and the systems that store, transport, and process it; and 2) know the threats you face. To make sound decisions about information security, management must be informed about the various threats facing the organization, its people, applications, data, and information systems—that is, the enemy. In the context of information security, a **threat** is an object, person, or other entity that represents a constant danger to an asset.

To understand the wide range of threats that pervade the interconnected world, researchers have interviewed practicing information security personnel and examined information security literature on threats. While the categorizations may vary, threats are relatively well researched and, consequently, fairly well understood.

The 2004 Computer Security Institute/Federal Bureau of Investigation (CSI/FBI) Computer Crime and Security Survey is a representative study. The CSI/FBI study found that 79 percent of the organizations responding (primarily large corporations and government agencies) identified cyber security breaches within the last 12 months, a number that is on the decline. The study also found that 54 percent of these organizations reported financial losses, totaling over $141 million, due to computer security breaches. The number of respondents identifying unauthorized computer use was 53 percent, down from 56 percent in 2003.[3]

The categorization scheme shown in Table 2-1 consists of 12 general categories that represent a clear and present danger to an organization's people, information, and systems.[4] Each organization must prioritize the threats it faces, based on the particular security situation in which it operates, its organizational strategy regarding risk, and the exposure levels in which its assets operate. Chapter 4 covers these topics in more detail. Upon reviewing the right-hand column of Table 2-1, you may observe that many of the examples of threats (i.e., acts or failures) could be listed in more than one category. For example, an act of theft performed by a hacker falls into the category of deliberate acts of theft, but is also often accompanied by defacement actions to delay discovery and thus may also be placed within the category of deliberate acts of sabotage or vandalism.

Table 2-1 Threats to Information Security[5]

Categories of Threat	Examples
1. Acts of human error or failure	Accidents, employee mistakes
2. Compromises to intellectual property	Piracy, copyright infringement
3. Deliberate acts of espionage or trespass	Unauthorized access and/or data collection
4. Deliberate acts of information extortion	Blackmail or information disclosure
5. Deliberate acts of sabotage or vandalism	Destruction of systems or information
6. Deliberate acts of theft	Illegal confiscation of equipment or information
7. Deliberate software attacks	Viruses, worms, macros, denial-of-service
8. Forces of nature	Fire, flood, earthquake, lightning
9. Deviations in quality of service	ISP, power, or WAN service issues from service providers
10. Technical hardware failures or errors	Equipment failure
11. Technical software failures or errors	Bugs, code problems, unknown loopholes
12. Technological obsolescence	Antiquated or outdated technologies

Acts of Human Error or Failure

This category includes acts performed without intent or malicious purpose by an authorized user. When people use information systems, sometimes mistakes happen. Inexperience, improper training, and the making of incorrect assumptions are just a few circumstances that can cause these misadventures. Regardless of the cause, even innocuous and seemingly harmless mistakes can produce extensive damage with catastrophic results. For example, a simple keyboarding error can, as described below, cause worldwide Internet outages.

> In April 1997, the core of the Internet suffered a disaster. Internet service providers lost connectivity with other ISPs due to an error in a routine Internet router-table update process. The resulting outage effectively shut down a major portion of the Internet for at least twenty minutes. It has been estimated that about 45 percent of Internet users were affected. In July 1997, the Internet went through yet another more critical global shutdown for millions of users. An accidental upload of a corrupt database to the Internet's root domain servers occurred. Since this provides the ability to address hosts on the net by name (i.e., eds.com), it was impossible to send e-mail or access Web sites within the .com and .net domains for several hours. The .com domain comprises a majority of the commercial enterprise users of the Internet.[6]

One of the greatest threats to an organization's information security is the organization's own employees. Employees are the threat-agents closest to the organizational data. Because employees use data in everyday activities to conduct the organization's business, their mistakes represent a serious threat to the confidentiality, integrity, and availability of data—even, as Figure 2-1 suggests, relative to threats from outsiders. This is because employee mistakes can easily lead to the following: revelation of classified data, entry of erroneous data, accidental deletion or modification of data, storage of data in unprotected areas, and failure to protect information. Leaving classified information in unprotected areas, such as a desktop, Web site, or even the trash can, is as much a threat to the protection of the information as is the individual who seeks to exploit the information, because one person's carelessness can create a vulnerability and thus an opportunity that another person may not be able to pass up. However, if an individual damages or destroys data on purpose, the act belongs to a different threat category.

Much human error or failure can be prevented with training and ongoing awareness activities, but also with controls, ranging from simple procedures, such as requiring the user to type a critical command twice, to more complex procedures, such as the verification of commands by a second party. An example of the latter is the performance of key recovery actions in PKI systems. Many military applications have robust, dual-approval controls built in. Some systems that have a high potential for data loss or system outages use expert systems to monitor human actions and request confirmation for critical inputs.

Who is the biggest threat to your organization?

Dick Davis a.k.a.
"wannabe amateur hacker"

Harriet Allthumbs
employee
accidentally
deleted the one copy
of a critical report

Tom Twostory
convicted burglar

FIGURE 2-1   Acts of Human Error or Failure

Compromises to Intellectual Property

As will be discussed in detail in Chapter 3, many organizations create or support the development of intellectual property (IP) as part of their business operations. Intellectual property is defined as "the ownership of ideas and control over the tangible or virtual representation of those ideas. Use of another person's intellectual property may or may not involve royalty payments or permission, but should always include proper credit to the source."[7] Intellectual property includes trade secrets, copyrights, trademarks, and patents. Once intellectual property has been defined and properly identified, breaches to IP constitute a threat to the security of this information. Employees may have access privileges to the various types of IP, and may be required to use the IP to conduct day-to-day business.

Frequently an organization purchases or leases the IP of other organizations, and must abide by the purchase or licensing agreement for its fair and responsible use. The most common IP breach is the unlawful use or duplication of software-based intellectual property, more commonly known as **software piracy**. Many individuals and organizations do not purchase their software as often as they should. Because most software is licensed to a particular purchaser, its use is restricted to a single user or to a designated user in an organization. If the user copies the program to another computer without securing another license or transferring the license, he or she has violated the copyright. (See the Offline on Violating Software Licenses for more details.) Software licenses are strictly enforced by a number of regulatory and private organizations, and software publishers use several control mechanisms to prevent copyright infringement. In addition to the laws surrounding software piracy, two watchdog organizations investigate allegations of software abuse: Software & Information Industry Association (SIIA) at *www.siia.net*, formerly known as the Software Publishers Association, and the Business Software Alliance (BSA) at *www.bsa.org*. A recent BSA survey in July 2004 revealed that as much as a third of all software in use globally is pirated. Additional details on these organizations and how they operate to preserve IP rights are discussed in Chapter 3, "Legal, Ethical, and Professional Issues in Information Security."

Enforcement of copyright laws has been attempted through a number of technical security mechanisms, such as the using of digital watermarks and embedded code, the requiring of copyright codes, and even the intentional adding of bad sectors on software media. The most common reminder of the individual's obligation to fair and responsible use is the license agreement window that usually pops up during the installation of new software. This screen serves as the legal proof that the user has read and agrees to the license agreement. For a time, these license agreements were referred to as blow-by screens, as users found that if they hit the Enter key frequently during installation, these bothersome installation screens quickly vanished, allowing faster installation of the software. Now, it is more common to see a different type of acceptance screen, one that requires a response via mouse click, or pressing a key other than Enter.

Another effort to combat piracy is the online registration process. Individuals who install software are often asked or even required to register their software to obtain technical support, or full use. Some believe that this process compromises personal privacy, because individuals never really know exactly what information is obtained from their computer and sent to the software manufacturer.

OFFLINE

Violating Software Licenses

Adapted from "Bootlegged Software Could Cost Community College"[8]

By Natalie Patton, *Las Vegas Review Journal*, September 18, 1997.

Ever heard of the software police? The Washington-based Software Publishers Association (SPA) copyright watchdogs were tipped off that a community college in Las Vegas, Nevada was using copyrighted software in violation of the software licenses. The SPA spent months investigating the report. Academic Affairs Vice President Robert Silverman said the college was prepared to pay some license violation fines, but was unable to estimate the total amount of the fines. The college cut back on new faculty hires, and set aside over 1.3 million dollars in anticipation of the total cost.

The audit was intensive, examining every computer on campus, including faculty machines, lab machines, and the college president's computer. Peter Beruk, SPA's director of domestic antipiracy cases, said the decision to audit a reported violation is only made when there is overwhelming evidence to win a lawsuit, as the SPA has no policing authority, and can only bring civil actions. Most of the investigated organizations settle out of court, agreeing to pay the fines, to avoid costly court battles.

The process begins with an anonymous tip, usually from an individual inside the organization. Of the hundreds of tips the SPA receives each week, only a handful are selected for on-site visits. If the audited organizations have license violations they are required to destroy illegal copies, repurchase software they wish to keep (at double the retail price), and pay the cost of the illegal use.

In this case, the community college president suggested the blame for the community college's violations belonged to faculty and students who may have downloaded illegal copies of software from the Internet, or installed software on campus computers without permission. Some of the faculty suspected that the problem lay in the qualifications and credibility of the campus technology staff. The president promised to put additional staff and rules in place to prevent a reoccurrence of such license violations.

Deliberate Acts of Espionage or Trespass

Deliberate acts of espionage or trespass are a well-known and broad category of electronic and human activities that can breach the confidentiality of information. When an unauthorized individual gains access to the information an organization is trying to protect, that act is categorized as a deliberate act of espionage or trespass. Attackers can use many different methods to access the information stored in an information system. Some information gathering techniques are quite legal, for example, using a Web browser to perform market research. These legal techniques are called, collectively, **competitive intelligence**. When information gatherers employ techniques that cross the threshold of what is legal or ethical, they are conducting **industrial espionage**. Many countries considered allies of the United States engage in industrial espionage against American organizations. When foreign governments are involved, these activities are actually considered espionage and a threat to national security. Some forms of espionage are relatively low-tech. One example, called **shoulder surfing**, is pictured in Figure 2-2. This technique is used in public or semipublic settings when individuals gather information they are not authorized to have by looking over another individual's shoulder or viewing the information from a distance. Instances of shoulder surfing occur at computer terminals, desks, ATM machines, public phones, or other places where a person is accessing confidential information. There is unwritten etiquette among professionals who address information security in the workplace. When someone can see another person entering personal or private information into a system, the first person should look away politely as the information is entered. Failure to do so constitutes not only a breach of etiquette, but is considered an affront to privacy as well as a threat to the security of the confidential information.

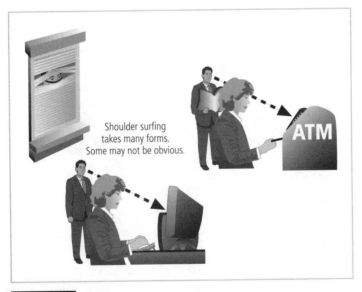

Shoulder surfing takes many forms. Some may not be obvious.

FIGURE 2-2 Shoulder Surfing

Acts of **trespass** can lead to unauthorized real or virtual actions that enable information gatherers to enter premises or systems they have not been authorized to enter. Controls are sometimes implemented to mark the boundaries of an organization's virtual territory. These boundaries give notice to trespassers that they are encroaching on the organization's cyberspace. Sound principles of authentication and authorization can help organizations protect valuable information and systems. These control methods and technologies employ multiple layers or factors to protect against unauthorized access.

The classic perpetrator of *deliberate acts of espionage* or *trespass* is the hacker. **Hackers** are "people who use and create computer software [to] gain access to information illegally."[9] Hackers are frequently glamorized in fictional accounts as people who stealthily manipulate a maze of computer networks, systems, and data to find the information that solves the mystery or saves the day. Television and motion pictures are inundated with images of hackers as heroes or heroines. However, the true life of the hacker is far more mundane (see Figure 2-3). In the gritty world of reality, a hacker frequently spends long hours examining the types and structures of the targeted systems and uses skill, guile, or fraud to attempt to bypass the controls placed around information that is the property of someone else.

There are generally two skill levels among hackers. The first is the **expert hacker**, sometimes called **elite hacker**, who develops software scripts and program exploits used by those in the second category, that of the novice, or **unskilled hacker**. The expert hacker is usually a master of several programming languages, networking protocols, and operating systems, and also exhibits a mastery of the technical environment of the chosen targeted system. As described in the Offline section titled "Hack PCWeek," expert hackers are extremely talented individuals who usually have lots of time and energy to devote to attempting to break into other people's information systems.

Once an expert hacker chooses a target, the likelihood that he or she will successfully enter the system is high. Fortunately for the many poorly protected organizations in the world, there are substantially fewer expert hackers than novice hackers.

Traditional hacker profile:
Age 13-18, male with limited parental supervision spends all his free time at the computer

Modern hacker profile:
Age 12-60, male or female, unknown background, with varying technological skill levels; may be internal or external to the organization

FIGURE 2-3 Hacker Profiles

Expert hackers are reported to be bored with attacking systems directly, and have turned their attention to writing software. These programs are automated exploits that allow novice hackers to act as **script kiddies**—hackers of limited skill who use expertly written software to attack a system—or **packet monkeys**—script kiddies who use automated exploits to engage in distributed denial-of-service attacks (described later in this chapter). The good news is that if an expert hacker can post a script tool where a script kiddie or packet monkey can find it, then systems and security administrators can find it, too. The developers of protection software and hardware and the service providers who keep defensive systems up to date also keep themselves informed of the latest in exploit scripts. As a result of preparation and continued vigilance, attacks conducted by scripts are usually predictable, and can be adequately defended against.

OFFLINE

Hack PCWeek

On September 20, 1999, PCWeek did the unthinkable: it set up two computers, one Linux-based, one Windows NT-based, and challenged members of the hacking community to be the first to crack either system, deface the posted Web page, and claim a $1000 reward. Four days later the Linux-based computer was hacked. Figure 2-4 shows the configuration of the *www.hackpcweek.com* Web site. The article below provides the technical details of how the hack was accomplished not by a compromise of the root operating system, but by the exploitation of an add-on CGI script with improper security checks.

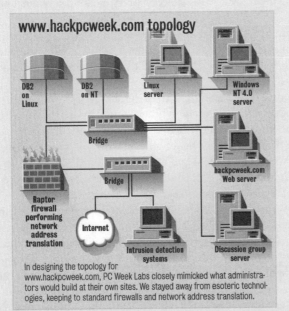

In designing the topology for www.hackpcweek.com, PC Week Labs closely mimicked what administrators would build at their own sites. We stayed away from esoteric technologies, keeping to standard firewalls and network address translation.

FIGURE 2-4 Hack PC Week Configuration

continued

"The Gibraltar Hack: Anatomy of a Break-in"[10]

By Pankaj Chowdhry, PCWeek Labs, *eWEEK*, October 11, 1999.

The hacker who first broke into the *www.hackpcweek.com* Web site hails, ironically, from Gibraltar—a location known as the Rock for its impregnability.

The hack of our site's Linux server, via CGI, was cleverly crafted and methodical. The culprit, Luis Mora, known publicly as Jfs, is certainly a cut above the average hacker, 95 percent of whom can be stopped by a good firewall. It's the 5 percent like Jfs that organizations need to worry about.

Jfs detailed the lengths to which he went to get into the system, a process that took him a relatively short 20 hours. Our analysis of the steps he took shows that administrators have a lot to be afraid of.

Jfs first did a standard vulnerability analysis, using a port scanner. Our servers were pretty well locked down, and Jfs didn't find anything except for HTTP port 80. He next looked for Web server fingerprints to find out what software we were running. Our circuit-level firewall was worth its weight in gold here.

After looking for the obvious stuff, Jfs began to map out our site, beginning with the directory structure. Using the HTML pages, he got a pretty good idea of what he was dealing with.

He identified the commercial application that was running on our system as PhotoAds, whose source code is available with the purchase of the product. Having come to dead ends at all the networking vulnerabilities, he decided to pay more attention to our commercial scripts.

With the PhotoAds source code in hand, Jfs tried the standard viewing of the configuration. But because of the server setup he could not get to it. He was able to see our environment configuration script, but this provided him with little useful information.

Undeterred, Jfs began trying to exploit server-side includes and mod_PERL embedded commands. He tried this in every field and found that a PERL regexp filtered out most input before it got into the HTML. He did, however, find one user-assigned variable that wasn't checked for malicious data. That was all he needed.

Jfs found that the ENV variable in the HTTP REFERER was left open. He tried to use a server-side include or mod_PERL embedded command to compromise the system. Unfortunately for him, neither of these services was configured on the machine.

He persisted, this time looking for holes in the PhotoAds CGI scripts. With an obviously extensive knowledge of PERL, he began looking at open() and system() calls.

He examined all of the variables and found only one to be of substance—the variable for the upload graphics-file name. If he could edit this name, he could write to any file on the system, including index.html—the home page.

The variable consisted of two elements, a directory variable and a file name variable. The directory variable was hard-coded in the config file, so that was useless.

The file name variable was filtered by a regexp, so Jfs couldn't upload just anything. In fact, files needed to end in .gif or .jpg to get through. Using *www.phrack.com* as a resource, Jfs figured out a string that would refer him to the home index.html page.

He couldn't use a post command to send the string because it strips out all percentage signs, a necessary component of the hack string. This left him with just a get command.

continued

Because we configured the upload image size to 0, Jfs was left with only the gif section of the code.

By examining the code for the script, Jfs found that the graphics width must be less than 350 pixels with a height less than 250 pixels. He got around this by manually setting the sixth through ninth bytes to ascii null.

He moved on, only to find that any uploaded files are automatically placed in another directory and renamed.

Jfs attempted to get around the rename function. After examining the script, he saw that there was no error checking on the rename function. This presented the opportunity he was looking for. Using his knowledge of Linux, he figured out that the way to get the script to process past the rename function was to give the script a bad file name that would be skipped, leaving the file with its original name.

Jfs knew that Linux has a standard maximum file name size of 1,024 bytes. However, he also had to create a number that matched the long file name, which was easy because of the faulty input checking.

The result was a hack that let Jfs overwrite any file in the file system that was owned by the same user as the CGI process. Unfortunately for him, the CGI process was owned by 'nobody,' and all of the HTML documents were owned by root. He had hit another dead end.

Using pretty sophisticated knowledge of C, Jfs tried to get an ELF executable into the server, but he had to manually manipulate the binaries because of length restrictions with the get command. This limited Jfs to 8,190 bytes. Because he already had a 1,024-character number, he was left with about 7,000 bytes to code the entire executable.

Jfs stripped out everything he could and managed to get it under the size requirements.

This didn't get him the files he needed, so he went after root access—the hacker's Holy Grail. Using the Bugtraq service, he found a cron exploit for which patches hadn't been applied. He modified the hack to get a suidroot. This got him root access—and the ability to change the home page to the chilling: "This site has been hacked. Jfs was here."

Game over.

In February 2000, a juvenile hacker named Mafiaboy, who had been responsible for a series of widely publicized denial-of-service attacks on prominent Web sites, pled guilty to 56 counts of computer mischief, and was sentenced to eight months in juvenile detention, and to pay $250 to charity.[11] His downfall came from his inability to cover his tracks by deleting the system logs that tracked his activity, and his need to brag about his exploits in chat rooms.

There are other terms for system rule breakers that may be less familiar. The term **cracker** is now commonly associated with an individual who "cracks" or removes software protection that is designed to prevent unauthorized duplication. With the removal of the copyright protection, the software can be easily distributed and installed. The terms hacker and cracker denote criminal intent.

A **phreaker** hacks the public telephone network to make free calls or disrupt services. Phreakers grew in fame in the 1970s, when they developed devices called blue boxes that enabled free calls from pay phones. Later, red boxes were developed to simulate the tones of coins falling in a pay phone, and finally black boxes emulated the line voltage. With the advent of digital communications, these boxes became practically obsolete. Even with the loss of the colored box technologies, phreakers continue to cause problems for all telephone systems.

The most notorious hacker in recent history is Kevin Mitnick, highlighted in the following Offline.

OFFLINE

Kevin Mitnick

Among the most notorious hackers to date is Kevin Mitnick. The son of divorced parents, Kevin Mitnick grew up in a lackluster middle-class environment. Kevin got his start as a phreaker, with a local group of juvenile enthusiasts. Eventually this group expanded their malicious activities into computer companies. After attacking and physically breaking into the Pacific Bell Computer Center for Mainframe Operations, the group was arrested when a former girlfriend of one of the members turned them in. A 17-year-old, Mitnick was convicted of the destruction of data and theft of equipment, and sentenced to three months in juvenile detention and a year's probation.

Mitnick spent the next few years sharpening his hacking and phreaking skills, and surviving run-ins with the police. He was arrested again in 1983 at the University of Southern California, where he was caught breaking into Pentagon computers over the ARPANET. He received six months in another juvenile prison. He disappeared a few years later, after a warrant was issued for his arrest for breaking into a credit agency computer database. In 1987, he was eventually convicted of using illegal telephone cards and sentenced to 36 months probation. His next hacking battle pitched him against the FBI. His knowledge of the telephone system frustrated their efforts to apprehend him until his best friend turned him in. His unusual defense of computer addiction resulted in a one-year prison sentence and six months counseling. By 1992, it seemed that Mitnick had reverted to a relatively normal life until an episode of illegal database use was traced back to him. After an FBI search of his residence, he was charged with illegally accessing a phone company's computer and associating with a former criminal associate. But this time Kevin Mitnick disappeared before his trial.[12]

In 1995, he was finally tracked down and arrested. Because he was a known flight risk, he was held without bail for nearly five years, eight months of it in solitary confinement. Afraid he would never get to trial, he eventually pleaded guilty to wire fraud, computer fraud, and intercepting communications. He is now free on probation, and was required, until January 2003, to get permission to travel or use any technology. His newest job is on the lecture circuit, where he speaks out in support of information security and against hacking.[13]

Deliberate Acts of Information Extortion

The threat of information extortion involves the possibility of an attacker or trusted insider stealing information from a computer system and demanding compensation for its return or for an agreement not to disclose the information. Extortion is common in credit card number theft. For example, Web-based retailer CD Universe was the victim of a theft of data files containing customer credit card information. The culprit was a Russian hacker named Maxus, who hacked the online vendor and stole several hundred thousand credit card numbers. When the company refused to pay the $100,000 blackmail, he posted the card numbers to a Web site, offering them to the criminal community. His Web site became so popular he had to restrict access.[14]

Another example of extortion occurred in June of 2000, when a student was charged with online blackmail. The student discovered how to download books from an online digital book company without paying. He threatened to release this information unless he was provided with "a sum equal to the retail value of the content on the company's Web site, a 2001 Volvo wagon, two digital audio players, and unlimited free downloads of the company's content."[15] Since a single conviction for using the Internet to send blackmail threats could result in two years in prison and fines up to $100,000, this student faced a maximum total of 36 years and fines up to $800,000 if convicted on all counts.

Deliberate Acts of Sabotage or Vandalism

Equally popular today are assaults on the electronic face of an organization—its Web site. This category of threat involves the deliberate sabotage of a computer system or business, or acts of vandalism to either destroy an asset or damage the image of an organization. These acts can range from petty vandalism by employees to organized sabotage against an organization.

Although not necessarily financially devastating, attacks on the image of an organization are serious. Organizations frequently rely on image to support the generation of revenue, and vandalism to a Web site can erode consumer confidence, thus reducing the organization's sales and net worth. For example, in the early hours of July 13, 2001, a group known as Fluffi Bunni left its mark on the front page of the SANS (SysAdmin, Audit, Network, Security) Institute, a cooperative research and education organization. This event was particularly embarrassing to SANS Institute management, since the Institute provides security instruction and certification. The defacement read, "Would you really trust these guys to teach you security?"[16]

There are innumerable reports of hackers accessing systems, and damaging or destroying critical data. Hacked Web sites once made front-page news, as the perpetrators intended. The impact of these acts has lessened as the volume has increased. The Web site that acts as the clearinghouse for many hacking reports, *Attrition.org*, has stopped cataloging all Web site defacements, because the sheer volume of the acts has outstripped the ability of the volunteers to keep the site up to date.[17]

Compared to Web site defacement, vandalism within a network is more malicious in intent and less public. Today, security experts are noticing a rise in another form of online vandalism, **hacktivist** or **cyberactivist** operations, which interfere with or disrupt systems to protest the operations, policies, or actions of an organization or government agency. For example:

> "In 1998, the Electronic Disturbance Theater (EDT) took the concept of electronic civil disobedience a step further. They organized a series of Web sit-ins, first against Mexican President Zedillo's Web site and later against President Clinton's White House Web site, the Pentagon, the School of the Americas, the Frankfurt Stock Exchange, and the Mexican Stock Exchange. The purpose was to demonstrate solidarity with the Mexican Zapatistas."[18]

Figure 2-5 illustrates how Greenpeace, a well-known environmental activist organization, once used its Web presence to recruit cyberactivists.

FIGURE 2-5 Cyber Activists Wanted

A much more sinister form of hacking is **cyberterrorism**. Cyberterrorists hack systems to conduct terrorist activities through network or Internet pathways. The United States and other governments are developing security measures intended to protect the critical computing and communications networks as well as the physical and power utility infrastructures. Here is a description of the coining and use of the term cyberterrorism:

> "In the 1980s, Barry Collin, a senior research fellow at the Institute for Security and Intelligence in California, coined the term 'cyberterrorism' to refer to the convergence of cyberspace and terrorism. Mark Pollitt, special agent for the FBI, offers a working definition: 'Cyberterrorism is the premeditated, politically motivated attacks against information, computer systems, computer programs, and data which result in violence against noncombatant targets by subnational groups or clandestine agents.'"[19]

Examples of cyberterrorism are currently limited to acts such as the defacement of NATO Web pages during the war in Kosovo. In fact some industry observers have taken the position that cyberterrorism is not a real threat, and instead is merely hype that distracts from the more concrete and pressing information security issues that do need attention.[20]

Occasionally, hackers and hacking do become matters of life and death. In some cases, the hacking lifestyle crosses paths with the darker alleys of the criminal underworld as indicated in the following:

> "But when Boris Floriciz was found hanging from a tree in a Berlin park on Oct. 22, his belt around his neck and his feet dragging the ground, it drew attention even outside the tight-knit world of hackers.
>
> His friends wonder whether he was caught up in the murkier side of the trade — one of spies, espionage, and black-market criminals. Was it suicide, as police suspect? Or homicide?
>
> At 26, Floriciz seemed headed for a great future. He'd just finished his computer science degree. International firms sought him as a consultant. He was happy, say his friends, who cannot believe he would take his own life.
>
> Floriciz's friends wonder if he had become a threat to someone on the wrong side of the business, leading to his death."[21]

Deliberate Acts of Theft

The threat of **theft**—the illegal taking of another's property—is a constant problem. Within an organization, property can be physical, electronic, or intellectual. The value of information suffers when it is copied and taken away without the owner's knowledge.

Physical theft can be controlled quite easily. A wide variety of measures can be used, from locked doors to trained security personnel and the installation of alarm systems. Electronic theft, however, is a more complex problem to manage and control. When someone steals a physical item, the loss is easily detected; after all, it has been removed and is no longer present. With the theft of electronic information, the evidence of a crime is not readily apparent. If thieves are clever and cover their tracks carefully, no one may ever know of the crime until it is far too late.

Deliberate Software Attacks

Perhaps the most familiar threat is the software attack. Deliberate software attacks occur when an individual or group designs software to attack a system. Most of this software is referred to as **malicious code** or **malicious software**, or sometimes **malware**. These software components or programs are designed to damage, destroy, or deny service to the target systems. Some of the more common instances of malicious code are viruses and worms, Trojan horses, logic bombs, and back doors.

Equally prominent among the recent incidences of malicious code are the denial-of-service attacks conducted by Mafiaboy (mentioned earlier) on Amazon.com, CNN.com, E*TRADE.com, ebay.com, Yahoo.com, Excite.com, and Dell.com. These software-based attacks lasted approximately four hours, and are reported to have caused millions of dollars in lost revenue.[22] The British Internet service provider Cloudnine is believed to be the first business "hacked out of existence" in a denial-of-service attack in January 2002. This attack was similar to denial-of-service attacks launched by Mafiaboy in February 2000.[23] The following are explanations of common malware threats.

Virus

A computer **virus** consists of segments of code that perform malicious actions. This code behaves very much like a virus pathogen attacking animals and plants, using the cell's own replication machinery to propagate and attack. The code attaches itself to the existing program and takes control of that program's access to the targeted computer. The virus-controlled target program then carries out the virus's plan, by replicating itself into additional targeted systems. Many times it's users that help virus code get into a system. Opening an infected e-mail or some other seemingly trivial action can cause anything from random messages popping up on a user's screen to the complete destruction of entire hard drives of data. Just as their namesakes are passed among living bodies, computer viruses are passed from machine to machine via physical media, e-mail, or other forms of computer data transmission. When these viruses infect a machine, they may immediately scan the local machine for e-mail applications, or even send themselves to every user in the e-mail address book.

One of the most common methods of virus transmission at the opening of the twenty-first century is via e-mail attachment files. Most organizations block e-mail attachments of certain types and also filter all e-mail for known virus strains. In earlier times, viruses were slow moving creatures that transferred viral payloads through the cumbersome movement of diskettes from system to system. Now, computers are networked, and e-mail programs prove to be fertile ground for computer viruses unless they are suitably controlled. The current software marketplace has several established vendors, such as Symantec Norton Anti-Virus and McAfee VirusScan, that provide applications to assist in the control of computer viruses.

There are several types of viruses. One is the **macro virus**, which is embedded in the automatically executing macro code common in word processors, spread sheets, and database applications. Another type, the **boot virus**, infects the key operating system files located in a computer's boot sector.

Worms

Named for the Tapeworm in John Brunner's novel *The Shockwave Rider*, a **worm** is a malicious program that replicates itself constantly, without requiring another program to provide a safe environment for replication. Worms can continue replicating themselves until they completely fill available resources, such as memory, hard drive space, and network bandwidth. Read the Offline on Robert Morris and the worm he created to learn about the damage a worm can cause. Code Red, Sircam, Nimda (admin spelled backwards), and Klez are examples of a class of worms that combines multiple modes of attack into a single package. Figure 2-6 shows sample e-mails containing the Nimda and Sircam worms. These newer worm variants contain multiple exploits that can use any of the many predefined distribution vectors to programmatically distribute the worm (see the section on polymorphism later in this chapter for more details). The Klez virus, shown in Figure 2-7, delivers a double-barreled payload: it has an attachment that contains the worm, and if the e-mail is viewed on an HTML-enabled browser, it attempts to deliver a macro virus. News-making attacks, such as MS-Blaster, MyDoom, and Netsky, are variants of the multifaceted attack worms and viruses that exploit weaknesses in the leading operating systems and applications.

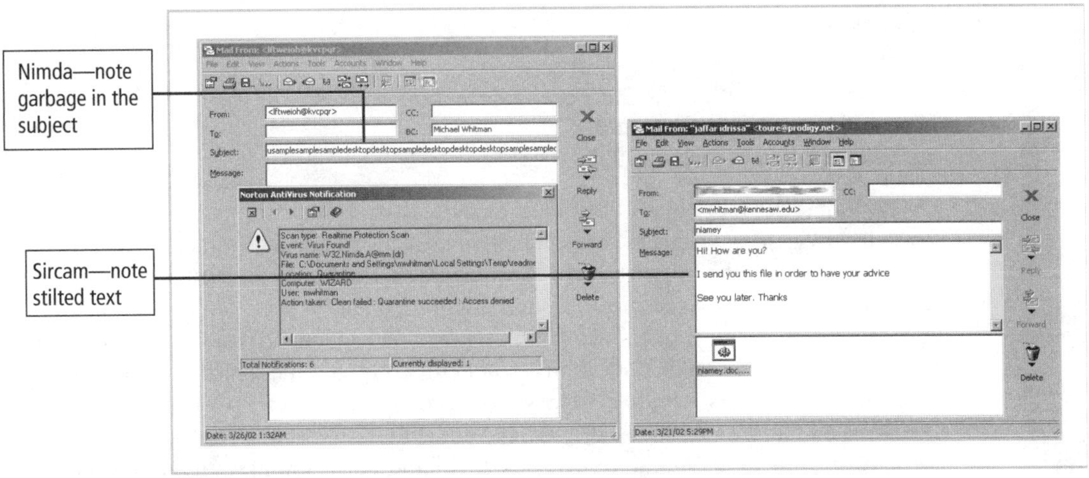

Nimda—note garbage in the subject

Sircam—note stilted text

FIGURE 2-6 Nimda and Sircam Viruses

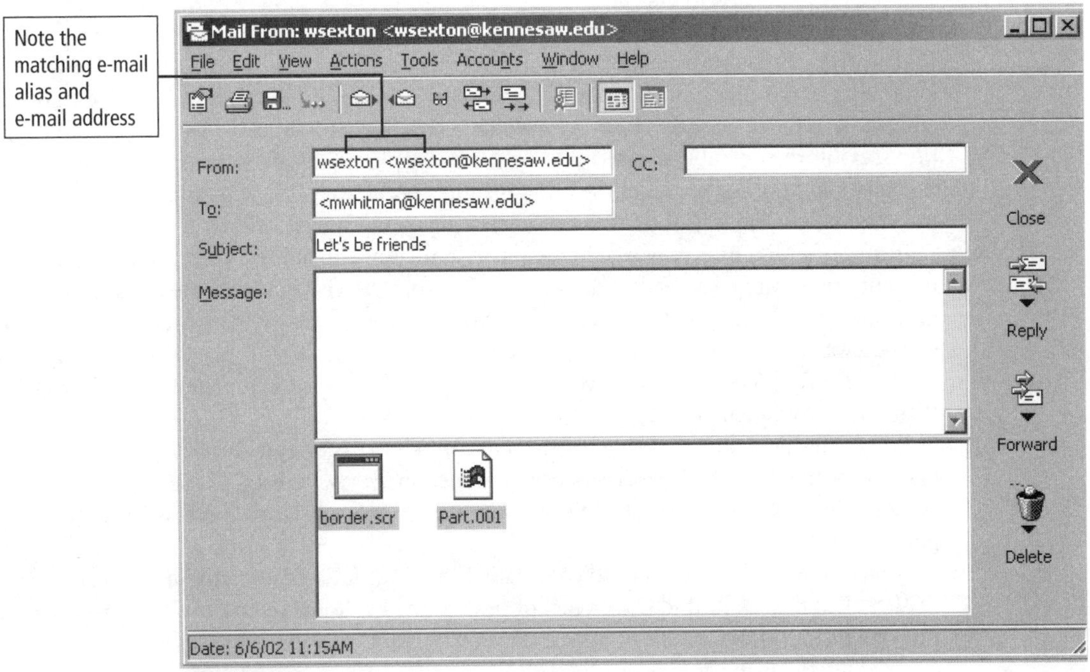

Note the matching e-mail alias and e-mail address

FIGURE 2-7 Klez Virus

The complex behavior of worms can be initiated with or without the user downloading or executing the file. Once the worm has infected a computer, it can redistribute itself to all e-mail addresses found on the infected system. Furthermore, a worm can deposit copies of itself onto all Web servers that the infected system can reach, so that users who subsequently visit those sites become infected. Worms also take advantage of open shares found on the network in which an infected system is located, placing working copies of the worm code onto the server so that users of those shares are likely to become infected.

OFFLINE

Robert Morris And The Internet Worm

"Zen and the Art of the Internet"[24]
By Brendan P. Kehoe, January 1992.

On November 2, 1988, Robert Morris, Jr., a graduate student in Computer Science at Cornell, wrote an experimental, self-replicating, self-propagating program called a worm and injected it into the Internet. He chose to release it from MIT, to disguise the fact that the worm came from Cornell. Morris soon discovered that the program was replicating and reinfecting machines at a much faster rate than he had anticipated—there was a bug. Ultimately, many machines at locations around the country either crashed or became 'catatonic.' When Morris realized what was happening, he contacted a friend at Harvard to discuss a solution. Eventually, they sent an anonymous message from Harvard over the network, instructing programmers how to kill the worm and prevent reinfection. However, because the network route was clogged, this message did not get through until it was too late. Computers were affected at many sites, including universities, military sites, and medical research facilities. The estimated cost of dealing with the worm at each installation ranged from $200 to more than $53,000.

The program took advantage of a hole in the debug mode of the UNIX *sendmail* program, which runs on a system and waits for other systems to connect to it and give it e-mail, and a hole in the finger daemon *fingerd*, which serves finger requests (a UNIX feature that provides information about users on the system). People at the University of California at Berkeley and MIT had copies of the program and were actively disassembling it (returning the program back into its source form) to try to figure out how it worked.

Teams of programmers worked nonstop to come up with at least a temporary fix, to prevent the continued spread of the worm. After about twelve hours, the team at Berkeley came up with steps that would help retard the spread of the payload. Another method was also discovered at Purdue and widely published. The information didn't get out as quickly as it could have, however, since so many sites had completely disconnected themselves from the network.

After a few days, things slowly began to return to normalcy and everyone wanted to know who had done it all. Morris was later named in *The New York Times* as the author (though this hadn't yet been officially proven, there was a substantial body of evidence pointing to Morris).

Robert T. Morris was convicted of violating the Computer Fraud and Abuse Act (Title 18), and sentenced to three years of probation, 400 hours of community service, a fine of $10,050, and the costs of his supervision. His appeal, filed in December 1990, was rejected the following March.

Reprinted with permission from Brendan Kehoe of the Zen Internet Group.

Trojan horses

Trojan horses are software programs that hide their true nature, and reveal their designed behavior only when activated. Trojan horses are frequently disguised as helpful, interesting, or necessary pieces of software, such as readme.exe files often included with shareware or freeware packages. Unfortunately, like their namesake in Greek legend, once Trojan horses are brought into a system, they become activated and can wreak havoc on the unsuspecting user. Figure 2-8 outlines a typical Trojan horse attack. Around January 20, 1999, Internet e-mail users began receiving e-mail with an attachment of a Trojan horse program named Happy99.exe. When the e-mail attachment was opened, a brief multimedia program displayed fireworks and the message "Happy 1999." While the fireworks display was running, the Trojan horse program was installing itself into the user's system. The program continued to propagate itself by following up every e-mail the user sent with a second e-mail to the same recipient that contained the Happy99 Trojan horse program.

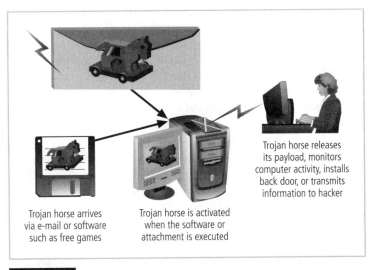

Trojan horse arrives via e-mail or software such as free games

Trojan horse is activated when the software or attachment is executed

Trojan horse releases its payload, monitors computer activity, installs back door, or transmits information to hacker

FIGURE 2-8   Trojan Horse Attack

Back Door or Trap Door

A virus or worm can have a payload that installs a **back door** or **trap door** component in a system, which allows the attacker to access the system at will with special privileges. Examples of these kinds of payloads include Subseven and Back Orifice.

Polymorphism

One of the biggest problems in fighting viruses and worms is the recent development of polymorphic threats. A **polymorphic threat** is one that changes its apparent shape over time, making it undetectable by techniques that look for preconfigured signatures. These viruses and worms actually evolve, changing their size and appearance to elude detection by antivirus software programs. This means that an e-mail generated by the virus may not match previous examples, making detection more of a challenge.

Virus and Worm Hoaxes

As frustrating as viruses and worms are, perhaps more time and money is spent on resolving **virus hoaxes**. Well-meaning people can disrupt the harmony and flow of an organization when they send random e-mails warning of dangerous viruses that are fictitious. When individuals fail to follow virus-reporting procedures, the network becomes overloaded, and much time and energy is wasted as users forward the warning message to everyone they know, post the message on bulletin boards, and try to update their antivirus protection software.

There are a number of resources on the Internet that allow individuals to research viruses to determine if they are fact or fiction. For the latest information on real threatening viruses and hoaxes, along with other relevant and current security information, visit the CERT Coordination Center at *www.cert.org*. For a more entertaining approach to the latest virus, worm, and hoax information, visit the Urban Legend Reference Pages at *www.snopes.com/inboxer/hoaxes/hoaxes.asp* or the Hoax Busters Web page at *hoaxbusters.ciac.org*.

Forces of Nature

Forces of nature, *force majeure*, or acts of God can pose some of the most dangerous threats imaginable, because they are unexpected and occur with very little warning. These threats, which include events such as fire, flood, earthquake, and lightning as well as volcanic eruption and insect infestation, can disrupt not only the lives of individuals, but also the storage, transmission, and use of information. Some of the more common threats in this group are presented in the list below.

- **Fire**: Usually meant in this context as a structural fire that damages the building housing the computing equipment that comprises all or part of the information system. Also encompasses smoke damage from a fire and/or water damage from sprinkler systems or firefighters. Can usually be mitigated with fire casualty insurance and/or business interruption insurance.

- **Flood**: An overflowing of water onto land that is normally dry, causing direct damage to all or part of the information system, or to the building that houses all or part of the information system. May also disrupt operations through interruptions in access to the buildings that house all or part of the information system. Can sometimes be mitigated with flood insurance and/or business interruption insurance.

- **Earthquake**: A sudden movement of the earth's crust caused by the release of stress accumulated along geologic faults, or by volcanic activity. Earthquakes can cause direct damage to all or part of the information system or, more often, to the building that houses it. May also disrupt operations through interruptions in access to the buildings that house all or part of the information system. Can sometimes be mitigated with specific casualty insurance and/or business interruption insurance, but is usually a separate policy.

- **Lightning**: An abrupt, discontinuous natural electric discharge in the atmosphere. Lightning usually directly damages all or part of the information system an/or its power distribution components. It can also cause fires or other damage to the building that houses all or part of the information system. May also disrupt operations through interruptions in access to the buildings that house all or part of the information system. Can usually be mitigated with multipurpose casualty insurance and/or business interruption insurance.

- **Landslide or mudslide**: The downward sliding of a mass of earth and rock directly damaging all or part of the information system or, more likely, the building that houses it. May also disrupt operations through interruptions in access to the buildings that house all or part of the information system. Can sometimes be mitigated with casualty insurance and/or business interruption insurance.

- **Tornado or severe windstorm**: A rotating column of air ranging in width from a few yards to more than a mile and whirling at destructively high speeds, usually accompanied by a funnel-shaped downward extension of a cumulonimbus cloud. Storms can directly damage all or part of the information system or, more likely, the building that houses it. May also disrupt operations through interruptions in access to the buildings that house all or part of the information system. Can sometimes be mitigated with casualty insurance and/or business interruption insurance.

- **Hurricane or typhoon**: A severe tropical cyclone originating in the equatorial regions of the Atlantic Ocean or Caribbean Sea or eastern regions of the Pacific Ocean (typhoon), traveling north, northwest, or northeast from its point of origin, and usually involving heavy rains. These storms can directly damage all or part of the information system or, more likely, the building that houses it. Organizations located in coastal or low-lying areas may experience flooding (see above). These storms may also disrupt operations through interruptions in access to the buildings that house all or part of the information system. Can sometimes be mitigated with casualty insurance and/or business interruption insurance.

- **Tsunami**: A very large ocean wave caused by an underwater earthquake or volcanic eruption. These events can directly damage all or part of the information system or, more likely, the building that houses it. Organizations located in coastal areas may experience tsunamis. Tsunamis may also cause disruption to operations through interruptions in access or electrical power to the buildings that house all or part of the information system. Can sometimes be mitigated with casualty insurance and/or business interruption insurance.

- **Electrostatic discharge (ESD)**: Usually static electricity and ESD are little more than a nuisance. Unfortunately, however, the mild static shock we receive when walking across a carpet can be costly or dangerous when it ignites flammable mixtures and damages costly electronic components. Static electricity can draw dust into clean-room environments or cause products to stick together. The cost of ESD-damaged electronic devices and interruptions to service can range from only a few cents to several millions of dollars for critical systems. Loss of production time in information processing due to ESD impact is significant. While not usually viewed as a threat, ESD can disrupt information systems, but it is not usually an insurable loss unless covered by business interruption insurance.

- **Dust contamination**: Some environments are not friendly to the hardware components of information systems. Because dust contamination can shorten the life of information systems or cause unplanned downtime, this threat can disrupt normal operations.

Since it is not possible to avoid force of nature threats, organizations must implement controls to limit damage, and they must also prepare contingency plans for continued operations, such as disaster recovery plans, business continuity plans, and incident response plans to limit losses in the face of these threats.

Deviations in Quality of Service

This category covers situations in which a product or service is not delivered to the organization as expected. Utility companies, service providers, and other value-adding organizations form a vast web of interconnected services. The organization's information system depends on the successful operation of many interdependent support systems, including power grids, telecom networks, parts suppliers, service vendors, and even the janitorial staff and garbage haulers. Any one of these support systems can be interrupted by storms, employee illnesses, or other unforeseen events. Threats in this category are manifest in attacks such as a backhoe taking out a fiber-optic link for an ISP. The backup provider may be online and in service, but may be able to supply only a fraction of the bandwidth the organization needs for full service. This degradation of service is a form of **availability disruption**. Internet service, communications, and power irregularities can dramatically affect the availability of information and systems.

Internet Service Issues

For organizations that rely heavily on the Internet and the World Wide Web to support continued operations, Internet service provider failures can considerably undermine the availability of information. Many organizations have sales staff and telecommuters working at remote locations. When these offsite employees cannot contact the host systems, manual procedures must be used to continue operations.

When an organization places its Web servers in the care of a Web hosting provider, that provider assumes responsibility for all Internet services as well as for the hardware and operating system software used to operate the Web site. These Web hosting services are usually arranged with an agreement providing minimum service levels known as a **Service Level Agreement (SLA)**. When a service provider fails to meet the SLA, the provider may accrue fines to cover losses incurred by the client, but these payments seldom cover the losses generated by the outage.

Communications and other Service Provider Issues

Other utility services can affect organizations as well. Among these are telephone, water, wastewater, trash pickup, cable television, natural or propane gas, and custodial services. The loss of these services can impair the ability of an organization to function. For instance, most facilities require water service to operate an air-conditioning system. Even in Minnesota in February, air-conditioning systems are needed to keep a modern facility operating. Alternatively, if the wastewater system fails, an organization might be prevented from allowing employees into the building. This would stop normal business operations.

Power Irregularities

Irregularities from power utilities are common and can lead to fluctuations such as power excesses, power shortages, and power losses. This can pose problems for organizations that provide inadequately conditioned power for their information systems equipment. In the U.S., we are "fed" 120-volt, 60-cycle power usually through 15 and 20 amp circuits. When voltage levels **spike** (experience a momentary increase), or **surge** (experience a prolonged increase), the extra voltage can severely damage or destroy equipment. Equally disruptive are power shortages from a lack of available power. A momentary low voltage or **sag**, or a more prolonged drop in voltage, known as a **brownout**, can cause systems to shut down or reset, or otherwise disrupt availability. Complete loss of power for a moment is known as a **fault**, and a more lengthy loss as a **blackout**. Because sensitive electronic equipment—especially networking equipment, computers, and computer-based systems—are susceptible to fluctuations, controls can be applied to them to manage power quality. With small computers and network systems, quality power-conditioning options such as surge suppressors can smooth out spikes. The more expensive uninterruptible power supply (UPS) can protect against spikes and surges as well as against sags and even blackouts of limited duration.

Technical Hardware Failures or Errors

Technical hardware failures or errors occur when a manufacturer distributes equipment containing a known or unknown flaw. These defects can cause the system to perform outside of expected parameters, resulting in unreliable service or lack of availability. Some errors are terminal, in that they result in the unrecoverable loss of the equipment. Some errors are intermittent, in that they only periodically manifest themselves, resulting in faults that are not easily repeated, and thus, equipment can sometimes stop working, or work in unexpected ways. Murphy's Law (and yes, there really was a Murphy) says that if something can possibly go wrong, it will.[25] In other words, it's not *if* something will fail, but when.

One of the best-known hardware failures is that of the Intel Pentium II chip (shown in Figure 2-9). The microchip had a defect that caused it to calculate erroneously in certain circumstances. Intel initially expressed little concern for the defect, stating that it would take an inordinate amount of time to identify a calculation that would interfere with the reliability of the results. Yet within days, popular computing journals were publishing a simple calculation (the division of 4195835 by 3145727 by a spreadsheet) that determined if an individual's machine contained the defective chip and thus the floating-point operation bug. The Pentium floating-point division bug (FDIV) led to a public relations disaster for Intel that resulted in its first-ever chip recall, and a loss of over $475 million. A few months later, disclosure of another bug known as the Dan-0411 flag erratum further eroded the chip manufacturer's public image.[26] In 1998, when Intel released its Xeon chip, it also had hardware errors. Intel said, "All new chips have bugs, and the process of debugging and improving performance inevitably continues even after a product is in the market."[27]

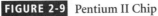

FIGURE 2-9 Pentium II Chip

Technical Software Failures or Errors

This category involves threats that come from purchasing software with unknown, hidden faults. Large quantities of computer code are written, debugged, published, and sold before all their bugs are detected and resolved. Sometimes, combinations of certain software and hardware reveal new bugs. These failures range from bugs to untested failure conditions. Sometimes these bugs are not errors, but rather purposeful shortcuts left by programmers for benign or malign reasons. Collectively, shortcut access routes into programs that bypass security checks are called trap doors and can cause serious security breaches.

In general, software bugs are so commonplace that entire Web sites are dedicated to documenting them. Among the most often used is Bugtraq, found at *http://www.securityfocus.com*, which provides both up-to-the-minute information on the latest security vulnerabilities, as well as a very thorough archive of past bugs.

Technological Obsolescence

Antiquated or outdated infrastructure can lead to unreliable and untrustworthy systems. Management must recognize that when technology becomes outdated, there is a risk of loss of data integrity from attacks. Management's strategic planning should always include an analysis of the technology currently in use. Ideally, proper planning by management should prevent technology from becoming obsolete, but when obsolescence is identified, management must take immediate action. IT professionals play a large role in the identification of probable obsolescence.

Recently, the software vendor Symantec retired support for a legacy version of its popular antivirus software, and organizations interested in continued product support were obliged to upgrade immediately to a different antivirus control software. In organizations where IT personnel had kept management informed of the coming retirement, these replacements were made more promptly and at lower cost than at organizations where the software was allowed to become obsolete.

Attacks

An **attack** is an act or action that takes advantage of a vulnerability to compromise a controlled system. It is accomplished by a **threat agent** that damages or steals an organization's information or physical asset. A **vulnerability** is an identified weakness in a controlled system, where controls are not present or are no longer effective. Unlike threats, which are always in existence, attacks exist when a specific act or action comes into play and may cause a potential loss. For example, the *threat* of damage from a thunderstorm is present during most of the summer for many places, but an *attack* and its associated risk of loss only exist for the duration of an actual thunderstorm. The following sections discuss each of the major types of attack used against controlled systems.

Malicious Code

The **malicious code** attack includes the execution of viruses, worms, Trojan horses, and active Web scripts with the intent to destroy or steal information. The state-of-the-art malicious code attack is the polymorphic, or multivector, worm. These attack programs use up to six known attack vectors to exploit a variety of vulnerabilities in commonly found information system devices. Perhaps the best illustration of such an attack remains the outbreak of Nimda in September 2001, which used five of the six vectors to spread itself with startling speed. TruSecure Corporation, an industry source for information security statistics and solutions, reports that Nimda spread to span the Internet address space of 14 countries in less than 25 minutes.[28] Table 2-2 outlines the six categories of known attack vectors.

Table 2-2 Attack Replication Vectors

Vector	Description
IP scan and attack	The infected system scans a random or local range of IP addresses and targets any of several vulnerabilities known to hackers or left over from previous exploits such as Code Red, Back Orifice, or PoizonBox.
Web browsing	If the infected system has write access to any Web pages, it makes all Web content files (.html, .asp, .cgi, and others) infectious, so that users who browse to those pages become infected.
Virus	Each infected machine infects certain common executable or script files on all computers to which it can write with virus code that can cause infection.
Unprotected shares	Using vulnerabilities in file systems and the way many organizations configure them, the infected machine copies the viral component to all locations it can reach.
Mass mail	By sending e-mail infections to addresses found in the address book, the infected machine infects many users, whose mail-reading programs also automatically run the program and infect other systems.
Simple Network Management Protocol (SNMP)	By using the widely known and common passwords that were employed in early versions of this protocol (which is used for remote management of network and computer devices), the attacking program can gain control of the device. Most vendors have closed these vulnerabilities with software upgrades.

Hoaxes

A more devious approach to attacking computer systems is the transmission of a virus hoax *with a real virus attached*. When the attack is masked in a seemingly legitimate message, unsuspecting users more readily distribute it. Even though these users are trying to do the right thing to avoid infection, they end up sending the attack on to their coworkers and friends and infecting many users along the way.

Back Doors

Using a known or previously unknown and newly discovered access mechanism, an attacker can gain access to a system or network resource through a back door. Sometimes these entries are left behind by system designers or maintenance staff, and thus referred to as trap doors.[29] A trap door is hard to detect, because very often the programmer who puts it in place also makes the access exempt from the usual audit logging features of the system.

Password Crack

Attempting to reverse-calculate a password is often called **cracking**. A cracking attack is a component of many dictionary attacks (to be covered shortly). It is used when a copy of the Security Account Manager (SAM) data file can be obtained. The SAM file contains the hashed representation of the user's password. A password can be hashed using the same algorithm and compared to the hashed results. If they are the same, the password has been cracked.

Brute Force

The application of computing and network resources to try every possible combination of options of a password is called a **brute force attack**. Since this is often an attempt to repeatedly guess passwords to commonly used accounts, it is sometimes called a **password attack**. If attackers can narrow the field of accounts to be attacked, they can devote more time and resources to attacking fewer accounts. That is one reason a recommended practice is to change account names for common accounts from the manufacturer's default.

While often effective against low-security systems, password attacks are often not useful against systems that have adopted the usual security practices recommended by manufacturers. Controls that limit the number of attempts allowed per unit of elapsed time are very effective at limiting brute force attacks. Defenses against brute force attacks are usually adopted early on in any security effort and are thoroughly covered in the SANS/FBI list of the top twenty most critical Internet security vulnerabilities.[30]

Dictionary

This is another form of the brute force attack noted above for guessing passwords. The **dictionary attack** narrows the field by selecting specific accounts to attack and uses a list of commonly used passwords (the dictionary) instead of random combinations. Organizations can use similar dictionaries to disallow passwords during the reset process and thus guard against easy-to-guess passwords. In addition, rules requiring additional numbers and/or special characters make the dictionary attack less effective.

Denial-of-Service (DoS) and Distributed Denial-of-Service (DDoS)

In a **denial-of-service (DoS)** attack, the attacker sends a large number of connection or information requests to a target (see Figure 2-10). So many requests are made that the target system cannot handle them along with other legitimate requests for service successfully. This may result in the system crashing, or simply becoming unable to perform ordinary functions. A **distributed denial-of-service (DDoS)** is an attack in which a coordinated stream of requests is launched against a target from many locations at the same time. Most DDoS attacks are preceded by a preparation phase in which many systems, perhaps thousands, are compromised. The compromised machines are turned into **zombies**, machines that are directed remotely (usually by a transmitted command) by the attacker to participate in the attack. DDoS attacks are the most difficult to defend against, and there are presently no controls that any single organization can apply. There are, however, some cooperative efforts to enable DDoS defenses among groups of service providers; among them is the Consensus Roadmap for Defeating Distributed Denial of Service Attacks.[31] To use a popular metaphor, DDoS is considered a weapon of mass destruction on the Internet.[32] The MyDoom worm attack of early 2004 was intended to be a distributed denial-of-service (DDoS) attack against *www.sco.com* (the Web site of a vendor of a UNIX operating system) that lasted from February 1, 2004 until February 12, 2004. Allegedly, the attack was payback for the SCO Group's perceived hostility toward the open-source Linux community.[33]

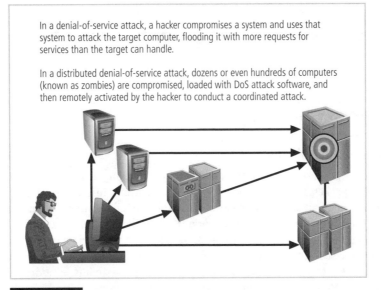

In a denial-of-service attack, a hacker compromises a system and uses that system to attack the target computer, flooding it with more requests for services than the target can handle.

In a distributed denial-of-service attack, dozens or even hundreds of computers (known as zombies) are compromised, loaded with DoS attack software, and then remotely activated by the hacker to conduct a coordinated attack.

FIGURE 2-10   Denial-of-Service Attacks

Any system connected to the Internet and providing TCP-based network services (such as a Web server, FTP server, or mail server) is potentially subject to denial-of-service attacks. Note that in addition to attacks launched at specific hosts, these attacks can also be launched against routers or other network server systems if these hosts enable (or turn on) other TCP services (e.g., echo). Even though such attacks make use of a fundamental element of the TCP protocol used by all systems, the consequences of the attacks may vary, depending on the system.[34]

Spoofing

Spoofing is a technique used to gain unauthorized access to computers, wherein the intruder sends messages to a computer that has an IP address that indicates that the messages are coming from a trusted host. To engage in IP spoofing, a hacker must first use a variety of techniques to find an IP address of a trusted host and then modify the packet headers (see Figure 2-11) so that it appears that the packets are coming from that host.[35] Newer routers and firewall arrangements can offer protection against IP spoofing.

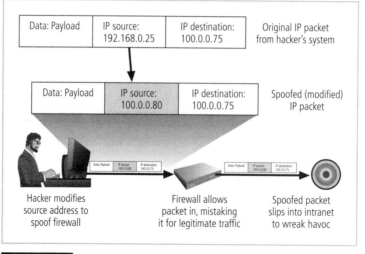

FIGURE 2-11 IP Spoofing

Man-in-the-Middle

In the well-known **man-in-the-middle** or **TCP hijacking attack**, an attacker monitors (or sniffs) packets from the network, modifies them, and inserts them back into the network. This type of attack uses IP spoofing (as explained above) to enable an attacker to impersonate another entity on the network. It allows the attacker to eavesdrop as well as to change, delete, reroute, add, forge, or divert data.[36] In a variant on the TCP hijacking session, the spoofing involves the interception of an encryption key exchange, which enables the hacker to act as an invisible man-in-the-middle—that is, eavesdropper—with regard to encrypted communications. Figure 2-12 illustrates these attacks by showing how a hacker uses public and private encryption keys to intercept messages. For more information on encrypted keys, see Chapter 8, "Cryptography."

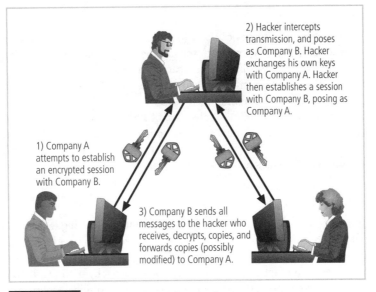

1) Company A attempts to establish an encrypted session with Company B.

2) Hacker intercepts transmission, and poses as Company B. Hacker exchanges his own keys with Company A. Hacker then establishes a session with Company B, posing as Company A.

3) Company B sends all messages to the hacker who receives, decrypts, copies, and forwards copies (possibly modified) to Company A.

FIGURE 2-12 Man-in-the-Middle Attack

Spam

Spam is unsolicited commercial e-mail. While many consider spam a trivial nuisance rather than an attack, it has been used as means to make malicious code attacks more effective. In March 2002, reports emerged of malicious code embedded in MP3 files that were included as attachments to spam.[37] The most significant consequence of spam on the modern organization, however, is the waste of both computer and human resources it causes by the flow of unwanted electronic mail. Many organizations attempt to cope with the flood of spam by using filtering technologies to stem the flow. Other organizations simply tell the users of the mail system to delete unwanted messages.

Mail Bombing

Another form of e-mail attack that is also a DoS is called a **mail bomb**, in which an attacker routes large quantities of e-mail to the target. This can be accomplished through social engineering (to be discussed shortly) or by exploiting various technical flaws in the Simple Mail Transport Protocol. The target of the attack receives unmanageably large volumes of unsolicited e-mail. By sending large e-mails with forged header information, attackers can take advantage of poorly configured e-mail systems on the Internet and trick them into sending many e-mails to an address chosen by the attacker. If many such systems are tricked into participating in the event, the target e-mail address is buried under thousands or even millions of unwanted e-mails.

Sniffers

A **sniffer** is a program or device that can monitor data traveling over a network. Sniffers can be used both for legitimate network management functions and for stealing information from a network. Unauthorized sniffers can be extremely dangerous to a network's security, because they are virtually impossible to detect and can be inserted almost anywhere. This makes them a favorite weapon in the hacker's arsenal. Sniffers often work on TCP/IP networks, where they're sometimes called **packet sniffers**.[38] Sniffers add risk to the network, because many systems and users send information on local networks in clear text. A sniffer program shows all the data going by, including passwords, the data inside files—such as word-processing documents—and screens full of sensitive data from applications.

Social Engineering

Within the context of information security, **social engineering** is the process of using social skills to convince people to reveal access credentials or other valuable information to the attacker. This can be done in several ways, and usually involves the perpetrator posing as a person higher in the organizational hierarchy than the victim. To prepare for this false representation, the perpetrator may have used social engineering against others in the organization to collect seemingly unrelated information that, when used together, makes the false representation more credible. For instance, anyone can call the main switchboard of a company and get the name of the CIO, but an attacker may find it just as easy to get even more information by calling others in the company and asserting his or her (albeit false) authority by mentioning the CIO's name. Social engineering attacks may involve individuals posing as new employees or as current employees pathetically requesting assistance to prevent getting fired. Sometimes attackers threaten, cajole, or beg to sway the target. Other variations are possible, as noted here in this excerpted advisory from The Computer Emergency Response Team/Coordination Center (CERT/CC):

> "CERT/CC has received several incident reports concerning users receiving requests to take an action that results in the capturing of their password. The request could come in the form of an e-mail message, a broadcast, or a telephone call. The latest ploy instructs the user to run a "test" program, previously installed by the intruder, which will prompt the user for his or her password. When the user executes the program, the user's name and password are e-mailed to a remote site. These messages can appear to be from a site administrator or root. In reality, they may have been sent by an individual at a remote site, who is trying to gain access or additional access to the local machine via the user's account."[39]

While this advisory may seem very trivial to some experienced users, the fact remains that *many* users have fallen for these tricks (refer to CERT Advisory CA-91.03). A similar social engineering attack called the Advance Fee Fraud (AFF), and internationally known as the "4-1-9" fraud, is named after a section of the Nigerian penal code. The perpetrators of 4-1-9 schemes often involve fictitious companies, such as the Nigerian National Petroleum Company. Alternatively, they may invent other entities, such as a bank, government agency, or a non-governmental organization. See Figure 2-13 for a sample letter from this type of scheme. This scam is notorious for stealing funds from gullible individuals, first by requiring those people who wish to participate in the proposed money-making venture to send money upfront, and then by soliciting an endless series of fees. These 4-1-9 schemes are even suspected to involve kidnapping, extortion, and murder, and they have, according to the Secret Service, bilked over $100 million from unsuspecting Americans lured into disclosing personal banking information. For more information, go to *www.secretservice.gov/alert419.shtml.*

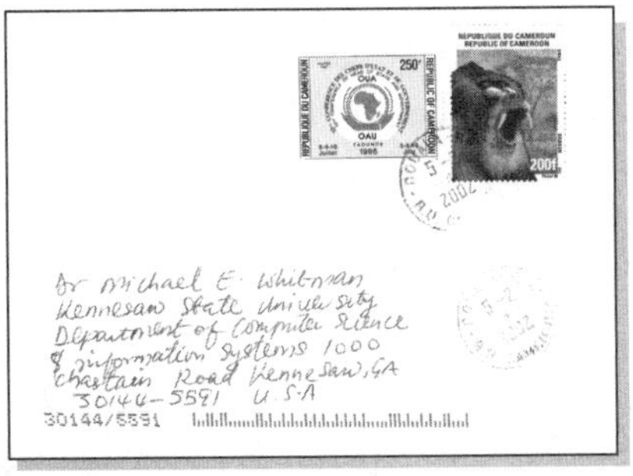

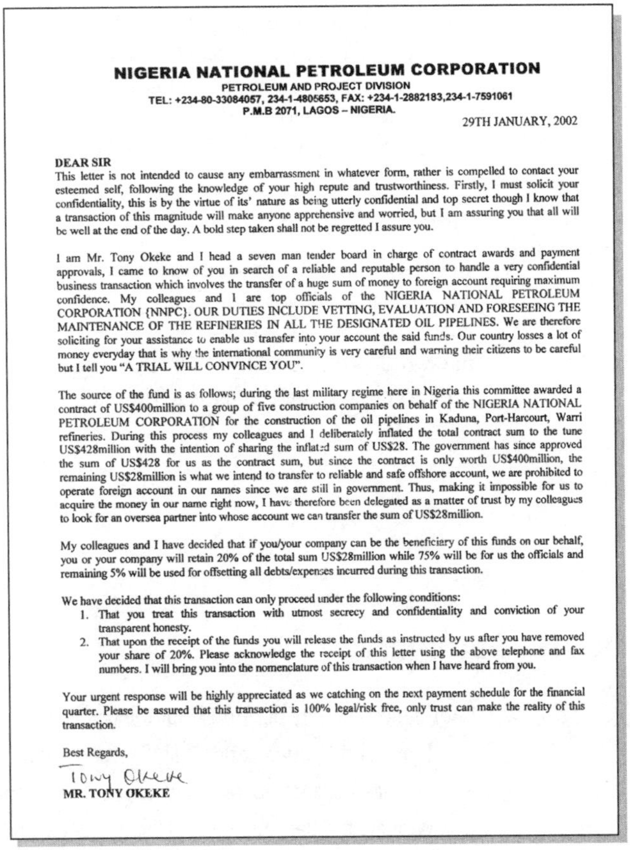

NIGERIA NATIONAL PETROLEUM CORPORATION
PETROLEUM AND PROJECT DIVISION
TEL: +234-80-33084057, 234-1-4805653, FAX: +234-1-2882183,234-1-7591061
P.M.B 2071, LAGOS – NIGERIA.

29TH JANUARY, 2002

DEAR SIR
This letter is not intended to cause any embarrassment in whatever form, rather is compelled to contact your esteemed self, following the knowledge of your high repute and trustworthiness. Firstly, I must solicit your confidentiality, this is by the virtue of its' nature as being utterly confidential and top secret though I know that a transaction of this magnitude will make anyone apprehensive and worried, but I am assuring you that all will be well at the end of the day. A bold step taken shall not be regretted I assure you.

I am Mr. Tony Okeke and I head a seven man tender board in charge of contract awards and payment approvals, I came to know of you in search of a reliable and reputable person to handle a very confidential business transaction which involves the transfer of a huge sum of money to foreign account requiring maximum confidence. My colleagues and I are top officials of the NIGERIA NATIONAL PETROLEUM CORPORATION {NNPC}. OUR DUTIES INCLUDE VETTING, EVALUATION AND FORESEEING THE MAINTENANCE OF THE REFINERIES IN ALL THE DESIGNATED OIL PIPELINES. We are therefore soliciting for your assistance to enable us transfer into your account the said funds. Our country losses a lot of money everyday that is why the international community is very careful and warning their citizens to be careful but I tell you "A TRIAL WILL CONVINCE YOU".

The source of the fund is as follows; during the last military regime here in Nigeria this committee awarded a contract of US$400million to a group of five construction companies on behalf of the NIGERIA NATIONAL PETROLEUM CORPORATION for the construction of the oil pipelines in Kaduna, Port-Harcourt, Warri refineries. During this process my colleagues and I deliberately inflated the total contract sum to the tune US$428million with the intention of sharing the inflated sum of US$28. The government has since approved the sum of US$428 for us as the contract sum, but since the contract is only worth US$400million, the remaining US$28million is what we intend to transfer to reliable and safe offshore account, we are prohibited to operate foreign account in our names since we are still in government. Thus, making it impossible for us to acquire the money in our name right now, I have therefore been delegated as a matter of trust by my colleagues to look for an oversea partner into whose account we can transfer the sum of US$28million.

My colleagues and I have decided that if you/your company can be the beneficiary of this funds on our behalf, you or your company will retain 20% of the total sum US$28million while 75% will be for us the officials and remaining 5% will be used for offsetting all debts/expenses incurred during this transaction.

We have decided that this transaction can only proceed under the following conditions:
1. That you treat this transaction with utmost secrecy and confidentiality and conviction of your transparent honesty.
2. That upon the receipt of the funds you will release the funds as instructed by us after you have removed your share of 20%. Please acknowledge the receipt of this letter using the above telephone and fax numbers. I will bring you into the nomenclature of this transaction when I have heard from you.

Your urgent response will be highly appreciated as we catching on the next payment schedule for the financial quarter. Please be assured that this transaction is 100% legal/risk free, only trust can make the reality of this transaction.

Best Regards,

Tony Okeke
MR. TONY OKEKE

FIGURE 2-13 Nigerian National Petroleum Company

The infamous hacker Kevin Mitnick (whose exploits are detailed in an Offline section in this chapter) once stated:

> "People are the weakest link. You can have the best technology; firewalls, intrusion-detection systems, biometric devices...and somebody can call an unsuspecting employee. That's all she wrote, baby. They got everything."[40]

Buffer Overflow

Buffers are used when there is a mismatch in the processing rates between two entities involved in a communication process. A **buffer overflow** is an application error that occurs when more data is sent to a buffer than it can handle. During a buffer overflow, the attacker can make the target system execute instructions, or the attacker can take advantage of some other unintended consequence of the failure. Sometimes this is limited to a denial-of-service attack, when the attacked system shuts down and is (until it's restarted) unavailable to users. In either case, data on the attacked system loses integrity.[41] In 1998, Microsoft encountered the following buffer overflow problem:

> "Microsoft acknowledged that if you type a res:// URL (a Microsoft-devised type of URL) which is longer than 256 characters in Internet Explorer 4.0, the browser will crash. No big deal, except that anything after the 256th character can be executed on the computer. This maneuver, known as a buffer overrun, is just about the oldest hacker trick in the book. Tack some malicious code (say, an executable version of the Pentium-crashing FooF code) onto the end of the URL, and you have the makings of a disaster."[42]

Timing Attack

Relatively new, the **timing attack** works by exploring the contents of a Web browser's cache. These attacks allow a Web designer to create a malicious form of cookie that is stored on the client's system. The cookie could allow the designer to collect information on how to access password-protected sites.[43] Another attack by the same name involves attempting to intercept cryptographic elements to determine keys and encryption algorithms.[44]

Chapter Summary

- Information security performs four important functions for an organization:
  - Protects the organization's ability to function
  - Enables the safe operation of applications implemented on the organization's IT systems
  - Protects the data the organization collects and uses
  - Safeguards the technology assets in use at the organization
- To make sound decisions about information security, management must be informed about threats facing the organization, its people, applications, data, and information systems.
- Threats, or dangers facing an organization's people, information, and systems, fall into the following twelve general categories:
  - Acts of Human Error or Failure—Acts performed without intent or malicious purpose by an authorized user (these are the reason why employees constitute one of the greatest threats to information security).
  - Compromises to Intellectual Property—Use of another person's intellectual property without proper payment or attribution to the source.
  - Deliberate Acts of Espionage or Trespass—Acts involving an unauthorized individual gaining access to the information an organization is trying to protect.
  - Deliberate Acts of Information Extortion—Acts involving an attacker or trusted insider stealing information from a computer system and demanding compensation for its return or for an agreement not to disclose the information.

- Deliberate Acts of Sabotage or Vandalism—Assaults on the electronic face of an organization—that is, its Web site.

- Deliberate Acts of Theft—The illegal taking of another's property.

- Deliberate Software Attacks—Attacks that occur when an individual or group designs and launches software, such as viruses and worms, to deliberately attack a system.

- Forces of Nature—Events resulting from forces of nature, *force majeure*, or acts of God and posing some of the most dangerous threats as they are often unexpected and can occur with very little warning.

- Deviations in Quality of Service—Situations in which a product or service is not delivered to the organization as expected.

- Technical Hardware Failures or Errors—Failures or errors that occur when a manufacturer distributes equipment containing a known or unknown flaw.

- Technical Software Failures or Errors—Failures or errors resulting from software with unknown, hidden faults.

- Technological Obsolescence—State of organization having infrastructure that is antiquated or outdated and can, therefore, lead to unreliable and untrustworthy systems.

- An **attack** is a deliberate act that takes advantage of a vulnerability to compromise a controlled system. It is accomplished by a **threat agent** that damages or steals an organization's information or physical asset. A **vulnerability** is an identified weakness in a controlled system, where controls are not present or are no longer effective. Major types of attack are:

  - Malicious code—Attacks that include the execution of viruses, worms, Trojan horses, and active Web scripts with the intent to destroy or steal information.

  - Back door—Attacks in which an attacker gains access to system or network resources through an access path that bypasses usual security controls.

  - Cracking—Attacks involving attempts to reverse-calculate a password; may use a brute force approach or a dictionary attack.

  - Denial-of-service (DoS)—Attacks in which the attacker sends such a large number of connection or information requests to a target that the target system cannot handle them. Distributed denial-of-service (DDoS) attacks involve the launching of a coordinated stream of requests against a target from many locations at the same time.

  - Spoofing—Attacks in which an intruder sends messages to a computer with an IP address that indicates that the message is coming from a trusted host.

  - Man-in-the-middle or TCP hijacking—Attacks in which an attacker sniffs packets from the network, modifies them, and inserts them back into the network.

  - Spam—Attacks involving sending unsolicited commercial e-mail.

  - Mail bomb—Attacks in which an attacker routes large quantities of e-mail to the target.

  - Sniffer—Programs or devices that can monitor data traveling over a network; unauthorized sniffers can be extremely dangerous to a network's security, because they are virtually impossible to detect and can be inserted almost anywhere.

  - Social engineering—Attacks in which an attacker uses social skills to convince people to reveal access credentials or other valuable information.

  - Buffer Overflow—Attacks involving an application error that occurs when more data is sent to a buffer than it can handle; during this error, the attacker can gain control over the target system, or take advantage of some other unintended consequence of the failure.

  - Timing attack—Attacks that work by exploring the contents of a Web browser's cache.

Review Questions

1. Why is information security a management problem? What can management do that technology cannot?

2. Why is data the most important asset an organization possesses? What other assets in the organization require protection?

3. It is important to protect data in motion (transmission) and data at rest (storage). In what other state must data be protected? In which of the three states is data most difficult to protect?

4. How does a threat to information security differ from an attack? How can the two overlap?

5. How can dual controls, such as two-person confirmation, reduce the threats from acts of human error and failure? What other controls can reduce this threat?

6. Why do employees constitute one of the greatest threats to information security?

7. What measures can individuals take to protect against shoulder surfing?

8. How has the perception of the hacker changed over recent years? What is the profile of a hacker today?

9. What is the difference between a skilled hacker and an unskilled hacker (other than the lack of skill)? How does the protection against each differ?

10. What are the various types of malware? How do worms differ from viruses? Do Trojan horses carry viruses or worms?

11. Why does polymorphism cause greater concern than traditional malware? How does it affect detection?

12. What is the most common form of violation of intellectual property? How does an organization protect against it? What agencies fight it?

13. What are the various types of *force majeure*? Which type might be of greatest concern to an organization in Las Vegas? Oklahoma City? Miami? Los Angeles?

14. How does technological obsolescence constitute a threat to information security? How can an organization protect against it?

15. What is the difference between an exploit and vulnerability?

16. What are the types of password attacks? What can a systems administrator do to protect against them?

17. What is the difference between a denial-of-service attack and a distributed denial-of-service attack? Which is potentially more dangerous and devastating? Why?

18. For a sniffer attack to succeed, what must the attacker do? How can an attacker gain access to a network to use the sniffer system?

19. What are some ways a social engineering hacker can attempt to gain information about a user's login and password? How would this type of attack differ if it were targeted towards an administrator's assistant versus a data-entry clerk?

20. What is a buffer overflow, and how is it used against a Web server?

Exercises

1. Consider the statement: an individual threat agent, like a hacker, can be represented in more than one threat category. If a hacker hacks into a network, copies a few files, defaces the Web page, and steals credit card numbers, how many different threat categories does this attack cover?

2. Using the Web, research Mafiaboy's exploits. When and how did he compromise sites? How was he caught?

3. Search the Web for the "The Official Phreaker's Manual." What information contained in this manual might help a security administrator to protect a communications system?

4. The chapter discussed many threats to information security. Using the Web, find at least two other sources of information on threats. Begin with *www.securitystats.com*.

5. Using the categories of threats mentioned in this chapter, as well as the various attacks described, review several newspapers and locate examples of each.

Case Exercises

Soon after the board of directors meeting, Charlie was promoted to Chief Information Security Officer, a new position that reports to the CIO Gladys Williams. That was created to provide leadership for SLS's efforts to improve its security profile.

Questions:

1. How do Fred, Gladys, and Charlie perceive the scope and scale of the new information security effort?

2. How will Fred measure success when he evaluates Gladys' performance for this project? How about Charlie's performance?

3. Which of the threats discussed in this chapter should receive Charlie's attention early in his planning process?

Endnotes

1. Daniel S. Levine. "One on One with Charles Cresson Wood of InfoSecurity Infrastructure." *Techbiz Online*. 12 October 2001. [Cited 14 February 2004]. Available from the World Wide Web <*http://www.sanfrancisco.bizjournals.com/sanfrancisco/stories/2001/10/15/newscolumn7.html*>.

2. SUN-TZU. "THE PRINCIPLES OF WARFARE - THE ART OF WAR," Chapter Three: Planning Attacks. Accessed 2/16/04 from <*http://www.sonshi.com/sun3.html*>.

3. Lawrence A. Gordon, Martin P. Loeb, William Lucyshyn, and Robert Richardson (2004). 2004 CSI/FBI Computer Crime and Security Survey. [Cited 21 June 2004]. Available from the World Wide Web <*http://www.gocsi.com*>.

4. Michael Whitman. "Enemy at the Gates: Threats to Information Security." *Communications of the ACM*, 46(8). August 2003, pp. 91-96.

5. Michael Whitman. "Enemy at the Gates: Threats to Information Security." *Communications of the ACM*, 46(8) August 2003, pp. 91-96.

6. James T. Kennedy. "Internet Intricacies: Don't Get Caught in the Net." *Contingency Planning & Management* **3**, no. 1, p. 12.

7. FOLDOC. "Intellectual Property." *FOLDOC Online*. 27 March 1997. [Cited 15 February 2004]. Available from the World Wide Web <*http://foldoc.doc.ic.ac.uk/foldoc/foldoc.cgi?query=intellectual+property*>.

8. Natalie Patton. "Bootlegged Software Could Cost Community College." *Las Vegas Review Journal Online*. 18 September 1997. [Cited 15 February 2004]. Available from the World Wide Web <*http://www.lvrj.com/lvrj_home/1997/Sep-18-Thu-1997/news/6072867.html*>.

9. Merriam-Webster. "hackers." *Merriam-Webster Online*. [Cited 15 February 2004]. Available from the World Wide Web <*http://www.m-w.com*>.

10. Pankaj Chowdhry. "The Gibraltar Hack: Anatomy of a Break-in." *PCWeek* 16, no. 41 (1999): 1, 22.

11. Linda Rosencrance. "Teen hacker 'Mafiaboy' sentenced." *ComputerWorld Online*. 15 February 2004. Available from the World Wide Web <*http://www.computerworld.com/securitytopics/security/story/0,10801,63823,00.html*>.

12. Excerpt from *Takedown*. "Kevin Mitnick." *Takedown Online*. [Cited 15 February 2004]. Available from the World Wide Web <*http://www.takedown.com/bio/mitnick1.html*>.

13. Reuters. "Hacker Legend Meets Former Target." *ZDNet Online*. 15 February 2004. Available from the World Wide Web <*http://www.zdnet.com/2100-1105-842318.html*>.

14. "Rebuffed Internet extortionist posts stolen credit card data." *CNN Online*. 10 January 2000. [Cited 16 February 2004]. Available from the World Wide Web <*http://www.cnn.com/2000/TECH/computing/01/10/credit.card.crack.2/*>.

15. Brian McWilliams. "PhD Student Arrested in Blackmail Attempt." *Internet News Online*. 25 May 2000. [Cited 15 February 2004]. Available from the World Wide Web <*http://www.internetnews.com/bus-news/article.php/380531*>.

16. Lawrence M. Walsh and Anne Saita. "Hacked Off: Black Hat and DefCon Served their Purpose, but Failed to Live up to Expectations." *Information Security Magazine Online*. August 2001. [Cited 15 February 2004]. Available from the World Wide Web <*http://www.infosecuritymag.com/articles/august01/departments_news.shtml*>.

17. Sam Costello. "Attrition.org stops mirroring Web site defacements." *ComputerWorld Online*. 22 May 2001. [Cited 15 February 2004]. Available from the World Wide Web. <*http://www.computerworld.com/securitytopics/security/story/0,10801,60769,00.html*>.

18. Dorothy E. Denning. "Activism, Hacktivism, and Cyberterrorism: The Internet as a Tool for Influencing Foreign Policy." *Info War Online*. 4 February 2000. [Cited 1 February 2002]. Available from the World Wide Web <*http://www.infowar.com/class_2/00/class2_020400b_j.shtml*>.

19. Dorothy E. Denning. "Activism, Hacktivism, and Cyberterrorism: The Internet as a Tool for Influencing Foreign Policy." *Info War Online.* 4 February 2000. [Cited 1 February 2002]. Available from the World Wide Web <*http://www.infowar.com/class_2/00/class2_020400b_j.shtml*>.

20. April Brousseau. "Cybersecurity Threat Evaluated." *2001 MEDiA Student Group Online.* [Cited 1 February 2002]. Available from the World Wide Web <*http://media.sa.utoronto.ca/jup460/april.pdf*>.

21. Infowar.com. "Hacker's Death: Murder or Suicide?" *Info War Online.* 2 December 1998. [Cited 1 February 2002]. Available from the World Wide Web <*http://www.infowar.com/hacker/hack_120298d_j.shtml*>.

22. D. Ian Hopper. "'Mafiaboy' Faces up to 3 Years in Prison." *CNN.com Online.* 19 April 2000. [Cited 15 February 2004]. Available from the World Wide Web <*http://www.cnn.com/2000/TECH/computing/04/19/dos.charges/index.html*>.

23. Bernhard Warner. "Internet Firm Hacked Out of Business." *Tech Update Online.* [Cited 15 February 2004]. Available from the World Wide Web <*http://www.techupdate.zdnet.com/techupdate/stories/main/0,14179,2844881,00.html*>.

24. Brendan P. Kehoe. *Zen and the Art of the Internet,* 1st Edition. January 1992. [Cited 15 February 2004]. Available from the World Wide Web <*http://www.cs.indiana.edu/docproject/zen/zen-1.0_10.html#SEC91*>.

25. "Murphy's Laws Site." [Cited 15 February 2004]. Available from the World Wide Web <*http://www.murphys-laws.com/*>.

26. Alexander Wolfe. "Intel Preps Plan to Bust Bugs in Pentium MPUs." *Electronic Engineering Times* no. 960 (June 1997): 1.

27. Roger Taylor. "Intel to Launch New Chip Despite Bug Reports." *Financial Times* (London), 25 June 1998, 52.

28. Trusecure. "Trusecure Successfully Defends Customers Against Goner Virus." *Trusecure Online.* 18 December 2001. [Cited 15 February 2004]. Available from the World Wide Web <*http://www.trusecure.com/company/press/release755.shtml*>.

29. SANS Institute. "Back Door NSA Glossary of Terms Used in Security and Intrusion Detection." *SANS Institute Online.* [Cited 15 February 2004]. Available from the World Wide Web <*http://www.sans.org/newlook/resources/glossary.html*>.

30. SANS Institute. "The Twenty Most Critical Internet Security Vulnerabilities (Updated): The Experts' Consensus." *SANS Institute Online.* 2 May 2002. [Cited 15 February 2004]. Available from the World Wide Web <*http://www.sans.org/top20.html*>.

31. SANS Institute. "Consensus Roadmap for Defeating Distributed Denial of Service Attacks: A Project of the Partnership for Critical Infrastructure Security." *SANS Institute Online.* 23 February 2000. [Cited 15 February 2004]. Available from the World Wide Web <*http://www.sans.org/dosstep/roadmap.php*>.

32. Paul Brooke. "DDoS: Internet Weapons of Mass Destruction." *Network Computing* 12, no. 1 (January 2001): 67.

33. Trend Micro. "WORM_MYDOOM.A." [Cited February 14, 2004]. Available from the World Wide Web <*http://www.trendmicro.com/vinfo/virusencyclo/default5.asp?VName=WORM_MYDOOM.A*>.

34. CERT® Advisory CA-1996-21 TCP SYN Flooding and IP Spoofing Attacks, CERT. "TCP SYN Flooding and IP Spoofing Attacks." advisory CA-1996-21.

35. Webopedia. "IP spoofing." *Webopedia Online.* 4 June 2002. [Cited 15 February 2004]. Available from the World Wide Web <*http://www.webopedia.com/TERM/I/IP_spoofing.html*>.

36. Bhavin Bharat Bhansali. "Man-In-The-Middle Attack: A Brief." *SANS Institute Online.* 16 February 2001. [Cited 15 February 2004]. Available from the World Wide Web *<http://www.giac.org/practical/gsec/Bhavin_Bhansali_GSEC.pdf>.*

37. James Pearce. "Security Expert Warns of MP3 Danger." *ZDNet News Online.* 18 March 2002. [Cited 15 February 2004]. Available from the World Wide Web *<http://zdnet.com.com/2100-1105-861995.html>.*

38. Webopedia. "sniffer." *Webopedia Online.* 5 February 2002. [Cited 15 February 2004]. Available from the World Wide Web *<http://www.webopedia.com/TERM/s/sniffer.html>.*

39. CERT® Advisory CA-1991-03 Unauthorized Password Change Requests Via Mail Messages, CERT. "Unauthorized Password Change Requests Via Mail Messages." advisory CA-1991-03.

40. Elinor Abreu. "Kevin Mitnick Bares All." *NetworkWorldFusion News Online.* 28 September 2000. [Cited 15 February 2004]. Available from the World Wide Web *<http://www.nwfusion.com/news/2000/0928mitnick.html>.*

41. Webopedia. "buffer overflow." *Webopedia Online.* 29 July 2003. [Cited 15 February 2004]. Available from the World Wide Web *<http://www.webopedia.com/TERM/b/buffer_overflow.html>.*

42. Scott Spanbauer. "Pentium Bug, Meet the IE 4.0 Flaw." *PC World* 16, no. 2 (February 1998): 55.

43. Princeton University. "Standard Feature of Web Browser Design Leaves Opening For Privacy Attacks." *Science Daily Online.* 8 December 2000. [Cited 15 February 2004]. Available from the World Wide Web *<http://www.sciencedaily.com/releases/2000/12/001208074325.htm>.*

44. Gaël Hachez, François Koeune, and Jean-Jacques Quisquater. "Timing attack: what can be achieved by a powerful adversary?" (Proceedings of the 20th symposium on Information Theory in the Benelux, May 1999), 63-70.

Legal, Ethical, and Professional Issues in Information Security

3

In civilized life, law floats in a sea of ethics.

EARL WARREN, CHIEF JUSTICE, U.S. SUPREME COURT, 12 NOVEMBER 1962

HENRY MAGRUDER MADE A MISTAKE: he left a CD at the coffee station. Later, Iris Majwubu was at the coffee station, topping off her coffee cup, hoping to wrap up her work on the current SQL code module before it was time to go home. As she turned to leave, she saw the unlabeled CD on the counter. Being the helpful sort, she picked it up, intending to return it to the person who'd left it behind.

Expecting to find perhaps the latest device drivers, or someone's work from the development team's office, Iris slipped the disk into the drive of her computer and ran a virus scan against its contents. She then opened the file explorer program. She had been correct in assuming the CD contained data files, lots of them. She opened a file at random, and names, addresses, and Social Security numbers scrolled down her screen. These were not the test records she expected; instead they looked more like critical payroll data. Concerned, she found a readme.txt file and opened it. It read:

```
Jill, see files on this disc. Hope they meet your
expectations. Wire money to my account as arranged.
Rest of data sent on payment.
```

Iris realized that someone was selling sensitive company data to an outside information broker. She looked back at the directory listing and saw that the files spanned the range of every department at Sequential Label and Supply—everything from customer lists to shipping invoices. She saw one file that she knew contained the credit card numbers for every Web customer the company supplied. She opened another file and saw that it stopped about halfway through the data. Whoever did this had split the data into two parts. That made sense: payment on delivery of the first half.

Now, who did this belong to? She opened up the file properties option on the readme.txt file. The file owner was listed as "hmagruder." That must be Henry Magruder, the developer two cubes over in the next aisle. Iris pondered her next action.

LEARNING OBJECTIVES:

Upon completion of this material, you should be able to:

- Use this chapter as a guide for future reference on laws, regulations, and professional organizations
- Differentiate between laws and ethics
- Identify major national laws that relate to the practice of information security
- Understand the role of culture as it applies to ethics in information security

Introduction

This chapter covers information security law and ethics. Although the two topics are intertwined, the first part of this chapter focuses on relevant legislation and regulation concerning the management of information in an organization. The second part of the chapter presents ethical issues for information security as well as a summary of professional organizations with established ethical codes. Use this chapter both as a reference to the legal aspects of information security and as an aide in planning your professional career.

As a future information security professional, you must understand the scope of an organization's legal and ethical responsibilities. The information security professional plays an important role in an organization's approach to controlling liability for privacy and security risks. In the modern litigious societies of the world, sometimes laws are enforced in civil courts where large damages are awarded to plaintiffs who bring suits against organizations. Sometimes these damages are assessed to set an example. To minimize these liabilities and reduce risks from electronic and physical threats, and to reduce all losses from legal action, information security practitioners must thoroughly understand the current legal environment, stay current with laws and regulations, and watch for new issues as they emerge. By educating the management and employees of an organization on their legal and ethical obligations and the proper use of information technology and information security, security professionals can help keep an organization focused on its primary objectives.

Law and Ethics in Information Security

In general individuals elect to trade some aspects of personal freedom for social order. As Jean-Jacques Rousseau explains in *The Social Contract Or Principles Of Political Right*[1] (1762), the rules the members of a society create to balance the right of the individual to self-determination with the needs of the society as a whole are called *laws*. **Laws** are rules that mandate or prohibit certain behavior in society; they are drawn from **ethics**, which define socially acceptable behaviors. The key difference between laws and ethics is that laws carry the sanctions of a governing authority and ethics do not. Ethics in turn are based on **cultural mores**: the fixed moral attitudes or customs of a particular group. Some ethics are recognized as universal. For example, murder, theft, assault, and arson are commonly accepted as actions that deviate from ethical and legal codes in the civilized world.

Types of Law

There are various categories of laws. **Civil law** represents a wide variety of laws that govern a nation or state. **Criminal law** addresses violations harmful to society and is actively enforced through prosecution by the state. **Tort law** enables individuals to seek recourse against others in the event of personal, physical, or financial injury. Torts are enforced via individual lawsuits rather than criminal prosecutions by the state. When someone brings a legal action under tort law, personal attorneys present the evidence and argue the details rather than representatives of the state, who prosecute criminal cases.

The categories of laws that affect the individual in the workplace are private law and public law. **Private law** regulates the relationship between the individual and the organization, and encompasses family law, commercial law, and labor law. **Public law** regulates the structure and administration of government agencies and their relationships with citizens, employees, and other governments, providing careful checks and balances. Examples of public law include criminal, administrative, and constitutional law.

Relevant U.S. Laws

Historically, the United States has been a leader in the development and implementation of information security legislation to prevent misuse and exploitation of information and information technology. The development of information security legislation contributes to a more reliable business environment, which, in turn, enables a stable economy. In this global leadership capacity, the U.S. has demonstrated a clear understanding of the problems facing the information security field and has specified penalties for individuals and organizations that fail to follow the requirements set forth in the U.S. civil statutes. The sections that follow present the most important U.S. laws that apply to information security.

General Computer Crime Laws

There are several key laws relevant to the field of information security. The **Computer Fraud and Abuse Act of 1986 (CFA Act)** is the cornerstone of many computer-related federal laws and enforcement efforts. It was amended in October 1996 by the **National Information Infrastructure Protection Act of 1996**, which modified several sections of the previous act and increased the penalties for selected crimes. The punishment for offenses prosecuted under this statute varies from fines to imprisonment up to 20 years, or both.

The severity of the penalty depends on the value of the information obtained and whether the offense is judged to have been committed:

1. For purposes of commercial advantage
2. For private financial gain
3. In furtherance of a criminal act

The previous law was further changed when the **U.S.A. Patriot Act of 2001** modified a wide range of existing laws to provide law enforcement agencies with broader latitude in order to combat terrorism-related activities. The laws modified by the Patriot Act include some of the earliest laws created to deal with electronic technology.

The **Communication Act of 1934** was revised by the **Telecommunications Deregulation and Competition Act of 1996**, which attempts to modernize the archaic terminology of the older act. These much-needed updates of terminology were included as part of the **Communications Decency Act of 1996 (CDA)**. The CDA was immediately ensnared in a thorny legal debate over the attempt to define indecency, which through major publicity efforts sponsored by the Internet Blue Ribbon Campaign and by the Electronic Freedom Frontier (*www.eff.org*), quickly reached the Supreme Court. Unfortunately, the subsequent Supreme Court ruling left weak and ineffective controls in place of the original, more aggressive and ambitious law.

Another key law is the **Computer Security Act of 1987**. It was one of the first attempts to protect federal computer systems by establishing minimum acceptable security practices. The National Bureau of Standards, in cooperation with the National Security Agency, became responsible for developing these security standards and guidelines.

Privacy

The issue of privacy has become one of the hottest topics in information security at the beginning of the 21st century. Many organizations are collecting, swapping, and selling personal information as a commodity, and many individuals are becoming aware of these practices and looking to governments for protection of their privacy. The ability to collect information on an individual, combine facts from separate sources, and merge it all with other information has resulted in databases of information that were previously impossible to set up. One technology that could be used by others to monitor or track private communications was the Clipper Chip. The Clipper Chip used an algorithm with a two-part key that was to be managed by two separate government agencies, and it was reportedly designed to protect individual communications while allowing the government to decrypt suspect transmissions.[2] This technology was the focus of discussion between advocates for personal privacy and those seeking to enable more effective law enforcement. Consequently, this technology was never implemented by the U.S. government.

In response to the pressure for privacy protection, the number of statutes addressing an individual's right to privacy has grown. It must be understood, however, that **privacy** in this context is not absolute freedom from observation, but rather is a more precise "state of being free from unsanctioned intrusion."[3] To help you better understand this rapidly evolving issue, some of the more relevant privacy laws are presented here.

Privacy of Customer Information

Part of the regulations represented in the U.S. legal code specify the responsibilities of common carriers (organizations that process or move data for hire) to protect the confidentiality of customer information, including that of other carriers. The **Privacy of**

Customer Information Section of the common carrier regulation specifies that any proprietary information shall be used explicitly for providing services, and not for any marketing purposes.[4] It also stipulates that carriers cannot disclose this information except when necessary to provide their services. The only other exception is when a customer requests the disclosure of information, and then the disclosure is restricted to that customer's information only. This law does allow for the use of aggregate information, as long as the same information is provided to all common carriers and all carriers possessing the information engage in fair competitive business practices. **Aggregate information** is created by combining pieces of data that are not considered private in themselves, but may raise privacy concerns when taken together. This is particularly important for customers whose data is collected in software updates and with cookies.

While the common carrier regulation described above regulates public carriers in the protection of an individual's privacy, **The Federal Privacy Act of 1974** regulates the government in the protection of individual privacy. The Federal Privacy Act was created to ensure that government agencies protect the privacy of individuals' and businesses' information and to hold those agencies responsible if any portion of this information is released without permission. The following agencies, regulated businesses, and individuals are exempted from some of the regulations so that they can perform their duties:

- Bureau of the Census
- National Archives and Records Administration
- Congress
- Comptroller General
- Federal courts with regard to specific issues using appropriate court orders
- Credit reporting agencies
- Individuals or organizations that demonstrate that information is necessary to protect the health or safety of that individual

The **Electronic Communications Privacy Act of 1986** is a collection of statutes that regulate the interception of wire, electronic, and oral communications. These statutes work in conjunction with the **Fourth Amendment of the U.S. Constitution**, which protects individuals from unlawful search and seizure.

The **Health Insurance Portability and Accountability Act Of 1996 (HIPAA)**, also known as the **Kennedy-Kassebaum Act**, is an attempt to protect the confidentiality and security of health-care data by establishing and enforcing standards and by standardizing electronic data interchange. HIPAA impacts all health-care organizations, including doctors' practices, health clinics, life insurers, and universities, as well as some organizations that have self-insured employee health programs. HIPAA specifies stiff penalties for organizations that fail to comply with the law, with fines up to $250,000 and/or 10 years imprisonment for knowingly misusing client information. Organizations had until April 14, 2003 to comply with the act, although extensions to this deadline have since been granted.[5]

How does HIPAA affect the field of information security? Beyond the basic privacy guidelines, the act requires organizations that retain health-care information to use information security mechanisms to protect this information, as well as policies and procedures to maintain this security. It also requires a comprehensive assessment of the organization's information security systems, policies, and procedures. Electronic signatures have become more prevalent, and HIPAA provides guidelines for the use of these signatures based on security standards that ensure message integrity, user authentication, and nonrepudiation. There is no specification of particular security technologies for each of the security requirements, only that security must be implemented to ensure the privacy of the health-care information.

The privacy standards of HIPAA severely restrict the dissemination and distribution of private health information without documented consent. The standards provide patients with the right to know who has access to their information and who has accessed it. The standards also restrict the use of health information to the minimum necessary for the health-care services required.

HIPAA has five fundamental principles:

1. Consumer control of medical information
2. Boundaries on the use of medical information
3. Accountability for the privacy of private information
4. Balance of public responsibility for the use of medical information for the greater good measured against impact to the individual
5. Security of health information

The **Financial Services Modernization Act** or **Gramm-Leach-Bliley Act of 1999** contains a number of provisions focusing on facilitating affiliation among banks, securities firms, and insurance companies. Specifically, this act requires all financial institutions to disclose their privacy policies on the sharing of nonpublic personal information. It also requires due notice to customers, so that they can request that their information not be shared with third parties. In addition, the act ensures that the privacy policies in effect in an organization are both fully disclosed when a customer initiates a business relationship, and distributed at least annually for the duration of the professional association.

This discussion of information security–related laws is supplemented in Table 3-1.

Table 3-1 Key U.S. Laws of Interest to Information Security Professionals

Act	Subject	Date	Web Resource Location	Description
Communications Act of 1934, updated by Telecommunications Deregulation and Competition Act of 1996	Telecommunications	1934 (amended 1996 and 2001)	*www.fcc.gov/Reports/ 1934new.pdf*	Regulates interstate and foreign telecommunications
Computer Fraud and Abuse Act (also known as Fraud and Related Activity in Connection with Computers (18 U.S.C. 1030)	Threats to computers	1986 (amended 1994, 1996, and 2001)	*www.usdoj.gov/ criminal/cybercrime/ 1030_new.html*	Defines and formalizes laws to counter threats from computer-related acts and offenses
Computer Security Act of 1987	Federal Agency Information Security	1987	*www.cio.gov/ Documents/ computer_security_ act_Jan_1998.html*	Requires all federal computer systems that contain classified information to have surety plans in place, and requires periodic security training for all individuals who operate, design, or manage such systems

Table 3-1   Key U.S. Laws of Interest to Information Security Professionals (continued)

Act	Subject	Date	Web Resource Location	Description
Economic Espionage Act of 1996	Trade secrets	1996	*www.ncix.gov/pubs/ online/eea_96.htm*	Designed to prevent abuse of information gained by an individual working in one company and employed by another
Electronic Communications Privacy Act Of 1986	Cryptography	1986	*http://www.cpsr.org/ cpsr/privacy/ communications/ wiretap/electronic_ commun_privacy_ act.txt*	Also referred to as the Federal Wiretapping Act; regulates interception and disclosure of electronic information
Federal Privacy Act Of 1974	Privacy	1974	*www.usdoj.gov/foia/ privstat.htm*	Governs federal agency use of personal information
Gramm-Leach-Bliley Act of 1999 (GLB) or Financial Services Modernization Act	Banking	1999	*www.senate.gov/~ banking/conf/*	Focuses on facilitating affiliation among banks, insurance, and securities firms; it has significant impact on the privacy of personal information used by these industries
Health Insurance Portability and Accountability Act (HIPAA)	Health care privacy	1996	*www.hhs.gov/ocr/ hipaa/*	Regulates collection, storage, and transmission of sensitive personal health care information
National Information Infrastructure Protection Act of 1996	Criminal intent	1996	*https://www.cnet. navy.mil/niipa.pdf*	Categorized crimes based on defendant's authority to access computer *and* criminal intent
Sarbanes-Oxley Act of 2002	Financial Reporting	2002	*http://news.findlaw.com/ hdocs/docs/gwbush/ sarbanesoxley072302.pdf*	Affects how public organizations and accounting firms deal with corporate governance, financial disclosure, and the practice of public accounting

Table 3-1 Key U.S. Laws of Interest to Information Security Professionals (continued)

Act	Subject	Date	Web Resource Location	Description
Security and Freedom Through Encryption Act of 1999	Use and sale of software that uses or enables encryption	1999	*http://thomas.loc.gov/ cgi-bin/query/z?c106: H.R.850.IH*	Clarifies use of encryption for people in the United States and permits all persons in the U.S. to buy or sell any encryption product and states that the government cannot require the use of any kind of key escrow system for encryption products.
U.S.A. Patriot Act of 2001 (H.R. 3162)	Terrorism	2001	*http://www.legal-database.com/patriot-act.htm*	Defines stiffer penalties for prosecution of terrorist crimes

Export and Espionage Laws

The discussion up to this point has been focused on domestic laws and issues. There are also considerations to be made for international issues. The need to ensure national security, and to protect trade secrets and a variety of other state and private assets, has led to several laws restricting what information and information management and security resources may be exported from the United States. These laws attempt to stem the theft of information by establishing strong penalties for related crimes. The Economic Espionage Act of 1996 and the Security and Freedom Through Encryption Act of 1999 are two laws that directly affect information security.

In an attempt to protect American ingenuity, intellectual property, and competitive advantage, Congress passed the **Economic Espionage Act (EEA)** in 1996. This law attempts to prevent trade secrets from being illegally shared.

The **Security And Freedom Through Encryption Act of 1999** provides guidance on the use of encryption, and provides measures of protection from government intervention. The acts include provisions that:

- Reinforce an individual's right to use or sell encryption algorithms, without concern for regulations requiring some form of key registration. Key registration is the storage of a cryptographic key (or its text equivalent) with another party to be used to break the encryption of data. This is often called "key escrow."
- Prohibit the federal government from requiring the use of encryption for contracts, grants, and other official documents, and correspondence.
- State that the use of encryption is not probable cause to suspect criminal activity.
- Relax export restrictions by amending the Export Administration Act of 1979.
- Provide additional penalties for the use of encryption in the commission of a criminal act.

As illustrated in Figure 3-1, the distribution of many software packages is restricted to approved organizations, governments, and countries.

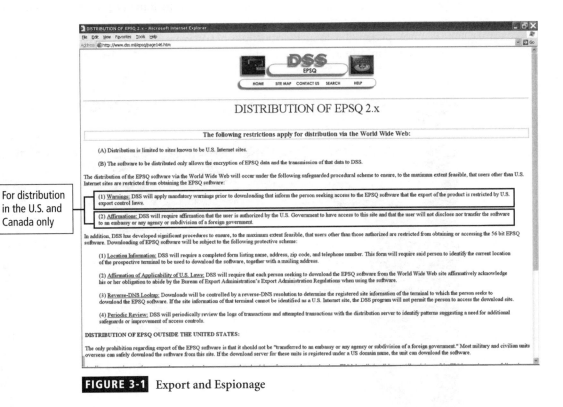

For distribution in the U.S. and Canada only

FIGURE 3-1 Export and Espionage

U.S. Copyright Law

Intellectual property is recognized as a protected asset in the United States. The U.S. copyright laws extend this privilege to the published word, including electronic formats. Fair use of copyrighted materials includes their use to support news reporting, teaching, scholarship, and a number of other related activities, so long as the use is for educational or library purposes, not for profit, and is not excessive. As long as proper acknowledgement is provided to the original author of such works, including a proper description of the location of source materials (citation), and the work is not represented as one's own, it is entirely permissible to include portions of someone else's work as reference. For more detailed information on copyright regulations, visit the U.S. Copyright Office Web site, shown in Figure 3-2.

FIGURE 3-2   The U.S. Copyright Office Web Site

Financial Reporting

The **Sarbanes-Oxley Act of 2002** is a critical piece of legislation that affects the executive management of publicly traded corporations and public accounting firms. This law, which is being implemented in phases, seeks to improve the reliability and accuracy of financial reporting, as well as increase the accountability of corporate governance, in publicly traded companies. Penalties for non-compliance range from fines to jail terms. Executives working in firms covered by this law will seek assurance on the reliability and quality of information systems from senior information technology managers. In turn, IT managers will likely ask information security managers to verify the confidentiality and integrity of those same information systems in a process known in the industry as sub-certification.

Freedom of Information Act of 1966 (FOIA)

The **Freedom of Information Act** allows any person to request access to federal agency records or information not determined to be a matter of national security. Agencies of the federal government are required to disclose any requested information on receipt of a written request. This requirement is enforceable in court. Some information is, however, protected from disclosure, and the act does not apply to state or local government agencies or to private businesses or individuals, although many states have their own version of the FOIA.

State And Local Regulations

In addition to the national and international restrictions placed on organizational use of computer technology, each state or locality may have a number of its own applicable laws and regulations. Information security professionals must, therefore, understand state laws and regulations and ensure that the organization's security policies and procedures comply with those laws and regulations.

For example, in 1991 the state of Georgia passed the **Georgia Computer Systems Protection Act**, which seeks to protect information, and which establishes penalties for the use of information technology to attack or exploit information systems.

International Laws and Legal Bodies

It is important for IT professionals and information security practitioners to realize that when their organizations do business on the Internet, they do business globally. As a result, these professionals must be sensitive to the laws and ethical values of many different cultures, societies, and countries. While it may be impossible to please all of the people all of the time, dealing with the laws of other states and nations is one area where it is certainly *not* easier to ask for forgiveness than for permission.

A number of different security bodies and laws are described in this section. Because of the political complexities of the relationships among nations, and the differences in culture, there are currently few international laws relating to privacy and information security. The laws discussed below are important, but are limited in their enforceability. The Web site of a typical American institution that deals in international law is shown in Figure 3-3.

FIGURE 3-3 The American Society of International Law Web Site

European Council Cyber-Crime Convention

The Council of Europe adopted the **European Council Cyber-Crime Convention** in 2001. It provides for the creation of an international task force to oversee a range of security functions associated with Internet activities for standardized technology laws across international borders. It also attempts to improve the effectiveness of international investigations into breaches of technology law. This convention has been well received by advocates of intellectual property rights because of its emphasis on copyright infringement prosecution. But even though thirty-four countries attended the signing in November, 2001, only six have actually ratified the Convention as of June 2004. These countries are Albania, Croatia, Estonia, Hungary, Lithuania, and Romania. In other words, no major nation has agreed to be bound by the Convention. The United States Senate is currently in the process of holding hearings on the Convention in order to decide whether the U.S. would be bound by its terms. Many supporters of individual rights are opposed to the adoption of the Convention because they think it unduly infringes on the rights of the individual to free speech and threatens the core civil liberties of U.S. residents. See Figure 3-4 for information on the European Union (EU) Law portal, which provides a convenient method to access more information about the legal environment in the EU.

As is true with much of the complex legislation at the international level, the Cyber-Crime Convention lacks any realistic provisions for enforcement. The overall goal of the convention is to simplify the acquisition of information for law enforcement agencies in certain types of international crimes. It also simplifies the extradition process. The convention has more than its share of skeptics, who see it as an ambiguous attempt to control a complex problem. Adversaries of the convention are afraid that it could create more problems than it solves. The product of a number of governments, the convention tends to favor the interests of national agencies over the rights of businesses, organizations, and individuals.

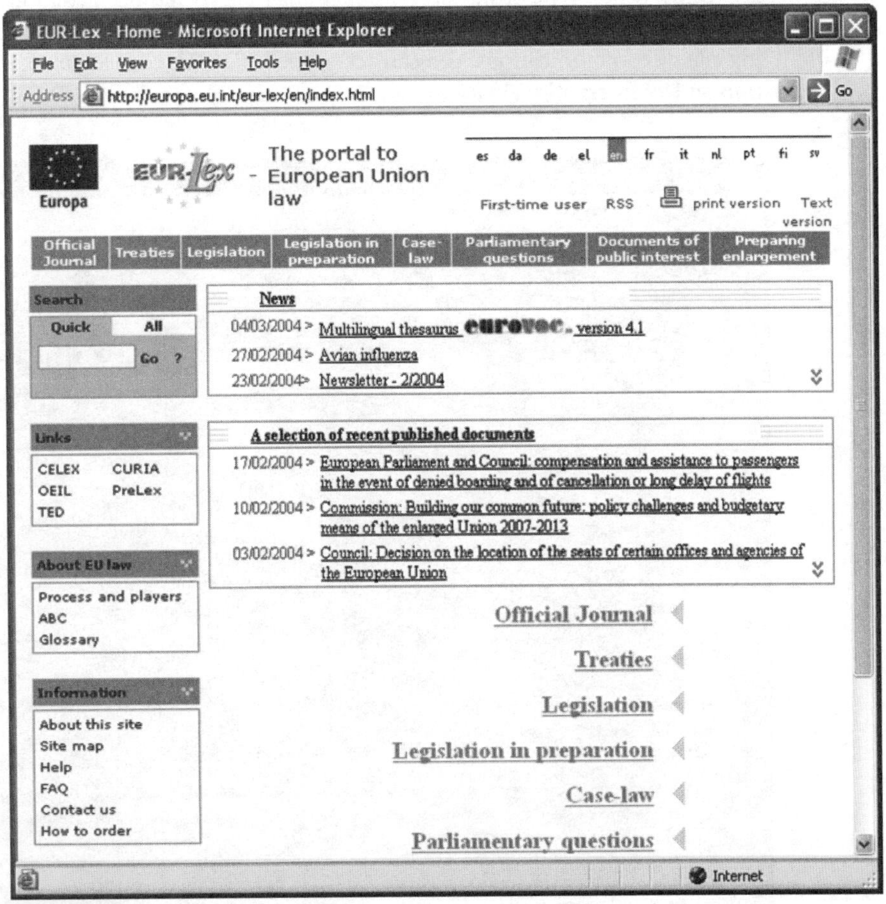

FIGURE 3-4 The EU Law Portal

Digital Millennium Copyright Act (DMCA)

The Digital Millennium Copyright Act (DMCA) is the American contribution to an international effort to reduce the impact of copyright, trademark, and privacy infringement, especially when accomplished via the removal of technological copyright protection measures. This American law was created in response to the 1995 adoption of **Directive 95/46/EC** by the European Union, which added further protection to individuals with regard to the processing of personal data and the free movement of such data. The United Kingdom has also already implemented a version of this law called the **Database Right**, in order to comply with Directive 95/46/EC.

United Nations Charter

To some degree the **United Nations Charter** makes provisions for information security during information warfare. **Information Warfare (IW)** involves the use of information technology by a sovereign state to conduct organized and lawful military operations. IW is a relatively new type of warfare, although the military has been conducting electronic warfare and counter warfare operations for decades by jamming, intercepting, and spoofing enemy communications. You can access the UN's Web site (Figure 3-5) for information on UN International Law.

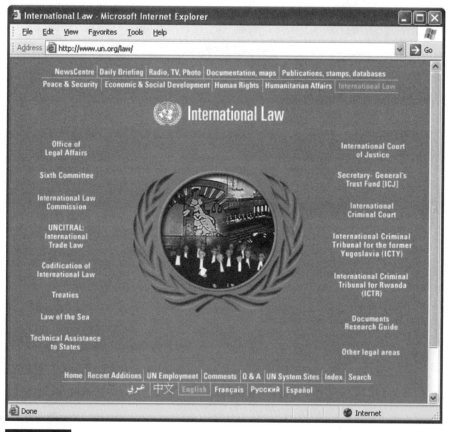

FIGURE 3-5   The UN International Law Web Site

Policy Versus Law

The sections above discuss the information security legal environment, both in the United States and on the international scene. Information security professionals must remain informed and up to date on this external legal environment. Within an organization, information security professionals help maintain security via the establishment and enforcement of policies. These **policies**—a body of expectations that describe acceptable and unacceptable employee behaviors in the workplace—function as organizational laws, complete with penalties, judicial practices, and sanctions to require compliance. Because these policies function as laws, they must be crafted with the same care, to ensure that the policies are complete, appropriate, and fairly applied to everyone in the workplace. The difference between a policy and a law, however, is that ignorance of a policy is an acceptable defense. Thus, for a policy to become enforceable, it must be:

- Distributed to all individuals who are expected to comply with it
- Readily available for employee reference
- Easily understood, with multilanguage translations and provisions for visually impaired or literacy-impaired employees
- Acknowledged by the employee, usually by means of a signed form

Only when all of these conditions are met can an organization appropriately penalize, without fear of legal retribution, employees who violate the policy.

Ethics and Information Security

Any discussion of ethics must deal with conflicts about the role of ethics and morality in the workplace. Information security professionals in organizations may be faced with an additional challenge. Many outside of their profession look to them to take a leadership role in the realm of ethical workplace behavior—in other words, to lead by example. Many professional groups have explicit rules governing ethical behavior in the workplace. For example, doctors and lawyers who commit an egregious violation of their professions' canons of conduct can be removed from practice. Unlike the medical and legal fields, however, the information technology field in general and the information security field in particular do not have a binding code of ethics. Instead, professional associations (such as the Association for Computing Machinery and the Information Systems Security Association) and accreditation agencies (such as ISC2) work to establish the profession's ethical codes of conduct. While these professional organizations can prescribe ethical conduct, they do not always have the authority to banish violators from practicing their trade. To begin exploring some of the ethical issues particular to information security, take a look at the Ten Commandments of Computer Ethics in the following Offline.

OFFLINE

The Ten Commandments of Computer Ethics [6]

From The Computer Ethics Institute

1. Thou shalt not use a computer to harm other people.
2. Thou shalt not interfere with other people's computer work.
3. Thou shalt not snoop around in other people's computer files.
4. Thou shalt not use a computer to steal.
5. Thou shalt not use a computer to bear false witness.
6. Thou shalt not copy or use proprietary software for which you have not paid.
7. Thou shalt not use other people's computer resources without authorization or proper compensation.
8. Thou shalt not appropriate other people's intellectual output.
9. Thou shalt think about the social consequences of the program you are writing or the system you are designing.
10. Thou shalt always use a computer in ways that ensure consideration and respect for your fellow humans.

Ethical Differences Across Cultures

Cultural differences can make it difficult to determine what is and is not ethical—especially when considering the use of computers. Studies on ethics and computer use reveal that individuals of different nationalities have different perspectives; difficulties arise when one nationality's ethical behavior conflicts with the ethics of another national group. For example, to Western cultures, many of the ways in which Asian cultures use computer technology is software piracy.[7] This ethical conflict arises out of Asian traditions of collective ownership, which clash with the protection of intellectual property. Approximately 90 percent of all software is created in the United States. Some countries are more relaxed with intellectual property copy restrictions than others.

A recent study, published by Dr. Michael Whitman of Kennesaw State University in the *Journal of International Business Studies*, has examined computer use ethics among nine nations: Singapore, Hong Kong, the United States, England, Australia, Sweden, Wales, and the Netherlands.[8] This study selected a number of computer-use vignettes (see the Offline titled "The Use of Scenarios in Computer Ethics Studies") and presented them to students in universities in these nine nations. This study did not categorize or classify the responses as ethical or unethical. Instead, the responses only indicated a degree of ethical sensitivity or knowledge about the performance of the individuals in the short case studies. The scenarios were grouped into three categories of ethical computer use: software license infringement, illicit use, and misuse of corporate resources.

Software License Infringement

The topic of software license infringement or piracy is routinely covered by the popular press. Overall, most of the nations studied by Dr. Whitman had similar attitudes toward software piracy. Statistically speaking, only the United States and the Netherlands had attitudes that differed substantially from those of all other countries examined. The United States was significantly less tolerant of piracy, while the Netherlands was significantly more permissive. Although a number of studies have reported that the Pacific Rim countries of Singapore and Hong Kong are hotbeds of software piracy, this study found their tolerance for copyright infringement to be moderate, as were the attitudes of England, Wales, Australia, and Sweden. What this could mean is that the individuals surveyed *understood* what software license infringement was but felt either that their use was not piracy, or that their society permitted this piracy in some way. Peer pressure, the lack of legal disincentives, the lack of punitive measures, or any one of a number of other reasons could also explain why these alleged piracy centers were not oblivious to intellectual property laws. Even though the Netherlands displayed a more permissive attitude towards piracy, it only ranked third in piracy rates of the countries surveyed in this study.

Illicit Use

The individuals studied unilaterally condemned viruses, hacking, and other forms of system abuse as unacceptable behavior. There were, however, differences among the groups as to just how tolerant individuals were. Students from Singapore and Hong Kong proved to be significantly more tolerant than those from the United States, Wales, England, and Australia. Sweden and the Netherlands were also significantly more tolerant than Wales and Australia but significantly less tolerant than Hong Kong. The low overall degree of tolerance for illicit system use may be a function of the easy association between the common crimes of breaking and entering, trespassing, theft, and destruction of property to their computer-related counterparts.

Misuse of Corporate Resources

The scenarios used to examine the levels of tolerance in this category each represented a different degree of noncompany use of corporate assets without indicating what the company's established policy toward personal use of company resources was. In general, individuals displayed a rather lenient view of personal use of company equipment. Only Singapore and Hong Kong view personal use of company equipment as unethical. There were several substantial differences in this category, with the Netherlands reporting the most lenient view. With the exceptions of Singapore and Hong Kong, it is apparent that many individuals, regardless of cultural background, feel that if an organization does not specifically forbid personal use of its computing resources, such use is acceptable. It is interesting to note that only the two Asian samples, Singapore and Hong Kong, reported generally intolerant attitudes toward personal use of organizational computing resources. The reasons behind this are unknown.

Overall, the researchers found that there is a general agreement among nationalities as to what is acceptable or unacceptable computer use. There is, however, a range of views within the acknowledgement of ethical versus unethical behavior as to whether or not some actions are moderately or highly acceptable. This set of studies underscores the intercultural similarities that exist as much as they describe the differences between cultures. It also shows little support for the popular media's portrayal of Asians as having a propensity to steal digital content. In fact, the Hong Kong and Singapore respondents did not show the most ethical flexibility among the nationalities studied. Higher piracy rates in Singapore and Hong Kong may be less a function of ethical difference and more the result of fewer legal and financial disincentives to engage in software copyright infringement. The only country that consistently ranked as least likely to honor copyrights of content creators was the Netherlands. However, this does not appear to result in copyright violations; although the Netherlands has a higher piracy rate than some nations, it still ranks behind Singapore and Hong Kong.[9]

When considering ethical issues of information security, it is useful to judge practical situations. The Offline box on scenarios in computer ethics is designed to challenge your judgment and get you thinking.

OFFLINE

The Use of Scenarios in Computer Ethics Studies

Adapted from "Cross-National Differences in Computer-Use Ethics: A Nine Country Study" By Michael E. Whitman, Anthony M. Townsend, and Anthony R. Hendrickson, *The Journal of International Business Studies*.

The following vignettes can be used in an open and frank discussion of computer ethics. Review each scenario carefully and respond to each question using the following statement, choosing the description you feel most appropriate: *I feel the actions of this individual were (very ethical / ethical / neither ethical nor unethical / unethical / very unethical).* Then, justify your response.

Ethical Decision Evaluation

Note: These scenarios are based on published works by Professor Whitman and Professor David Paradice.

1. A scientist developed a theory that required proof through the construction of a computer model. He hired a computer programmer to build the model, and the theory was shown to be correct. The scientist won several awards for the development of the theory, but he never acknowledged the contribution of the computer programmer.
   The scientist's failure to acknowledge the computer programmer was:

2. The owner of a small business needed a computer-based accounting system. One day, he identified the various inputs and outputs he felt were required to satisfy his needs. Then he showed his design to a computer programmer and asked the programmer if she could implement such a system. The programmer knew she could implement the system because she had developed much more sophisticated systems in the past. In fact, she felt this design was rather crude and would soon need several major revisions. But she didn't say anything about her feelings, because the business owner didn't ask her and she thought she might be the one hired to implement the needed revisions later.
   The programmer's decision not to point out the design flaws was:

3. A student suspected and found a loophole in the university computer's security system that allowed him access to other students' records. He told the system administrator about the loophole, but continued to access others' records until the problem was corrected two weeks later.
   The student's action in searching for the loophole was:
   The student's action in continuing to access others' records for two weeks was:
   The system administrator's failure to correct the problem sooner was:

continued

4. A computer user called a mail-order software company to order a particular accounting system. When he received his order, he found that the store had accidentally sent him a very expensive word-processing program as well as the accounting package that he had ordered. The invoice listed only the accounting package. The user decided to keep the word-processing package.

   The user's decision to keep the word-processing package was:

5. A programmer at a bank realized that he had accidentally overdrawn his checking account. He made a small adjustment in the bank's accounting system so that his account would not have the additional service charge assessed. As soon as he deposited funds that made his balance positive again, he corrected the bank's accounting system.

   The programmer's modification of the accounting system was:

6. A computer programmer enjoyed building small computer applications (programs) to give his friends. He would frequently go to his office on Saturday when no one was working and use his employer's computer to develop applications. He did not hide the fact that he was going into the building; he had to sign a register at a security desk each time he entered.

   The programmer's use of the company computer was:

7. A computer programmer built small computer applications (programs) in order to sell them. This was not his main source of income. He worked for a moderately sized computer vendor. He would frequently go to his office on Saturday when no one was working and use his employer's computer to develop applications. He did not hide the fact that he was going into the building; he had to sign a register at a security desk each time he entered.

   The programmer's use of the company computer was:

8. A student enrolled in a computer class was also employed at a local business part-time. Frequently her homework in the class involved using popular word-processing and spreadsheet packages. Occasionally she worked on her homework on the office computer at her part-time job, on her coffee or meal breaks.

   The student's use of the company computer was:

   If the student had worked on her homework during "company time" (not during a break), the student's use of the company computer would have been:

9. A student at a university learned to use an expensive spreadsheet program in her accounting class. The student would go to the university microcomputer lab and use the software to complete her assignment. Signs were posted in the lab indicating that copying software was forbidden. One day, she decided to copy the software anyway to complete her work assignments at home.

   If the student destroyed her copy of the software at the end of the term, her action in copying the software was:

   If the student forgot to destroy her copy of the software at the end of the term, her action in copying the software was:

   If the student never intended to destroy her copy of the software at the end of the term, her action in copying the software was:

continued

10. A student at a university found out that one of the local computer bulletin boards contained a "pirate" section (a section containing a collection of illegally copied software programs). He subscribed to the board, and proceeded to download several games and professional programs, which he then distributed to several of his friends.

    The student's actions in downloading the games were:

    The student's actions in downloading the programs were:

    The student's actions in sharing the programs and games with his friends were:

11. State College charges its departments for computer time usage on the campus mainframe. A student had access to the university computer system because a class she was taking required extensive computer usage. The student enjoyed playing games on the computer, and frequently had to request extra computer funds from her professor in order to complete her assignments.

    The student's use of the computer to play games was:

12. An engineer needed a program to perform a series of complicated calculations. He found a computer programmer capable of writing the program, but would only hire the programmer if he agreed to share any liability that may result from an error in the engineer's calculations. The programmer said he would be willing to assume any liability due to a malfunction of the program, but was unwilling to share any liability due to an error in the engineer's calculations.

    The programmer's position in this situation is:

    The engineer's position in this situation is:

13. A manager of a company that sells computer-processing services bought similar services from a competitor. She used her access to the competitor's computer to try to break the security system, identify other customers, and cause the system to "crash" (cause loss of service to others). She used the service for over a year and always paid her bills promptly.

    The manager's actions were:

14. One day, a student programmer decided to write a virus program. Virus programs usually make copies of themselves on other disks automatically, so the virus can spread to unsuspecting users. The student wrote a program that caused the microcomputer to ignore every fifth command entered by a user. The student took his program to the university computing lab and installed it on one of the microcomputers. Before long, the virus spread to hundreds of users.

    The student's action of infecting hundreds of users' disks was:

    If the virus program output the message "Have a nice day," then the student's action of infecting hundreds of users' disks would have been:

    If the virus erased files, then the student's action of infecting hundreds of users' files would have been:

Ethics and Education

Differences in the ethics of computer use are not exclusively international. Differences are found among individuals within the same country, within the same social class, and within the same company. Key studies reveal that the overriding factor in leveling the ethical perceptions within a small population is education. Employees must be trained and kept aware of a number of topics related to information security, not the least of which are the expected behaviors of an ethical employee. This is especially important in information security, as many employees may not have the formal technical training to understand that their behavior is unethical or even illegal. Proper ethical and legal training is vital to creating an informed, well prepared, and low-risk system user.

Deterrence to Unethical and Illegal Behavior

Whatever the cause of illegal, immoral, or unethical behavior, one thing is certain: it is the responsibility of information security personnel to do everything in their power to deter these acts and to use policy, education and training, and technology to protect information and systems. Many security professionals understand the technology aspect of protection but underestimate the value of policy. There are three general categories of unethical and illegal behavior:

- **Ignorance:** As mentioned earlier, ignorance of the law is no excuse, however ignorance of policy and procedures is. The first method of deterrence is education. This is accomplished through designing, publishing, and disseminating organization policies and relevant laws, and also gaining the agreement of all members of the organization to comply with these policies and laws. Reminders, training, and awareness programs keep the policy information in front of the individual, and thus better support retention and compliance.

- **Accident:** Individuals with authorization and privileges to manage information within the organization are most likely to cause harm or damage by accident. Careful planning and control helps prevent accidental modification to systems and data.

- **Intent:** Criminal or unethical intent goes to the state of mind of the individual performing the act. Intent is often the cornerstone of legal defense, when it becomes necessary to determine whether or not the offender acted out of ignorance, by accident, or with specific intent to cause harm or damage. Those with intent to cause harm or damage are best controlled by means of litigation, prosecution, and technical controls. If individuals have the will, ability, and intent to commit crimes, they probably will.

Deterrence

Deterrence is the best method for preventing an illegal or unethical activity. Laws, policies, and technical controls are all examples of deterrents. However, it is generally agreed that laws and policies and their associated penalties only deter if three conditions are present:

- **Fear of penalty:** The individual intending to commit the act must fear the penalty. Threats of informal reprimand or verbal warnings may not have the same impact as the threat of imprisonment or forfeiture of pay.

- **Probability of being caught:** The individual has to believe there is a strong possibility of being caught performing the illegal or unethical act. Penalties can be severe, but the penalty will not deter the behavior unless there is an expectation of being caught.

- **Probability of penalty being administered:** The individual must believe that the penalty will in fact be administered.

Codes of Ethics and Professional Organizations

A number of professional organizations have established codes of conduct or codes of ethics that members are expected to follow. Codes of ethics can have a positive effect on an individual's judgment regarding computer use.[10] Unfortunately, many employers do not encourage their employees to join these professional organizations. But individuals who have earned some level of certification or professional accreditation can be deterred from ethical lapses by the threat of loss of accreditation or certification due to a violation of a code of conduct. Loss of certification or accreditation can dramatically reduce the individual's marketability and earning power.

It is the responsibility of security professionals to act ethically and according to the policies and procedures of their employers, their professional organizations, and the laws of society. It is likewise the organization's responsibility to develop, disseminate, and enforce its policies. Following is a discussion of professional organizations and where they fit into the ethical landscape. Table 3-2 provides an overview of these organizations. Many of these organizations offer certification programs that require the applicants to subscribe formally to the ethical codes. The subject of professional certification is discussed in Chapter 11.

Table 3-2   Professional Organizations of Interest to Information Security Professionals

Professional Organization	Web Resource Location	Description	Focus
Association of Computing Machinery	*www.acm.org*	Code of 24 imperatives of personal ethical responsibilities of security professionals	Ethics of security professionals
Computer Security Division of the National Institute of Standards and Technology	*csrc.nist.gov*	Raising awareness of information technology security, especially in new and emerging technologies	Dissemination of national information on information security
Computer Security Institute	*www.gocsi.com*	Policy development, risk analysis, security awareness, and other vital aspects of information protection; practical insights into the technical problems of network security	Individual training courses and tracks (not certification)
Information Systems Audit and Control Association	*www.isaca.org*	One process area and six subject areas that focus on auditing, information security, business process analysis, and IS planning	Tasks and knowledge required of the information systems audit professional

Table 3-2 Professional Organizations of Interest to Information Security Professionals (continued)

Professional Organization	Web Resource Location	Description	Focus
Information Systems Security Association	*www.issa.org*	Professional association of information systems security professionals; provides education forums, publications, and peer networking for members	Professional security information sharing
Internet Society	*www.isoc.org*	Professional association of individuals and organizations with an interest in the promotion of the growth and leadership for the Internet	Internet leadership and development
International Information Systems Security Certification Consortium (ISC)^2	*www.isc2.org*	International Consortium dedicated to improving the quality of security professionals	Requires certificants to follow its published code of ethics
SANS Institutes Global Information Assurance Certification	*www.giac.org*	Twelve individual technical certifications that can be tied into six tracks, or culminate in the capstone GIAC Security Engineer certification	Requires certificants to follow its published code of ethics

Major Professional Organizations for IT

The ethical codes of a few of the major professional organizations for IT are examined in the following paragraphs.

Association of Computing Machinery (ACM): The ACM (*www.acm.org*) is a respected professional society that was established in 1947 as "the world's first educational and scientific computing society." It is one of the few organizations that strongly promotes education and provides discounts for student members. The ACM's code of ethics requires members to perform their duties in a manner befitting an ethical computing professional. The code contains specific references to protecting the confidentiality of information, causing no harm (with specific references to viruses), protecting the privacy of others, and respecting the intellectual property and copyrights of others. The ACM also publishes a wide variety of professional computing publications, including the highly regarded *Communications of the ACM*.

International Information Systems Security Certification Consortium, Inc. (ISC)^2: The (ISC)^2 (*www.isc2.org*) is a nonprofit organization that focuses on the development and implementation of information security certifications and credentials. The (ISC)^2 manages a body of knowledge on information security and administers and evaluates examinations for information security certifications. Currently, the (ISC)^2 offers professional certifications in the information security arena. The code of ethics put forth by (ISC)^2 is primarily designed for information security professionals who have earned a certification from (ISC)^2. This code focuses on four mandatory canons: "Protect society, the commonwealth, and the infrastructure; act honorably, honestly, justly, responsibly, and legally; provide diligent and competent service to principals; and advance and protect the profession."[11] Through this code, (ISC)^2 seeks to provide sound guidance that promotes reliance on the ethicality and trustworthiness of the information security professional as the guardian of information and systems.

System Administration, Networking, and Security Institute (SANS): SANS (*www.sans.org*) is a professional organization with a large membership dedicated to the protection of information and systems. Founded in 1989, SANS is a professional research and education cooperative organization with a current membership of more than 156,000 security professionals, auditors, system administrators, and network administrators. SANS offers a set of certifications called the Global Information Assurance Certification, or GIAC. All professionals certified by GIAC are required to make an acknowledgement that certification and the privileges that come from it carry a corresponding obligation to uphold the GIAC Code of Ethics. Those certificate holders that do not conform to this code face punishment, and may lose GIAC certification.

Information Systems Audit and Control Association (ISACA): ISACA (*www.isaca.org*) is a professional association with a focus on auditing, control, and security. The membership comprises both technical and managerial professionals. ISACA focuses on providing IT control practices and standards. Although this organization does not focus exclusively on information security, it does include many information security components within its areas of concentration. ISACA also has a code of ethics for its professionals, and it requires many of the same high standards for ethical performance as the other organizations and certifications.

Computer Security Institute (CSI): CSI (*www.gocsi.com*) provides information and training to support the computer, networking, and information security professional. Established in 1974, CSI sponsors a number of conferences and is well known for its annual computer threat survey developed in cooperation with the FBI. While the CSI does not have a code of ethics, the organization has argued for the adoption of ethical behavior among practicing information security professionals.

Information Systems Security Association (ISSA): The ISSA (*www.issa.org*) is a nonprofit society of information security professionals. As a professional association, its primary mission is to bring together qualified information security practitioners for information exchange and educational development. ISSA provides a number of scheduled conferences, meetings, publications, and information resources to promote information security awareness and education. ISSA also promotes a code of ethics, similar in content to those of (ISC)^2, ISACA, and the ACM, whose focus is "promoting management practices that will ensure the confidentiality, integrity, and availability of organizational information resources."[12]

Other Security Organizations

There are a number of professional and private societies and organizations that, while not as large and prestigious as those noted earlier, play a key role in the development and dissemination of ethical information security practices and technologies. A few of them are presented here:

The **Internet Society (ISOC)** *(www.isoc.org)* is a nonprofit, nongovernmental, international organization for professionals. It promotes the development and implementation of education, standards, policy, and education and training to promote the Internet. At the time of this writing, global membership is free. While the organization as a whole does not actively promote ethical practices education, standards, and policy, there are a number of ISOC organizations that do actively review and promote these issues; one of these is the **Internet Engineering Task Force (IETF)**. The IETF consists of individuals from the computing, networking, and telecommunications industries and is responsible for developing the Internet's technical foundations. Standards developed through the IETF are then reviewed by the Internet Engineering Steering Group (IESG), with appeal to the Internet Architecture Board, and promulgated by the Internet Society as international standards. Standards are reviewed and published through Requests for Comments (RFCs) and may be viewed at *www.rfc-editor.org*, as well as through numerous mirror sites. These RFCs are rich sources of information on the development and standardization of commonly used protocols for both the Internet and related technologies.

The **Computer Security Division (CSD)** of the National Institute for Standards and Technology, or NIST, has a resource center known as the Computer Security Resource Center (CSRC). While CSD does not promote an ethical standard or viewpoint, this organization does promote industry best practices and is an almost necessary reference for any current or aspiring information security professional. Also, its Web site *(csrc.nist.gov)* houses one of the most comprehensive sets of publicly available information on information security topics.

The **CERT Coordination Center,** or CERT/CC *(www.cert.org)*, is a center of Internet security expertise and is located at the Software Engineering Institute, a federally funded research and development center operated by Carnegie Mellon University. The CERT/CC studies security issues and provides publications and alerts to help educate the public to the threats facing information security. The center also provides training and expertise in the handling of computer incidents. CERT/CC acts both as research center and outside consultant in the areas of incident response and security practices and programs development.

The **Computer Professionals for Social Responsibility (CPSR)** is a public organization for anyone generally concerned with the impact of computer technology on society. CPSR promotes ethical and responsible development and use of computing, and seeks to inform public and private policy and lawmakers on this subject. It acts as a watchdog for the development of ethical computing.

Key U.S. Federal Agencies

There are a number of key U.S. federal agencies charged with the protection of American information resources and the investigation of threats to, or attacks on, these resources. These include the Department of Homeland Security (DHS), the Federal Bureau of Investigation's National Infrastructure Protection Center (NIPC), the National Security Administration (see Figure 3-6), and the U.S. Secret Service.

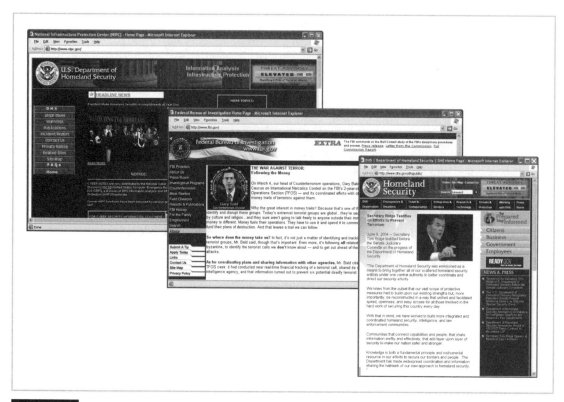

FIGURE 3-6 DHS, FBI, and NIPC Home Pages

The **Department of Homeland Security (DHS)** was created in 2003 through the Homeland Security Act of 2002, which was passed in response to the events of September 11, 2001. DHS is made up of five directorates, or divisions, through which it carries out its mission of protecting the people as well as the physical and informational assets of the United States. Of these, the Directorate of Information & Infrastructure works to create and enhance capabilities used to discover and respond to attacks on national information systems and critical infrastructure. The Science and Technology Directorate is responsible for research and development activities in support of homeland defense. This effort is guided by a continuing examination of the vulnerabilities throughout the national infrastructure, and it sponsors the emerging best practices developed to counter the threats and weaknesses in the system.

In addition, the Directorate of Information & Infrastructure promotes research and development of software and technology that will protect information systems and databases used throughout the national computer infrastructure. It continues to develop dissemination models for the promotion of current best practices for protection through the following affiliated agencies and groups:

- National Infrastructure Protection Center
- Federal Computer Incident Response Center
- SANS Institute
- CERT Coordination Center

Working with DHS, The Federal Bureau of Investigation's **National Infrastructure Protection Center (NIPC)**, at *www.nipc.gov*, was established in 1998 and serves as the U.S. government's center for threat assessment, warning, investigation, and response to threats or attacks against critical U.S. infrastructures. A key part of the NIPC's efforts to educate, train, inform, and involve the business and public sector in information security is the National InfraGard Program. Established in January 2001, the **National InfraGard Program** began as a cooperative effort between the FBI's Cleveland Field Office and local technology professionals. The FBI sought assistance in determining a more effective method of protecting critical national information resources. The resulting cooperative formed the first InfraGard chapter as a formal effort to combat both cyber and physical threats. Since then, every field office has established an InfraGard chapter, and collaborates with public and private organizations and the academic community to share information about attacks, vulnerabilities, and threats. The National InfraGard Program serves its members in four basic ways:

- By maintaining an intrusion alert network using encrypted e-mail
- By maintaining a secure Web site for communication about suspicious activity or intrusions
- Through local chapter activities
- By operating a help desk for questions

InfraGard's dominant contribution is the free exchange of information to and from the private sector in the areas of threats and attacks on information resources.

Another key federal agency is the **National Security Agency (NSA)**. The NSA is:

"...the Nation's cryptologic organization. It coordinates, directs, and performs highly specialized activities to protect U.S. information systems and produce foreign intelligence information...It is also one of the most important centers of foreign language analysis and research within the Government."[13]

The NSA (see Figure 3-7) is responsible for signal intelligence and information system security. The NSA's Information Assurance Directorate (IAD) provides information security "solutions including the technologies, specifications and criteria, products, product configurations, tools, standards, operational doctrine, and support activities needed to implement the protect, detect and report, and respond elements of cyber defense."[14] The IAD also develops and promotes an Information Assurance Framework Forum in cooperation with commercial organizations and academic researchers. This framework provides strategic guidance as well as technical specifications for security solutions. IAD's Common Criteria is a set of standards designed to promote understanding of information security.

Prominent among the NSA's efforts and activities in the information security arena are the Information Security Outreach programs. The NSA recognizes universities that not only offer information security education, but ones that have also integrated information security philosophies and efforts into the internal operations of the schools. These recognized "Centers of Excellence in Information Assurance Education" receive the honor of displaying the recognition as well as being acknowledged on the NSA's Web site. Additionally, the NSA has a program to certify curriculum in information security. The Information Assurance Courseware Evaluation process examines information security courses in an institution and, if accepted, provides a three-year accreditation. Graduates of these programs receive certificates that indicate this accreditation.

FIGURE 3-7 The National Security Agency Home Page

The **U.S. Secret Service** is a department within the Department of the Treasury. In addition to its well-known mission of providing protective services for key members of the U.S. government, the Secret Service is also charged with the detection and arrest of any person committing a United States federal offense relating to computer fraud and false identification crimes. This represents an extension of the original mission of protecting U.S. currency to areas of communications fraud and abuse—a logical extension, given that the communications networks of the U.S. carry more funds than all of the armored cars in the world combined. Protect the networks and protect the data, and you protect the money, stocks, and other financial transactions. For more information on the Secret Service, see its Web site (shown in Figure 3-8).

FIGURE 3-8 The Secret Service Web Site

Organizational Liability and the Need for Counsel

What if an organization does not demand or even encourage strong ethical behavior from its employees? What if an organization does not behave ethically? Even if there is no breach of criminal law, there is still the issue of liability. **Liability** is the legal obligation of an entity that extends beyond criminal or contract law; it includes the legal obligation to make **restitution**, or to compensate, for wrongs committed by an organization or its employees. The bottom line is that if an employee, acting with or without the authorization of the organization, performs an illegal or unethical act that causes some degree of harm, the organization can be held financially liable for that action. An organization increases its liability if it refuses to take measures known as due care. **Due care** has been taken when an organization makes sure that every employee knows what is acceptable or unacceptable behavior, and knows the consequences of illegal or unethical actions. **Due diligence** requires that an organization make a valid effort to protect others and continually maintain this level of effort. Given the Internet's global reach, those who could be injured or wronged by an organization's members could be anywhere, in any state, any country around the world. Under the U.S. legal system, any court can impose its authority over an individual or organization if it can establish **jurisdiction**—jurisdiction being the court's right to hear a case if the wrong was committed in its territory or involving its citizenry. This is sometimes referred to as **long arm jurisdiction**—the long arm of the law reaching across the country or around the world to pull an accused individual into its court systems. Trying a case in the injured party's home area is usually favorable to the injured party.[15]

Chapter Summary

- Laws are formally adopted rules for acceptable behavior in modern society. Ethics are socially acceptable behaviors. The key difference between laws and ethics is that laws carry the sanction of a governing authority and ethics do not.

- Organizations formalize desired behaviors in documents called policies. Policies must be read and agreed to before they are binding.

- Civil law represents a wide variety of laws that are used to govern a nation or state. Criminal law addresses violations that harm society and are enforced by agents of the state or nation. Tort law is conducted by means of individual lawsuits rather than criminal prosecution by the state.

- Private law focuses on individual relationships, public law addresses regulatory agencies.

- The Federal Privacy Act of 1974 regulates the government in the protection of individual privacy.

- The Electronic Communications Privacy Act of 1986 is a collection of statutes that regulate the interception of wire, electronic, and oral communications.

- The Health Insurance Portability and Accountability Act of 1996 is an attempt to protect the confidentiality and security of health-care data by establishing and enforcing standards, and by standardizing electronic data interchange.

- The desire to protect national security, trade secrets, and a variety of other state and private assets has led to several laws restricting what information and information management and security resources may be exported from the United States.

- Intellectual property is recognized as a protected asset in this country. U.S. copyright law extends this privilege to the published word, including electronic media.

- Studies have determined that individuals of differing nationalities have differing perspectives on ethical practices regarding the use of computer technology.

- Deterrence can prevent an illegal or unethical activity from occurring. Deterrence requires significant penalties, a high probability of apprehension, and an expectation of enforcement of penalties.

- As part of an effort to encourage positive ethics, a number of professional organizations have established codes of conduct or codes of ethics that their members are expected to follow.

- There are a number of U.S. federal agencies responsible for protecting American information resources and investigating threats to, or attacks on, these resources.

Review Questions

1. What is the difference between criminal law and civil law?

2. What is tort law, and what does it enable an individual to accomplish?

3. What are the primary examples of public law?

4. Which law amended the Computer Fraud and Abuse Act of 1986, and what did it change?

5. What is the constitutionality status of the Communications Decency Act?

6. What is privacy in an information security context?

7. What is another name for the Kennedy-Kassebaum Act (1996), and why is it important to organizations that are not in the health-care industry?

8. If you work for a financial service organization such as a bank or credit union, which law from 1999 affects your use of customer data? What other impacts does it have?

9. Which law from 1997 provides guidance on the use of encryption?

10. What is intellectual property (IP)? Is it afforded the same protection in every country of the world? What laws currently protect it in the United States and Europe?

11. How will the Sarbanes-Oxley Act of 2002 affect information security managers?

12. What is a policy? How does it differ from a law?

13. What are the three general categories of unethical and illegal behavior?

14. What is the best method for preventing an illegal or unethical activity?

15. Of the organizations listed in this chapter, which has been established for the longest time? When was it founded?

16. Of the organizations listed in this chapter, which is focused on auditing and control?

17. Of the organizations listed in this chapter, which sponsors a program called Global Information Assurance Certification (GIAC)?

18. What is due care? Why would an organization want to make sure it exercises due care in its usual course of operations?

19. What can be done to deter someone from committing a crime?

20. How does due diligence differ from due care? Why are both important?

Exercises

1. What does CISSP stand for? If a person has achieved the CISSP, use the Internet to determine what ethical rules they have agreed to follow.

2. For what kind of information security jobs does the NSA recruit? Use the Internet to visit its Web page and find out.

3. Using the resources available in your library, find out what laws your state has passed to prosecute computer crime.

4. Using the Web, go to *www.eff.org*. What are the current top concerns of this organization?

5. Using the ethical scenarios presented in the chapter, finish each of the incomplete statements, and bring your answers to class to compare your answers with those of your peers.

Case Exercises

Iris called the company security hotline. The hotline was an anonymous way to report any suspicious activity or abuse of company policy, although Iris chose to identify herself. The next morning, she was called to a meeting with an investigator from corporate security, which led to more meetings with others in corporate security, and then finally a meeting with the Director of Human Resources and Gladys Williams, the CIO of SLS.

Questions:

1. Was Iris justified in determining who the owner of the CD was?
2. Should Iris have approached Henry directly, or was the hotline the most effective way to take action?
3. Should Iris have placed the CD back at the coffee station and forgotten the whole thing? Would that response have been ethical on her part?

Endnotes

1. John B. Noone. *Rousseau's Social Contract: A Conceptual Analysis* Athens: University Of Georgia Press, 1981.
2. *EPIC.* "*The Clipper Chip.*" [Cited 6 March 2004]. Available from the World Wide Web <*http://www.epic.org/crypto/clipper/*>.
3. American Heritage Dictionary. "privacy." *The American Heritage Dictionary of the English Language Online.* [Cited 6 March 2004]. Available from the World Wide Web <*http://www.bartleby.com/cgi-bin/texis/webinator/ahdsearch?search_type=enty&query= privacy&db=ahd&Submit=Search*>.
4. Legal Information Institute. *Privacy of Customer Information,* title 47, sec. 222. [Cited 6 March 2004]. Available from the World Wide Web <*http://www4.law.cornell.edu/uscode/ 47/222.html*>.
5. HIPAAAdvisory. "HIPAA primer." *HIPAAAdvisory Online.* [Cited 6 March 2004]. Available from the World Wide Web <*http://www.hipaadvisory.com/regs/*>.
6. The Computer Ethics Institutite. "The 10 Commandments of Computer Ethics." *CEI Online.* 16 April 2001. Available from the World Wide Web <*http://www.cpsr.org/ program/ethics/cei.html*>.
7. Inquirer. "Software Piracy in Asia Exposed." *The Inquirer Online.* 27 January 2002. [Cited 6 March 2004]. Available from the World Wide Web <*http://www.theinquirer.net/piracy1.htm*>.
8. Michael E. Whitman, Anthony M. Townsend, and Anthony R. Hendrickson. "Cross-National Differences in Computer-Use Ethics: A Nine Country Study." *The Journal of International Business Studies* 30, no. 4 (1999): 673–687.
9. Michael E. Whitman, Anthony M. Townsend, and Anthony R. Hendrickson. "Cross-National Differences in Computer-Use Ethics: A Nine Country Study." *The Journal of International Business Studies* 30, no. 4 (1999): 673–687.
10. Susan J. Harrington. "The Effects of Codes of Ethics and Personal Denial of Responsibility on Computer Abuse Judgment and Intentions." *MIS Quarterly* 20, no. 3 (September 1996): 257–278.

11. International Information Systems Security Certification Consortium, Inc. "(ISC)^2 Code of Ethics." *ISC^2 Online.* [Cited 6 March 2004]. Available from the World Wide Web *<http://www.isc2.org/cgi/content.cgi?category=12>.*

12. ISSA. "ISSA Code of Ethics." *ISSA Online.* [Cited 6 March 2004]. Available from the World Wide Web *<http://www.issa.org/codeofethics.html>.*

13. The National Security Agency. *Introduction to NSA/CSS.* [Cited 6 March 2004]. Available from the World Wide Web *<http://www.nsa.gov/about/index.cfm >.*

14. The National Security Agency. *Information Assurance,* [Cited 6 March 2004]. Available from the World Wide Web *<http://www.nsa.gov/ia/>.*

15. Robert J. Alberts, Anthony M. Townsend, and Michael E. Whitman. "The Threat of Long-arm Jurisdiction to Electronic Commerce." *Communications of the ACM* 41, no. 12 (December 1998): 15–20.

4

Risk Management

CHARLIE MOODY CALLED the meeting to order. The conference room was full of developers, systems analysts, IT managers, business users, and business managers.

"All right everyone, let's get started. Welcome to the kick-off meeting of the Sequential Label and Supply Information Security Task Force. That's the name of our new project team, and we're here today to talk about our objectives and to review the initial work plan."

"Why are all of the users here?" asked the manager of sales. "Isn't security a problem for the IT department?"

Charlie explained, "Well, that used to be the case, but we've come to realize that information security is about managing the risk of using automated systems, which involves almost everyone in the company. In order to make our systems more secure, we will need the participation of people from all departments."

Charlie continued, "I hope everyone has read the packets we sent out last week with the legal requirements we face in our industry and the background articles on threats and attacks. Today we'll begin the process of identifying and classifying all of the information technology risks that face our organization. This includes everything from fires and floods that could disrupt our business to criminal hackers who might try to steal or destroy our data. Once we identify and classify the risks facing our assets, we can discuss how to reduce or eliminate these risks by establishing controls. Which controls we actually apply will depend on the costs and benefits of each control."

"Wow, Charlie!" said Amy Windahl from the back of the room. "I'm sure we need to do it—I was hit by the last attack, just as everyone here was—but we have hundreds of systems."

"It's more like thousands," said Charlie. He went on, "That's why we have so many people on this team and why the team includes members of every department."

Charlie continued, "Okay, everyone, please open your packets and take out the project plan with the work list showing teams, tasks, and schedules. Any questions before we start reviewing the work plan?"

LEARNING OBJECTIVES:

Upon completion of this material, you should be able to:

- Define risk management, risk identification, and risk control
- Understand how risk is identified and assessed
- Assess risk based on probability of occurrence and impact on an organization
- Grasp the fundamental aspects of documenting risk through the creation of a risk assessment
- Describe the risk mitigation strategy options for controlling risks
- Identify the categories that can be used to classify controls
- Recognize the conceptual frameworks that exist for evaluating risk controls and be able to formulate a cost benefit analysis
- Understand how to maintain and perpetuate risk controls

Introduction

The formal process of identifying and controlling the risks facing an organization is called risk management. This process is made up of two major undertakings: risk identification and risk control. The first of these, **risk identification**, is the process of examining and documenting the security posture of an organization's information technology and the risks it faces. Risk assessment is the documentation of the results of risk identification. The second major undertaking, **risk control**, is the process of applying controls to reduce the risks to an organization's data and information systems. The various components of risk management and their relationship to each other are shown in Figure 4-1.

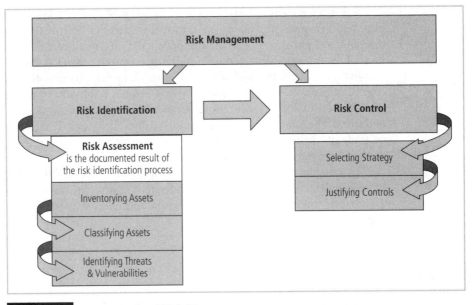

FIGURE 4-1   Components of Risk Management

As an aspiring information security professional, you have a key role to play in risk management. Among the communities of interest, the general management of the organization must structure the IT and information security functions to lead a successful defense of the organization's information assets—information and data, hardware, software, procedures, and people. The IT community must serve the information technology needs of the broader organization and at the same time leverage the special skills and insights of the information security community. The information security team must lead the way with skill, professionalism, and flexibility as it works with the other communities of interest to appropriately balance the usefulness and security of the information system.

In the early days of information technology, corporations used IT systems mainly to gain a definitive advantage over the competition. Establishing a competitive business model, method, or technique allowed an organization to provide a product or service that was superior and created a **competitive advantage**. This earlier model has given way to one in which all competitors have reached a certain level of automation. IT is now readily available to all organizations that make the investment, allowing competitors to react quickly to changes in the market. In this highly competitive environment, organizations cannot expect the implementation of new technologies to provide a competitive lead over others in the industry. Instead, the concept of **competitive disadvantage** has emerged: the need to avoid falling behind the competition. Effective IT-enabled organizations quickly absorb emerging technologies now, not to gain or maintain competitive advantage, but to avoid loss of market share due to an inability to maintain the highly responsive services required in today's marketplaces.

To keep up with the competition, organizations must design and create safe environments in which business processes and procedures can function. These environments must maintain confidentiality and privacy and assure the integrity of organizational data—objectives that are met through the application of the principles of risk management.

Risk management is the process of identifying vulnerabilities in an organization's information systems and taking carefully reasoned steps to ensure the confidentiality, integrity, and availability of all the components in the organization's information system. Each of the three elements in the C.I.A. triangle, introduced in Chapter 1, is an essential part of every IT organization's ability to sustain long-term competitiveness. When an organization depends on IT-based systems to remain viable, information security and the discipline of risk management move beyond theoretical discussions and become an integral part of the economic basis for making business decisions. These decisions are based on trade-offs between the costs of applying information systems controls and the benefits realized from the operation of secured, available systems.

This chapter explores a variety of control approaches, and follows with a discussion of how controls can be categorized to understand control processes and details better. The chapter finishes with a section on maintaining effective controls in the modern IT organization.

An Overview of Risk Management

An observation made over 2,400 years ago by Chinese General Sun Tzu has direct relevance to information security today.

> "If you know the enemy and know yourself, you need not fear the result of a hundred battles. If you know yourself but not the enemy, for every victory gained you will also suffer a defeat. If you know neither the enemy nor yourself, you will succumb in every battle."[1]

Consider for a moment the similarities between information security and warfare. Information security managers and technicians are the defenders of information. The many threats discussed in Chapter 2 are constantly attacking the defenses surrounding information assets. Defenses are built in layers, by placing safeguard upon safeguard. You attempt to prevent, protect, detect, and recover from attack after attack after attack. Moreover, organizations are legally prevented from switching to offense, and the attackers themselves have no need to expend their resources on defense. In order to be victorious, you must, therefore, know yourself and know the enemy.

Know Yourself

First, you must identify, examine, and understand the information and systems currently in place within your organization. This is self-evident. To protect *assets*, which are defined here as information and the systems that use, store, and transmit information, you must understand what they are, how they add value to the organization, and to which vulnerabilities they are susceptible. Once you know what you have, you can identify what you are already doing to protect it. Just because you have a control in place to protect an asset does not necessarily mean that the asset is protected. Frequently, organizations implement control mechanisms, but then neglect the necessary periodic review, revision, and maintenance. The policies, education and training programs, and technologies that protect information must be carefully maintained and administered to ensure that they are still effective.

Know the Enemy

Informed of your organization's assets and weaknesses, you move on to Sun Tzu's second step: know the enemy. This means identifying, examining, and understanding the *threats* facing the organization. You must determine those threat aspects that most directly affect the organization and the security of the organization's information assets. You can then use your understanding of these aspects to create a list of threats prioritized by how important each asset is to the organization.

The Roles of the Communities of Interest

In an organization, it is the responsibility of each community of interest to manage the risks that organization encounters. Each community of interest has a role to play, as outlined below.

Information Security

Since the members of the information security community best understand the threats and attacks that introduce risk into the organization, they often take a leadership role in addressing risk.

Management and Users

When properly trained and kept aware of the threats the organization faces, these groups play a part in the early detection and response process. Management must also ensure that sufficient resources (money and personnel) are allocated to the information security and information technology groups to meet the security needs of the organization. Users work with the systems and the data and are therefore well positioned to understand the value these information assets offer the organization and which assets among the many in use are the most valuable.

Information Technology

This group must build secure systems and operate them safely. For example, IT operations ensure good backups to control the risk from hard drive failures. The IT community can evaluate both valuation and threat perspectives to management during the risk management process.

All of the communities of interest must work together to address all levels of risk, which range from disasters that can devastate the whole organization to the smallest employee mistakes. The three communities of interest are also responsible for the following:

- Evaluating the risk controls
- Determining which control options are cost effective for the organization
- Acquiring or installing the needed controls
- Overseeing that the controls remain effective

It is essential that all three communities of interest conduct periodic management reviews. The first focus of management review is asset inventory. On a regular basis, management must verify the completeness and accuracy of the asset inventory. In addition, organizations must review and verify the threats and vulnerabilities that have been identified as dangerous to the asset inventory, as well as the current controls and mitigation strategies. The cost effectiveness of each control should be reviewed as well, and the decisions on deployment of controls revisited. Further, managers of all levels must regularly verify the ongoing effectiveness of every control deployed. For example, a sales manager might assess control procedures by going through the office before the workday starts and picking up all the papers from every desk in the sales department. When the workers showed up, the manager could inform them that a fire had been simulated and all of their papers had been destroyed and that each worker must now follow the disaster recovery procedures to assess the effectiveness of the procedures and suggest corrections.

The first phase of risk management, risk identification, is discussed in the following section.

Risk Identification

A risk management strategy calls on the information security professionals to know their organizations' information assets through identifying, classifying, and prioritizing them. Assets are the targets of various threats and threat agents, and the goal is to protect the assets from the threats. Once the organizational assets have been identified, a threat identification process is undertaken. The circumstances and settings of each information asset are examined to identify vulnerabilities. When vulnerabilities are found, controls are identified and assessed as to their capability to limit possible losses in the eventuality of attack.

The process of risk identification begins with the identification of the organization's information assets and an assessment of their value. The subsequent components of this process are shown in Figure 4-2.

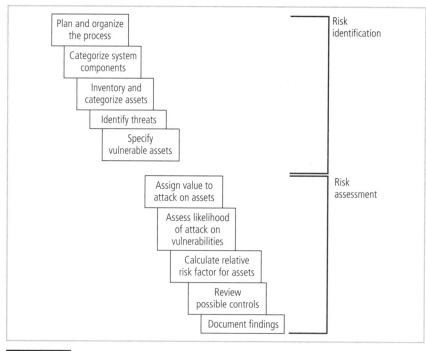

FIGURE 4-2 Components of Risk Identification

Asset Identification and Valuation

This iterative process begins with the identification of assets, including all of the elements of an organization's system, such as people, procedures, data and information, software, hardware, and networking elements. Then, you classify and categorize the assets, adding details as you dig deeper into the analysis.

TABLE 4-1 Categorizing the Components of an Information System

Traditional System Components	SecSDLC and Risk Management System Components	
People	Employees	Trusted employees Other staff
	Nonemployees	People at trusted organizations Strangers
Procedures	Procedures	IT and business standard procedures IT and business sensitive procedures
Data	Information	Transmission Processing Storage
Software	Software	Applications Operating systems Security components
Hardware	System devices and peripherals	Systems and peripherals Security devices
	Networking components	Intranet components Internet or DMZ components

Table 4-1 compares the categorizations found within a standard information system (people, procedures, data and information, software, and hardware) with those found in an enhanced version, which incorporates risk management and the SecSDLC approach. As you can see, the SecSDLC/risk management categorization introduces a number of new subdivisions:

- People include employees and nonemployees. There are two subcategories of employees: those who hold trusted roles and have correspondingly greater authority and accountability, and other staff who have assignments without special privileges. Nonemployees include contractors and consultants, members of other organizations with which the organization has a trust relationship, and strangers.

- Procedures fall into two categories: IT and business standard procedures, and IT and business sensitive procedures. The business sensitive procedures are those that may assist a threat agent in crafting an attack against the organization or that have some other content or feature that may introduce risk to the organization. One example of the loss of a sensitive procedure is the theft of the documentation for the E911 system from Bellsouth.[2] In this case, the documentation revealed certain aspects of the inner workings of a critical phone system.

- Data components have been expanded to account for the management of information in all states: transmission, processing, and storage. These expanded categories solve the problem posed by the term *data*, which is usually associated with databases, and does not bring to mind the full range of modalities of data and information used by a modern organization.

- Software components can be assigned to one of three categories: applications, operating systems, or security components. Software components that provide security controls may span the range of operating systems and applications categories, but are differentiated by the fact that they are part of the information security control environment and must be protected more thoroughly than other systems components.

- Hardware is assigned to one of two categories: the usual systems devices and their peripherals, and the devices that are part of information security control systems. The latter must be protected more thoroughly than the former.

- Hardware components have been separated into two categories: devices and peripherals, and networks. Since networking subsystems are often the focal point of attacks against the system, they should be considered as special cases rather than combined with general hardware and software components.

People, Procedures, and Data Asset Identification

Identifying human resources, documentation, and data information is more difficult than identifying hardware and software assets. People with knowledge, experience, and judgment should be assigned the task. As the assets of people, procedures, and data are identified, they should also be recorded using a reliable data-handling process. Whatever record keeping mechanism is used, be sure it has the flexibility to allow the specification of attributes particular to the type of asset. Some attributes are unique to a class of elements. When deciding which information assets to track, consider including the following asset attributes:

- People: Position name/number/ID (try to avoid names and stick to identifying positions, roles, or functions); supervisor; security clearance level; special skills
- Procedures: Description; intended purpose; relationship to software, hardware, and networking elements; storage location for reference; storage location for update
- Data: Classification; owner, creator, and manager; size of data structure; data structure used (sequential or relational); online or offline; location; backup procedures employed

As the data-tracking process is developed, consider carefully how much data should be tracked and for which specific assets. Most large organizations find that that they can only effectively track a few valuable facts about the most critical devices. For instance, a company may only track the IP address, server name, and device type for the mission-critical servers used by the company. They may forego the tracking of more detailed facts on all devices and completely forego the tracking of desktop or laptop systems.

Hardware, Software, and Network Asset Identification

What attributes of each of these information assets should be tracked? It depends on the needs of the organization and its risk management efforts, as well as the preferences and needs of the management of the information security and information technology communities. When deciding which information assets to track, you may want to consider including the asset attributes listed below:

- Name: Use the device or program name that is most common. Organizations may have several names for the same product. For example, a software product might have a nickname that people within the company use while the product is in development, as well as a formal name used by marketing and vendors. No matter how many names you track and how you select a name, always define what each name means for each group that uses the information. You should adopt naming standards that do not convey information to potential system attackers. For instance, a server named CASH1 or HQ_FINANCE may entice attackers to take a shortcut to those systems and go for the valuables first.

- IP address: This is useful for network devices and servers, but does not usually apply to software. You can, however, use a relational database and track software instances on specific servers or networking devices. Also note that many organizations use the dynamic host control protocol (DHCP) within TCP/IP that reassigns IP numbers to devices as needed, making the use of IP numbers as part of the asset identification process problematic. IP address use in inventory is usually limited to those devices that use static IP addresses.

- Media access control (MAC) address: MAC addresses are sometimes called electronic serial numbers or hardware addresses. As part of the TCP/IP standard, all network interface hardware devices have a unique number. The MAC address number is used by the network operating system as a means to identify a specific network device. It is used by the client's network software to recognize traffic that it must process. In most settings, MAC addresses can be a useful way to track connectivity. They can, however, be spoofed by some hardware and software combinations.

- Element type: Document the function of each element by listing its type. For hardware, you can develop a list of possible element types, such as servers, desktops, networking devices, or test equipment, to whatever degree of detail you require. For software elements, you may choose to develop a list of types that includes operating systems, custom applications by type (accounting, HR, or payroll to name a few), packaged applications, and specialty applications, such as firewall programs. The needs of the organization determine the degree of specificity. Types may, in fact, be recorded at two or more levels of specificity. Record one attribute that classifies the asset at a high level and then add attributes for more detail. For example, one server might be listed as:
  - DeviceClass = S (server)
  - DeviceOS = W2K (Windows 2000)
  - DeviceCapacity = AS (advanced server)

- Serial number: For hardware devices, the serial number can uniquely identify a specific device. Some software vendors also assign a software serial number to each instance of the program licensed by the organization.

- Manufacturer name: Record the manufacturer of the device or software component. This can be useful when responding to incidents that involve these devices or when certain manufacturers announce specific vulnerabilities.

- Manufacturer's model number or part number: Record the model or part number of the element. This record of exactly what the element is can be very useful in later analysis of vulnerabilities, because some vulnerability instances only apply to specific models of certain devices and software components.

- Software version, update revision, or FCO number: Whenever possible, document the specific software or firmware revision number and, for hardware devices, the current **field change order (FCO)** number. An FCO is an authorization issued by an organization for the repair, modification, or update of a piece of equipment. The equipment is not returned to the manufacturer, but is usually repaired at the customer's location, often by a third party. Documenting the revision number and FCO is particularly important for networking devices that function mainly through the software running on them. For example, firewall devices often have three versions: an operating system (OS) version, a software version, and a basic input/output system (BIOS) firmware version. Depending on your needs, you may have to track each of those version numbers.

- Physical location: Note where this element is located physically. This may not apply to software elements, but some organizations have license terms that specify where software can be used.

- Logical location: Note where this element can be found on the organization's network. The logical location is most useful for networking devices and indicates the logical network where the device is connected.

- Controlling entity: Identify which organizational unit controls the element. Sometimes a remote location's onsite staff controls a networking device, and at other times the central networks team controls other devices of the same make and model. You should try to differentiate which group or unit controls each specific element, because that group may want a voice in how much risk that device can tolerate and how much expense they can sustain to add controls.

Automated Risk Management Tools

Automated tools can sometimes identify the system elements that make up the hardware, software, and network components. For example, many organizations use automated asset inventory systems. The inventory listing is usually available in a database, or can be exported to a database for custom information on security assets. Once stored, the inventory listing must be kept current, often by means of a tool that periodically refreshes the data.

When you move to the later steps of risk management, which involve calculations of loss and projections of costs, the case for the use of automated risk management tools for tracking information assets becomes stronger. At this point in the process, however, simple word-processing, spreadsheet, and database tools can provide adequate record keeping.

Information Asset Classification

Some organizations further subdivide the categories listed in Table 4-1. For example, the category of Internet components can be subdivided into servers, networking devices (routers, hubs, switches), protection devices (firewalls, proxies), and cabling. Each of the other categories can be similarly further subdivided as needed by the organization.

In addition to these subdivisions, it is advisable to add another dimension to represent the sensitivity and security priority of the data and the devices that store, transmit, and process the data. Many organizations already have data classification schemes. Examples of these kinds of classifications are confidential data, internal data, and public data. Informal organizations may have to organize themselves to create a usable data classification model. The other side of the data classification scheme is the personnel security clearance structure, which determines the level of information individuals are authorized to view based on what each person needs to know.

No matter how an organization chooses to identify the various components of systems, it is most important that the classification of components be specific enough to allow determination of priority levels. This is necessary because the next step is to rank the components based on criteria established by the categorization. It is also important that the categories be comprehensive and mutually exclusive. *Comprehensive* means that all information assets must fit in the list somewhere, and *mutually exclusive* means that an information asset should fit in only one category. For example, suppose an organization has a public key infrastructure certificate authority, which is a software application that provides cryptographic key management services. Using a purely technical standard, an analysis team could categorize the certificate authority in the asset list of Table 4-1 as software, and within the software category as either an application or a security component. A certificate authority should actually be categorized as a software security component, since it is part of the security infrastructure and must be protected carefully. To simplify the categorization of elements that could be placed in a number of slots, it is essential to establish a clear and comprehensive set of categories.

Information Asset Valuation

As each asset is assigned to its category, posing a number of questions assists in developing the weighting criteria to be used for information asset valuation or impact evaluation. As each question is asked and answered, you should prepare a worksheet like the one shown in Figure 4-3 to collect your answers for later analysis. Before beginning the inventory process, the organization should determine which criteria can best be used to establish the value of the information assets. Among the criteria to be considered are:

- Which information asset is the most critical to the success of the organization? When determining the relative importance of each asset, refer to the organization's mission statement or statement of objectives. From that source, determine which elements of the organization are essential to meeting the organization's objectives, which elements support the objectives, and which are merely adjuncts. For example, a manufacturing company that makes aircraft engines finds that the process control systems controlling the machine tools on the assembly line are of the first order of importance. Although shipping and receiving data-entry consoles are important to those functions, they may be less critical if alternatives are available or can be easily arranged. Another example is an online organization such as Amazon.com. The Web servers that advertise Amazon's products and receive orders 24 hours a day are essential to the critical success of the business, whereas the desktop systems used by the company's customer service department to answer customer e-mails are not nearly as important.

System Name: ___SLS E-Commerce_____
Date Evaluated: _February 2006__
Evaluated By: ___D. Jones_____

Information assets	Data classification	Impact to profitability
Information Transmitted:		
EDI Document Set 1—Logistics BOL to outsourcer (outbound)	Confidential	High
EDI Document Set 2—Supplier orders (outbound)	Confidential	High
EDI Document Set 2—Supplier fulfillment advice (inbound)	Confidential	Medium
Customer order via SSL (inbound)	Confidential	Critical
Customer service Request via e-mail (inbound)	Private	Medium
DMZ Assets:		
Edge Router	Public	Critical
Web server #1—home page and core site	Public	Critical
Web server #2—Application server	Private	Critical

Notes: BOL: Bill of Lading:
    DMZ: Demilitarized Zone
    EDI: Electronic Data Interchange
    SSL: Secure Sockets Layer

FIGURE 4-3   Example Inventory Worksheet

- Which information asset generates the most revenue? You can also determine which information assets are critical by evaluating how much of the organization's revenue depends on a particular asset, or for nonprofit organizations, by identifying which information assets are most critical to service delivery. In some organizations, different systems are in place for each line of business or service offering. Which of these play the biggest role in generating revenue or delivering services?

- Which information asset generates the most profitability? Organizations should evaluate how much of the organization's profitability depends on a particular asset. For instance, at Amazon.com, some servers support the sales operations and other servers support the auction process, while yet other servers support the customer review database. Which of these servers contribute most to the profitability of the business? Although important, the customer review database server really does not directly add to profitability—at least not at the high volumes that the sales operations servers do. Note, however, that some services may have large revenue values, but are operating on such thin or nonexistent margins that they do not generate a profit. Nonprofit organizations can determine what percentage of their clientele receives services from the information asset being evaluated.

- Which information asset would be the most expensive to replace? Sometimes an information asset acquires special value because it is unique. If an enterprise still uses a Model-129 keypunch machine, for example, to create special punch card entries for a critical batch run, that machine may be worth more than its cost, since there may no longer be spare parts or service providers available for it. Another example is a specialty device with a long acquisition lead time because of manufacturing or transportation requirements. Such a device has a unique value to the organization. After the organization has identified this unique value, it can address ways to control the risk of losing access to the unique asset. An organization can also control the risk of loss for this kind of asset by buying and storing a backup device.

- Which information asset would be the most expensive to protect? In this case, you are looking at the cost of providing controls. Some assets are by their nature difficult to protect. Finding a complete answer to this question may have to be delayed beyond the risk identification phase of the process, because the costs of controls cannot be computed until the controls are identified, and that is a later step in this process. But information about the difficulty of establishing controls should be collected in the identification phase.

- Which information asset would be the most embarrassing or cause the greatest liability if revealed? Almost every organization is aware of its *image* in the local, national, and international spheres. For many organizations, the compromising of certain assets could prove especially damaging to this image—not to mention simply embarrassing. The image of Microsoft, for example, was tarnished when one of its employees became a victim of the QAZ Trojan capability and the latest version of Microsoft Office was stolen.[3]

In addition to those just listed, there are other company-specific criteria that may add value to the asset evaluation process. They should be identified, documented, and added to the process. To finalize this step of the information asset identification process, each organization should assign a weight to each asset based on the answers to the various chosen questions. These weighted values might use a numeric process, as shown below in Table 4-2.

Listing Assets in Order of Importance

Once the process of inventorying and assessing value is complete, you can calculate the relative importance of each asset using a straightforward process known as *weighted factor analysis*, as shown in Table 4-2. In this process, each information asset is assigned a score for each critical factor. In the example shown in Table 4-2, these scores range from 0.1 to 1.0, which is the range of values recommended by NIST SP800-30, a document published by the National Institute of Standards and Technology and entitled *Risk Management for Information Technology Systems*. In addition, each critical factor is also assigned a weight (ranging from 1 to 100) to show that criteria's assigned importance for the organization.

TABLE 4-2   Example of a Weighted Factor Analysis Worksheet

Information Asset	Criteria 1: Impact to Revenue	Criteria 2: Impact to Profitability	Criteria 3: Impact to Public Image	Weighted score
Criterion Weight (1-100) *Must total 100*	30	40	30	
EDI Document Set 1— Logistics BOL to outsourcer (outbound)	0.8	0.9	0.5	75
EDI Document Set 2— Supplier orders (outbound)	0.8	0.9	0.6	78
EDI Document Set 2— Supplier fulfillment advice (inbound)	0.4	0.5	0.3	41
Customer order via SSL (inbound)	1.0	1.0	1.0	100
Customer service request via e-mail (inbound)	0.4	0.4	0.9	55

Notes: EDI: Electronic Data Interchange
SSL: Secure Sockets Layer

A quick review of Table 4-2 shows that the Customer order via SSL (inbound) data flow is the most important asset on this worksheet with a weighted score of 100, and that the EDI Document Set 2—Supplier fulfillment advice (inbound) is the least critical, with a score of 41.

Data Classification and Management

Corporate and military organizations use a variety of classification schemes. Georgia-Pacific Corporation (G-P) uses a corporate **data classification scheme** throughout the company that helps secure confidentiality and integrity of information.

The G-P information classification scheme has three categories: confidential, internal, and external. Information owners are responsible for classifying the information assets for which they are responsible. At least once a year, information owners must review information classifications to ensure the information is still classified correctly and the appropriate access controls are in place.

The information classifications are as follows:

- Confidential: Used for the most sensitive Georgia-Pacific information that must be tightly controlled, even within the company. Access to information with this classification is strictly on a need-to-know basis or as required by the terms of a contract. Information with this classification may also be referred to as "sensitive" or "proprietary."

- Internal: Used for all internal information that does not meet the criteria for the confidential category and is to be viewed only by G-P employees, authorized contractors, and other third parties.

- External: All information that has been approved by management for public release.[4]

As you might expect, the U.S. military classification scheme has a more complex categorization system than is required by most corporations. The military is perhaps the best-known user of data classification schemes. In order to maintain the protection of the confidentiality of information, the military has invested heavily in INFOSEC (information security), OPSEC (operations security), and COMSEC (communications security). In fact, many of the developments in data communications and information security are the result of military-sponsored research and development. For most information, the military uses a five-level classification scheme: Unclassified, Sensitive But Unclassified (i.e., For Official Use Only), Confidential, Secret, and Top Secret. Each of these is defined below.[5]

- Unclassified Data: Information that can generally be distributed to the public without any threat to U.S. national interests.

- Sensitive But Unclassified (SBU) Data: "Any information of which the loss, misuse, or unauthorized access to, or modification of might adversely affect U.S. national interests, the conduct of Department of Defense (DoD) programs, or the privacy of DoD personnel." Common classifications in this category include For Official Use Only, Not for Public Release, or For Internal Use Only.

- Confidential Data: "Any information or material the unauthorized disclosure of which reasonably could be expected to cause damage to the national security. Examples of damage include the compromise of information that indicates strength of ground, air, and naval forces in the United States and overseas areas; disclosure of technical information used for training, maintenance, and inspection of classified munitions of war; revelation of performance characteristics, test data, design, and production data on munitions of war."

- Secret: "Any information or material the unauthorized disclosure of which reasonably could be expected to cause serious damage to the national security. Examples of serious damage include disruption of foreign relations significantly affecting the national security; significant impairment of a program or policy directly related to the national security; revelation of significant military plans or intelligence operations; compromise of significant military plans or intelligence operations; and compromise of significant scientific or technological developments relating to national security."

- Top Secret Data: "Any information or material the unauthorized disclosure of which reasonably could be expected to cause exceptionally grave damage to the national security. Examples of exceptionally grave damage include armed hostilities against the United States or its allies; disruption of foreign relations vitally affecting the national security; the compromise of vital national defense plans or complex cryptologic and communications intelligence systems; the revelation of sensitive intelligence operations; and the disclosure of scientific or technological developments vital to national security." This classification comes with the general expectation of "crib-to-grave" protection, meaning that any individual entrusted with top-secret information is expected to retain this level of confidence for his or her lifetime.

The military also has some specialty classification ratings, such as Personnel Information and Evaluation Reports, to protect related areas of information. Federal agencies such as the FBI and CIA also use specialty classification schemes, like Need-to-Know, and Named Projects. Obviously, Need-to-Know allows access to information by individuals who need the information to perform their work. Named Projects are clearance levels based on a scheme similar to Need-to-Know. When an operation, project, or set of classified data is created, the project is assigned a code name, such as Phoenix. Next, a list of authorized individuals is created and assigned to either the Need-to-Know or Named Projects category, and the list is maintained to enable the restriction of access to these categories of material.

Most organizations do not need the detailed level of classification used by the military or federal agencies. However, organizations may find it necessary to classify data to provide protection. A simple scheme can allow an organization to protect such sensitive information as marketing or research data, personnel data, customer data, and general internal communications. Or, a scheme such as the following could be adopted:

- Public: Information for general public dissemination, such as an advertisement or public release.
- For Official Use Only: Information that is not particularly sensitive, but not for public release, such as internal communications.
- Sensitive: Information important to the business that could embarrass the company or cause loss of market share if revealed.
- Classified: Information of the utmost secrecy to the organization, disclosure of which could severely impact the well-being of the organization.

Security Clearances

The other side of the data classification scheme is the personnel **security clearance** structure. In organizations that require security clearances, each user of data must be assigned a single authorization level that indicates the level of classification he or she is authorized to view. This is usually accomplished by assigning each employee to a named role, such as data entry clerk, development programmer, information security analyst, or even CIO. Most organizations have a set of roles and the accompanying security clearances associated with each role. Overriding an employee's security clearance is the fundamental principle of **need-to-know** as described earlier. Regardless of security clearance, employees are not simply allowed to view any and all data that falls within their level of clearance. Before someone can access a specific set of data, the need-to-know requirement must be met. This extra level of protection ensures that the confidentiality of information is properly maintained.

Management of Classified Data

Management of classified data includes its storage, distribution, portability, and destruction. All information that is not unclassified or public must be clearly marked as such; see the examples from the military shown in Figure 4-4. The military also uses color-coordinated cover sheets to protect classified information from the casual observer. In addition, each classified document should contain the appropriate designation at the top and bottom of each page. When classified data is stored, it must be available only to authorized individuals. This usually requires locking file cabinets, safes, or other such protective devices for hard copies and systems. When an individual carries classified information, it should be inconspicuous, as in a locked briefcase or portfolio.

FIGURE 4-4 Military Data Classification Cover Sheets

One control policy that can be difficult to enforce is the clean desk policy. A **clean desk policy** requires that employees secure all information in appropriate storage containers at the end of each day. When copies of classified information are no longer valuable or excess copies exist, proper care should be taken to destroy them, usually after double signature verification, by means of shredding, burning, or transferring to a service offering authorized document destruction. It is important to enforce policies to ensure that no classified information is disposed of in trash or recycling areas. There are individuals who search trash and recycling—a practice known as **dumpster diving**—to retrieve information that could embarrass a company or compromise information security.

Threat Identification

After identifying and performing a preliminary classification of an organization's information assets, the analysis phase moves on to an examination of the threats facing the organization. As you discovered in Chapter 2, a wide variety of threats face an organization and its information and information systems. The realistic threats need to be investigated further while the unimportant threats are set aside. If you assume every threat can and will attack every information asset, the project scope will quickly become so complex it will overwhelm the ability to plan.

Identify and Prioritize Threats and Threat Agents

The threats to information security that you learned about in Chapter 2 are shown here in Table 4-3.

TABLE 4-3   Threats to Information Security[6]

Threat	Example
Act of human error or failure	Accidents, employee mistakes
Compromises to intellectual property	Piracy, copyright infringement
Deliberate acts of espionage or trespass	Unauthorized access and data collection
Deliberate acts of information extortion	Blackmail for information disclosure
Deliberate acts of sabotage or vandalism	Destruction of systems or information
Deliberate acts of theft	Illegal confiscation of equipment or information
Deliberate software attacks	Viruses, worms, macros, denial of service
Forces of nature	Fire, flood, earthquake, lightning
Quality of service deviations from service providers	Power and WAN quality of service issues
Technical hardware failures or errors	Equipment failure
Technical software failures or errors	Bugs, code problems, unknown loopholes
Technological obsolescence	Antiquated or outdated technologies

©2003 ACM, Inc., Included here by permission.

Each of the threats from Table 4-1 must be examined to assess its potential to endanger the organization. This examination is known as a **threat assessment**. You can address each threat with a few basic questions, as follows:

- Which threats present a danger to an organization's assets in the given environment? Not all threats have the potential to affect every organization. The organization examines each category in Table 4-3 and determines if any of the categories do not apply. While it is unlikely that an entire category of threats can be eliminated, such elimination speeds up later steps of the process. (Take a look at the Offline entitled "Threats to Information Security" to see what threats leading CIOs identified for their organizations.) Once an organization has determined which threats apply, the security team brainstorms for particular examples of threats within each category. These specific threats are examined to determine if any do not apply to the organization. For example, a company with offices in the 12th floor of a high-rise in Denver, Colorado, is not subject to flooding. Similarly, a firm with an office in Oklahoma City, Oklahoma, should not be concerned with landslides. With this methodology, specific threats may be eliminated because of very low probability.

■ Which threats represent the most danger to the organization's information? The degree of danger a threat presents is difficult to assess. Danger may be simply the probability of a threat attacking the organization, or it can represent the amount of damage the threat could create. It can also represent the frequency with which an attack can occur. Since this is a preliminary assessment, the analysis is limited to examining the existing level of preparedness, as well as improving the strategy of information security. The results represent a quick overview of the components involved.

As you will discover later in this chapter, you can use both quantitative and qualitative measures to rank values. Since information in this case is preliminary, the security team may wish to rank threats subjectively in order of danger. Alternatively, the organization may simply rate each of the threats on a scale of one to five, with one designating threats that are not significant and five designating threats that are highly significant.

■ How much would it cost to recover from a successful attack? One of the calculations that guides corporate spending on controls is the cost of recovery operations in the event of a successful attack. At this preliminary phase, it is not necessary to conduct a detailed assessment of the costs associated with recovering from a particular attack. You might find a simpler technique quite sufficient to allow investigators to continue with the process. For example, you could subjectively rank or list the threats based on the cost to recover. Or you could assign a rating for each of the threats on a scale of one to five, with one designating not expensive at all and five designating extremely expensive. You could, if the information were available, assign a raw value to the cost, e.g., $5K, $10K, or $2M. In other words, the goal of this phase is to provide a rough assessment of the cost to recover operations should the attack interrupt normal business operations and require recovery. It may not be possible to assign a specific value, which is why the ranking or rating options are so popular.

■ Which of the threats would require the greatest expenditure to prevent? Just as in the previous question, another factor that affects the level of danger posed by a particular threat is the cost of protecting the organization against the threat. Some threats, such as malicious code, have nominal costs of protection. Other threats have very high levels of costs for protection, such as forces of nature. As a result, the amount of time and money invested in protecting against a particular threat is moderated by the amount of time and money required to fully protect against that particular threat. Here again you can begin by ranking, rating, or attempting to quantify the level of effort or expense it would take to defend an asset from a particular threat. The ranking might use the same techniques outlined above in calculating recovery costs. Take a look at the Offline entitled "Expenditures for Threats to Information Security" to see how some top executives recently handled this issue.

By posing and answering these questions, you establish a framework for the discussion of threat assessment. This list of questions may not cover everything that affects the information security threat assessment. If an organization has specific guidelines or policies, these should influence the process and require the posing of additional questions. This list can be easily expanded to include additional requirements.

OFFLINE

Threats to Information Security—Survey of Industry

Adapted from "Enemy at the Gates: Threats to Information Security"[7]
By Michael E. Whitman, Communications of the ACM, August 2003

What are the threats to information security according to top computing executives? A recent study by Professor Michael Whitman asked that very question. Based on the categories of threats presented earlier, over 1000 top computing executives were asked to rate each threat category on a scale of not significant to very significant. The data was converted to a five-point scale with five representing very significant. You can see in Table 4-4 that the mean of the threats ranged from 3.99 to 2.45.

CIOs were also asked to identify the top five threats to their organizations. This was converted into a weight, with five points for a first place vote, and so on to one point for a fifth place vote. The sum of weights is presented under the Weight heading in Table 4-4. The two ratings were combined into a weighted rank.

Table 4-4 Weighted Ranks of Threats to Information Security

Threat	Mean	Std. Dev	Weight	Weighted Rank
1. Deliberate software attacks	3.99	1.03	546	**2178.3**
2. Technical software failures or errors	3.16	1.13	358	**1129.9**
3. Acts of human error or failure	3.15	1.11	350	**1101.0**
4. Deliberate acts of espionage or trespass	3.22	1.37	324	**1043.6**
5. Deliberate acts of sabotage or vandalism	3.15	1.37	306	**962.6**
6. Technical hardware failures or errors	3.00	1.18	314	**942.0**
7. Deliberate acts of theft	3.07	1.30	226	**694.5**
8. Forces of nature	2.80	1.09	218	**610.9**
9. Compromises to intellectual property	2.72	1.21	181	**494.8**
10. Quality of service deviations from service providers	2.65	1.06	164	**433.9**
11. Technological obsolescence	2.71	1.11	158	**427.9**
12. Deliberate acts of information extortion	2.45	1.42	92	**225.2**

continued

Another popular study also examines threats to information security. The Computer Security Institute in cooperation with the Federal Bureau of Investigation conducts an annual study of computer crime. Table 4-5 shows the results of the CSI/FBI study from the last five years.

The number of successful attacks continues the declining trend started in 2001. In the 2004 CSI/FBI study, every surveyed company reported some number of Web site incidents. Most reporting organizations, representing 89% of respondents, indicated their organization had from one to five Web site incidents in the previous 12 months. Whether a company catches an attack and is then willing to report the attack is another matter entirely. In any case, the fact is, almost every company has been attacked. Whether or not that attack was successful depends on the company's security efforts.

Table 4-5   CSI/FBI Survey Results for Types of Attack or Misuse (2000-2004)[8]

Types of Attack or Misuse	2004	2003	2002	2001	2000
1. Virus	78%	85%	94%	85%	90%
2. Insider abuse of Net access	59%	80%	78%	91%	79%
3. Laptop	49%	55%	64%	60%	69%
4. System penetration	39%	36%	40%	40%	25%
5. Unauthorized access by insiders	37%	45%	38%	49%	71%
6. Denial of service	17%	42%	40%	36%	27%
7. Abuse of wireless	15%	(new category for 2004)			
8. Theft of proprietary info	10%	21%	20%	26%	20%
9. Misuse of public Web applications	10%	(new category for 2004)			
10. Web site defacement	7%	(new category for 2004)			
11. Sabotage	5%	21%	8%	18%	17%
12. Financial fraud	5%	15%	12%	12%	11%
13. Telecom fraud	5%	10%	9%	10%	11%
14. Telecom eavesdropping	—*	6%	6%	10%	7%
15. Active wiretap	—*	1%	1%	2%	1%

* item dropped in 2004 survey
All text, excluding the "CSI/FBI Survey Results for Attack of Misuse,"
©2003 ACM, Inc., Included here by permission.

OFFLINE

Expenditures for Threats to Information Security

Adapted from "Enemy at the Gates: Threats to Information Security"[9]
By Michael E. Whitman, Communications of the ACM, August 2003

A recent study by Professor Michael Whitman asked top computing executives to determine the priorities for expenditures for threats to information security. The respondents indicated their top five expenditures. These ratings were used to create a rank order of the expenses. The results are presented in Table 4-6.

Table 4-6 Weighted Ranking of Top Threat-Driven Expenditures

Threats	Weighted Ranking
1. Deliberate software attacks	12.7
2. Acts of human error or failure	7.6
3. Technical software failures or errors	7.0
4. Technical hardware failures or errors	6.0
5. Quality of service deviations from service providers	4.9
6. Deliberate acts of espionage or trespass	4.7
7. Deliberate acts of theft	4.1
8. Deliberate acts of sabotage or vandalism	4.0
9. Technological obsolescence	3.3
10. Forces of nature	3.0
11. Compromises to intellectual property	2.2
12. Deliberate acts of information extortion	1.0

Vulnerability Identification

Once you have identified the organization's information assets and documented some criteria for beginning to assess the threats it faces, you then review each information asset for each threat it faces and create a list of vulnerabilities. What are vulnerabilities? They are specific avenues that threat agents can exploit to attack an information asset. They are chinks in the armor of the information asset—a flaw or weakness in an information asset, security procedure, design, or control that could be exercised either accidentally or on purpose to breach security. For example, suppose the edge router in an organization's DMZ is the asset. The threats to the possible vulnerabilities of this router would be analyzed as shown in Table 4-7.

TABLE 4-7   Vulnerability Assessment of a Hypothetical DMZ Router

Threat	Possible Vulnerabilities
Deliberate software attacks	▪ Internet protocol is vulnerable to denial of service. ▪ Outsider IP fingerprinting activities can reveal sensitive information unless suitable controls are implemented.
Acts of human error or failure	▪ Employees or contractors may cause outage if configuration errors are made.
Technical software failures or errors	▪ Vendor-supplied routing software could fail and cause an outage.
Technical hardware failures or errors	▪ Hardware can fail and cause an outage.
Quality of service deviations from service providers	▪ Power system failures are always possible. ▪ Unless suitable electrical power conditioning is provided, failure is probable over time.
Deliberate acts of espionage or trespass	▪ This information asset has little intrinsic value, but other assets protected by this device could be attacked if it is compromised.
Deliberate theft	▪ This information asset has little intrinsic value, but other assets protected by this device could be attacked if it is compromised.
Deliberate acts of sabotage or vandalism	▪ Internet protocol is vulnerable to denial of service. ▪ This device may be subject to defacement or cache poisoning.
Technological obsolescence	▪ If this asset is not reviewed and periodically updated, it may fall too far behind its vendor support model to be kept in service.
Forces of nature	▪ All information assets in the organization are subject to forces of nature, unless suitable controls are provided.
Compromises to intellectual property	▪ This information asset has little intrinsic value, but other assets protected by this device could be attacked if it is compromised.
Deliberate acts of information extortion	▪ This information asset has little intrinsic value, but other assets protected by this device could be attacked if it is compromised.

Now, you examine how each of the threats that are possible or likely could be perpetrated, and list the organization's assets and their vulnerabilities. The list is usually long and shows all the vulnerabilities of the information asset. Some threats manifest themselves in multiple ways, yielding multiple vulnerabilities for that threat. The process of listing vulnerabilities is somewhat subjective and is based on the experience and knowledge of the people creating the list. Therefore, the process works best when groups of people with diverse backgrounds within the organization work iteratively in a series of brainstorming sessions. For instance, the team that reviews the vulnerabilities for networking equipment should include the networking specialists, the systems management team that operates the network, the information security risk specialist, and even technically proficient users of the system.

At the end of the risk identification process, you have a list of assets and their vulnerabilities. This list, along with any supporting documentation, is the starting point for the next step, risk assessment.

Risk Assessment

Now that you have identified the organization's information assets, and the threats and vulnerabilities, you can assess the relative risk for each of the vulnerabilities. This is accomplished by a process called **risk assessment**. Risk assessment assigns a risk rating or score to each information asset. While this number does not mean anything in absolute terms, it is useful in gauging the relative risk to each vulnerable information asset and facilitates the development of comparative ratings later in the risk control process.

Introduction to Risk Assessment

Figure 4-5 shows the factors that go into the risk-rating estimate for each of the vulnerabilities.

Risk is
the **likelihood** of the occurrence of a vulnerability
multiplied by
the **value** of the information asset
minus
the percentage of risk mitigated by **current controls**
plus
the **uncertainty** of current knowledge of the vulnerability

FIGURE 4-5 Factors of Risk

It is important to note that the goal at this point is to create a method for evaluating the relative risk of each of the listed vulnerabilities. Chapter 5 describes methods to determine more accurate and detailed costs of each of the vulnerabilities, as well as projected expenses for the variety of controls that can reduce the risk for each of them. For now, use the simpler risk model described in Figure 4-5 to evaluate the risk for each information asset. The next section presents the factors that are used to calculate the relative risk for each vulnerability.

Likelihood

Likelihood is the probability that a specific vulnerability within an organization will be successfully attacked.[10] In risk assessment, you assign a numeric value to the likelihood of a vulnerability being successfully exploited. The National Institute of Standards and Technology recommends in Special Publication 800-30 that likelihood vulnerabilities be assigned a number between 0.1 for low and 1.0 for high. Thus, for example, being struck by a meteorite while indoors would be rated 0.1. At the other extreme, receiving at least one e-mail containing a virus or worm in the next year would be rated 1.0. You could also choose to use a number between 1 and 100, but zero is not used, since vulnerabilities with a zero likelihood have been removed from the asset/vulnerability list. Whatever rating system you decide on for assigning likelihood, use professionalism, experience, and judgment—and use the rating model you select consistently. Whenever possible, use external references for likelihood values that have been reviewed and adjusted for your specific circumstances. Many asset/vulnerability combinations have sources for likelihood, for example:

- The likelihood of a fire has been estimated actuarially for each type of structure.
- The likelihood that any given e-mail contains a virus or worm has been researched.
- The number of network attacks can be forecast based on how many network addresses the organization has assigned.

Valuation of Information Assets

Using the information obtained during the information asset identification steps, you can now assign weighted scores for the value to the organization of each information asset. The actual number used can vary with the needs of the organization. Some groups use a scale of 1 to 100, with 100 reserved for those information assets the loss of which would stop company operations within a few minutes. Other scales, including the one recommended by NIST SP 800-30, use assigned weights in broad categories, assigning all important assets a value of 100, all low-criticality assets a value of 1, and all others a medium value of 50. Still other groups use a scale of 1 to 10, or assigned values of 1, 3, and 5 to represent low, medium, and high-valued assets. You can also create weight values for your specific needs. To be effective, the values must be assigned by asking the questions described in the previous section of this chapter, "Identify and Prioritize Threats and Threat Agents." These questions are restated below:

- Which threats present a danger to an organization's assets in the given environment?
- Which threats represent the most danger to the organization's information?
- How much would it cost to recover from a successful attack?
- Which of the threats would require the greatest expenditure to prevent?

After reevaluating these questions, you must use the background information from the risk identification process and illuminate that information by posing one additional question:

- Which of the questions posed above for each information asset is the most important to the protection of information of the organization?

This question helps to set priorities in the assessment of vulnerabilities. Which is the most important to the organization, the cost to recover from a threat attack, the cost to protect against a threat attack—or generally, which of the threats has the highest probability of successful attack? Additional questions may also be asked. Again, you are looking at threats the organization faces in its current state; however, this information will be valuable in later stages as you begin to design the final security solution. Once these questions are answered, you move to the next step in the process: examining how current controls can reduce the risk faced by specific vulnerabilities.

If a vulnerability is fully managed by an existing control, it no longer needs to be considered for additional controls and can be set aside. If it is partially controlled, estimate what percentage of the vulnerability has been controlled.

It is not possible to know everything about each vulnerability, such as how likely it is to occur or how great an impact a successful attack would have. The degree that a current control can reduce risk is also subject to estimation error. You must now apply judgment to add a factor into the equation to allow for an estimation of the uncertainty of the information.

Risk Determination

For the purpose of relative risk assessment, risk *equals* likelihood of vulnerability occurrence *times* value (or impact) *minus* percentage risk already controlled *plus* an element of uncertainty as illustrated in Figure 4-5. For example:

- Information asset A has a value score of 50 and has one vulnerability: Vulnerability 1 has a likelihood of 1.0 with no current controls; and you estimate that assumptions and data are 90% accurate.
- Information asset B has a value score of 100 and has two vulnerabilities: Vulnerability 2 has a likelihood of 0.5 with a current control that addresses 50% of its risk; vulnerability 3 has a likelihood of 0.1 with no current controls. You estimate that assumptions and data are 80% accurate.

The resulting ranked list of risk ratings for the three vulnerabilities is:

- Asset A: Vulnerability 1 rated as $55 = (50 \times 1.0) - 0\% + 10\%$ where
  $55 = (50 \times 1.0) - ((50 \times 1.0) \times 0.0) + ((50 \times 1.0) \times 0.1)$
  $55 = 50 - 0 + 5$
- Asset B: Vulnerability 2 rated as $35 = (100 \times 0.5) - 50\% + 20\%$ where
  $35 = (100 \times 0.5) - ((100 \times 0.5) \times 0.5) + ((100 \times 0.5) \times 0.2)$
  $35 = 50 - 25 + 10$
- Asset B: Vulnerability 3 rated as $12 = (100 \times 0.1) - 0\% + 20\%$ where
  $12 = (100 \times 0.1) - ((100 \times 0.1) \times 0.0) + ((100 \times 0.1) \times 0.2)$
  $12 = 10 - 0 + 2$

Identify Possible Controls

For each threat and its associated vulnerabilities that have residual risk, create a preliminary list of control ideas. **Residual risk** is the risk that remains to the information asset even after the existing control has been applied.

As you discovered in Chapter 1, controls, safeguards, and countermeasures are terms used to represent security mechanisms, policies, and procedures. These mechanisms, policies, and procedures counter attacks, reduce risk, resolve vulnerabilities, and otherwise improve the general state of security within an organization.

As was presented in the NSTISSC model in Chapter 1, there are three general categories of controls: policies, programs, and technologies. *Policies* are documents that specify an organization's approach to security. There are four types of security policies: general security policy, program security policy, issue-specific policies, and systems-specific policies. Each type of policy is outlined in this section, and covered in additional detail in Chapter 5. The *general security policy* is an executive-level document that outlines the organization's approach and attitude towards information security and relates the strategic value of information security within the organization. This document, typically created by the CIO in conjunction with the CEO and CISO, sets the tone for all subsequent security activities. The *program security policy* is a planning document that outlines the process of implementing security in the organization. This policy is the blueprint for the analysis, design, and implementation of security. *Issue-specific policies* address the specific implementations or applications of which users should be aware. These policies are typically developed to provide detailed instructions and restrictions associated with security issues. Examples include policies for Internet use, e-mail, and access to the building. Finally, *systems-specific policies* address the particular use of certain systems. This could include firewall configuration policies, systems access policies, and other technical configuration areas. *Programs* are activities performed within the organization to improve security. These include security education, training, and awareness programs. Chapter 5 covers the details of these types of programs. Security *technologies* are the technical implementations of the policies defined by the organization. Chapters 6, 7, and 8 present a more detailed description of the various technologies used in security implementations.

Access Controls

One particular application of controls is **access controls**, which specifically addresses admission of a user into a trusted area of the organization. These areas can include information systems, physically restricted areas such as computer rooms, and even the organization in its entirety. Access controls usually consist of a combination of policies, programs, and technologies.

Types of Access Controls

There are a number of ways to control access. Access controls can be mandatory, nondiscretionary, or discretionary. Each of these approaches addresses a group of controls used to regulate access to a particular type or collection of information, as explained below.

Mandatory access controls (MACs): MACs are structured and coordinated with a data classification scheme. **Mandatory access controls** give users and data owners limited control over access to information resources. In a data classification scheme, each collection of information is rated. Next, each user is rated to specify the level of information the user may access. These ratings are often referred to as sensitivity levels, and these sensitivity levels indicate the level of confidentiality the information requires. A variation of this form of access control is called **lattice-based access control**, in which users are assigned a matrix of authorizations for particular areas of access. The level of authorization may vary between levels, depending on the classification authorizations individuals possess for each group of information or resources. The lattice structure contains subjects and objects, and the boundaries associated with each pair are demarcated. Lattice-based control specifies the level of access each subject has to each object, if any. With this type of control, the column of attributes associated with a particular object (such as a printer) is referred to as an **access control list (ACL).** The row of attributes associated with a particular subject (such as a user) is referred to as a **capabilities table**.

Nondiscretionary controls: **Nondiscretionary controls** controls are managed by a central authority in the organization and can be based on an individual's role—**role-based controls**—or a specified set of tasks the individual is assigned—**task-based controls**. Task-based controls can also be based on lists maintained on subjects or objects. Role-based controls are tied to the role a user performs in an organization, and task-based controls are tied to a particular assignment or responsibility. The role and task controls make it easier to maintain the controls and restrictions associated with a particular role or task, especially if the individual performing the role or task changes often. Instead of constantly assigning and revoking the particular privileges of individuals who come and go, the administrator simply assigns the associated access rights to the role or task, and then whenever individuals are associated with that role or task, they automatically receive the corresponding access. When their turns are over, they are removed from the role or task, and the access is revoked.

Discretionary access controls (DAC): **Discretionary access controls** are implemented at the discretion or option of the data user. The ability to share resources in a peer-to-peer configuration allows users to control and possibly provide access to information or resources at their disposal. The users can allow general, unrestricted access, or they can allow specific individuals or sets of individuals to access these resources. For example, a user has a hard drive containing information to be shared with office coworkers. This user can elect to allow access to specific individuals by providing access, by name, in the share control function. Figure 4-6 shows an example of a discretionary access control from a peer-to-peer network using Microsoft Windows.

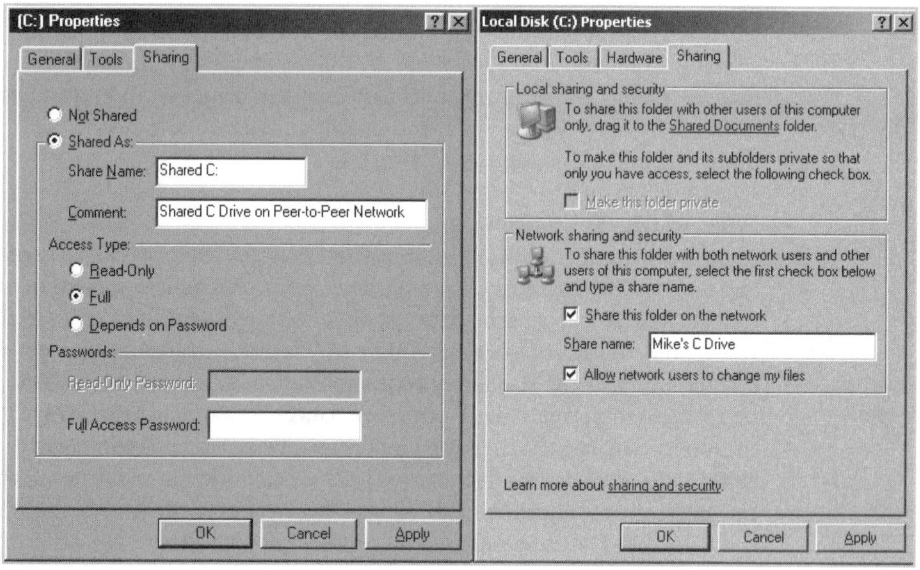

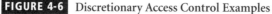

FIGURE 4-6 Discretionary Access Control Examples

Documenting the Results of Risk Assessment

By the end of the risk assessment process, you probably have in hand a collection of long lists of information assets with data about each of them. The goal of this process so far has been to identify the information assets of the organization that have specific vulnerabilities and list them, ranked according to those most needing protection. In preparing this list, you collected and preserved a wealth of factual information about the assets, the threats they face, and the vulnerabilities they expose. You should also have collected some information about the controls that are already in place. The final summarized document is the ranked vulnerability risk worksheet, a sample of which is shown in Table 4-8. A review of this worksheet shows similarities to the weighted factor analysis worksheet shown in Table 4-2. The worksheet shown in Table 4-8 is organized as follows:

- Asset: List each vulnerable asset.
- Asset Impact: Show the results for this asset from the weighted factor analysis worksheet. In the example, this is a number from 1 to 100.
- Vulnerability: List each uncontrolled vulnerability.
- Vulnerability Likelihood: State the likelihood of the realization of the vulnerability by a threat-agent, as noted in the vulnerability analysis step. In the example, the number is from 0.1 to 1.0.
- Risk-Rating Factor: Enter the figure calculated from the asset impact multiplied by likelihood. In the example, the calculation yields a number from 1 to 100.

TABLE 4-8   Ranked Vulnerability Risk Worksheet

Asset	Asset Impact or Relative Value	Vulnerability	Vulnerability Likelihood	Risk-Rating Factor
Customer service request via e-mail (inbound)	55	E-mail disruption due to hardware failure	0.2	11
Customer order via SSL (inbound)	100	Lost orders due to web server hardware failure	0.1	10
Customer order via SSL (inbound)	100	Lost orders due to Web server or ISP service failure	0.1	10
Customer service request via e-mail (inbound)	55	E-mail disruption due to SMTP mail relay attack	0.1	5.5
Customer service request via e-mail (inbound)	55	E-mail disruption due to ISP service failure	0.1	5.5
Customer order via SSL (inbound)	100	Lost orders due to Web server denial-of-service attack	0.025	2.5
Customer order via SSL (inbound)	100	Lost orders due to Web server software failure	0.01	1

SSL: Secure sockets layer

You may be surprised that the most pressing risk in Table 4-8 is represented by the vulnerable mail server. Even though the information asset represented by the customer service e-mail has an impact rating of only 55, the relatively high likelihood of a hardware failure makes it the most pressing problem.

Now that you have completed the risk identification process, what should the documentation package for this process look like? In other words, what are the deliverables from this phase of the project? The process you develop for risk identification should include designating what function the reports serve, who is responsible for preparing the reports, and who reviews them. The ranked vulnerability risk worksheet is the initial working document for the next step in the risk management process: assessing and controlling risk. Table 4-9 shows a sample list of the worksheets that might be prepared by the information security project team. Note that another method used to present the results of the risk assessment process is shown in Chapter 12 in the planning and risk assessment section of the information security maintenance process.

TABLE 4-9 Risk Identification and Assessment Deliverables

Deliverable	Purpose
Information asset classification worksheet	Assembles information about information assets and their impact on or value to the organization
Weighted criteria analysis worksheet	Assigns ranked value or impact weight to each information asset
Ranked vulnerability risk worksheet	Assigns ranked value of risk rating for each uncontrolled asset-vulnerability pair

Risk Control Strategies

When organizational management has determined that risks from information security threats are creating a competitive disadvantage, they empower the information technology and information security communities of interest to control the risks. Once the project team for information security development has created the ranked vulnerability worksheet, the team must choose one of four basic strategies to control each of the risks that result from these vulnerabilities. The four strategies discussed are:

- Apply safeguards that eliminate or reduce the remaining uncontrolled risks for the vulnerability (avoidance).
- Transfer the risk to other areas or to outside entities (transference).
- Reduce the impact should the vulnerability be exploited (mitigation).
- Understand the consequences and accept the risk without control or mitigation (acceptance).

Avoidance

Avoidance is the risk control strategy that attempts to prevent the exploitation of the vulnerability. This is the preferred approach, and is accomplished by means of countering threats, removing vulnerabilities in assets, limiting access to assets, and adding protective safeguards.

There are three common methods of risk avoidance: avoidance through application of policy, avoidance through application of training and education, and avoidance through application of technology.

Application of Policy

This approach allows management to mandate that certain procedures are always followed. For example, if the organization needs to control password use more tightly, a policy requiring passwords on all IT systems can be implemented. Note that policy alone may not be enough, and effective management always couples changes in policy with training and education or the application of technology, or both.

Training and Education

As explained in earlier chapters, policy must be communicated to employees. In addition, new technology often requires training. Awareness, training, and education are essential if employees are to exhibit safe and controlled behavior.

Applying Technology

In the real world of information security, technical solutions are often required to assure that risk is reduced. To continue the earlier example, passwords can be used with most modern operating systems, but some system administrators may not configure systems to use passwords. If, however, policy requires passwords, and the administrators are both aware of the requirement and trained to implement it, the technical control is successfully used.

Implementing Avoidance

Risks may be avoided by countering the threats facing an asset or by eliminating the exposure of a particular asset. Eliminating a threat is a difficult proposition, but it is possible. For example, when an organization becomes susceptible to cyberactivism (the use of computer-related technologies to advance a political agenda), it must take steps to avoid potential attacks. Recently McDonald's Corporation sought to reduce risks to its image by imposing stricter conditions on egg suppliers regarding the health and welfare of chickens.[11] This had been a source of contention between animal rights activists and the corporation for many years. This strategy accords with other changes made by McDonald's to meet demands from animal rights activists to improve relationships with these groups.

Another method of risk management that falls under the category of avoidance is the implementation of security controls and safeguards to deflect attacks on systems and therefore minimize the probability that an attack will be successful. An organization with dial-in access vulnerability, for example, may choose to implement a control or safeguard for that service. An authentication procedure based on a cryptographic technology, such as RADIUS (Remote Authentication Dial-In User Service) or another protocol or product, would provide sufficient control.[12] On the other hand, the organization may choose to eliminate the dial-in system and service to avoid the potential risk.

OFFLINE

The Human Firewall Project[13]

By The Human Firewall Council, July 2002

A consortium of security experts from government, private industry, associations, and nonprofit organizations known as the Human Firewall Council is directing the Human Firewall campaign. The goal of the Council is to help educate people in organizations about how better to protect information assets from the perspective of changing human behavior. The creation of a "human firewall" complements the usual technical firewalls and other network security devices and software designed to safeguard an enterprise.

Here are the eight essential steps to building a human firewall:

1. Get top management buy-in and commitment. The Gartner Group has identified three major questions that executives and boards of directors need to answer when confronting information security issues:
   - Is our security policy enforced fairly, consistently, and legally across the organization?
   - Would our employees, contractors, and partners know if a security violation were being committed?
   - Would they know what to do about it if they did recognize a security violation?
2. Assign and clarify roles and responsibilities.
3. Create an action plan with a budget.
4. Develop and/or update information security policies.
5. Develop an organization-wide security awareness/education program.
6. Measure the progress of your security awareness/education efforts.
7. Adapt and improve your security awareness/education programs according to progress/feedback.
8. Develop an information security incident response team and plan.

To see where the Human Firewall Council places people in the layers of defenses surrounding information, examine Figure 4-7.

continued

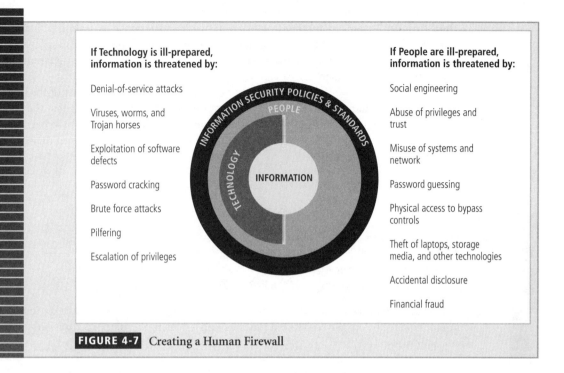

If Technology is ill-prepared, information is threatened by:

Denial-of-service attacks

Viruses, worms, and Trojan horses

Exploitation of software defects

Password cracking

Brute force attacks

Pilfering

Escalation of privileges

If People are ill-prepared, information is threatened by:

Social engineering

Abuse of privileges and trust

Misuse of systems and network

Password guessing

Physical access to bypass controls

Theft of laptops, storage media, and other technologies

Accidental disclosure

Financial fraud

INFORMATION SECURITY POLICIES & STANDARDS

PEOPLE

TECHNOLOGY

INFORMATION

FIGURE 4-7 Creating a Human Firewall

Transference

Transference is the control approach that attempts to shift the risk to other assets, other processes, or other organizations. This may be accomplished through rethinking how services are offered, revising deployment models, outsourcing to other organizations, purchasing insurance, or implementing service contracts with providers.

In the popular book *In Search of Excellence*, management consultants Tom Peters and Robert Waterman present a series of case studies of high-performing corporations. One of the eight characteristics of excellent organizations is that they "stick to their knitting. They stay reasonably close to the business they know."[14] This means that a company such as Kodak, a manufacturer of photographic equipment and chemicals, focuses on photographic equipment and chemicals. A company such as General Motors focuses on the design and construction of cars and trucks. Neither company spends strategic energies on the technology of Web site development. They focus energy and resources on what they do best while relying on consultants or contractors for other types of expertise.

This principle should be considered whenever an organization begins to expand its operations, including information and systems management, and even information security. If an organization does not already have quality security management and administration experience, it should hire individuals or firms that provide such expertise. For example, many organizations want Web services, including Web presences, domain name registration, and domain and Web hosting. Rather than implementing their own servers and hiring their own Webmasters, Web systems administrators, and specialized security experts, savvy organizations hire an ISP or a consulting organization to provide these products and services for them.

This allows the organization to transfer the risks associated with the management of these complex systems to another organization that has experience in dealing with those risks. A side benefit of specific contract arrangements is that the provider is responsible for disaster recovery, and through service level agreements is responsible for guaranteeing server and Web site availability.

Outsourcing, however, is not without its own risks. It is up to the owner of the information asset, IT management, and the information security team to ensure that the disaster recovery requirements of the outsourcing contract are sufficient and have been met *before* they are needed for recovery efforts. If the outsourcer has failed to meet the contract terms, the consequences may be far worse than expected.

OFFLINE

Top 10 Information Security Mistakes Made by Individuals

Adapted from "Top 10 Security Mistakes"[15]
By Alan S. Horowitz, *Computerworld*, July 9, 2001.

The following compilation was developed by security experts to represent mistakes most commonly made by employees—often unknowingly—which put their organization's information assets at risk:

1. Passwords on Post-it Notes
2. Leaving unattended computers on
3. Opening e-mail attachments from strangers
4. Poor password etiquette
5. Laptops on the loose (unsecured laptops that are easily stolen)
6. Blabbermouths (people who talk about passwords)
7. Plug and play (technology that enables hardware devices to be installed and configured without the protection provided by people who perform installations)
8. Unreported security violations
9. Always behind the times (the patch procrastinator)
10. Not watching for dangers *inside* the organization

Mitigation

Mitigation is the control approach that attempts to reduce the impact caused by the exploitation of vulnerability through planning and preparation. This approach includes three types of plans: the incident response plan (IRP), the disaster recovery plan (DRP), and the business continuity plan (BCP). Each of these plans depends on the ability to detect and respond to an attack as quickly as possible and relies on the existence and quality of the other plans. Mitigation begins with the early detection that an attack is in progress and the ability of the organization to respond quickly, efficiently, and effectively.

Incident Response Plan

The actions an organization can and perhaps should take while the incident is in progress should be defined in a document referred to as the *incident response plan (IRP)*. The IRP provides answers to questions victims might pose in the midst of an incident, such as "What do I do now?" For example, a systems administrator may notice that someone is copying information from the server without authorization, signaling violation of policy by a potential hacker or an unauthorized employee. What should the administrator do first? Whom should they contact? What should they document? The IRP supplies the answers.

For example, in the event of a serious virus or worm outbreak, the IRP may be used to assess the likelihood of imminent damage and to inform key decision makers in the various communities of interest (IT, information security, organization management, and users). The IRP also enables the organization to take coordinated action that is either predefined and specific, or *ad hoc* and reactive.

Disaster Recovery Plan

The most common of the mitigation procedures is the *disaster recovery plan (DRP)*. Although media backup strategies are an integral part of the disaster recovery plan, the overall program includes the entire spectrum of activities used to recover from an incident. DRP can include strategies to limit losses before and during the disaster. These strategies are fully deployed once the disaster has stopped. DRPs usually include all preparations for the recovery process, strategies to limit losses during the disaster, and detailed steps to follow when the smoke clears, the dust settles, or the floodwaters recede.

DRP and IRP planning overlap to a degree. In many regards, the DRP is the subsection of the IRP that covers disastrous events. The IRP is also flexible enough to be useful in situations that are near disasters but still require coordinated, planned actions. While some DRP and IRP decisions and actions are the same, their urgency and results can differ dramatically. The DRP focuses more on preparations completed before and actions taken after the incident, whereas the IRP focuses on intelligence gathering, information analysis, coordinated decision making, and urgent, concrete actions.

Business Continuity Plan

The third type of planning document within the mitigation strategy is the *business continuity plan (BCP)*. The BCP is the most strategic and long term of the three plans. It encompasses the continuation of business activities if a catastrophic event occurs, such as the loss of an entire database, building, or operations center. The BCP includes planning the steps necessary to ensure the continuation of the organization when the scope or scale of a disaster exceeds the ability of the DRP to restore operations. This can include preparation steps for activation of secondary data centers, hot sites, or business recovery sites. These are covered in more detail in Chapter 5. These systems enable the organization to continue operations with minimal disruption of service. Many companies offer this service as a contingency against disastrous events such as fires, floods, earthquakes, and most natural disasters.

Table 4-10 summarizes each of the mitigation plans, and supplies examples.

TABLE 4-10 Summaries of Mitigation Plans

Plan	Description	Example	When Deployed	Timeframe
Incident Response Plan (IRP)	Actions an organization takes during incidents (attacks)	▪ List of steps to be taken during disaster ▪ Intelligence gathering ▪ Information analysis	As incident or disaster unfolds	Immediate and real-time reaction
Disaster Recovery Plan (DRP)	Preparations for recovery should a disaster occur; strategies to limit losses before and during disaster; step-by-step instructions to regain normalcy	▪ Procedures for the recovery of lost data ▪ Procedures for the reestablishment of lost services ▪ Shutdown procedures to protect systems and data	Immediately after the incident is labeled a disaster	Short-term recovery
Business Continuity Plan (BCP)	Steps to ensure continuation of the overall business when the scale of a disaster exceeds the DRP's ability to restore operations	▪ Preparation steps for activation of secondary data centers ▪ Establishment of a hot site in a remote location	Immediately after the disaster is determined to affect the continued operations of the organization	Long-term operation

Acceptance

In contrast to mitigation, acceptance of risk is the choice to do nothing to protect a vulnerability and to accept the outcome of its exploitation. This may or may not be a conscious business decision. The only industry-recognized valid use of this strategy occurs when the organization has:

▪ Determined the level of risk
▪ Assessed the probability of attack
▪ Estimated the potential damage that could occur from attacks
▪ Performed a thorough cost benefit analysis
▪ Evaluated controls using each appropriate type of feasibility
▪ Decided that the particular function, service, information, or asset did not justify the cost of protection

This control, or rather lack of control, is based on the conclusion that the cost of protecting an asset does not justify the security expenditure. For example, suppose it would cost an organization $100,000 per year to protect a server. The security assessment determined that for $10,000 the organization could replace the information contained in the server, replace the server itself, and cover associated recovery costs. In this case, management may be satisfied with taking its chances and saving the money that would normally be spent on protecting this asset.

If every vulnerability identified in the organization is handled through acceptance, it may reflect an organization's inability to conduct proactive security activities and an apathetic approach to security in general. It is not acceptable for an organization to adopt a policy that ignorance is bliss and hope to avoid litigation by pleading ignorance of its obligation to protect employee and customer information. It is also unacceptable for management to hope that if they don't try to protect information, the opposition will assume that there is little to be gained by an attack. The risks far outweigh the benefits of this approach, which usually ends in regret, as the exploitation of the vulnerabilities causes a seemingly unending series of information security lapses. Acceptance as a strategy is often mistakenly chosen based on the school of fish justification—that sharks will not come after a small fish in a school of other small fish. But this reasoning can be very risky.

Now that you understand the four strategies that are used to control risk, you need to learn the next step in the process: selection of the proper strategy to defend the specific vulnerability of a specific information asset.

Selecting a Risk Control Strategy

Risk control involves selecting one of the four risk control strategies for each vulnerability. The flowchart shown in Figure 4-8 guides you through the process of deciding how to proceed with one of the four strategies. As shown in the diagram, after the information system is designed, you question whether the protected system has vulnerabilities and can be exploited. If the answer is yes, and a viable threat exists, you begin to examine what the attacker would gain from a successful attack. To determine if the risk is acceptable or not, you estimate the expected loss the organization will incur if the risk is exploited.

For further guidance, some rules of thumb on strategy selection are presented below. When weighing the benefits of the different strategies, keep in mind that the level of threat and value of the asset should play a major role in strategy selection.

- When a vulnerability (flaw or weakness) exists: Implement security controls to reduce the likelihood of a vulnerability being exercised.
- When a vulnerability can be exploited: Apply layered protections, architectural designs, and administrative controls to minimize the risk or prevent occurrence.
- When the attacker's cost is less than his potential gain: Apply protections to increase the attacker's cost (e.g., use system controls to limit what a system user can access and do, thereby significantly reducing an attacker's gain).
- When potential loss is substantial: Apply design principles, architectural designs, and technical and nontechnical protections to limit the extent of the attack, thereby reducing the potential for loss.

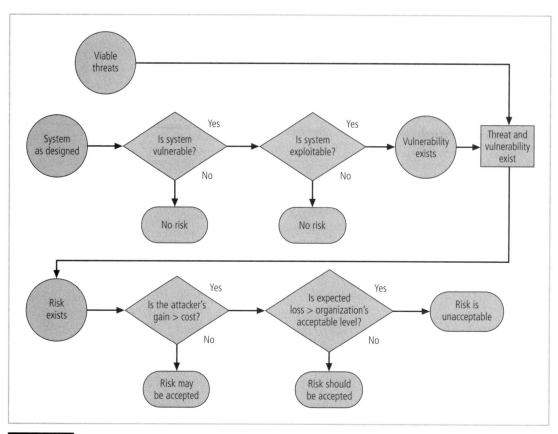

FIGURE 4-8 Risk Handling Decision Points

Evaluation, Assessment, and Maintenance of Risk Controls

Once a control strategy has been implemented, it should be monitored and measured on an ongoing basis to determine the effectiveness of the security controls and the accuracy of the estimate of the residual risk. Figure 4-9 shows how this cyclical process is continuously used to ensure that risks are controlled. Note that there is no exit from this cycle; it is a process that continues for as long as the organization continues to function.

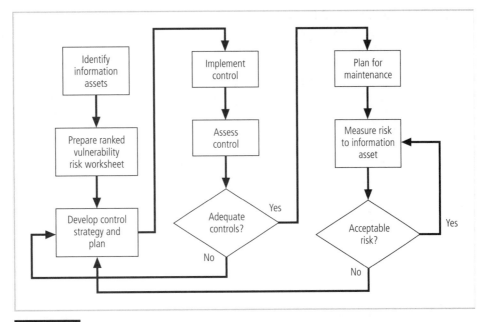

FIGURE 4-9 Risk Control Cycle

Categories of Controls

Controlling risk through avoidance, mitigation, or transference may be accomplished by implementing controls or safeguards. To help you approach this topic, four ways to categorize controls have been identified:

- Control function
- Architectural layer
- Strategy layer
- Information security principle

While there are certainly additional ways to categorize controls and safeguards, these four categories effectively introduce the process and provide an opportunity to present information about the varieties of controls currently in use.

Control Function

Controls or safeguards designed to defend systems are either preventive or detective. **Preventive controls** stop attempts to exploit a vulnerability by implementing enforcement of an organizational policy or a security principle, such as authentication or confidentiality. Preventive controls use a technical procedure, such as encryption, or some combination of technical means and enforcement methods. **Detective controls** warn organizations of violations of security principles, organizational policies, or attempts to exploit vulnerabilities. Detective controls use techniques such as audit trails, intrusion detection, and configuration monitoring.

Architectural Layer

Some controls apply to one or more layers of an organization's technical architecture. Controls can be classified by the layer or layers in which they provide control. Some controls, such as firewalls, operate at the interface between architectural layers, such as between the external network and the extranet, or between the organization's WAN and the LAN for a specific facility. Other controls, such as an organizational policy to always use nine or more characters for all passwords and SNMP shared-device passwords (or community strings), operate at all of the architectural layers, from external networks through and including specific applications. In general, the following entities are commonly regarded as distinct layers in an organization's information architecture:

- Organizational policy
- External networks
- Extranets (or demilitarized zones)
- Intranets (WANs and LANs)
- Network devices that interface network zones (switches, routers, firewalls, and hubs)
- Systems (computers for mainframe, server, and desktop use)
- Applications

Strategy Layer

Controls are sometimes classified by the risk control strategy they operate within: avoidance, mitigation, or transference.

Characteristics of Secure Information

Controls can also be classified according to which of the commonly accepted characteristics of secure information they are intended to assure, as follows:

- Confidentiality: The control assures the confidentiality of organizational data when it is stored, processed, or transmitted. An example of this type of control is the use of Secure Sockets Layer (SSL) encryption technology to secure Web content as it moves from Web server to browser.

- Integrity: The control assures that the information asset properly, completely, and correctly receives, processes, stores, and retrieves data in a consistent and correct manner. An example of this type of control is the use of parity or cyclical redundancy checks in data transmission protocols. Another example is the use of a product, such as Tripwire, that monitors the contents and structure of critical system files for unauthorized change.

- Availability: The control assures ongoing access to critical information assets. An example of this kind of control is the deployment of a network operations center using a sophisticated network monitoring tool set, such as Tivoli or OpenView, to assure optimum availability of network resources.

- Authentication: The control assures that the entity (person or computer) accessing information assets is in fact the stated entity. Examples of this include the use of cryptographic certificates to establish SSL connections, or the use of cryptographic hardware tokens such as SecurID cards as a second authentication of identity.

- Authorization: The control assures that a specific user (person or computer) has been specifically and explicitly authorized to access, update, or delete the contents of an information asset. An example of this control is the activation and use of access control lists and authorization groups in the Windows networking environment. Another example is the use of a database authorization scheme to verify the designated users for each function.

- Accountability: The control assures that every activity undertaken can be attributed to a specific named person or automated process. An example is the use of audit logs to track when each user logged in and logged out of each computer.
- Privacy: The control assures that the procedures to access, update, or remove personally identifiable information comply with the applicable laws and policies for that kind of information.

Feasibility Studies

Before deciding on the strategy (avoidance, transference, mitigation, or acceptance) for a specific vulnerability, all the economic and noneconomic consequences of the vulnerability facing the information asset must be explored. This is an attempt to answer the question, "What are the actual and perceived advantages of implementing a control as opposed to the actual and perceived disadvantages of implementing the control?"

There are a number of ways to determine the advantage of a specific control. The primary means is to determine the value of the information assets to be protected from the vulnerability. There are also many choices when an organization is faced with the daunting task of determining the disadvantages associated with specific controls for avoidance, transference, or mitigation of risk. The following sections discuss some of the more commonly used techniques for making these choices. Note that some of these techniques involve dollar expenses and savings implied from economic cost avoidance, and others deal with noneconomic feasibility criteria. **Cost avoidance** is the process of avoiding the financial impact of an incident by implementing a control.

Cost Benefit Analysis (CBA)

The approach most commonly considered for a project of information security controls and safeguards is the economic feasibility of implementation. While a number of alternatives for solving a problem may exist, they may not all have the same economic feasibility. Most organizations can spend only a reasonable amount of time and money on information security, and the definition of reasonable differs from organization to organization, and even from manager to manager. Organizations are urged to begin the cost benefit analysis by evaluating the worth of the information assets to be protected and the loss in value if those information assets were compromised by the exploitation of a specific vulnerability. It is only common sense that an organization should not spend more to protect an asset than the asset is worth. The formal process to document this decision making process is called a **cost benefit analysis** or an **economic feasibility study**.

Just as it is difficult to determine the value of information, it is also difficult to determine the cost of safeguards. Some of the items that affect the cost of a control or safeguard include:

- Cost of development or acquisition (purchase cost) of hardware, software, and services
- Training fees (cost to train personnel)
- Cost of implementation (cost to install, configure, and test hardware, software, and services)
- Service costs (vendor fees for maintenance and upgrades)
- Cost of maintenance (labor expense to verify and continually test, maintain, and update)

Benefit is the value that an organization realizes by using controls to prevent losses associated with a specific vulnerability. The amount of the benefit is usually determined by valuing the information asset or assets exposed by the vulnerability and then determining how much of that value is at risk, and how much risk there is for the asset. A benefit may be expressed as a reduction in the annualized loss expectancy, which is defined later in this chapter.

Asset valuation is the process of assigning financial value or worth to each information asset. Some argue that it is virtually impossible to determine the true value of information and information-bearing assets accurately. Perhaps this is one reason why insurance underwriters currently have no definitive valuation tables for assigning worth to information assets. The value of information differs within organizations and between organizations, depending both on the characteristics of the information and the perceived value of that information to each organization. Much of the work of assigning value to assets can draw on the information asset inventory and assessment that was prepared for the risk identification process completed earlier in this chapter.

The valuation of assets involves estimation of real and perceived costs associated with design, development, installation, maintenance, protection, recovery, and defense against loss and litigation. These estimates are calculated for every set of information-bearing systems or information assets. Some component costs are simple to determine, such as the cost to replace a network switch or the hardware needed for a specific class of server. Other costs are almost impossible to determine accurately, for example, the dollar value of the loss in market share if information on new product offerings is released prematurely and a company loses its competitive edge. A further complication is the value that some information assets acquire over time that is beyond the **intrinsic value** of the asset under consideration. The higher **acquired value** is the more appropriate value in most cases.

Some of the components of asset valuation include:

- Value retained from the cost of creating the information asset: Information is created or acquired at some cost to the organization. The cost can be calculated or estimated. One category of the cost of creating an asset is software development, and another is data collection and processing. Many organizations have developed extensive cost-accounting practices to capture the costs associated with the collection and processing of data, as well as the costs of the software development and maintenance activities. For software development, cost includes the cost of the blood, sweat, and tears of many people designing, testing, and resolving problems in the systems development life cycle for each application and system. The effort draws mainly on IT personnel but includes the user and general management community and sometimes the information security staff. In today's marketplace, with average programmer salaries of almost $29 per hour and contractor expenses even higher, the average cost to complete a moderately sized application quickly escalates.[16] For example, multimedia-based training averages 350 hours of development for each hour of training.[17] That's over $10,000 per hour for multimedia-based training software.

- Value retained from past maintenance of the information asset: It is estimated that for every dollar spent to develop an application or to acquire and process data stored by the organization, many more dollars are spent on maintenance over the useful life of the data or software. If actual costs have not been recorded, the cost can be estimated in terms of the amount and level of the human resources necessary to continually update, support, modify, and service the applications and systems associated with a particular set of information.

- Value implied by the cost of replacing the information: Another important cost associated with the loss or damage to information is the cost associated with replacing or restoring the information. This includes the human resource time needed to reconstruct, restore, or regenerate the information from backups, independent transactions logs, or even hardcopies of data sources. Most organizations rely on routine media backups to protect their information. If you find yourself estimating recovery costs, keep in mind that employees are occupied with routine work, and you may have to hire contractors for this effort. Also, loss of real-time information may not be recoverable from a previous tape backup, unless journaling capabilities were built into the system process. To replace information in the system, the various sources of the information may have to be reconstructed, and the data reentered into the system and validated for accurate representation of the original data. This restoration can take longer than the time it took to create the data.

- Value from providing the information: Different from the cost of developing or maintaining the information is the cost of providing the information to the users who need it. This includes the value associated with the delivery of the information through databases, networks, and hardware and software systems. It also includes the cost of the infrastructure necessary to provide access and control of the information.

- Value incurred from the cost of protecting the information: Here is a recursive dilemma, which is the value of an asset is based in part on the cost of protecting it. The amount of money spent to protect an asset is based in part on the value of the asset. While this is a seemingly unsolvable circle of logic, it is possible to estimate the value of the protection for an information asset to better understand the value associated with its potential loss. For the values listed above, it is easy to calculate a specific value. With this and the following values, the result is likely be an estimate of cost.

- Value to owners: How much is your Social Security number worth to you? Or your telephone number? It can be quite a daunting task to place a value on information. In addition to the costs associated with the information described above, what is the increase in the value of information above and beyond its cost? A market researcher collects data from a company's sales figures and determines that there is a strong market potential for a certain age group with a certain demographic value for a new product offering. While the cost associated with the creation of this new information may be small, how much is the new information actually worth? It could be worth millions if it successfully defines a new market share. The value of information to an organization, or how much of the organization's bottom line is directly attributable to the information, may be impossible to estimate. However, it is vital to understand the overall cost of protecting this information in order to understand its value. Here again, estimating value may be the only method possible.

- Value of intellectual property: Related to the value of information is the specific consideration of the value of intellectual property. The value of a new product or service to a customer may be unknowable. How much would a cancer patient pay for a cure? How much would a shopper pay for a new type of cheese? What is the value of an advertising jingle? All of these could represent the intellectual property of an organization, yet their valuation is complex. A related but separate consideration is intellectual properties known as trade secrets. These intellectual information assets are so valuable that they are literally the primary assets of some organizations.

■ Value to adversaries: Also related to this analysis is the value of information to the organization's competition or adversaries. How much would it be worth to an organization to know what the competition is up to? Many organizations now have established departments that deal in competitive intelligence and are responsible for assessing and estimating the activities of the organization's competition or opposition. Even organizations in traditionally not-for-profit industries can benefit from understanding what is going on in political, business, and competitive organizations. Stories of industrial espionage abound, including the urban legend of Company A encouraging its employees to hire on as janitors at Company B. As custodians, the employees could snoop through open terminals, photograph and photocopy key unsecured documents, and rifle through internal trash and recycling bins. Such legends highlight the value information can have to the right individuals. Similar are stories of disgruntled employees, soon to be terminated, stealing information and presenting it to competitive organizations to gain favor and new employment. Those considering such a tactic should reflect on this: would you trust someone who stole from your competition to gain a job with your company? Most everyone assumes that saboteurs repeat their activities whenever they become disgruntled.

■ Loss of productivity while the information assets are unavailable: Many times, electrical power may be interrupted. Although the effective use of UPS equipment can prevent a power outage from causing the loss of existing data, outages still may lead to data loss in that they render system users unable to complete work that would create additional information. Worse yet, workers may resort to other activities until power is restored. Although a power outage is not an example of an attack that damages information, it is an instance in which a threat (deviations in quality of service from service providers) affects the productivity of an organization. The hours of wasted employee time, the cost of using alternatives, and the general lack of productivity can severely set back a critical operation or process.

■ Loss of revenue while information assets are unavailable: Have you ever been in a retail store when your credit card wouldn't scan? How many times did salespeople rescan before resorting to entering the numbers manually? How long did it take to enter the numbers manually in contrast to the quick swipe? What if the credit card verification process was offline? Did the store have a manual process for validating or processing credit card payment in the absence of the familiar approval system? Many organizations have all but abandoned manual backups for automated processes. There are situations in which businesses turn away customers because their automated payment systems are inoperative. While this is typically a failure of management to prepare (disaster recovery planning), it clearly illustrates the potential loss of revenue when information and information systems are unavailable. In today's marketplace, most grocery stores no longer label each item with the price, because the UPC scanners and the related databases calculate the costs and inventory levels dynamically. Without these systems, could your grocery store sell goods? How much would they lose if they could not? It has been estimated that "43 percent of all businesses that close their doors due to a disaster or crisis, even for one day, never reopen them again. An additional 28 percent fail during the next three to five years."[18] Now imagine what would happen if, instead of a grocery store, an online book retailer such as Amazon.com were to suffer a power outage. The entire operation would instantly be shut down. Or consider what would happen if Amazon's offering system remained operational, but its payment systems went offline? In this case, customers would be able to make selections, but not check out. Either way, the organization would lose revenue. While the dot com businesses may be more susceptible to loss of information as a loss of revenue, most organizations would not be able to conduct business if certain pieces of information were unavailable.

The organization must be able to place a dollar value on each collection of information and the information assets it owns. This value is based on the answers to these questions:

- How much did it cost to create or acquire this information?
- How much would it cost to recreate or recover this information?
- How much does it cost to maintain this information?
- How much is this information worth to the organization?
- How much is this information worth to the competition?

Once an organization has estimated the worth of various assets, it can begin to examine the potential loss that could occur from the exploitation of vulnerability or a threat occurrence. This process results in the estimate of potential loss per risk. The questions that must be asked here include:

- What damage could occur, and what financial impact would it have?
- What would it cost to recover from the attack, in addition to the financial impact of damage?
- What is the single loss expectancy for each risk?

A **single loss expectancy (SLE)** is the calculation of the value associated with the most likely loss from an attack. It is a calculation based on the value of the asset and the **exposure factor (EF)**, which is the expected percentage of loss that would occur from a particular attack, as follows:

$$\text{SLE} = \textbf{asset value x exposure factor (EF)}$$

where EF equals the percentage loss that would occur from a given vulnerability being exploited.

For example, if a Web site has an estimated value of $1,000,000 (value determined by asset valuation), and a deliberate act of sabotage or vandalism (hacker defacement) scenario indicates that 10% of the Web site would be damaged or destroyed after such an attack, then the SLE for this Web site would be $1,000,000 x .10 = $100,000. This estimate is then used to calculate another value, annual loss expectance, which will be discussed shortly.

As difficult as it is to estimate the value of information, the estimation of the probability of a threat occurrence or attack is even more difficult. There are not always tables, books, or records that indicate the frequency or probability of any given attack. There are sources available for some asset-threat pairs. For instance, the likelihood of a tornado or thunderstorm destroying a building of a specific type of construction within a specified region of the country is available to insurance underwriters. In most cases, however, an organization can rely only on its internal information to calculate the security of its information assets. Even if the network, systems, and security administrators have been actively and accurately tracking these occurrences, the organization's information is sketchy at best. As a result, this information is usually estimated. In most cases, the probability of a threat occurring is usually a loosely derived table indicating the probability of an attack from each threat type within a given time frame (for example, once every

10 years). This value is commonly referred to as the **annualized rate of occurrence (ARO)**. ARO is simply how often you expect a specific type of attack to occur. As you learned earlier in this chapter, many attacks occur much more frequently than every year or two. For example, a successful deliberate act of sabotage or vandalism might occur about once every two years, in which case the ARO would be 50% (.50), whereas some kinds of network attacks can occur multiple times per second. To standardize calculations, you convert the rate to a yearly (annualized) value. This is expressed as the probability of a threat occurrence.

Once each asset's worth is known, the next step is to ascertain how much loss is expected from a single expected attack, and how often these attacks occur. Once those values are established, the equation can be completed to determine the overall lost potential per risk. This is usually determined through an **annualized loss expectancy (ALE)**, which is calculated from the ARO and SLE, as shown here:

$$ALE = SLE \times ARO$$

Using the example of the Web site that might suffer a deliberate act of sabotage or vandalism and thus has an SLE of $100,000 and an ARO of .50, the ALE would be calculated as follows:

$$ALE = \$100,000 \times .50$$

$$ALE = \$50,000$$

This indicates that unless the organization increases the level of security on its Web site, it can expect to lose $50,000 per year, every year. Armed with such a figure, the organization's information security design team can justify expenditure for controls and safeguards and deliver a budgeted value for planning purposes. Note that sometimes noneconomic factors are considered in this process, so that in some cases even when ALE amounts are not huge, control budgets can be justified.

The Cost Benefit Analysis (CBA) Formula

In its simplest definition, CBA (or economic feasibility) determines whether or not the control alternative being evaluated is worth the associated cost incurred to control the specific vulnerability. CBAs may be calculated before a control or safeguard is implemented to determine if the control is worth implementing. CBAs can also be calculated after controls have been implemented and have been functioning for a time. Observation over time adds precision to the evaluation of the benefits of the safeguard and the determination of whether the safeguard is functioning as intended. While many CBA techniques exist, the CBA is most easily calculated using the ALE from earlier assessments before the implementation of the proposed control, which is known as ALE(prior). Subtract the revised ALE, estimated based on control being in place, known as ALE(post). Complete the calculation by subtracting the **annualized cost of the safeguard (ACS)**.

$$CBA = ALE(prior) - ALE(post) - ACS$$

Once the controls are implemented, it is crucial to continue to examine their benefits to determine when the controls must be upgraded, supplemented, or replaced. As Frederick Avolio states in his article "Best Practices in Network Security":

> Security is an investment, not an expense. Investing in computer and network security measures that meet changing business requirements and risks makes it possible to satisfy changing business requirements without hurting the business' viability.[19]

Benchmarking

Instead of determining the financial value of information and then implementing security as an acceptable percentage of that value, an organization could take a different approach to risk management, and look to peer organizations for benchmarks. **Benchmarking** is the process of seeking out and studying the practices used in other organizations that produce results you would like to duplicate in your organization. An organization typically benchmarks by selecting a measure with which it may compare itself to the other organizations in its market. The organization then measures the difference between the way it conducts business and the way the other organizations conduct business. The industry Web site Best Practices Online puts it this way:

> Benchmarking can yield great benefits in the education of executives and the realized performance improvements of operations. In addition, benchmarking can be used to determine strategic areas of opportunity. In general, it is the application of what is learned in benchmarking that delivers the marked and impressive results so often noted. The determination of benchmarks allows one to make a direct comparison. Any identified gaps are improvement areas.[20]

When benchmarking, an organization typically uses one of two types of measures to compare practices: metrics-based measures or process-based measures.

Metrics-based measures are comparisons based on numerical standards, such as:

- Numbers of successful attacks
- Staff-hours spent on systems protection
- Dollars spent on protection
- Numbers of security personnel
- Estimated value in dollars of the information lost in successful attacks
- Loss in productivity hours associated with successful attacks

An organization uses numerical standards like these to rank competing organizations with a similar size or market to its own and then determines how it measures up to the competitors. The difference between an organization's measures and those of others is often referred to as a **performance gap**. Performance gaps provide insight into the areas that an organization should work on to improve its security postures and defenses.

The other measures commonly used in benchmarking are **process-based measures**. Process-based measures are generally less focused on numbers and more strategic than metrics-based measures. For each of the areas the organization is interested in benchmarking, process-based measures enable the organization to examine the activities an individual company performs in pursuit of its goal, rather than the specifics of how goals are attained. The primary focus is *the method* the organization uses to accomplish a particular process, rather than the outcome.

In information security, two categories of benchmarks are used: standards of due care and due diligence, and best practices. Within best practices, the **gold standard** is a subcategory of practices that are typically viewed as "the best of the best." Each of these is described in the following sections.

For legal reasons, an organization may be forced to adopt a certain minimum level of security, as discussed in Chapter 3. When organizations adopt levels of security for a legal defense, they may need to show that they have done what any *prudent* organization would do in similar circumstances. This is referred to as a **standard of due care**. It is insufficient to implement these standards and then ignore them. The application of controls at or above the prescribed levels and the maintenance of those standards of due care show that the organization has performed due diligence. **Due diligence** is the demonstration that the organization is diligent in ensuring that the implemented standards continue to provide the required level of protection. Failure to support a standard of due care or due diligence can open an organization to legal liability, provided it can be shown that the organization was negligent in its application or lack of application of information protection. This is especially important in areas in which the organization maintains information about customers, including medical, legal, or other personal data.

The security protection an organization is expected to maintain is complex and broad in scope. It may, therefore, be physically impossible to be the "best in class" in any or all categories. Based on the budgets assigned to the protection of information, it may also be financially impossible to provide a level of security equal to organizations with greater revenues. Sometimes organizations want to implement the best, most technologically advanced, most secure levels of protection, but for financial or other reasons they cannot. Such organizations should remember the adage, "Good security now is better than perfect security never."[21] It would also be counterproductive to establish costly, state-of-the-art security in one area, only to leave other areas exposed. Organizations must make sure they have met a reasonable level of security across the board, protecting all information, before beginning to improve individual areas to reach a higher standard, such as best practices.

Security efforts that seek to provide a superior level of performance in the protection of information are referred to as **best business practices** or simply **best practices** or **recommended practices**. Even the standards promoted on the Internet as requests for comments (RFCs) have best practices (see *www.rfc-editor.org/categories/rfc-best.html*). Best security practices are those security efforts that are among the best in the industry, balancing the need for access to information with adequate protection. Best practices seek to provide as much security as possible for information and systems while maintaining a solid degree of fiscal responsibility. Companies with best practices may not be the best in every area, but may simply have established an extremely high quality or successful security effort in one or more areas. Benchmarking best practices is accomplished by means of the metrics-based or process-based measures described earlier. The federal government has established a Web site through which government agencies can share best practices in the area of information security with other agencies (see *http://fasp.nist.gov*). This project is known as the Federal Agency Security Project (FASP). It was the result of

> the Federal Chief Information Officer Council's Federal Best Security Practices (BSP) pilot effort to identify, evaluate, and disseminate best practices for computer information protection and security... The FASP site contains agency policies, procedures, and practices; the CIO pilot BSPs; and a Frequently-Asked-Questions (FAQ) section.[22]

While few commercial equivalents exist at this time, many of the government's BSPs are applicable to the areas of security in both the public and the private sector. The FASP has collected sample policies, strategies, and other practice-related documents, which are presented for use as guidelines.

Even the best business practices are not sufficient for some organizations. These organizations prefer to set the standard by implementing the most protective, supportive, and yet fiscally responsible standards they can. They strive toward the gold standard. The gold standard is a defining level of performance that demonstrates one company's industrial leadership, quality, and concern for the protection of information. The implementation of this level of security requires a great amount of support, both in financial and personnel resources. While there is limited public information on best practices, there is virtually no published criteria for the gold standard. The gold standard represents an almost unobtainable level of security, unsurpassed in industry. Many vendors claim to offer a gold standard in one product or service, but this is predominantly marketing hype.

You can sometimes get advice about how to select control strategies from government sources. For some organizations that operate in industries that are regulated by governmental agencies, government recommendations are, in effect, requirements. For other organizations, government regulations are excellent sources for information about what other organizations may be doing or are required to do in controlling information security risks.

Applying Best Practices

The preceding sections have presented a number of sources you can consider when applying standards to your organization. You can study the documented best practice processes or procedures that have been shown to be effective and are thus recommended by a person or organization and evaluate how they apply to your organization. When considering best practices for adoption, consider the following:

- Does your organization resemble the identified target organization with the best practice under consideration? Is your organization in a similar industry as the target? Keep in mind that a strategy that works well in manufacturing organizations often has little bearing in a nonprofit organization. Does your organization face similar challenges as the target? If your organization has no functioning information security program, a best practice target that assumes you start with a functioning program is not useful. Is your organizational structure similar to the target's? Obviously, a best practice proposed for a small home office setting is not appropriate to help design control strategies for a multinational company.

- Are the resources your organization can expend similar to those identified with the best practice? If your approach is significantly limited by resources, it is not useful to submit a best practice proposal that assumes unlimited funding and does not specify items that are too expensive to implement.

- Is your organization in a similar threat environment as that proposed in the best practice? A proposal of best practice from months and even weeks ago may not be appropriate for the current threat environment. Think of the best practices for Internet connectivity that are required in the modern organization at the opening of the twenty-first century and compare them to the best practices of five years earlier.

Another source for best practices information is the CERT Web site (*www.cert.org/ security-improvement/*), which presents a number of security improvement modules and practices in HTML and PDF format. Similarly, Microsoft has published a set of best security practices at its Web site (*www.microsoft.com/privacy/safeinternet/security/best_practices/default.htm*). Microsoft focuses on seven key areas for their best practices:

1. Use antivirus software.
2. Use strong passwords.
3. Verify your software security settings.
4. Update product security.
5. Build personal firewalls.
6. Back up early and often.
7. Protect against power surges and loss.

In support of security efforts, Microsoft offers "The Ten Immutable Laws of Security"[23] as follows:

Law #1: If a bad guy can persuade you to run his program on your computer, it's not your computer anymore.

Law #2: If a bad guy can alter the operating system on your computer, it's not your computer anymore.

Law #3: If a bad guy has unrestricted physical access to your computer, it's not your computer anymore.

Law #4: If you allow a bad guy to upload programs to your Web site, it's not your Web site anymore.

Law #5: Weak passwords trump strong security.

Law #6: A machine is only as secure as the administrator is trustworthy.

Law #7: Encrypted data is only as secure as the decryption key.

Law #8: An out-of-date virus scanner is only marginally better than no virus scanner at all.

Law #9: Absolute anonymity isn't practical, in real life or on the Web.

Law #10: Technology is not a panacea.

Problems with Applying Benchmarking and Best Practices

The biggest problem with benchmarking and best practices in information security is that organizations don't talk to each other. A successful attack is viewed as an organizational failure. Because valuable lessons are not recorded, disseminated, and evaluated, the entire industry suffers. However, with the increased attention paid to security, more and more security administrators are joining professional associations and societies (such as the Information Systems Security Association), sharing stories, and publishing the lessons learned. Individual security administrators are more often submitting sanitized versions of attacks (from which specific details that could identify the targeted organization have been removed) to security journals. But again, most organizations refuse even to acknowledge, much less publicize, the occurrence of successful attacks.

Another problem with benchmarking is that no two organizations are identical. Even if two organizations are producing products or services in the same market, their sizes, compositions, management philosophies, organizational cultures, technological infrastructures, and budgets for security may differ dramatically. Thus, even if these organizations did exchange specific information, it may not apply in a different context. What organizations seek most are lessons they can apply, rather than specific technologies they should adopt. This emphasizes the fact that security is a managerial problem, not a technical one. If it were a technical problem, implementing the same technology would solve the problem regardless of industry or organizational composition. Because it is a managerial and people problem, the number and types of variables that impact the security of the organization can differ radically in any two businesses.

A third problem is that best practices are a moving target. What worked well two years ago may be completely worthless against today's threats. Security practices must keep abreast of new threats in addition to the methods, techniques, policies, guidelines, educational and training approaches, and technologies used to combat the threats.

One last issue to consider is that simply knowing what was going on in the information security industry in recent years through the use of benchmarking research doesn't necessarily prepare a practitioner for what to do next. It is said that those who cannot remember the past are condemned to repeat it. In security, those who do not prepare for the attacks of the past see them occur again and again. However, preparing for past threats does not safeguard against new and different challenges ahead. It is important to be as prepared as possible and then focus efforts on monitoring the communications and new listings that are popular among systems and security administrators to determine what is new and how to prepare for it.

Baselining

Related to the concept of benchmarking is the process of baselining. A **baseline** is a "value or profile of a performance metric against which changes in the performance metric can be usefully compared."[24] An example is the establishment of the number of attacks per week the organization is experiencing. In the future, this baseline can serve as a reference point to determine if the average number of attacks is increasing or decreasing. **Baselining** is the analysis of measures against established standards. In information security, baselining is the comparison of security activities and events against the organization's future performance. In a sense, baselining can provide the foundation for internal benchmarking. The information gathered for an organization's first risk assessment becomes the baseline for future comparisons. Therefore, the initial baseline must be carefully established.

When baselining, it is useful to have a guide to the overall process. The National Institute of Standards and Technology has two publications specifically written to support these activities:

- Security SP 800-27 Engineering Principles for Information Technology Security (A Baseline for Achieving Security), June 2001
- SP 800-26 Security Self-Assessment Guide for Information Technology Systems, November 2001

Both of these documents are available at *http://csrc.nist.gov/publications/nistpubs/index.html.*

Other Feasibility Studies

In addition to the methods discussed above, which are frequently used to document feasibility, there are other approaches to consider. In the previous sections, the concepts of economic feasibility or using baselines or benchmarks were used to justify proposals for information security controls. When an analyst moves to the next step of measuring how ready an organization is for these controls, he or she must determine the proposal's organizational, operational, technical, and political feasibility. The methods for these types of feasibility evaluations are discussed in the following sections.

Organizational Feasibility

Organizational feasibility examines how well the proposed information security alternatives will contribute to the efficiency, effectiveness, and overall operation of an organization. In other words, the proposed control approach for the vulnerability must contribute to the organization's strategic objectives. Above and beyond the impact on the bottom line, the organization must determine how the proposed alternatives contribute to the business objectives of the organization. Does the implementation align with the strategic planning for the information systems? Or does it require deviation from the planned expansion and management of the current systems? The organization should not invest in technology that changes the fundamental ability of the organization to explore certain avenues and opportunities. For example, suppose that a university decides to implement a new firewall without considering the organizational feasibility of this project. Consequently, it takes a few months for the technology group to learn enough about the firewall to completely configure it. Then, a few months after the implementation begins, it is discovered that the firewall in its current configuration does not permit outgoing Web-streamed media. If one of the business goals of the university is the pursuit of distance-learning opportunities, and the firewall prevents the pursuit of that goal, the firewall has failed the organizational feasibility measure and should be modified or replaced.

Operational Feasibility

Operational feasibility addresses several key areas not covered in the other feasibility measures. **Operational feasibility** addresses user acceptance and support, management acceptance and support, and the overall requirements of the organization's stakeholders. Operational feasibility is also known as **behavioral feasibility**, because it measures the behavior of users. One of the fundamental principles of systems development is obtaining user buy-in on a project. If the users do not accept a new technology, policy, or program, it will fail. Users may not openly oppose a change, but the result may be the same. If users do not support a control, they will find ways of disabling or otherwise circumventing it, thereby creating yet another vulnerability. One of the most common methods for obtaining user acceptance and support is through user involvement. User involvement can be obtained via three simple steps: communicate, educate, and involve.

Organizations should *communicate* with system users throughout the development of the security program, letting them know that change is occurring. This includes communicating the timetables and schedules of implementation, plus the dates, times, and locations of upcoming briefings and training. Those making the changes should let those being affected know the purpose of the proposed changes, and how these changes will enable everyone to work more securely. In addition, organizations should make efforts to design training to *educate* employees about how to work under the new constraints and avoid any negative impact on performance. One of the most frustrating things from users' perspective is the implementation of a new program that prevents them from accomplishing their duties, with only a promise of eventual training. Those making changes must also *involve* users by asking them what they want from the new systems and what they will tolerate from the new systems, and by including selected representatives from the various constituencies in the development process. Adherence to these three simple steps of communication, education, and involvement can reduce *resistance* to change and build *resilience* for change—that ethereal quality that allows workers not only to tolerate constant change, but also to accept it as a necessary part of the job.

Technical Feasibility

In addition to the straightforward feasibilities associated with the economic costs and benefits of the controls, the project team must also consider the technical feasibilities associated with the design, implementation, and management of controls. Some safeguards, especially technology-based safeguards, are extremely difficult to implement, configure, and manage. **Technical feasibility** examines whether or not the organization has or can acquire the technology necessary to implement and support the control alternatives. Does the organization have the hardware and software necessary to support a new firewall system? If not, can it be obtained? Technical feasibility also examines whether the organization has the technological expertise to manage the new technology. Does the organization have a staff of individuals qualified (and possibly certified) to install and manage a new firewall system? If not, can staff be spared from their current obligations to attend formal training and education programs to prepare them to administer the new systems? Or must personnel be hired? In the current job environment, how difficult is it to find qualified personnel? These issues must be examined in detail before the acquisition of a new set of controls. Many organizations rush into the acquisition of new safeguards, without completely examining the associated requirements.

Political Feasibility

For some organizations, the most significant feasibility evaluated may be political. Politics is often defined as the art of the possible.[25] Within organizations, **political feasibility** defines what can and cannot occur based on the consensus and relationships between the communities of interest. The limits placed on an organization's actions or behaviors by the information security controls must fit within the realm of the possible before they can be effectively implemented, and that realm includes the availability of staff resources.

In some cases, resources are provided to the information security community directly under a budget apportionment model. The management and professionals involved in information security then allocate the resources to activities and projects using processes of their own design.

In other organizations, resources are first allocated to the IT community of interest, and the information security team must compete for these resources. In some cases, cost benefit analysis and other forms of justification discussed previously in this chapter are used in an allocation process to make rational decisions about the relative merit of various activities and projects. Unfortunately in some settings, these decisions are politically charged and are not made according to the pursuit of the greater organizational goals.

Another methodology for budget allocation requires the information security team to propose and justify use of the resources for activities and projects in the context of the entire organization. This requires that arguments for information security spending articulate the benefit of the expense for the whole organization, so that members of the organizational communities of interest can understand its value.

Risk Management Discussion Points

Not every organization has the collective will or budget to manage each vulnerability by applying controls, and therefore each organization must define the level of risk it is willing to live with.

Risk Appetite

Risk appetite defines the quantity and nature of risk that organizations are willing to accept as they evaluate the tradeoffs between perfect security and unlimited accessibility. For instance, a financial services company, regulated by government and conservative by nature, may seek to apply every reasonable control and even some invasive controls to protect its information assets. Other, non-regulated organizations may also be conservative by nature, seeking to avoid the negative publicity associated with the perceived loss of integrity from the exploitation of a vulnerability. Thus, a firewall vendor may install a set of firewall rules that are far stricter than normal because the negative consequence of being hacked would be catastrophic in the eyes of its customers. Other organizations may take on dangerous risks through ignorance. The reasoned approach to risk is one that balances the expense (in terms of finance and the usability of information assets) of controlling vulnerabilities against the losses possible if these vulnerabilities were exploited.

As mentioned in Chapter 1, James Anderson, vice president of information security at Inovant, the world's largest commercial processor of financial payment transactions, believes that information security in today's enterprise is a "well-informed sense of assurance that the information risks and controls are in balance." The key for the organization is to find the balance in its decision-making processes and in its feasibility analyses, therefore assuring that an organization's risk appetite is based on experience and facts and not on ignorance or wishful thinking.

Residual Risk

Even when vulnerabilities have been controlled as much as possible, there is often still some risk that has not been completely removed, shifted, or planned for. This remainder is called residual risk. To express it another way, "residual risk is a combined function of (1) a threat less the effect of threat-reducing safeguards, (2) a vulnerability less the effect of vulnerability-reducing safeguards, and (3) an asset less the effect of asset value-reducing safeguards."[26] Figure 4-10 illustrates how residual risk remains after safeguards are implemented.

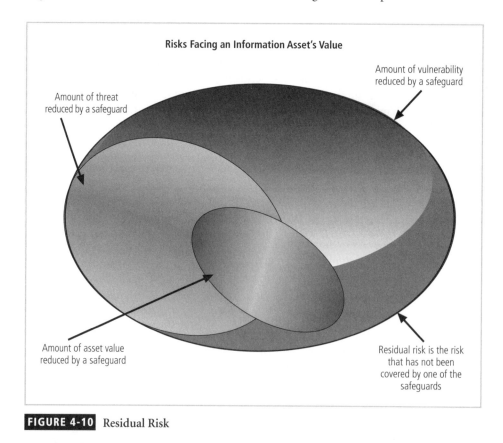

Risks Facing an Information Asset's Value

Amount of vulnerability reduced by a safeguard

Amount of threat reduced by a safeguard

Amount of asset value reduced by a safeguard

Residual risk is the risk that has not been covered by one of the safeguards

FIGURE 4-10   Residual Risk

The significance of residual risk must be judged within the context of the organization. Although it is counterintuitive, the goal of information security is not to bring residual risk to zero; it is to bring residual risk into line with an organization's comfort zone or risk appetite. If decision makers have been informed of uncontrolled risks and the proper authority groups within the communities of interest have decided to leave residual risk in place, the information security program has accomplished its primary goal.

Documenting Results

The results from risk assessment activities can be delivered in a number of ways: a report on a systematic approach to risk control, a project-based risk assessment, or a topic-specific risk assessment.

When the organization is pursuing an overall risk management program, it requires a systematic report that enumerates the opportunities for controlling risk. In this report, a series of proposed controls are documented, each of which has been justified by one or more feasibility or rationalization approaches. At a minimum, each information asset-threat pair should have a documented control strategy that clearly identifies any residual risk remaining after the proposed strategy has been executed. Furthermore, each control strategy should articulate which of the four fundamental risk-reducing approaches will be used or how they might be combined, and how that should justify the findings by referencing the feasibility studies. Additional preparatory work for project management should be included where available.

Another option for a systematic report is to document the outcome of the control strategy for each information asset-threat pair in an action plan. This action plan includes concrete tasks, each with accountability assigned to an organizational unit or to an individual. It may also include hardware and software requirements, budget estimates, and detailed timelines to activate the project management activities needed to implement the control.

On some occasions, the risk assessment will be prepared for a specific IT project. Sometimes this is completed at the request of the project manager of an IT project, either because it is required by organizational policy or because it is good project management practice. On some occasions, the project risk assessment may be requested by auditors or senior management if they perceive that an IT project has sidestepped the organization's information security objectives. The project risk assessment should identify the sources of risk in the finished IT system, with suggestions for remedial controls, as well as those risks that might impede the completion of the project. For example, a new application usually requires a project risk assessment at system design time and then periodically as the project evolves toward completion.

Lastly, when management requires details about a specific information system topic and the risk it poses to the organization, risk assessment may be documented in a topic-specific report. These are usually demand reports that are prepared at the direction of senior management and are focused on a narrow area of information systems operational risk. For example, a newly emergent vulnerability is reported to management, which then asks for a specific risk assessment. A more complete treatment of the process of documenting the results of risk management activities is presented in Chapter 12 under the subject of *risk assessments*.

Recommended Practices in Controlling Risk

If an organization is faced with a situation that indicates a control strategy that will require a maximum budget of $50,000, the planned expenditures must be justified and budget authorities must be convinced to spend up to *$50,000 to protect a particular asset from an identified threat.* Unfortunately, most budget authorities focus on trying to cut a percentage of the total figure to save the organization money. This underlines the importance of developing strong justifications for specific action plans and providing concrete estimates in those plans.

Another factor to consider is that each control or safeguard affects more than one asset-threat pair. If a new $50,000 firewall is installed to protect the Internet connection infrastructure from the threat posed by hackers launching port-scanning attacks, the same firewall may protect this Internet connection infrastructure from other threats and attacks. In addition, the firewall may protect other information assets from other threats and attacks. The final choice of proposed controls may be a balanced mixture of controls that provide the greatest value to as many asset-threat pairs as possible. This reveals another facet of the problem: information security professionals manage a dynamic matrix covering a broad range of threats, information assets, controls, and identified vulnerabilities. Each time a control is added to the matrix, it undoubtedly changes the ALE for the information asset vulnerability for which it has been designed, and it also may alter the ALE for other information asset vulnerabilities. To put it more simply, if you put in one safeguard, you decrease the risk associated with all subsequent control evaluations. To make matters even more complex, the action of implementing a control may change the values assigned or calculated in a prior estimate.

Between the impossible task associated with the valuation of information assets and the dynamic nature of the ALE calculations, it's no wonder organizations are looking for a way to implement controls that doesn't involve such complex, inexact, and dynamic calculations. This leads to an ongoing search for ways to design security architectures that go beyond the direct application of specific controls, in which each is justified for a specific information asset vulnerability, to safeguards that can be applied to several vulnerabilities at once. Some of the alternatives that have been and continue to be developed are discussed in the following sections.

Qualitative Measures

The spectrum of steps described previously was performed with actual values or estimates. This is known as a **quantitative assessment**. However, an organization could determine that it cannot put specific numbers on these values. Fortunately, it is possible to repeat these steps using an evaluation process, called **qualitative assessment,** that is based on characteristics that do not use numerical measures. For example, instead of placing a value of once every 10 years for the ARO, the organization could list all possible attacks on a particular set of information and rate each by the probability of occurrence. This could be accomplished using scales rather than specific estimates. A sample scale could include none, representing no chance of occurrence, then low, medium, high, up to very high, representing almost certain occurrence. Organizations may, of course, prefer other scales: A-Z, 0-10, 1-5, or 0-20. Using scales also relieves the organization from the difficulty of determining exact values. Many of these same scales can be used in any situation requiring a value, even in asset valuation. For example, instead of estimating that a particular piece of information is worth $1,000,000, you can value information on a scale of 1-20, with 1 indicating relatively worthless information, and 20 indicating extremely critical information, such as a certain soda manufacturer's secret recipe or those 11 herbs and spices of a popular fried chicken vendor.

Delphi Technique

How do you calculate the values and scales of either qualitative or quantitative assessment? An individual can pull the information together based on personal experience, but two heads are better than one. And a team of heads is better than only two. One technique for accurately estimating scales and values is the Delphi technique. The **Delphi technique**, named for the oracle at Delphi, is a process whereby a group rates or ranks a set of information. The individual responses are compiled and then returned to the group for another iteration. This process continues until the entire group is satisfied with the result. This technique can be applied to the development of scales, asset valuation, asset or threat ranking, or any decision that can benefit from the input of more than one decision maker.

Chapter Summary

- Risk management examines and documents the current information technology security being used in an organization. It is the process of identifying vulnerabilities in an organization's information systems and taking carefully reasoned steps to assure the confidentiality, integrity, and availability of all of the components in the information systems.

- A key component of a risk management strategy is the identification, classification, and prioritization of the information assets in the organization.

- The human resources, documentation, and data information assets of an organization are not as easily identified and documented as tangible assets, such as hardware and software.

- After identifying and performing a preliminary classification of information assets, the threats facing an organization should be examined. There are 12 categories of threats to information security.

- To fully understand each threat and the impact it can have on the organization, each identified threat must be examined through a threat assessment process.

- The goal of risk assessment is the assignment of a risk rating or score that represents the relative risk for a specific vulnerability of a specific information asset.

- Once the vulnerabilities are identified and ranked, the organization must choose a strategy to control the risks resulting from these vulnerabilities. The four control strategies are avoidance, transference, mitigation, and acceptance.

- The economic feasibility study is used to determine the costs associated with protecting an asset. The formal documentation process of feasibility is called a cost benefit analysis.

- Benchmarking is an alternative method to the economic feasibility analysis that seeks out and studies the practices used in other organizations that produce the results desired in an organization.

- The goal of information security is to bring residual risk, the amount of risk unaccounted for after the application of controls and other risk management strategies, to an acceptable level.

Review Questions

1. What is risk management? Why is the identification of risks, by listing assets and their vulnerabilities, so important to the risk management process?

2. According to Sun Tzu, what two key understandings must you achieve to be successful in battle?

3. Who is responsible for risk management in an organization? Which community of interest usually takes the lead in information security risk management?

4. In risk management strategies, why must periodic review be a part of the process?

5. Why do networking components need more examination from an information security perspective than from a systems development perspective?

6. What value would an automated asset inventory system have for the risk identification process?

7. What information attribute is often of great value for local networks that use static addressing?

8. Which is more important to the systems components classification scheme: that the asset identification list be comprehensive or mutually exclusive?

9. What's the difference between an asset's ability to generate revenue and its ability to generate profit?

10. What are vulnerabilities? How do you identify them?

11. What is competitive disadvantage? Why has it emerged as a factor?

12. What are the four strategies for controlling risk?

13. Describe risk avoidance. Name three common methods of risk avoidance.

14. Describe risk transference. Describe how outsourcing can be used for risk transference.

15. Describe risk mitigation. What three planning approaches are discussed in the text as opportunities to mitigate risk?

16. How is an incident response plan different from a disaster recovery plan?

17. What is risk appetite? Explain why risk appetite varies from organization to organization.

18. What is a cost benefit analysis?

19. What is the definition of single loss expectancy? What is annual loss expectancy?

20. What is residual risk?

Exercises

1. If an organization has three information assets to evaluate for risk management, as shown in the accompanying data, which vulnerability should be evaluated for additional controls first? Which one should be evaluated last?

   Data for Exercise 1:

   - Switch L47 connects a network to the Internet. It has two vulnerabilities: it is susceptible to hardware failure at a likelihood of 0.2, and it is subject to an SNMP buffer overflow attack at a likelihood of 0.1. This switch has an impact rating of 90 and has no current controls in place. You are 75% certain of the assumptions and data.
   - Server WebSrv6 hosts a company Web site and performs e-commerce transactions. It has a Web server version that can be attacked by sending it invalid Unicode values. The likelihood of that attack is estimated at 0.1. The server has been assigned an impact value of 100, and a control has been implanted that reduces the impact of the vulnerability by 75%. You are 80% certain of the assumptions and data.
   - Operators use an MGMT45 control console to monitor operations in the server room. It has no passwords and is susceptible to unlogged misuse by the operators. Estimates show the likelihood of misuse is 0.1. There are no controls in place on this asset; it has an impact rating of 5. You are 90% certain of the assumptions and data.

2. Using the data classification scheme presented in this chapter, identify and classify the information contained in your personal computer or personal digital assistant. Based on the potential for misuse or embarrassment, what information would be confidential, sensitive but unclassified, or for public release?

3. Suppose XYZ Software Company has a new application development project, with projected revenues of $1,200,000. Using the following table, calculate the ARO and ALE for each threat category that XYZ Software Company faces for this project.

Threat Category	Cost per Incident (SLE)	Frequency of Occurrence
Programmer mistakes	$5,000	1 per week
Loss of intellectual property	$75,000	1 per year
Software piracy	$500	1 per week
Theft of information (hacker)	$2,500	1 per quarter
Theft of information (employee)	$5,000	1 per six months
Web defacement	$500	1 per month
Theft of equipment	$5,000	1 per year
Viruses, worms, Trojan horses	$1,500	1 per week
Denial-of-service attacks	$2,500	1 per quarter
Earthquake	$250,000	1 per 20 years
Flood	$250,000	1 per 10 years
Fire	$500,000	1 per 10 years

4. How might XYZ Software Company arrive at the values in the above table? For each entry, describe the process of determining the cost per incident and frequency of occurrence.

5. Assume a year has passed and XYZ has improved security by applying a number of controls. Using the information from Exercise 3 and the following table, calculate the post-control ARO and ALE for each threat category listed.

Threat Category	Cost per Incident	Frequency of Occurrence	Cost of Control	Type of Control
Programmer mistakes	$5,000	1 per month	$20,000	Training
Loss of intellectual property	$75,000	1 per 2 years	$15,000	Firewall/IDS
Software piracy	$500	1 per month	$30,000	Firewall/IDS
Theft of information (hacker)	$2,500	1 per 6 months	$15,000	Firewall/IDS
Theft of information (employee)	$5,000	1 per year	$15,000	Physical security
Web defacement	$500	1 per quarter	$10,000	Firewall
Theft of equipment	$5,000	1 per 2 years	$15,000	Physical security
Viruses, worms, Trojan horses	$1,500	1 per month	$15,000	Anti-virus
Denial-of-service attacks	$2,500	1 per 6 months	$10,000	Firewall
Earthquake	$250,000	1 per 20 years	$5,000	Insurance/backups
Flood	$50,000	1 per 10 years	$10,000	Insurance/backups
Fire	$100,000	1 per 10 years	$10,000	Insurance/backups

Why have some values changed in the columns Cost per Incident, and Frequency of Occurrence? How could a control affect one, but not the other?

Assume the values in the Cost of Control column presented in the table for Exercise 5 were those unique costs directly associated with protecting against that threat. In other words, don't worry about overlapping costs between controls. Calculate the CBA for the planned risk control approach for each threat category. For each threat category, determine if the proposed control is worth the costs.

Case Exercises

As Charlie wrapped up the meeting, he ticked off a few key reminders for everyone involved in the asset identification project.

"Okay, everyone, before we finish, please remember that you should try to make your asset lists complete, but be sure to focus your attention on the more valuable assets first. Also, remember that we evaluate our assets based on business impact to profitability first, and then economic cost of replacement. Make sure you check with me about any questions that come up. We will schedule our next meeting in two weeks, so please have your draft inventories ready."

Questions:

1. Did Charlie effectively organize the work before the meeting? Why or why not? Make a list of the important issues you think should be covered by the work plan. For each issue, provide a short explanation.

2. Will the company get useful information from the team it has assembled? Why or why not?

3. Why might some attendees resist the goals of the meeting? Does it seem that each person invited was briefed on the importance of the event and the issues behind it?

Endnotes

1. Sun Tzu. *The Art of War*, trans. Samuel B. Griffith. (Oxford: Oxford University Press, 1988) p. 84.

2. Mike Godwin. "When Copying Isn't Theft." *Electronic Frontier Foundation Online.* [Cited 20 March 2004]. Available from the World Wide Web <*http://www.eff.org/IP/ phrack_riggs_neidorf_godwin.article*>.

3. Ted Bridis and Rebecca Buckman. "Microsoft Hacked! Code Stolen?" *ZDNet News Online.* 20 March 2004. [Cited 17 June 2002]. Available from the World Wide Web <*http://zdnet.com.com/2100-11-525083.html*>.

4. Adapted from the Georgia-Pacific Corporation Practices Guide.

5. U.S. Army, Fort Gordon. *School of Information Technology* AR 350-1. [Cited 20 March 2004]. Available from the World Wide Web <*http://atzhssweb.gordon.army.mil/otd/ c2protect/iaso/Army/AR%20380-5/chapter1.htm*>.

6. Michael E. Whitman, "Enemy at the Gates: Threats to Information Security." *Communications of the ACM*, 46(8) August, 2003, pp. 91–95.

7. Michael E. Whitman. "Enemy at the Gates: Threats to Information Security." *Communications of the ACM*, 46(8) August, 2003, pp. 91–95.

8. Lawrence A. Gordon, Martin P. Loeb, William Lucyshyn, and Robert Richardson (2004). 2004 CSI/FBI Computer Crime and Security Survey. [Cited 21 June 2004]. Available from the World Wide Web <*http://www.gocsi.com*>.

9. Michael E. Whitman. "Enemy at the Gates: Threats to Information Security." *Communications of the ACM*, 46(8) August 2003, pp. 91–95.

10. National Institute of Standards and Technology. *Risk Management Guide for Information Technology Systems.* SP 800-30. (January 2002).

11. Jack M. Greenberg. "Corporate Press Release: First Worldwide Social Responsibility Report." *McDonald's Corporation Online.* 15 April 2002. [Cited 20 June 2003]. Available from the World Wide Web <*http://164.109.33.187/corp/values/socialrespons/ sr_report.html*>.

12. 37th IETF. "Remote Authentication Dial-In User Service (RADIUS) Charter." (proceedings at the 37th IETF meeting, San Jose, Calif., December 1996) [Cited 20 March 2004]. Available from the World Wide Web <*http://www.ietf.org/proceedings/96dec/charters/ radius-charter.html*>.

13. HumanFirewall.org. "Building a Human Firewall." *Human Firewall Online 2001.* [Cited 20 March 2004]. Available from the World Wide Web <*http://www.humanfirewall.org*>.

14. Thomas J. Peters and, Robert H. Waterman. *In Search of Excellence: Lessons from America's Best Run Companies.* (New York: Harper and Row, © 1982).

15. Alan S. Horowitz. "Top 10 Security Mistakes." *ComputerWorld.* (Framingham) 35, no. 28 (9 July 2001): 38.

16. Shannon Cochran. "The Top Ten Cities for Programmers." *Dr. Dobb's Journal Online.* October 2000. [Cited 19 June 2002]. Available from the World Wide Web <*http://www.ddj.com/documents/s=880/ddj0010l/*>.

17. Shelley Hesse. "Guidelines for Your First Authorware Project." *Multimedia Enterprise Online.* [Cited 20 March 2004]. Available from the World Wide Web <*http://www.media-enterprise.com/articles/aw_guidelines.htm*>.

18. Peter Gourlay. "Playing it Safe." *U.S. Business Review Online.* December 2001. [Cited 19 June 2002]. Available from the World Wide Web <*http://www.usbusiness-review.com/ 0112/02.html*>.

19. Frederick M. Avolio. "Best Practices in Network Security." *Network Computing* 11, no. 5 (20 March 2000): 60–66.

20. Best Practices, LLC. "What is Benchmarking?" *Best Practices Online.* [Cited 20 March 2004]. Available from the World Wide Web <*http://www.best-in-class.com/site_tools/faq.htm#benchmarking*>.

21. Frederick M. Avolio. "Best Practices in Network Security." *Network Computing* 11, no. 5 (20 March 2000): 60–66.

22. National Institute of Standards and Technology. *Computer Security Resource Center* (Gaithersburg, June 2002). Available from the World Wide Web <*http://fasp.nist.gov*>.

23. The Microsoft Security Response Center. *The Ten Immutable Laws of Security?* (Redmond, July 2002). Available from the World Wide Web <*http://www.microsoft.com/technet/treeview/default.asp?url=/technet/columns/security/10imlaws.asp*>.

24. Philip Carden. "Network Baselining and Performance Management." *Network Computing Online* [Cited 20 March 2004]. Available from the World Wide Web <*http://www.networkcomputing.com/netdesign/base1.html*>.

25. Thomas Mann. "Politics is often defined as the art of the possible." (speech in the Library of Congress, Washington, D.C., 29 May 1945).

26. Gamma Secure Systems Limited. "First Measure Your Risk." *Gamma Online.* 2 January 2002. [Cited 20 March 2004]. Aavailable from the World Wide Web <*http://www.gammassl.co.uk/inforisk/*>.

Planning for Security

5

Begin with the end in mind.

STEPHEN COVEY, AUTHOR OF *SEVEN HABITS OF HIGHLY EFFECTIVE PEOPLE*

CHARLIE MOODY FLIPPED HIS JACKET collar up to cover his ears. The spray blowing over him from the fire hoses was cold and was icing the cars that lined the street where he stood watching his office building burn. The warehouse and shipping dock were not gone, only severely damaged by smoke and water. He tried to hide his dismay by turning to speak to Fred Chin.

"Look at the bright side," said Charlie. "At least we can get the new server that we have been putting off."

Fred shook his head. "Charlie, you must be dreaming. We don't have enough insurance for a full replacement of everything we've lost."

Charlie was stunned. The offices were gone, and all the computer systems, servers, and desktops were melted slag, and he was going to have to try to rebuild without all the resources he needed. At least he had good backups, or so he hoped. He thought hard, trying to remember the last time the off-site backup tapes had been tested.

He wondered where all the network design diagrams were. He knew he could call his network provider to order new circuits as soon as Fred found some new office space. But where were all the circuit specs? The only copy had been in a drawer in his office, the office that wasn't there anymore. This was not going to be fun. He would have to call directory assistance just to get the phone number for his boss, Gladys Williams, the CIO.

Charlie heard a buzzing noise off to his left. He turned to see the flashing numbers of his alarm clock. Relief flooded over him as he realized it was just another nightmare and Sequential Label and Supply had not really burned down. He turned on the light to make some notes for himself to go over with his staff later in the morning. Charlie was going to make some changes to the company contingency plans *today*.

LEARNING OBJECTIVES:

Upon completion of this material, you should be able to:

- Describe management's role in the development, maintenance, and enforcement of information security policy, standards, practices, procedures, and guidelines
- Understand what an information security blueprint is, what its major components are, and how it is used to support the information security program
- Understand how an organization institutionalizes its policies, standards, and practices using education, training, and awareness programs
- Explain what contingency planning is and how incident response planning, disaster recovery planning, and business continuity plans are related to contingency planning

Introduction

The creation of an information security program begins with the creation and/or review of the organization's information security policies, standards, and practices. Then, the selection or creation of information security architecture and the development and use of a detailed information security blueprint will create the plan for future success. This blueprint for the organization's information security efforts can be realized only if it operates in conjunction with the organization's information security policy. Without policy, blueprints, and planning, the organization will be unable to meet the information security needs of the various communities of interest. The role of planning in the modern organization is hard to overemphasize. All but the smallest of organizations undertake at least some planning: strategic planning to manage the allocation of resources, and contingency planning to prepare for the uncertainties of the business environment.

Information Security Policy, Standards, and Practices

Management from all communities of interest, including general staff, information technology, and information security, must consider policies as the basis for all information security planning, design, and deployment. Policies direct how issues should be addressed and technologies should be used. Policies do not specify the proper operation of equipment or software—this information should be placed in the standards, procedures, and practices of users' manuals and systems documentation. In addition, *policy should never contradict law*, because this can create a significant liability for the organization. For a sidebar discussion of this issue, see the Offline box regarding Arthur Andersen.

OFFLINE

"I obstructed justice," testified David B. Duncan, the former chief outside auditor of Enron Corp. He told a federal jury that he knew he had committed a crime when he instructed his colleagues at Arthur Andersen LLP to destroy documents as their energy client collapsed. "I instructed people on the engagement team to follow a document-retention policy which I knew would result in the destruction of documents." Duncan was fired by Andersen in January after an internal probe revealed that the company shredded documents and deleted e-mail messages related to Enron. He pleaded guilty to a single count of obstruction of justice, under a plea agreement that could result in up to 10 years in prison.[1]

By now most of the free world is familiar with the Enron/Andersen Consulting fiasco. The Enron Energy Corporation was found to have lied about its financial records, specifically about its reported profits. Enron was also accused of a host of dubious business practices, including concealing financial losses and debts.

The depth and breadth of the fraud was so great that at least one executive committed suicide rather than face criminal charges. Also, as described above, one of the company's accounting firms, world renowned Arthur Andersen Consulting, contributed to the problem by shredding literally tons of financial documents, in an attempt to hide the problem. Andersen claimed this was its policy.

Policy that conflicts with law is by definition illegal; and therefore following such a policy is a criminal act. In the Enron/Andersen scandal, people went to jail claiming they were simply following policy. And they might have gotten away with it, if they actually had followed policy, because the Andersen policy for document retention stated that staff must keep work papers for six years before they can destroy them. But client-related files, such as correspondence or other records, are only kept "until not useful." Managers and individual partners keeping such material in client folders or other files should "purge" the documents, the policy states. But in cases of threatened litigation, Andersen staff must not destroy "related information."[2] A subsequent update to the policy was interpreted as a mandate to shred all but the most basic working papers as soon as possible unless precluded by an order for legal discovery.

And so the shredding party began. A big part of the problem was that the policy wasn't followed consistently—that is, this shredding began right *after* Andersen found out that Enron was to be investigated for fraudulent business practices, which indicated that the consulting firm had decided to cover its tracks, and those of its benevolent business partner.

Now people are going to jail, one is dead, and everyone claims they were just following policy.

Quality security programs begin and end with policy.[3] Because information security is primarily a management problem, not a technical one, policy obliges personnel to function in a manner that adds to the security of information assets, rather than as a threat to those assets. It is interesting to note that security policies are the least expensive control to execute, but the most difficult to implement *properly*. They are the lowest cost in that they involve only the time and effort of the management team to create, approve, and communicate. Even if the management team decides to hire an outside consultant to assist in the development of policy, the costs are minimal compared to those of technical controls. However, shaping policy is difficult because it must:

- Never conflict with laws
- Stand up in court, if challenged
- Be properly administered through dissemination and documented acceptance

Definitions

Before examining the various types of information security policies, it is important to understand exactly what policy is and how it can and should be used.

A **policy** is a plan or course of action used by an organization to convey instructions from its senior-most management to those who make decisions, take actions, and perform other duties on behalf of the organization. Policies are organizational laws in that they dictate acceptable and unacceptable behavior within the context of the organization's culture. Like laws, policies must define what is right, and what is wrong, what the penalties are for violating policy, and what the appeal process is. (These topics are explored further in the following sections.) **Standards**, on the other hand, are more detailed statements of what must be done to comply with policy. They have the same requirements for compliance as policies. The level of acceptance of standards may be informal, as in **de facto standards**. Or standards may be published, scrutinized, and ratified by a group, as in formal or **de jure standards**. Finally, practices, procedures, and guidelines effectively explain how to comply with policy. Figure 5-1 shows policies as the force that drives standards, which in turn drive practices, procedures, and guidelines.

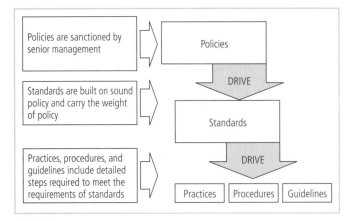

FIGURE 5-1   Policies, Standards, and Practices

Policies are written to support the mission, vision, and strategic planning of an organization. The **mission** of an organization is a written statement of an organization's purpose. The **vision** of an organization is a written statement about the organization's goals—where will the organization be in five years? In ten? **Strategic planning** is the process of moving the organization towards its vision.

To be effective, a policy must be disseminated by all means possible, including printed personnel manuals, organization intranets, and periodic supplements. All members of the organization must read, understand, and agree to the policies. At the same time, policies should be considered living documents, in that they require constant modification and maintenance as the needs of the organization evolve.

The meaning of the term **security policy** depends on its context. Governmental agencies discuss security policy in terms of national security and national policies to deal with foreign states. A security policy can also represent a credit card agency's policy for processing credit card numbers. In general, a security policy is a set of rules that protect an organization's assets. An **information security policy** provides rules for the protection of the information assets of the organization. As stated in Chapter 1, the task of information security professionals is to protect the confidentiality, integrity, and availability of information and information systems, whether in the state of transmission, storage, or processing. This is accomplished by applying policy, education and training programs, and technology.

Management must define three types of security policy according to The National Institute of Standards and Technology's Special Publication 800-14 (a publication that will be discussed in much greater detail later in this chapter):

1. General or security program policies
2. Issue-specific security policies
3. Systems-specific security policies

Each of these management policies is examined in greater detail in the pages that follow.

Enterprise Information Security Policy (EISP)

An **enterprise information security policy (EISP)** is also known as a general security policy, IT security policy, or information security policy. The EISP is based on and directly supports the mission, vision, and direction of the organization and sets the strategic direction, scope, and tone for all security efforts. The EISP is an executive-level document, usually drafted by, or in cooperation with, the chief information officer of the organization. This policy is usually two to ten pages long and shapes the philosophy of security in the IT environment. The EISP does not usually require continuous modification, unless there is a change in the strategic direction of the organization.

The EISP guides the development, implementation, and management of the security program. It contains the requirements to be met by the information security blueprint or framework. It defines the purpose, scope, constraints, and applicability of the security program in the organization. It also assigns responsibilities for the various areas of security, including systems administration, maintenance of the information security policies, and the practices and responsibilities of the users. Finally, it addresses legal compliance. According to the National Institute of Standards, the EISP typically addresses compliance in two areas:

1) General compliance to ensure meeting the requirements to establish a program and the responsibilities assigned therein to various organizational components and
2) the use of specified penalties and disciplinary action.[4]

When the EISP has been developed, the CISO (or chief information security officer) begins forming the security team and initiating the necessary changes to the information security program.

Issue-Specific Security Policy (ISSP)

As an organization executes various technologies and processes to support routine operations, guidelines are needed to instruct employees to use these technologies and processes properly. In general, the **issue-specific security policy**, or **ISSP**, 1) addresses specific areas of technology as listed below, 2) requires frequent updates, and 3) contains a statement on the organization's position on a specific issue.[5] An ISSP may cover the following topics, among others:

- Electronic mail
- Use of the Internet
- Specific minimum configurations of computers to defend against worms and viruses
- Prohibitions against hacking or testing organization security controls
- Home use of company-owned computer equipment
- Use of personal equipment on company networks
- Use of telecommunications technologies (FAX and phone)
- Use of photocopy equipment

There are a number of approaches to take when creating and managing ISSPs within an organization. Three of the most common are to create the following types of ISSP documents:

1. Independent ISSP documents, each tailored to a specific issue
2. A single comprehensive ISSP document covering all issues
3. A modular ISSP document that unifies policy creation and administration, while maintaining each specific issue's requirements

The independent document approach to take when creating and managing ISSPs typically has a scattershot effect. Each department responsible for a particular application of technology creates a policy governing its use, management, and control. This approach to creating ISSPs may fail to cover all of the necessary issues, and can lead to poor policy distribution, management, and enforcement.

The single comprehensive policy approach is centrally managed and controlled. With formal procedures for the management of ISSPs in place, the comprehensive policy approach establishes guidelines for overall coverage of necessary issues and clearly identifies processes for the dissemination, enforcement, and review of these guidelines. Usually, these policies are developed by those responsible for managing the information technology resources. Unfortunately, these policies tend to overgeneralize the issues and skip over vulnerabilities.

The optimal balance between the independent and comprehensive ISSP approaches is the modular approach. It is also centrally managed and controlled but tailored to the individual technology issues. The modular approach provides a balance between issue orientation and policy management. The policies created with this approach comprise individual modules, each created and updated by individuals responsible for the issues addressed. These individuals report to a central policy administration group that incorporates specific issues into an overall comprehensive policy.

Figure 5-2 is an outline of a sample ISSP, which can be used as a model. An organization should add to this structure the specific details that dictate security procedures not covered by these general guidelines.

Considerations for an Effective Telecommunications Use Policy

1. Statement of policy
   a. Scope and applicability
   b. Definition of technology addressed
   c. Responsibilities
2. Authorized access and usage of equipment
   a. User access
   b. Fair and responsible use
   c. Protection of privacy
3. Prohibited usage of equipment
   a. Disruptive use or misuse
   b. Criminal use
   c. Offensive or harassing materials
   d. Copyrighted, licensed, or other intellectual property
   e. Other restrictions
4. Systems management
   a. Management of stored materials
   b. Employer monitoring
   c. Virus protection
   d. Physical security
   e. Encryption
5. Violations of policy
   a. Procedures for reporting violations
   b. Penalties for violations
6. Policy review and modification
   a. Scheduled review of policy and procedures for modification
7. Limitations of liability
   a. Statements of liability or disclaimers

FIGURE 5-2 Elements of an Issue-Specific Security Policy Statement[6]

The components of each of the major categories presented in the sample issue-specific policy shown in Figure 5-2 are discussed below. Even though the details may vary from policy to policy and some sections of a modular policy may be combined, it is essential for management to address and complete each section.

Statement of Policy

The policy should begin with a clear statement of purpose. Consider a policy that covers the issue of fair and responsible use of the WWW and the Internet. The introductory section of this policy should outline these topics: What is the scope of this policy? Who is responsible and accountable for policy implementation? What technologies and issues does it address?

Authorized Access and Usage of Equipment

This section of the policy statement addresses *who* can use the technology governed by the policy, and *what* it can be used for. Remember that an organization's information systems are the exclusive property of the organization, and users have no particular rights of use. Each technology and process is provided for business operations. Use for any other purpose constitutes misuse of equipment. This section defines "fair and responsible use" of equipment and other organizational assets, and should also address key legal issues, such as protection of personal information and privacy.

Prohibited Usage of Equipment

While the policy section described above detailed what the issue or technology *can* be used for, this section outlines what it *cannot* be used for. Unless a particular use is clearly prohibited, the organization cannot penalize its employees for misuse. The following can be prohibited: personal use, disruptive use or misuse, criminal use, offensive or harassing materials, and infringement of copyrighted, licensed, or other intellectual property. As an alternative approach, categories 2 and 3 of Figure 5-2 can be collapsed into a single category— appropriate use. Many organizations use an ISSP titled "Appropriate Use" to cover both categories.

Systems Management

There may be some overlap between an ISSP and a systems-specific policy (to be discussed shortly), but the systems management section of the ISSP policy statement focuses on the users' relationship to systems management. Specific rules from management include regulating the use of e-mail, the storage of materials, authorized monitoring of employees, and the physical and electronic scrutiny of e-mail and other electronic documents. It is important that all such responsibilities are designated as belonging to either the systems administrator or the users, otherwise both parties may infer that the responsibility belongs to the other party.

Violations of Policy

Once guidelines on equipment use have been outlined and responsibilities have been assigned, the individuals to whom the policy applies must understand the penalties and repercussions of violating the policy. Violations of policy should carry appropriate, not draconian, penalties. This section of the policy statement should contain not only the specifics of the penalties for each category of violation but also instructions on how individuals in the organization can report observed or suspected violations. Many individuals feel that powerful individuals in the organization can discriminate, single out, or otherwise retaliate against someone who reports violations. Allowing anonymous submissions is often the only way to convince individual users to report the unauthorized activities of other, more influential employees.

Policy Review and Modification

Because any document is only as good as its frequency of review, each policy should contain procedures and a timetable for periodic review. As the needs and technologies change in the organization, so must the policies that govern their use. This section should contain a specific methodology for the review and modification of the policy, to ensure that users do not begin circumventing it as it grows obsolete.

Limitations of Liability

The final consideration listed in Figure 5-2 is a general statement of liability or set of disclaimers. If an individual employee is caught conducting illegal activities with organizational equipment or assets, management does not want the organization held liable. So the policy should state that if employees violate a company policy or any law using company technologies, the company will not protect them, and the company is not liable for its actions. It is inferred that such a violation would be without knowledge or authorization by the organization.

Systems-Specific Policy (SysSP)

While issue-specific policies are formalized as written documents to be distributed to users and agreed to in writing, **systems specific security policies (SysSPs)** are frequently codified as standards and procedures to be used when configuring or maintaining systems. An example of a systems-specific policy is an access control list that defines which users may and may not access a particular system, complete with the levels of access for each authorized user. Systems-specific policies can be organized into two general groups:

1. **Access control lists (ACLs)**: Lists, matrices, and capability tables governing the rights and privileges of a particular user to a particular system. As indicated earlier, an ACL is a list of access rights used by file storage systems, object brokers, or other network communications devices to determine which individuals or groups may access an object that it controls. (As you probably know from previous coursework, object brokers are system components that handle message requests between the software components of a system.) A similar list, which is also associated with users and groups, is called a **capability table**. This specifies which subjects and objects a user or group can access. Capability tables are frequently complex matrices, rather than simple lists or tables.
2. **Configuration rules**: The specific configuration codes entered into security systems to guide the execution of the system when information is passing through it.

ACL Policies

As illustrated in Figures 5-3 and 5-4, both the Novell Netware 5.x/6.x and the Microsoft Windows families of systems translate ACLs into sets of configurations that administrators use to control access to their respective systems. The level of detail may differ from system to system, but in general ACLs allow a configuration to restrict access from anyone and anywhere. Restrictions can be set for a particular user, computer, time, duration—even a particular file. This specificity provides powerful control to the administrator. In general ACLs regulate the who, what, when, and where of access:

- *Who* can use the system
- *What* authorized users can access
- *When* authorized users can access the system
- *Where* authorized users can access the system from

The *who* of ACL access may be determined by an individual person's identity or that person's membership in a group of people with the same access privileges. Determining *what* users are permitted to access can include restrictions on the various attributes of the system resources, such as the type of resource (printers, files, communication devices, or applications), name of the resource, or the location of the resource. Access is controlled by adjusting the resource privileges for the person or group to one of Read, Write, Create, Modify, Delete, Compare, or Copy for the specific resource. To control *when* access is allowed, some organizations choose to implement time-of-day and/or day-of-week restrictions for some network or system resources. For the control of *where* resources can be accessed from, many network-connected assets have restrictions placed on them to block remote usage and also have some levels of access that are restricted to locally connected users. When these various ACL options are applied cumulatively, the organization has the ability to describe fully how its resources can be used.

In some systems, these lists of ACL rules are known as *capability tables, user profiles,* or *user policies*. They specify what the user can and cannot do on the resources within that system. Figures 5-3 and 5-4 show how the ACL security model has been implemented by Novell and Microsoft operating systems.

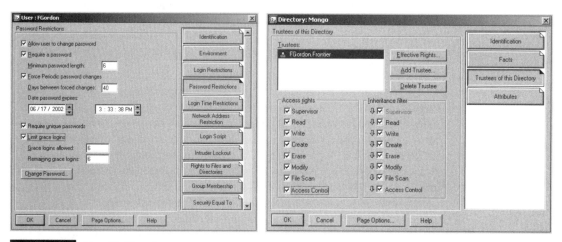

FIGURE 5-3   Novell's Use of ACLs

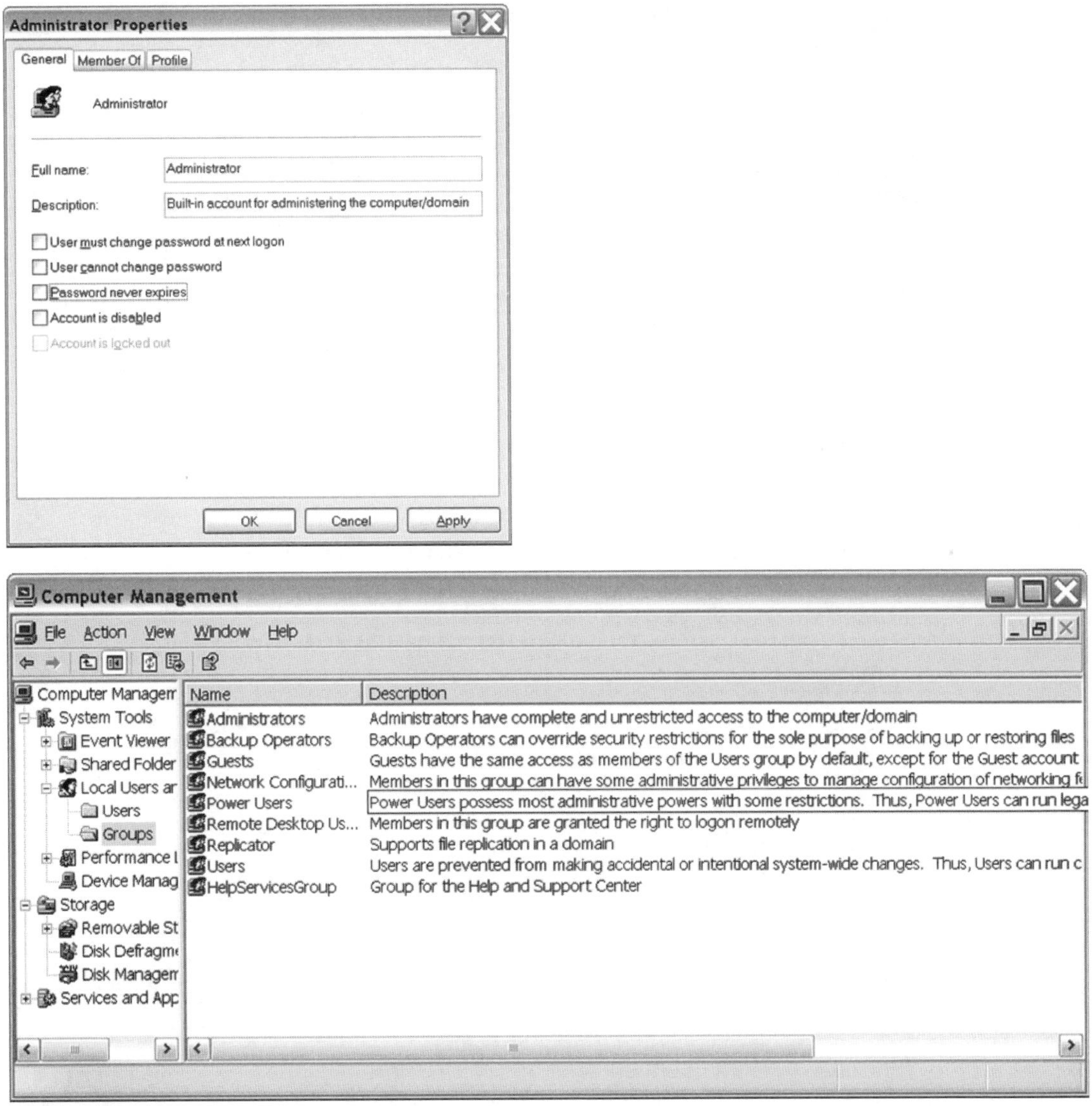

FIGURE 5-4 Microsoft Windows XP Use of ACLs

Rule Policies

Rule policies are more specific to the operation of a system than ACLs and may or may not deal with users directly. Many security systems require specific configuration scripts that tell the systems what actions to perform on each set of information they process. Examples of these systems include firewalls, intrusion detection systems, and proxy servers. The examples in Figures 5-5 and 5-6 show how network security policy has been implemented by Check Point in a firewall rule set and by Tripwire in an IDS rule set.

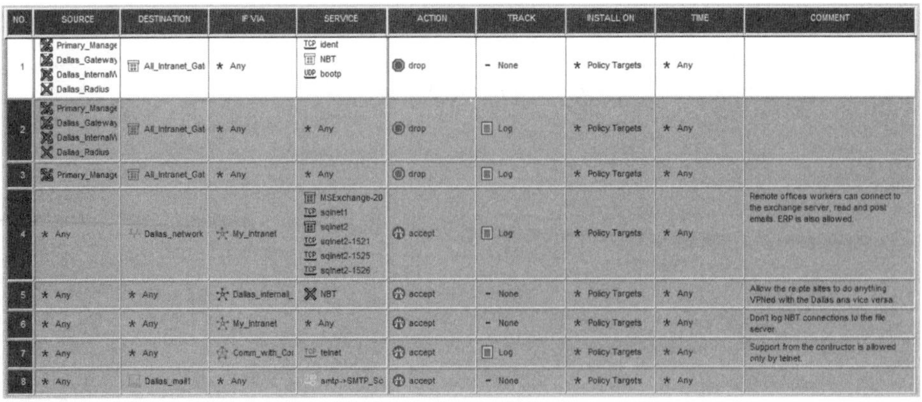

NO.	SOURCE	DESTINATION	IF VIA	SERVICE	ACTION	TRACK	INSTALL ON	TIME	COMMENT
1	Primary_Manage Dallas_Gateway Dallas_InternalV Dallas_Radius	All_Intranet_Gat	* Any	TCP ident NBT UDP bootp	drop	- None	* Policy Targets	* Any	
2	Primary_Manage Dallas_Gateway Dallas_InternalV Dallas_Radius	All_Intranet_Gat	* Any	* Any	drop	Log	* Policy Targets	* Any	
3	Primary_Manage	All_Intranet_Gat	* Any	* Any	drop	Log	* Policy Targets	* Any	
4	* Any	Dallas_network	My_Intranet	MSExchange-20 TCP sqlnet1 sqlnet2 TCP sqlnet2-1521 TCP sqlnet2-1525 TCP sqlnet2-1526	accept	Log	* Policy Targets	* Any	Remote offices workers can connect to the exchange server, read and post emails. ERP is also allowed.
5	* Any	* Any	Dallas_internal_	NBT	accept	- None	* Policy Targets	* Any	Allow the re.pte sites to do anything VPNed with the Dallas ans vice versa
6	* Any	* Any	My_Intranet	* Any	accept	- None	* Policy Targets	* Any	Don't log NBT connections to the file server
7	* Any	* Any	Comm_with_Co	TCP telnet	accept	Log	* Policy Targets	* Any	Support from the contructor is allowed only by telnet.
8	* Any	Dallas_mail1	* Any	smtp->SMTP_Sc	accept	- None	* Policy Targets	* Any	

VPN-1/Firewall-1 Policy Editor courtesy of Check Point Software Technologies Ltd.

FIGURE 5-5 Check Point VPN-1/Firewall-1 Policy Editor

```
###################################################################
# This Policy was created by the Tripwire Policy Resource Center  #
# Created on: Mon Mar 25 21:54:27 GMT 2002                        #
# Copyright (C) 2001, Tripwire Inc. Reprinted with permission     #
###################################################################
@@section global
SYSTEMDRIVE="C:" ;
BOOTDRIVE="C:" ;
SYSTEMROOT="C:\\Winnt" ;
PROGRAMFILES="C:\\Program Files" '
IE5="C:\\Program Files\\Plus!\\Microsoft Internet" ;
# Email Recipients # #
SIG_HIGHEST_MAILRECIPIENTS  = "Administrator" ;
SIG_HIGH_MAILRECIPIENTS     = "Administrator" ;
SIG_MED_MAILRECIPIENTS      = "Administrator" ;
SIG_LOW_MAILRECIPIENTS      = "Administrator" ;
# Security Levels # #
SIG_LOW       = 33 ;     # Non-critical files that are of minimal security impact
SIG_MED       = 66 ;     # Non-critical files that are of segnificant security impact
SIG_HIGH      = 100;     # Critical files that are significant points of vulnerability
SIG_HIGHEST   = 1000;    # Super-critical files. Mostly used for the TCB section.
@@section NTFS
{
 rulename = "IE 5.01 Registry keys",
 severity = $ (SIG_HIGHEST),
 emailto  = $ (SIG_HIGHEST_MAILRECIPIENTS),
 recurse  = true
}
{
 $ (HKLM_CCS_SM_CBadApps)                              -> $ (REG_SEC_HIGHEST) ;
 $ (HKLM_CRYPT)                                        -> $ (REG_SEC_HIGHEST) ;
 $ (HKLM_CRYPTINIT)                                    -> $ (REG_SEC_HIGHEST) ;
 $ (HKLMCRYPTMSG)                                      -> $ (REG_SEC_HIGHEST) ;
 $ (HKLM_CRYPTSIGN)                                    -> $ (REG_SEC_HIGHEST) ;
 $ (HKLM_EventSystem)                                  -> $ (REG_SEC_HIGHEST) ;
 $ (HKLM_SW_IE_Setup)                                  -> $ (REG_SEC_HIGHEST) ;
 $ (HKLM_WHM)                                          -> $ (REG_SEC_HIGHEST) ;
 $ (HKLM_WIE)                                          -> $ (REG_SEC_HIGHEST) ;
 $ (HKLM_WIE_INF_Setup)                                -> $ (REG_SEC_HIGHEST) ;
 $ (HKLM_WMM)                                          -> $ (REG_SEC_HIGHEST) ;
}
```

FIGURE 5-6 Tripwire Use of Rules

```
#        Snippet Name: A Nimda Virus Rule                      # #
#        Snippet Author: support@tripwire.com                  # #
#      Snippet Version: 1.0.0     # #
#              Nimda#     # #
@@section NTFS
{
rulename = "Nimda File Scan",
Severity = 100
}
{
$ (SYSTEMROOT)\ZaCker.vbs -> $ (IgnoreNone);
$ (SYSTEMROOT)\MixDaLaL.vbs -> $ (IgnoreNone);
$ (SYSTEMDIR)\ZaCker.vbs -> $ (IgnoreNone);
$ (SYSTEMDIR)\MixDaLaLa.vbs -> $ (IgnoreNone);
}
```

Courtesy of Tripwire®, Inc.

FIGURE 5-6 Tripwire Use of Rules (continued)

Policy Management

Policies are living documents that must be managed and nurtured, as they constantly change and grow. It is unacceptable to create such an important set of documents and then shelve them. These documents must be properly disseminated (distributed, read, understood, and agreed to) and managed. How they are managed relates directly to the policy management section of the issue-specific policy indicated earlier. Good management practices for policy development and maintenance make for a more resilient organization. For example, all policies, including security policies, undergo tremendous stress when corporate mergers and divestitures occur. These situations induce high rates of change and create situations in which employees are faced with uncertainty and many distractions. These types of changes may also result in system vulnerabilities being exposed if, for instance, inconsistent security policies are being implemented in different parts of the new, merged organization. When two companies merge but retain separate policies, the difficulty of implementing security controls that minimize risks increases. Likewise, when one company with unified policies splits in two, each new company may require different policies.

To remain viable, security policies must have an individual responsible for reviews, a schedule of reviews, a method for making recommendations for reviews, and a specific policy issuance and revision date. Each of these is examined in additional detail below.

Responsible Individual

Just as information systems and information security projects must have a champion and manager, so must policies. The policy champion and manager is called the **policy administrator**. Typically the policy administrator is a mid-level staff member and is responsible for the creation, revision, distribution, and storage of the policy. Note that the policy administrator does not necessarily have to be a technically oriented person. While much of the background for practicing information security professionals requires extensive technical knowledge, the particular area of policy management and policy administration requires only a moderate level of technical background. It is good practice, however, for these individuals to actively solicit input both from the technically adept information security experts and from the business-focused managers in each community of interest when making revisions to security policies. This individual should also notify all affected members of the organization when the policy is modified.

It is disheartening when a policy that required hundreds of staff-hours to develop and document is ignored. Thus, someone must be responsible for making sure that the policy and all subsequent revisions are placed into the hands of those individuals who are held accountable for its implementation. The policy administrator must be clearly identified on the policy document as the primary point of contact for additional information or for revision suggestions to the policy.

Schedule of Reviews

Policies can only retain their effectiveness in a changing environment if they are periodically reviewed for currency and accuracy and modified to reflect these changes. Policies that are not kept current can become liabilities for the organization, as outdated rules are enforced (or not), and new requirements are ignored. In order for the organization to demonstrate due diligence, it must demonstrate that it is actively trying to meet the requirements of the market in which it operates. This applies equally to both public (government, academic, and nonprofit) and private (commercial and for-profit) organizations. A properly organized schedule of reviews should be defined and published as part of the document. Typically a policy should be reviewed at least annually to ensure that it is still an effective control.

Review Procedures and Practices

To facilitate policy reviews, the policy manager should implement a mechanism by which individuals can comfortably make recommendations for revisions. Recommendation methods can involve e-mail, office mail, and an anonymous drop box. If the policy is controversial, the policy administrator may feel that anonymous submission of information is the best way to determine staff opinions. Many employees feel intimidated by management and hesitate to voice honest opinions about a policy unless they can do so anonymously. Once the policy has come up for review, all comments should be examined and management-approved improvements should be implemented. Additional review methods can involve including representative users in the revision process and allowing direct comment on the revision of the policy. In reality, most policies are drafted by a single, responsible individual and are then reviewed by a higher-level manager. But even this method should not preclude the collection and review of employee input.

Policy and Revision Date

The simple action of dating the policy is often skipped over. When policies are drafted and published without a date, confusion can arise when users of the policy are unaware of the policy's age or status. If policies are not reviewed and kept current, or if members of the organization are following undated versions, disastrous results and legal headaches can ensue. These problems are particularly common in a high-turnover environment. It is, therefore, important that the policy contain the date of origin, along with the date(s) of any revisions. Some policies may also need a **sunset clause** indicating their expiration date. This can be particularly important for policies governing information use in short-term business associations or agencies that are involved with the organization. Establishing a policy end date prevents a temporary policy from mistakenly becoming permanent, and it also enables an organization to gain experience with a given policy before adopting it permanently—and thus perhaps avoid making a mistake.

Automated Policy Management

A final topic for this section is the emergence, in recent years, of a new category of software for managing information security policies. This type of software was developed in response to needs articulated by information security practitioners. While there have been many software products that meet the need for a specific technical control, there is now software to meet the need for automating some of the busywork of policy management. Automation can streamline the repetitive steps of writing policy, tracking the workflow of policy approvals, publishing policy once it is written and approved, and tracking when individuals have read the policy. Using techniques from computer-based training and testing, organizations can train staff members and also improve the organization's awareness program. To quote the marketing literature from NetIQ Corporation:

> SOFTWARE THAT PUTS YOU IN CONTROL OF SECURITY POLICY CREATION, DISTRIBUTION, EDUCATION, AND TRACKING FOR COMPLIANCE.
>
> VigilEnt Policy Center now makes it possible to manage security policy dynamically so that you can create, distribute, educate, and track understanding of your information security policies for all employees in your organization. It enables you to keep policies up-to-date, change them quickly as needed, and ensure that they are being understood properly, all through a new automated, interactive, Web-based software application.[7]

Information Classification

The classification of information, as you learned earlier in this book, is an important facet of policy and is also a control for the protection of information in general. In other words, policies are classified. The same protection scheme created to prevent production data from accidental release to the wrong party should be applied to policies, in order to keep them freely available, but only within the organization. Many company policies are at least classified as "for internal use only." As such, they should not be left where they could be inadvertently thrown away, picked up, or observed by unauthorized individuals outside the organization. With the increase in incidences of shoulder surfing and dumpster diving, organizations should pay increased attention to securing access to sensitive policy materials. Suppose, for example, that an intruder surmised from an unsecured copy of the policy document that tape backups are made at midnight and then carried off-site to an administrator's home. This individual could then obtain valuable data without even setting foot in the organization or accessing the organization's systems directly.

Related to document classification and the requirement to protect policies is the clean desk policy. Consider the following scenario. In an organization that has properly implemented a data classification scheme, an average administrator may deal with a number of different types of information throughout a busy day. If, at the end of a given day, the administrator were to leave this information unsecured, this could create an opportunity for the accidental or intentional disclosure of the information to individuals still in the building. In today's open office environments, most employees work from cubicles and do not have a door to secure their workspaces, so it may be beneficial to implement a clean desk policy. A **clean desk policy** stipulates that at the end of the business day, all classified information must be properly stored and secured. Secure storage could include file cabinets, desk drawers, or other controlled access areas. As is evident from the photograph of the desk of one of the authors (Figure 5-7), this type of policy is generally not a requirement in academia.

FIGURE 5-7 Clean Desk Policy Violation?

Once an organization has developed its information security policies and standards, it is time for the information security community to begin developing the blueprint for the information security program. It should be noted that if one or more components of policies, standards, or practices are missing before or during the development of the blueprint, management must determine if such an omission is acceptable to the organization.

The Information Security Blueprint

After the information security team has inventoried the organization's information assets and assessed and prioritized the threats to those assets, it will conduct a series of risk assessments using quantitative or qualitative analyses, as well as feasibility studies and cost benefit analyses. These assessments, which include determining each asset's current protection level, will be used to decide whether or not to proceed with any given control. Armed with a general idea of the vulnerabilities in the information technology systems of the organization, the security team develops a design blueprint for security, which is used to implement the security program.

This **security blueprint** is the basis for the design, selection, and implementation of all security policies, education and training programs, and technological controls. The security blueprint is a more detailed version of the **security framework,** which is an outline of the overall information security strategy for the organization and a roadmap for planned changes to the information security environment of the organization. The blueprint should specify the tasks to be accomplished and the order in which they are to be realized and serve as a scalable, upgradeable, and comprehensive plan for the information security needs for coming years.

One approach to selecting a methodology by which to develop an information security blueprint is to adapt or adopt a published model or framework for information security. This framework can be an outline of steps involved in designing and later implementing information security in the organization. There are a number of published information security frameworks, including those from government sources presented later in this chapter. Because each information security environment is unique, the security team may need to modify or adapt pieces from several frameworks. Experience teaches you that what works well for one organization may not precisely fit another. Therefore, each implementation may need modification or even redesign before it suits the needs of a particular asset-threat problem.

ISO 17799/BS7799

One of the most widely referenced and often discussed security models is the *Information Technology – Code of Practice for Information Security Management*, which was originally published as the British Standard BS7799. In 2000, this Code of Practice was adopted as an international standard framework for information security by the International Organization for Standardization (ISO) and the International Electrotechnical Commission (IEC) as ISO/IEC 17799. While the details of ISO/IEC 17799 are available only through purchase of the standard, its structure and general organization are well known. For a summary description, see Figure 5-8. For more details on ISO/IEC Sections, see *http://www.iso17799software.com/what.htm*.

Content Outline
1. Organizational Security Policy
2. Organizational Security Infrastructure
3. Asset Classification and Control
4. Personnel Security
5. Physical and Environmental Security
6. Communications and Operations Management
7. System Access Control
8. System Development and Maintenance
9. Business Continuity Planning
10. Compliance

FIGURE 5-8 Ten Sections of ISO/IEC 17799[8]

The stated purpose of ISO/IEC 17799 is to "give recommendations for information security management for use by those who are responsible for initiating, implementing, or maintaining security in their organization. It is intended to provide a common basis for developing organizational security standards and effective security management practice and to provide confidence in inter-organizational dealings."[9] This International Standard is actually drawn from only the first volume of the two-volume British Standard 7799. Volume 2 of BS7799 picks up where ISO/IEC 17799 leaves off. Where Volume 1 of BS7799 and ISO/IEC 17799 are focused on a broad overview of the various areas of security, providing information on 127 controls over ten broad areas, Volume 2 of BS7799 provides information on how to implement Volume 1 and ISO/IEC 17799 and how to set up an information security management system (ISMS). The overall methodology for this process and its major steps are presented in Figure 5-9.

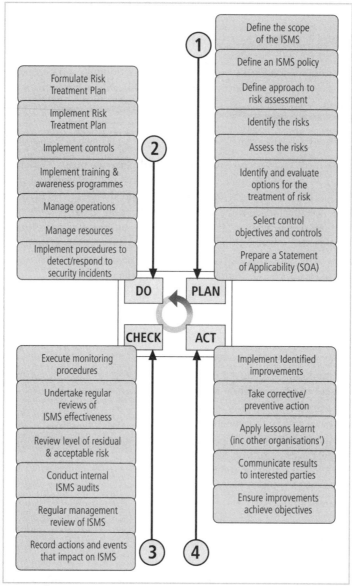

Courtesy of Gamma Secure Systems

FIGURE 5-9 BS7799:2 Major Process Steps[10]

In the United Kingdom, correct implementation of these standards (both volumes), as determined by a BS7799 certified evaluator, is used to obtain system (ISMS) certification and accreditation. Several countries including the United States, Germany, and Japan have not adopted 17799. They claim that there are several fundamental problems, which include:

- The global information security community has not defined any justification for a code of practice as identified in the ISO/IEC 17799.

- ISO/IEC 17799 lacks "the necessary measurement precision of a technical standard." [11]
- There is no reason to believe that ISO/IEC 17799 is more useful than any other approach.
- ISO/IEC 17799 is not as complete as other frameworks.
- ISO/IEC 17799 is perceived to have been hurriedly prepared given the tremendous impact its adoption could have on industry information security controls.[12]

ISO/IEC 17799 is an interesting framework for information security, but aside from those relatively few U.S. organizations that operate in the European Union (or are otherwise obliged to meet its terms), most U.S. organizations are not expected to comply with this standard.

NIST Security Models

Another possible approach is described in the many documents available from the Computer Security Resource Center of the National Institute for Standards and Technology (*csrc.nist.gov*). Because the NIST documents are publicly available at no charge and have been available for some time, they have been broadly reviewed by government and industry professionals, and are among the references cited by the federal government when it decided not to select the ISO/IEC 17799 standards. The following NIST documents can assist in the design of a security framework:

- SP 800-12: *An Introduction to Computer Security: The NIST Handbook*
- SP 800-14: *Generally Accepted Security Principles and Practices for Securing Information Technology Systems*
- SP 800-18: *The Guide for Developing Security Plans for Information Technology Systems*
- SP 800-26: *Security Self-Assessment Guide for Information Technology Systems*
- SP 800-30: *Risk Management for Information Technology Systems*

Many of these documents have been referenced in earlier chapters as sources of information for the management of security. The following sections examine these documents in more detail as they apply to the blueprint for information security.

NIST Special Publication SP 800-12

SP 800-12, *An Introduction to Computer Security: The NIST Handbook*, is an excellent reference and guide for the security manager or administrator in the routine management of information security. It provides little guidance, however, on design and implementation of new security systems, and therefore should be used only as a valuable precursor to understanding an information security blueprint.

NIST Special Publication 800-14

Generally Accepted Principles and Practices for Securing Information Technology Systems provides best practices and security principles that can direct the security team in the development of a security blueprint. In addition to detailing security best practices across the spectrum of security areas, it provides philosophical principles that the security team should integrate into the entire information security process. Figure 5-10 presents the table of contents of the NIST SP 800-14. The document can guide the development of the security framework and should be combined with other NIST publications providing the necessary structure to the entire security process.

NIST SP 800-14 Generally Accepted Principles and Practices
for Securing Information Technology Systems
Table of Contents

2. Generally Accepted System Security Principles
   2.1 Computer Security Supports the Mission of the Organization
   2.2 Computer Security is an Integral Element of Sound Management
   2.3 Computer Security Should Be Cost-Effective
   2.4 Systems Owners Have Security Responsibilities Outside Their Own Organizations
   2.5 Computer Security Responsibilities and Accountability Should Be Made Explicit
   2.6 Computer Security Requires a Comprehensive and Integrated Approach
   2.7 Computer Security Should Be Periodically Reassessed
   2.8 Computer Security is Constrained by Societal Factors
3. Common IT Security Practices
   3.1 Policy
       3.1.1 Program Policy
       3.1.2 Issue-Specific Policy
       3.1.3 System-Specific Policy
       3.1.4 All Policies
   3.2 Program Management
       3.2.1 Central Security Program
       3.2.2 System-Level Program
   3.3 Risk Management
       3.3.1 Risk Assessment
       3.3.2 Risk Mitigation
       3.3.3 Uncertainty Analysis
   3.4 Life Cycle Planning
       3.4.1 Security Plan
       3.4.2 Initiation Phase
       3.4.3 Development/Acquisition Phase
       3.4.4 Implementation Phase
       3.4.5 Operation/Maintenance Phase
       3.4.6 Disposal Phase
   3.5 Personnel/User Issues
       3.5.1 Staffing
       3.5.2 User Administration
   3.6 Preparing for Contingencies and Disasters
       3.6.1 Business Plan
       3.6.2 Identify Resources
       3.6.3 Develop Scenarios
       3.6.4 Develop Strategies
       3.6.5 Test and Revise Plan
   3.7 Computer Security Incident Handling
       3.7.1 Uses of a Capability
       3.7.2 Characteristics
   3.8 Awareness and Training
   3.9 Security Considerations in Computer Support and Operations
   3.10 Physical and Environmental Security
   3.11 Identification and Authentication
       3.11.1 Identification
       3.11.2 Authentication
       3.11.3 Passwords
       3.11.4 Advanced Authentication
   3.12 Logical Access Control
       3.12.1 Access Criteria
       3.12.2 Access Control Mechanisms
   3.13 Audit Trails
       3.13.1 Contents of Audit Trail Records
       3.13.2 Audit Trail Security
       3.13.3 Audit Trail Reviews
       3.13.4 Keystroke Monitoring
   3.14 Cryptography

FIGURE 5-10 NIST SP 800-14 Table of Contents[13]

The scope of NIST SP 800-14 is broad. It is important to consider each of the security principles it presents, and therefore the following sections examine some of the more significant points in more detail:

2.1 Security Supports the Mission of the Organization: Failure to develop an information security system based on the organization's mission, vision, and culture guarantees the failure of the information security program.

2.2 Security Is an Integral Element of Sound Management: Effective management includes planning, organizing, leading, and controlling. Security enhances these areas by supporting the planning function when information security policies provide input into the organization initiatives. Information security specifically supports the controlling function, as security controls support sound management by means of the enforcement of both managerial and security policies.

2.3 Security Should Be Cost-Effective: The costs of information security should be considered part of the cost of doing business, much like the cost of the computers, networks, and voice communications systems. These are not profit-generating areas of the organization and may not lead to competitive advantages. Information security should justify its own costs. Security measures that do not justify cost benefit levels must have a strong business case (such as a legal requirement) to warrant their use.

2.4 Systems Owners Have Security Responsibilities Outside Their Own Organizations: Whenever systems store and use information from customers, patients, clients, partners, and others, the security of this information becomes a serious responsibility for the owner of the systems.

2.5 Security Responsibilities and Accountability Should Be Made Explicit: Policy documents should clearly identify the security responsibilities of users, administrators, and managers. To be legally binding, this information must be documented, disseminated, read, understood, and agreed to. As noted in Chapter 3, ignorance of the law is no excuse, but ignorance of policy is. Regarding the law, the organization should also detail the relevance of laws to issue-specific security policies. These details should be distributed to users, administrators, and managers to assist them in complying with their responsibilities.

2.6 Security Requires a Comprehensive and Integrated Approach: Security personnel alone cannot effectively implement security. As emphasized throughout this textbook, *security is everyone's responsibility*. The three communities of interest (information technology management and professionals, information security management and professionals, as well as the users, managers, administrators, and other stakeholders of the broader organization) should participate in the process of developing a comprehensive information security program.

2.7 Security Should Be Periodically Reassessed: Information security that is implemented and then ignored is considered negligent, the organization having not demonstrated due diligence. Security is an ongoing process. It cannot be implemented and then expected to function independently without constant maintenance and change. To be effective against a constantly shifting set of threats and constantly changing user base, the security process must be periodically repeated. Continuous analyses of threats, assets, and controls must be conducted and new blueprints developed. Only thorough preparation, design, implementation, eternal vigilance, and ongoing maintenance can secure the organization's information assets.

2.8 Security Is Constrained by Societal Factors: There are a number of factors that influence the implementation and maintenance of security. Legal demands, shareholder requirements, even business practices affect the implementation of security controls and safeguards. For example, security professionals generally prefer to isolate information assets from the Internet, which is the leading avenue of threats to the assets, but the business requirements of the organization may preclude this control measure.

Figure 5-11 presents the "Principles for Securing Information Technology Systems," which is part of NIST SP 800-14. You can use this document to make sure the key elements needed for a successful effort are factored into the design of an information security program and to produce a blueprint for an effective security architecture.

Principles for Securing Information Technology Systems
NIST SP 800-14 Generally Accepted Principles and Practices
for Securing Information Technology Systems

Principle 1.   Establish a sound security policy as the foundation for design.
Principle 2.   Treat security as an integral part of the overall system design.
Principle 3.   Clearly delineate the physical and logical security boundaries governed by associated security policies.
Principle 4.   Reduce risk to an acceptable level.
Principle 5.   Assume that external systems are insecure.
Principle 6.   Identify potential trade-offs between reducing risk and increased costs and decrease in other aspects of operational effectiveness.
Principle 7.   Implement layered security (ensure no single point of vulnerability).
Principle 8.   Implement tailored system security measures to meet organizational security goals.
Principle 9.   Strive for simplicity.
Principle 10. Design and operate an IT system to limit vulnerability and to be resilient in response.
Principle 11. Minimize the system elements to be trusted.
Principle 12. Implement security through a combination of measures distributed physically and logically.
Principle 13. Provide assurance that the system is, and continues to be, resilient in the face of expected threats.
Principle 14. Limit or contain vulnerabilities.
Principle 15. Formulate security measures to address multiple overlapping information domains.
Principle 16. Isolate public access systems from mission critical resources (e.g., data, processes, etc.).
Principle 17. Use boundary mechanisms to separate computing systems and network infrastructures.
Principle 18. Where possible, base security on open standards for portability and interoperability.
Principle 19. Use common language in developing security requirements.
Principle 20. Design and implement audit mechanisms to detect unauthorized use and to support incident investigations.
Principle 21. Design security to allow for regular adoption of new technology, including a secure and logical technology upgrade process.
Principle 22. Authenticate users and processes to ensure appropriate access control decisions both within and across domains.
Principle 23. Use unique identities to ensure accountability.
Principle 24. Implement least privilege.
Principle 25. Do not implement unnecessary security mechanisms.
Principle 26. Protect information while being processed, in transit, and in storage.
Principle 27. Strive for operational ease of use.
Principle 28. Develop and exercise contingency or disaster recovery procedures to ensure appropriate availability.
Principle 29. Consider custom products to achieve adequate security.
Principle 30. Ensure proper security in the shutdown or disposal of a system.
Principle 31. Protect against all likely classes of "attacks."
Principle 32. Identify and prevent common errors and vulnerabilities.
Principle 33. Ensure that developers are trained in how to develop secure software.

FIGURE 5-11   Principles from NIST SP 800-14[14]

NIST Special Publication 800-18

The Guide for Developing Security Plans for Information Technology Systems can be used as the foundation for a comprehensive security blueprint and framework. This publication provides detailed methods for assessing, designing, and implementing controls and plans for applications of varying size. SP 800-18 can serve as a useful guide to the activities described in this chapter and as an aid in the planning process. It also includes templates for major application security plans. As with any publication of this scope and magnitude, SP 800-18 must be customized to fit the particular needs of an organization. The table of contents for Publication 800-18 is presented in Figure 5-12.

Guide for Developing Security Plans for Information Technology Systems
Table of Contents

2. System Analysis
  2.1 System Boundaries
  2.2 Multiple Similar Systems
  2.3 System Category
    2.3.1 Major Applications
    2.3.2 General Support System
3. Plan Development – All Systems
  3.1 Plan Control
  3.2 System Identification
    3.2.1 System Name/Title
    3.2.2 Responsible Organization
    3.2.3 Information Contact(s)
    3.2.4 Assignment of Security Responsibility
  3.3 System Operational Status
  3.4 General Description/Purpose
  3.5 System Environment
  3.6 System Interconnection/Information Sharing
  3.7 Sensitivity of Information Handled
    3.7.1 Laws, Regulations, and Policies Affecting the System
    3.7.2 General Description of Sensitivity
4. Management Controls
  4.1 Risk Assessment and Management
  4.2 Review of Security Controls
  4.3 Rules of Behavior
  4.4 Planning for Security in the Life Cycle
    4.4.1 Initiation Phase
    4.4.2 Development/Acquisition Phase
    4.4.3 Implementation Phase
    4.4.4 Operation/Maintenance Phase
    4.4.5 Disposal Phase
  4.5 Authorize Processing
5. Operational Controls
  5.MA. Major Application – Operational Controls
  5.MA.1 Personnel Security
  5.MA.2 Physical and Environmental Protection
    5.MA.2.1 Explanation of Physical and Environment Security
    5.MA.2.2 Computer Room Example
  5.MA.3 Production, Input/Output Controls
  5.MA.4 Contingency Planning
  5.MA.5 Application Software Maintenance Controls
  5.MA.6 Data Integrity/Validation Controls
  5.MA.7 Documentation
  5.MA.8 Security Awareness and Training
6.MA Major Application - Technical Controls
  6.MA.1 Identification and Authentication
    6.MA.1.1 Identification
    6.MA.1.2 Authentication
  6.MA.2 Logical Access Controls (Authorization/Access Controls)
  6.MA.3 Public Access Controls
  6.MA.4 Audit Trails
5.GSS General Support System – Operational Controls
  5.GSS.1 Personnel Controls
  5.GSS.2 Physical and Environmental Protection
    5.GSS.2.1 Explanation of Physical and Environment Security
    5.GSS.2.2 Computer Room Example
  5.GSS.3 Production, Input/Output Controls
  5.GSS.4 Contingency Planning (Continuity of Support)
  5.GSS.5 Hardware and System Software Maintenance Controls
  5.GSS.6 Integrity Controls
  5.GSS.7 Documentation
  5.GSS.8 Security Awareness and Training
  5.GSS.9 Incident Response Capability
6.GSS General Support System - Technical Controls
  6.GSS.1 Identification and Authentication
    6.GSS.1.1 Identification
    6.GSS.1.2 Authentication
  6.GSS.2 Logical Access Controls (Authorization/Access Controls)
  6.GSS.3 Audit Trails

FIGURE 5-12 NIST SP 800-18[15]

IETF Security Architecture

The Security Area Working Group acts as an advisory board for the protocols and areas developed and promoted by the Internet Society and the Internet Engineering Task Force (IETF), and while the group endorses no specific information security architecture, one of its requests for comment (RFC), RFC 2196: *Site Security Handbook*, provides a good functional discussion of important security issues. RFC 2196: *Site Security Handbook* covers five basic areas of security with detailed discussions on development and implementation. There are also chapters on such important topics as security policies, security technical architecture, security services, and security incident handling.

The chapter on architecture begins with a discussion of the importance of security policies, and expands into an examination of services, access controls, and other relevant areas. The table of contents for the RFC 2196: *Site Security Handbook* is represented in the Figure 5-13.

RFC 2196: Site Security Handbook
Table of Contents

1. Introduction
   1.1   Purpose of this Work
   1.2   Audience
   1.3   Definitions
   1.4   Related Work
   1.5   Basic Approach
   1.6   Risk Assessment
2. Security Policies
   2.1   What is a Security Policy and Why Have One?
   2.2   What Makes a Good Security Policy?
   2.3   Keeping the Policy Flexible
3. Architecture
   3.1   Objectives
   3.2   Network and Service Configuration
   3.3   Firewalls
4. Security Services and Procedures
   4.1   Authentication
   4.2   Confidentiality
   4.3   Integrity
   4.4   Authorization
   4.5   Access
   4.6   Auditing
   4.7   Securing Backups
5. Security Incident Handling
   5.1   Preparing and Planning for Incident Handling
   5.2   Notification and Points of Contact
   5.3   Identifying an Incident
   5.4   Handling an Incident
   5.5   Aftermath of an Incident
   5.6   Responsibilities
6. Ongoing Activities
7. Tools and Locations
8. Mailing Lists and Other Resources
9. References

FIGURE 5-13   RFC 2196: Table of Contents[16]

VISA International Security Model

VISA International promotes strong security measures in its business associates and has established guidelines for the security of its information systems. VISA has developed two important documents that improve and regulate its information systems: "Security Assessment Process" and "Agreed Upon Procedures." Both documents provide specific instructions on the use of the VISA Cardholder Information Security Program.[17] The "Security Assessment Process" document is a series of recommendations for the detailed examination of an organization's systems with the eventual goal of integration into the VISA systems. The "Agreed Upon Procedures" document outlines the policies and technologies required for security systems that carry the sensitive cardholder information to and from VISA systems. Using the two documents, a security team can develop a sound strategy for the design of good security architecture. The only downside to this approach is the specific focus on systems that can or do integrate with VISA's systems with the explicit purpose of carrying the aforementioned cardholder information.

Baselining and Best Business Practices

As you learned in Chapter 4, baselining and best practices are solid methods for collecting security practices. Baselining and best practices don't provide a complete methodology for the design and implementation of all the practices needed by an organization; however, it is possible to piece together the desired outcome of the security process, and therefore to work backwards toward an effective design. The Federal Agency Security Practices (FASP) site, *fasp.nist.gov*, is a popular place to look up best practices. FASP is designed to provide best practices for public agencies, but these practices can be adapted easily to private institutions. The documents found in this site include specific examples of key policies and planning documents, implementation strategies for key technologies, and position descriptions for key security personnel. Of particular value is the section on program management, which includes the following:

- A summary guide: public law, executive orders, and policy documents
- Position description for computer system security officer
- Position description for information security officer
- Position description for computer specialist
- Sample of an information technology (IT) security staffing plan for a large service application (LSA)
- Sample of information technology (IT) security program policy
- Security handbook and standard operating procedures
- Telecommuting and mobile computer security policy

In the later stages of creating an information security blueprint, these policy documents are particularly useful.

A number of other public and semipublic institutions provide information on best practices—one of these groups is the Internet Security Task Force (*www.ca.com/ISTF*). This task force is a collection of parties, both public and private, with a shared interest in the security of the Internet. The parties provide recommendations for security implementations. Another widely referenced source is the Computer Emergency Response Team (CERT) at Carnegie Mellon University (*www.cert.org*). Although detailed and specific, CERT promotes a series of security modules with links to practices and implementation that represents a security methodology.

Professional societies often provide information on best practices for their members. The Technology Manager's Forum (*www.techforum.com*) has an annual best practice award in a number of areas, including information security. The Information Security Forum (*www.isfsecuritystandard.com*) has a free publication titled "Standard of Good Practice." This publication outlines information security best practices.

Many organizations hold seminars and classes on best practices for implementing security. For example, the Information Systems Audit and Control Association (*www.isaca.com*) hosts seminars on a routine basis. Similarly, the International Association of Professional Security Consultants (*www.iapsc.org*) has a listing of best practices, as does the Global Grid Forum (*www.gridforum.org*). At minimum, information security professionals can peruse Web portals for posted security best practices. There are several free portals dedicated to security that have collections of best practices, such as SearchSecurity.com, and NIST's Computer Resources Center. These are but a few of the many public and private organizations that promote solid best security practices. Investing a few hours searching the Web reveals dozens of locations for additional information.

Finding information on security design is the easy part. Sorting through the collected mass of information, documents, and publications can take a substantial investment in time and human resources. In the end, each organization needs a clear methodology for the creation of the framework leading to a blueprint for the development of a security system. The hybrid framework outlined in the following section fulfills that need.

Hybrid Framework for a Blueprint of an Information Security System

This section presents a hybrid framework, or a general outline of a methodology that organizations can use to create a security system blueprint as they fill in the implementation details to address the components of a solid information security plan.

Each of the topics in the Self-Assessment Guide shown in Figure 5-14 emerged from SP 800-26. The discussion that follows in this section has been filtered with the current knowledge and experience of information security professionals. This discussion of the framework of security also includes philosophical components of the Human Firewall Project,[18] which maintain that people, not technology, are the primary defenders of information assets in an information security program, and are uniquely responsible for their protection.

NIST SP 800-26 Security Self-Assessment Guide
for Information Technology Systems

Management Controls
1. Risk Management
2. Review of Security Controls
3. Life Cycle Maintenance
4. Authorization of Processing (Certification and Accreditation)
5. System Security Plan

Operational Controls
6. Personnel Security
7. Physical Security
8. Production, Input/Output Controls
9. Contingency Planning
10. Hardware and Systems Software
11. Data Integrity
12. Documentation
13. Security Awareness, Training, and Education
14. Incident Response Capability

Technical Controls
15. Identification and Authentication
16. Logical Access Controls
17. Audit Trails

FIGURE 5-14 NIST SP 800-26 Table of Contents[19]

The spheres of security, shown in Figure 5-15, are the foundation of the security framework. Generally speaking, the spheres of security illustrate how information is under attack from a variety of sources. The sphere of use, at the left in Figure 5-15, illustrates the ways in which people access information; for example, people read hard copies of documents and can also access information through systems. Information, as the most important asset in this model, is at the center of the sphere. Information is always at risk from attacks through the people and computer systems that have access to the information. Networks and the Internet represent indirect threats, as exemplified by the fact that a person attempting to access information from the Internet must first go through the local networks and then access systems that contain the information. The sphere of protection, at the right in Figure 5-15, illustrates that between each layer of the sphere of use there must exist a layer of protection to prevent access to the inner layer from the outer layer. Each shaded band is a layer of protection and control. For example, the items labeled "Policy & law" and "Education & training" are located between people and the information. Controls are also implemented between systems and the information, between networks and the computer systems, and between the Internet and internal networks. This reinforces the concept of defense in depth. As illustrated in the sphere of protection, a variety of controls can be used to protect the information. The items of control shown in the figure are not intended to be comprehensive but rather illustrate individual safeguards that can protect the various systems that are located closer to the center of the sphere. However, because people can directly access each ring as well as the information at the core of the model, the side of the sphere of protection that attempts to control access by relying on people requires a different approach to security than the side that uses technology. In fact, the people within the organization must become a layer of security, a **human firewall** that protects the information from unauthorized access and use. The members of the organization must become a safeguard, which is effectively trained, implemented, and maintained, or else they too will represent a threat to the information.

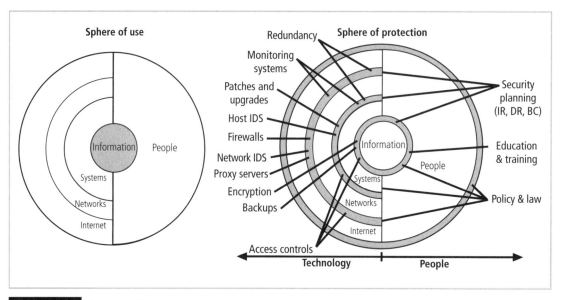

FIGURE 5-15 Spheres of Security

Information security is designed and implemented in three layers: policies, people (education, training, and awareness programs), and technology. While the design and implementation of the people layer and the technology layer overlap, both must follow the sound management policies discussed earlier in this chapter. Each of the layers constitutes controls and safeguards that are put into place to protect the information and information system assets that the organization values. The order of the controls within the layers follows the prioritization scheme developed in Chapter 4. But before any controls and safeguards are put into place, the policies defining the management philosophies that guide the security process must already be in place.

As shown in Figure 5-14, safeguards provide three levels of control: managerial, operational, and technical. Each of these is examined in detail below.

Managerial controls cover security processes that are designed by strategic planners and implemented by the security administration of the organization. The topics listed under management controls set the direction and scope of the security process and provide detailed instructions for its conduct. Management controls address the design and implementation of the security planning process and security program management. They also address risk management and security control reviews, discussed in Chapters 4.

Management controls further describe the necessity and scope of legal compliance and the maintenance of the entire security life cycle.

Operational controls deal with the operational functionality of security in the organization. They include management functions and lower-level planning, such as disaster recovery and incident response planning. Operational controls also address personnel security, physical security, and the protection of production inputs and outputs. In addition, operational controls guide the development of education, training, and awareness programs for users, administrators, and management. Finally, they address hardware and software systems maintenance and the integrity of data.

Technical controls address the tactical and technical issues related to designing and implementing security in the organization, as well as issues related to examining and selecting the technologies appropriate to protecting information. While operational controls address specific operational issues, such as developing and integrating controls into the business functions, technical controls address the specifics of technology selection and the acquisition (make or buy) of certain technical components. They also include logical access controls, such as identification, authentication, authorization, and accountability. Technical controls also address the development and implementation of audit trails for accountability. In addition, these controls cover cryptography to protect information in storage and transit. Finally, they include the classification of assets and users, to facilitate the authorization levels needed.

Using the three sets of controls just described, the organization should be able to specify controls to cover the entire spectrum of safeguards, from strategic to tactical, and from managerial to technical.

Design of Security Architecture

To inform the discussion of information security program architecture and to illustrate industry best practices, the following sections outline a few key security architectural components. Many of these components are examined in detail in later chapters that cover technical controls, but an overview is provided here because being able to assess whether a framework and/or blueprint are on target to meet an organization's needs requires a working knowledge of these security architecture components.

Defense in Depth

One of the basic tenets of security architectures is the implementation of security in layers. This layered approach is called **defense in depth**. Defense in depth requires that the organization establish sufficient security controls and safeguards so that an intruder faces multiple layers of control. These layers of control can be organized into policy, training and education, and technology, as per the NSTISSC model presented in Chapter 1. While policy itself may not prevent attacks, it certainly prepares the organization to handle them. Coupled with other layers, policy can deter attacks. Training and education are similar. Technology is also implemented in layers, with detection equipment working in tandem with reaction technology, all operating behind access control mechanisms. Implementing multiple types of technology and thereby preventing the failure of one system from compromising the security of the information is referred to as **redundancy**. Redundancy can be implemented at a number of points throughout the security architecture, such as firewalls, proxy servers, and access controls. Figure 5-16 illustrates the concept of building controls in multiple, sometimes redundant layers. The figure shows the use of firewalls and intrusion detection systems (IDS) that use both packet-level rules (shown as the header in the diagram) and data content analysis (shown as 0100101011 in the diagram). More information on firewalls and intrusion detection systems is presented in Chapters 6 and 7, respectively.

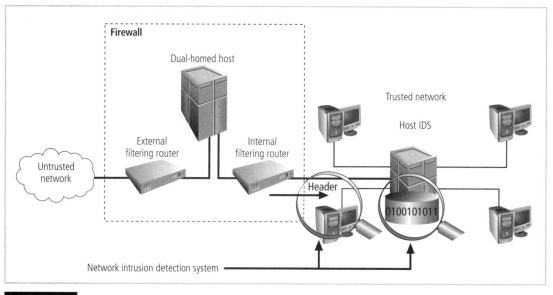

FIGURE 5-16 Defense in Depth

Security Perimeter

A perimeter is the boundary of an area. A **security perimeter** defines the edge between the outer limit of an organization's security and the beginning of the outside world. A security perimeter is the first level of security that protects all internal systems from outside threats, as pictured in Figure 5-17. Unfortunately, the perimeter does not protect against internal attacks from employee threats or on-site physical threats. There can be both an electronic security perimeter, usually at the organization's exterior network or Internet connection, and a physical security perimeter, usually at the gate to the organization's offices. Both require perimeter security. Security perimeters can effectively be implemented as multiple technologies that segregate the protected information from those who would attack it. Within security perimeters the organization can establish **security domains,** or areas of trust within which users can freely communicate. The assumption is that if individuals have access to one system within a security domain, they have authorized access to all systems within that particular domain. The presence and nature of the security perimeter is an essential element of the overall security framework, and the details of implementing the perimeter make up a great deal of the particulars of the completed security blueprint. The key components used for planning the perimeter are presented in the following sections on firewalls, DMZs, proxy servers, and intrusion detection systems. A more complete presentation on the technologies of information security are presented later in the book (in Chapters 6, 7, and 8).

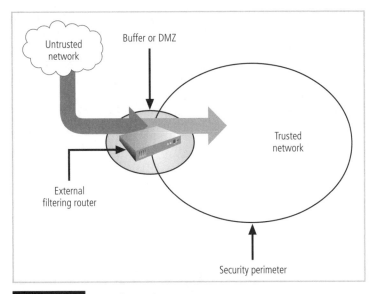

FIGURE 5-17 Security Perimeters

Key Technology Components

Some other key technology components in an information security architecture are firewalls, DMZs, proxy servers, and intrusion detection systems.

Firewalls. A **firewall** is a device that selectively discriminates against information flowing into or out of the organization. A firewall is usually a computing device, or a specially configured computer that allows or prevents information from entering or exiting the defined area based on a set of predefined rules. Firewalls are usually placed on the security perimeter, just behind or as part of a **gateway router**. While the gateway router is primarily designed to connect the organization's systems to the outside world, it too can be used as the front-line defense against attacks, as it can be configured to allow only a few types of protocols to enter. There are a number of types of firewalls, which are usually classified by the level of information they can filter. Firewalls can be packet filtering, stateful packet filtering, proxy, or application level. A firewall can be a single device or a **firewall subnet**, which consists of multiple firewalls creating a buffer between the outside and inside networks. Thus, firewalls can be used to create security perimeters like the one shown in Figure 5-17.

DMZs. A buffer against outside attacks is frequently referred to as a **demilitarized zone (DMZ)**. The DMZ is a no-man's-land between the inside and outside networks; it is also where some organizations place Web servers. These servers provide access to organizational Web pages, without allowing Web requests to enter the interior networks.

Proxy Servers. An alternative approach to the strategies of using a firewall subnet or a DMZ is to use a **proxy server**, or **proxy firewall**. A proxy server performs actions on behalf of another system. When deployed, a proxy server is configured to look like a Web server and is assigned the domain name that users would be expecting to find for the system and its services. When an outside client requests a particular Web page, the proxy server receives the request as if it were the subject of the request, then asks for the same information from the true Web server (acting as a proxy for the requestor), and then responds to the request as a proxy for the true Web server. This gives requestors the response they need without allowing them to gain direct access to the internal and more sensitive server. The proxy server may be hardened and become a bastion host placed in the public area of the network, or it might be placed within the firewall subnet or the DMZ for added protection. For more frequently accessed Web pages, proxy servers can cache or temporarily store the page, and thus are sometimes called **cache servers**. Figure 5-18 shows a representative example of a configuration using a proxy.

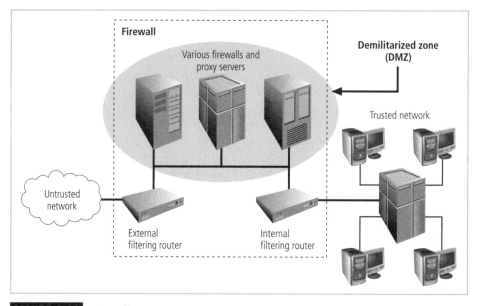

FIGURE 5-18   Firewalls, Proxy Servers, and DMZs

Intrusion Detection Systems (IDSs). In an effort to detect unauthorized activity within the inner network or on individual machines, an organization may wish to implement **intrusion detection systems (IDSs)**. IDSs come in two versions, with hybrids possible. **Host-based IDSs** are usually installed on the machines they protect to monitor the status of various files stored on those machines. The IDS learns the configuration of the system, assigns priorities to various files depending on their value, and can then alert the administrator of suspicious activity. **Network-based IDSs** look at patterns of network traffic and attempt to detect unusual activity based on previous baselines. This could include packets coming into the organization's networks with addresses from machines already within the organization (IP spoofing). It could also include high volumes of traffic going to outside addresses (as in cases of data theft) or coming into the network (as in a denial of service attack). Both host- and network-based IDSs require a database of previous activity. In the case of host-based IDSs, the system can create a database of file attributes, as well as maintain a catalog of common attack signatures. Network-based IDSs can use a similar catalog of common attack signatures and develop databases of "normal" activity for comparison with future activity. IDSs can be used together for the maximum level of security for a particular network and set of systems. Figure 5-19 shows an example of an intrusion detection system.

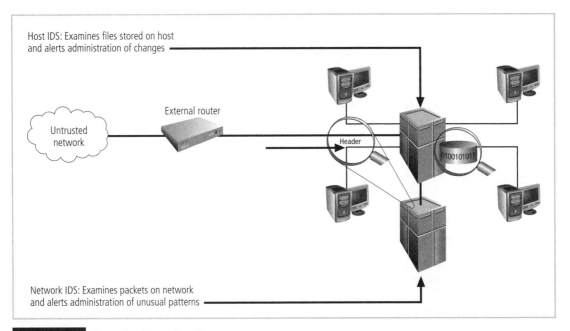

Host IDS: Examines files stored on host and alerts administration of changes

External router

Untrusted network

Header

0100101011

Network IDS: Examines packets on network and alerts administration of unusual patterns

FIGURE 5-19 Intrusion Detection Systems

This cursory overview of technology components is meant to provide sufficient understanding to allow a decision maker to determine what should be implemented and when to bring in additional expertise to better craft the security design. Chapters 6, 7, and 8 examine in detail the implementation of various information security technologies.

After your organization has selected a model, created a framework, and fleshed it out into a blueprint for implementation, you should make sure your planning includes the steps needed to create a training and awareness program that increases information security knowledge and visibility and enables people across the organization to work in secure ways that enhance the safety of the organization's information assets.

Security Education, Training, and Awareness Program

As soon as the general security policy and its approach to security in the organization has been drafted, policies to implement a **security education, training, and awareness (SETA)** program should naturally follow. The SETA program is the responsibility of the CISO and is a control measure designed to reduce the incidences of accidental security breaches by employees. Employee errors are among the top threats to information assets. As a result, it is worth expending the organization's resources to develop programs to combat this threat. SETA programs are designed to supplement the general education and training programs that many organizations have in place to educate staff on information security. For example, if an organization detects that many employees are opening e-mail attachments inappropriately, those employees must be retrained. As a matter of good practice, systems development life cycles must include user training during the implementation phase. Employee training should be managed so that there is some assurance that all employees are properly trained. Security education and training is designed to build on the general knowledge that employees possess to do their jobs and to focus on ways to work securely.

The SETA program consists of three elements: security education, security training, and security awareness. An organization may not be capable of or willing to undertake all three of these elements; in this case, it may outsource elements to local educational institutions. The purpose of SETA is to enhance security by:

- Improving awareness of the need to protect system resources
- Developing skills and knowledge so computer users can perform their jobs more securely
- Building in-depth knowledge, as needed, to design, implement, or operate security programs for organizations and systems[20]

Table 5-1 compares the features of security education, training, and awareness within the organization.

Table 5-1   Comparative Framework of SETA (from NIST SP800-12[21])

	Education	Training	Awareness
Attribute	Why	How	What
Level	Insight	Knowledge	Information
Objective	Understanding	Skill	Exposure
Teaching method	Theoretical instruction ■ Discussion seminar ■ Background reading ■ Hands-on practice	Practical instruction ■ Lecture ■ Case study workshop ■ Posters	Media ■ Videos ■ Newsletters
Test measure	Essay (interpret learning)	Problem solving (apply learning)	■ True or false ■ Multiple choice (identify learning)
Impact timeframe	Long-term	Intermediate	Short-term

Security Education

Everyone in an organization needs to be trained and aware of information security, but not every member of the organization needs a formal degree or certificate in information security. When management agrees that formal education is appropriate, an employee can investigate available courses from local institutions of higher learning or continuing education. A number of universities have formal coursework in information security. For those interested in researching formal information security programs, there are resources available, such as the NSA-identified Centers of Excellence in Information Assurance Education (*www.nsa.gov/isso/programs/nietp/newspg1.htm*). The Centers of Excellence program identifies outstanding universities with both coursework in information security and an integrated view of information security in the institution itself. Other local resources can also provide security education information, such as Kennesaw State's Center for Information Security Education (*http://infosec.kennesaw.edu*).

Security Training

Security training involves providing members of the organization with detailed information and hands-on instruction to prepare them to perform their duties securely. Management of information security can develop customized in-house training or outsource the training program.

An alternative to formal training programs are industry training conferences and programs offered through professional agencies such as SANS (*www.sans.org*), ISC2 (*www.isc2.org*), ISSA (*www.issa.org*), and CSI (*www.gocsi.org*). Many of these programs are too technical for the average employee, but may be perfect for the continuing education requirements of information security professionals.

There are a number of available resources for conducting SETA programs that offer assistance in the form of sample topics and structures for security classes. For organizations, the Computer Security Resource Center at NIST provides several useful documents free of charge in their special publications area (*http://csrc.nist.gov*).

Security Awareness

One of the least frequently implemented, but most beneficial programs is the security awareness program. A security awareness program is designed to keep information security at the forefront of users' minds as they work day to day. These programs don't have to be complicated or expensive. Good programs can include newsletters, security posters (see Figure 5-20 for an example), videos, bulletin boards, flyers, and trinkets (or promotional items like these can be included with other training programs). Trinkets can include security slogans printed on mouse pads, coffee cups, T-shirts, pens, or any object frequently used during the workday that reminds employees of security. In addition, a good security awareness program requires a dedicated individual willing to invest the time and effort into promoting the program, and a champion willing to provide the needed financial support.

The security newsletter is the most cost-effective method of disseminating security information and news to the employee. Newsletters can be hard copy, e-mail, or intranet-based. Newsletter topics can include new threats to the organization's information assets, the schedule for upcoming security classes, and the addition of new security personnel. The goal is to keep the idea of information security in users' minds and to stimulate users to care about security. If a security awareness program is not actively implemented, employees may begin to neglect security matters and the risk of employee accidents and failures is likely to increase.

FIGURE 5-20   Information Security Awareness at Kennesaw State University

Continuity Strategies

A key role for all managers is planning. Managers in the IT and information security communities are usually called on to provide strategic planning to assure the continuous availability of information systems.[22] Unfortunately for managers, however, the probability that some form of attack will occur, whether from inside or outside, intentional or accidental, human or nonhuman, annoying or catastrophic factors, is very high. Thus, managers from each community of interest within the organization must be ready to act when a successful attack occurs.

There are various types of plans for events of this type: business continuity plans (BCPs), disaster recovery plans (DRPs), incident response plans (IRPs), and contingency plans (CPs). In some organizations, these might be handled as a single plan. In large, complex organizations, each of these named plans may represent separate but related planning functions that differ in scope, applicability, and design. In a small organization, the security administrator (or systems administrator) may have one simple plan that consists of a straightforward set of media backup and recovery strategies, and a few service agreements from the company's service providers. But the sad reality is that many organizations have a level of planning that is woefully deficient.

This chapter classifies incident response, disaster recovery, and business continuity planning as components of contingency planning, as shown in Figure 5-21. A **contingency plan (CP)** is prepared by the organization to anticipate, react to, and recover from events that threaten the security of information and information assets in the organization, and, subsequently, to restore the organization to normal modes of business operations. The discussion of CP begins with an explanation of the difference among its various elements, and an examination of the points at which each element is brought into play.

Organizations need to develop disaster recovery plans, incident response plans, and business continuity plans as subsets of an overall CP. An **incident** is any clearly identified attack on the organization's information assets that would threaten the assets' confidentiality, integrity, or availability. An **incident response plan (IRP)** deals with the identification, classification, response, and recovery from an incident. A **disaster recovery plan (DRP)** deals with the preparation for and recovery from a disaster, whether natural or man-made. A **business continuity plan (BCP)** ensures that critical business functions continue, if a catastrophic incident or disaster occurs. The primary functions of these three types of planning are as follows:

- The IRP focuses on immediate response, but if the attack escalates or is disastrous (e.g., fire, flood, earthquake, or total blackout) the process moves on to disaster recovery and BCP.
- The DRP typically focuses on restoring systems at the original site after disasters occur, and as such is closely associated with BCP.
- The BCP occurs concurrently with DRP when the damage is major or long term, requiring more than simple restoration of information and information resources. The BCP establishes critical business functions at an alternate site.

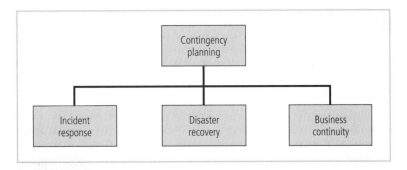

FIGURE 5-21 Components of Contingency Planning

Some experts argue that the DRPs and BCPs are so closely linked that they are indistinguishable. However, each has a distinct role and planning requirement. The following sections detail the tasks necessary for each of these three types of plans. You can also further distinguish among the three types of planning by examining when each comes into play during the life of an incident. Figure 5-22 shows a sample sequence of events and the overlap between when each plan comes into play. Disaster recovery activities typically continue even after the organization has resumed operations at the original site.

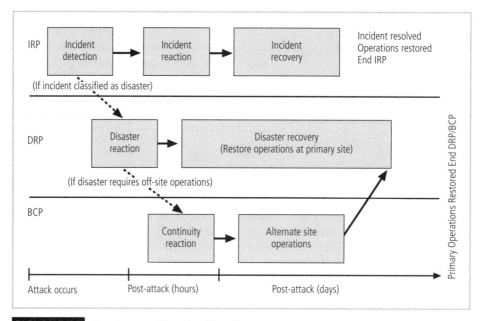

FIGURE 5-22 Contingency Planning Timeline

As the individual components of contingency planning are described, you may notice that contingency planning has many similarities with the risk management process. The CP is a microcosm of risk management activities, and it focuses on the specific steps required to return all information assets to the level at which they were functioning before the incident or disaster. As a result, the planning process closely emulates the process of risk management.

Before any planning can begin, an assigned person or a planning team has to get the process started. In the usual case, a contingency planning team is assembled for that purpose. A roster for this team may consist of the following members:

- Champion: As with any strategic function, the CP project must have a high-level manager to support, promote, and endorse the findings of the project. In a CP project, this could be the CIO, or ideally the CEO.

- Project manager: A champion provides the strategic vision and the linkage to the power structure of the organization, but someone has to manage the project. A project manager, possibly a midlevel manager or even the CISO, must lead the project and make sure a sound project planning process is used, a complete and useful project plan is developed, and project resources are prudently managed to reach the goals of the project.

- Team members: The team members for this project should be the managers or their representatives from the various communities of interest: business, information technology, and information security. Representative business managers, familiar with the operations of their respective functional areas, should supply details on their activities and provide insight into the criticality of their functions to the overall sustainability of the business. Information technology managers on the project team should be familiar with the systems that could be at risk and with the IRPs, DRPs, and BCPs that are needed to provide technical content within the planning process. Information security managers must oversee the security planning of the project and provide information on the threats, vulnerabilities, attacks, and recovery requirements needed in the planning process.

The major project work modules performed by the contingency planning project team are shown in Figure 5-23. As you read the remainder of this chapter, it may help you to look back at this diagram, since many of the upcoming sections correspond to the steps depicted in the diagram.

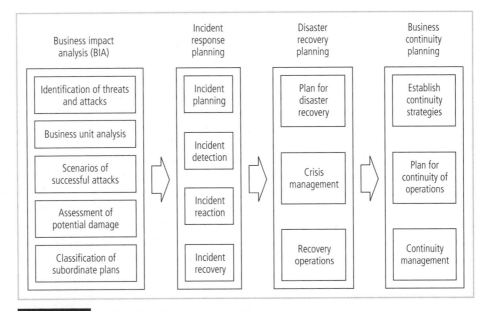

FIGURE 5-23   Major Steps in Contingency Planning

Business Impact Analysis

The first phase in the development of the CP process is the **business impact analysis (BIA)**. A BIA is an investigation and assessment of the impact that various attacks can have on the organization. BIA takes up where the risk assessment process leaves off. It begins with the prioritized list of threats and vulnerabilities identified in the risk management process from Chapter 4 and adds critical information. The BIA is a crucial component of the initial planning stages, as it provides detailed scenarios of the potential impact each attack could have on the organization. The BIA therefore adds insight into what the organization must do to respond to attack, minimize the damage from the attack, recover from the effects, and return to normal operations. One of the fundamental differences between a BIA and the risk management processes discussed in Chapter 4 is that the risk management approach identifies the threats, vulnerabilities, and attacks to determine what controls can protect the information. The BIA assumes that these controls have been bypassed, have failed, or are otherwise ineffective in stopping the attack, and that the attack is successful. The question asked at this point is, *if* the attack succeeds, *what* do you do then? Obviously the organization's security team does everything in its power to stop these attacks, but as you have seen, some attacks, such as natural disasters, deviations from service providers, acts of human failure or error, and deliberate acts of sabotage and vandalism, may be unstoppable.

The CP team conducts the BIA in the following stages, which are shown in Figure 5-23 and described in the sections that follow:

1. Threat attack identification and prioritization
2. Business unit analysis
3. Attack success scenario development
4. Potential damage assessment
5. Subordinate plan classification

Threat Attack Identification and Prioritization

If this section sounds familiar, it's because you learned about identifying and prioritizing the threats facing the organization in the discussion of risk assessment earlier in this book. Organizations that have completed this process need only update the threat list with the latest developments and add one additional piece of information, the attack profile. An **attack profile** is a detailed description of the activities that occur during an attack. The content items in an attack profile, shown in Table 5-2, include preliminary indications of an attack, as well as actions and outcomes. These profiles must be developed for every serious threat the organization faces, natural or man-made, deliberate or accidental. It is as important to know what the typical hacker's profile is as it is to know how employees make errors in data entry, or what weather conditions indicate the threat of an imminent tornado or hurricane. The attack profile is useful in later planning stages to provide indicators of attacks. It is used here to determine the extent of damage that could result to a business unit if a given attack were successful.

Table 5-2   Attack Profile

Date of analysis	June 21, 2006
Attack name and description	Mako worm
Threat and probable threat agent	Malicious code via automated attack
Known or possible vulnerabilities	All desktop systems not updated with all latest patches
Likely precursor activities or indicators	Attachments to e-mails
Likely attack activities or indicators of attack in progress	Systems sending e-mails to entries from address book, activity on port 80 without browser being used
Information assets at risk from this attack	All desktop and server systems are at risk
Damage or loss to information assets likely from this attack	Business partners and others connected to our networks
Other assets at risk from this attack	
Damage or loss to other assets likely from this attack	Will vary depending on severity, minimum disruption will be need to repair worm infection

Business Unit Analysis

The second major task within the BIA is the analysis and prioritization of business functions within the organization. This series of tasks serves to identify and prioritize the functions within the organization's units (departments, sections, divisions, groups, or other such units) to determine which are most vital to the continued operations of the organization. Each unit must also be independently evaluated to determine how important its functions are to the organization as a whole. For example, recovery operations would probably focus on the IT department and network operation before addressing the personnel department and hiring activities. Likewise, it is more urgent to reinstate a manufacturing company's assembly line function than the maintenance tracking system for that assembly line. This is not to say that personnel functions and assembly line maintenance are not important to the business; but the reality is that if the organization's main revenue-producing operations cannot be restored quickly, there may be no need for other functions.

Attack Success Scenario Development

Once the threat attack profiles have been developed and the business functions prioritized, the business impact analysis team must create a series of scenarios depicting the impact of a successful attack from each threat on each prioritized functional area. This can be a long and detailed process, as threats that succeed can affect many functions. Attack profiles should include scenarios depicting a typical attack with details on the method of attack, the indicators of attack, and the broad consequences. Once the attack profiles are completed, the business function details can be integrated with the attack profiles. Then attack success scenarios with more detail are added to the attack profile, including alternate outcomes. These alternate outcomes should describe a best, worst, and most likely case that could result from each type of attack on a particular business functional area. This level of detail allows planners to address each business function in turn.

Potential Damage Assessment

From the attack success scenarios developed above, the BIA planning team must estimate the cost of the best, worst, and most likely cases. At this stage, you are *not* determining how much to spend on the protection of information assets, since this was analyzed during the risk management activities. Instead, you are identifying what must be done to recover from each possible case. These costs include the actions of the response team(s), which are described in subsequent sections, as they act to recover quickly and effectively from an incident or disaster. These cost estimates can also inform management representatives from all the organization's communities of interest of the importance of the planning and recovery efforts. The final result of the assessment is referred to as an **attack scenario end case**.

Subordinate Plan Classification

Once the potential damage has been assessed, and each scenario and attack scenario end case has been evaluated, a subordinate plan must be developed or identified from among existing plans already in place. These subordinate plans take into account the identification of, reaction to, and recovery from each attack scenario. An attack scenario end case is categorized either as disastrous or not disastrous. Most attacks are not disastrous and therefore fall into the category of incident response. Those scenarios that do qualify as disastrous are addressed in the disaster recovery plan. The qualifying difference is whether or not an organization is able to take effective action during the attack to combat its effects. Attack end cases that are disastrous find members of the organization waiting out the attack with hopes to recover effectively after it is over. In a typical disaster recovery operation, the lives and welfare of the employees are the most important priority *during* the attack, as most disasters are fires, floods, hurricanes, and tornadoes. Please note that there are attacks that are not natural disasters that fit this category as well, for example:

- Electrical blackouts
- Attacks on service providers that result in a loss of communications to the organization (either telephone or Internet)
- Massive, malicious code attacks that sweep through an organization before they can be contained

The bottom line is that each scenario should be classified as a probable incident or disaster, and then the corresponding actions required to respond to the scenario should be built into either the IRP or DRP.

Incident Response Planning

As described in the sections below, incident response planning covers the identification of, classification of, and response to an incident. The IRP is made up of activities that are to be performed when an incident has been identified. Before developing such a plan, you should understand the philosophical approach to incident response planning.

What is an incident? What is incident response? As stated earlier, an incident is an attack against an information asset that poses a clear threat to the confidentiality, integrity, or availability of information resources. If an action that threatens information occurs and is completed, the action is classified as an incident. All of the threats identified in earlier chapters could result in attacks that would be classified as information security incidents. For purposes of this discussion, however, attacks are only classified as incidents if they have the following characteristics:

- They are directed against information assets.
- They have a realistic chance of success.
- They could threaten the confidentiality, integrity, or availability of information resources.

Incident response (IR) is therefore the set of activities taken to plan for, detect, and correct the impact of an incident on information assets. Prevention is purposefully omitted, as this activity is more a function of information security in general than of incident response. In other words, IR is more reactive than proactive, with the exception of the planning that must occur to prepare the IR teams to be ready to react to an incident.

IR consists of the following four phases:

1. Planning
2. Detection
3. Reaction
4. Recovery

Before examining each of these phases, consider the following scenario from the not too distant past:

The Second Armored Cavalry Regiment (ACR) was the oldest cavalry regiment on continuous active duty until it was decommissioned in 1994. The 2nd ACR served as the vanguard of the first Armored Division in the sweep of Iraqi forces during the 1991 Gulf War. Before Desert Shield, the 2nd ACR was, for many years, responsible for the patrol and protection of the West German, East German, and Czechoslovakian border. This mission was carried out by placing one troop from each of the three front line squadrons in various border patrol camps along the border. Each of these border troops conducted constant surveillance of the border, ready to give early warning of potential border violations, political incidents, and even hostile invasions. Within the border camp, the border troop consisted of either a cavalry troop with 12 M3A1 Bradley Fighting Vehicles and 9 M1A1 Abrams Main Battle Tanks, or a tank company, with 14 M1A1s. Occasionally, units from outside the ACR took a shift on the border, but it was ultimately the 2nd ACR's responsibility to guard this stretch of territory.

The unit occupying the border camp was required to organize a series of elements capable of deploying in reaction to an incident on the border—be it a border crossing by a political defector or an invasion by a military force. The smallest such element was the "reaction force" made up of eight to ten soldiers manning two battle vehicles (Bradleys or Abrams). It was required to be ready to deploy to an area outside the base within 15 minutes in order to combat a foe or report on the incident. While the routine patrols were conducted in HMMWVs (Hummers), the reaction elements had to deploy in battle vehicles. The next larger element was the "reaction platoon," the remainder of the reaction force's platoon (two additional Abrams, or four additional Bradleys, and 8 to 20 additional soldiers) that had to be ready to deploy within 30 minutes. Had the incident warranted it, the entire troop had to be prepared to depart base within one hour. This deployment was rehearsed daily by the reaction force, weekly by the reaction platoon, and at least twice during border camp by the entire troop.

What does this scenario illustrate? An incident is an incident. The employees in an organization responding to a security incident are of course not expected to deploy fully armed to engage in combat against a physical threat. But the preparation and planning required to respond to an information security incident is not entirely different from that required to respond to a military incident; in both cases, the same careful attention to detail must be paid, each potential threat scenario must be examined, and a number of responses commensurate with the level of the incident must be developed.

Incident Planning

Planning for incidents is the first step in the overall process of incident response planning. Planning for an incident requires a detailed understanding of the scenarios developed for the BIA. With this information in hand, the planning team can develop a series of predefined responses that guide the organization's incident response (IR) team and information security staff. The predefined responses enable the organization to react quickly and effectively to the detected incident. This assumes two things: first, the organization has an IR team, and second, the organization can detect the incident.

The IR team consists of those individuals who must be present to handle the systems and functional areas that can minimize the impact of an incident as it takes place. Picture the military movies you have seen in which some form of attack has occurred on the United States. If the movies were accurate in their portrayal of IR teams, they would have shown the IR team verifying the threat, determining the appropriate response, and coordinating the actions necessary to deal with the situation.

Incident Response Plan

The process of planned team responses in the military can be used to guide the process of incident response. The planners should develop a set of documents that guide the actions of each involved individual who reacts to and recovers from the incident. These plans must be properly organized and stored to be available when and where needed, and in a useful format. An example of such a document is presented later in this chapter in a section titled "Model for a Consolidated Contingency Plan."

Format and Content. The IR plan must be organized in such a way to support, rather than impede, quick and easy access to required information. This can be accomplished through a number of measures, the simplest of which is to create a directory of incidents with tabbed sections for each incident. To respond to an incident, the responder simply opens the binder, flips to the appropriate section, and follows the clearly outlined procedures for an assigned role. This requires the planners to develop the detailed procedures necessary to respond to each incident—procedures that must include both the actions to take *during* the incident, as well as the actions to take *after* the incident. In addition, the document should contain information to prepare the staff for the incident by providing procedures to perform *before* the incident.

Storage. Where is the IR plan stored? Note that the information in the IR plan should be protected as sensitive information. If attackers gain knowledge of how a company responds to a particular incident, they can improve their chances of success in the attack. On the other hand, the organization needs to have this information readily available to the individuals who must respond to the incident. This typically means storing the IR plan within arm's reach of the information assets that must be modified or manipulated during or immediately after the attack. The binder could be stored adjacent to the administrator's workstation, or in a bookcase in the server room. The bottom line is that the individuals responding to the incident should not have to search frantically for the needed information.

Testing. A plan untested is not a useful plan. Or in the military vernacular, "Train as you fight, and fight as you train." Even if an organization has what appears on paper to be an effective IR plan, the procedures that come from the plan may be ineffective unless the plan has been practiced or tested. Testing a plan can be done in many different ways, using one or more testing strategies. Five testing strategies that are often used are presented here.[23]

1. Checklist: Copies of the IR plan are distributed to each individual with a role to play during an actual incident. These individuals each review the plan and create a checklist of correct and incorrect components. Although not a true test, the making of this checklist is an important step in reviewing the document before it is actually needed.
2. Structured walk-through: In a walk-through, each involved individual practices the steps he or she will take during an actual event. This can consist of an "on-the-ground" walk-through, in which everyone discusses his or her actions at each particular location and juncture, or it can be more of a "talk-through," in which all involved individuals sit around a conference table and discuss in turn how they would act as the incident unfolded.

3. Simulation: The next step up is a simulation of an incident. Here, each involved individual works individually, rather than in conference, simulating the performance of each task required to react to and recover from a simulated incident. The simulation stops short of the actual physical tasks required, such as installing the backup, or disconnecting a communications circuit. The major difference between a walk-through and a simulation is the independence of the individual performers in a simulation, as they work on their own tasks and assume responsibility for identifying the faults in their own procedures.

4. Parallel: Yet another test, larger in scope and intensity, is the parallel test. In the parallel test, individuals act as if an actual incident occurred, performing their required tasks and executing the necessary procedures. The difference is that the normal operations of the business do not stop. The business continues to function, even though the IR team acts to contain the test incident. Great care must be taken to ensure that the procedures performed do not halt the operations of the business functions, and thereby create an actual incident.

5. Full interruption: The final, most comprehensive and realistic test is to react to an incident as if it were real. In a full interruption, the individuals follow each and every procedure, including the interruption of service, restoration of data from backups, and notification of appropriate individuals as discussed in subsequent sections. This is often performed after normal business hours in organizations that cannot afford to disrupt or simulate the disruption of business functions for the purposes of the test. This is the best practice the team can get, but is unfortunately too risky for most businesses.

At a minimum, organizations should conduct periodic walk-throughs (or talk-throughs) of the IR plan. As quickly as business and information resources change, a failure to update the IR plan can result in an inability to react effectively to an incident, or possibly cause greater damage than the incident itself. If this sounds like a major training effort, note the sayings below from the author Richard Marcinko, a former Navy SEAL—these remarks have been paraphrased (and somewhat sanitized) for your edification.[24]

- The more you sweat in training, the less you bleed in combat.
- Training and preparation hurt.
- Lead from the front, not the rear.
- You don't have to like it, just do it.
- Keep it simple.
- Never assume.
- You are paid for your results, not your methods.

Incident Detection

Individuals sometimes notify systems administrators, security administrators, or their managers of an unusual occurrence. This is most often a complaint to the help desk from one or more users about a technology service. These complaints are often collected by the help desk and can include reports such as "the system is acting unusual," "programs are slow," "my computer is acting weird," or "data is not available." Incident detection relies on either a human or automated system, which is often the help desk staff, to identify an unusual occurrence and to classify it properly as an incident. The mechanisms that could potentially detect an incident include intrusion detection systems (both host-based and network-based), virus detection software, systems administrators, and even end users. Intrusion detection systems and virus detection software are examined in detail in later chapters. This chapter focuses on the human element.

In defining an incident as any clearly identified attack on the organization's information assets, the emphasis should fall on *clearly identified*. An ambiguously identified attack could be an actual attack, a problem with heavy network traffic, or even the client's computer malfunctioning. Only by carefully training the user, the help desk, and all security personnel on the analysis and identification of attacks can the organization hope to identify and classify an incident quickly. Once an attack is properly identified, the organization can effectively execute the corresponding procedures from the IR plan. Thus, **incident classification** is the process of examining a potential incident, or **incident candidate**, and determining whether or not the candidate constitutes an actual incident. Who does this? Anyone with the appropriate level of knowledge can classify an incident. Typically a help desk operator brings the issue forward to a help desk supervisor, the security manager, or a designated incident watch manager. Once a candidate has been classified as a valid incident, the responsible manager must decide whether to implement the incident response plan.

Incident Indicators. There are a number of occurrences that could signal the presence of an incident candidate. Unfortunately many of these are similar to the actions of an overloaded network, computer, or server, and some are similar to the normal operation of these information assets. Other incident candidates are similar to the actions of a misbehaving computing system, software package, or other less serious threat. Donald Pipkin, an IT security expert, identifies three categories of incident indicators: possible, probable, and definite.[25]

Possible indicators. The four types of events described below are possible indicators of incidents:

1. Presence of unfamiliar files: If users report discovering files in their home directories or on their office computers, or administrators find files that do not seem to have been placed in a logical location or that were not created by an authorized user, the presence of these files may signal the occurrence of an incident.
2. Presence or execution of unknown programs or processes: Similar to the presence of unfamiliar files, if users or administrators detect unfamiliar programs running, or processes executing on office machines or network servers, this could be an incident.
3. Unusual consumption of computing resources: Many computer operating systems can monitor the consumption of resources. Windows 2000 and XP, as well as many UNIX variants, allow users and administrators to monitor CPU and memory consumption. Most computers can monitor hard drive space. Servers maintain logs of file creation and storage. The sudden consumption of resources, spikes, or drops, can be indicators of candidate incidents—or that a user has finally cleaned out some shared drives.
4. Unusual system crashes: Some computer systems crash on a regular basis. Older operating systems running newer programs are notorious for locking up or rebooting whenever the OS is unable to execute a requested process or service. Many people are familiar with these systems' error messages, such as *Unrecoverable Application Error* and *General Protection Fault*, and many other unfortunate users have seen the infamous *NT Blue Screen of Death*. But if a computer-based system seems to be crashing, hanging, rebooting, or freezing more than usual, it could be a candidate incident.

Probable indicators. The four types of events described below are probable indicators of incidents:

1. Activities at unexpected times: If traffic levels on the organization's network exceed the measured baseline values, there is a probability that an incident is underway. If this surge in activity occurs at times when few members of the organization are at

work, the probability that it is an actual incident is much higher. Similarly, if systems are accessing drives, such as floppies and CD-ROMs, when the end user is not using them, an incident may be occurring.

2. Presence of new accounts: Periodic review of user accounts can reveal an account (or accounts) that the administrator does not remember creating, or accounts that are not logged in the administrator's journal. Even one unlogged new account is a candidate incident. An unlogged new account with root or other special privileges has an even higher probability of being an actual incident.

3. Reported attacks: If users of the system report a suspected attack, there is a high probability that an incident is underway or has already occurred. When considering the probability of an attack, you should consider the technical sophistication of the person making the report.

4. Notification from IDS: If the organization has installed host-based or network-based intrusion detection systems, and if they are correctly configured, the notification from the IDS could indicate a strong likelihood that an incident is in progress. The problem with most IDSs is that they are seldom configured optimally, and even when they are, they tend to issue high levels of false positives or false alarms. It is then up to the administrator to determine whether the notification is real or the result of a routine operation by a user or other administrator.

Definite indicators. The five types of events described below are definite indicators of incidents. Definite indicators of incidents are those activities which clearly signal that an incident is in progress or has occurred.

1. Use of dormant accounts: Many network servers maintain default accounts that came with the system from the manufacturer. Although industry best practices indicate that these accounts should be changed or removed, some organizations ignore these practices by making the default accounts inactive. In addition, systems may have any number of accounts that are not actively used, such as those of previous employees, employees on extended vacation or sabbatical, or dummy accounts set up to support system testing. If any of these dormant accounts suddenly becomes active without a change in status for the underlying user, this most probably indicates that an incident occurred.

2. Changes to logs: The smart administrator backs up systems logs as well as systems data. As part of a routine incident scan, these logs may be compared to the online version to determine if they have been modified. If they have been modified, and the systems administrator cannot determine explicitly that an authorized individual modified them, an incident has occurred.

3. Presence of hacker tools: The authors of this textbook have had a number of hacker tools installed or stored on their office computers. These are used periodically to scan internal computers and networks to determine what the hacker can see. They are also used to support research into attack profiles. Every time the authors' computers are booted, the antivirus program detects these tools as threats to the systems. If the authors did not positively know that they themselves had installed the tools, the presence of these tools would constitute an incident. Many organizations have policies that explicitly prohibit the installation of such tools without the written permission from the CISO. Installing these tools without the proper authorization is a policy violation and subject to discipline. Most organizations that have sponsored and approved penetration-testing operations require that all tools in this category be confined to specific systems that are not used on the general network unless active penetration testing is underway.

4. Notifications by partner or peer: Not all incidents can be directly detected. Many organizations have business partners, upstream and downstream value chain associations, and even hierarchical superior or subordinate organizations. If one of these organizations indicates that it is being attacked, and that the attackers are using your computing systems, an incident has occurred or is in progress.

5. Notification by hacker: Some hackers enjoy taunting their victims. If your Web page suddenly begins displaying a "gotcha" from a hacker, it's an incident. If you receive an e-mail from a hacker containing information from your "secured" corporate e-mail, it's an incident. If you receive an extortion request for money in exchange for your customers' credit card files, it's an incident.

Predefined situations. There are also several predefined situations that signal an automatic incident. These include:

1. Loss of availability: Information or information systems become unavailable.
2. Loss of integrity: Users report corrupt data files, garbage where data should be, or data that just looks wrong.
3. Loss of confidentiality: You are notified of sensitive information leaks, or that information you thought was protected has been disclosed.
4. Violation of policy: If organizational policies addressing information or information security have been violated, an incident has occurred.
5. Violation of law: If the law has been broken, and the organization's information assets were involved, an incident has occurred.

When Does an Incident Become a Disaster? An event can be categorized as a disaster when the following happens: 1) the organization is unable to mitigate the impact of an incident during the incident, and 2) the level of damage or destruction is so severe that the organization is unable to recover quickly. The difference may be subtle. It is up to the organization to decide which incidents are classified as disasters and therefore receive the appropriate level of response.

Incident Reaction

Once an incident has been classified as such, the organization moves from detection to reaction. **Incident reaction** consists of actions outlined in the IRP that guide the organization in attempting to stop the incident, mitigate the impact of the incident, and provide information for recovery from the incident. These actions take place as soon as the incident itself is over. In reacting to the incident there are a number of actions that must occur quickly, including notification of key personnel and documentation of the incident. These must have been prioritized and documented in the IRP for quick use in the heat of the moment.

Notification of Key Personnel. As soon as the help desk, end user, or systems administrator determines that an incident is in progress, he or she must immediately notify the right people in the right order. Most organizations, including the military, maintain an alert roster for just such an emergency. An **alert roster** is a document containing contact information for the individuals to be notified in the event of an incident. There are two ways to activate an alert roster: sequential and hierarchical. A **sequential roster** is activated as a contact person calls each person on the roster. A **hierarchical roster** is activated as the first person calls a few other people on the roster, who in turn call a few other people. Each has its advantages and disadvantages. The hierarchical is quicker, with more people calling at the same time, but the message may get distorted, as it is passed from person to person. The sequential is more accurate, as the contact person provides each person with the same message, but it takes longer.

The **alert message** is a scripted description of the incident, usually just enough information so that each individual knows what portion of the IRP to implement, and not enough to slow down the notification process. It is important to mention that not everyone is on the alert roster, only those individuals who must respond to the incident. The alert roster, as with any document, must be maintained and tested to ensure accuracy. The notification process must be periodically rehearsed to assure it is effective and efficient.

There are other personnel who must also be notified but may not be part of the scripted alert notification process, because they are not needed until preliminary information has been collected and analyzed. Management must be notified, of course, but not so early that, should the incident prove to be a false or minor alarm, the notification causes undue panic, and not so late that the media or other external sources learn of the incident before management, and thereby cause embarrassment. Some incidents are disclosed to the employees in general, as a lesson in security, and some are not, as a measure of security. Other organizations may need to be notified if the incident spreads beyond the initial target organization's information resources, or if the incident is part of a larger-scale assault. An example of a larger-scale assault is Mafiaboy's DDoS attack on multiple Web-based vendors in late 1999. In such cases, it is up to the IRP development team to determine whom to notify and when to offer guidance about additional notification steps to be taken.

Documenting an Incident. As soon as an incident, or disaster, has been declared, key personnel must be notified and the documentation of the unfolding event begun. There are many reasons for documenting the event. First, documenting the event in the organization's records is important because it enables an organization to learn what happened, how it happened, and what actions were taken. The documentation records the who, what, when, where, why, and how of the event. Therefore, it can serve as a case study that the organization can use to determine if the right actions were taken and if these actions were actually effective. Second, documenting the event can prove, should there ever be a question, that the organization did everything possible to prevent the spread of the incident. From a legal standpoint, the standards of due care protect the organization in cases where an incident affects individuals inside and outside the organization or other organizations that use the targeted organization's systems. Lastly, the documentation of an incident can also be used to run a simulation in future training sessions on future versions of the IRP.

Incident Containment Strategies

One of the most critical components of incident reaction is to stop the incident or contain its scope or impact. Unfortunately, the most direct means of containment, which is simply "cutting the wire," is often not an option for many organizations, thus an organization must choose among alternative containment strategies. Incident containment strategies vary depending on the incident, and on the amount of damage it causes or may cause. However, before an incident can be contained, the affected areas of the information and information systems must be determined. This is not the time to conduct a detailed analysis of the affected areas; that type of analysis is typically performed after the fact in the forensics process. You need, instead, to identify what information and systems have been involved in the incident to determine what kind of containment strategy is best and which systems or networks need to be contained. In general, incident containment strategies focus on two tasks: stopping the incident and recovering control of the systems.

The organization can stop the incident and attempt to recover control through a number of strategies:

- If the incident originates outside the organization, the simplest and most straightforward approach is to sever the affected communication circuits. However, if the organization's lifeblood runs through that circuit, it may not be feasible to take so drastic a measure. If the incident does not threaten the most critical functional areas, it may be more feasible simply to monitor the incident and contain it in another way. One approach used by some organizations is to apply filtering rules dynamically to limit certain types of network access. For example, if a threat agent is attacking a network by exploiting a vulnerability in the Simple Network Management Protocol (SNMP), applying a blocking filter for the commonly used IP ports for that vulnerability stops the attack without compromising other services on the network. Depending on the nature of the attack and the technical capabilities of the organization, *ad hoc* controls such as these can sometimes be used to gain valuable time to devise a more permanent control strategy.
- If the incident is using compromised accounts, those accounts can be disabled.
- If the incident is coming in through a firewall, the firewall can be reconfigured to block that particular traffic.
- If the incident is using a particular service or process, that process or service can be disabled temporarily.
- If the incident is using the organization's e-mail system to propagate itself, it may be feasible to take down the application or server that supports e-mail.

The ultimate containment option, reserved for only the most drastic of scenarios, involves a full stop of all computers and network devices in the organization. Obviously, this step is taken only when all control of the infrastructure has been lost, and the only hope is to preserve the data stored on the computers with the idea that this data can be used in the future to restore operations.

The bottom line is that containment consists of isolating the affected channels, processes, services, or computers, and removing the losses. Taking down the entire system, servers, and network may accomplish this. The incident response manager informed by the guidance of the IRP determines the length of the interruption.

Incident Recovery

Once the incident has been contained and control of the systems regained, the next stage of the IRP must be immediately executed. This is recovery from the incident. As with reaction to the incident, the first task is to identify the human resources needed for the recovery and launch them into action. Almost simultaneously with identifying and notifying the staff, the full extent of the damage must be assessed. Assessment provides the information necessary to determine what must be done to restore the system to a fully functional state. Next, the process of computer forensics determines how the incident occurred and what happened. These facts emerge as the incident is reconstructed from the data recorded before and during the incident. Next the organization repairs vulnerabilities, addresses any shortcomings in safeguards, and restores the data and services of the systems.

Prioritization of Efforts. As the dust from the incident settles, a natural state of confusion and disbelief follows. This is often referred to as post-traumatic stress disorder or PTSD. One does not have to be involved in a military battle to suffer from this ailment. The fallout from stressful workplace activity is well-documented and the common view is that cyber attacks as well as conflicts of all kinds affect everyone involved. The important thing is to get everyone moving and focused on the task ahead: the restoration of the systems. Each individual involved should begin recovery operations based on the appropriate section of the IRP.

Damage Assessment. The military calls it *battlefield damage assessment*. The medical field calls it *triage*. Whatever the terminology used, **incident damage assessment** is the rapid determination of the scope of the breach of the confidentiality, integrity, and availability of information and information assets during or just following an incident. The process of damage assessment may take mere moments or it may take days or weeks depending on the extent of the damage. The damage caused by an incident can range from minor—a curious hacker snooped around—to extremely severe—a credit card number theft, or the infection of hundreds of computer systems by a worm or virus.

There are several sources of information on the type, scope, and extent of damage. These include system logs, intrusion detection logs, configuration logs and documents, the documentation from the incident response, and the results of a detailed assessment of systems and data storage. Based on these logs and documentation, the IR team must begin to examine the current state of the information and systems and compare them to a known state. Related to the task of incident damage assessment is the field of computer forensics. **Computer forensics** is the process of collecting, analyzing, and preserving computer-related evidence. **Evidence** is the physical object or documented information that proves an action occurred or identifies the intent of a perpetrator. Computer evidence must be carefully collected, documented, and maintained to be acceptable in formal or informal proceedings. Organizations may have informal proceedings when dealing with internal violations of policy or standards of conduct. They may also need to use evidence in formal administrative or legal proceedings, should a perpetrator be brought to justice. Sometimes the fallout from an incident lands in a courtroom for a civil trial. Each of these circumstances requires that individuals who examine the damage incurred receive special training, so that if an incident becomes part of a crime or results in a civil action, the individuals are adequately prepared to participate.

Recovery. Once the extent of the damage has been determined, the recovery process can begin in earnest. The recovery process involves much more than the simple restoration of stolen, damaged, or destroyed data files. It involves the following steps:[26]

1. Identify the vulnerabilities that allowed the incident to occur and spread. Resolve them.
2. Address the safeguards that failed to stop or limit the incident, or were missing from the system in the first place. Install, replace, or upgrade them.
3. Evaluate monitoring capabilities (if present). Improve their detection and reporting methods, or simply install new monitoring capabilities.
4. Restore the data from backups. See the Technical Details boxes on the following topics for more information: 1) data storage and management, 2) system backups and recovery, and 3) RAID. Restoration requires the IR team to understand the backup strategy used by the organization, restore the data contained in backups, and then recreate the data that was created or modified since the last backup.

5. Restore the services and processes in use. Compromised services and processes must be examined, cleaned, and then restored. If services or processes were interrupted during the process of regaining control of the systems, they need to be brought back online.

6. Continuously monitor the system. If an incident happened once, it could easily happen again. Just because the current incident is over doesn't mean the organization is in the clear. Hackers frequently boast of their abilities in chat rooms and dare their peers to match their efforts. If word gets out, others may be tempted to try their hands at the same or different attacks. It is therefore important to maintain vigilance during the entire IR process.

7. Restore the confidence of the members of the organization's communities of interest. It may be advisable to issue a short memorandum outlining the incident, and assuring everyone that the incident was handled and the damage controlled. If the incident was minor, say so. If the incident was major or severely damaged the systems or data, reassure the users that they can expect operations to return to normal shortly. The objective is not to placate or lie, but to prevent panic or confusion from causing additional disruptions to the operations of the organization.

Before returning to routine duties, the IR team must conduct an **after-action review** or AAR. The after-action review is a detailed examination of the events that occurred from first detection to final recovery. All key players review their notes, and verify that the IR documentation is accurate and precise. All team members review their actions during the incident and identify areas in which the IR plan worked, didn't work, or should improve. This allows the team to update the IRP while the needed changes are fresh in their minds. The AAR is documented and can serve as a training case for future staff. It also brings to a close the actions of the IR team.

TECHNICAL DETAILS

Data Storage and Management

To better understand what goes on during incident response or disaster recovery data restoration, you should understand how system backups are created.

Data backup is a complex operation and involves selecting the backup type, establishing backup schedules, and even duplicating data automatically using a variety of redundant array of inexpensive drives (RAID) structures. For more details, see the Technical Details box on RAID.

There are three basic types of backups: full, differential, and incremental. A **full backup** is just that, a full and complete backup of the entire system, including all applications, operating systems components, and data. The advantage of a full backup is that it takes a comprehensive snapshot of the organization's system. The primary disadvantages are that it requires large media to store such a large file, and the backup can be time consuming. A **differential backup** is the storage of all files that have changed or been added since the last full backup. The differential backup works faster and uses less storage space than the full backup, but each daily differential backup is larger and slower than that of the day before. For example, if you conduct a full backup on Sunday, then Monday's backup contains all the files that have changed since Sunday, and Tuesday's backup contains all

continued

the files that have changed since Sunday as well, including Monday. By Friday, the file size has grown substantially. Also, if one backup is corrupt, the previous day's backup contains almost all of the same information. The third type of backup is the incremental backup. The **incremental backup** only archives the files that have been modified that day, and thus requires less space and time than the differential. The downside to incremental backups is that if an incident occurs, multiple backups would be needed to restore the full system.

The first component of a backup and recovery system is the scheduling of the backups, coupled with the storage of these backups. The most common schedule is a daily on-site incremental or differential backup, with a weekly off-site full backup. Most backups are conducted during twilight hours, when systems activity is lowest, and the probability of user interruption is limited. There are also some other popular methods for selecting the files to back up. These include grandfather/father/son and Towers of Hanoi (see the Technical Details box on the general strategies of backups and recovery).

Regardless of the strategy employed, some fundamental advice must be heeded. All on-site and off-site storage must be secured. It is common practice to use fireproof safes or filing cabinets to store tapes. The off-site storage in particular must be in a safe location, such as a safety deposit box in a bank or a professional backup and recovery service. The trunk of the administrator's car is not considered secure off-site storage. It is also important to provide a conditioned environment for the tapes, preferably an airtight, humidity-free, static-free storage container. Each tape must be clearly labeled, and write-protected. Because tapes frequently wear out, it is important to retire them periodically and introduce new media.

Backup Media. The brief overview of backup media and strategies in the Technical Details sections of this chapter provides additional insight into the backup management process. Most common types of backup media include digital audio tapes (DAT), quarter-inch cartridge drives (QIC), 8mm tape, and digital linear tape (DLT). Each type of tape has its restrictions and advantages. Backups can also be performed to CD-ROM and DVD options (CD-R, CD-RW, and DVD-RW), specialized drives (Zip, Jaz, and Bernouli), or tape arrays.

TECHNICAL DETAILS

System Backups and Recovery—General Strategies

Two of the more popular methods for selecting the files to back up are outlined below.

Grandfather, father, son: Assuming that backups are taken every night, with five tapes used every week, this method is based on a 15-tape strategy.

The first week uses the first five tapes (set A).

The second week uses the second five tapes (set B).

The third week uses a third set of five tapes (set C).

The fourth week, the set A tapes are reused.

continued

The fifth week, the set B tapes are reused.

The sixth week, the set C tapes are reused.

Every second or third month, a set of tapes is taken out of the cycle for permanent storage and a new set is brought in. This method equalizes the wear and tear on the tapes, and helps to prevent tape failure.

Towers of Hanoi: The Towers of Hanoi is more complex and is actually based on mathematical principles. With this method, different tapes are used with different frequencies. This strategy assumes a five-tape per week strategy, with a backup each night.

The first night tape A is used.

The second night tape B is used.

The third night tape A is reused.

The fourth night tape C is used.

The fifth night tape A is reused.

The sixth night tape B is reused.

The seventh night tape A is reused.

The eighth night tape D is used.

The ninth night tape A is reused.

The tenth night tape B is reused.

The eleventh night tape A is reused.

The twelfth night tape C is reused.

The thirteenth night tape A is reused.

The fourteenth night tape B is reused.

The fifteenth night tape A is reused.

The sixteenth night tape E is used.

Tape A is used for incremental backups after its first use and must be monitored closely as it tends to wear out faster than the other tapes.

TECHNICAL DETAILS

System Backups and Recovery—RAID

One form of data backup for online usage is the **Redundant Array of Inexpensive Drives (RAID)** system. Unlike tape backups, RAID uses a number of hard drives to store information across multiple drive units. This spreads out data and minimizes the impact of a single drive failure. There are nine established RAID configurations:

RAID Level 0. This is not a form of redundant storage. RAID 0 creates one larger logical volume across several available hard disk drives and stores the data in segments, called stripes, across all the disk drives in the array. This is also often called **disk striping** without parity and is frequently used to combine smaller drive volumes into fewer, larger volumes. Unfortunately, failure of one drive may make all data inaccessible.

RAID Level 1. Commonly called **disk mirroring**, RAID Level 1 uses twin drives in a computer system. The computer records all data to both drives simultaneously, providing a backup if the primary drive fails. It's a rather expensive and inefficient use of

continued

media. A variation of mirroring is called **disk duplexing**. With mirroring, the same drive controller manages both drives, but with disk duplexing each drive has its own controller. Mirroring is often used to create duplicate copies of operating system volumes for high-availability systems.

RAID Level 2. This is a specialized form of disk striping with parity, and is not widely used. It uses a specialized parity coding mechanism known as the Hamming Code to store stripes of data on multiple data drives and corresponding redundant error correction on separate error correcting drives. This approach allows the reconstruction of data in the event some of the data or redundant parity information is lost. There are no commercial implementations of RAID Level 2.

RAID Levels 3 and 4. RAID 3 is byte-level and RAID 4 is block-level striping of data in which the data is stored in segments on dedicated data drives, and parity information is stored on a separate drive. As with RAID 0, one large volume is used for the data, but the parity drive operates independently to provide error recovery.

RAID LEVEL 5. This form of RAID is most commonly used in organizations that balance safety and redundancy against the costs of acquiring and operating the systems. It is similar to RAID 3 and 4 in that it stripes the data across multiple drives, but there is no dedicated parity drive. Instead, segments of data are interleaved with parity data and are written across all of the drives in the set. RAID 5 drives can also be **hot swapped**, meaning they can be replaced without taking the entire system down.

RAID Level 6. This is a combination of RAID 1 and RAID 5.

RAID Level 7. This is a variation on RAID 5 in which the array works as a single virtual drive. RAID Level 7 is sometimes performed by running special software over RAID 5 hardware.

RAID Level 10. This is a combination of RAID 1 and RAID 0.

Additional redundancy can be provided by mirroring entire servers called redundant servers or **server fault tolerance** (SFTIII in Novell).

Automated Response

New series of technologies and capabilities are emerging in the field of incident response. Some of these build on traditional strategies and extend their capabilities and functions. Although traditional systems were configured to detect incidents and then notify the human administrator, new systems can respond to the incident threat autonomously, based on preconfigured options. A more complete discussion of these technologies is presented in Chapter 7.

The downsides of current automated response systems may outweigh their benefits. Legal issues associated with tracking individuals through the systems of others have yet to be resolved. What if the hacker that is backtracked is actually a compromised system running an automated attack? What are the legal liabilities of a counterattack? How can security administrators condemn a hacker, when they themselves may have illegally hacked systems to track the hacker? These issues are complex but must be resolved to give the security professionals better tools to combat incidents.

Disaster Recovery Planning

As discussed in the beginning of this chapter, disaster recovery planning (DRP) is planning the preparation for and recovery from a disaster, whether natural or man-made. The contingency planning team must make the distinction between disasters and incidents. It may not be possible to make this distinction until an attack occurs; often an event that is initially classified as an incident is later determined to be a disaster. When this happens, the organization may change how it is responding and take action to secure its most valuable assets to preserve value for the longer term even at the risk of more disruption in the short term. Again, the key emphasis of a DRP is to reestablish operations at the primary site, the location at which the organization performs its business. The goal is to make things whole or as they were before the disaster.

The Disaster Recovery Plan

Similar in structure to the IRP, the DRP provides detailed guidance in the event of a disaster. It is organized by the type or nature of the anticipated disaster and specifies recovery procedures during and after a disaster. It also provides details on the roles and responsibilities of the various individuals involved in the disaster recovery effort, and identifies the personnel and agencies that must be notified. Just as the IRP must be tested, so must the DRP, using the same testing mechanisms. At a minimum, the DRP must be reviewed during a walk-through or talk-through on a periodic basis.

Many of the same precepts of incident response apply to disaster recovery:

1. There must be a clear establishment of priorities. The first priority is always the preservation of human life. Data and systems immediately fall to the wayside if the disaster threatens the lives, health, or welfare of the employees of the organization or members of the community in which the organization operates. Only after all employees and neighbors have been safeguarded can the disaster recovery team attend to nonhuman asset protection.

2. There must be a clear delegation of roles and responsibilities. Everyone who is assigned to the DR team should be aware of his or her expected actions during a disaster. Some people are responsible for coordinating with local authorities, such as fire, police, and medical staff. Others are responsible for the evacuation of personnel, if required. And still others are tasked simply to pack up and leave.

3. Someone must initiate the alert roster and notify key personnel. Those to be notified may be the fire, police, or medical authorities mentioned earlier. They may also include insurance agencies, disaster teams like the Red Cross, and management teams.

4. Someone must be tasked with the documentation of the disaster. Just as in an IR reaction, someone must begin recording what happened to serve as a basis for later determination of why and how the event occurred.

5. If and only if it is possible, attempts must be made to mitigate the impact of the disaster on the operations of the organization. If everyone is safe, and all needed authorities have been notified, some individuals can be tasked with the evacuation of physical assets. Some can be responsible for making sure all systems are securely shut down to prevent further loss of data.

Crisis Management

Disasters are, of course, larger in scale and less manageable than incidents, but the planning processes are the same, and in many cases are conducted simultaneously. What may truly distinguish the incident from the disaster are the actions of the response teams. An incident response team typically rushes to duty stations or to the office from home. The first act is to reach for the IRP to begin reacting. A disaster recovery team may not have the luxury of flipping through a binder to see what must be done. The disaster recovery personnel must know their responses without any supporting documentation. This is a function of preparation, training, and rehearsal. You probably all remember the frequent fire, tornado, or hurricane drills—and even the occasional nuclear blast drills—from your public school days. Just because you move from school to the business world doesn't lessen the threat of a fire or other disaster. As a result, DRP rehearsals are just as important now as then.

The actions taken during and after a disaster are referred to as **crisis management**. Crisis management differs dramatically from incident response, as it focuses first and foremost on the people involved. Secondly, it addresses the viability of the business. The disaster recovery team works closely with the crisis management team. According to Gartner Research, the crisis management team is:

> "responsible for managing the event from an enterprise perspective and covers the following major activities:
>
> - Supporting personnel and their loved ones during the crisis
> - Determining the event's impact on normal business operations and, if necessary, making a disaster declaration
> - Keeping the public informed about the event and the actions being taken to ensure the recovery of personnel and the enterprise
> - Communicating with major customers, suppliers, partners, regulatory agencies, industry organizations, the media, and other interested parties."[27]

The crisis management team should establish a base of operations or command center to support communications until the disaster has ended. The crisis management team includes individuals from all functional areas of the organization to facilitate communications and cooperation. Some key areas of crisis management include:

- Verifying personnel head count: Everyone must be accounted for, including those on vacations, leaves of absence, and business trips.
- Checking the alert roster: Alert rosters and general personnel phone lists are used to notify individuals whose assistance may be needed, or simply to tell employees not to report to work, until the disaster is over.
- Checking emergency information cards: It is important that each employee has in his possession two types of emergency information cards. The first is personal emergency information that lists whom to notify in case of an emergency (next of kin), medical conditions, and a form of identification. The second type is a set of instructions on what to do in the event of an emergency. This mini-snapshot of the disaster recovery plan should contain, at a minimum, a contact number or hot line, emergency services numbers (fire, police, medical), evacuation and assembly locations (storm shelters, for example), the name and number of the disaster recovery coordinator, and any other needed information.

Crisis management must balance the needs of the employees with the needs of the business in providing personnel with support for personal and family issues during disasters.

Recovery Operations

Reaction to a disaster can vary so widely that it is impossible to describe the process with any accuracy. As a result, it is up to each organization to examine the scenarios developed at the start of contingency planning, and determine how to respond.

Should the physical facilities be spared after the disaster, the disaster recovery team should begin the restoration of systems and data to reestablish full operational capability. If the organization's facilities do not survive, alternative actions must be taken until new facilities can be acquired. When a disaster threatens the viability of the organization at the primary site, the disaster recovery process transitions into the process of business continuity planning.

Business Continuity Planning

Business continuity planning prepares an organization to reestablish critical business operations during a disaster that affects operations at the primary site. If a disaster has rendered the current location unusable for continued operations, there must be a plan to allow the business to continue to function. Not every business needs such a plan or such facilities. Small companies or fiscally sound organizations may have the latitude simply to cease operations until the physical facilities can be restored. But organizations such as manufacturing and retail may not have this option, because they depend on physical types of commerce and may not be able to relocate operations.

Developing Continuity Programs

Once the incident response plans and disaster recovery plans are in place, the organization needs to consider finding temporary facilities to support the continued viability of the business in the event of a disaster. The development of the BCP is somewhat simpler than that of the IRP or DRP, in that it consists primarily of selecting a continuity strategy and integrating the off-site data storage and recovery functions into this strategy. Some of the components of the BCP could already be integral to the normal operations of the organization, such as an off-site backup service. Others require special consideration and negotiation. The first part of business continuity planning is performed when the joint DRP/BCP plan is developed. The identification of critical business functions and the resources needed to support them is the cornerstone of BCP. When a disaster strikes, these functions are the first to be reestablished at the alternate site. The contingency planning team needs to appoint a group of individuals to evaluate and compare the various alternatives available, and recommend which strategy should be selected and implemented. The strategy selected usually involves some form of off-site facility, which should be inspected, configured, secured, and tested on a periodic basis. The selection should be reviewed periodically to determine if a superior alternative has emerged or if the organization needs a different solution.

Continuity Strategies

There are a number of strategies from which an organization can choose when planning for business continuity. The determining factor in selection between these options is usually cost. In general there are three exclusive options: hot sites, warm sites, and cold sites; and three shared functions: time-share, service bureaus, and mutual agreements.

Hot Sites. A **hot site** is a fully configured computer facility, with all services, communications links, and physical plant operations including heating and air conditioning. Hot sites duplicate computing resources, peripherals, phone systems, applications, and workstations. A hot site is the pinnacle of contingency planning, a duplicate facility that needs only the latest data backups and the personnel to function as a fully operational twin of the original. When needed, a hot site can be operational in a matter of minutes, and in some cases may be built to perform a fail-over seamlessly by picking up the processing load from a failing site. The hot site is therefore the most expensive alternative available. Other disadvantages include the need to provide maintenance for all the systems and equipment in the hot site, as well as physical and information security. However, if the organization desires a 24/7 capability for near real-time recovery, the hot site is the way to go.

Warm Sites. The next step down from the hot site is the warm site. A **warm site** provides many of the same services and options of the hot site. However, it typically does not include the actual applications the company needs, or the applications may not yet be installed and configured. A warm site frequently includes computing equipment and peripherals with servers but not client workstations. A warm site has many of the advantages of a hot site, but at a lower cost. The downside is that it requires hours, if not days, to make a warm site fully functional.

Cold Sites. The final dedicated site option is the cold site. A **cold site** provides only rudimentary services and facilities. No computer hardware or peripherals are provided. All communications services must be installed after the site is occupied. Basically a cold site is an empty room with heating, air conditioning, and electricity. Everything else is an option. Although the obvious disadvantages may preclude selection, a cold site is better than nothing. The main advantage of cold sites over hot and warm sites is in the area of cost. Furthermore, if the warm or hot site is based on a shared capability, not having to contend with organizations sharing space and equipment should a widespread disaster occur may make the cold site a more controllable option even if it is slower to be brought into action. In spite of these advantages, some organizations feel it would be easier to lease a new space on short notice than pay maintenance fees on a cold site.

Time-shares. The first of the three sharing options is the time-share. Just as the name indicates, a **time-share** is a hot, warm, or cold site that is leased in conjunction with a business partner or sister organization. The time-share allows the organization to maintain a disaster recovery and business continuity option, but at a reduced overall cost. The advantages are identical to the type of site selected (hot, warm, or cold). The primary disadvantage is the possibility that more than one organization involved in the time-share may need the facility simultaneously. Other disadvantages include the need to stock the facility with the equipment and data from all organizations involved, the negotiations for arranging the time-share, and associated agreements, should one or more parties decide to cancel the agreement or to sublease its options. This option is much like agreeing to co-lease an apartment with a group of friends. One can only hope the organizations remain on amiable terms, as they would all have physical access to each other's data.

Service Bureaus. A **service bureau** is an agency that provides a service for a fee. In the case of disaster recovery and continuity planning, the service is the agreement to provide physical facilities in the event of a disaster. These types of agencies also frequently provide off-site data storage for a fee. With service bureaus, contracts can be carefully created, specifying exactly what the organization needs, without the need to reserve dedicated facilities. A service agreement usually guarantees space when needed, even if the service bureau has to acquire additional space in the event of a widespread disaster. This option is much like the rental car clause in your car insurance policy. The disadvantage is that it is a service, and must be renegotiated periodically. Also, using a service bureau can be quite expensive.

Mutual Agreements. A **mutual agreement** is a contract between two or more organizations that specifies how each will assist the other in the event of a disaster. It stipulates that each organization is obligated to provide the necessary facilities, resources, and services until the receiving organization is able to recover from the disaster. This type of arrangement is much like moving in with relatives or even friends: it doesn't take long to outstay your welcome. While this may seem like a viable solution, many organizations balk at the idea of having to fund (even in the short term) duplicate services and resources should the other agreeing parties need them. The arrangement is ideal if you need the assistance, but not if you are the host. Still, mutual agreements between divisions of the same parent company, between subordinate and superior organizations, or between business partners may be a cost-effective solution.

Other Options. There are also some specialized alternatives available, such as a rolling mobile site configured in the payload area of a tractor or trailer, or externally stored resources. These can consist of a rental storage area containing duplicate or second-generation equipment to be extracted in the event of an emergency. An organization can also contract with a prefabricated building contractor for immediate, temporary facilities (mobile offices) to be placed on site in the event of a disaster. At any rate, these alternatives should be considered when evaluating strategy options.

Off-Site Disaster Data Storage. To get these types of sites to be up and running quickly, the organization must be able to move data into the new site's systems. There are a number of options for getting operations up and running quickly, and some of these options can be used for purposes other than restoration of continuity. These include electronic vaulting, remote journaling, and database shadowing. These options are discussed in detail below and, of course, are in addition to the traditional backup methods mentioned earlier.

- Electronic vaulting: The transfer of large batches of data to an off-site facility is called **electronic vaulting**. This transfer is usually conducted through leased lines, or services provided for a fee. The receiving server archives the data until the next electronic vaulting process is received. Some disaster recovery companies specialize in electronic vaulting services.

- Remote journaling: The transfer of live transactions to an off-site facility is called **remote journaling**. It differs from electronic vaulting in that 1) only transactions are transferred, not archived data, and 2) the transfer is in real-time. Electronic vaulting is much like a traditional backup, with a dump of data to the off-site storage, but remote journaling involves activities on a systems level, much like server fault tolerance, with the data written to two locations simultaneously.

- Database shadowing: An improvement to the process of remote journaling, **database shadowing** not only processes duplicate, real-time data storage, but also duplicates the databases at the remote site to multiple servers. It combines the server fault tolerance mentioned earlier with remote journaling, writing three or more copies of the database simultaneously.

Model for a Consolidated Contingency Plan

To facilitate understanding of the structure and use of the incident response and disaster recovery plans, this section presents a comprehensive model that incorporates the basics of each type of planning in a single document. It is not uncommon for small- to medium-sized organizations to use such a document. The single document set supports concise planning and encourages smaller organizations to develop, test, and use IR and DR plans. The model presented is based on analyses of disaster recovery and incident response plans of dozens of organizations.

The Planning Document

The first document created for the IR and DR document set is the incident reaction document. The key players in an organization, typically the top computing executive, systems administrators, security administrator, and a few functional area managers, get together to develop the IR and DR plan. The first task is to establish the responsibility for managing the document, which typically falls to the security administrator. A secretary is appointed to document the activities and results of the planning session. First, independent incident response and disaster recovery teams are formed. For this model, the two groups include the same individuals as the planning committee, plus additional systems administrators. Next, the roles and responsibilities are outlined for each team member. At this point, general responsibilities are being addressed, not procedural activities. The alert roster is developed as are lists of critical agencies, should they be needed.

Next, the group identifies and prioritizes threats to the organization's information and information systems. Because of the integrated nature of the IR, DR, and BCP, the overall contingency planning process addresses areas within each. These are the six steps in the consolidated contingency planning process:[28]

1. Identifying the mission- or business-critical functions: The organization identifies those areas of operation that must continue in a disaster to enable the organization to operate. These must be prioritized from most critical to least critical to allow optimal allocation of resources (time, money, and personnel) in the event of a disaster.

2. Identifying the resources that support the critical functions: For each function, the organization identifies the resources required by that function to be successful. These resources can include people, computing capability, applications, data, services, physical infrastructure, and documentation.

3. Anticipating potential contingencies or disasters: The organization brainstorms potential disasters and determines what functions they would affect.

4. Selecting contingency planning strategies: The organization identifies methods of dealing with each anticipated scenario and outlines a plan to prepare for and react to the disaster.

Armed with this information, the actual consolidated plan begins to take shape. For each incident scenario, three sets of procedures are created and documented:

- The procedures that must be performed *during the incident*. These procedures are grouped and assigned to individuals. The planning committee begins to draft a set of these function-specific procedures.

- The procedures that must be performed immediately *after the incident has ceased*. Again, separate functional areas may be assigned different procedures.

- The procedures that must be performed to *prepare for the incident*. These are the details of the data backup schedules, the disaster recovery preparation, training schedules, testing plans, copies of service agreements, and business continuity plans if any.

At this level, the business continuity plan can consist simply of additional material about a service bureau that can store off-site data via electronic vaulting with an agreement to provide office space and lease equipment as needed.

Finally, the IR portion of the plan is assembled. Sections detailing the organization's DRP and BCP efforts are placed after the incident response sections. Critical information as outlined in these planning sections is recorded, including information on alternate sites. Figure 5-24 shows some specific formats for the contingency plan. Multiple copies for each functional area are created, catalogued, and signed out to responsible individuals.

5. Implementing the contingency strategies: The organization signs contracts, acquires services, and implements backup programs that integrate the new strategy into the organization's routine operations.

6. Testing and revising the strategy: The organization periodically tests and revises the plan.

These are the words that all contingency planners live by: *plan for the worst and hope for the best*.

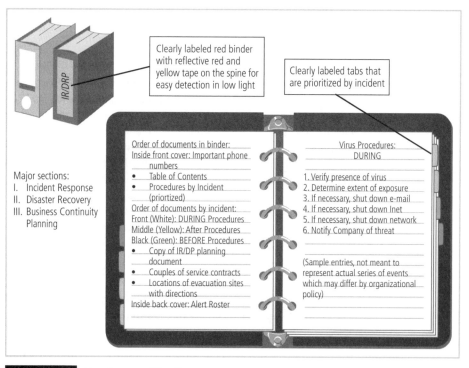

Clearly labeled red binder with reflective red and yellow tape on the spine for easy detection in low light

Clearly labeled tabs that are prioritized by incident

IR/DRP

Major sections:
I. Incident Response
II. Disaster Recovery
III. Business Continuity Planning

Order of documents in binder:
Inside front cover: Important phone numbers
• Table of Contents
• Procedures by Incident (priortized)
Order of documents by incident:
Front (White): DURING Procedures
Middle (Yellow): After Procedures
Black (Green): BEFORE Procedures
• Copy of IR/DP planning document
• Couples of service contracts
• Locations of evacuation sites with directions
Inside back cover: Alert Roster

Virus Procedures:
DURING

1. Verify presence of virus
2. Determine extent of exposure
3. If necessary, shut down e-mail
4. If necessary, shut down Inet
5. If necessary, shut down network
6. Notify Company of threat

(Sample entries, not meant to represent actual series of events which may differ by organizational policy)

FIGURE 5-24   Contingency Plan Format

Law Enforcement Involvement

There may come a time when an incident, whether an attack or a breach of policy, constitutes a violation of law. Perhaps what was originally believed to be an accident turns out to be an attempt at corporate espionage, sabotage, or theft. When an organization considers involving law enforcement, there are several questions that must be answered. When should the organization get law enforcement involved? What level of law enforcement agency should be involved—local, state, or federal? What happens when a law enforcement agency is involved? Some of these questions are best answered by the organization's legal department. But what if the organization doesn't have a legal department, or the security administrators are unable to contact the legal department in the midst of an attack?

Federal Authorities

Selecting which level of law enforcement to involve depends in part on the type of crime suspected. The Federal Bureau of Investigation deals with many computer crimes that are categorized as felonies. There are other federal agencies available to deal with various criminal activity, including the U.S. Secret Service for crimes involving U.S. currency, counterfeiting, credit cards, and identity theft. The U.S. Treasury Department has a bank fraud investigation unit, and the Securities and Exchange Commission has investigation and fraud control units as well. However, because of the heavy load of cases these agencies must handle, they typically give priority to incidents that affect the national critical infrastructure or that have significant economic impact. The FBI Web site states that the FBI Computer Intrusion Squad pursues "the investigation of cyber-based attacks, primarily unauthorized access (intrusion) and denial-of-service, directed at the major components of this country's critical information, military, and economic infrastructures. Critical infrastructure includes the nation's power grids and power-supply systems, transportation control systems, money transfer and accounting systems, defense-related systems, and telecommunications networks. Additionally, the Squad investigates cyber attacks directed at private industry and public institutions that maintain information vital to national security and/or the economic success of the nation."[29] In other words, if the crime isn't directed at or doesn't affect the national infrastructure, the FBI may not be able to assist as effectively as state or local agencies. As a rule of thumb, however, if the crime crosses state lines, it's a federal matter. The FBI may also become involved at the request of a state agency, if it has available personnel.

State Investigative Services

Many states have their own version of the FBI. In Georgia, it's called the Georgia Bureau of Investigation, and in other states it may be a division of the State Police. (FYI: in Texas, it is the legendary Texas Rangers.) The GBI arrests individuals, serves warrants, and enforces laws that regulate property owned by the state or any state agency. The GBI also assists local law enforcement officials in pursuing criminals and enforcing state laws. Some organizations may reside in states whose investigative offices do not have a special agency dedicated to computer crime. If, in these cases, there is a state law pertinent to computer crimes, the state agency itself handles the case. The state agency also comes in when its assistance is requested by a local law enforcement office, and in some cases when it is requested by businesses or nonprofit agencies.

Local Law Enforcement

Each county and city has its own law enforcement agency. These agencies enforce all local and state laws and handle suspects and security crime scenes for state and federal cases. Local law enforcement agencies seldom have a computer crimes task force, but the investigative (detective) units are quite capable of processing crime scenes, and handling most common criminal activities, such as physical theft or trespassing, damage to property, and the apprehension and processing of suspects of computer related crimes.

Benefits and Drawbacks of Law Enforcement Involvement

Involving law enforcement agencies has both advantages and disadvantages. The agencies may be much better able to process evidence than a particular organization. In fact, unless the security forces in the organization have been trained in processing evidence and computer forensics, they may do more harm than good in extracting the necessary information to legally convict a suspected criminal. Law enforcement agencies are also prepared to handle the warrants and subpoenas necessary to documenting a case. They are also adept at obtaining statements from witnesses, affidavits, and other required documents. Law enforcement personnel can be a security administrator's greatest ally in the war on computer crime. It is therefore important to get to know your local and state officials charged with enforcing information security laws, before you have to make a call announcing a suspected crime. Most state and federal agencies even offer awareness programs, including guest speakers at conferences, and programs like the InfraGard program of the FBI's National Information Protection Center (*www.infragard.net/*). These agents appreciate the challenges facing security administrators, who often have a law enforcement background.

On the downside, once a law enforcement agency takes over a case, the organization loses complete control over the chain of events, the collection of information and evidence, and the prosecution of suspects. Someone the organization believes to deserve censure and dismissal may face criminal charges, whose prosecution may make public the intricate details of their crimes. The organization may not be informed about the progress of the case for weeks or even months. Equipment vital to the organization's business may be tagged as evidence, to be removed, stored, and preserved until it can be examined for possible support for the criminal case.

However, if an organization detects a criminal act, it is legally obligated to involve the appropriate law enforcement officials. Failure to do so can subject the organization and its officers to prosecution as accessories to the crimes, or as impeding the course of an investigation. It is up to the security administrator to ask questions of their law enforcement counterparts to determine when each agency wishes to be involved, and specifically which crimes are to be addressed by each agency.

Chapter Summary

- There are a number of published information security frameworks, such as those from government organizations as well as those from private organizations and professional societies, that supply information on best practices for their members.

- The hybrid framework is a methodology that organizations can use to fill in the implementation details to create a security system blueprint and address almost all of the components of a solid information security plan.

- One of the foundations of security architectures is the requirement to implement security in layers. This layered approach is referred to as defense in depth.

- A security perimeter defines the edge between the outer limit of an organization's security and the beginning of the outside world. In an effort to detect unauthorized activity within the inner network or on individual machines, an organization may wish to implement Intrusion Detection Systems (IDS).

- Management must consider policies as the basis for all information security planning, design, and deployment. Policies direct how issues should be addressed and technologies used.

- Standards are more detailed than policies and describe steps to be taken for an organization to conform to policies.

- Management must define three types of security policy: general or security program policy, issue-specific security policies, and systems-specific security policies.

- Policy documents must be properly managed. Good management practices require an individual responsible for reviews, a schedule of reviews, a method for making recommendations for reviews, and a policy issuance and revision date.

- Information security policy is best disseminated in a comprehensive security education, training, and awareness (SETA) program. One of the least frequently implemented but most beneficial programs is the security awareness program. A security awareness program is designed to keep information security at the forefront of the users' minds.

- Contingency planning (CP) comprises a set of plans designed to ensure the effective reaction to and recovery from an attack and the subsequent restoration to normal modes of business operations.

- There are six steps to contingency planning: identifying the mission- or business-critical functions, identifying the resources that support the critical functions, anticipating potential contingencies or disasters, selecting contingency planning strategies, implementing the contingency strategies, and testing and revising the strategy.

- Organizations must develop disaster recovery plans, incident response plans, and business continuity plans using the business impact analysis process, which consists of five stages: identification and prioritization of the threat attack, business unit analysis and prioritization, attack success scenario development, potential damage assessment, and subordinate plan classification.

- Incident response planning consists of four phases: incident planning, incident detection, incident reaction, and incident recovery.

- Disaster recovery planning outlines the response to and recovery from a disaster, whether natural or man-made.

- It is important to understand when and if to involve law enforcement. Getting to know local and state law enforcement can assist in these decisions.

Review Questions

1. How can a security framework assist in the design and implementation of a security infrastructure?

2. Where can a security administrator go to find information on established security frameworks?

3. What are the inherent problems with ISO 17799, and why hasn't the U.S. adopted it? What are the recommended alternatives?

4. What documents are available from the NIST Computer Resource Center, and how can they support the development of a security framework?

5. Can an organization that does not use the VISA cardholder protection system in conjunction with the processing of credit cards benefit from VISA's security framework? How?

6. What benefit can a private, for-profit agency derive from best practices designed for federal agencies?

7. What resources are available on the Web that can aid an organization in developing best practices as part of a security framework?

8. Briefly describe management, operational, and technical controls, and explain when each would be applied as part of a security framework?

9. What are the differences between a policy, a standard, and a practice? What are the three types of security policies? Where would each be used? What type of policy would be needed to guide use of the Web? E-mail? Office equipment for personal use?

10. Who is ultimately responsible for managing a technology? Who is responsible for enforcing policy that affects the use of a technology?

11. What is contingency planning? How is it different from routine management planning? What are the components of contingency planning?

12. When is IRP used?

13. When is DRP used?

14. When is BCP used? How do you determine when to use IRP, DRP, or BCP plans?

15. What are the five elements of a business impact analysis?

16. What are Pipkin's three categories of incident indicators?

17. What is containment, and why is it part of the planning process?

18. What is computer forensics? When are the results of computer forensics used?

19. What is an after-action review? When is it performed? Why is it done?

20. List and describe the six continuity strategies identified in the text.

Exercises

1. Using a graphics program, design several security awareness posters on the following themes: updating antivirus signatures, protecting sensitive information, watching out for e-mail viruses, prohibiting use of company equipment for personal matters, changing and protecting passwords, avoiding social engineering, and protecting software copyrights. What other areas can you come up with?

2. Search the Web for a listing of security education and training programs in your area. Keep a list and see which category has the most examples. See if you can determine the costs associated with each example. Which do you feel would be more cost effective in terms of both time and money?

3. Search the Web for examples of issue-specific security policies. What types of policies can you find? Draft a simple issue-specific policy using the format provided in the text that outlines "Fair and Responsible Use of College Computers" and is based on the rules and regulations you have been provided with in your institution. Does your school have a similar policy? Does it contain all the elements listed in the text?

4. Use your library or the Web to find a reported natural disaster that occurred at least 180 days ago. From the news accounts, determine if local or national officials had prepared disaster plans and if these plans were used. See if you can determine how the plans helped the officials improve the response to the disaster. How do the plans help the recovery?

5. Classify each of the following occurrences as an incident or disaster. If an occurrence is a disaster, determine whether or not business continuity plans would be called into play.

   a. A hacker gets into the network and deletes files from a server.
   b. A fire breaks out in the storeroom and sets off sprinklers on that floor. Some computers are damaged, but the fire is contained.
   c. A tornado hits a local power company, and the company will be without power for three to five days.
   d. Employees go on strike, and the company could be without critical workers for weeks.
   e. A disgruntled employee takes a critical server home, sneaking it out after hours.

   For each of the scenarios (a–e), describe the steps necessary to restore operations. Indicate whether or not law enforcement would be involved.

Case Exercises

Charlie sat at his desk the morning after his nightmare. He had answered the most pressing e-mail in his Inbox and had a piping hot cup of coffee at his elbow. He looked down at a blank legal pad ready to make notes about what to do in case his nightmare became reality.

Questions:

1. What would be the first note you would write down if you were Charlie?
2. What else should be on Charlie's list?

Endnotes

1. Johnson, Carrie (2002). "Enron Auditor Admits Crime. Andersen's Duncan Ordered Shredding." May 14, viewed online 3/30/04 at <*http://foi.missouri.edu/enronandetal/ duncantest1.html*>.
2. Beltran, Luisa (2002). "Andersen exec: shredding began after e-mail." January 21, 2002. Viewed online 3/15/04 at <*http://money.cnn.com/2002/01/21/companies/enron_odom/*>.
3. Charles Cresson Wood. "Integrated Approach Includes Information Security." *Security* 37, no. 2 (February 2000): 43–44.
4. National Institute of Standards and Technology. *An Introduction to Computer Security: The NIST Handbook.* SP 800-12.
5. National Institute of Standards and Technology. *An Introduction to Computer Security: The NIST Handbook.* SP 800-12.
6. Robert J. Aalberts, Anthony M. Townsend, and Michael E. Whitman. "Considerations for an Effective Telecommunications Use Policy." *Communications of the ACM* 42, no. 6 (June 1999): 101–109.
7. NetIQ Security Technologies, Inc. "Enterprise Security Infrastructure Solution." *NetIQ Online.* [Cited 25 March 2004]. Available from the World Wide Web <*http://www.netiq.com/products/*>.
8. National Institute of Standards and Technology. *Information Security Management, Code of Practice for Information Security Management.* ISO/IEC 17799. (6 December 2001).
9. National Institute of Standards and Technology. *Information Security Management, Code of Practice for Information Security Management.* ISO/IEC 17799. (6 December 2001).
10. National Institute of Standards and Technology. *Information Security Management, Code of Practice for Information Security Management.* ISO/IEC 17799. (6 December 2001).

11. National Institute of Standards and Technology. *Information Security Management, Code of Practice for Information Security Management.* ISO/IEC 17799. (6 December 2001).

12. National Institute of Standards and Technology. *Information Security Management, Code of Practice for Information Security Management.* ISO/IEC 17799. (6 December 2001).

13. National Institute of Standards and Technology. *Generally Accepted Principles and Practices for Securing Information Technology Systems.* SP 800-14. (September 1996).

14. National Institute of Standards and Technology, *Generally Accepted Principles and Practices for Securing Information Technology Systems.* SP 800-14. (September 1996).

15. National Institute of Standards and Technology, *Guide for Developing Security Plans for Information Technology Systems.* SP 800-18. December 1998.

16. B. Fraser, *Site Security Handbook - RFC 2196,* (September 1997) WWW Document; [Cited 26 March 2004], *http://www.ietf.org/rfc/rfc2196.txt.*

17. Visa, "Cardholder Information Security Program," Visa Online, [Cited 24 June 2002]; available from the World Wide Web *http://www.usa.visa.com/business/merchants/ cisp_index.html.*

18. HumanFirewall.org, "Building a Human Firewall," *Human Firewall Online,* (2001) WWW Document; [Cited 26 March 2004]; available from the World Wide Web *http://www.humanfirewall.org/.*

19. Marianne Swanson, *Security Self-Assessment Guide for Information Technology Systems - NIST Special Publication 800-26,* (November 2001) WWW Document, [Cited 26 March 2004], *http://csrc.nist.gov/publications/nistpubs/800-26/sp800-26.pdf.*

20. National Institute of Standards and Technology, *An Introduction to Computer Security: The NIST Handbook.* SP 800-12.

21. National Institute of Standards and Technology, *An Introduction to Computer Security: The NIST Handbook.* SP 800-12.

22. William R. King and Paul Gray, *The Management of Information Systems* (Chicago: Dryden Press, 1989), 359.

23. Ronald L. Krutz and Russell Dean Vines, *The CISSP Prep Guide: Mastering the Ten Domains of Computer Security* (New York: John Wiley and Sons Inc., 2001), 288.

24. Richard Marcinko and John Weisman, *Designation Gold* (New York: Pocket Books, 1998), preface.

25. D. L. Pipkin, *Information Security: Protecting the Global Enterprise.* (Upper Saddle River, NJ: Prentice Hall 2000) 256.

26. D. L. Pipkin, *Information Security: Protecting the Global Enterprise.* (Upper Saddle River, NJ: Prentice Hall, 2000), 285.

27. Roberta Witty, "What is Crisis Management?" *Gartner Online* (19 September 2001) [Cited 26 June 2002]; available from the World Wide Web *http://security1.gartner.com/ story.php.id.152.jsp.*

28. NIST, "Special Publication 800-12 An Introduction to Computer Security: The NIST Handbook," (October 1995); accessed 02/10/2002. *http://csrc.nist.gov/publications/ nistpubs/800-12/.*

29. Federal Bureau of Investigation, *Technology Crimes,* (San Francisco); available from the World Wide Web *http://www.fbi.gov/contact/fo/sanfran/sfcomputer.htm.*

Security Technology: Firewalls and VPNs

6

People are the missing link to improving information security.
Technology alone can't solve the challenges of information security.

THE HUMAN FIREWALL COUNCIL

KELVIN URICH CAME INTO THE MEETING ROOM a few minutes late. He took an empty chair at the conference table, flipped open his notepad, and went straight to the point. "Okay, folks, I am scheduled to present the plan to Charlie Moody and the IT planning staff in two weeks. I noticed from the last project status report that you still do not have a consensus for the Internet connection architecture. Without that, we have not selected a technical approach and have not even started costing the project and planning for deployment. We cannot make acquisition and operating budgets, and I will look very silly at the presentation. What seems to be the problem?"

Laverne Nguyen replied, "Well, we seem to have developed a difference of opinion among the members of the architecture team. Some of us want to set up a screened subnet with bastion hosts, and some of the others want to use a screened subnet with proxy servers. That decision will affect the way we specify the new application and Web servers."

Miller Harrison, a contractor brought in to help with this project, picked up where Laverne had left off. "We can't seem to be able to move beyond this impasse, but we have done all the planning up to that point."

"Laverne, what does the consultant's report say?"

Laverne answered. "She proposed two alternative designs and noted that a decision will have to be made between them 'at a later date'."

Miller looked sour.

Kelvin said, "Sounds like we need to make a decision, and soon. Get a conference room reserved for tomorrow, ask the consultant if she can come in for a few hours first thing, and let everyone on the architecture team know we will meet from 8 to 11 on this matter. Now, here is how I think we should prepare for the meeting."

LEARNING OBJECTIVES:

Upon completion of this material, you should be able to:

- Understand the role of physical design in the implementation of a comprehensive security program
- Understand firewall technology and the various approaches to firewall implementation
- Identify the various approaches to remote and dial-up access protection—that is, how these connection methods can be controlled to assure confidentiality of information, and the authentication and authorization of users
- Understand content filtering technology
- Describe the technology that enables the use of Virtual Private Networks

Introduction

As one of the methods of control that go into a well-planned information security program, technical controls are essential in enforcing policy for many IT functions that do not involve direct human control. Networks and computer systems make millions of decisions every second and operate in ways and at speeds that people cannot control in real time. Technical control solutions, properly implemented, can improve an organization's ability to balance the often conflicting objectives of making information more readily and widely available against increasing the information's levels of confidentiality and integrity. This chapter, along with Chapters 7 and 8, describes how many of the more common technical control solutions function, and also explains how they fit into the physical design of an information security program. Those students who want to acquire expertise on the configuration and maintenance of these types of technology-based control systems will require additional education and training in these areas.

Physical Design

In general, the physical design of an information security program is made up of two parts: security technologies (presented in Chapters 6, 7, and 8) and physical security (covered in Chapter 9). Physical design extends the logical design of the information security program—which is found in the information security blueprint and the contingency planning elements—and makes it ready for implementation. Physical design encompasses the selection and implementation of technologies and processes that mitigate risk from threats to the information assets of an organization. Specifically, the physical design process:

- Selects specific technologies to support the information security blueprint
- Identifies complete technical solutions based on these technologies, including deployment, operations, and maintenance elements, to improve the security of the environment
- Designs physical security measures to support the technical solution
- Prepares project plans for the implementation phase that follows

Firewalls

In the commercial and residential construction of buildings, firewalls are concrete or masonry walls that run from the basement through the roof, to prevent a fire from jumping from one section of the building to another. In the construction of aircraft and automobiles, a firewall is an insulated metal barrier that keeps the hot and dangerous moving parts of the motor separate from the inflammable interior where the passengers sit. A **firewall** in an information security program is similar to a building's firewall in that it prevents specific types of information from moving between the outside world, known as the **untrusted network** (e.g., the Internet), and the inside world, known as the **trusted network**. The firewall may be a separate computer system, a software service running on an existing router or server, or a separate network containing a number of supporting devices.

Firewall Categorization Methods

Firewalls can be categorized by processing mode, development era, or structure. There are five major processing-mode categories of firewalls: packet filtering firewalls, application gateways, circuit gateways, MAC layer firewalls, and hybrids.[1] Hybrid firewalls use a combination of the other three methods, and in practice, most firewalls fall into this category, since most use multiple approaches within the same device. Firewalls categorized by which level of technology they employ are identified by generation, with the later generations being more complex and more recently developed. Firewalls categorized by intended structure are typically divided into categories including residential- or commercial-grade, hardware-based, software-based, or appliance-based devices.

Firewalls Categorized by Processing Mode

As mentioned, the five processing modes are:

- Packet filtering
- Application gateways
- Circuit gateways
- MAC layer firewalls
- Hybrids

Packet Filtering.   The first type of firewall is the **packet filtering firewall**, or simply filtering firewall. Filtering firewalls examine the header information of data packets that come into a network. A packet filtering firewall installed on a TCP/IP based network typically functions at the IP level and determines whether to drop a packet (deny) or forward it to the next network connection (allow) based on the rules programmed into the firewall. Packet filtering firewalls examine every incoming packet header and can selectively filter packets based on header information such as destination address, source address, packet type, and other key information. Figure 6-1 shows the structure of an IP packet.

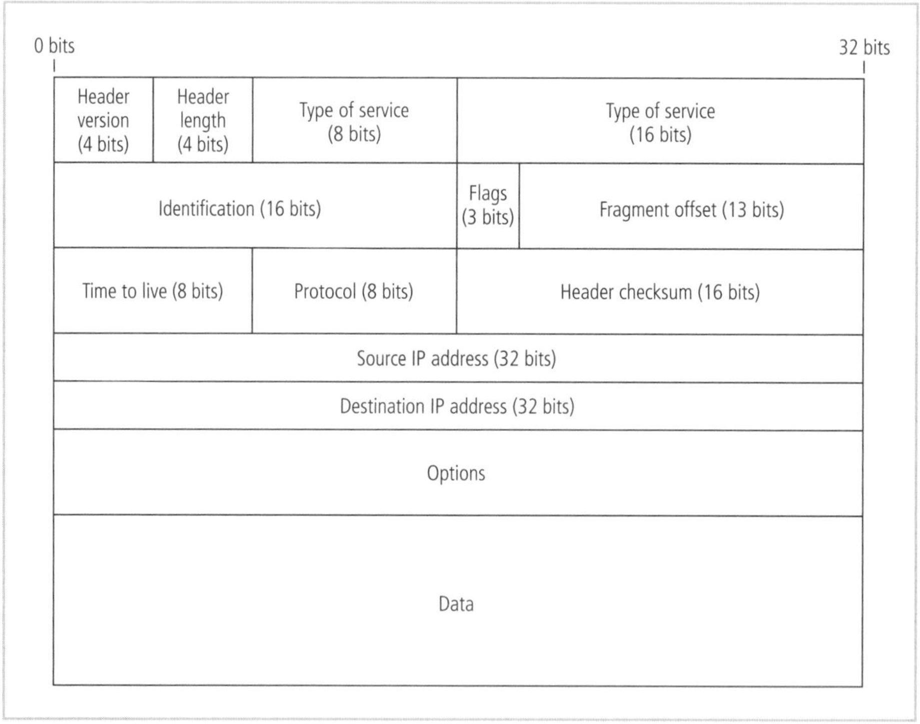

0 bits				32 bits
Header version (4 bits)	Header length (4 bits)	Type of service (8 bits)	Type of service (16 bits)	
Identification (16 bits)			Flags (3 bits)	Fragment offset (13 bits)
Time to live (8 bits)		Protocol (8 bits)	Header checksum (16 bits)	
Source IP address (32 bits)				
Destination IP address (32 bits)				
Options				
Data				

FIGURE 6-1 IP Packet Structure

Packet filtering firewalls scan network data packets looking for compliance with or violation of the rules of the firewall's database. Filtering firewalls inspect packets at the network layer, or Layer 3, of the OSI model. If the device finds a packet that matches a restriction, it stops the packet from traveling from one network to another.

The restrictions most commonly implemented in packet filtering firewalls are based on a combination of the following:

- IP source and destination address
- Direction (inbound or outbound)
- Transmission Control Protocol (TCP) or User Datagram Protocol (UDP) source and destination port requests

A packet's content will vary in structure, depending on the nature of the packet. The two primary service types are TCP and UDP (as noted above). Figures 6-2 and 6-3 show the structures of these two major elements of the combined protocol known as TCP/IP.

FIGURE 6-2 TCP Packet Structure

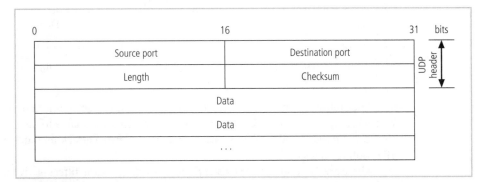

FIGURE 6-3 UDP Datagram Structure

Simple firewall models examine two aspects of the packet header: the destination and source address. They enforce **address restrictions**, rules designed to prohibit packets with certain addresses or partial addresses from passing through the device. They accomplish this through access control lists (ACLs), which are created and modified by the firewall administrators. Figure 6-4 shows how a packet filtering router can be used as a simple firewall to filter data packets from inbound connections and allow outbound connections unrestricted access to the public network.

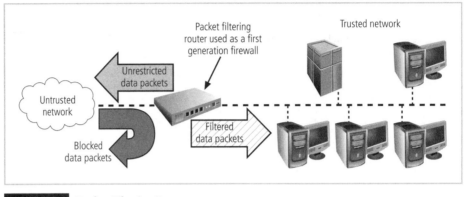

FIGURE 6-4   Packet Filtering Router

For an example of an address restriction scheme, consider Table 6-1. If an administrator were to configure a simple rule based on the content of Table 6-1, any attempt to connect that was made by an external computer or network device in the 192.168.*.* address range (192.168.0.0-192.168.255.255) would be allowed. The ability to restrict a specific service, rather than just a range of IP addresses, is available in a more advanced version of this first generation firewall. Additional details on firewall rules and configuration are presented in a later section of this chapter.

TABLE 6-1   Sample Firewall Rule and Format

Source Address	Destination Address	Service (HTTP, SMTP, FTP, Telnet)	Action (Allow or Deny)
172.16.x.x	10.10.x.x	Any	Deny
192.168.x.x	10.10.10.25	HTTP	Allow
192.168.0.1	10.10.10.10	FTP	Allow

The ability to restrict a specific service is now considered standard in most routers and is invisible to the user. Unfortunately, such systems are unable to detect the modification of packet headers, which occurs in some advanced attack methods, including IP spoofing attacks.

There are three subsets of packet filtering firewalls: static filtering, dynamic filtering, and stateful inspection.

Static filtering: Static filtering requires that the filtering rules governing how the firewall decides which packets are allowed and which are denied are developed and installed. This type of filtering is common in network routers and gateways.

Dynamic filtering: Dynamic filtering allows the firewall to react to an emergent event and update or create rules to deal with the event. This reaction could be positive, as in allowing an internal user to engage in a specific activity upon request, or negative, as in dropping all packets from a particular address when an increase in the presence of a particular type of malformed packet is detected. While static filtering firewalls allow entire sets of one type of packet to enter in response to authorized requests, the **dynamic packet filtering firewall** allows only a particular packet with a particular source, destination, and port address to enter through the firewall. It does this by opening and closing "doors" in the firewall based on the information contained in the packet header, which makes dynamic packet filters an intermediate form, between traditional static packet filters and application proxies (which are described later).

Stateful inspection: **Stateful inspection firewalls**, also called stateful firewalls, keep track of each network connection between internal and external systems using a **state table**. A state table tracks the state and context of each packet in the conversation by recording which station sent what packet and when. Like first generation firewalls, stateful inspection firewalls perform packet filtering, but they take it a step further. Whereas simple packet filtering firewalls only allow or deny certain packets based on their address, a stateful firewall can block incoming packets that are not responses to internal requests. If the stateful firewall receives an incoming packet that it cannot match in its state table, it defaults to its ACL to determine whether to allow the packet to pass. The primary disadvantage of this type of firewall is the additional processing required to manage and verify packets against the state table, which can leave the system vulnerable to a DoS or DDoS attack. In such an attack, the firewall system receives a large number of external packets, which slows the firewall because it attempts to compare all of the incoming packets first to the state table and then to the ACL. On the positive side, these firewalls can track connectionless packet traffic, such as UDP and remote procedure calls (RPC) traffic. Dynamic stateful filtering firewalls keep a dynamic state table to make changes (within predefined limits) to the filtering rules based on events as they happen. A state table looks similar to a firewall rule set but has additional information, as shown in Table 6-2. The state table contains the familiar source IP and port, and destination IP and port, but adds information on the protocol used (i.e., UDP or TCP), total time in seconds, and time remaining in seconds. Many state table implementations allow a connection to remain in place for up to 60 minutes without any activity before the state entry is deleted. The example shown in Table 6-2 shows this in the column labeled *Total Time*. The time remaining column shows a countdown of the time that is left until the entry is deleted.

TABLE 6-2   State Table Entries

Source Address	Source Port	Destination Address	Destination Port	Time Remaining in Seconds	Total Time in Seconds	Protocol
192.168.2.5	1028	10.10.10.7	80	2725	3600	TCP

Application Gateways. The **application gateway**, also known as an **application-level firewall** or **application firewall**, is frequently installed on a dedicated computer, separate from the filtering router, but is commonly used in conjunction with a filtering router. The application firewall is also known as a **proxy server**, since it runs special software that acts as a proxy for a service request. For example, an organization that runs a Web server can avoid exposing the server to direct traffic from users by installing a proxy server, configured with the registered domain's URL. This proxy server will then receive requests for

Web pages, access the Web server on behalf of the external client, and return the requested pages to the users. These servers can store the most recently accessed pages in their internal cache, and are thus also called cache servers. The benefits from this type of implementation are significant. For one, since the proxy server is often placed in an unsecured area of the network or is placed in the demilitarized zone (DMZ)—an intermediate area between a trusted network and an untrusted network—it, rather than the Web server, is exposed to the higher levels of risk from the less trusted networks. Additional filtering routers can be implemented behind the proxy server, limiting access to the more secure internal system, and thereby further protecting internal systems.

One common example of an application-level firewall (or proxy server) is a firewall that blocks all requests for and responses to requests for Web pages and services from the internal computers of an organization, and instead makes all such requests and responses go to intermediate computers (or proxies) in the less protected areas of the organization's network. This technique of using proxy servers is still widely used to implement electronic commerce functions, although most users of this technology have upgraded to take advantage of the DMZ approach discussed below.

The primary disadvantage of application-level firewalls is that they are designed for a specific protocol and cannot easily be reconfigured to protect against attacks on other protocols. Since application firewalls work at the application layer (hence the name), they are typically restricted to a single application (e.g., FTP, Telnet, HTTP, SMTP, SNMP). The processing time and resources necessary to read each packet down to the application layer diminishes the ability of these firewalls to handle multiple types of applications.

Circuit Gateways.   The **circuit gateway firewall** operates at the transport layer. Again, connections are authorized based on addresses. Like filtering firewalls, circuit gateway firewalls do not usually look at data traffic flowing between one network and another, but they do prevent direct connections between one network and another. They accomplish this by creating tunnels connecting specific processes or systems on each side of the firewall, and then allow only authorized traffic, such as a specific type of TCP connection for only authorized users, in these tunnels. A circuit gateway is a firewall component often included in the category of application gateway, but it is in fact a separate type of firewall. Writing for NIST in SP 800-110, John Wack describes the operation of a circuit gateway as follows: "A *circuit-level gateway* relays TCP connections but does no extra processing or filtering of the protocol. For example, the use of a TELNET application server is a circuit-level gateway operation, since once the connection between the source and destination is established, the firewall simply passes bytes between the systems without further evaluation of the packet contents. Another example of a circuit-level gateway would be for NNTP, in which the NNTP server would connect to the firewall, and then internal systems' NNTP clients would connect to the firewall. The firewall would, again, simply pass bytes."[2]

MAC Layer Firewalls.   While not as well known or widely referenced as the firewall approaches above, MAC layer firewalls are designed to operate at the media access control layer of the OSI network mode. This gives these firewalls the ability to consider the specific host computer's identity in its filtering decisions. Using this approach, the MAC addresses of specific host computers are linked to ACL entries that identify the specific types of packets that can be sent to each host, and all other traffic is blocked.

Figure 6-5 shows where in the OSI model each of the firewall processing modes inspects data.

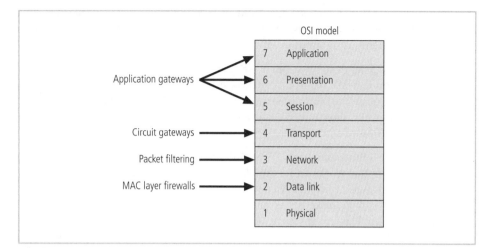

FIGURE 6-5 Firewall Types and the OSI Model

Hybrid Firewalls.   Hybrid firewalls combine the elements of other types of firewalls—that is, the elements of packet filtering and proxy services, or of packet filtering and circuit gateways. Alternately, a hybrid firewall system may actually consist of two separate firewall devices; each is a separate firewall system, but they are connected so that they work in tandem. For example, a hybrid firewall system might include a packet filtering firewall that is set up to screen all acceptable requests then pass the requests to a proxy server, which, in turn, requests services from a Web server deep inside the organization's networks. An added advantage to the hybrid firewall approach is that it enables an organization to make a security improvement without completely replacing its existing firewalls.

Firewalls Categorized by Development Generation
The first generation of firewall devices consists of routers that perform only simple packet filtering operations. More recent generations of firewalls offer increasingly complex capabilities, including the increased security and convenience of creating a DMZ—"demilitarized zone." At the present time, there are five generally recognized generations of firewalls, and these generations can be implemented in a wide variety of architectures.

First Generation.   **First generation** firewalls are static packet filtering firewalls—that is, simple networking devices that filter packets according to their headers as the packets travel to and from the organization's networks.

Second Generation.   **Second generation** firewalls are application-level firewalls or proxy servers—that is, dedicated systems that are separate from the filtering router and that provide intermediate services for requestors.

Third Generation.   **Third generation** firewalls are stateful inspection firewalls, which, as you may recall, monitor network connections between internal and external systems using state tables.

Fourth Generation.   While static filtering firewalls, such as first and third generation firewalls, allow entire sets of one type of packet to enter in response to authorized requests, the **fourth generation** firewalls, which are also known as dynamic packet filtering firewalls, allow only a particular packet with a particular source, destination, and port address to enter.

Fifth Generation.   The **fifth generation** firewall is the **kernel proxy**, a specialized form that works under the Windows NT Executive, which is the kernel of Windows NT. This type of firewall evaluates packets at multiple layers of the protocol stack, by checking security in the kernel as data is passed up and down the stack. Cisco implements this technology in the security kernel of its Centri Firewall. The Cisco security kernel contains three component technologies:[3] the Interceptor/Packet Analyzer, the Security Verification ENgine (SVEN), and Kernel Proxies. The Interceptor captures packets arriving at the firewall server and passes them to the Packet Analyzer, which reads the header information, extracts signature data, and passes both the data and the packets to the SVEN. The SVEN receives this information and determines whether to drop the packet, map it to an existing session, or create a new session. If a current session exists, the SVEN passes the information through a custom-built protocol stack created specifically for that session. The temporary protocol stack uses a customized implementation of the approach widely known as Network Address Translation (NAT). The SVEN enforces the security policy that is configured into the Kernel Proxy as it inspects each packet.

Firewalls Categorized by Structure

Firewalls can also be categorized by the structures used to implement them. Most commercial-grade firewalls are dedicated *appliances*. That is, they are stand-alone units running on fully customized computing platforms that provide both the physical network connection and firmware programming necessary to perform their function, whatever that function (static packet filtering, application proxy, etc.) may be. Some firewall appliances use highly customized, sometimes proprietary hardware systems that are developed exclusively as firewall devices. Other commercial firewall systems are actually off-the-shelf general purpose computer systems. These computers then use custom application software running either over standard operating systems like Windows or Linux/Unix or on specialized variants of these operating systems. Most small office or residential-grade firewalls are either simplified dedicated appliances running on computing devices, or application software installed directly on the user's computer.

Commercial-Grade Firewall Appliances.   Firewall appliances are stand-alone, self-contained combinations of computing hardware and software. These devices frequently have many of the features of a general-purpose computer with the addition of firmware-based instructions that increase their reliability and performance and minimize the likelihood of being compromised. The customized software operating system that drives the device can be periodically upgraded, but can only be modified using a direct physical connection or after using extensive authentication and authorization protocols. The firewall rule sets are stored in non-volatile memory, and thus they can be changed by technical staff when necessary but are available each time the device is restarted.

These appliances may be manufactured from stripped-down general purpose computer systems, and/or designed to run a customized version of a general-purpose operating system. These variant operating systems are tuned to meet the type of firewall activity built into the application software that provides the firewall functionality.

Commercial-Grade Firewall Systems. A commercial-grade firewall system consists of application software that is configured for the requirements of the firewall application and running on a general-purpose computer. Organizations can install firewall software on an existing general purpose computer system, or they can purchase hardware that has been configured to the specifications that yield optimum performance for the firewall software. These systems exploit the fact that firewalls are essentially application software packages that use common general-purpose network connections to move data from one network to another.

Small Office/Home Office (SOHO) Firewall Appliances. As more and more small businesses and residences obtain fast Internet connections with digital subscriber lines (DSL) or cable modem connections, they become more and more vulnerable to attacks. What many small business and work-from-home users don't realize is that, unlike dial-up connections, these high-speed services are always on and thus the computers connected to them are constantly connected. These computers are, therefore, much more likely to show up on the scanning actions performed by hackers than if they were only connected for the duration of a dial-up session. Coupled with the typically lax security capabilities of home computing operating systems like Windows 95, Windows 98 and even Windows Millennium Edition, most of these systems are wide open to outside intrusion. Even Windows XP Home Edition, a home computing operating system which can be securely configured, is often a soft target since few users bother to learn how to configure it securely. Just as organizations must protect their information, residential users must also implement some form of firewall to prevent loss, damage, or disclosure of personal information.

One of the most effective methods of improving computing security in the SOHO setting is through the implementation of a SOHO or residential-grade firewall. These devices, also known as broadband gateways or DSL/cable modem routers, connect the user's local area network or a specific computer system to the Internetworking device—in this case, the cable modem or DSL router provided by the Internet service provider (ISP). The SOHO firewall serves first as a stateful firewall to enable inside to outside access and can be configured to allow limited TCP/IP port forwarding and/or screened subnet capabilities (see the later sections of this chapter for definitions of these terms).

In recent years, the broadband router devices that can function as packet filtering firewalls have been enhanced to combine the features of wireless access points (WAPs) as well as small stackable LAN switches in a single device. These convenient combination devices give the residential/SOHO user the strong protection that comes from the use of Network Address Translation (NAT) services. NAT assigns non-routing local addresses to the computer systems in the local area network and uses the single ISP assigned address to communicate with the Internet. Since the internal computers are not visible to the public network, they are very much less likely to be scanned or compromised. Many users implement these devices primarily to allow multiple internal users to share a single external Internet connection. Figure 6-6 shows a few examples of the SOHO firewall devices currently available on the market.

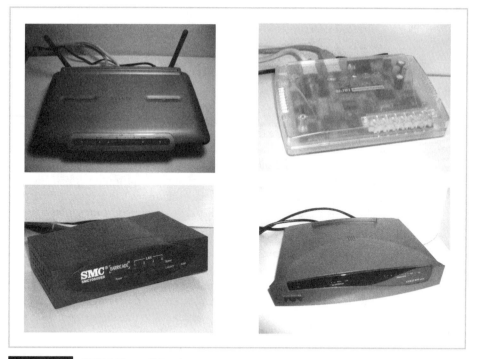

FIGURE 6-6   SOHO Firewall Devices

Many of these firewalls provide more than simple NAT services. As illustrated in Figures 6-7 through 6-10, some SOHO/residential firewalls include packet filtering, port filtering, and simple intrusion detection systems, and some can even restrict access to specific MAC addresses. Users may be able to configure port forwarding and enable outside users to access specific TCP or UDP ports on specific computers on the protected network.

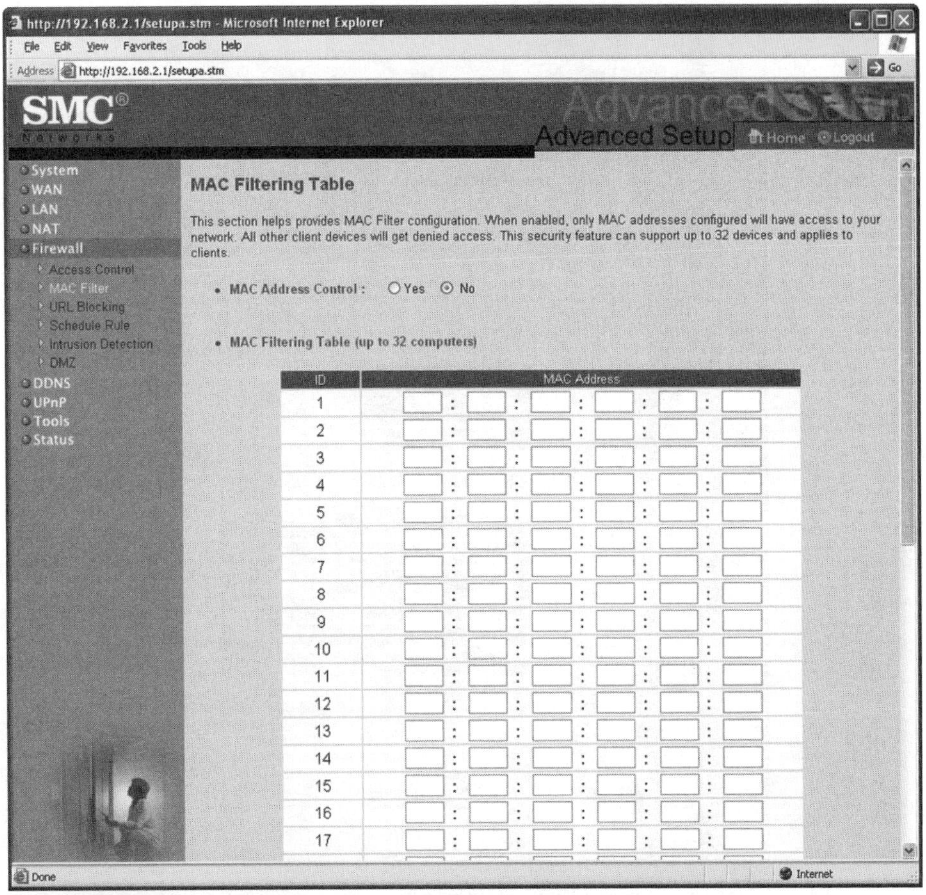

FIGURE 6-7   Barricade MAC Address Restriction Screen

Figure 6-7 is an example of the setup screen from the SMC Barricade residential broadband router that can be used to identify which computers inside the trusted network may access the Internet.

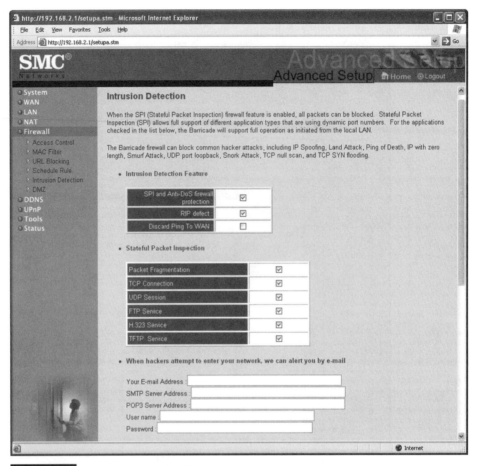

FIGURE 6-8   Barricade Intrusion Detection Configuration Screen

Some firewall devices are manufactured to provide a limited intrusion detection capability. (Intrusion detection is a topic covered in detail in Chapter 7.) Figure 6-8 shows the configuration screen from the SMC Barricade residential broadband router that enables the intrusion detection feature. When enabled, this feature will detect specific, albeit limited, attempts to compromise the protected network. In addition to recording intrusion attempts, the router can be made to use the contact information provided on this configuration screen to notify the firewall administrator of the occurrence of an intrusion attempt.

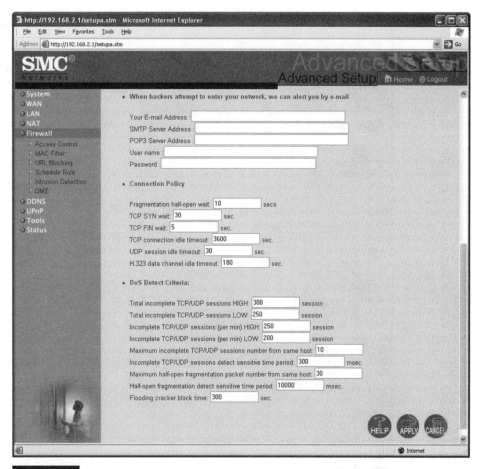

FIGURE 6-9   Barricade Intrusion Detection Configuration Screen Continued

Figure 6-9 shows a continuation of the configuration screen for the intrusion detection feature. Note that the intrusion criteria are limited in number, but the actual threshold levels of the various activities detected can be customized by the administrator.

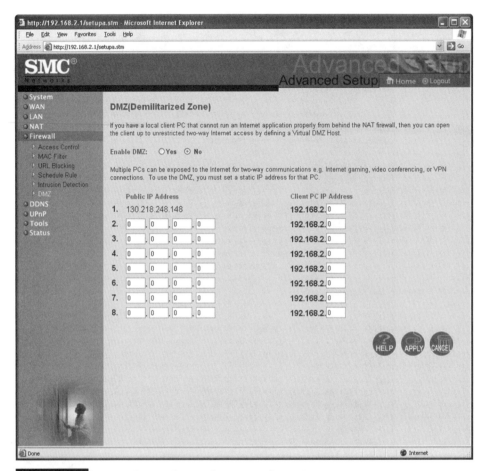

FIGURE 6-10 Barricade Demilitarized Zone Configuration Screen

Figure 6-10 illustrates that even simple residential firewalls can be used to create a logical screened subnetwork (often called a demilitarized zone, or DMZ) that can provide Web services. This screen shows how the Barricade can be configured to allow Internet clients access to servers inside the trusted network. The network administrator is expected to ensure that the exposed servers are sufficiently secured for this type of exposure.

Residential-Grade Firewall Software. Another method of protecting the residential user is to install a software firewall directly on the user's system. Many people have elected to implement these residential-grade software-based firewalls, but, unfortunately, they may not be as fully protected as they think. The majority of individuals who implement a software-based firewall use one of the products listed in Table 6-3. This list represents a selection of applications that claim to detect and prevent intrusion into the user's system, without affecting usability. The problem is that many of the applications on the list provide free versions of their software that are not fully functional, yet many users implement them thinking their systems are sufficiently protected. But the old adage of you get what you pay for certainly applies to software in this category. Thus, users who implement less-capable software often find that it delivers less complete protection. Some of these applications combine firewall services with other protections like antivirus, or intrusion detection.

Table 6-3 Common Software Firewalls

NetGuard and Esafe Desktop from Aladdin
Zone Labs ZoneAlarm
Kerio Personal Firewall
Agnitum Outpost Firewall
Sygate Personal Firewall
Deerfield Personal Firewall
Norton Personal Firewall
Black Ice Defender from NetworkICE
Tiny Personal Firewall

There are limits to the level of configurability and protection that software firewalls can provide. Many of the applications on this list have very limited configuration options ranging from none to low to medium to high security. With only three or four levels of configuration, users may find that the application becomes increasingly difficult to use in everyday situations. They find themselves sacrificing security for usability, as the application constantly asks for instruction on whether to allow a particular application, packet, or service to connect internally or externally. The Microsoft Windows 2000 and XP versions of Internet Explorer have a similar configuration with settings that allow users to choose from a list of preconfigured options, or choose a custom setting with a more detailed security configuration.

Software vs. Hardware: The SOHO Firewall Debate.   So which type of firewall should the residential user implement? There are many users who swear by their software firewalls. Personal experience will produce a variety of opinionated perspectives. Ask yourself this question: *Where* would you rather defend against a hacker? With the software option, the hacker is inside your computer, battling with a piece of software (free software, in many cases) that may not have been correctly installed, configured, patched, upgraded, or designed. If the software happens to have a known vulnerability, the hacker could bypass it and then have unrestricted access to your system. With the hardware device, even if the hacker manages to crash the firewall system, your computer and information are still safely behind the now disabled connection, which is assigned a nonroutable IP address making it virtually impossible to reach from the outside. A former student of one of the authors responded to this debate by installing a hardware firewall, and then visiting a hacker chat room. He challenged the group to penetrate his system. A few days later, he received an e-mail from a hacker claiming to have accessed his system. The hacker included a graphic of a screen showing a C:\ prompt, which he claimed was from the student's system. After doing a bit of research, the student found out that the firewall had an image stored in firmware that was designed to distract attackers. It was an image of a command window with a DOS prompt. The hardware (NAT) solution had withstood the challenge.

Firewall Architectures

Each of the firewall devices noted earlier can be configured in a number of network connection architectures. These approaches are sometimes mutually exclusive and sometimes can be combined.

The configuration that works best for a particular organization depends on three factors: the objectives of the network, the organization's ability to develop and implement the architectures, and the budget available for the function. Although literally hundreds of variations exist, there are four common architectural implementations of firewalls. These implementations are packet filtering routers, screened host firewalls, dual-homed firewalls, and screened subnet firewalls. Each of these is examined in more detail in the following sections.

Packet Filtering Routers

Most organizations with an Internet connection have some form of a router as the interface to the Internet at the perimeter between the organization's internal networks and the external service provider. Many of these routers can be configured to reject packets that the organization does not allow into the network. This is a simple but effective way to lower the organization's risk from external attack. The drawbacks to this type of system include a lack of auditing and strong authentication. Also, the complexity of the access control lists used to filter the packets can grow and degrade network performance. Figure 6-4 (shown earlier in this chapter) is an example of this type of architecture.

Screened Host Firewalls

The next type of architecture combines the packet filtering router with a separate, dedicated firewall, such as an application proxy server. This approach allows the router to pre-screen packets to minimize the network traffic and load on the internal proxy. The application proxy examines an application layer protocol, such as HTTP, and performs the proxy services. This separate host is often referred to as a **bastion host**; it can be a rich target for external attacks, and should be very thoroughly secured. Even though the bastion host/application proxy actually contains only cached copies of the internal Web documents, it can still present a promising target, because compromise of the bastion host can disclose the configuration of internal networks and possibly provide external sources with internal information. Since the bastion host stands as a sole defender on the network perimeter, it is also commonly referred to as the **sacrificial host**. To its advantage, this configuration requires the external attack to compromise two separate systems, before the attack can access internal data. In this way, the bastion host protects the data more fully than the router alone. Figure 6-11 shows a typical configuration of a screened host architectural approach.

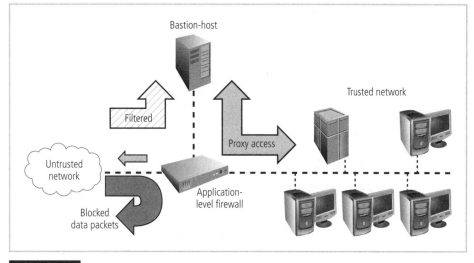

Bastion-host

Trusted network

Filtered

Proxy access

Untrusted network

Application-level firewall

Blocked data packets

FIGURE 6-11 Screened Host Firewall

Dual-Homed Host Firewalls

The next step up in firewall architectural complexity is the dual-homed host. When this architectural approach is used, the bastion host contains two NICs (network interface cards) rather than one, as in the bastion host configuration. One NIC is connected to the external network, and one is connected to the internal network, providing an additional layer of protection. With two NICs, all traffic *must* physically go through the firewall to move between the internal and external networks. Implementation of this architecture often makes use of NAT. As described earlier in this chapter, NAT is a method of mapping real, valid, external IP addresses to special ranges of non-routable internal IP addresses, thereby creating yet another barrier to intrusion from external attackers. The internal addresses used by NAT consist of three different ranges. Organizations that need Class A addresses can use the 10.x.x.x range, which has over 16.5 million usable addresses. Organizations that need Class B addresses can use the 192.168.x.x range, which has over 65,500 addresses. Finally, organizations with smaller needs, such as those needing only a few Class C addresses, can use the 172.16.0.0 to 172.16.15.0 range, which has 16 Class C addresses or about 4000 usable addresses. See Table 6-4 for a recap of the IP address ranges reserved for non-public networks. Messages sent with internal addresses within these three reserved ranges cannot be routed externally, so that if a computer with one of these internal-use addresses is directly connected to the external network, and avoids the NAT server, its traffic cannot be routed on the public network. Taking advantage of this, NAT prevents external attacks from reaching internal machines with addresses in specified ranges. If the NAT server is a multi-homed bastion host, it translates between the true, external IP addresses assigned to the organization by public network naming authorities and the internally assigned, non-routable IP addresses. NAT translates by dynamically assigning addresses to internal communications and tracking the conversations with sessions to determine which incoming message is a response to which outgoing traffic. Figure 6-12 shows a typical configuration of a dual-homed host firewall that uses NAT and proxy access to protect the internal network.

Table 6-4   Reserved Non-Routable Address Ranges

Class	From	To	CIDR Mask	Decimal Mask
Class "A" or 24 Bit	10.0.0.0	10.255.255.255	/8	255.0.0.0
Class "B" or 20 Bit	172.16.0.0	172.31.255.255	/12 or /16	255.240.0.0 or 255.255.0.0
Class "C" or 16 Bit	192.168.0.0	192.168.255.255	/16 or /24	255.255.0.0 or 255.255.255.0

Another benefit of a dual-homed host is its ability to translate between many different protocols at their respective data link layers, including Ethernet, Token Ring, Fiber Distributed Data Interface (FDDI), and Asynchronous Transfer Method (ATM). On the downside, if this dual-homed host is compromised, it can disable the connection to the external network, and as traffic volume increases, it can become overloaded. Compared to more complex solutions, however, this architecture provides strong overall protection with minimal expense.

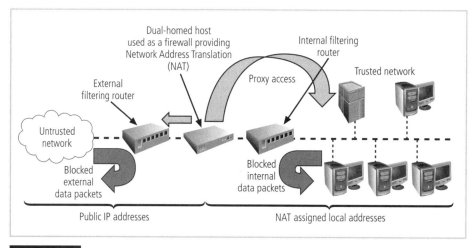

FIGURE 6-12   Dual-Homed Host Firewall

Screened Subnet Firewalls (with DMZ)

The dominant architecture used today is the screened subnet firewall. The architecture of a screened subnet firewall provides a DMZ. The DMZ can be a dedicated port on the firewall device linking a single bastion host, or it can be connected to a screened subnet, as shown in Figure 6-13. Until recently, servers providing services through an untrusted network were commonly placed in the DMZ. Examples of these include Web servers, file transfer protocol (FTP) servers, and certain database servers. More recent strategies using proxy servers have provided much more secure solutions.

A common arrangement finds the subnet firewall consisting of two or more internal bastion hosts behind a packet filtering router, with each host protecting the trusted network. There are many variants of the screened subnet architecture. The first general model consists of two filtering routers, with one or more dual-homed bastion hosts between them. In the second general model, as illustrated in Figure 6-13, the connections are routed as follows:

- Connections from the outside or untrusted network are routed through an external filtering router.
- Connections from the outside or untrusted network are routed into—and then out of—a routing firewall to the separate network segment known as the DMZ.
- Connections into the trusted internal network are allowed only from the DMZ bastion host servers.

The screened subnet is an entire network segment that performs two functions: it protects the DMZ systems and information from outside threats by providing a network of intermediate security (more secure than the general public networks but less secure than the internal network); and it protects the internal networks by limiting how external connections can gain access to internal systems. Although extremely secure, the screened subnet can be expensive to implement and complex to configure and manage. The value of the information it protects must justify the cost.

Another facet of the DMZ is the creation of an area of known as an extranet. An extranet is a segment of the DMZ where additional authentication and authorization controls are put into place to provide services that are not available to the general public. An example would be an online retailer that allows anyone to browse the product catalog and place items into a shopping cart, but will require extra authentication and authorization when the customer is ready to check out and place an order.

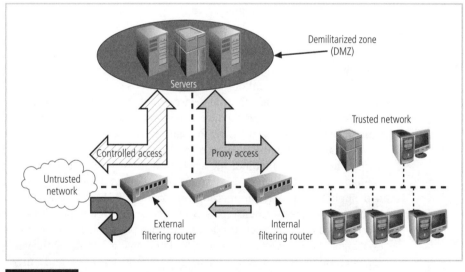

FIGURE 6-13   Screened Subnet (DMZ)

SOCKS Servers

Deserving of brief special attention is the SOCKS firewall implementation. SOCKS is the protocol for handling TCP traffic through a proxy server. The SOCKS system is a proprietary circuit-level proxy server that places special SOCKS client-side agents on each workstation. The general approach is to place the filtering requirements on the individual workstation rather than on a single point of defense (and thus point of failure). This frees the entry router from filtering responsibilities, but it then requires each workstation to be managed as a firewall detection and protection device. A SOCKS system can require support and management resources beyond those usually encountered for traditional firewalls since it is used to configure and manage hundreds of individual clients, as opposed to a single device or small set of devices.

Selecting the Right Firewall

When selecting the best firewall for an organization, you should consider a number of factors. The most important of these is the extent to which the firewall design provides the desired protection. When evaluating a firewall, questions should be created that cover the following topics:[4]

1. What type of firewall technology offers the right balance between protection and cost for the needs of the organization?
2. What features are included in the base price? What features are available at extra cost? Are all cost factors known?
3. How easy is it to set up and configure the firewall? How accessible are the staff technicians who can competently configure the firewall?
4. Can the candidate firewall adapt to the growing network in the target organization?

The second most important issue is cost. Cost may keep a certain make, model, or type out of reach for a particular security solution. As with all security decisions, certain compromises may be necessary in order to provide a viable solution under the budgetary constraints stipulated by management.

Configuring and Managing Firewalls

Once the firewall architecture and technology have been selected, the initial configuration and ongoing management of the firewall(s) needs to be considered. Good policy and practice dictates that each firewall device, whether a filtering router, bastion host, or other firewall implementation, must have its own set of configuration rules that regulate its actions. In theory, packet filtering firewalls use a rule set made up of simple statements that regulate source and destination addresses identifying the type of requests and/or the ports to be used and that indicate whether to allow or deny the request. In actuality, the configuration of firewall policies can be complex and difficult. IT professionals familiar with application programming can appreciate the problems associated with debugging both syntax errors and logic errors. Syntax errors in firewall policies are usually easy to identify, as the systems alert the administrator to incorrectly configured policies. However, logic errors, such as allowing instead of denying, specifying the wrong port or service type, and using the wrong switch, are another story. These and a myriad of other simple mistakes can take a device designed to protect users' communications and turn it into one giant choke point. A choke point that restricts all communications or an incorrectly configured rule can cause other unexpected results. For example, novice firewall administrators often improperly configure a virus-screening e-mail gateway (think of this as a type of e-mail firewall), which, instead of screening e-mail for malicious code, results in the blocking of all incoming e-mail and causes, understandably, a great deal of frustration among users.

Configuring firewall policies is as much an art as it is a science. Each configuration rule must be carefully crafted, debugged, tested, and placed into the access control list in the proper sequence. The process of writing good, correctly sequenced firewall rules ensures that the actions taken comply with the organization's policy. The process also makes sure that those rules that can be evaluated quickly and govern broad access are performed before those that may take longer to evaluate and affect fewer cases, which, in turn, ensures that the analysis is completed as quickly as possible for the largest number of requests. When configuring firewalls, keep one thing in mind: when security rules conflict with the performance of business, security often loses. If users can't work because of a security restriction, the security administration is usually told, in no uncertain terms, to remove the safeguard. In other words, organizations are much more willing to live with potential risk than certain failure. The following sections describe the best practices most commonly used in firewalls and the best ways to configure the rules that support firewalls.

Best Practices for Firewalls

This section outlines some of the best practices for firewall use.[5] Note that these rules are not presented in any particular sequence. For sequencing of rules, refer to the next section.

- All traffic from the trusted network is allowed out. This allows members of the organization to access the services they need. Filtering and logging of outbound traffic is possible when indicated by specific organizational policies.

- The firewall device is never directly accessible from the public network for configuration or management purposes. Almost all administrative access to the firewall device is denied to internal users as well. Only authorized firewall administrators access the device through secure authentication mechanisms, with preference for a method that is based on cryptographically strong authentication and uses two-factor access control techniques.

- Simple Mail Transport Protocol (SMTP) data is allowed to pass through the firewall, but it should all be routed to a well-configured SMTP gateway to filter and route messaging traffic securely.

- All Internet Control Message Protocol (ICMP) data should be denied. Known as the Ping service, ICMP is a common method for hacker reconnaissance and should be turned off to prevent snooping.

- Telnet (terminal emulation) access to all internal servers from the public networks should be blocked. At the very least, Telnet access to the organization's Domain Name Service (DNS) server should be blocked to prevent illegal zone transfers, and to prevent hackers from taking down the organization's entire network. If internal users need to come into an organization's network from outside the firewall, the organization should enable them to use a Virtual Private Network (VPN) client, or other secure system that provides a reasonable level of authentication.

- When Web services are offered outside the firewall, HTTP traffic should be denied from reaching your internal networks through the use of some form of proxy access or DMZ architecture. That way, if any employees are running Web servers for internal use on their desktops, the services are invisible to the outside Internet. If the Web server is behind the firewall, allow HTTP or HTTPS (also known as Secure Sockets Layer or SSL[6]) through for the Internet at large to view it. The best solution is to place the Web servers containing critical data inside the network and use proxy services from a DMZ (screened network segment), and also to restrict Web traffic bound for internal network addresses in response to only those requests that originated from internal addresses. This restriction can be accomplished through NAT or other stateful inspection or proxy server firewall approaches. All other incoming HTTP traffic should be blocked. If the Web servers only contain advertising, they should be placed in the DMZ and rebuilt on a timed schedule or when—not *if*, but *when*—they are compromised.

Firewall Rules

As noted earlier in this chapter, firewalls operate by examining a data packet and performing a comparison with some predetermined logical rules. The logic is based on a set of guidelines programmed in by a firewall administrator, or created dynamically and based on outgoing requests for information. This logical set is most commonly referred to as firewall rules, rule base, or firewall logic. Most firewalls use packet header information to determine whether a specific packet should be allowed to pass through or should be dropped. In order to better understand more complex rules, it is important to be able to create simple rules and understand how they interact. In the exercise that follows, many of the rules are based on the best practices outlined earlier. For the purposes of this discussion, assume a network configuration as illustrated in Figure 6-14, with an internal and an external filtering firewall. In the exercise, the rules for both firewalls will be discussed, and a recap at the end of the exercise will show the complete rule sets for each filtering firewall.

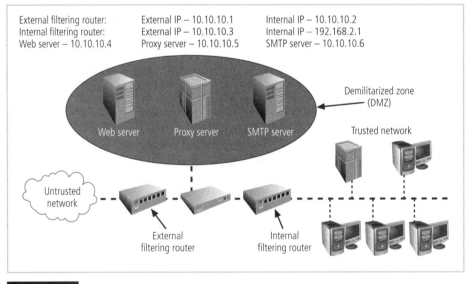

External filtering router: External IP – 10.10.10.1   Internal IP – 10.10.10.2
Internal filtering router: External IP – 10.10.10.3   Internal IP – 192.168.2.1
Web server – 10.10.10.4   Proxy server – 10.10.10.5   SMTP server – 10.10.10.6

FIGURE 6-14   Example Network Configuration

Some firewalls can filter packets by the name of a particular protocol as opposed to the protocol's usual port numbers. For instance, Telnet protocol packets usually go to TCP port 23, but can sometimes be redirected to another much higher port number in an attempt to conceal the activity. The System (or Well-Known) Ports are those from 0 through 1023, User (or Registered) Ports are those from 1024 through 49151, and

Dynamic (or Private) Ports are those from 49152 through 65535 (see *http://www.iana.org/ assignments/port-numbers* for more information).

The following example uses the port numbers associated with several well-known protocols to build a rule base. The port numbers to be used are listed in Table 6-5. Note that this is not an exhaustive list. For a detailed list, see the above URL.

TABLE 6-5 Select Well-Known Port Numbers

Port Number	Protocol
7	Echo
20	File Transfer [Default Data] – (FTP)
21	File Transfer [Control] – (FTP)
23	Telnet
25	Simple Mail Transfer Protocol – (SMTP)
53	Domain Name Services – (DNS)
80	Hypertext Transfer Protocol – (HTTP)
110	Post Office Protocol version 3 – (POP3)
161	Simple Network Management Protocol – (SNMP)

Rule Set 1: Responses to internal requests are allowed. In most firewall implementations, it is desirable to allow a response to an internal request for information. In dynamic or stateful firewalls, this is most easily accomplished by matching the incoming traffic to an outgoing request in a state table. In simple packet filtering, this can be accomplished with the following rule for the External Filtering Router. (Note that the network address for the destination ends with .0; some firewalls use a notation of .X instead.)

TABLE 6-6 Rule Set 1

Source Address	Source Port	Destination Address	Destination Port	Action
Any	Any	10.10.10.0	>1023	Allow

From Table 6-6, you can see that this rule states that *any* incoming packet (with any source address and from any source port) that is destined for the internal network (whose destination address is 10.10.10.0) and for a destination port greater than 1023 (that is, any port out of the number range for the well-known ports) is allowed to enter. Why allow all such packets? While outgoing communications request information from a specific port (i.e., a port 80 request for a Web page), the response is assigned a number outside the well-known port range. If multiple browser windows are open at the same time, each window can request a packet from a Web site, and the response is directed to a specific destination port, allowing the browser and Web server to keep each conversation separate. While this rule is sufficient for the external router (firewall), it is dangerous simply to allow any traffic in just because it is destined to a high port range. A better solution is to have the internal firewall router use state tables that track connections and prevent dangerous packets from entering this upper port range.

Rule Set 2: The firewall device is never accessible directly from the public network. If hackers can directly access the firewall, they may be able to modify or delete rules and allow unwanted traffic through. For the same reason, the firewall itself should never be allowed to access other network devices directly. If hackers compromise the firewall and then use its permissions to access other servers or clients, they may cause additional damage or mischief. The rules shown in Table 6-7 prohibit anyone from directly accessing the firewall and the firewall from directly accessing any other devices. Note that this example is for the external filtering router/firewall only. Similar rules should be crafted for the internal router. Why are there separate rules for each IP address? The 10.10.10.*1* address regulates external access to and by the firewall, while the 10.10.10.*2* address regulates internal access. Not all hackers are outside the firewall!

TABLE 6-7   Rule Set 2

Source Address	Source Port	Destination Address	Destination Port	Action
Any	Any	10.10.10.1	Any	Deny
Any	Any	10.10.10.2	Any	Deny
10.10.10.1	Any	Any	Any	Deny
10.10.10.2	Any	Any	Any	Deny

Rule Set 3: All traffic from the trusted network is allowed out. As a general rule it is wise not to restrict outgoing traffic, unless a separate router is configured to handle this traffic. Assuming most of the potentially dangerous traffic is inbound, screening outgoing traffic is just more work for the firewalls. This level of trust is fine for most organizations. If the organization wants control over outbound traffic, it should use a separate router. The rule shown in Table 6-8 allows internal communications out.

TABLE 6-8   Rule Set 3

Source Address	Source Port	Destination Address	Destination Port	Action
10.10.10.0	Any	Any	Any	Allow

Why should rule set 3 come after rule set 1 and 2? It makes sense to allow the rules that unambiguously impact the most traffic to be earlier in the list. The more rules a firewall must process to find one that applies to the current packet, the slower the firewall will run. Therefore, most widely applicable rules should come first since the first rule that applies to any given packet will be applied.

Rule Set 4: The rule set for the Simple Mail Transport Protocol (SMTP) data is shown in Table 6-9. As shown, the packets governed by this rule are allowed to pass through the firewall, but are all routed to a well-configured SMTP gateway. It is important that e-mail traffic reach your e-mail server, and *only* your e-mail server. Some hackers try to disguise dangerous packets as e-mail traffic to fool a firewall. If such packets can reach only the e-mail server, and the e-mail server has been properly configured, the rest of the network ought to be safe.

TABLE 6-9 Rule Set 4

Source Address	Source Port	Destination Address	Destination Port	Action
Any	Any	10.10.10.6	25	Allow

Rule Set 5: All Internet Control Message Protocol (ICMP) data should be denied. Pings, formally known as ICMP Echo requests, are used by internal systems administrators to ensure that clients and servers can reach and communicate. There is virtually no legitimate use for ICMP outside the network, except to test the perimeter routers. ICMP uses port 7 to request a response to a query (e.g., "Are you there?") and can be the first indicator of a malicious attack. It's best to make all directly connected networking devices "black holes" to external probes. Traceroute uses a variation on the ICMP Echo requests, so restricting this one port provides protection against two types of probes. Allowing internal users to use ICMP requires configuring two rules, as shown in Table 6-10.

TABLE 6-10 Rule Set 5

Source Address	Source Port	Destination Address	Destination Port	Action
10.10.10.0	Any	Any	7	Allow
Any	Any	10.10.10.0	7	Deny

The first of these two rules allows internal administrators (and users) to use Ping. Note that this rule is unnecessary if internal permissions rules like those in rule set 2 is used. The second rule in Table 6-10 does not allow anyone else to use Ping. Remember that rules are processed in order. If an internal user needs to Ping an internal or external address, the firewall allows the packet and stops processing the rules. If the request does not come from an internal source, then it bypasses the first rule and moves to the second.

Rule Set 6: Telnet (terminal emulation) access to all internal servers from the public networks should be blocked. Though not used much in Windows environments, Telnet is still useful to systems administrators on Unix/Linux systems. But the presence of external requests for Telnet services can indicate a potential attack. Allowing internal use of Telnet requires the same type of initial permission rule you use with Ping. See Table 6-11. Note that this rule is unnecessary if internal permissions rules like those in rule set 2 is used.

TABLE 6-11 Rule Set 6

Source Address	Source Port	Destination Address	Destination Port	Action
10.10.10.0	Any	10.10.10.0	23	Allow
Any	Any	10.10.10.0	23	Deny

Rule Set 7: When Web services are offered outside the firewall, HTTP traffic should be denied from reaching the internal networks through the use of some form of proxy access or DMZ architecture. With a Web server in the DMZ you simply allow HTTP to access the Web server, and use rule set 8, the Cleanup rule, (which will be described shortly) to prevent any other access. In order to keep the Web server inside the internal network, direct all HTTP requests to the proxy server, and configure the internal filtering router/firewall only to allow the proxy server to access the internal Web server. The rule shown in Table 6-12 illustrates the first example.

TABLE 6-12   Rule Set 7a

Source Address	Source Port	Destination Address	Destination Port	Action
Any	Any	10.10.10.4	80	Allow

This rule accomplishes two things: it allows HTTP traffic to reach the Web server, and it prevents non-HTTP traffic from reaching the Web server. It does the latter through the Cleanup rule (Rule 8). If someone tries to access the Web server with non-HTTP traffic (other than port 80), then the firewall skips this rule and goes to the next.

Proxy server rules allow an organization to restrict all access to a device. The external firewall would be configured as shown in Table 6-13.

TABLE 6-13   Rule Set 7b

Source Address	Source Port	Destination Address	Destination Port	Action
Any	Any	10.10.10.5	80	Allow

The effective use of a proxy server of course requires the DNS entries to be configured as if the proxy server were the Web server. The proxy server would then be configured to repackage any HTTP request packets into a new packet and retransmit to the Web server inside the firewall. Allowing for the retransmission of the repackaged request requires the rule shown in Table 6-14 to enable the proxy server at 10.10.10.5 to send to the internal router, presuming the IP address for the internal Web server is 192.168.2.4.

TABLE 6-14   Rule Set 7c

Source Address	Source Port	Destination Address	Destination Port	Action
10.10.10.5	80	192.168.2.4	80	Allow

The restriction on the source address then prevents anyone else from accessing the Web server from outside the internal filtering router/firewall.

Rule Set 8: The Cleanup Rule. As a general practice in firewall rule construction, if a request for a service is not explicitly allowed by policy, that request should be denied by a rule. The rule shown in Table 6-15 implements this practice and blocks any requests that aren't explicitly allowed by other rules.

TABLE 6-15   Rule Set 8

Source Address	Source Port	Destination Address	Destination Port	Action
Any	Any	Any	Any	Deny

Additional rules restricting access to specific servers or devices can be added, but they must be sequenced before the cleanup rule. Order is extremely important, as misplacement of a particular rule can result in unforeseen results. One organization installed a new $50,000 firewall, only to discover that the security the firewall provided was too perfect—that is, nothing was allowed in, and nothing was allowed out! It wasn't until the firewall administrators realized that the rule base was out of sequence that the problem was resolved.

Tables 6-16 and 6-17 show the rule sets, in their proper sequences, for both the external and internal firewalls.

TABLE 6-16   External Filtering Firewall Rule Set

Rule #	Source Address	Source Port	Destination Address	Destination Port	Action
1	Any	Any	10.10.10.0	>1023	Allow
2	Any	Any	10.10.10.1	Any	Deny
3	Any	Any	10.10.10.2	Any	Deny
4	10.10.10.1	Any	Any	Any	Deny
5	10.10.10.2	Any	Any	Any	Deny
6	10.10.10.0	Any	Any	Any	Allow
7	Any	Any	10.10.10.6	25	Allow
8	Any	Any	10.10.10.0	7	Deny
9	Any	Any	10.10.10.0	23	Deny
10	Any	Any	10.10.10.4	80	Allow
11	Any	Any	Any	Any	Deny

Note that the rule allowing responses to internal communications comes first (appearing in Table 6-16 as Rule #1), followed by the four rules prohibiting direct communications to or from the firewall (Rules #2-5 in Table 6-16). After this comes the rule stating that all outgoing internal communications are allowed, followed by the rules governing access to the SMTP server, and denial of Ping, Telnet access, and access to the HTTP server. If heavy traffic to the HTTP server is expected, move the HTTP server rule closer to the top (for example, into the position of Rule #2), which would expedite rule processing for external communications. The final rule in Table 6-16 denies any other types of communications.

TABLE 6-17   Internal Filtering Firewall Rule Set

Rule #	Source Address	Source Port	Destination Address	Destination Port	Action
1	Any	Any	10.10.10.0	>1023	Allow
2	Any	Any	10.10.10.3	Any	Deny
3	Any	Any	192.168.2.1	Any	Deny
4	10.10.10.3	Any	Any	Any	Deny
5	192.168.2.1	Any	Any	Any	Deny
6	192.168.2.0	Any	Any	Any	Allow
7	10.10.10.5	Any	192.168.2.0	Any	Allow
8	Any	Any	Any	Any	Deny

Note the similarities and differences in the two rule sets. The internal filtering router/firewall rule set, shown in Table 6-17, has to both protect against traffic to and allow traffic from the internal network (192.168.2.0). Most of the rules in Table 6-17 are similar to those in Table 6-16: allowing responses to internal communications (Rule #1); denying communications to/from the firewall itself (Rules #2-5); and allowing all outbound internal traffic (Rule #6). Note that there is no permissible traffic from the DMZ systems, except as in Rule #1. Why isn't there a comparable rule for the 192.168.2.1 subnet? Because this is an unrouteable network, external communications are handled by the NAT server, which maps internal (192.168.2.0) addresses to external (10.10.10.0) addresses. This prevents a hacker from compromising one of the internal boxes and accessing the internal network with it. The exception is the proxy server (Rule #7 in Table 6-17), which should be very carefully configured. If the organization does not need the proxy server, as in cases where all externally accessible services are provided from machines in the DMZ, then Rule #7 is not needed. Note that there are no Ping and Telnet rules in Table 6-17. This is because the external firewall filters these external requests out. The last rule, Rule #8, provides cleanup.

Content Filters

Another utility that can contribute to the protection of the organization's systems from misuse and unintentional denial-of-service, and is often closely associated with firewalls, is the **content filter**. A content filter is a software filter—technically not a firewall—that allows administrators to restrict access to content from within a network. It is essentially a set of scripts or programs that restricts user access to certain networking protocols and Internet locations, or restricts users from receiving general types or specific examples of Internet content. Some refer to content filters as **reverse firewalls**, as their primary focus is to restrict internal access to external material. In most common implementation models, the content filter has two components: rating and filtering. The rating is like a set of firewall rules for Web sites, and is common in residential content filters. The rating can be complex, with multiple access control settings for different levels of the organization, or it can be simple, with a basic allow/deny scheme like that of a firewall. The filtering is a method used to restrict specific access requests to the identified resources, which may be

Web sites, servers, or whatever resources the content filter administrator configures. This is sort of a reverse access control list (technically speaking, a capability table), in that whereas an access control list normally records a set of users that have access to resources, this control list records resources which the user cannot access.

The first types of content filters were systems designed to restrict access to specific Web sites, and were stand-alone software applications. These could be configured in either an exclusive or inclusive manner. In an exclusive mode, certain sites are specifically excluded. The problem with this approach is that there may be thousands of Web sites that an organization wants to exclude, and more might be added every hour. The inclusive mode works off of a list of sites that are specifically permitted. In order to have a site added to the list, the user must submit a request to the content filter manager, which could be time-consuming and restrict business operations. Newer models of content filters are protocol-based, examining content as it is dynamically displayed and restricting or permitting access based on a logical interpretation of content.

The most common content filters restrict users from accessing Web sites with obvious non-business related material, such as pornography, or deny incoming spam e-mail. Content filters can be small add-on software programs for the home or office, such as Net-Nanny or SurfControl, or corporate applications, such as the Novell Border Manager. The benefit of implementing content filters is the assurance that employees are not distracted by non-business material and cannot waste organizational time and resources. The downside is that these systems require extensive configuration and on-going maintenance to keep the list of unacceptable destinations or the source addresses for incoming restricted e-mail up-to-date. Some newer content filtering applications (like newer antivirus programs) come with a service of downloadable files that update the database of restrictions. These applications work by matching either a list of disapproved or approved Web sites and by matching key content words, such as "nude" and "sex." Creators of restricted content have, of course, realized this and work to bypass the restrictions by suppressing these types of trip words, thus creating additional problems for networking and security professionals.

Protecting Remote Connections

The networks that organizations create are seldom used only by people at that location. When connections are made between one network and another, the connections are arranged and managed carefully. Installing such network connections requires using leased lines or other data channels provided by common carriers, and therefore these connections are usually permanent and secured under the requirements of a formal service agreement. But when individuals—whether they be employees from home, contract workers hired for specific assignments, or other workers who are traveling—seek to connect to an organization's network(s), a more flexible option must be provided. In the past, organizations provided these remote connections exclusively through dial-up services like Remote Authentication Service (RAS). Since the Internet has become more widespread in recent years, other options such as Virtual Private Networks (VPNs) have become more popular.

Dial-Up

Before the Internet emerged, organizations created private networks and allowed individuals and other organizations to connect to them using dial-up or leased line connections. (In the current networking environment, where Internet connections are quite common, dial-up access and leased lines from customer networks are used less frequently.) The connections between company networks and the Internet use firewalls to safeguard that interface. Although connections via dial-up and leased lines are becoming less popular, they are still quite common. And it is a widely held view that these unsecured, dial-up connection points represent a substantial exposure to attack. An attacker who suspects that an organization has dial-up lines can use a device called a war dialer to locate the connection points. A **war dialer** is an automatic phone-dialing program that dials every number in a configured range (e.g., 555-1000 to 555-2000), and checks to see if a person, answering machine, or modem picks up. If a modem answers, the war dialer program makes a note of the number and then moves to the next target number. The attacker then attempts to hack into the network via the identified modem connection using a variety of techniques. Dial-up network connectivity is usually less sophisticated than that deployed with Internet connections. For the most part, simple username and password schemes are the only means of authentication. However, some technologies, such as RADIUS systems, TACACS, and CHAP password systems, have improved the authentication process, and there are even systems now that use strong encryption. Authenticating technologies such as RADIUS, TACACS, Kerberos, and SESAME are discussed below.

RADIUS and TACACS

RADIUS and TACACS are systems that authenticate the credentials of users who are trying to access an organization's network via a dial-up connection. Typical dial-up systems place the responsibility for the authentication of users on the system directly connected to the modems. If there are multiple points of entry into the dial-up system, this authentication system can become difficult to manage. The **RADIUS (Remote Authentication Dial-In User Service)** system centralizes the management of user authentication by placing the responsibility for authenticating each user in the central RADIUS server. When a remote access server (RAS) receives a request for a network connection from a dial-up client, it passes the request along with the user's credentials to the RADIUS server. RADIUS then validates the credentials and passes the resulting decision (accept or deny) back to the accepting remote access server. Figure 6-15 shows the typical configuration of an RAS system.

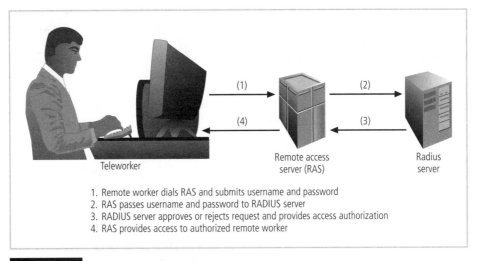

1. Remote worker dials RAS and submits username and password
2. RAS passes username and password to RADIUS server
3. RADIUS server approves or rejects request and provides access authorization
4. RAS provides access to authorized remote worker

FIGURE 6-15 RADIUS Configuration

Similar in function to the RADIUS system is the **Terminal Access Controller Access Control System (TACACS).** TACACS is another remote access authorization system that is based on a client/server configuration. Like RADIUS, it contains a centralized database, and it validates the user's credentials at this TACACS server. There are three versions of TACACS: TACACS, Extended TACACS, and TACACS+. The original version combines authentication and authorization services. The extended version separates the steps needed to provide authentication of the individual or system attempting access from the steps needed to authorize that the authenticated individual or system is able to make this type of connection. The extended version then keeps records that show that the action of granting access has accountability and that the access attempt is linked to a specific individual or system. The plus version uses dynamic passwords and incorporates two-factor authentication.

Securing Authentication with Kerberos

Two authentication systems can be implemented to provide secure third-party authentication: Kerberos and Sesame. **Kerberos**—named after the three-headed dog of Greek mythology (spelled Cerberus in Latin), which guarded the gates to the underworld—uses symmetric key encryption to validate an individual user to various network resources. Kerberos keeps a database containing the private keys of clients and servers—in the case of a client, this key is simply the client's encrypted password. Network services running on servers in the network register with Kerberos, as do the clients that use those services. The Kerberos system knows these private keys and can authenticate one network node (client or server) to another. For example, Kerberos can authenticate a user once—at the time the user logs in to a client computer—and then, at a later time during that session, it can authorize the user to have access to a printer without requiring the user to take any additional action. Kerberos also generates temporary session keys, which are private keys given to the two parties in a conversation. The session key is used to encrypt all communications between these two parties. Typically a user logs into the network, is authenticated to the Kerberos system, and is then authenticated to other resources on the network by the Kerberos system itself.

Kerberos consists of three interacting services, all of which use a database library:

1. Authentication server (AS), which is a Kerberos server that authenticates clients and servers.
2. Key Distribution Center (KDC), which generates and issues session keys.
3. Kerberos ticket granting service (TGS), which provides tickets to clients who request services. In Kerberos a **ticket** is an identification card for a particular client that verifies to the server that the client is requesting services and that the client is a valid member of the Kerberos system and therefore authorized to receive services. The ticket consists of the client's name and network address, a ticket validation starting and ending time, and the session key, all encrypted in the private key of the server from which the client is requesting services.

Kerberos is based on the following principles:

- The KDC knows the secret keys of all clients and servers on the network.
- The KDC initially exchanges information with the client and server by using these secret keys.
- Kerberos authenticates a client to a requested service on a server through TGS and by issuing temporary session keys for communications between the client and KDC, the server and KDC, and the client and server.
- Communications then take place between the client and server using these temporary session keys. [7]

Figures 6-16 and 6-17 illustrate this process.

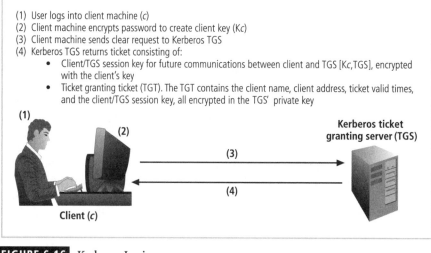

(1) User logs into client machine (*c*)
(2) Client machine encrypts password to create client key (K*c*)
(3) Client machine sends clear request to Kerberos TGS
(4) Kerberos TGS returns ticket consisting of:
  - Client/TGS session key for future communications between client and TGS [K*c*,TGS], encrypted with the client's key
  - Ticket granting ticket (TGT). The TGT contains the client name, client address, ticket valid times, and the client/TGS session key, all encrypted in the TGS' private key

Kerberos ticket granting server (TGS)

Client (*c*)

FIGURE 6-16   Kerberos Login

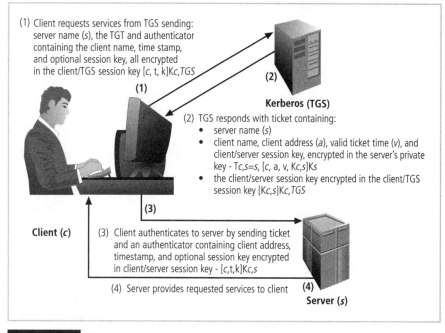

(1) Client requests services from TGS sending: server name (s), the TGT and authenticator containing the client name, time stamp, and optional session key, all encrypted in the client/TGS session key [c, t, k]Kc,TGS

Kerberos (TGS)

(2) TGS responds with ticket containing:
- server name (s)
- client name, client address (a), valid ticket time (v), and client/server session key, encrypted in the server's private key - Tc,s=s, [c, a, v, Kc,s]Ks
- the client/server session key encrypted in the client/TGS session key [Kc,s]Kc,TGS

Client (c)

(3) Client authenticates to server by sending ticket and an authenticator containing client address, timestamp, and optional session key encrypted in client/server session key - [c,t,k]Kc,s

(4) Server provides requested services to client

Server (s)

FIGURE 6-17 Kerberos Request for Services

Kerberos may be obtained free of charge from MIT at *http://web.mit.edu/is/help/ kerberos/*, but if you use it, be aware of some fundamental problems. If the Kerberos servers are subjected to denial-of-service attacks, no client can request services. If the Kerberos servers, service providers, or clients' machines are compromised, their private key information may also be compromised.

Sesame

The Secure European System for Applications in a Multivendor Environment (SESAME) is the result of a European research and development project partly funded by the European Commission. SESAME is similar to Kerberos in that the user is first authenticated to an authentication server and receives a token. The token is then presented to a privilege attribute server (instead of a ticket granting service as in Kerberos) as proof of identity to gain a privilege attribute certificate (PAC). The PAC is like the ticket in Kerberos; however, a PAC conforms to the standards of the European Computer Manufacturers Association (ECMA) and the International Organization for Standardization/International Telecommunications Union (ISO/ITU-T). The balances of the differences lie in the security protocols and distribution methods used. SESAME uses public key encryption to distribute secret keys. SESAME also builds on the Kerberos model by adding additional and more sophisticated access control features, more scalable encryption systems, as well as improved manageability, auditing features, and the delegation of responsibility for allowing access.

Virtual Private Networks (VPNs)

Virtual Private Networks are implementations of cryptographic technology (which you learn about in Chapter 8 of this book). A **Virtual Private Network (VPN)** is a private and secure network connection between systems that uses the data communication capability of an unsecured and public network. The Virtual Private Network Consortium (VPNC) (*www.vpnc.org*) defines a VPN as "a private data network that makes use of the public telecommunication infrastructure, maintaining privacy through the use of a tunneling protocol and security procedures."[8] VPNs are commonly used to extend securely an organization's internal network connections to remote locations beyond the trusted network. The VPNC defines three VPN technologies: trusted VPNs, secure VPNs, and hybrid VPNs. A **trusted VPN**, also known as a legacy VPN, uses leased circuits from a service provider and conducts packet switching over these leased circuits. The organization must trust the service provider, who provides contractual assurance that no one else is allowed to use these circuits and that the circuits are properly maintained and protected—hence the name *trusted* VPN.[9] **Secure VPNs** use security protocols and encrypt traffic transmitted across unsecured public networks like the Internet. A **hybrid VPN** combines the two, providing encrypted transmissions (as in secure VPN) over some or all of a trusted VPN network.

A VPN that proposes to offer a secure and reliable capability while relying on public networks must accomplish the following, regardless of the specific technologies and protocols being used:

- *Encapsulation* of incoming and outgoing data, wherein the native protocol of the client is embedded within the frames of a protocol that can be routed over the public network as well as be usable by the server network environment.

- *Encryption* of incoming and outgoing data to keep the data contents private while in transit over the public network but usable by the client and server computers and/or the local networks on both ends of the VPN connection.

- *Authentication* of the remote computer and, perhaps, the remote user as well. Authentication and the subsequent authorization of the user to perform specific actions are predicated on accurate and reliable identification of the remote system and/or user.

In the most common implementation, a VPN allows a user to turn the Internet into a private network. As you know, the Internet is anything but private. However, using the tunneling approach an individual or organization can set up tunneling points across the Internet and send encrypted data back and forth, using the IP-packet-within-an-IP-packet method to transmit data safely and securely. VPNs are simple to set up and maintain and usually require only that the tunneling points be dual-homed—that is, connecting a private network to the Internet or to another outside connection point. There is VPN support built into most Microsoft server software, including NT and 2000, as well as client support for VPN services built into XP. While true private network services connections can cost hundreds of thousands of dollars to lease, configure, and maintain, a VPN can cost next to nothing. There are a number of ways to implement a VPN. IPSec, the dominant protocol used in VPNs, uses either transport mode or tunnel mode. IPSec can be used as a stand-alone protocol, or coupled with the Layer 2 Tunneling Protocol (L2TP).

Transport Mode

In transport mode, the data within an IP packet is encrypted, but the header information is not. This allows the user to establish a secure link directly with the remote host, encrypting only the data contents of the packet. The downside to this implementation is that packet eavesdroppers can still determine the destination system. Once an attacker knows the destination, he or she may be able to compromise one of the end nodes and acquire the packet information from it. On the other hand, transport mode eliminates the need for special servers and tunneling software, and allows the end users to transmit traffic from anywhere. This is especially useful for traveling or telecommuting employees. Figure 6-18 illustrates the transport mode methods of implementing VPNs.

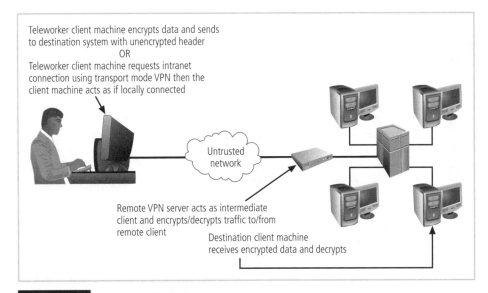

FIGURE 6-18   Transport Mode VPN

There are two popular uses for transport mode VPNs. The first is the end-to-end transport of encrypted data. In this model, two end users can communicate directly, encrypting and decrypting their communications as needed. Each machine acts as the end node VPN server and client. In the second, a remote access worker or teleworker connects to an office network over the Internet by connecting to a VPN server on the perimeter. This allows the teleworker's system to work as if it were part of the local area network. The VPN server in this example acts as an intermediate node, encrypting traffic from the secure intranet and transmitting it to the remote client, and decrypting traffic from the remote client and transmitting it to its final destination. This model frequently allows the remote system to act as its own VPN server, which is a weakness, since most work-at-home employees are not provided with the same level of physical and logical security they would be if they worked in the office.

OFFLINE

VPN vs. Dial-Up[10]

Modern organizations can no longer afford to have their knowledge workers "chained" to hardwired local networks and resources. The increase in broadband home services and public Wi-Fi networks has increased use of VPN technologies, enabling remote connections to the organization's network to be established from remote locations, as when, for example, employees work from home or are traveling on business trips. Road warriors can now access their corporate e-mail and local network resources from wherever they happen to be.

Remote access falls into three broad categories: 1) connections with full network access, where the remote computer acts as if it were a node on the organization's network; 2) feature-based connections, where users need access to specific, discrete network features like e-mail or file transfers; and 3) connections that allow remote control of a personal computer, usually in the worker's permanent office. It is the first category of connections that now use VPN instead of the traditional dial-up access based on dedicated inbound phone lines.

In the past, mobile workers used Remote Access Servers (RAS) over dial-up or ISDN leased lines to connect to company networks from remote locations (that is, when they were working from home or traveling). All things considered, RAS was probably more secure than the current practice of using a VPN, as the connection was made on a truly private network. However, RAS is expensive because it depends on dedicated phone circuits, specialized equipment, and aging infrastructure.

The alternative is VPN, which makes use of the public Internet. It is a solution that offers industrial-grade security. VPN today uses two different approaches to the technology—IPSec and Secure Sockets Layer (SSL). IPSec is more secure but is more expensive and requires more effort to administer. SSL is already available on most common Internet browsers and offers broader compatibility without requiring special software on the client computer. While SSL-based VPN has a certain attractiveness on account of its wide applicability and lower cost, it is not a perfect solution. The fact that it can be used nearly anywhere makes losses from user lapses and purposeful abuse more likely.

Tunnel Mode

In tunnel mode, the organization establishes two perimeter tunnel servers. These servers serve as the encryption points, encrypting all traffic that will traverse an unsecured network. In tunnel mode, the entire client packet is encrypted and added as the data portion of a packet addressed from one tunneling server and to another. The receiving server decrypts the packet and sends it to the final address. The primary benefit to this model is that an intercepted packet reveals nothing about the true destination system.

One example of a tunnel mode VPN is provided with Microsoft's Internet Security and Acceleration (ISA) Server. With ISA Server, an organization can establish a gateway-to-gateway tunnel, encapsulating data within the tunnel. ISA can use the Point to Point Tunneling Protocol (PPTP), Layer 2 Tunneling Protocol (L2TP), or Internet Security Protocol (IPSec) technologies. Additional detail on these protocols is provided in Chapter 8. Figure 6-19 shows an example of tunnel mode VPN implementation. On the client end, a user with Windows 2000 or XP can establish a VPN by configuring his or her system to connect to a VPN server. The process is straightforward. First, connect to the Internet through an ISP or direct network connection. Second, establish the link with the remote VPN server. Figure 6-20 shows the connection screens used to configure the VPN link.

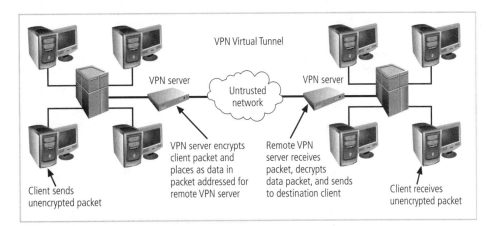

FIGURE 6-19   Tunnel Mode VPN

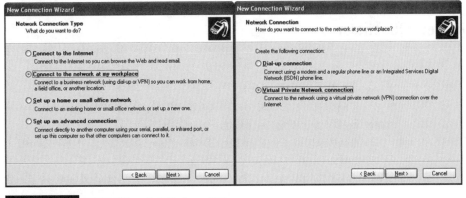

FIGURE 6-20   VPN Client in Windows XP

Chapter Summary

- A firewall as part of an information security program is any device that prevents a specific type of information from moving between the outside network, known as the untrusted network, and the inside network, known as the trusted network.

- Firewalls can be categorized into five groupings: packet filtering, circuit gateways, MAC layers, application gateways, and hybrid firewalls.

- Packet filtering firewalls can be implemented as static filtering, dynamic filtering, and stateful inspection firewalls.

- Firewalls are often categorized by the generation of the technology with which they are implemented, which can range from the first to the fifth generations.

- Firewalls can be categorized by the structural approach used for the implementation, including commercial appliances, commercial systems, residential/SOHO appliances, and residential software firewalls.

- There are four common architectural implementations of firewalls: packet filtering routers, screened host firewalls, dual-homed firewalls, and screened subnet firewalls.

- Content filtering can improve security and assist organizations in improving the manageability of the use of technology.

- Firewalls operate by evaluating data packet contents against logical rules. This logical set is most commonly referred to as firewall rules, rule base, or firewall logic.

- Dial-up protection mechanisms help secure those organizations that use modems for remote connectivity. Kerberos and SESAME are authentication technologies that add security to this technology.

- Virtual Private Network technology can be used to enable remote offices and users to connect to private networks securely over public networks.

Review Questions

1. What is the typical relationship among the untrusted network, the firewall, and the trusted network?

2. What is the relationship between a TCP and UDP packet? Will any specific transaction usually involve both types of packets?

3. How is an application layer firewall different from a packet filtering firewall? Why is an application layer firewall sometimes called a proxy server?

4. How is static filtering different from dynamic filtering of packets? Which is perceived to offer improved security?

5. What is stateful inspection? How is state information maintained during a network connection or transaction?

6. What is a circuit gateway. and how does it differ from the other forms of firewalls?

7. What special function does a cache server perform? Why is this useful for larger organizations?

8. Describe how the various types of firewalls interact with the network traffic at various levels of the OSI model.

9. What is a hybrid firewall?

10. List the five generations of firewall technology. Which generations are still in common use?

11. How does a commercial-grade firewall appliance differ from a commercial-grade firewall system? Why is this difference significant?

12. Explain the basic technology that makes residential/SOHO firewall appliances effective in protecting a local network. Why is this usually adequate for protection?

13. What key features point up the superiority of residential/SOHO firewall appliances over personal computer-based firewall software?

14. How do screened host architectures for firewalls differ from screened subnet firewall architectures? Which of these offers more security for the information assets that remain on the trusted network?

15. What a sacrificial host? What is a bastion host?

16. What is a DMZ? Is this really a good name, considering the function this type of subnet performs?

17. What are the three questions that frame the discussion about selecting a firewall for a specific organization?

18. What is RADIUS? What advantage does it have over TACACS?

19. What is a content filter? Where is it placed in the network to gain the best result for the organization?

20. What is a VPN? What are some reasons it is widely popular in many organizations?

Exercises

1. Using the Web, search for "personal software firewalls." Examine the various alternatives available and compare their functionality, cost, features, and type of protection. Create a weighted ranking according to your own evaluation of the features and specifications of each software package.

2. Using Figure 6-14, create rule(s) necessary for both the internal and external firewalls to allow a remote user to access an internal machine from the Internet using the software Timbuktu. This requires researching the ports used by this software packet.

3. Using Figure 6-14, suppose management wants to create a "server farm" inside the internal network that is configured to allow a proxy firewall in the DMZ to access an internal Web server (rather than a Web server in the DMZ). What additional concerns need to be addressed for this implementation?

4. Using the Internet, determine what applications are commercially available to secure dial-up access points.

5. Using a Microsoft XP or 2000 system, open Internet Explorer. Open Internet Options under the Tools menu. Examine the contents of the Security and Privacy tabs. How can these tabs be configured to provide: a) content filtering, and b) protection from unwanted items like cookies?

Case Exercises

The next morning at 8 o'clock, Kelvin called the meeting to order.

The first person to address the group was the network design consultant, Susan Hamir. She reviewed the critical points from her earlier design report, going over the options it had presented and outlining the tradeoffs in those design choices.

When she finished, she sat down and Kelvin addressed the group again: "We need to break the logjam on this design issue. We have all the right people in this room to make the right choice for the company. Now here are the questions I want us to consider over the next three hours." Kelvin hit the key on his PC to show a slide with a list of discussion questions on the projector screen.

Questions:

1. What questions do you think Kelvin should have included on his slide to start the discussion?

2. If the questions to be answered were broken down into two categories, they would be cost vs. maintaining high security while keeping flexibility. Which is most important for SLS?

Endnotes

1. Avolio, Frederic. Firewalls and Internet Security, the Second Hundred (Internet) Years WWW Document. Accessed 2/6/04. Available from the World Wide Web <*http://www.cisco.com/warp/public/759/ipj_2-2/ipj_2-2_fis1.html*>.

2. Wack, John. "Circuit-Level Gateways" WWW Document, Accessed 2/6/04. Available from the World Wide Web <*http://csrc.nist.gov/publications/nistpubs/800-10/node53.html*>.

3. Cisco Systems, Inc. "Inside the Cisco Centri Firewall." Cisco Online [Cited 1 July 2002]. Available from the World Wide Web <*http://www.cisco.com/univercd/cc/td/doc/product/iaabu/centri4/user/scf4ch5.htm#xtocid157876*>.

4. Elron Software, Inc.. "Choosing the Best Firewall for Your Growing Network." Elron Online. 22 April 2002. [Cited 1 July 2002]. Available from the World Wide Web <*http://www.elronsoftware.com/connection/story67a.html*>.

5. Laura Taylor. "Guidelines for Configuring your Firewall Rule-Set." Tech Update Online. 12 April 2001. [Cited 1 July 2002]. Available from the World Wide Web <*http://techupdate.zdnet.com/techupdate/stories/main/0,14179,2707159,00.html*>.

6. SSL from Webopedia.com. Retrieved July 8, 2004. Available from the World Wide Web <*http://www.webopedia.com/TERM/S/SSL.html*>.

7. Krutz, Ronald L. and Vines, Russell Dean. *The CISSP Prep Guide: Mastering the Ten Domains of Computer Security.* (New York: John Wiley and Sons Inc., 2001), 40.

8. VPN Consortium (2004) VPN Technologies: Definitions and Requirements. Viewed online March 12, 2004. Available from the World Wide Web <*http://www.vpnc.org/vpn-technologies.html*>.

9. VPN Consortium (2004) VPN Technologies: Definitions and Requirements, Viewed online 3.12.04 at *http://www.vpnc.org/vpn-technologies.html*.

10. Oo Gin Lee, "Reach for the remote," Asia Computer Weekly. Singapore: Dec 3, 2003. (1).

7

Security Technology: Intrusion Detection, Access Control, and other Security Tools

> Do not wait; the time will never be *just right.* Start where you stand, and work with whatever tools you may have at your command, and better tools will be found as you go along.
>
> **NAPOLEON HILL (1883-1970)**
> **FOUNDER OF** *THE SCIENCE OF SUCCESS*

MILLER HARRISON WAS GOING TO MAKE THEM SORRY, and make them pay. Earlier today, his contract at SLS had been terminated, and he'd been sent home. Oh sure, the big shot manager, Charlie Moody, had said Miller would still get paid for the two weeks remaining in his contract, and that the decision was based on "changes in the project and evolving needs as project work continued," but Miller knew better. He knew he'd been let go because of that know-nothing Kelvin and his simpering lapdog Laverne Nguyen. And now he was going to show them and everyone else at SLS who knew more about security.

Miller remembered from the days before he became an information security consultant that the secret to hacking into a network successfully was knowing that it required the same patience, attention to detail, and dogged determination that defending a network did. He also remembered that the first step in a typical hacking protocol was footprinting—that is, getting a fully annotated diagram of the network. Luckily for him, Miller could skip this first step, because, as he had been working at SLS for a number of weeks, he had been given a network diagram, and even though this diagram was not supposed to leave the workplace, he had brought a copy home last week when Laverne first started trying to tell him how to do his job.

After they let him go today, Miller's supervisor from the consulting firm had made him turn in his company laptop right away and then actually had the nerve to search his briefcase.

By this time, however, Miller had—again, luckily for him—already stashed all the files and access codes he needed to wage an attack.

Ready to start, he activated his VPN client to connect to the SLS network. He realized almost immediately that Charlie Moody had also confiscated the crypto-token that enabled him to use the VPN for remote access to SLS. No problem, Miller decided. If the front door was locked, he would try the back door. He opened up a modem dialing program and typed in the dial-up number for SLS he had gotten from the network administrator last week. After the usual caterwauling sounds, the dialer established the connection. Miller readied himself to begin his retribution against the SLS servers. His fingers were poised above the keyboard when he saw a prompt.

SLS Inc. Company Use Only. Unauthorized use is prohibited and subject to prosecution.

Enter Passphrase:

Miller realized that the SLS security team had rerouted all dial-up requests to be authenticated through the same RADIUS services that the VPN used. Thus, he was locked out of the back door too. But Miller moved on to his next option, which was to use another back door of his very own. This was also another little "precaution" he'd taken last week before he'd been booted from his job. The back door consisted of a zombie program he'd installed to run on the company's extranet Quality Assurance server. No one at SLS took the QA server seriously since it did not store any production data. In fact, the server wasn't even subject to all the change control procedures that were applied to other systems on the extranet. Miller activated the control program he used to remotely control the zombie program and typed in the IP address of the computer where the zombie was running. No response. He opened up a command window and Pinged the zombie. The computer at that address answered each Ping promptly, which meant the computer itself was alive and well. Miller checked the UDP port number the zombie in his notebook used and ran an Nmap scan against that single computer for that port. The UDP port the zombie control dialogue used was closed tight. He cursed the firewall, the policy that controlled it and the technicians that kept it up to date.

With all of his pre-planned payback cut off at the edge of SLS's network, he decided to continue his hack by going back to the usual first step in his hacking protocol—in other words, to get a detailed fingerprinting of all SLS Internet addresses. Since the front and both back doors were locked, it was time to get a new floor plan. His next action was to launch a simple network port scanner on his Linux laptop. He restarted Nmap and configured it to scan the entire IP address range for SLS's extranet. With a single keystroke, he unleashed the port scanner against the SLS network.

LEARNING OBJECTIVES:

Upon completion of this material, you should be able to:

- Identify and describe the categories and operating models of intrusion detection systems
- Identify and describe honey pots, honey nets, and padded cell systems
- List and define the major categories of scanning and analysis tools, and describe the specific tools used within each of these categories
- Discuss various approaches to access control, including the use of biometric access mechanisms

Introduction

Chapter 6 began the discussion on the physical design of an information security program by covering firewalls, dial-up protection mechanisms, content filtering, and VPNs. This chapter builds on that discussion by describing some other technologies—namely, intrusion detection systems; honey pots, honey nets, and padded cell systems; scanning and analysis tools; and access control—that organizations can use to secure their information assets.

The fact that information security is a discipline that relies on people in addition to technical controls to improve the protection of an organization's information assets cannot be overemphasized. Yet as noted in Chapter 6, technical solutions, properly implemented, can enhance the confidentiality, integrity, and availability of an organization's information assets.

In order to understand the technologies discussed in this chapter, especially the intrusion detection systems, you must first understand the nature of the event they attempt to detect. An **intrusion** is a type of attack on information assets in which the instigator attempts to gain entry into a system or disrupt the normal operations of a system with, almost always, the intent to do malicious harm. Even when such attacks are self propagating, as in the case of viruses and distributed denial of services, they were almost always instigated by an individual whose purpose is to harm an organization. Often, the difference between types of intrusions lies with the attacker: some intruders don't care which organizations they harm and prefer to remain anonymous, while others, like Mafiaboy, crave the notoriety associated with breaking in.

Incident response is the identification of, classification of, response to, and recovery from an incident. The literature in the area of incident response discusses the subject in terms of prevention, detection, reaction, and correction. Intrusion *prevention* consists of activities that seek to deter an intrusion from occurring. Some important intrusion prevention activities are writing and implementing good enterprise information security policy, planning and performing effective information security programs, installing and testing technology-based information security countermeasures (such as firewalls and intrusion detection systems), and conducting and measuring the effectiveness of employee training and awareness activities. Intrusion *detection* consists of procedures and systems that are created and operated to detect system intrusions. This includes the mechanisms an organization implements to limit the number of false positive alarms while ensuring the detection of true intrusion events. Intrusion *reaction* encompasses the actions an organization undertakes when an intrusion event is detected. These actions seek to limit the loss from an intrusion and initiate procedures for returning operations to a normal state as rapidly as possible. Intrusion *correction* activities finalize the restoration of operations to a normal state, and by seeking to identify the source and method of the intrusion in order to ensure that the same type of attack cannot occur again, they return to intrusion prevention—thus closing the incident response loop.

In addition to intrusion detection systems, this chapter also covers honey pots and padded cell systems, scanning and analysis tools, and access control technologies. Honey pots and padded cell systems are mechanisms used to attempt to channel or redirect attackers whereas the intrusion detection systems record their actions and notify the system owner. In order to understand how attackers take advantage of network protocol and system weaknesses, you must learn about the specialized scanning and analysis tools they use to detect these weaknesses. The first line of defense against all attackers is an understanding of the basic access control technology built into information systems.

Intrusion Detection Systems (IDSs)

Information security **intrusion detection systems (IDSs)** were first commercially available in the late 1990s. An IDS works like a burglar alarm in that it detects a violation of its configuration (analogous to an opened or broken window) and activates an alarm. This alarm can be audible and/or visual (producing noise and lights, respectively), or it can be silent (taking the form of an e-mail message or pager alert). With almost all IDSs, system administrators can choose the configuration of the various alerts and the associated alarm levels for each type of alert. Many IDSs enable administrators to configure the systems to notify them directly of trouble via e-mail or pagers. The systems can also be configured—again like a burglar alarm—to notify an external security service organization of a "break-in." The configurations that enable IDSs to provide such customized levels of detection and response are quite complex. A valuable source of information for more detailed study about IDS is National Institute of Standards and Technology (NIST) Special Publication 800-31, "Intrusion Detection Systems," written by Rebecca Bace and Peter Mell and available through the NIST's Computer Security Resource Center at *http://csrc.nist.gov*.

IDS Terminology

In order to understand IDS operational behavior, you must first become familiar with some terminology that is unique to the field of IDSs. The following is a compilation of relevant IDS-related terms and definitions that were drawn from the marketing literature of a well-known information security company, TruSecure, but are representative across the industry:

- **Alert** or **Alarm:** An indication that a system has just been attacked and/or continues to be under attack. IDSs create alerts or alarms to notify administrators that an attack is or was occurring and may have been successful. Alerts and alarms may take the form of audible signals, e-mail messages, pager notifications, pop-up windows, or log entries (these are merely written, i.e., they do not involve taking any action).

- **False Attack Stimulus**: An event that triggers alarms and causes a false positive when no actual attacks are in progress. Testing scenarios that evaluate the configuration of IDSs may use false attack stimuli to determine if the IDSs can distinguish between these stimuli and real attacks.

- **False Negative**: The failure of an IDS system to react to an actual attack event. Of all failures, this is the most grievous, for the very purpose of an IDS is to detect attacks.

- **False Positive**: An alarm or alert that indicates that an attack is in progress or that an attack has successfully occurred when in fact there was no such attack. A false positive alert can sometimes be produced when an IDS mistakes normal system operations/activity for an attack. False positives tend to make users insensitive to alarms, and will reduce their quickness and degree of reaction to actual intrusion events through the process of desensitization to alarms and alerts. This can make users less inclined, and therefore slow, to react when an actual intrusion occurs.

- **Noise**: The ongoing activity from alarm events that are accurate and noteworthy but not necessarily significant as potentially successful attacks. Unsuccessful attacks are the most common source of noise in IDSs, and some of these may not even be attacks at all, but rather employees or other users of the local network simply experimenting with scanning and enumeration tools without any intent to do harm. The issue faced regarding noise is that most of the intrusion events detected are not malicious and have no significant chance of causing a loss.

- **Site Policy**: The rules and configuration guidelines governing the implementation and operation of IDSs within the organization.

- **Site Policy Awareness**: An IDS's ability to dynamically modify its site policies in reaction or response to environmental activity. A so-called *Smart* IDS can adapt its reaction activities based on both guidance learned over time from the administrator and circumstances present in the local environment. Using a device of this nature, the IDS administrator acquires logs of events that fit a specific profile instead of being alerted about minor changes, such as when a file is changed or a user login fails. Another advantage of using a Smart IDS is that the IDS knows when it does *not* need to alert the administrator—this would be the case when an attack using a known and documented exploit is made against systems that the IDS knows are patched against that specific kind of attack. When the IDS can accept multiple response profiles based on changing attack scenarios and environmental values, it can be made much more useful.

- **True Attack Stimulus**: An event that triggers alarms and causes an IDS to react as if a real attack is in progress. The event may be an actual attack, in which an attacker is at work on a system compromise attempt, or it may be a drill, in which security personnel are using hacker tools to conduct tests of a network segment.

- **Confidence Value**: A value associated with an IDS's ability to detect and identify an attack correctly. The confidence value an organization places in the IDS is based on experience and past performance measurements. The confidence value, which is a type of *fuzzy logic*, provides an additional piece of information to assist the administrator in determining whether an attack alert is indicating that an actual attack in progress, or whether the IDS is reacting to false attack stimuli and creating a false positive. For example, if a system deemed capable of reporting a denial-of-service attack with 90% confidence sends an alert, there is a high probability that an actual attack is occurring.

- **Alarm Filtering**: The process of classifying the attack alerts that an IDS produces in order to distinguish/sort false positives from actual attacks more efficiently. Once an IDS has been installed and configured, the administrator can set up alarm filtering by first running the system for a while to track what types of false positives it generates and then adjusting the classification of certain alarms. For example, the administrator may set the IDS to discard certain alarms that he or she knows are produced by false attack stimuli or normal network operations. Alarm filters are similar to packet filters in that they can filter items by their source or destination IP addresses, but they have the additional capability of being able to filter by operating systems, confidence values, alarm type, or alarm severity.
- **Alarm Clustering**: A consolidation of almost identical alarms into a single higher-level alarm. This consolidation will reduce the total number of alarms generated, thereby reducing administrative overhead, and will also indicate a relationship between the individual alarm elements.
- **Alarm Compaction**: Alarm clustering that is based on frequency, similarity in attack signature, similarity in attack target, or other similarities. Like the previous form of alarm clustering, this will reduce the total number of alarms generated, thereby reducing administrative overhead, and will also indicate a relationship between the individual alarm elements when they have specific similar attributes.

Why Use an IDS?

According to the NIST's documentation on industry best practices, there are several compelling reasons to acquire and use an IDS:

1. To prevent problem behaviors by increasing the perceived risk of discovery and punishment for those who would attack or otherwise abuse the system

2. To detect attacks and other security violations that are not prevented by other security measures

3. To detect and deal with the preambles to attacks (commonly experienced as network probes and other 'doorknob rattling' activities)

4. To document the existing threat to an organization

5. To act as quality control for security design and administration, especially of large and complex enterprises

6. To provide useful information about intrusions that do take place, allowing improved diagnosis, recovery, and correction of causative factors[1]

One of the best reasons why organizations should install an IDS is that these systems can serve as straightforward deterrent measures, by increasing the fear of detection and discovery among would-be attackers. If internal and external users know that an organization has an intrusion detection system, they are less likely to probe or attempt to compromise it, just as criminals are much less likely to break into a house that has been clearly marked as having a burglar alarm.

The second reason for installing an IDS is to cover the organization when its network fails to protect itself against known vulnerabilities or is unable to respond to a rapidly changing threat environment. There are many factors that can delay or undermine an organization's ability to make its systems safe from attack and subsequent loss. For example, even though popular information security technologies such as scanning tools (to be discussed later in this chapter) allow security administrators to evaluate the readiness of their systems, they may still fail to detect or correct a known deficiency, or may perform the vulnerability-detection process too infrequently. In addition, even when a vulnerability is detected in a timely manner, it cannot always be corrected quickly. Also, because such corrective measures usually involve the administrator installing patches and upgrades, they are subject to delays caused by fluctuation in the administrator's workload. To further complicate the matter, sometimes there are services that are known to be vulnerable, but they are so essential to ongoing operations that they cannot be disabled or otherwise protected in the short term. At such times—that is, when there is a known vulnerability or deficiency in the system—an IDS can be particularly effective, as it can be set up to detect attacks or attempts to exploit existing weaknesses. By, in effect, guarding these vulnerabilities, IDS can become an important part of the strategy of defense in depth.

The next reason why IDSs are useful is that they can help administrators detect the preambles to attacks. Most attacks begin with an organized and thorough probing of the organization's network environment and its defenses. This initial estimation of the defensive state of an organization's networks and systems is called *doorknob rattling* and is conducted first through activities collectively known as *footprinting* (which involves gathering information about the organization and its network activities and the subsequent process of identifying network assets), and then through another set of activities collectively known as *fingerprinting* (in which network locales are scanned for active systems, and then the network services offered by the host systems on that network are identified). When a system is capable of detecting the early warning signs of footprinting and fingerprinting, much as neighborhood watch volunteers might be capable of detecting potential burglars who are casing their neighborhoods by skulking through and testing doors and windows, then the administrators may have time to prepare for a potential attack or to take actions to minimize potential losses from an attack.

A fourth reason for acquiring an IDS is documentation. In order to justify the expenses associated with implementing security technology like an IDS (and other controls such as firewalls), security professionals frequently have to make a business case. Since projects to deploy these technologies are often very expensive, almost all organizations require that project proponents document the threat from which the organization must be protected. The most frequent method used for doing this is to collect data on the attacks that are currently occurring in the organization and other similar organizations. While such data can be found in published reports or journal articles, first-hand measurements and analysis of the organization's own local network data are likely to be the most persuasive. As it happens, one means of collecting such data is by using IDS. Thus, IDSs are self-justifying systems—that is, they can serve to document the scope of the threat(s) an organization faces and thus produce data that can help administrators persuade management that additional expenditures in information security technologies (e.g., IDSs) are not only warranted, but critical for the ongoing protection of information assets. Measuring attack information with a freeware IDS tool (such as snort) may be a way to begin this process of documentation.

Another reason that supports the use of an IDS relates to the concepts of quality assurance and continuous improvement, which are both well known to most senior managers. In terms of quality control, IDSs support the concept of defense in depth, for they can consistently pick up information about attacks that have successfully compromised the outer layers of information security controls—that is, compromised controls such as a firewall. This information can be used to identify and repair emergent or residual flaws in the security and network architectures, and thus help the organization expedite its incident response process and make other such continuous improvements.

A final reason for installing an IDS is that even if an IDS fails to prevent an intrusion, it can still assist in the after-attack review by helping a system administrator collect information on how the attack occurred, what the intruder accomplished, and which methods the attacker employed. This information can be used, as discussed in the preceding paragraph, to remedy deficiencies as well as trigger the improvement process to prepare the organization's network environment for future attacks. The IDS may also provide forensic information that may be useful as evidence, should the attacker be caught and criminal or civil legal proceedings pursued. In the case of handling forensic information, an organization should follow commonly accepted and legally mandated procedures for handling evidence. Foremost among these is that the information collected should be stored in a location and manner that precludes its subsequent modification. Other legal requirements and plans the organization has for the use of the data may warrant additional storage and handling constraints. As such, an organization may find it useful to consult with legal counsel when determining policy governing this situation.[2]

Types of IDSs and Detection Methods

IDSs operate as network-based, host-based, or application-based systems. A network-based IDS is focused on protecting network information assets. A host-based version is focused on protecting the server or host's information assets. Figure 7-1 shows an example that monitors both network connection activity and current information states on host servers. The application-based model works on one or more host systems that support a single application and is oriented to defend that specific application from special forms of attack. Regardless of whether they operate at the network, host, or application level, all IDSs use one of two detection methods: signature-based or statistical anomaly-based. Each of these approaches to intrusion detection is examined in detail in the following sections.

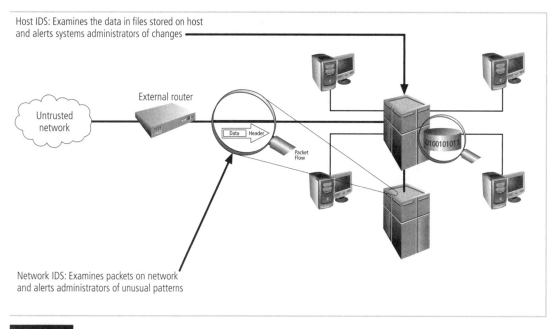

Host IDS: Examines the data in files stored on host and alerts systems administrators of changes

External router

Untrusted network

Data   Header

Packet Flow

0100101011

Network IDS: Examines packets on network and alerts administrators of unusual patterns

FIGURE 7-1   Intrusion Detection Systems

Network-Based IDS

A **network-based IDS (NIDS)** resides on a computer or appliance connected to a segment of an organization's network and monitors network traffic on that network segment, looking for indications of ongoing or successful attacks. When a situation occurs that the NIDS is programmed to recognize as an attack, it responds by sending notifications to administrators. When examining the packets transmitted through an organization's networks, a NIDS looks for attack patterns within network traffic such as large collections of related items that are of a certain type, which could indicate that a denial-of-service attack is underway, or the exchange of a series of related packets in a certain pattern, which could indicate that a port scan is in progress. A NIDS can detect many more types of attacks than a host-based IDS, but to do so, it requires a much more complex configuration and maintenance program.

A NIDS is installed at a specific place in the network (such as on the inside of an edge router) from where it is possible to watch the traffic going into and out of a particular network segment. The NIDS can be deployed to watch a specific grouping of host computers on a specific network segment, or it may be installed to monitor all traffic between the systems that make up an entire network. When placed next to a hub, switch, or other key networking device, the NIDS may use that device's monitoring port. The **monitoring port**, also known as a switched port analysis (SPAN) port or mirror port, is a specially configured connection on a network device that is capable of viewing all of the traffic that moves through the entire device. In the early '90s, before switches became the popular choice for connecting networks in a shared-collision domain, hubs were used. Hubs received traffic from one node, and retransmitted it to all other nodes. This configuration allowed any device connected to the hub to monitor all traffic passing through the hub. Unfortunately, it also represented a security risk, since anyone connected to the hub could monitor all the traffic that moved through that network segment. More recently, switches have been deployed on most networks, and they, unlike hubs, create dedicated point-to-point links between their ports. These links create a higher level of transmission security and privacy, and effectively prevent anyone from being able to capture, and thus eavesdrop on, the traffic passing through the switch. Unfortunately, however, this ability to capture the traffic is necessary for the use of an IDS. Thus, monitoring ports are required. These connections enable network administrators to collect traffic from across the network for analysis by the IDS as well as for occasional use in diagnosing network faults and measuring network performance.

Figure 7-2 shows a sample screen from Demarc Pure Secure (see *www.demarc.com*) displaying events generated by the Snort Network IDS Engine (see *www.snort.org*).

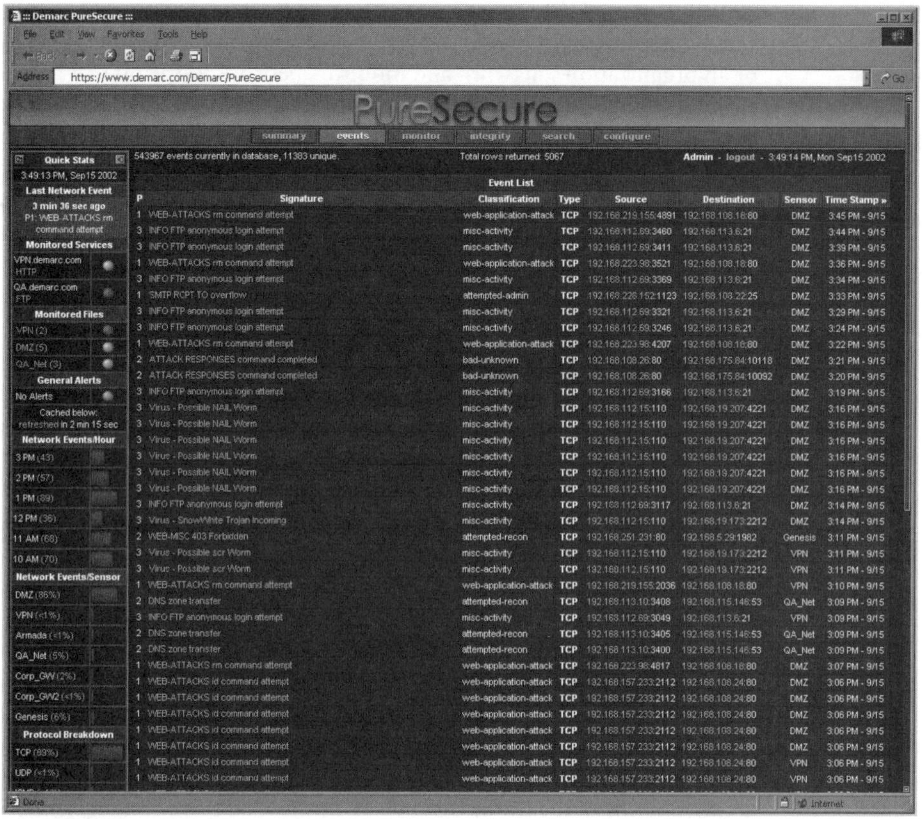

Courtesy Demarc Security, Inc.

FIGURE 7-2   Demarc Pure Secure Total Intrusion Detection

NIDS Signature Matching.   To determine whether or not an attack has occurred or may be underway, NIDSs must look for attack patterns by comparing measured activity to known signatures in their knowledge base. This is accomplished by the comparison of captured network traffic using a special implementation of the TCP/IP stack that reassembles the packets and applies protocol stack verification, application protocol verification, and/or other verification and comparison techniques.

In the process of **protocol stack verification**, the NIDSs look for invalid data packets—i.e., packets that are malformed under the rules of the TCP/IP protocol. A data packet is verified when its configuration matches that defined by the various Internet protocols (e.g., TCP, UDP, IP). The elements of the protocols in use (IP, TCP, UDP, and application layers such as HTTP) are combined in a complete set called the *protocol stack* when the software is implemented in an operating system or application. Many types of intrusions, especially DoS and DDoS attacks, rely on the creation of improperly formed packets to take advantage of weaknesses in the protocol stack in certain operating systems or applications.

In **application protocol verification**, the higher-order protocols (e.g., HTTP, FTP, Telnet) are examined for unexpected packet behavior, or improper use. Sometimes an intrusion involves the arrival of valid protocol packets but in excessive quantities (in the case of the Tiny Fragment Packet attack, the packets are also excessively fragmented).

While the protocol stack verification looks for violations in the protocol packet *structure*, the application protocol verification looks for violations in the protocol packet *use*. One example of this kind of attack is DNS cache poisoning, in which valid packets exploit poorly configured DNS servers to inject false information to corrupt the servers' answers to routine DNS queries from other systems on the network. Unfortunately, however, this higher-order examination of traffic can have the same effect on an IDS as it can on a firewall—that is, it slows the throughput of the system. As such, it may be necessary to have more than one NIDS installed, with one of them performing protocol stack verification and one performing application protocol verification.

Advantages and Disadvantages of NIDSs. The following is a summary, taken from Bace and Mell, of the advantages and disadvantages of NIDSs:

Advantages:

1. Good network design and placement of NIDS devices can enable an organization to use a few devices to monitor a large network.
2. NIDSs are usually passive devices and can be deployed into existing networks with little or no disruption to normal network operations.
3. NIDSs are not usually susceptible to direct attack and, in fact, may not be detectable by attackers.[3]

Disadvantages:

1. A NIDS can become overwhelmed by network volume and fail to recognize attacks it might otherwise have detected. Some IDS vendors are accommodating the need for ever faster network performance by improving the processing of detection algorithms in dedicated hardware circuits to gain a performance advantage. Additional efforts to optimize rule set processing may also reduce overall effectiveness in detecting attacks.
2. NIDSs require access to all traffic to be monitored. The broad use of switched Ethernet networks has replaced the ubiquity of shared collision domain hubs. Since many switches have limited or no monitoring port capability, some networks are not capable of providing aggregate data for analysis by a NIDS. Even when switches do provide monitoring ports, they may not be able to mirror all activity with a consistent and reliable time sequence.
3. NIDSs cannot analyze encrypted packets, making some of the network traffic invisible to the process. The increasing use of encryption that hides the contents of some or all of the packet by some network services (such as SSL, SSH, and VPN) limits the effectiveness of NIDSs.
4. NIDSs cannot reliably ascertain if an attack was successful or not. This requires the network administrator to be engaged in an ongoing effort to evaluate the results of the logs of suspicious network activity.
5. Some forms of attack are not easily discerned by NIDSs, specifically those involving fragmented packets. In fact, some NIDSs are particularly susceptible to malformed packets and may become unstable and stop functioning.[4]

Host-Based IDS

A **host-based IDS (HIDS)** works differently from a network-based version of IDS. While a network-based IDS resides on a network segment and monitors activities across that segment, a host-based IDS resides on a particular computer or server, known as the host, and monitors activity only on that system. HIDSs are also known as **system integrity verifiers**[5] as they benchmark and monitor the status of key system files and detect when an intruder creates, modifies, or deletes monitored files. A HIDS is also capable of monitoring system configuration databases, such as Windows registries, in addition to stored configuration files like .ini, .cfg, and .dat files. Most HIDSs work on the principle of configuration or change management, which means they record the sizes, locations, and other attributes of system files. The HIDS then triggers an alert when one of the following changes occurs: file attributes change, new files are created, or existing files are deleted. A HIDS can also monitor systems logs for predefined events. The HIDS examines these files and logs to determine if an attack is underway or has occurred, and if the attack is succeeding or was successful. The HIDS will maintain its own log file so that even when hackers successfully modify files on the target system to cover their tracks, the HIDS can provide an independent audit trail of the attack. Once properly configured, a HIDS is very reliable. The only time a HIDS produces a false positive alert is when an authorized change occurs for a monitored file. This action can be quickly reviewed by an administrator and dismissed as acceptable. The administrator may choose then to disregard subsequent changes to the same set of files. If properly configured, a HIDS can also detect when an individual user attempts to modify or exceed his or her access authorization and give him or herself higher privileges.

A HIDS has an advantage over NIDS in that it can usually be installed in such a way that it can access information that is encrypted when traveling over the network. For this reason, a HIDS is able to use the content of otherwise encrypted communications to make decisions about possible or successful attacks. Since the HIDS has a mission to detect intrusion activity on one computer system, all the traffic it needs to make that decision is coming to the system where the HIDS is running. The nature of the network packet delivery, whether switched or in a shared-collision domain, is not a factor.

A HIDS relies on the classification of files into various categories and then applies various notification actions, depending on the rules in the HIDS configuration. Most HIDSs provide only a few general levels of alert notification. For example, an administrator can configure a HIDS to treat the following types of changes as reportable security events: changes in a system folder (e.g., in C:\Windows or C:\WINNT); and changes within a security-related application (such as C:\TripWire). In other words, administrators can configure the system to alert on any changes within a critical data folder. The configuration rules may classify changes to a specific application folder (e.g., C:\Program Files\Office) as being normal, and hence unreportable. Administrators can configure the system to log all activity but to page them or e-mail them only if a reportable security event occurs. Although this change-based system seems simplistic, it seems to suit most administrators, who, in general, become concerned only if unauthorized changes occur in specific and sensitive areas of the host file system. Applications frequently modify their internal files, such as dictionaries and configuration templates, and users are constantly updating their data files. Unless a HIDS is very specifically configured, these actions can generate a large volume of false alarms.

Managed HIDSs can monitor multiple computers simultaneously. They do this by creating a configuration file on each monitored host and by making each HIDS report back to a master console system, which is usually located on the system administrator's computer. This master console monitors the information provided from the managed hosts and notifies the administrator when it senses recognizable attack conditions. Figure 7-3 provides a sample screen from Tripwire, a popular host-based IDS (see *www.tripwire.com*).

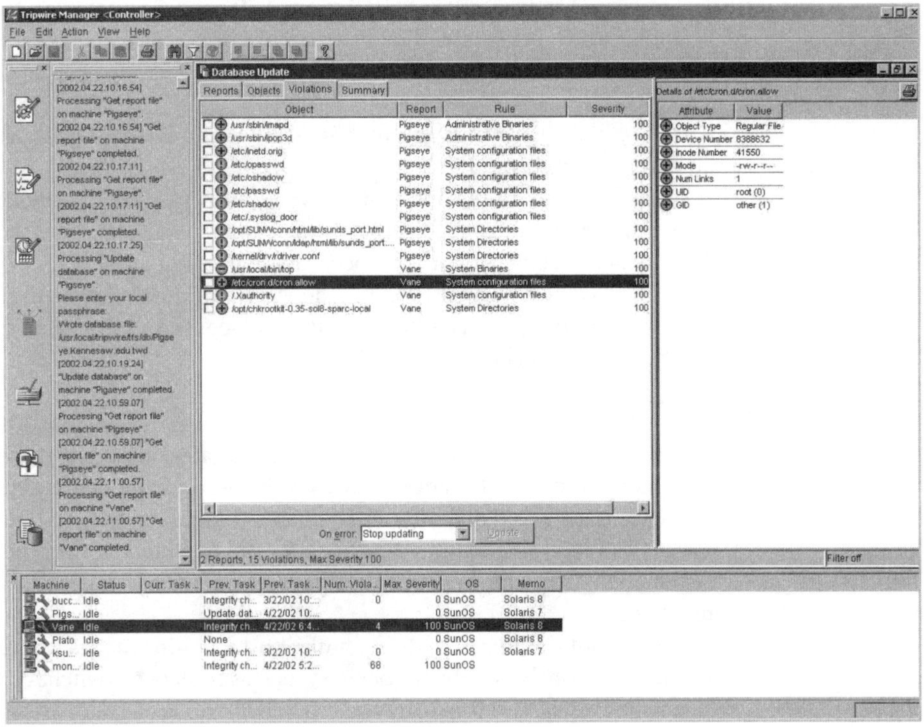

Courtesy of Tripwire®

FIGURE 7-3 Tripwire HIDS

In configuring a HIDS, the system administrator must begin by identifying and categorizing folders and files. One of the most common methods is to designate folders using a pattern of red, yellow, and green categories. Critical systems components are coded red, and usually include the system registry and any folders containing the OS kernel, and application software. Critically important data should also be included in the red category. Support components, such as device drivers and other relatively important files, are generally coded yellow; and user data is usually coded green. This is not to suggest that user data is unimportant, but in practical and strategic terms, monitoring changes to user data does have a lower priority. One reason for this is that users are often assigned storage space that they are expected to use routinely to maintain and back up their documents, files, and images; another reason is that user data files are expected to change frequently—that is, as users make modifications. Systems kernel files, on the other hand, should only change during upgrades or installations. Categorizing critical systems components at a different level from less important files will ensure that the level of response to change will be in proportion to the level of priority. Should the three-tier system be overly simplistic for an organization, there are systems that allow for an alternative scale of 0-100, with 100 being most mission-critical and zero being unimportant. It is not unusual, however, for these types of scales to be overly refined and result in confusion regarding, for example, the prioritization of responses to level 67 and 68 intrusions. Sometimes simpler is better.

Advantages and Disadvantages of HIDSs. The following is a summary, taken from Bace and Mell, of the advantages and disadvantages of HIDSs:

Advantages:

1. A HIDS can detect local events on host systems and also detect attacks that may elude a network-based IDS.
2. A HIDS functions on the host system, where encrypted traffic will have been decrypted and is available for processing.
3. The use of switched network protocols does not affect a HIDS.
4. A HIDS can detect inconsistencies in how applications and systems programs were used by examining the records stored in audit logs. This can enable it to detect some types of attacks, including Trojan Horse programs.[6]

Disadvantages:

1. HIDSs pose more management issues since they are configured and managed on each monitored host. This means that it will require more management effort to install, configure, and operate a HIDS than a comparably sized NIDS solution.
2. A HIDS is vulnerable both to direct attacks and to attacks against the host operating system. Either circumstance can result in the compromise and/or loss of HIDS functionality.
3. A HIDS is not optimized to detect multi-host scanning, nor is it able to detect the scanning of non-host network devices, such as routers or switches. Unless complex correlation analysis is provided, the HIDS will not be aware of attacks that span multiple devices in the network.
4. A HIDS is susceptible to some denial-of-service attacks.
5. A HIDS can use large amounts of disk space to retain the host OS audit logs; and to function properly, it may require disk capacity to be added to the system.
6. A HIDS can inflict a performance overhead on its host systems, and in some cases may reduce system performance below acceptable levels.[7]

Application-Based IDS

A refinement of the host-based IDS is the **application-based IDS (AppIDS)**. Whereas the HIDS examines a single system for file modification, the application-based IDS examines an application for abnormal events. It usually does this examination by looking at the files created by the application and looking for anomalous occurrences such as users exceeding their authorization, invalid file executions, or other activities that would indicate that there is a problem in the normal interaction between the users, the application, and the data. By tracking the interaction between users and applications, the AppIDS is able to trace specific activity back to individual users. One unique advantage of the AppIDS is its ability to view encrypted data. Since the AppIDS interfaces with data as it is processed by an application, and any encrypted data that enters an application is decrypted by the application itself, an AppIDS does not need to become involved in the decryption process. This allows an AppIDS to examine the encryption/decryption process and identify any potential anomalies in data handling or user access.

According to the Missouri State Information Infrastructure Protection Agency, "application-based IDS may be configured to intercept the following types of requests and use them in combinations and sequences to constitute an application's normal behavior:

- File System (file read or write)
- Network (packet events at the driver (NDIS) or transport (TDI) level)
- Configuration (read or write to the registry on Windows)
- Execution Space (write to memory not owned by the requesting application; for example, attempts to inject a shared library DLL into another process)"[8]

Advantages and Disadvantages of AppIDSs. The following is a summary, taken from Bace and Mell, of the advantages and disadvantages of AppIDSs:

Advantages:

1. An AppIDS is aware of specific users and can observe the interaction between the application and the user. This allows the AppIDS to attribute unauthorized activities to specific and known users.
2. An AppIDS is able to operate even when incoming data is encrypted since it is able to operate at the point in the process when the data has been decrypted by applications and has not been re-encrypted for storage.

Disadvantages:

1. AppIDSs may be more susceptible to attack than other IDS approaches, since applications are often less well protected than network and host OS components.
2. AppIDSs are less capable of detecting software tampering and may be taken in by Trojan Horse code or other forms of spoofing. It is usually recommended that AppIDS be used in combination with HIDS and NIDS.[9]

Signature-Based IDS

The preceding sections described where the IDS system should be placed for the purpose of monitoring a network, a host, or an application. Another important differentiation among IDSs is based on detection methods—in other words, on how the IDS should make decisions about intrusion activity. Two detection methods dominate: the signature-based approach and the statistical-anomaly approach. A **signature-based IDS** (sometimes called a **knowledge-based IDS**) examines data traffic in search of patterns that match known **signatures**—that is, preconfigured, predetermined attack patterns. Signature-based IDS technology is widely used because many attacks have clear and distinct signatures, for example: (1) footprinting and fingerprinting activities, described in detail earlier in this chapter, have an attack pattern that includes the use of ICMP, DNS querying, and e-mail routing analysis; (2) exploits involve a specific attack sequence designed to take advantage of a vulnerability to gain access to a system; (3) denial-of-service (DoS) and distributed denial-of-service (DDoS) attacks, during which the attacker tries to prevent the normal usage of a system, entail overloading the system with requests so that the system's ability to process them efficiently is compromised/disrupted and it begins denying services to authorized users.[10]

The problem with the signature-based approach is that as new attack strategies are identified the IDS's database of signatures must be continually updated. Failure to keep this database current can allow attacks that use new strategies to succeed. An IDS that uses signature-based methods works in ways much like most antivirus software. In fact, antivirus software is often classified as a form of signature-based IDS. This is why experts tell users that if they don't keep their antivirus software updated, it will not work as effectively. Another weakness of the signature-based method is the time frame over which attacks occur. If attackers are purposefully slow and methodical, they may slip undetected through this type of IDS because their actions will not match those of their signatures, which often include the time allowed between steps in the attack. The only way for a signature-based IDS to resolve this vulnerability is for it to collect and analyze data over longer periods of time, a process that requires substantially larger data storage capability and additional processing capacity.

Statistical Anomaly-Based IDS

Another approach for detecting intrusions is based on the frequency with which certain network activities take place. The **statistical anomaly-based IDS (stat IDS)** or **behavior-based IDS** collects statistical summaries by observing traffic that is known to be normal. This normal period of evaluation establishes a performance baseline. Once the baseline is established, the stat IDS will periodically sample network activity, and, using statistical methods, compare the sampled network activity to this baseline. When the measured activity is outside the baseline parameters, it is said to exceed the **clipping level**; at this point, the IDS will trigger an alert to notify the administrator. The data that is measured from the normal traffic and is used to prepare the baseline can include variables such as host memory or CPU usage, network packet types, and packet quantities. The measured activity is considered to be outside the baseline parameters (and thus will trigger an alert) when there is an anomaly, or inconsistency, in the comparison of these variables.

The advantage of the statistical anomaly-based approach is that the IDS can detect new types of attacks, for it is looking for abnormal activity of any type. Unfortunately, however, these systems require much more overhead and processing capacity than signature-based ones, as they must constantly compare patterns of activity against the baseline. Another drawback is that these systems may not detect minor changes to system variables and may generate many false positives. If the actions of the users or systems on a network vary widely, with periods of low activity interspersed with periods of frantic packet exchange, this type of IDS may not be suitable, because the dramatic swings from one level to another will almost certainly generate false alarms. Because of its complexity and impact on the overhead computing load of the host computer as well as the number of false positives it can generate, this type of IDS is less commonly used than the signature-based type.

Log File Monitors

A **log file monitor (LFM)** is an approach to IDS that is similar to the NIDS. Using LFM, the system reviews the log files generated by servers, network devices, and even other IDSs. These systems look for patterns and signatures in the log files that may indicate that an attack or intrusion is in process or has already succeeded. While an individual host IDS is only able to look at the activity in one system, the LFM is able to look at multiple log files from a number of different systems. The patterns that signify an attack can be subtle and hard to distinguish when one system is examined in isolation, but they may be much easier to identify when the entire network and its systems are viewed holistically. Of course this holistic approach will require the allocation of considerable resources since it will involve the collection, movement, storage, and analysis of very large quantities of log data.

IDS Response Behavior

Each IDS will respond to external stimulation in different ways, depending on its configuration and function. Some may respond in active ways, collecting additional information about the intrusion, modifying the network environment, or even taking action against the intrusion. Others may respond in passive ways, setting off alarms or notifications, collecting passive data through SNMP traps, and the like.

Response Options for an IDS

Once an IDS detects an anomalous network situation, it has a number of options, depending on the policy and objectives of the organization that has configured it as well as the capabilities of the organization's system. In configuring an IDS's responses to alerts, the system administrator must exercise care to ensure that a response to an attack (or potential attack) does not compound the problem or create a situation that is more disastrous than that of a successful attack. For example, if a NIDS reacts to a suspected DoS attack by severing the network connection, the NIDS has just accomplished what the attacker had hoped. If the attacker discovers that this is the default response to a particular kind of attack, all he or she has to do is repeatedly attack the system at intervals in order to have the organization's own IDS response interrupt its normal business operations. An analogy to this approach would be the case of a potential car thief who walks up to a desirable target in the early hours of a morning, strikes the car's bumper with a rolled up newspaper, and then ducks into the bushes. When the car alarm is triggered, the car owner wakes up, checks the car, determines there is no danger, resets the alarm, and goes back to bed. The thief then repeats the triggering actions every half hour or so until the owner gets so frustrated that he or she disables the alarm, believing it to be malfunctioning. The thief is now free to steal the car without worrying about triggering the alarm.

IDS responses can be classified as active or passive. An active response is one in which a definitive action is initiated when certain types of alerts are triggered. These automated responses include collecting additional information, changing or modifying the environment, and taking action against the intruders. In contrast, IDSs with passive response options simply report the information they have already collected and wait for the administrator to take actions. Generally, the administrator chooses a course of action after he or she has analyzed the collected data, and thus with passive-response IDSs, the administrator becomes the active component of the overall system. The latter is currently the most common implementation, although most systems allow some active options that are kept disabled by default.

The following list illustrates some of the responses an IDS can be configured to produce. Note that some of these are unique to a network-based or a host-based IDS, while others are applicable to both.[11]

- Audible / visual alarm: The IDS can trigger a .wav file, beep, whistle, siren, or other audible or visual notification to alert the administrator of an attack. The most common type of such notifications is the computer pop-up window. This display can be configured with color indicators and specific messages, and it can also contain specifics as to what type of attack is suspected, the tools used in the attack, the level of confidence the system has in its own determination, and the addresses and/or locations of the systems involved.

- SNMP traps and plug-ins: The Simple Network Management Protocol contains trap functions, which allow a device to send a message to the SNMP management console to indicate that a certain threshold has been crossed, either positively or negatively. The IDS can execute this trap, telling the SNMP console an event has occurred. Some of the advantages of this operation include the relatively standard implementation of SNMP in networking devices, the ability to configure the network system to use SNMP traps in this manner, the ability to use systems specifically to handle SNMP traffic, including IDS traps, and the ability to use standard communications networks.

- E-mail message: The IDS can e-mail an individual to notify him or her of an event. Many administrators use personal digital assistants (PDAs) to check their e-mail frequently, thus have access to immediate global notification. Organizations should use caution in relying on e-mail systems as the primary means of communication between the IDS and security personnel, for not only is e-mail inherently fraught with reliability issues, but an intruder may compromise the e-mail system and block the sending of any such notification messages.

- Page or phone message: The IDS can be configured to dial a phone number, producing either an alphanumeric page or a modem noise on a phone call.

- Log entry: The IDS can enter information about the event (e.g., addresses, time, systems involved, protocol information, etc.) into an IDS system log file, or operating system log file. These files can be stored on separate servers to prevent skilled attackers from deleting entries about their intrusions and thus hiding the details of their attack.

- Evidentiary packet dump: Those organizations that have a need for legal uses of the IDS data may choose to record all log data in a special way. This method will allow the organization to perform further analysis on the data and also submit the data as evidence in a future civil or criminal case. Once the data has been written using a cryptographic hashing algorithm (discussed in detail in Chapter 8), it becomes evidentiary documentation—that is, suitable for criminal or civil court use. This packet logging can, however, be resource-intensive, especially in denial-of-service attacks.

- Take action against the intruder: It has become possible, although not advisable, to take action against an intruder. Known as trap and trace, back-hacking, or traceback, this response option involves configuring intrusion detection systems to conduct a trace on the data leaving the attacked site and heading to the systems instigating the attacks. The idea here is that once these attacking systems are identified, some form of counterattack can be initiated. While this sounds tempting, it is ill-advised and may not be legal. An organization only owns a network to its perimeter, and conducting traces or back-hacking to systems outside that perimeter may make the organization just as criminally liable as the individual(s) who began the attack. In addition, it is not uncommon for an attacker to compromise an intermediary system and use that system to conduct the attack. If an organization attempts a back-hack and winds up damaging or destroying data on the intermediary system, it has, in effect, attacked an innocent third party, and will therefore be regarded, in the eyes of that party, as an attacker. The matter can be further complicated if the hacker has used address spoofing, a means by which the attacker can freely change the address headers on the source fields in the IP headers and make the destination address recipients think the packets are coming from one location, when in reality they are coming from somewhere else. Any organization planning to configure any sort of retaliation effort into an automated intrusion detection system is strongly encouraged to seek legal counsel.

- Launch program: An IDS can be configured to execute a specific program when it detects specific types of attacks. A number of vendors have specialized tracking, tracing, and response software that could be part of an organization's intrusion response strategy.
- Reconfigure firewall: An IDS could send a command to the firewall to filter out suspected packets by IP address, port, or protocol. (It is, unfortunately, still possible for a skilled attacker to break in by simply spoofing a different address, shifting to a different port, or changing the protocols used in the attack.) While it may not be easy, an IDS can block or deter intrusions by one of the following methods:
  - Establishing a block for all traffic from the suspected attacker's IP address, or even from the entire source network from which the attacker appears to be operating. This blocking might be set for a specific period of time and be reset to normal rules after that period has expired.
  - Establishing a block for specific TCP or UDP port traffic from the suspected attacker's address or source network, blocking only the services that seem to be under attack.
  - Blocking all traffic to or from a network interface (such as the organization's Internet connection) if the severity of the suspected attack warrants that level of response.[12]
- Terminate session: Terminating the session by using the TCP/IP protocol specified packet *TCP close* is a simple process. Some attacks would be deterred or blocked by session termination, but others would simply continue when the attacker issues a new session request.
- Terminate connection: The last resort for an IDS under attack would be to terminate the organization's internal or external connections. Smart switches can cut traffic to/from a specific port, should that connection be linked to a system that is malfunctioning or otherwise interfering with efficient network operations. As indicated earlier, this response should be the last resort to protect information, as it may be the very goal of the attacker.

[The following sections are drawn from NIST SP 800-31 "Intrusion Detection Systems"]

Reporting and Archiving Capabilities

Many, if not all, commercial IDSs provide capabilities to generate routine reports and other detailed information documents. Some of these can output reports of system events and intrusions detected over a particular reporting period (for example, a week or a month). Some provide statistics or logs generated by the IDSs in formats suitable for inclusion in database systems or for use in report generating packages.

Failsafe Considerations for IDS Responses

Another factor for consideration when considering IDS architectures and products is the failsafe features included by the design and/or product. Failsafe features are those design features meant to protect the IDSs from being circumvented or defeated by an attacker. These represent a necessary difference between standard system management tools and security management tools. There are several areas that require failsafe measures. For instance, IDSs need to provide silent, reliable monitoring of attackers. Should the response function of an IDS break this silence by broadcasting alarms and alerts in plaintext over the monitored network, it would allow attackers to detect the presence of the IDS. Worse yet, the attackers can directly target the IDS as part of the attack on the victim system. Encrypted tunnels or other cryptographic measures used to hide and authenticate IDS communications are excellent ways to secure and ensure the reliability of the IDS.

Selecting IDS Approaches and Products

The wide array of intrusion detection products available today addresses a broad range of organizational security goals and considerations. Given that range of products and features, the process of selecting products that represent the best fit for any specific organization's needs is challenging. The following questions may be useful when preparing a specification for acquiring and deploying an intrusion detection product.

Technical and Policy Considerations

In order to determine which IDS would best meet the needs of a specific organization's environment, first consider that environment, in technical, physical, and political terms.

What Is Your Systems Environment? The first hurdle a potential IDS must clear is that of functioning in your systems environment. This is important, for if an IDS is not designed to accommodate the information sources that are available on your systems, it will not be able to see anything that goes on in your systems, whether that activity is an attack or it is normal activity.

- What are the technical specifications of your systems environment?
  First, specify the technical attributes of your systems environment. Examples of information specified here would include network diagrams and maps specifying the number and locations of hosts; operating systems for each host; the number and types of network devices such as routers, bridges, and switches; number and types of terminal servers and dial-up connections; and descriptors of any network servers, including types, configurations, and application software and versions running on each. If you run an enterprise network management system, specify it here.

- What are the technical specifications of your current security protections?
  Once you have described the technical attributes of your systems environment, describe the security protections you already have in place. Specify numbers, types, and locations of network firewalls, identification and authentication servers, data and link encryptors, antivirus packages, access control products, specialized security hardware (such as crypto accelerator hardware for Web servers), Virtual Private Networks, and any other security mechanisms on your systems.

- What are the goals of your enterprise?
  Some IDSs have been developed to accommodate the special needs of certain industries or market niches such as electronic commerce, health care, or financial markets. Define the functional goals of your enterprise (there can be several goals associated with a single organization) that are supported by your systems.

- How formal is the system environment and management culture in your organization?
  Organizational styles vary, depending on the function of the organization and its traditional culture. For instance, military or other organizations that deal with national security issues tend to operate with a high degree of formality, especially when contrasted with university or other academic environments. Some IDSs offer features that support enforcement of formal use policies, with configuration screens that accept formal expressions of policy, and extensive reporting capabilities that do detailed reporting of policy violations.

What Are Your Security Goals and Objectives? Once you've specified the technical landscape of your organization's systems as well as the existing security mechanisms, it's time to articulate the goals and objectives you wish to attain by using an IDS.

- Is the primary concern of your organization protecting from threats originating outside your organization?

  Perhaps the easiest way to specify security goals is by categorizing your organization's threat concerns. Identify the concerns that your organization has regarding threats that originate outside the organization.

- Is your organization concerned about insider attack?

  Repeat the last step, this time addressing concerns about threats that originate from within your organization, encompassing not only the user who attacks the system from within (such as a shipping clerk who attempts to access and alter the payroll system) but also the authorized user who oversteps his privileges thereby violating organizational security policy or laws (a customer service agent who, driven by curiosity, accesses earnings and payroll records for public figures).

- Does your organization want to use the output of your IDS to determine new needs?

  System usage monitoring is sometimes provided as a generic system management tool to determine when system assets require upgrading or replacement. When such monitoring is performed by an IDS, the needs for upgrade can show up as anomalous levels of user activity.

- Does your organization want to use an IDS to maintain managerial control (non-security related) over network usage?

  In some organizations, there are system use policies that target user behaviors that may be classified as personnel management rather than system security issues. These might include accessing Web sites that provide content of questionable taste or value (such as pornography) or using organizational systems to send e-mail or other messages for the purpose of harassing individuals. Some IDSs provide features that accommodate detecting such violations of management controls.

What Is Your Existing Security Policy? At this time, you should review your existing organization security policy. This will serve as the template against which features of your IDS will be configured. As such, you may find you need to augment the policy, or else derive the following items from it.

- How is it structured?

  It is helpful to articulate the goals outlined in the security policy in terms of the standard security goals (integrity, confidentiality, and availability) as well as more generic management goals (privacy, protection from liability, manageability).

- What are the general job descriptions of your system users?

  List the general job functions of system users (there are commonly several functions assigned to a single user) as well as the data and network accesses that each function requires.

- Does the policy include reasonable use policies or other management provisions?

  As mentioned above, many organizations have system use policies included as part of security policies.

■ Has your organization defined processes for dealing with specific policy violations? It is helpful to have a clear idea of what the organization wishes to do when the IDS detects that a policy has been violated. If the organization doesn't intend to react to such violations, it may not make sense to configure the IDS to detect them. If, on the other hand, the organization wishes to actively respond to such violations, the IDS's operational staff should be informed of the organization's response policy so that they can deal with alarms in an appropriate manner.

Organizational Requirements and Constraints

Your organization's operational goals, constraints, and culture will affect the selection of the IDS and other security tools and technologies to protect your systems. Consider these organizational requirements and limitations.

What Are Requirements that Are Levied from Outside the Organization?

■ Is your organization subject to oversight or review by another organization? If so, does that oversight authority require IDSs or other specific system security resources?

■ Are there requirements for public access to information on your organization's systems? Do regulations or statutes require that information on your system be accessible by the public during certain hours of the day, or during certain date or time intervals?

■ Are there other security-specific requirements levied by law? Are there legal requirements for protection of personal information (such as earnings information or medical records) stored on your systems? Are there legal requirements for investigation of security violations that divulge or endanger that information?

■ Are there internal audit requirements for security best practices or due diligence? Do any of these audit requirements specify functions that the IDSs must provide or support?

■ Is the system subject to accreditation? If so, what is the accreditation authority's requirement for IDSs or other security protection?

■ Are there requirements for law enforcement investigation and resolution of security incidents? Do these specify any IDS functions, especially those having to do with collection and protection of IDS logs as evidence?

What Are Your Organization's Resource Constraints? IDSs can protect the systems of an organization, but at a price. It makes little sense to incur additional expense for IDS features if your organization does not have sufficient systems or personnel to use them and take advantage of the alerts generated by the system.

■ What is the budget for acquisition and life cycle support of intrusion detection hardware, software, and infrastructure? Remember here that the acquisition of IDS software is not the only element that counts toward the total cost of ownership; you may also have to acquire a system on which to run the software, specialized assistance in installing and configuring the system, and training your personnel. Ongoing operations may also require additional staff or outside contractors.

■ Is there sufficient existing staff to monitor an intrusion detection system full time? Some IDSs are designed under the assumption that systems personnel will attend them around the clock. If you do not anticipate having such personnel available, you may wish to explore those systems that accommodate less than full-time attendance or else consider systems that are designed for unattended use.

- Does your organization have authority to instigate changes based on the findings of an intrusion detection system? It is critical that you and your organization be clear about what you plan to do with the problems uncovered by an IDS. If you are not empowered to handle the incidents that arise as a result of the monitoring, you should consider coordinating your selection and configuration of the IDS with the party who is empowered.

IDSs Product Features and Quality

Is the Product Sufficiently Scalable for Your Environment? As mentioned before in this document, many IDSs are not able to scale to large or widely distributed enterprise network environments.

How Has the Product Been Tested? Simply asserting that an IDS has certain capabilities is not sufficient to demonstrate that those capabilities are real. You should request additional demonstration of the suitability of a particular IDS to your environment and goals.

- Has the product been tested against functional requirements? Ask the vendor about the assumptions made regarding the goals and constraints of customer environments.
- Has the product been tested against attack? Ask vendors for details of the security testing to which its products have been subjected. If the product includes network-based vulnerability assessment features, ask also whether test routines that produce system crashes or other denials of service have been identified and flagged in system documentation and interfaces.

What Is the User Level of Expertise Targeted by the Product? Different IDS vendors target users with different levels of technical and security expertise. Ask the vendor what their assumptions are regarding the users of their products.

Is the Product Designed to Evolve as the Organization Grows? One product design goal that will enhance its value to your organization over time is the ability to adapt to your needs over time.

- Can the product adapt to growth in user expertise? Ask here whether the IDS's interface can be configured (with shortcut keys, customizable alarm features, and custom signatures) on the fly. Ask also whether these features are documented and supported.
- Can the product adapt to growth and change of the organization's systems infrastructure? This question has to do with the ability of the IDS to scale to an expanding and increasingly diverse network. Most vendors have experience in adapting their products as target networks grow. Ask also about commitments to support new protocol standards and platform types.
- Can the product adapt to growth and change of the security threat environment? This question is especially critical given the current Internet threat environment, in which 30-40 new attacks are posted to the Web every month.

What Are the Support Provisions for the Product? Like other systems, IDSs require maintenance and support over time. These needs should be identified and prepared in a written report.

- What are commitments for product installation and configuration support? Many vendors provide expert assistance to customers in installing and configuring IDSs; others expect that your own staff will handle these functions, and provide only telephone or e-mail help desk functions.

- What are commitments for ongoing product support? In this area, ask about the vendor's commitment to supporting your use of their IDS product.
- Are subscriptions to signature updates included? As most IDSs are misuse-detectors, the value of the product is only as good as the signature database against which events are analyzed. Most vendors provide subscriptions to signature updates for some period of time (a year is typical).
- How often are subscriptions updated? In today's threat environment, in which 30-40 new attacks are published every month, this is a critical question.
- How quickly after a new attack is made public will the vendor ship a new signature? If you are using IDSs to protect highly visible or heavily traveled Internet sites, it is especially critical that you receive the signatures for new attacks as soon as possible.
- Are software updates included? Most IDSs are software products and therefore subject to bugs and revisions. Ask the vendor about software update and bug patch support, and determine to what extent they are included in the product you purchase.
- How quickly will software updates and patches be issued after a problem is reported to the vendor? As software bugs in IDSs can allow attackers to nullify their protective effect, it is extremely important that problems be fixed, reliably and quickly.
- Are technical support services included? What is the cost? In this category, technical support services mean vendor assistance in tuning or adapting your IDS to accommodate special needs, be they monitoring a custom or legacy system within your enterprise, or reporting IDS results in a custom protocol or format.
- What are the contact provisions for contacting technical support (e-mail, telephone, online chat, web-based reporting)? The contact provisions will likely tell you whether these technical support services are accessible enough to support incident handling or other time-sensitive needs.
- Are there any guarantees associated with the IDS? As in other software products, IDSs traditionally have few guarantees associated with them; however, in an attempt to gain market share, some vendors are initiating guarantee programs.
- What training resources does the vendor provide as part of the product? Once an IDS is selected, installed, and configured, it must still be operated by your personnel. In order for these people to make optimal use of the IDS, they should be trained in its use. Some vendors provide this training as part of the product package.
- What additional training resources are available from the vendor and at what cost? In the case that the IDS's vendor does not provide training as part of the IDS package, you should budget appropriately to train your operational personnel.

Strengths and Limitations of IDSs

Although intrusion detection systems are a valuable addition to an organization's security infrastructure, there are things they do well, and other things they do not do well. As you plan the security strategy for your organization's systems, it is important for you to understand what IDSs should be trusted to do and what goals might be better served by other types of security mechanisms.

Strengths of Intrusion Detection Systems

Intrusion detection systems perform the following functions well:

- Monitoring and analysis of system events and user behaviors
- Testing the security states of system configurations

- Baselining the security state of a system, then tracking any changes to that baseline
- Recognizing patterns of system events that correspond to known attacks
- Recognizing patterns of activity that statistically vary from normal activity
- Managing operating system audit and logging mechanisms and the data they generate
- Alerting appropriate staff by appropriate means when attacks are detected
- Measuring enforcement of security policies encoded in the analysis engine
- Providing default information security policies
- Allowing non-security experts to perform important security monitoring functions

Limitations of Intrusion Detection Systems

Intrusion detection systems cannot perform the following functions:

- Compensating for weak or missing security mechanisms in the protection infrastructure. Such mechanisms include firewalls, identification and authentication, link encryption, access control mechanisms, and virus detection and eradication.
- Instantaneously detecting, reporting, and responding to an attack, when there is a heavy network or processing load
- Detecting newly published attacks or variants of existing attacks
- Effectively responding to attacks launched by sophisticated attackers
- Automatically investigating attacks without human intervention
- Resisting attacks that are intended to defeat or circumvent them
- Compensating for problems with the fidelity of information sources
- Dealing effectively with switched networks

[The preceding sections were drawn from NIST SP 800-31 "Intrusion Detection Systems"]

Deployment and Implementation of an IDS

Deploying and implementing an IDS is not always a straightforward task. The strategy for deploying an IDS should consider a number of factors, the foremost being how the IDS will be managed and where it should be placed. These factors will determine the number of administrators needed to install, configure, and monitor the IDS, as well as the number of management workstations, the size of the storage needed for retention of the data generated by the systems, and the ability of the organization to detect and respond to remote threats.

IDS Control Strategies

An IDS can be implemented via one of three basic control strategies. A control strategy determines how an organization exerts influence and maintains the configuration of an IDS. It will also determine how the input and output of the IDS is to be managed. The three commonly utilized control strategies are centralized, partially distributed, and fully distributed. The IT industry has been exploring technologies and practices to enable the distribution of computer processing cycles and data storage for many years. These explorations have long considered the advantages and disadvantages of the centralized strategy versus those of strategies with varying degrees of distribution. In the early days of computing, all systems were fully centralized, resulting in a control strategy that provided high levels of security and control, as well as efficiencies in resource allocation and management. During the '80s and '90s, with the rapid growth in networking and computing capabilities, the IT industry's ideas about how to arrange computing systems swung to the other end of the pendulum—that is, the trend was to implement a fully distributed strategy. In the mid-'90s, however, the high costs of a fully distributed architecture became apparent, and the IT industry shifted toward a mixed strategy of partially distributed control. A strategy of partial distribution, where some features and components are distributed and others are centrally controlled, has now emerged as the recognized recommended practice for IT systems in general and for IDS control systems in particular.

Centralized Control Strategy. As illustrated in Figure 7-4, with a **centralized IDS control strategy** all IDS control functions are implemented and managed in a central location. This is indicated in the figure with the large square symbol labeled "IDS Console." The IDS console includes the management software, which collects information from the remote sensors (appearing in the figure as triangular symbols), analyzes the systems or networks monitored, and makes the determination as to whether the current situation has deviated from the preconfigured baseline. All reporting features are also implemented and managed from this central location. The primary advantages of this strategy are related to cost and control. With one central implementation, there is one management system, one place to go to monitor the status of the systems or networks, one location for reports, and one set of administrative management. This centralization of IDS management supports specialization in tasks, since all managers are either located near the IDS management console or can acquire an authenticated remote connection to it, and technicians are located near the remote sensors. This means that each person can focus specifically on the assigned task at hand. In addition, the central control group can evaluate the systems and networks as a whole, and since it can compare pieces of information from all sensors, the group is better positioned to recognize a large-scale attack.

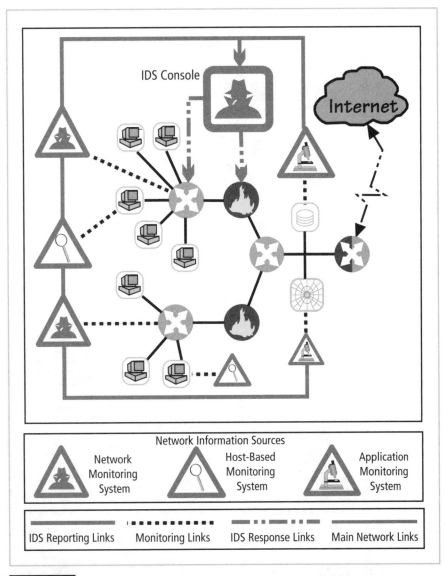

FIGURE 7-4 Centralized IDS Control[13]

Fully Distributed Control Strategy. As presented in Figure 7-5, a **fully distributed IDS control strategy** is the opposite of the centralized strategy. Note in the figure that all control functions (which appear as small square symbols enclosing a computer icon) are applied at the physical location of each IDS component. Each monitoring site uses its own paired sensors to perform its own control functions to achieve the necessary detection, reaction, and response functions. Thus, each sensor/agent is best configured to deal with its own environment. Since the IDSs do not have to wait for a response from a centralized control facility, their reaction to individual attacks is greatly speeded up.

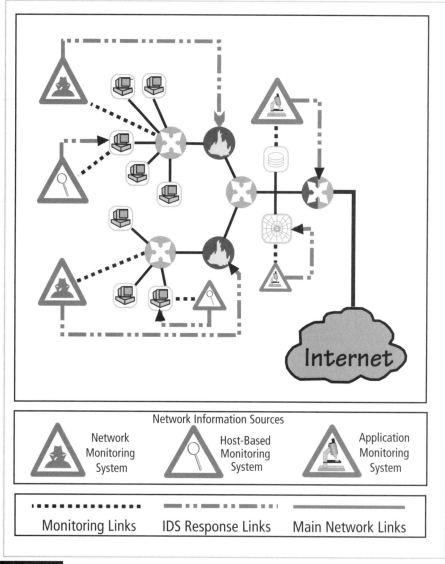

FIGURE 7-5 Fully Distributed IDS Control[14]

Partially Distributed Control Strategy. Finally, a **partially distributed IDS control strategy**, as depicted in Figure 7-6, combines the best of the other two strategies. While the individual agents can still analyze and respond to local threats, their reporting to a hierarchical central facility enables the organization to detect widespread attacks. This blended approach to reporting is one of the more effective methods of detecting intelligent attackers, especially those who probe an organization through multiple points of entry, trying to scope out the systems' configurations and weaknesses, before they launch a concerted attack. The partially distributed control strategy also allows the organization to optimize for economy of scale in the implementation of key management software and personnel, especially in the reporting areas. When the organization can create a pool of security managers to evaluate reports from multiple distributed IDS systems, it becomes better able to detect these distributed attacks before they become unmanageable.

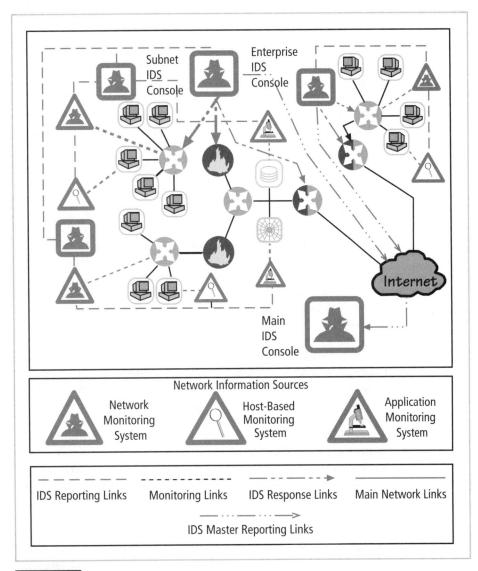

Network Information Sources

| Network Monitoring System | Host-Based Monitoring System | Application Monitoring System |

IDS Reporting Links   Monitoring Links   IDS Response Links   Main Network Links

IDS Master Reporting Links

FIGURE 7-6 Partially Distributed IDS Control[15]

IDS Deployment Overview

Like the decision regarding control strategies, the decisions about where to locate the elements of the intrusion detection systems can be an art in itself. Given the highly technical skills required to implement and configure IDSs and the imperfection of the technology, great care must be made in the decisions about where to locate the components, both in their physical connection to the network and host devices and in how they will be logically connected to each other and the IDS administration team. Since IDSs are designed to detect, report, and even react to anomalous stimuli, placing IDSs in an area where such traffic is common can result in excessive reporting. Moreover, the administrators monitoring systems located in such areas can become desensitized to the high level of information flow and may fail to detect actual attacks in progress.

As an organization selects an IDS and prepares for implementation, planners must select a deployment strategy that is based on a careful analysis of the organization's information security requirements and that integrates with the organization's existing IT infrastructure but, at the same time, causes minimal impact. After all, the purpose of the IDS is to detect anomalous situations—not create them. One consideration for implementation is the skill level of the personnel required to install, configure, and maintain the systems. An IDS is a complex system in that it involves numerous remote monitoring agents (on both individual systems and networks) that require proper configuration to gain the proper authentication and authorization. As the IDS is deployed, each component should be installed, configured, fine-tuned, tested, and monitored. A problem in any step of the deployment process may produce a range of problems—from a minor inconvenience to a network-wide disaster. Thus, both the individuals installing the IDS and the individuals using and managing the system require proper training.

NIDS and HIDS can be used in tandem to cover both the individual systems that connect to an organization's networks and the networks themselves. To do this, it is important for an organization to use a phased implementation strategy so as not to impact the entire organization all at once. A phased implementation strategy also allows security technicians to resolve the problems that do arise without compromising the very information security the IDS is installed to protect. In terms of sequencing the implementation, first the organization should implement the network-based IDS, as they are less problematic and easier to configure than their host-based counterparts. After the NIDSs are configured and running without issue, the HIDSs can be installed to protect the critical systems on the host server. Next, after both are considered operational, it would be advantageous to scan the network with a vulnerability scanner like Nmap or Nessus to determine if a) the scanners pick up anything new or unusual, and b) if the IDS can detect the scans.

Deploying Network-Based IDSs. As discussed above, the placement of the sensor agents is critical to the operation of all IDSs, but this is especially critical in the case of Network IDSs. NIST recommends four locations for NIDS sensors:

Location 1: Behind each external firewall, in the network DMZ (See Figure 7-7, location 1)

Advantages:

- IDS sees attacks that originate from the outside world and may penetrate the network's perimeter defenses.
- IDS can identify problems with the network firewall policy or performance.
- IDS sees attacks that might target the Web server or ftp server, both of which commonly reside in this DMZ.
- Even if the incoming attack is not detected, the IDS can sometimes recognize, in the outgoing traffic, patterns that suggest that the server has been compromised.

Location 2: Outside an external firewall (See Figure 7-7, location 2)

Advantages:

- IDS documents the number of attacks originating on the Internet that target the network.
- IDS documents the types of attacks originating on the Internet that target the network.

Location 3: On major network backbones (See Figure 7-7, location 3)

Advantages:

- IDS monitors a large amount of a network's traffic, thus increasing its chances of spotting attacks.
- IDS detects unauthorized activity by authorized users within the organization's security perimeter.

Location: On critical subnets (See Figure 7-7, location 4)

Advantages:

- IDS detects attacks targeting critical systems and resources.
- Location allows organizations with limited resources to focus these resources on the network assets considered of greatest value.[16]

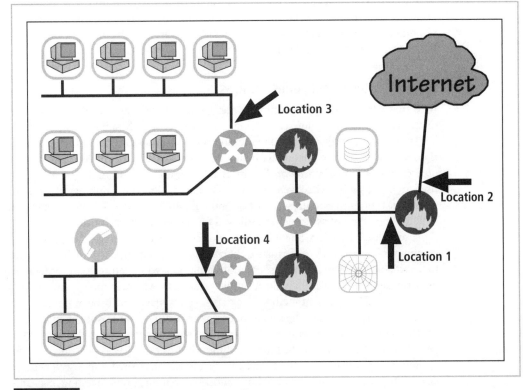

FIGURE 7-7   Network IDS Sensor Locations[17]

Deploying Host-Based IDSs. The proper implementation of HIDSs can be a painstaking and time-consuming task, as each HIDS must be custom configured to its host systems. Deployment begins with implementing the most critical systems first. This poses a dilemma for the deployment team, since the first systems to be implemented are mission-critical and any problems in the installation could be catastrophic to the organization. As such, it may be beneficial to practice an implementation on one or more test servers configured on a network segment that resembles the mission-critical systems. Practicing will help the installation team gain experience and also help determine if the installation might trigger any unusual events. Gaining an edge on the learning curve by training on non-production systems will benefit the overall deployment process by reducing the risk of unforeseen complications.

Installation continues until either all systems are installed, or the organization reaches the planned degree of coverage it is willing to live with, with regard to the number of systems or percentage of network traffic. Lastly, to provide ease of management, control, and reporting, each HIDS should, as discussed earlier, be configured to interact with a central management console.

Just as technicians can install the HIDS in off-line systems to develop expertise and identify potential problems, users and managers can gain expertise and understanding of the operation of the HIDS by using a test facility. This test facility could use the off-line systems configured by the technicians, but also be connected to the organization's backbone to allow the HIDS to process actual network traffic. This setup will also enable technicians to create a baseline of normal traffic for the organization. During the system testing process, training scenarios can be developed that will enable users to recognize and respond to common attack situations. Finally, to ensure effective and efficient operation, the management team can establish policy for the operation and monitoring of the HIDS.

Measuring the Effectiveness of IDSs

IDSs are evaluated using two dominant metrics: first, administrators evaluate the number of attacks detected in a known collection of probes; second, the administrators examine the level of use, commonly measured in megabits per second of network traffic, at which the IDSs fail. An evaluation of an IDS might read something like this: *at 100 Mb/s, the IDS was able to detect 97% of directed attacks.* This is a dramatic change from the previous method used for assessing IDS effectiveness, which was based on the total number of signatures the system was currently running—a sort of "more is better" approach. Unfortunately, this evaluation method of assessment was flawed for several reasons. Not all IDSs use simple signature-based detection. Some systems, as discussed earlier, can use the almost infinite combination of network performance characteristics of statistical-anomaly-based detection to detect a potential attack. Also, some more sophisticated signature-based systems actually use *fewer* signatures/rules than older, simpler versions—which, in direct contrast to the signature-based assessment method, suggests that less may actually be more. The recognition that the size of the signature base is an insufficient measure of an IDS's effectiveness led to the development of stress test measurements for evaluating IDS performance. These only work, however, if the administrator has a collection of known negative and positive actions that can be proven to elicit a desired response. Since developing this collection can be tedious, most IDS vendors provide testing mechanisms that verify that their systems are performing as expected. Some of these testing processes will enable the administrator to:

- Record and retransmit packets from a real virus or worm scan
- Record and retransmit packets from a real virus or worm scan with incomplete TCP/IP session connections (missing SYN packets)
- Conduct a real virus or worm scan against an invulnerable system

This last measure is important, since future IDSs will probably include much more detailed information about the overall site configuration. According to experts in the field, "it may be necessary for the IDSs to be able to actively probe a potentially vulnerable machine, in order to either pre-load its configuration with correct information, or perform a retroactive assessment. An IDS that performed some kind of actual system assessment would be a complete failure in today's generic testing labs, which focus on replaying attacks and scans against nonexistent machines."[18]

With the rapid growth in technology, each new generation of IDSs will require new testing methodologies. However, the measured values that will continue to be of interest to IDS administrators and managers will, most certainly, include some assessment of how much traffic the IDS can handle, the numbers of false positives and false negatives it generates, and a measure of the IDS's ability to detect actual attacks. Vendors of IDS systems could also include a report of the alarms sent and the relative accuracy of the system in correctly matching the alarm level to the true seriousness of the threat. Some planned metrics for IDSs may include the flexibility of signatures and detection policy customization.

IDS administrators may soon be able to purchase tools that test IDS effectiveness. Until these tools are available from a neutral third party, the diagnostics from the IDS vendors will always be suspect. No matter how reliable the vendor, no vendor would provide a test their system would fail.

One note of caution: there may be a strong tendency among IDS administrators to use common vulnerability assessment tools, like Nmap or Nessus, to evaluate the capabilities of an IDS. While this may seem like a good idea, it will in fact not work as expected, because most IDS systems are equipped to recognize the differences between a locally implemented vulnerability assessment tool and a true attack.

In order to perform a true assessment of the effectiveness of IDS systems, the test process should be as realistic as possible in its simulation of an actual event. This means coupling realistic traffic loads with realistic levels of attacks. One cannot expect an IDS to respond to a few packet probes as if they represent a denial-of-service attack. In one reported example, a program was used to create a synthetic load of network traffic made up of many TCP sessions, with each session consisting of a SYN (or synchronization) packet, a series of data, and ACK (or acknowledgement) packets, but no FIN or connection termination packets. Of the several IDS systems tested, one of them crashed due to lack of resources while it waited for the sessions to be closed. Another IDS passed the test with flying colors because it did not perform state tracking on the connections. Neither of the tested IDS systems worked as expected, but the one that didn't perform state tracking was able to stay operational and was, therefore, given a better score on the test.[19]

Honey Pots, Honey Nets, and Padded Cell Systems

A class of powerful security tools that go beyond routine intrusion detection is known variously as honey pots, honey nets, or padded cell systems. To realize why these tools are not yet widely used, you must understand how these products differ from a traditional IDS. **Honey pots** are decoy systems designed to lure potential attackers away from critical systems and encourage attacks against the themselves. Indeed, these systems are created for the sole purpose of deceiving potential attackers. In the industry, they are also known as decoys, lures, and fly-traps. When a collection of honey pots connects several honey pot systems on a subnet, it may be called a **honey net**. A honey pot system (or in the case of a honey net, an entire subnetwork) contains pseudo-services that emulate well-known services but is configured in ways that make it look vulnerable—that is, easily subject to attacks. This combination of attractants (i.e., attractive features such as the presence of both well-known services and vulnerabilities) is meant to lure potential attackers into committing an attack, and thereby revealing their existence—the idea being that once organizations have detected these attackers, they can better defend their networks against future attacks against real assets. In sum, honey pots are designed to:

- Divert an attacker from accessing critical systems
- Collect information about the attacker's activity
- Encourage the attacker to stay on the system long enough for administrators to document the event and, perhaps, respond

Honey pot systems are filled with information that is designed to appear valuable (hence the name honey pots), but this information is fabricated and would not even be useful to a legitimate user of the system. Thus, any time a honey pot is accessed, this constitutes suspicious activity. Honey pots are instrumented with sensitive monitors and event loggers that detect these attempts to access the system and collect information about the potential attacker's activities. A screenshot from a simple IDS that specializes in honey pot techniques, called Deception Toolkit, is shown in Figure 7-8. This screenshot shows the configuration of the honey pot as it is waiting for an attack.

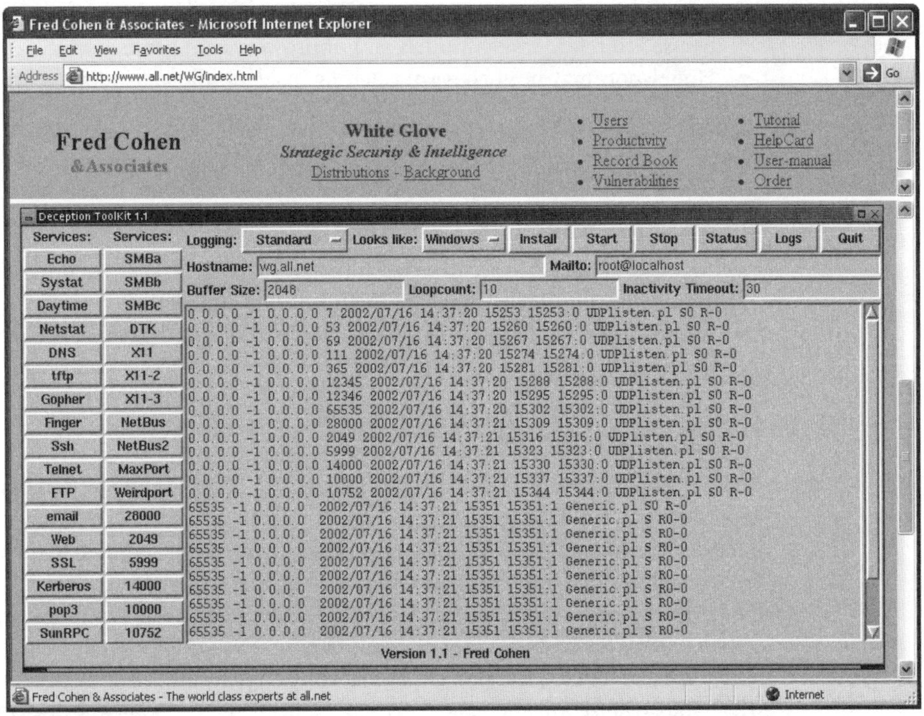

FIGURE 7-8 Deception Toolkit

Padded cells take a different approach. A **padded cell** is a honey pot that has been protected so that that it cannot be easily compromised. In other words, a padded cell is a hardened honey pot. In addition to attracting attackers with tempting data, a padded cell operates in tandem with a traditional IDS. When the IDS detects attackers, it seamlessly transfers them to a special simulated environment where they can cause no harm—the nature of this host environment is what gives the approach its name, padded cell. As in honey pots, this environment can be filled with interesting data, some of which can be designed to convince an attacker that the attack is going according to plan. Like honey pots, padded cells are well-instrumented and offer unique opportunities for a would-be victim organization to monitor the actions of an attacker.

IDS researchers have used padded cell and honey pot systems since the late 1980s, but until recently no commercial versions of these products were available. It is important to seek guidance from legal counsel before deciding to use either of these systems in your operational environment, since using an attractant and then launching a back-hack or counterstrike might be construed as an illegal action and make the organization subject to a lawsuit or a criminal complaint.

The advantages and disadvantages of using the honey pot or padded cell approach are summarized below:

Advantages:

- Attackers can be diverted to targets that they cannot damage.
- Administrators have time to decide how to respond to an attacker.

- Attackers' actions can be easily and more extensively monitored, and the records can be used to refine threat models and improve system protections.
- Honey pots may be effective at catching insiders who are snooping around a network.

Disadvantages:

- The legal implications of using such devices are not well defined.
- Honey pots and padded cells have not yet been shown to be generally useful security technologies.
- An expert attacker, once diverted into a decoy system, may become angry and launch a more hostile attack against an organization's systems.
- Administrators and security managers will need a high level of expertise to use these systems.[20]

Trap and Trace Systems

An extension of the attractant-based technologies in the preceding section, trap and trace applications are growing in popularity. These systems, often simply referred to as **trap and trace**, use a combination of techniques to detect an intrusion and then to trace incidents back to their sources. The trap usually consists of a honey pot or padded cell and an alarm. While the intruders are distracted, or trapped, by what they perceive to be successful intrusions, the system notifies the administrator of their presence. The trace feature is an extension to the honey pot or padded cell approach. Similar in concept to caller ID, the trace is a process by which the organization attempts to determine the identity of someone discovered in unauthorized areas of the network or systems. If this individual turns out to be someone inside the organization, the administrators are completely within their power to track the individual down and turn them over to internal or external authorities. If the individual is outside the security perimeter of the organization, then numerous legal issues arise. One of the most popular professional trap and trace software suites is ManHunt, by Recourse Technologies (*www.recourse.com*). It includes a companion product, ManTrap, which is the honey pot application and thus presents a virtual network running from a single server. ManHunt is an intrusion detection system with the capability of initiating a track back function that can trace a detected intruder as far as the administrator wishes. Although administrators usually trace an intruder back to their organization's information security boundary, it is possible, with this technology, for them to coordinate with an ISP that has similar technology and thus hand off a trace to an upstream neighbor.

On the surface, trap and trace systems seem like an ideal solution. Security is no longer limited to defense. Now the security administrators can go on the offense. They can track down the perpetrators and turn them over to the appropriate authorities. Under the guise of justice, some less scrupulous administrators may even be tempted to **back-hack**, or hack into a hacker's system to find out as much as possible about the hacker. Vigilante justice would be a more appropriate term for these activities, which are in fact deemed unethical by most codes of professional conduct. In tracking the hacker, administrators may end up wandering through other organizations' systems, especially when the wily hacker may have used IP spoofing, compromised systems, or a myriad of other techniques to throw trackers off the trail. The result is that the administrator becomes a hacker himself, and therefore defeats the purpose of catching hackers.

There are more legal drawbacks to trap and trace. The trap portion frequently involves the use of honey pots or honey nets. When using honey pots and honey nets, administrators should be careful not to cross the line between enticement and entrapment. **Enticement** is the process of attracting attention to a system by placing tantalizing bits of information in key locations. **Entrapment** is the action of luring an individual into committing a crime to get a conviction. Enticement is legal and ethical, whereas entrapment is not. It is difficult to gauge the effect such a system can have on the average user, especially if the individual has been nudged into looking at the information. Administrators should also be wary of the *wasp trap syndrome*. In this syndrome, a concerned homeowner installs a wasp trap in his back yard to trap the few insects he sees flying about. Because these traps use scented bait, however, they wind up attracting far more wasps than were originally present. Security administrators should keep the wasp trap syndrome in mind before implementing honey pots, honey nets, padded cells, or trap and trace systems.

Active Intrusion Prevention

Some organizations would like to do more than simply wait for the next attack and implement active countermeasures to stop attacks. One tool that provides active intrusion prevention is known as LaBrea (*http://www.labreatechnologies.com*). LaBrea works by taking up the unused IP address space within a network. When LaBrea notes an ARP request, it checks to see if the IP address requested is actually valid on the network. If the address is not currently being used by a real computer or network device, LaBrea will pretend to be a computer at that IP address and allow the attacker to complete the TCP/IP connection request, known as the three-way handshake. Once the handshake is complete, LaBrea will change the TCP sliding window size down to a low number to hold the TCP connection from the attacker open for many hours, days, or even months. Holding the connection open but inactive greatly slows down network-based worms and other attacks. It allows the LaBrea system time then to notify the system and network administrators about the anomalous behavior on the network.

Scanning and Analysis Tools

In order to secure a network, it is imperative that someone in the organization knows exactly where the network needs securing. This may sound like a simple and intuitive statement; however, many companies skip this step. They install a simple perimeter firewall, and then, lulled into a sense of security by this single layer of defense, they rest on their laurels. To truly assess the risk within a computing environment, one must deploy technical controls using a strategy of defense in depth. A strategy based on the concept of defense in depth is likely to include intrusion detection systems (IDS), active vulnerability scanners, passive vulnerability scanners, automated log analyzers, and protocol analyzers (commonly referred to as sniffers). As you've learned, the first item in this list, the IDS, helps to secure networks by detecting intrusions; the remaining items in the list also help secure networks, but they do this by helping administrators identify where the network needs securing. More specifically, scanner and analysis tools can find vulnerabilities in systems, holes in security components, and unsecured aspects of the network.

Although some information security experts may not perceive them as defensive tools, scanners, sniffers, and other such vulnerability analysis tools can be invaluable to security administrators because they enable administrators to see what the attacker sees. Some of these tools are extremely complex and others are rather simple. The tools can also range from being expensive commercial products to those that are freely available at no cost. Many of the best scanning and analysis tools are those that the attacker community has developed, and are available free on the Web. Good administrators should have several hacking Web sites bookmarked and should try to keep up with chat room discussions on new vulnerabilities, recent conquests, and favorite assault techniques. There is nothing wrong with a security administrator using the tools that potential attackers use in order to examine his or her defenses and find areas that require additional attention. In the military, there is a long and distinguished history of generals inspecting the troops under their command before battle, walking down the line checking out the equipment and mental preparedness of each soldier. In a similar way, the security administrator can use vulnerability analysis tools to inspect the units (host computers and network devices) under his or her command. A word of caution, though, should be heeded: many of these scanning and analysis tools have distinct signatures, and some Internet service providers (ISPs) scan for these signatures. If the ISP discovers someone using hacker tools, it can pull that person's access privileges. As such, it is probably best for administrators first to establish a working relationship with their ISPs and notify the ISP of their plans.

Scanning tools are, as mentioned earlier, typically used as part of an attack protocol to collect information that an attacker would need to launch a successful attack. The **attack protocol** is a series of steps or processes used by an attacker, in a logical sequence, to launch an attack against a target system or network. One of the preparatory parts of the attack protocol is the collection of publicly available information about a potential target, a process known as footprinting. **Footprinting** is the organized research of the Internet addresses owned or controlled by a target organization. The attacker uses public Internet data sources to perform keyword searches to identify the network addresses of the organization. This research is augmented by browsing the organization's Web pages. Web pages usually contain quantities of information about internal systems, individuals developing Web pages, and other tidbits, which can be used for social engineering attacks. The *View Source* option on most popular Web browsers allows the user to see the source code behind the graphics. A number of details in the source code of the Web page can provide clues to potential attackers and give them insight into the configuration of an internal network, such as the locations and directories for Common Gateway Interface (CGI) script bins and the names or possibly addresses of computers and servers. In addition, public business Web sites (such as Forbes, or Yahoo Business) will often reveal information about company structure, commonly used company names, and other information that attackers find useful. Furthermore, common search engines will allow attackers to query for any site that links to their proposed target. By doing a little bit of initial Internet research into a company, an attacker can often find additional Internet locations that are not commonly associated with the company—that is, Business to Business (B2B) partners and subsidiaries. Armed with this information, the attacker can find the "weakest link" into the target network.

For an example, consider Company X, which has a large datacenter located in Atlanta. The datacenter has been secured, and thus it will be very hard for an attacker to break into the datacenter via the Internet. However, the attacker has run a "link:" query on the search engine *www.altavista.com* and found a small Web server that links to Company X's main Web server. After further investigation, the attacker learns that the small Web server was set up by an administrator at a remote facility and that the remote facility has, via its own leased lines, an unrestricted internal link into Company X's corporate datacenter. The attacker can now attack the weaker site at the remote facility and use this compromised network—which is an internal network—to attack the true target. While it may seem trite or cliché, the phrase *a chain is only as strong as its weakest link* is very relevant to network and computer security. If a company has a trusted network connection in place with 15 business partners, even one weak business partner can compromise all 16 networks.

To assist in the footprint intelligence collection process, another type of scanner can be used. This is an enhanced Web scanner that, among other things, can scan entire Web sites for valuable pieces of information, such as server names and e-mail addresses. One such scanner is called Sam Spade, the details of which can be found at *www.samspade.org*. A sample screenshot from Sam Spade is shown in Figure 7-9. Sam Spade can also do a host of other scans and probes, such as sending multiple ICMP information requests (Pings), attempting to retrieve multiple and cross-zoned DNS queries, and performing network analysis queries (known, from the commonly used UNIX command for performing the analysis, as traceroutes). All of these are powerful diagnostic and hacking activities. Sam Spade is not, however, considered to be hackerware (or hacker-oriented software), but rather it is a utility that happens to be useful to network administrators and miscreants alike.

For Linux or BSD systems, there is a tool called "wget" that allows a remote individual to "mirror" entire Web sites. With this tool, attackers can copy an entire Web site and then go through the source HTML, JavaScript, and Web-based forms at their leisure, collecting and collating all of the data from the source code that will be useful to them for their attack.

FIGURE 7-9 Sam Spade

The next phase of the attack protocol is a second intelligence or data-gathering process called **fingerprinting**. This is a systematic survey of all of the target organization's Internet addresses (which were collected during the footprinting phase described above); the survey is conducted to ascertain the network services offered by the hosts in that range. By using the tools discussed in the next section, fingerprinting reveals useful information about the internal structure and operational nature of the target system or network for the anticipated attack. Since these tools were created to find vulnerabilities in systems and networks quickly and with a minimum of effort, they are valuable for the network defender since they can quickly pinpoint the parts of the systems or network that need a prompt repair to close the vulnerability.

Port Scanners

Port scanning utilities (or **port scanners**) are tools used by both attackers and defenders to identify (or fingerprint) the computers that are active on a network, as well as the ports and services active on those computers, the functions and roles the machines are fulfilling, and other useful information. These tools can scan for specific types of computers, protocols, or resources, or their scans can be generic. It is helpful to understand the environment that exists in the network you are using, so that you can use the tool most suited to the data collection task at hand. For instance, if you are trying to identify a Windows computer in a typical network, a built-in feature of the operating system, nbtstat, may be able to get the answer you need very quickly, without requiring the installation of a scanner. This tool will not work on other types of networks, however, so you must know your tools in order to make the best use of the features of each.

The more specific the scanner is, the better it can give attackers and defenders information that is detailed and will be useful later. However, it is also recommended that you keep a generic, broad-based scanner in your toolbox as well. This helps to locate and identify rogue nodes on the network that administrators may be unaware of. Probably the most popular port scanner is Nmap, which runs on both Unix and Windows systems. You can find out more about Nmap at *http://www.insecure.org*.

A port is a network channel or connection point in a data communications system. Within the TCP/IP networking protocol, TCP and User Datagram Protocol (UDP) port numbers differentiate the multiple communication channels that are used to connect to the network services being offered on the same network device. Each application within TCP/IP has a unique port number assigned. Some have default ports but can also use other ports. Some of the well-known port numbers are presented in Table 7-1. In all, there are 65,536 port numbers in use for TCP and another 65,536 port numbers for UDP. Services using the TCP/IP protocol can run on any port; however, the services with reserved ports generally run on ports 1–1023. Port 0 is not used. Ports greater than 1023 are typically referred to as ephemeral ports and may be randomly allocated to server and client processes.

Why secure open ports? Simply put, an open port can be used by an attacker to send commands to a computer, potentially gain access to a server, and possibly exert control over a networking device. The general rule of thumb is to remove from service or secure any port not absolutely necessary to conducting business. For example, if a business doesn't host Web services, there may be no need for port 80 to be available on its servers.

TABLE 7-1 Commonly Used Port Numbers

TCP Port Numbers	TCP Service
20 and 21	File Transfer Protocol (FTP)
22	Secure Shell (SSH)
23	Telnet
25	Simple Mail Transfer Protocol (SMTP)
53	Domain Name Services (DNS)
67 and 68	Dynamic Host Configuration Protocol (DHCP)
80	Hypertext Transfer Protocol (HTTP)
110	Post Office Protocol (POP3)
161	Simple Network Management Protocol (SNMP)
194	IRC chat port (used for device sharing)
443	HTTP over SSL
8080	Used for proxy services

Firewall Analysis Tools

Understanding exactly where an organization's firewall is located and what the existing rule sets on the firewall do are very important steps for any security administrator. There are several tools that automate the remote discovery of firewall rules and assist the administrator (or attacker) in analyzing the rules to determine exactly what they allow and what they reject.

The Nmap tool mentioned earlier has some advanced options that are useful for firewall analysis. The Nmap option called *Idle scanning* (which is run with the -I switch) will allow the Nmap user to bounce your scan across a firewall by using one of the IDLE DMZ hosts as the initiator of the scan. More specifically, as most operating systems do not use truly random IP packet identification numbers (IP IDs), if there is more than one host in the DMZ and one host uses non-random IP IDs, then the attacker can query the server (server X) and obtain the currently used IP ID as well as the known algorithm for incrementing the IP IDs. The attacker can then spoof a packet that is allegedly from server X and destined for an internal IP address behind the firewall. If the port is open on the internal machine, the internal machine will reply to server X with a SYN-ACK packet, which will force server X to respond with a TCP RESET packet. In responding with the TCP RESET, server X increments its IP ID number. The attacker can now query server X a second time to see if the IP ID has incremented. If it has, the attacker knows that the internal machine is alive and that the internal machine has the queried service port open. In a nutshell, running the Nmap Idle scan allows an attacker to scan an internal network as if he or she were physically located on a trusted machine inside the DMZ.

Another tool that can be used to analyze firewalls is Firewalk. Written by noted author and network security expert Mike Schiffman, Firewalk uses incrementing Time-To-Live (TTL) packets to determine the path into a network as well as the default firewall policy. Running Firewalk against a target machine will reveal where routers and firewalls are filtering traffic to the target host. More information on Firewalk can be obtained from *http://www.packetfactory.net/*.

A final firewall analysis tool worth mentioning is HPING, which is a modified Ping client. It supports multiple protocols and has a command-line means of specifying nearly any of the Ping parameters. For instance, you can use HPING with modified TTL values to determine the infrastructure of a DMZ. You can use HPING with specific ICMP flags in order to bypass poorly configured firewalls (i.e., firewalls that allow all ICMP traffic to pass through) and find internal systems. HPING can be found at *http://www.hping.org/*.

Incidentally, administrators who feel wary of using the same tools that attackers use should remember two important points: regardless of the nature of the tool that is used to validate or analyze a firewall's configuration, it is the intent of the user that will dictate how the information gathered will be used; in order to defend a computer or network well, it is necessary to understand the ways it can be attacked. Thus, a tool that can help close up an open or poorly configured firewall will help the network defender minimize the risk from attack.

Operating System Detection Tools

Detecting a target computer's operating system is very valuable to an attacker, because once the OS is known, all of the vulnerabilities to which it is susceptible can easily be determined. There are many tools that use networking protocols to determine a remote computer's OS. One specific tool worth mentioning is XProbe, which uses ICMP to determine the remote OS. This tool can be found at *http://www.sys-security.com/html/projects/X.html*. When it's run, XProbe sends a lot of different ICMP queries against the target host. As reply packets are received, XProbe matches these responses from the target's TCP/IP stack with its own internal database of known responses. As most OSs have a unique way of responding to ICMP requests, Xprobe is very reliable in finding matches and thus detecting the operating systems of remote computers. System and network administrators should take note of this, and plan to restrict the use of ICMP through their organization's firewalls and, when possible, within its internal networks.

Vulnerability Scanners

Active vulnerability scanners scan networks for highly detailed information. An *active* scanner is one that initiates traffic on the network in order to determine security holes. As a class, this type of scanner identifies exposed usernames and groups, shows open network shares, and exposes configuration problems and other vulnerabilities in servers. An example of a vulnerability scanner is GFI LANguard Network Security Scanner (NSS), which is available as freeware for non-commercial use. Another example of a vulnerability scanner is Nessus, which is a professional freeware utility that uses IP packets to determine the hosts available on the network, the services (ports) they are offering, the operating system and OS version they are running, the type of packet filters and firewalls in use, and dozens of other characteristics of the network. Figures 7-10 and 7-11 show sample LANguard and Nessus result screens.

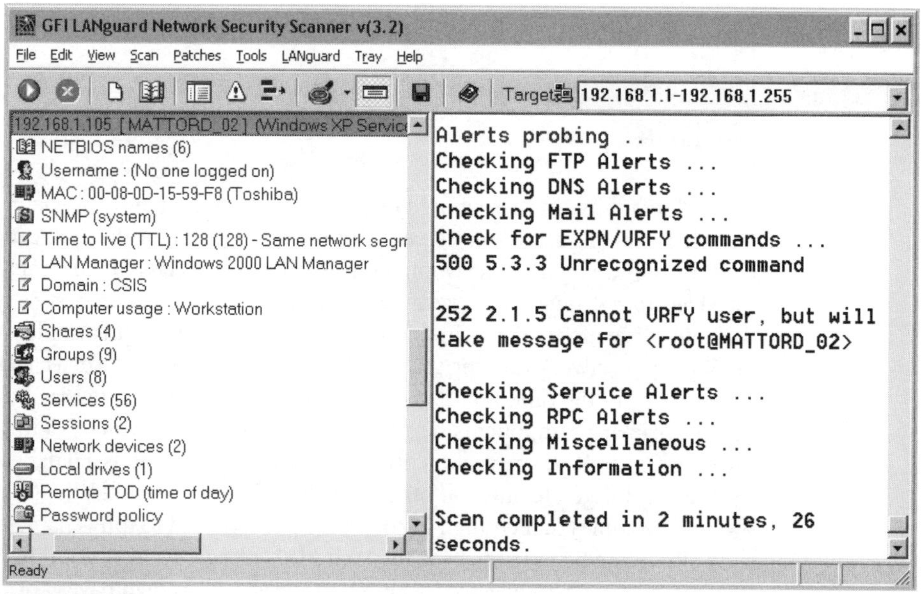

FIGURE 7-10   LANguard

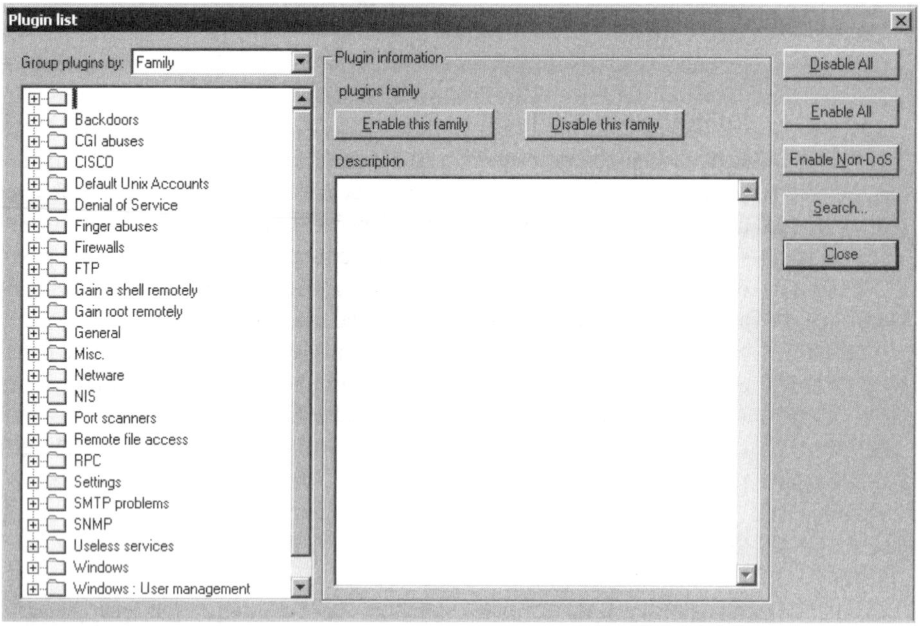

FIGURE 7-11 Nessus

Vulnerability scanners should be proficient in finding known, documented holes. But what happens if the Web server is from a new vendor, or the application was developed by an internal development team? There is a class of vulnerability scanners called *blackbox* scanners, or *fuzzers*. Fuzz testing is a straightforward testing technique that looks for vulnerabilities in a program or protocol by feeding random input to the program or a network running the protocol. Vulnerabilities can be detected by measuring the outcome of the random inputs. One example of a fuzz scanner is SPIKE, which has two primary components. The first is the SPIKE Proxy, which is a full-blown proxy server. As Web site visitors utilize the proxy, SPIKE builds a database of each of the traversed pages, forms, and other Web-specific information. When the Web site owner determines that enough history has been collected to fully characterize the Web sites, SPIKE can be used to check the Web site for bugs—that is, administrators can use the usage history collected by SPIKE to traverse all known pages, forms, active programs (e.g., asp, cgi-bin), etc., and can test the system by attempting overflows, SQL injection, cross-site scripting, and many other classes of Web attacks.

SPIKE also has a core functionality to fuzz any protocol that utilizes TCP/IP. By sniffing a session and building a SPIKE script, or building a full-blown C program using the SPIKE API, a user can simulate and "fuzz" nearly any protocol. Figure 7-12 shows the Spike PROXY configuration screen. Figure 7-13 shows a sample SPIKE script being prepared to fuzz the ISAKAMP protocol (which is used by VPNs). Figure 7-14 shows the SPIKE program, generic_send_udp, fuzzing an IKE server using the aforementioned SPIKE script. As you can see, SPIKE can be used to quickly fuzz and find weaknesses in nearly any protocol.

Similar in function, the previously mentioned Nessus scanner has a class of attacks called *DESTRUCTIVE*. If enabled, Nessus will attempt common overflow techniques against a target host. Fuzzers or blackbox scanners and Nessus in destructive mode can be very dangerous tools and should only be used in a lab environment. In fact, these tools are so powerful that even system defenders who use them are not likely to use them in the most aggressive modes on their production networks. At the time of this writing, the most popular scanners seem to be Nessus (a commercial version of Nessus for Windows is available), retina, and Internet Scanner. The Nessus scanner is available at no cost; the other two require a license fee.

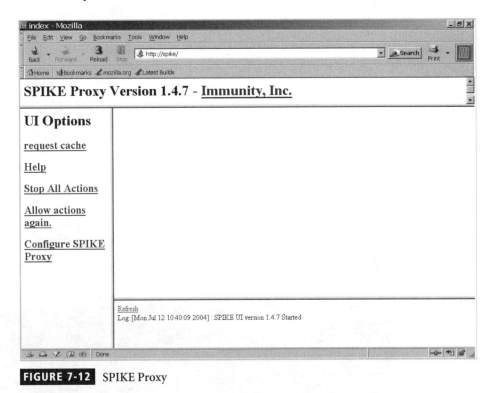

FIGURE 7-12 SPIKE Proxy

FIGURE 7-13 SPIKE In Action

FIGURE 7-14 SPIKE vs. IKE

Often times, some members of an organization will require proof that a system is actually vulnerable to a certain attack. They may require such proof in order to avoid having system administrators attempt to repair systems that are not in fact broken, or because they have not yet built a satisfactory relationship with the vulnerability assessment team. In these instances, there exists a class of scanners that will actually exploit the remote machine and allow the vulnerability analyst (sometimes called a penetration tester) to create an account, modify a Web page, or view data. These tools can be very dangerous and should only be used when absolutely necessary. Three tools that can perform this action are Core Impact, Immunity's CANVAS, and the Metasploit Framework.

Of these three tools, only the Metasploit Framework is available without a license fee. The Metasploit Framework is a collection of exploits coupled with an interface that allows the penetration tester to automate the custom exploitation of vulnerable systems. So, for instance, if you wished to exploit a Microsoft Exchange server and run a single command (perhaps add the user "security" into the administrators group), the tool would allow you to customize the overflow in this manner. See Figure 7-15 for a screenshot of the Metasploit Framework in action.

FIGURE 7-15 Metasploit

A **passive vulnerability scanner** is one that listens in on the network and determines vulnerable versions of both server and client software. At the time of this writing, there are two primary vendors offering this type of scanning solution: Tenable Network Security with its NeVO product and Sourcefire with its RNA product. Passive scanners are advantageous in that they do not require vulnerability analysts to get approval prior for testing. These tools simply monitor the network connections to and from a server to gain a list of vulnerable applications. Furthermore, passive vulnerability scanners have the ability to find client-side vulnerabilities that are typically not found in active scanners. For instance, an active scanner operating without DOMAIN Admin rights would be unable to determine the version of Internet Explorer running on a desktop machine, whereas a passive scanner will be able to make that determination by observing the traffic to and from the client. See Figure 7-16 for a screenshot of the NeVO passive vulnerability scanner running on Windows XP.

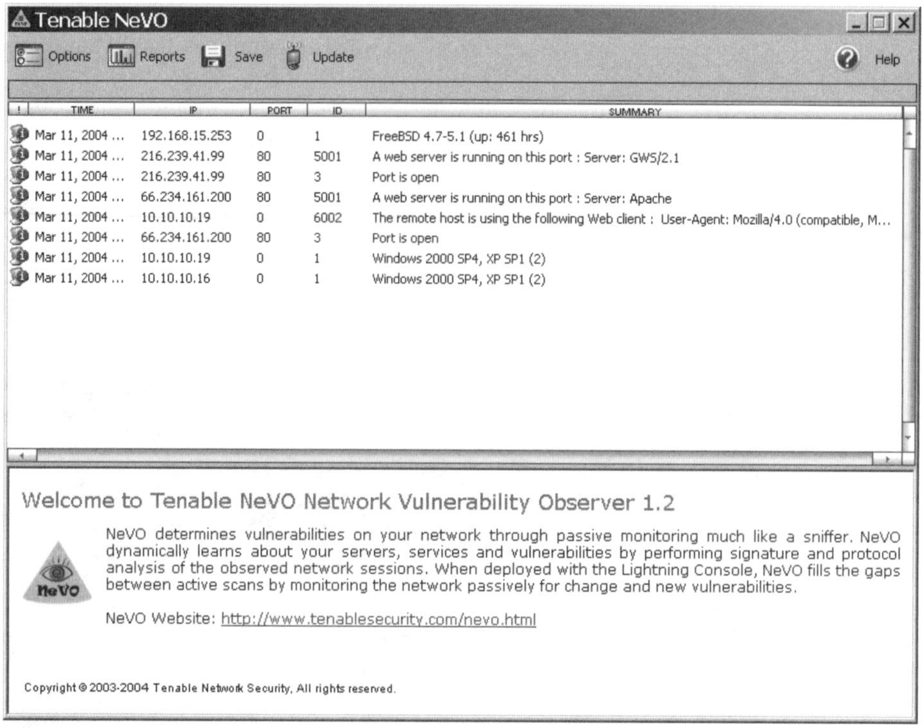

FIGURE 7-16 NeVO

Table 7-2 provides World Wide Web addresses for the products mentioned in the vulnerability scanners section.

Table 7-2 Vulnerability Scanner Products and Web Pages

Product	Web Page
Nessus	*http://www.nessus.org*
Nessus for Windows	*http://www.tenablesecurity.com*
GFI LANguard Network Security Scanner	*http://www.gfi.com/languard*
SPIKE - SPIKEproxy	*http://www.immunitysec.com*
Retina	*http://www.eeye.com*
Internet Scanner	*http://www.iss.net*
Core Impact	*http://www.coresecurity.com/home/home.php*
CANVAS	*http://www.immunitysec.com/CANVAS*
Metasploit Framework	*http://metasploit.com*

Packet Sniffers

Another tool worth mentioning here is the packet sniffer. A **packet sniffer** (sometimes called a network protocol analyzer) is a network tool that collects copies of packets from the network and analyzes them. It can provide a network administrator with valuable information for diagnosing and resolving networking issues. In the wrong hands, however, a sniffer can be used to eavesdrop on network traffic. There are both commercial and open-source sniffers—more specifically, sniffer is a commercial product, and snort is open-source software. An excellent free, client-based network protocol analyzer is Ethereal (*www.ethereal.com*). Ethereal allows the administrator to examine data from both live network traffic and captured traffic. Ethereal has several features, including a language filter and TCP session reconstruction utility. Figure 7-17 shows a sample screen from Ethereal. Typically, to use these types of programs most effectively, the user must be connected to a network from a central location. Simply tapping into an Internet connection floods you with more data than can be readily processed, and technically constitutes a violation of the wiretapping act. To use a packet sniffer legally, the administrator must: 1) be on a network that the organization owns, 2) be under direct authorization of the owners of the network, and 3) have knowledge and consent of the content creators. If all three conditions are met, the administrator can selectively collect and analyze packets to identify and diagnose problems on the network. Conditions one and two are self-explanatory. The third, consent, is usually handled by having all system users sign a release when they are issued a user ID and passwords. Incidentally, these three items are the same requirements for employee monitoring in general, and packet sniffing should be construed as a form of employee monitoring.

Many administrators feel that they are safe from sniffer attacks when their computing environment is primarily a switched network environment. This couldn't be farther from the truth. There are a number of open-source sniffers that support alternate networking approaches that can, in turn, enable packet sniffing in a switched network environment. Two of these alternate networking approaches are ARP-spoofing and session hijacking (which uses tools like ettercap). To secure data in transit across any network, organizations must use encryption to be assured of content privacy.

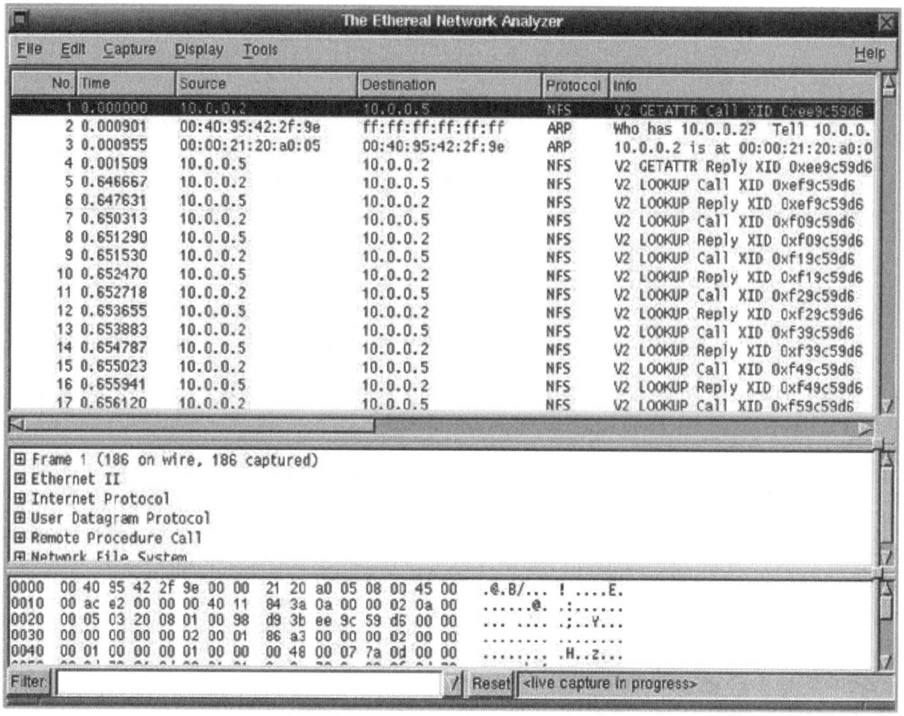

FIGURE 7-17 Ethereal

Wireless Security Tools

802.11 wireless networks have sprung up as subnets on nearly all large networks. A wireless connection, while convenient, has many potential security holes. An organization that spends all of its time securing the wired network and leaves wireless networks to operate in any manner is opening itself up for a security breach. As a security professional, you must assess the risk of wireless networks. A wireless security toolkit should include the ability to sniff wireless traffic, scan wireless hosts, and assess the level of privacy or confidentiality afforded on the wireless network. There is a suite of tools from dachb0den labs (*http://www.dachb0den.com/projects/bsd-airtools.html*) called bsd-airtools that automates all of the items noted above. The tools included within the bsd-airtools toolset are an access point detection tool, a sniffer, and a tool called dstumbler to crack Wired Equivalent Protocol (WEP) encryption keys. A Windows version of the dstumbler tool called NetStumbler is also offered as freeware and can be found at *http://www.netstumbler.org*. Figure 7-18 shows NetStumbler being run from a Windows XP machine. Another wireless tool worth mentioning is AirSnare. AirSnare is a free tool that can be run on a low-end wireless workstation. AirSnare monitors the airwaves for any new devices or Access Points. When it finds one, AirSnare will sound an alarm alerting the administrators that a new, potentially dangerous, wireless apparatus is attempting access on a closed wireless network. Figure 7-19 shows AirSnare in action.

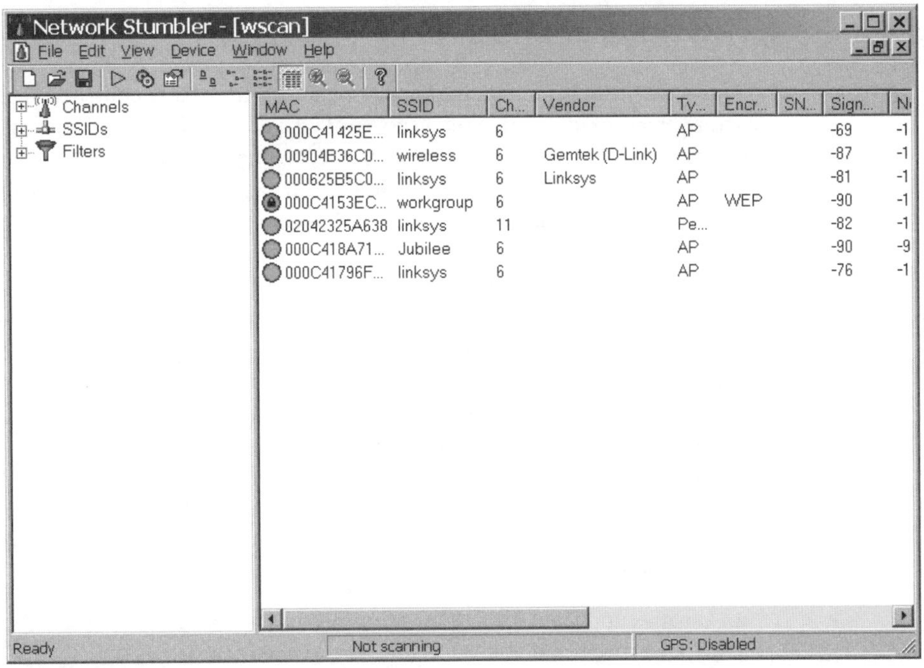

FIGURE 7-18 NetStumbler

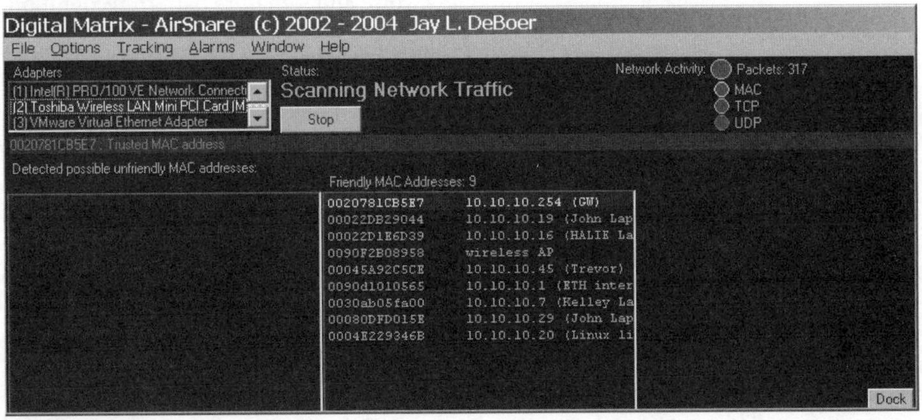

FIGURE 7-19 AirSnare

The tools discussed so far help the attacker and the defender prepare themselves to complete the next steps in the attack protocol: attack, compromise, and exploit. These steps are beyond the scope of this text, for they are usually covered in more advanced classes on computer and network attack and defense.

Access Control Devices

This section examines technologies associated with **access control**. When a prospective user, referred to in the area of access control as a **supplicant**, seeks to use a protected system, logically access a protected service, or physically enter a protected space, he or she must engage in authentication and authorization activities to establish his or her identity and verify that he or she has permission to complete the requested activity. A successful access control system includes a number of components, depending on the system's needs for authentication and authorization. Occasionally a system will have a need for strong authentication when verifying a supplicant's identity. **Strong authentication** requires at least two of the forms of authentication listed below to authenticate the supplicant's identity. Routine authentication has traditionally made use of only one form; and in many cases, this happens to be of the "What a supplicant knows" variety. This is why many systems familiar to us require a user ID and password (both examples of something known to the user) for authentication. When a second factor is required to verify the supplicant's identify, this is frequently a physical device, i.e., something the supplicant *has*, such as an ATM card or smart card. In terms of access control, there are four general forms of authentication to consider:

- What a supplicant knows: for example, user IDs and passphrases
- What a supplicant has: often tokens and smart cards
- Who a supplicant is: fingerprints, hand topography, hand geometry, retinal and iris recognition
- What a supplicant produces: voice and signature pattern recognition

The technology to manage authentication based on what a supplicant knows is widely integrated into the networking and security software systems in use across the IT industry. The last three forms of authentication are usually implemented as some form of identification technology and added to systems that require higher degrees of authentication.

Authentication

Authentication is the validation of a supplicant's identity. There are four general ways in which authentication is carried out. Each of these is discussed in detail in the following sections.

What a Supplicant Knows

This area of authentication deals with what the supplicant knows—for example, a password, passphrase, or other unique authentication code, such as a personal identification number (or PIN)—that could confirm his or her identity.

A **password** is a private word or combination of characters that only the user should know. One of the biggest debates in the information security industry concerns the complexity of passwords. On the one hand, a password should be difficult to guess, which means it cannot be a series of letters or word that is easily associated with the user, such as the name of the user's spouse, child, or pet. Nor should a password be a series of numbers commonly associated with the user, such as a phone number, Social Security number, or birth date. On the other hand, the password must be something the user can easily remember, which means it should be short or commonly associated with something the user can remember.

A **passphrase** is a series of characters, typically longer than a password, from which a **virtual password** is derived. For example, while a typical password might be "23skedoo," a typical passphrase can be "MayTheForceBeWithYouAlways," which can also be represented as "MTFBWYA."

What a Supplicant Has

The second area of authentication addresses something the supplicant carries in his or her possession—that is, something they have. These include **dumb cards**, such as ID cards or ATM cards with magnetic stripes containing the digital (and often encrypted) user personal identification number (PIN), against which the number a user inputs is compared. An improved version of the dumb card is the **smart card**, which contains a computer chip that can verify and validate a number of pieces of information instead of just a PIN. Another device often used is the token, a card or key fob with a computer chip and a liquid crystal display that shows a computer-generated number used to support remote login authentication. Tokens are synchronous or asynchronous. Once **synchronous tokens** are synchronized with a server, both devices (server and token) use the same time or a time-based database to generate a number that is displayed and entered during the user login phase. **Asynchronous tokens** use a challenge-response system, in which the server challenges the supplicant during login with a numerical sequence. The supplicant places this sequence into the token and receives a response. The prospective user then enters the response into the system to gain access. This system does not require the synchronization of the synchronous token system and therefore does not require the server and all the tokens to maintain the same exact time setting.

Who a Supplicant Is

The third area of authentication deals with a characteristic of the supplicant's person—that is, something they are. This process of using body measurements is known as biometrics. Biometrics includes:

- Fingerprint comparison of the supplicant's actual fingerprint to a stored fingerprint
- Palm print comparison of the supplicant's actual palm print to a stored palm print
- Hand geometry comparison of the supplicant's actual hand to a stored measurement
- Facial recognition using a photographic ID card, in which a human security guard compares the supplicant's face to a photo
- Facial recognition using a digital camera, in which a supplicant's face is compared to a stored image
- Retinal print comparison of the supplicant's actual retina to a stored image
- Iris pattern comparison of the supplicant's actual iris to a stored image

Among all possible biometrics, only three human characteristics are usually considered truly unique:

- Fingerprints
- Retina of the eye (blood vessel pattern)
- Iris of the eye (random pattern of features found in the iris including: freckles, pits, striations, vasculature, coronas, and crypts)

Figure 7-20 depicts some of these human recognition characteristics.

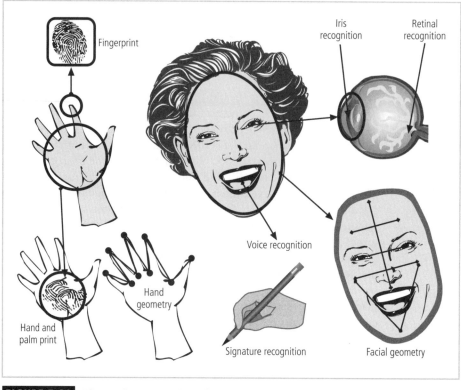

FIGURE 7-20 Biometric Recognition Characteristics

Most of the technologies that scan human characteristics convert these images to some form of minutiae. **Minutiae** are unique points of reference that are digitized and stored in an encrypted format when the user's system access credentials are created. Each subsequent access attempt results in a measurement that is compared with the encoded value to determine if the user is who he or she claims to be. A problem with this method is that some human characteristics can change over time, due to normal development, injury, or illness. This situation requires system designers to create fallback or failsafe authentication mechanisms to be used when the primary biometric procedure fails.

What a Supplicant Produces

The fourth and final area of authentication addresses something the supplicant performs or something he or she produces. This includes technology in the areas of signature recognition and voice recognition. Signature recognition has become commonplace. Retail stores use signature recognition, or at least signature capture, for authentication during a purchase. The customer signs his or her signature on a digital pad with a special stylus that captures the signature. The signature is digitized and either simply saved for future reference, or compared with a signature on a database for validation. Currently, the technology for signature capturing is much more widely accepted than that for signature comparison, because signatures change due to a number of factors, including age, fatigue, and the speed with which the signature is written.

Voice recognition works in a similar fashion in that an initial voiceprint of the user reciting a phrase is captured and stored. Later, when the user attempts to access the system, the authentication process will require the user to speak this same phrase so that the technology can compare the current voiceprint against the stored value.

Effectiveness of Biometrics

Biometric technologies are evaluated on three basic criteria: first, the false reject rate, which is the percentage of supplicants who are in fact authorized users but are denied access; second, the false accept rate, which is the percentage of supplicants who are unauthorized users but are granted access; finally, the crossover error rate, which is the level at which the number of false rejections equals the false acceptances. Each of these is examined in detail in the following sections.

False Reject Rate

The **false reject rate** is the percentage of or value associated with the rate at which supplicants who are authentic users are denied or prevented access to authorized areas as a result of a failure in the biometric device. This error rate is also known as a Type I error. While a nuisance to supplicants who are authorized users, this error rate is probably the one that least concerns security professionals since rejection of an authorized individual represents no threat to security, but is simply an impedance to authenticated use. As a result, the false reject rate is often ignored until it increases to a level high enough to irritate supplicants who, subsequently, begin complaining. Most people have experienced the frustration of having a frequently used credit card or ATM card fail to perform because of problems with the magnetic strip. In the field of biometrics, similar problems can occur when a system fails to pick up the various information points it uses to authenticate a prospective user properly.

False Accept Rate

The **false accept rate** is the percentage of or value associated with the rate at which supplicants who are not legitimate users are allowed access to systems or areas as a result of a failure in the biometric device. This error rate is also known as a Type II error. This type of error is unacceptable to security professionals, as it represents a clear breach of access.

Crossover Error Rate (CER)

The **crossover error rate (CER)** is the level at which the number of false rejections equals the false acceptances, also known as the equal error rate. This is possibly the most common and important overall measure of the accuracy of a biometric system. Most biometric systems can be adjusted to compensate for both false positive and false negative errors. Adjustment to one extreme creates a system that requires perfect matches and results in high false rejects, but almost no false accepts. Adjustment to the other extreme produces low false rejects, but high false accepts. The trick is to find the balance between providing the requisite level of security and minimizing the frustration level of authentic users. Thus, the optimal setting is found to be somewhere near the point at which these two error rates are equal—that is, at the crossover error rate or CER. CERs are used to compare various biometrics and may vary by manufacturer. A biometric device that provides a CER of 1% is a device for which the failure rate for false rejection and the failure rate for false acceptance are identical, at 1% failure of each type. A device with a CER of 1% is considered superior to a device with a CER of 5%.

Acceptability of Biometrics

As you've learned, a balance must be struck between how acceptable a security system is to its users and how effective it is in maintaining security. Many the biometric systems that are highly reliable and effective are considered somewhat intrusive to users. As a result, many information security professionals, in an effort to avoid confrontation and possible user boycott of the biometric controls, don't implement them. Table 7-3 shows how certain biometrics rank in terms of effectiveness and acceptance. Interestingly, the order of effectiveness is nearly exactly opposite the order of acceptance.

TABLE 7-3 Ranking of Effectiveness and Acceptance[21]

Effectiveness of Biometric Authentication Systems—Ranked from Most Secure to Least Secure	Acceptance of Biometric Authentication Systems—Ranked from Most Accepted to Least Accepted
Retina pattern recognition	Keystroke pattern recognition
Fingerprint recognition	Signature recognition
Handprint recognition	Voice pattern recognition
Voice pattern recognition	Handprint recognition
Keystroke pattern recognition	Fingerprint recognition
Signature recognition	Retina pattern recognition

Chapter Summary

- An intrusion detection system (IDS) works like a burglar alarm in that it detects a violation of its configuration (corresponding to an opened or broken window) and activates an alarm.

- A network-based IDS (NIDS) monitors network traffic, and when a predefined event occurs, it responds and notifies the appropriate administrator. A host-based IDS (HIDS) is a system that resides on a particular computer or server and monitors activity on that system.

- Signature-based IDSs, also known as knowledge-based IDSs, examine data traffic for patterns that match signatures, which are preconfigured, predetermined attack patterns. Statistical anomaly-based IDSs, also known as behavior-based IDSs, collect data from normal traffic and establish a baseline. When an activity is found to be outside the baseline parameters (or clipping level), these IDSs activate an alarm to notify the administrator.

- Selecting IDS products that best fit an organization's specific needs is a challenging and complex process.

- Honey pots are decoy systems, which means they are designed to lure potential attackers away from critical systems. In the security industry, these systems are also known as decoys, lures, or fly-traps. Two variations on this technology are known as honey nets and padded cell systems.

- Scanning and analysis tools are used to pinpoint vulnerabilities in systems, holes in security components, and unsecured aspects of the network. Although these tools are used by attackers, they can also be used by an administrator not only to learn more about his/her own system but also to identify and repair system weaknesses before they result in losses.

- Authentication is the validation of a prospective user's (or supplicant's) identity. Authentication depends on one or more of four factors: what a supplicant knows, what a supplicant has, who a supplicant is, and what a supplicant produces. The use of one authentication factor is necessary for access to almost all systems. Strong authentication uses two or more authentication factors. Biometric technologies are evaluated on three basic criteria: the false reject rate, the false accept rate, and the crossover error rate.

Review Questions

1. What common security system is an IDS most like? In what ways are these systems similar?
2. How does a false positive alarm differ from a false negative one? From a security perspective, which is least desirable?
3. How does a network-based IDS differ from a host-based IDS?
4. How does a signature-based IDS differ from a behavior-based IDS?
5. What is a monitoring (or SPAN) port? What is it used for?
6. List and describe the three control strategies proposed for IDS control.
7. What is a honey pot? How is it different from a honey net?
8. How does a padded cell system differ from a honey pot?
9. What is network footprinting? What is network fingerprinting? How are they related?
10. Why do many organizations ban port scanning activities on their internal networks? Why would ISPs ban outbound port scanning by their customers?

11. What is an open port? Why is it important to limit the number of open ports a system has to only those that are absolutely essential?

12. What is a vulnerability scanner? How is it used to improve security?

13. What is the difference between active and passive vulnerability scanners?

14. What kind of data and information can be found using a packet sniffer?

15. What capabilities should a wireless security toolkit include?

16. List and describe the four general forms of authentication.

17. Are any biometric recognition characteristics considered more reliable than others? Which are the most reliable?

18. What is a false reject rate? What is a false accept rate? How are they related to the crossover error rate?

19. What is the most widely accepted biometric authorization technology noted in the text? Why do you think this technology is so acceptable to users?

20. What is the most effective biometric authorization technology noted in the text? Why do you think this technology is deemed to be most effective by security professionals?

Exercises

1. A key feature of hybrid IDS systems is event correlation. After researching event correlation online, define the following terms as they are used in this process: compression, suppression, and generalization.

2. ZoneAlarm is a PC-based firewall and IDS tool. Visit the product manufacturer at *www.zonelabs.com*, and find the product specification for the IDS features of ZoneAlarm. Which of the ZoneAlarm products offer these features?

3. Using the Internet, search for commercial IDS systems. What classification systems and descriptions are used, and how can these be used to compare the features and components of each IDS? Create a comparison spreadsheet identifying the classification systems you find.

4. Use the Internet to find vendors of thumbprint and iris scanning tools. Which of these tools is more economical? Which of these is least intrusive?

5. There are several online passphrase generators available. Locate at least two of them on the Internet, and try them out. What did you observe?

Case Exercises

Returning to Miller Harrison and his attempts to hack into the SLS network, we find that he is still working his way down his attack protocol.

Nmap started out as it usually did: giving the program identification and version number. Then it started reporting back on the first host in the SLS network. It reported all of the open ports on this server. Then the program moved on to a second host and began reporting back the open ports on that system, too. Once it reached the third host, however, it suddenly stopped.

Miller restarted Nmap, using the last host IP as the starting point for the next scan. No response. He opened up another command window and tried to Ping the first host he had just port-scanned. No luck. He tried to Ping the SLS firewall. Nothing. He happened to know the IP address for the SLS edge router. He Pinged that and got the same result. He had been blackholed—meaning his IP address had been put on a list of addresses from which the SLS edge router would no longer accept packets. This was, ironically, his own doing. The IDS he had been helping SLS configure seemed to be working just fine at the moment. His attempt to hack the SLS network was shut down cold.

Questions:

1. Do you think Miller is out of options as he pursues his vendetta? If you think there are additional actions he could take in his effort to damage the SLS network, what are they?

2. Suppose a system administrator at SLS happened to read the details of this case. What steps should he or she take to improve the company's information security program?

Endnotes

1. Bace, Rebecca and Mell, Peter (2001). "Intrusion Detection Systems." NIST Special Publication 800-31, November. Viewed online on 2/15/04. Available from the World Wide Web <*http://csrc.nist.gov/publications/nistpubs/800-31/sp800-31.pdf.*>

2. Ibid.

3. Ibid.

4. Ibid.

5. Graham, Robert (2000). "FAQ: Intrusion Detection Systems." March. Viewed online on 2/25/04. Available from the World Wibe Web <*http://www.robertgraham.com/pubs/network-intrusion-detection.html#1.1*>.

6. Bace, Rebecca and Mell, Peter (2001). "Intrusion Detection Systems." NIST Special Publication 800-31, November. Viewed online on 2/15/04. Available from the World Wide Web <*http://csrc.nist.gov/publications/nistpubs/800-31/sp800-31.pdf*>.

7. Ibid.

8. Application-Based IDS, Compliance Component. Viewed online on 3/21/2004. Available on the World Wide Web <*http://siipc.mo.gov/PortalVB/ uploads/CC%20-%20Application%20Based%20IDS%2004-03-03.doc*>.

9. Bace, Rebecca and Mell, Peter (2001). "Intrusion Detection Systems." NIST Special Publication 800-31, November. Viewed online on 2/15/04. Available on the World Wide Web <*http://csrc.nist.gov/publications/nistpubs/800-31/sp800-31.pdf*>.

10. Graham, Robert (2000). "FAQ: Intrusion Detection Systems." March. Viewed online on 2/25/04. Available on the World Wide Web <*http://www.robertgraham.com/pubs/network-intrusion-detection.html*>.

11. Ibid.

12. Bace, Rebecca and Mell, Peter (2001). "Intrusion Detection Systems." NIST Special Publication 800-31, November. Viewed online on 2/15/04. Available on the World Wide Web <*http://csrc.nist.gov/publications/nistpubs/800-31/sp800-31.pdf*>.

13. Ibid.

14. Ibid.

15. Ibid.

16. Ibid.

17. Ibid.

18. Ranum, Marcus J. (2003) "False Positives: A User's Guide to Making Sense of IDS Alarms" for ICSA Labs IDSC. February. Viewed online on 3/15/04. Available on the World Wide Web <*http://www.icsalabs.com/html/communities/ids/whitepaper/FalsePositives.pdf*>.

19. Ibid.

20. Bace, Rebecca and Mell, Peter (2001). "Intrusion Detection Systems." NIST Special
     Publication 800-31, November. Viewed online on 2/15/04. Available on the World Wide Web
     <http://csrc.nist.gov/publications/ nistpubs/800-31/sp800-31.pdf>.
21. Harold F. Tipton and Micki Krause. *Handbook of Information Security Management.*
     (Boca Raton, LA: CRC Press LLC, 1998), 39–41.

Cryptography

> Yet it may roundly be asserted that human ingenuity cannot concoct a cipher which human ingenuity cannot resolve.
> **EDGAR ALLAN POE, THE GOLD BUG**

PETER HAYES, CFO OF SEQUENTIAL LABEL AND SUPPLY, OPENED AN E-MAIL from the manager of the accounting department. He saw that the e-mail had an attachment—probably a spreadsheet or a report of some kind. From the icon associated with the attached file, he knew it was an encrypted file. He saved the file to his computer's hard drive and then double-clicked on the icon to open it.

The operating system of his computer recognized that the file he was opening was encrypted and started the decryption program, which promptly asked Peter for his passphrase. Peter's mind went blank. He couldn't remember the passphrase. "Oh, good grief!" he said to himself aloud, reaching for his phone.

"Charlie, good, you're still here. I'm having trouble with a file in my e-mail program. My computer is prompting me for my passphrase, and I think I forgot it."

"Uh-oh," said Charlie.

"What do you mean 'Uh-oh'?" Peter asked.

"I mean you're S - O - L," Charlie replied. "Simply outta luck."

"Out of luck?" said Peter. "Why? Can't you do something? I have quite a few files saved on my computer that are encrypted with this PGP program. I need my files."

Charlie let him finish, then said, "Peter, do you recall how I told you it was important to remember your passphrase?" Charlie heard a sigh on the other end of the line, but decided to ignore it. "And do you remember I said that PGP is only free for individuals and that you weren't supposed to use it for company files since we didn't buy a license for the company? We only set that program up on your PC for your personal mail—for when your sister wanted to send you some financial records. When did you start using it for company business?"

"Well," Peter answered, "one of my staff had some financials that were going to be ready a few weeks ago while I was traveling. I swapped public keys with him before I left, and then he sent the files to me securely by e-mail while I was in Dallas. It worked out great. So that week I encrypted quite a few files. Now I can't get to any of them just because I can't seem to remember my passphrase." There was a long pause, when he said, "Can you hack it for me?"

Charlie chuckled a bit and then said, "Sure, Peter, no problem. Send me the files and I'll put the biggest server we have to work on it. Since we set you up in PGP with 128-bit 3DES, I should be able to apply a little brute force and crack the key to get the plaintext in two or three hundred million years or so."

LEARNING OBJECTIVES:

Upon completion of this material, you should be able to:

- Describe the most significant events and discoveries from the history of cryptology
- Understand the basic principles of cryptography
- Understand the operating principles of the most popular tools in the area of cryptography
- List and explain the major protocols used for secure communications
- Understand the nature and execution of the dominant methods of attack used against cryptosystems

Introduction

The science of cryptography is not as enigmatic as you might think. A variety of techniques related to cryptography are used regularly in everyday life. For example, open your newspaper to the entertainment section and you'll find the daily cryptogram, which is a word puzzle that makes a game out of unscrambling letters to find a hidden message. Also, although it is a dying art, many secretaries still use stenography, a coded form of documentation, to take rapid dictation from their managers. Finally, a form of cryptography is used even in the hobby of knitting, where directions are written in a coded form, in such patterns as K1P1 (knit 1, pearl 1), that only an initiate would be able to understand. Most of the examples above demonstrate the use of cryptography as a means of efficiently and rapidly conveying information. These aspects are only one important element of the science of cryptography. For the purposes of this chapter, the discussion of cryptography will be expanded to include the protection and verification of transmitted information.

In order to understand cryptography and its uses, you must become familiar with a number of key terms that are used across the information technology industry. The science of encryption, known as **cryptology**, encompasses *cryptography* and *cryptanalysis*. **Cryptography**, which comes from the Greek words *kryptos*, meaning "hidden," and *graphein*, meaning "to write," is the process of making and using codes to secure the transmission of information. Cryptanalysis is the process of obtaining the original message (called the **plaintext**) from an encrypted message (called the **ciphertext**) without knowing the algorithms and keys used to perform the encryption. **Encryption** is the process of converting an original message into a form that is unreadable to unauthorized individuals—that is, to anyone without the tools to convert the encrypted message back to its original format. **Decryption** is the process of converting the ciphertext into a message that conveys readily understood meaning.

The field of cryptology is so complex it can fill many volumes. As a result, this textbook seeks to provide only the most general overview of cryptology and some limited detail on the tools of cryptography. The early sections of this chapter, namely "A Short History of Cryptology," "Principles of Cryptography," and "Cryptography Tools," provide some background on cryptology and general definitions of the key concepts of cryptography, and discuss the usage of common cryptographic tools. Later sections discuss common cryptographic protocols and describe some of the attacks possible against cryptosystems.

A Short History of Cryptology

The creation and use of cryptology has a long history among the cultures of the world. Table 8-1 provides an overview of the history of cryptosystems.

TABLE 8-1 History of Cryptology

1900 B.C.	Egyptian scribes used nonstandard hieroglyphs while inscribing clay tablets; this is the first documented use of written cryptography.
1500 B.C.	Mesopotamian cryptography surpassed that of the Egyptians. This is demonstrated in a tablet that was discovered to contain an encrypted formula for pottery glazes; the tablet used special symbols that appear to have different meanings from the usual symbols used elsewhere.
500 B.C.	Hebrew scribes writing the book of Jeremiah used a reversed alphabet substitution cipher known as the ATBASH.
487 B.C.	The Spartans of Greece developed the Skytale, a system consisting of a strip of papyrus wrapped around a wooden staff. Messages were written down the length of the staff, and the papyrus was unwrapped. The decryption process involved wrapping the papyrus around a shaft of similar diameter.
50 B.C.	Julius Caesar used a simple substitution cipher to secure military and government communications. To form an encrypted text, Caesar shifted the letter of the alphabet three places. In addition to this monoalphabetic substitution cipher, Caesar strengthened his encryption by substituting Greek letters for Latin letters.
Fourth and fifth centuries	The Kama Sutra of Vatsayana listed cryptography as the 44th and 45th of the 64 arts (yogas) that men and women should practice: *44) The art of understanding writing in cipher, and the writing of words in a peculiar way; 45)The art of speaking by changing the forms of the word.*

TABLE 8-1 History of Cryptology (continued)

725	Abu 'Abd al-Rahman al-Khalil ibn Ahman ibn 'Amr ibn Tammam al Farahidi al-Zadi al Yahmadi wrote a text (now lost) of cryptography; he also solved a Greek cryptogram by guessing the plaintext introduction.
855	Abu Wahshiyyaan-Nabati, a scholar, published several cipher alphabets that were used for encrypted writings of magic formulas.
1250	Roger Bacon, an English monk, wrote *Epistle of Roger Bacon on the Secret Works of Art and of Nature and Also on the Nullity of Magic*, in which he described several simple ciphers.
1392	*The Equatorie of the Planetis*, an early text possibly written by Geoffrey Chaucer, contained a passage in a simple substitution cipher.
1412	Subhalasha, a 14-volume Arabic encyclopedia, contained a section on cryptography, including both substitution and transposition ciphers, and ciphers with multiple substitutions, a technique that had never been used before.
1466	Leon Battista Alberti is considered the Father of Western cryptography because on his work with polyalphabetic substitution; he also designed a cipher disk.
1518	Johannes Trithemius wrote the first printed book on cryptography and invented a steganographic cipher, in which each letter was represented as a word taken from a succession of columns. He also described a polyalphabetic encryption method using a rectangular substitution format that is now commonly used. He is credited with the introduction of the method of changing substitution alphabets with each letter as it is deciphered.
1553	Giovan Batista Belaso introduced the idea of the passphrase (password) as a key for encryption; this polyalphabetic encryption method is misnamed for another person who later used the technique and thus is called "The Vigenère Cipher" today.
1563	Giovanni Battista Porta wrote a classification text on encryption methods, categorizing them as transposition, substitution, and symbol substitution.
1623	Sir Francis Bacon described an encryption method by employing one of the first uses of steganography; he encrypted his messages by slightly changing the typeface of a random text so that each letter of the cipher was hidden within the text's letters.
1790s	Thomas Jefferson created a 26-letter wheel cipher, which he used for official communications while ambassador to France; the concept of the wheel cipher would be reinvented in 1854, and again in 1913.
1854	Charles Babbage appears to have reinvented Thomas Jefferson's wheel cipher.
1861–5	During the U.S. Civil War, Union forces used a substitution encryption method based on specific words, and the Confederacy used a polyalphabetic cipher whose solution had been published before the start of the Civil War.

TABLE 8-1   History of Cryptology (continued)

1914–17	World War I: The Germans, British, and French used a series of transposition and substitution ciphers in radio communications throughout the war. All sides spent considerable effort in trying to intercept and decode communications, and thereby brought about the birth of the science of cryptanalysis. British cryptographers broke the Zimmerman Telegram, in which the Germans offered Mexico U.S. territory in return for Mexico's support. This decryption helped to bring the United States into the war.
1917	William Frederick Friedman, the father of U.S. cryptanalysis, and his wife, Elizabeth, were employed as civilian cryptanalysts by the U.S. government. Friedman later founded a school for cryptanalysis in Riverbank, Illinois.
1917	Gilbert S. Vernam, an AT&T employee, invented a polyalphabetic cipher machine that used a non-repeating random key.
1919	Hugo Alexander Koch filed a patent in the Netherlands for a rotor-based cipher machine; in 1927, Koch assigned the patent rights to Arthur Scherbius, the inventor of the Enigma Machine, which was a mechanical substitution cipher.
1927–33	During Prohibition, criminals in the U.S. began using cryptography to maintain the privacy of messages used in criminal activities.
1937	The Japanese developed the Purple machine, which was based on principles similar to those of Enigma and used mechanical relays from telephone systems to encrypt diplomatic messages. By late 1940, a team headed by William Friedman had broken the code generated by this machine and constructed a machine that could quickly decode Purple's ciphers.
1939–42	The fact that the Allies secretly broke the Enigma cipher undoubtedly shortened World War II.
1942	Navajo *Windtalkers* entered World War II; in addition to speaking a language that was unknown outside a relatively small group within the United States, the Navajos developed code words for subjects and ideas that did not exist in their native tongue.
1948	Claude Shannon suggested using frequency and statistical analysis in the solution of substitution ciphers.
1970	Dr. Horst Feistel led an IBM research team in the development of the Lucifer cipher.
1976	A design based upon Lucifer was chosen by the U.S. National Security Agency as the Data Encryption Standard and found worldwide acceptance.
1976	Whitefield Diffie and Martin Hellman introduced the idea of public key cryptography.
1977	Ronald Rivest, Adi Shamir, and Leonard Adleman developed a practical public key cipher for both confidentiality and digital signatures; the RSA family of computer encryption algorithms was born.

TABLE 8-1	History of Cryptology (continued)
1978	The initial RSA algorithm was published in the Communication of ACM.
1991	Phil Zimmermann released the first version of PGP (Pretty Good Privacy); PGP was released as freeware and became the worldwide standard for public cryptosystems.
2000	Rijndael's cipher was selected as the Advanced Encryption Standard.

Principles of Cryptography

Historically, cryptography was used in manual applications, such as handwriting. But with the emergence of automated technologies in the 20th century, the need for encryption in the IT environment vastly increased. Today, many common IT tools use embedded encryption technologies to protect sensitive information within applications. For example, all the popular Web browsers use built-in encryption features that enable users to perform secure e-commerce applications, such as online banking and Web shopping.

Basic Encryption Definitions

To understand the fundamentals of cryptography, you must become familiar with the following definitions:

- **Algorithm:** The programmatic steps used to convert an unencrypted message into an encrypted sequence of bits that represent the message; sometimes used as a reference to the programs that enable the cryptographic processes
- **Cipher** or **cryptosystem:** An encryption method or process encompassing the algorithm, key(s) or cryptovariable(s), and procedures used to perform encryption and decryption
- **Ciphertext** or **cryptogram:** The unintelligible encrypted or encoded message resulting from an encryption
- **Code:** The process of converting components (words or phrases) of an unencrypted message into encrypted components
- **Decipher:** To decrypt or convert ciphertext into the equivalent plaintext
- **Encipher:** To encrypt or convert plaintext into the equivalent ciphertext
- **Key** or **cryptovariable:** The information used in conjunction with an algorithm to create the ciphertext from the plaintext or derive the plaintext from the ciphertext; the key can be a series of bits used by a computer program, or it can be a passphrase used by humans that is then converted into a series of bits for use in the computer program
- **Keyspace:** The entire range of values that can possibly be used to construct an individual key
- **Link encryption:** A series of encryptions and decryptions between a number of systems, wherein each system in a network decrypts the message sent to it and then reencrypts it using different keys and sends it to the next neighbor, and this process continues until the message reaches the final destination

- **Plaintext** or **cleartext:** The original unencrypted message that is encrypted; also the name given to the results of a message that has been successfully decrypted
- **Steganography:** The process of hiding messages—for example, messages can be hidden within the digital encoding of a picture or graphic
- **Work factor:** The amount of effort (usually in hours) required to perform cryptanalysis on an encoded message so that it may be decrypted when the key or algorithm (or both) are unknown

Cipher Methods

A plaintext can be encrypted through one of two methods, the bit stream method or the block cipher method. With the bit stream method, each bit in the plaintext is transformed into a cipher bit one bit at a time. In the case of the block cipher method, the message is divided into blocks, for example, sets of 8-, 16-, 32-, or 64-bit blocks, and then each block of plaintext bits is transformed into an encrypted block of cipher bits using an algorithm and a key. Bit stream methods most commonly use algorithm functions like the exclusive OR operation (XOR), whereas block methods can use substitution, transposition, XOR, or some combination of these operations, as described in the following sections. As you read on, you should note that most encryption methods using computer systems will operate on data at the level of its binary digits (bits), but some operations may operate at the byte or character level.

Elements of Cryptosystems

Cryptosystems are made up of a number of elements or components. These are usually algorithms and data handling techniques as well as procedures and process steps, which are combined in multiple ways to meet a given organization's need to ensure confidentiality and provide specialized authentication and authorization for its business processes. In the sections that follow, you will first read about the technical aspects of a number of cryptographic techniques, often called ciphers. The chapter will continue with an exploration of some of the tools commonly used to implement cryptographic systems in the world of business. The discussion will then proceed to the security protocols used to bring communications security to the Internet and the world of e-commerce. Finally, the chapter will conclude with a discussion of the attacks that are often found being used against cryptosystems. Along the way, you will also encounter a number of Technical Details boxes that cover advanced material. Be sure to check with your instructor about how your course will include the Technical Details material.

Substitution Cipher

When using a **substitution cipher**, you substitute one value for another. For example, you can substitute a letter in the alphabet with the letter three values to the right. Or, you may substitute one bit for another bit that is four places to its left. A three-character substitution to the right would result in the following transformation of the standard English alphabet:

Initial alphabet yields	ABCDEFGHIJKLMNOPQRSTUVWXYZ
Encryption alphabet	DEFGHIJKLMNOPQRSTUVWXYZABC

Within this substitution scheme, the plaintext MOM would be encrypted into the ciphertext PRP.

This is a simple enough method by itself but very powerful if combined with other operations. Incidentally, this type of substitution is based on a **monoalphabetic substitution**, since it only uses one alphabet. More advanced substitution ciphers use two or more alphabets, and are referred to as **polyalphabetic substitutions**.

To continue the previous example, consider the following block of text:

Plaintext =	ABCDEFGHIJKLMNOPQRSTUVWXYZ
Substitution cipher 1 =	DEFGHIJKLMNOPQRSTUVWXYZABC
Substitution cipher 2 =	GHIJKLMNOPQRSTUVWXYZABCDEF
Substitution cipher 3 =	JKLMNOPQRSTUVWXYZABCDEFGHI
Substitution cipher 4 =	MNOPQRSTUVWXYZABCDEFGHIJKL

The first row here is the plaintext, and the next four rows are four sets of substitution ciphers, which taken together constitute a **single polyalphabetic** substitution cipher. To encode the word TEXT with this cipher, you substitute a letter from the second row for the first letter in TEXT, a letter from the third row for the second letter, and so on—a process that yields the ciphertext WKGF. Note how the plaintext letter T is transformed into a W or a F, depending on its order of appearance in the plaintext. Complexities like these make this type of encryption substantially more difficult to decipher when one doesn't have the algorithm (in this case, the rows of ciphers) and the key, which is the method used (in this case the use of the second row for first letter, third for second, and so on). A logical extension to this process would be to randomize the cipher rows completely in order to create a more complex operation.

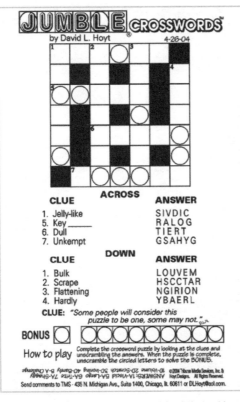

Source: http://www.tmsfeatures.com/samples/daily_jumble_xword/dly_xword1.pdf

FIGURE 8-1 Daily cryptogram

One example of a substitution cipher is the cryptogram in the daily newspaper (see Figure 8-1); another is the once famous *Radio Orphan Annie decoder pin* (shown in Figure 8-2), which consisted of two alphabetic rings that could be rotated to a predetermined pairing to form a simple substitution cipher. The device was made to be worn as a pin so one could always be at the ready. As mentioned in Table 8-1, Caesar reportedly used a three-position shift to the right to encrypt his messages (so A became D, B became E, and so on), thus this particular substitution cipher was given his name—the *Caesar Cipher*.

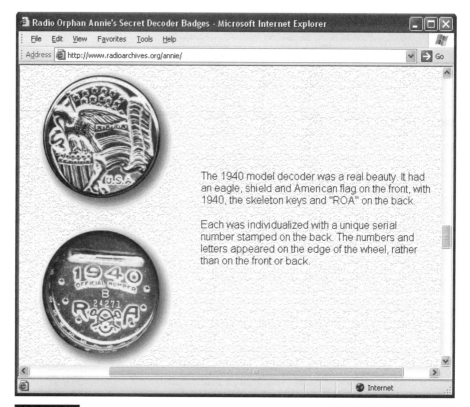

The 1940 model decoder was a real beauty. It had an eagle, shield and American flag on the front, with 1940, the skeleton keys and "ROA" on the back.

Each was individualized with a unique serial number stamped on the back. The numbers and letters appeared on the edge of the wheel, rather than on the front or back.

FIGURE 8-2   Radio Orphan Annie's Decoder Pin

An advanced type of substitution cipher that uses a **simple polyalphabetic** code is the **Vigenère cipher**. The cipher is implemented using the Vigenère Square. which is made up of 26 distinct cipher alphabets. Table 8-2 illustrates the setup of the Vigenère Square. In the header row, the alphabet is written in its normal order. In each subsequent row, the alphabet is shifted one letter to the right until a 26 X 26 block of letters is formed. There are a number of ways to use the Vigenère square. You could perform an encryption by simply starting in the first row and finding a substitute for the first letter of plaintext, and then moving down the rows for each subsequent letter of plaintext. With this method, the word SECURITY in plaintext would become TGFYWOAG in ciphertext.

TABLE 8-2 The Vigenère Square

	A	B	C	D	E	F	G	H	I	J	K	L	M	N	O	P	Q	R	S	T	U	V	W	X	Y	Z
1	B	C	D	E	F	G	H	I	J	K	L	M	N	O	P	Q	R	S	T	U	V	W	X	Y	Z	A
2	C	D	E	F	G	H	I	J	K	L	M	N	O	P	Q	R	S	T	U	V	W	X	Y	Z	A	B
3	D	E	F	G	H	I	J	K	L	M	N	O	P	Q	R	S	T	U	V	W	X	Y	Z	A	B	C
4	E	F	G	H	I	J	K	L	M	N	O	P	Q	R	S	T	U	V	W	X	Y	Z	A	B	C	D
5	F	G	H	I	J	K	L	M	N	O	P	Q	R	S	T	U	V	W	X	Y	Z	A	B	C	D	E
6	G	H	I	J	K	L	M	N	O	P	Q	R	S	T	U	V	W	X	Y	Z	A	B	C	D	E	F
7	H	I	J	K	L	M	N	O	P	Q	R	S	T	U	V	W	X	Y	Z	A	B	C	D	E	F	G
8	I	J	K	L	M	N	O	P	Q	R	S	T	U	V	W	X	Y	Z	A	B	C	D	E	F	G	H
9	J	K	L	M	N	O	P	Q	R	S	T	U	V	W	X	Y	Z	A	B	C	D	E	F	G	H	I
10	K	L	M	N	O	P	Q	R	S	T	U	V	W	X	Y	Z	A	B	C	D	E	F	G	H	I	J
11	L	M	N	O	P	Q	R	S	T	U	V	W	X	Y	Z	A	B	C	D	E	F	G	H	I	J	K
12	M	N	O	P	Q	R	S	T	U	V	W	X	Y	Z	A	B	C	D	E	F	G	H	I	J	K	L
13	N	O	P	Q	R	S	T	U	V	W	X	Y	Z	A	B	C	D	E	F	G	H	I	J	K	L	M
14	O	P	Q	R	S	T	U	V	W	X	Y	Z	A	B	C	D	E	F	G	H	I	J	K	L	M	N
15	P	Q	R	S	T	U	V	W	X	Y	Z	A	B	C	D	E	F	G	H	I	J	K	L	M	N	O
16	Q	R	S	T	U	V	W	X	Y	Z	A	B	C	D	E	F	G	H	I	J	K	L	M	N	O	P
17	R	S	T	U	V	W	X	Y	Z	A	B	C	D	E	F	G	H	I	J	K	L	M	N	O	P	Q
18	S	T	U	V	W	X	Y	Z	A	B	C	D	E	F	G	H	I	J	K	L	M	N	O	P	Q	R
19	T	U	V	W	X	Y	Z	A	B	C	D	E	F	G	H	I	J	K	L	M	N	O	P	Q	R	S
20	U	V	W	X	Y	Z	A	B	C	D	E	F	G	H	I	J	K	L	M	N	O	P	Q	R	S	T
21	V	W	X	Y	Z	A	B	C	D	E	F	G	H	I	J	K	L	M	N	O	P	Q	R	S	T	U
22	W	X	Y	Z	A	B	C	D	E	F	G	H	I	J	K	L	M	N	O	P	Q	R	S	T	U	V
23	X	Y	Z	A	B	C	D	E	F	G	H	I	J	K	L	M	N	O	P	Q	R	S	T	U	V	W
24	Y	Z	A	B	C	D	E	F	G	H	I	J	K	L	M	N	O	P	Q	R	S	T	U	V	W	X
25	Z	A	B	C	D	E	F	G	H	I	J	K	L	M	N	O	P	Q	R	S	T	U	V	W	X	Y
26	A	B	C	D	E	F	G	H	I	J	K	L	M	N	O	P	Q	R	S	T	U	V	W	X	Y	Z

A much more sophisticated way to use the Vigenère Square would be to use a keyword to represent the shift. To accomplish this, you would begin by writing a keyword above the plaintext message. For example, suppose the plaintext message was "`SACK GAUL SPARE NO ONE`" and the keyword was `ITALY`. We thus end up with the following:

```
ITALYITALYITALYITA
SACKGAULSPARENOONE
```

The idea behind this is that you will now use the keyword letter and the message (plaintext) letter below it in combination. Returning to the Vigenère Square, notice how the first column of text, like the first row, forms the normal alphabet. To perform the substitution of the message, start with first combination of keyword and message letters, IS. Use the keyword letter to locate the column, and the message letter to find the row, and then look for the letter at their intersection. Thus, for column "I" and row "S," you will find the ciphertext letter "A". After you follow this procedure for each of the letters in the message, you will produce the encrypted ciphertext `ATCVEINLDNIKEYMWGE`. Curiously, one weakness of this method is that any keyword-message letter combination containing an "A" row or column will reproduce the plaintext message letter. For example, the third letter in the plaintext message, the C (of SACK), has a combination of AC, and thus is unchanged in the ciphertext. To minimize the effects of this weakness, you should avoid choosing a keyword that contains the letter "A."

Transposition Cipher

The next type of cipher operation is the transposition. Just like the substitution operation, the transposition cipher is simple to understand, but it can, if properly used, produce ciphertext that is complex to decipher. In contrast to the substitution cipher, however, the **transposition cipher** (or **permutation cipher**) simply rearranges the values within a block to create the ciphertext. This can be done at the bit level or at the byte (character) level. For an example, consider the following transposition key pattern.

Key pattern: $1{\rightarrow}4$, $2{\rightarrow}8$, $3{\rightarrow}1$, $4{\rightarrow}5$, $5{\rightarrow}7$, $6{\rightarrow}2$, $7{\rightarrow}6$, $8{\rightarrow}3$

In this key, the bit or byte (character) in position 1 (with position 1 being at the far *right*) moves to position 4 (counting from the right), and the bit or byte in position 2 moves to position 8, and so on.

The following rows show the numbering of bit locations for this key; the plaintext message `00100101011010111001010101010100`, which is broken into 8-bit blocks for ease of discussion; and the ciphertext that is produced when the transposition key depicted above is applied to the plaintext:

Bit locations:	87654321	87654321	87654321	87654321
Plaintext 8-bit blocks:	00100101	01101011	10010101	01010100
Ciphertext:	00001011	10111010	01001101	01100001

Reading from right to left in the example above, the first bit of plaintext (position 1 of the first byte) becomes the fourth bit (in position 4) of the first byte of the ciphertext. Similarly, the second bit of the plaintext (position 2) becomes the eighth bit (position 8) of the ciphertext, and so on.

To examine further how this transposition key works, let's see its effects on a plaintext message comprised of letters instead of bits. Replacing the 8-bit block of plaintext with the example plaintext message presented earlier, "SACK GAUL SPARE NO ONE," yields the following:

```
Letter locations:    87654321|87654321|87654321|87654321|
Plaintext:           SACKGAUL|SPARENOO|NE      |         |
Key:                 Same key as above, but characters transposed, not bits.
Ciphertext:          UKAGLSCA|ORPEOSAN|  E   N |         |
```

Here, reading again from right to left, the letter in position 1 of the first block of plaintext, "L", becomes the letter at position 4 in the ciphertext. In other words, the "L" that is the 8th letter of the plaintext is the "L" at the 5th letter of the ciphertext. The letter in position 2 of the first block of plaintext, "U", becomes the letter at position 8 in the ciphertext. In other words, the "U" that is the 7th letter of the plaintext is the "U" at the 1st letter of the ciphertext. This process continues using the specified pattern.

In addition to being credited with inventing a substitution cipher, Julius Caesar was associated with an early version of the transposition cipher. As part of the Caesar block cipher, a courier would carry a message that when read normally would be unintelligible. However, the receiver of the message would know to fit the text to a prime number square (in practice, this meant that if there were fewer than 25 characters, the receiver would use a 5 x 5 square). For example, suppose you were the receiver and the ciphertext shown below arrived at your doorstep. Since it was from Caesar, you would know to make a square of 5 columns and 5 rows, and then to write the letters of the message into the square, filling the slots from left to right, top to bottom. Also, when you'd finished doing this, you'd know to read the message the opposite direction—that is, from top to bottom, left to right.

```
Ciphertext:          SGS_NAAPNECUAO KLR        EO
                     S G S _ N
                     A A P N E
                     C U A O
                     K L R _ _
                     _ _ E O _
```

Reading from top to bottom, left to right reveals the plaintext "SACK GAUL SPARE NO ONE".

When mechanical and electronic cryptosystems became more widely used, transposition ciphers and substitution ciphers began to be used in combinations to produce highly secure encryption processes. To make the encryption even stronger (more difficult to cryptanalyze) the keys and block sizes can be made much larger (up to 64 or 128 bits in size), which produces substantially more complex substitutions or transpositions.

Exclusive OR

The **exclusive OR operation (XOR)** is a function of Boolean algebra in which two bits are compared, and if the two bits are identical, the result is a binary 0. If the two bits are not the same, the result is a binary 1. XOR encryption is a very simple symmetric cipher that is used in many applications where security is not a defined requirement. Table 8-3 shows a truth table for XOR with the results of all the possible combinations of two bits.

TABLE 8-3 XOR Truth Table

First Bit	Second Bit	Result
0	0	0
0	1	1
1	0	1
1	1	0

To see how XOR works, let's consider an example in which the plaintext we will start with is the word "CAT". The binary representation of the plaintext is "01110000 01100101 1000000". In order to encrypt the plaintext, a key value should be selected. In this case, the bit pattern for the letter "V" (10000101) will be used and repeated for each character to be encrypted. Performing the XOR operation on the two bit streams (the plaintext and the key) will produce the following result:

TABLE 8-4 Example XOR Encryption

CAT as bits	0 1 1 1 0 0 0 0 0 1 1 0 0 1 0 1 1 0 0 0 0 0 0 0
VVV as key	1 0 0 0 0 1 0 1 1 0 0 0 0 1 0 1 1 0 0 0 0 1 0 1
Cipher	0 1 1 1 0 1 0 1 1 1 1 0 0 0 0 0 0 0 0 0 0 1 0 1

The row of Table 8-4 labeled "Cipher" contains the bit stream that will be transmitted; when this cipher is received, it can be decrypted using the key value of "V". Note that the XOR encryption method is very simple to implement and equally simple to break. The XOR encryption method should not be used by itself when an organization is transmitting or storing data that needs protection. Actual encryption algorithms used to protect data typically use the XOR operator as part of a more complex encryption process, thus understanding XOR encryption is a necessary step on the path to becoming a cryptologist.

Often, one can combine the XOR operation with a block cipher operation to produce a simple but powerful operation. Consider the example that follows, the first row of which shows a character message "5E5+•" requiring encryption. The second row shows this message in binary notation. In order to apply an 8-bit block cipher method, the binary message is broken into 8-bit blocks in the row labeled "Message Blocks." The fourth row shows the 8-bit key (01010101) chosen for the encryption. To encrypt the message, you must perform the XOR operation on each 8-bit block by using the XOR function on the message bit and the key bit to determine the bits of the ciphertext until the entire message is enciphered. The result is shown in the row labeled "Ciphertext". This ciphertext can now be sent to a receiver, who will be able to decipher the message by simply knowing the algorithm (XOR) and the key (01010101).

Message (text):	"5E5+•"
Message (binary):	0011010101000101001101010010101110010101
Message blocks:	00110101 01000101 00110101 00101011 10010101
Key:	01010101 01010101 01010101 01010101 01010101
Ciphertext:	01100000 00010000 01100000 01111110 11000000

If the receiver cannot apply the key to the ciphertext and derive the original message, either the cipher was applied with an incorrect key or the cryptosystem was not used correctly.

Vernam Cipher

Also known as the one-time pad, the **Vernam cipher**, which was developed at AT&T, uses a set of characters only one time for each encryption process (hence, the name one-time pad). The pad in the name comes from the days of manual encryption and decryption when the key values for each ciphering session were prepared by hand and bound into an easy-to-use form—i.e., a pad of paper. To perform the Vernam cipher encryption operation, the pad values are added to numeric values that represent the plaintext that needs to be encrypted. So, each character of the plaintext is turned into a number and a pad value for that position is added to it. The resulting sum for that character is then converted back to a ciphertext letter for transmission. If the sum of the two values exceeds 26, then 26 is subtracted from the total. (Note that the process of keeping a computed number within a specific range is called a modulo; thus, requiring that all numbers be in the range 1-26 is referred to as Modulo 26. In Modulo 26, if a number is larger than 26, then 26 is repeatedly subtracted from it until the number is in the proper range.)

To examine the Vernam cipher and its use of modulo, consider the following example, which uses the familiar "SACK GAUL SPARE NO ONE" as plaintext. In the first step of this encryption process, the letter "S" will be converted into the number 19 (because it is the 19th letter of the alphabet), and the same conversion will be applied to the rest of the letters of the plaintext message, as shown below.

Plaintext:	S	A	C	K	G	A	U	L	S	P	A	R	E	N	O	O	N	E
Plaintext value:	19	01	03	11	07	01	21	12	19	16	01	18	05	14	15	15	14	05
One-time pad text:	F	P	Q	R	N	S	B	I	E	H	T	Z	L	A	C	D	G	J
One time pad value:	06	16	17	18	14	19	02	09	05	08	20	26	12	01	03	04	07	10
Sum of plaintext and pad:	25	17	20	29	21	20	23	21	24	24	21	44	17	15	18	19	21	15
After modulo Subtraction:				03								18						
Ciphertext:	Y	Q	T	C	U	T	W	U	X	X	U	R	Q	O	R	S	U	O

Rows three and four in the example above show, respectively, the one-time pad text that was chosen for this encryption and the one time pad value. As you can see, the pad value is, like the plaintext value, derived by considering the position of each pad text letter in the alphabet, thus the pad text letter "F" is assigned the position number of 06. This conversion process is repeated for the entire one-time pad text. Next, the plaintext value and the one time pad value are added together—the first such sum is 25. Since 25 is in the range of 1 to 26, no Modulo-26 subtraction is required. The sum remains 25, and yields the ciphertext "Y", as shown above. Skipping ahead to the fourth character of the plaintext, "K", we find that the plaintext value for it is 11. The pad text is "R" and the pad value is 18. Adding 11 and 18 will result in a sum of 29. Since 29 is larger than 26, 26 is subtracted from it, which yields the value 3. The ciphertext for this plaintext character will then be the third letter of the alphabet, "C".

Decryption of any ciphertext generated from a one-time pad will require either knowledge of the pad values or the use of elaborate and (the encrypting party hopes) very difficult cryptanalysis. Using the pad values and the ciphertext, the decryption process would happen as follows; "Y" becomes the number 25 from which we subtract the pad value for the first letter of the message, 06. This yields a value of 19, or the letter

"S". This pattern continues until the fourth letter of the ciphertext where the ciphertext letter is "C" and the pad value is 18. Subtracting 18 from 3 will give a difference of negative 15. Since modulo-26 is employed, it requires that all numbers are in the range of 1–26, we must *add* 26 to the negative 15. This operations gives a sum of 11, which means that fourth letter of the message is "K".

Book or Running Key Cipher

One encryption method made popular by spy movies involves using the text in a book as the key to decrypt a message. The ciphertext consists of a list of codes representing the page number, line number, and word number of the plaintext word. The algorithm is the mechanical process of looking up the references from the ciphertext and converting each reference to a word by using the ciphertext's value and the key (the book). For example, from a copy of a particular popular novel, one may send the message: 259,19,8; 22,3,8; 375,7,4; 394,17,2. Although almost any book will work just fine, dictionaries and thesauruses are typically the most popular sources as they can guarantee having almost every word that might be needed. Returning to the example, the receiver must first know which novel is used—in this case, suppose it is the science fiction novel, *A Fire Upon the Deep*, the 1992 TOR edition. To decrypt the ciphertext, the receiver would acquire the book and begin by turning to page 259, finding line 19, and selecting the eighth word in that line (which happens to be "sack"). Then the receiver would go to page 22, line 3, and select the eighth word again, and so forth. For this example, the resulting message will be "SACK ISLAND SHARP PATH". If dictionaries are used, the message would be made up of only the page number and the number of the word on the page. An even more sophisticated version might use multiple books, perhaps even in a particular sequence for each word or phrase.

Hash Functions

In addition to ciphers, another important encryption technique that is often incorporated into cryptosystems is the hash function. **Hash functions** are mathematical algorithms that generate a message summary or digest (sometimes called a fingerprint) to confirm the identity of a specific message and to confirm that there have not been any changes to the content. While not directly related to the creation of a ciphertext, hash functions are used to confirm message identity and integrity, both of which are critical functions in e-commerce.

Hash algorithms are publicly known functions that create a hash value, also known as a message digest, by converting variable-length messages into a single fixed-length value. The **message digest** is a *fingerprint* of the author's message that is to be compared with the receiver's locally calculated hash of the same message. If both hashes are identical after transmission, the message has arrived without modification. Hash functions are considered one-way operations in that the message will always provide the same hash value if it is the same message, but the hash value itself cannot be used to determine the contents of the message.

Hashing functions do not require the use of keys, but a **message authentication code (MAC)**, which is a key-dependent, and one-way hash function, may be attached to a message to allow only specific recipients to access the message digest. The MAC is essentially a one-way hash value that is encrypted with a symmetric key. The recipients must possess the key to access the message digest and to confirm message integrity.

Because hash functions are one-way, they are used in password verification systems to confirm the identity of the user. In such systems, the hash value, or message digest, is calculated based upon the originally issued password, and this message digest is stored for later comparison. When the user logs on for the next session, the system calculates a hash value based on the user's inputted password. The newly calculated hash value is compared against the stored value to confirm identity.

The **Secure Hash Standard (SHS)** is a standard issued by the National Institute of Standards and Technology (NIST). Standard document FIPS 180-1 specifies SHA-1 (Secure Hash Algorithm 1) as a secure algorithm for computing a condensed representation of a message or data file. SHA-1 produces a 160-bit message digest, which can then be used as an input to a digital signature algorithm. SHA-1 is based on principles modeled after MD4 (which is part of the MDx family of hash algorithms created by Ronald Rivest). New hash algorithms (SHA-256, SHA-384, and SHA-512) have been proposed by NIST as standards for 128, 192, and 256 bits, respectively. The number of bits used in the hash algorithm is a measurement of the strength of the algorithm against collision attacks. SHA-256 is essentially a 256-bit block cipher algorithm that creates a key by encrypting the intermediate hash value with the message block functioning as the key. The compression function operates on each 512-bit message block and a 256-bit intermediate message digest.[1]

Cryptographic Algorithms

In general, cryptographic algorithms are often grouped into two broad categories—symmetric and asymmetric—but in practice, today's popular cryptosystems use a hybrid combination of symmetric and asymmetric algorithms. Symmetric and asymmetric algorithms can be distinguished by the types of keys they use for encryption and decryption operations. The upcoming section discusses both of these algorithms, and includes Technical Details boxes that provide supplemental information on cryptographic notation and advanced encryption standards.

Symmetric Encryption.   A method of encryption that requires the same **secret key** to encipher and decipher the message is known as **private key encryption** or **symmetric encryption.** Symmetric encryption methods use mathematical operations that can be programmed into extremely fast computing algorithms so that the encryption and decryption processes are done quickly by even small computers. As you can see in Figure 8-3, one of the challenges is that both the sender and the receiver must have the secret key. Also, if either copy of the key falls into the wrong hands, messages can be decrypted by others and the sender and intended receiver may not know the message was intercepted. The primary challenge of symmetric key encryption is getting the key to the receiver, a process that must be conducted out of band (meaning through a channel or band other than the one carrying the ciphertext) to avoid interception.

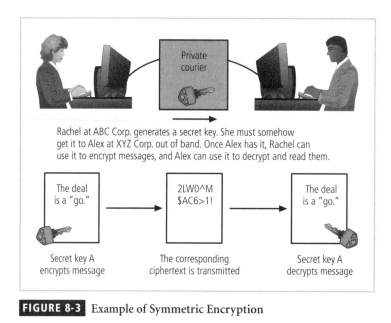

Rachel at ABC Corp. generates a secret key. She must somehow get it to Alex at XYZ Corp. out of band. Once Alex has it, Rachel can use it to encrypt messages, and Alex can use it to decrypt and read them.

| The deal is a "go." | 2LW0^M $AC6>1! | The deal is a "go." |

Secret key A encrypts message → The corresponding ciphertext is transmitted → Secret key A decrypts message

FIGURE 8-3 Example of Symmetric Encryption

TECHNICAL DETAILS BOX

Cryptographic Notation

The notation used to describe the encryption process varies, depending on its source. The notation chosen for the discussion in this text uses the letter M to represent the original message, C to represent the ending ciphertext, and E to represent the encryption process: thus, $E(M) = C$.[2] This formula represents the application of encryption (E) to a message (M) to create ciphertext (C). Also in this notation scheme, the letter D represents the decryption or deciphering process, thus the formula $D[E(M)] = M$ states that if you decipher (D) an enciphered message (E(M)), you should get the original message (M). This could also be stated as $D[C]=M$, or the deciphering of the ciphertext (remember that $C=E(M)$) results in the original message M. Finally, the letter K is used to represent the key, therefore $E(M,K) = C$ suggests that encrypting (E) the message (M) with the key (K) results in the ciphertext (C). Similarly, $D(C,K) = D[E(M,K),K] = M$, or deciphering the ciphertext with key K results in the original plaintext message—or, to translate this formula even more precisely, deciphering with key K the message encrypted with key K results in the original message.

To encrypt a plaintext set of data, you can use one of two methods: bit stream and block cipher. With the bit stream method, each bit is transformed into a cipher bit, one after the other. With the block cipher method, the message is divided into blocks, e.g., 8-, 16-, 32-, or 64-bit blocks, and then each block is transformed using the algorithm and key. Bit stream methods most commonly use algorithm functions like XOR, whereas block methods can use XOR, transposition, or substitution.

There are a number of popular symmetric encryption cryptosystems. One of the most widely known is the **Data Encryption Standard (DES)**, which was developed by IBM and is based on the company's Lucifer algorithm, which uses a key length of 128 bits. As implemented, DES uses a 64-bit block size and a 56-bit key. DES was adopted by NIST in 1976 as a federal standard for encryption of non-classified information. With this approval, DES became widely employed in commercial applications as the encryption standard of choice. DES enjoyed increasing popularity for almost 20 years, until 1997, when users realized that using a 56-bit key size was no longer sufficient as an acceptable level of secure communications. And soon enough, in 1998, a group called the Electronic Frontier Foundation (www.eff.org), using a specially designed computer, broke a DES key in less than three days (just over 56 hours, to be precise). Since then, it has been theorized that a dedicated attack supported by the proper hardware (thus, not even a specialized computer like that of Electronic Frontier Foundation) can break a DES key in less than four hours.

As DES became known as being too weak for highly classified communications, **Triple DES (3DES)** was created to provide a level of security far beyond that of DES. 3DES was an advanced application of DES, and was in fact originally designed to replace DES. While 3DES did deliver on its promise of encryption strength beyond DES, it too was soon proven too weak to survive indefinitely—especially as computing power continued to double every 18 months. Within just a few years, 3DES needed to be replaced.

TECHNICAL DETAILS BOX

Triple DES, (3DES)

As it was demonstrated that DES was not strong enough for highly classified communications, 3DES was created to provide a level of security far beyond that of standard DES. (In between, there was a 2DES; however, it was statistically shown that the double DES did not provide significantly stronger security than that of DES.) 3DES takes three 64-bit keys for an overall key length of 192 bits. Triple DES encryption is the same as that of standard DES; however, it is repeated three times. Triple DES can be employed using two or three keys, and a combination of encryption or decryption to obtain additional security. The most common implementations involve encrypting and/or decrypting with two or three different keys, a process that is described below. 3DES employs 48 rounds in its encryption computation, generating ciphers that are approximately 2^{56} (72 quadrillion) times stronger than standard DES ciphers but require only three times longer to process. One example of 3DES encryption is illustrated here:

1. In the first operation, 3DES encrypts the message with key 1, then decrypts it with key 2, and then it encrypts it again with key 1. In cryptographic notation terms, this would be [E{D[E(M,K1)],K2},K1]. Decrypting with a different key is essentially another encryption, but it reverses the application of the traditional encryption operations.
2. In the second operation, 3DES encrypts the message with key 1, then it encrypts it again with key 2, and then it encrypts it a third time with key 1 again, or [E{E[E(M,K1)],K2},K1].
3. In the third operation, 3DES encrypts the message three times with three different keys; [E{E[E(M,K1)],K2},K3]. This is the most secure level of encryption possible with 3DES.

The successor to 3DES is **Advanced Encryption Standard (AES)**. AES is a Federal Information Processing Standard (FIPS) that specifies a cryptographic algorithm that is used within the U.S. government to protect information at federal agencies that are not a part of the national defense infrastructure. (Agencies that are considered a part of national defense use other, more secure methods of encryption, which are provided by the National Security Agency.) The requirements for AES stipulate that the algorithm should be unclassified, publicly disclosed, and available royalty-free worldwide. AES has been developed to replace both DES and 3DES. While 3DES remains an approved algorithm for some uses, its expected useful life is limited. Historically, cryptographic standards approved by FIPS have been adopted on a voluntary basis by organizations outside government entities. The AES selection process involved cooperation between the U.S. government, private industry, and academia from around the world. AES was approved by the Secretary of Commerce as the official federal governmental standard on May 26, 2002.

The AES implements a block cipher called the Rijndael Block Cipher with a variable block length and a key length of 128, 192, or 256 bits. Experts estimate that the special computer used by the Electronic Frontier Foundation to crack DES within a couple of days would require approximately 4,698,864 quintillion years (4,698,864,000,000,000,000,000,000) to crack AES. To learn more about the AES, see the Technical Details box entitled "Advanced Encryption Standard (AES)."

TECHNICAL DETAILS BOX

Advanced Encryption Standard (AES)

Of the many ciphers that were submitted (from across the world) for consideration in the AES selection process, five finalists were chosen: MARS, RC6, Rijndael, Serpent, and Twofish. On October 2, 2000, NIST announced the selection of Rijndael as the cipher to be used as the basis for the AES, and this block cipher was approved by the Secretary of Commerce as the official federal governmental standard as of May 26, 2002.

The AES version of Rijndael can use a multiple round based system. Depending on the key size, the number of rounds varies between 9 and 13: for a 128-bit key, 9 rounds plus one end round are used; for a 192-bit key, 11 rounds plus one end round are used; and for a 256-bit key, 13 rounds plus one end round are used. Once Rijndael was adopted as the AES, the ability to use variable sized blocks was standardized to a single 128-bit block for simplicity.

There are four steps within each Rijndael round, and these are described in "The Advanced Encryption Standard (Rijndael)" by John Savard as follows:

1. The Byte Sub step. Each byte of the block is replaced by its substitute in an S-box (substitution box). [*Author's Note: The S-box consists of a table of computed values, the calculation of which is beyond the scope of this text.*]

2. The Shift Row step. Considering the block to be made up of bytes 1 to 16, these bytes are arranged in a rectangle, and shifted as follows:

```
from                to
1   5   9  13       1   5   9  13
2   6  10  14       6  10  14   2
3   7  11  15      11  15   3   7
4   8  12  16      16   4   8  12
```

Other shift tables are used for larger blocks.

3. The Mix Column step. Matrix multiplication is performed: each column is multiplied by the matrix:

```
2  3  1  1
1  2  3  1
1  1  2  3
3  1  1  2
```

4. The Add Round Key step. This simply XORs in the subkey for the current round. The extra final round omits the Mix Column step, but is otherwise the same as a regular round."[3]

Asymmetric Encryption.   Another category of encryption techniques is asymmetric encryption. Whereas the symmetric encryption systems are based on using a single key to both encrypt and decrypt a message, **asymmetric encryption** uses two different but related keys, and either key can be used to encrypt or decrypt the message. If, however, Key A is used to encrypt the message, only Key B can decrypt it, and if Key B is used to encrypt a message, only Key A can decrypt it. Asymmetric encryption can be used to provide elegant solutions to problems of secrecy and verification. This technique has its highest value when one key is used as a private key, which means that it is kept secret (much like the key of symmetric encryption), known only to the owner of the key pair, and the other key serves as a public key, which means that it is stored in a public location where anyone can use it. This is why the more common name for asymmetric encryption is **public key encryption**.

Consider the following example, illustrated in Figure 8-4. Alex at XYZ Corporation wants to send an encrypted message to Rachel at ABC Corporation. Alex goes to a public key registry and obtains Rachel's public key. Remember that the foundation of asymmetric encryption is that the same key cannot be used to both encrypt and decrypt the same message. So when Rachel's public key is used to encrypt the message, only Rachel's private key can be used to decrypt the message and that private key is held by Rachel alone. Similarly, if Rachel wants to respond to Alex's message, she goes to the registry where Alex's public key is held, and uses it to encrypt her message, which of course can only be read by Alex's private key. This approach, which keeps private keys secret and encourages the sharing of public keys in reliable directories, is an elegant solution to the key management problems found in symmetric key applications.

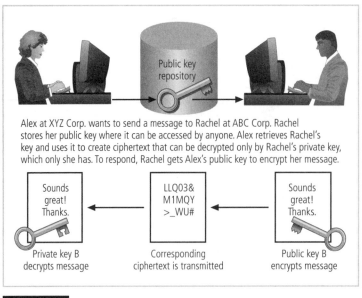

Alex at XYZ Corp. wants to send a message to Rachel at ABC Corp. Rachel stores her public key where it can be accessed by anyone. Alex retrieves Rachel's key and uses it to create ciphertext that can be decrypted only by Rachel's private key, which only she has. To respond, Rachel gets Alex's public key to encrypt her message.

FIGURE 8-4 Example of Asymmetric Encryption

Asymmetric algorithms are based on one-way functions. A one-way function is simple to compute in one direction, but complex to compute in the opposite. This is the foundation of public-key encryption. Public-key encryption is based on a hash value, which, as you learned earlier in this chapter, is calculated from an input number using a hashing algorithm. This hash value is essentially a summary of the original input values. It is virtually impossible to derive the original values without knowing how the values were used to create the hash value. For example, if you multiply 45 by 235 you get 10,575. This is simple enough. But if you are simply given the number 10,575, can you determine which two numbers were multiplied to determine this number? Now assume that each multiplier is 200 digits long and prime. The resulting multiplicative product would be up to 400 digits long. Imagine the time you'd need to factor that out. There is a shortcut, however. In mathematics, it is known as a trapdoor (which is different from the software trapdoor). A mathematical **trapdoor** is a "secret mechanism that enables you to easily accomplish the reverse function in a one-way function."[4] With a trapdoor, you can use a key to encrypt or decrypt the ciphertext, but not both, thus requiring two keys. The public key becomes be the true key, and the private key is to be derived from the public key using the trapdoor.

One of the most popular public key cryptosystems is RSA, whose name is derived from Rivest-Shamir-Adleman, the algorithm's developers. The **RSA algorithm** was the first public key encryption algorithm developed (in 1977) and published for commercial use. It is very popular and has been embedded in both Microsoft's and Netscape's Web browsers to enable them to provide security for e-commerce applications. The patented RSA algorithm has in fact become the de facto standard for public use encryption applications. To see how this algorithm works, see the Technical Details box entitled "RSA Algorithm."

TECHNICAL DETAILS BOX

RSA Algorithm

If you understand modulo mathematics, you can appreciate the complexities of the RSA algorithm. The security of the RSA algorithm is based on the computational difficulty of factoring large composite numbers and computing the *e^{th} roots modulo*, a composite number for a specified odd integer *e*. Encryption in RSA is accomplished by raising the message *M* to a nonnegative integer power *e*. The product is then divided by the nonnegative modulus *n* (n should have a bit length of at least 1024 bits), and the remainder is the ciphertext *C*. This process results in one-way operation (shown below) when n is a very large number.

$$C = Me / mod\ n$$

In the decryption process, the ciphertext C is raised to the power d, a nonnegative integer, as follows:

$$d = e^{-1} mod\ ((p-1)(q-1))$$

C is then reduced by modulo n. In order for the recipient to calculate the decryption key, the p and q factors must be known. The modulus n, which is a composite number, is determined by multiplying two large nonnegative prime numbers, p and q:

$$n = p \infty q$$

In RSA's asymmetric algorithm, which is the basis of most modern Public Key Infrastructure (PKI) systems (a topic covered later in this chapter), the public and private keys are generated using the following procedure, which is from the RSA Corporation:

- "Choose two large prime numbers, p and q, of equal length, and compute p x q = n, which is the public modulus.
- Choose a random public key, e, so that e and (p-1)(q-1) are relatively prime.
- Compute e x d = 1 mod (p − 1)(q − 1), where d is the private key.
- Thus d = e-1mod[(p − 1)(q − 1)]."

where "(d, n) is the private key; (e, n) is the public key. P is encrypted to generate ciphertext C as $C = P^e$ mod n, and is decrypted to recover the plaintext, P as $P = C^d$ mod n."[5]

Essentially, the RSA algorithm can be divided into three steps:

1. *Key generation:* Prime factors p and q are statistically selected by a technique known as probabilistic primality testing and then multiplied together to form n. The encryption exponent e is selected, and the decryption exponent d is calculated.
2. *Encryption:* M is raised to the power of e, reduced by modulo n, and remainder C is the ciphertext.
3. *Decryption:* C is raised to the power of d and reduced by modulo n.

The sender publishes the public key, which consists of modulus n and exponent e. The remaining variables d, p, and q are kept secret.

A message can then be encrypted by:	$C = M^e$(recipient) mod n(recipient)
Digitally signed by:	$C' = M'^d$(sender) mod n(sender)
Verified by:	$M' = C'^e$(sender) mod n(sender)
Decrypted by:	$M = C^d$(recipient) mod n(recipient)

Example Problems

Because this Technical Details box presents complex information, the following sections contain practice examples to help you better understand the machinations of the various algorithms.

RSA Algorithm Example:[6] Work through the following steps to better understand how the RSA algorithm functions:

1. Choose randomly two large prime numbers: P, Q (usually P, Q > 10^100) → This means 10 to the power 100.
2. Compute:
   $N = P \times Q$
   $Z = (P - 1)(Q - 1)$
3. Choose a number relatively prime with Z and call it D.
   D < N; relatively prime means that D and Z have no common factors, except 1.
4. Find number E, such that → E × D = 1 mod Z.
5. The public key is: (N, E); the private Key is (N, D).
6. Create Cipher (Encrypted Text):
   C = | TEXT |E (MOD N)
   C → Encrypted text → this is the text that's transmitted
   | TEXT | → Plaintext to be encrypted (its numerical correspondent)
7. Decrypt the message:
   D = Plaintext = CD (MOD N), C = Ciphertext from part 6.

Note that it is almost impossible to obtain the private key, knowing the public key, and it's almost impossible to factor N into P and Q.

RSA Numerical Example:[13] Work through the following steps to better understand RSA Numericals:

1. Choose P = 3, Q = 11 (two prime numbers). Note that small numbers have been chosen for the example, so that you can easily work with them. In real life encryption, they are larger than 10^100.
2. $N = P \infty Q = 3 \infty 11 = 33; Z = (P-1)(Q-1) = 2 \infty 10 = 20$
3. Choose a number for D that is relatively prime with Z, for example, D = 7 → (20 and 7 have no common divisors, except 1).
4. E = ? such as E ∞ D = 1 MOD Z (1 MOD Z means that the remainder of E/D division is 1).
   $E \infty D / Z \rightarrow E \infty 7 / 20 \rightarrow E=3$
   Check E ∞ D / Z → 3 ∞ 7 / 20 → 21/20 → Remainder = 1
5. So, the public key is (N,E) = (33,3) → This key will be used to encrypt the message. The private key is (N,D) = (33,7) → This key will be used to decrypt the message.

English Alphabet and Corresponding Numbers for Each Letter:[7] In real life applications, the ASCII code is used to represent each of the characters of a message. For this example, the position of the letter in the alphabet is used instead to simplify the calculations: A = 01, B = 02, etc... Z = 26.

Encrypt The Word "Technology" as illustrated in Table 8-5:[8] Now you can use the corresponding numerical and the previous calculations to calculate values for the public key (N,E) = (33,3) and the private key (N,D) = (33,7).

Table 8-5 Encryption

Plaintext	Text value	(Text)^E	(Text)^E MOD N = Ciphertext
T	20	8000	8000 MOD 33 = 14
E	05	125	125 MOD 33 = 26
C	03	27	27 MOD 33 = 27
H	08	512	512 MOD 33 = 17
N	14	2744	2744 MOD 33 = 05
O	15	3375	3375 MOD 33 = 09
L	12	1728	1728 MOD 33 = 12
O	15	3375	3375 MOD 33 = 09
G	07	343	343 MOD 33 = 13
Y	25	15625	15625 MOD 33 = 16

So, the cipher (encrypted message) is: 14262717050912091316. This is what is transmitted over unreliable lines. Note that there are two digits per letter. To decrypt the transmitted message we apply the private key (^D) and re-MOD the product, the result of which is the numerical equivalent of the original plaintext.

Table 8-6 Encryption

Ciphertext	(Cipher)^D	(Cipher)^D MOD N = |Text|	Plaintext
14	105413504	105413504 MOD 33 = 20	T
26	8031810176	8031810176 MOD 33 = 05	E
27	10460353203	10460353203 MOD 33 = 03	C
17	410338673	410338673 MOD 33 = 08	H
05	78125	78125 MOD 33 = 14	N
09	4782969	4782969 MOD 33 = 15	O
12	35831808	35831808 MOD 33 = 12	L
09	4782969	4782969 MOD 33 = 15	O
13	62748517	62748517 MOD 33 = 07	G
16	268435456	268435456 MOD 33 = 25	Y

As you can see in Table 8-6, although very small P and Q numbers were used, the numbers required for decrypting the message are relatively large. Now you have a good idea of what kind of numbers are needed when P and Q are large (that is, in the 10^{100} range).

If P and Q are not big enough for the cipher to be secure, P and Q must be increased. The strength of this encryption algorithm relies on how difficult it is to factor P and Q from N if N is known. If N is not known, the algorithm is even harder to break, of course.

The problem with asymmetric encryption, as is shown by the example in Figure 8-4, is that holding a single conversation between two parties requires four keys. Moreover, if four organizations want to exchange communications frequently, each party must manage its private key and four public keys. In such scenarios, determining which public key is needed to encrypt a particular message can become a rather confusing problem, and with more organizations in the loop, the problem expands. This is why asymmetric encryption is sometimes regarded by experts as an inefficient endeavor. Compared to symmetric encryption, asymmetric encryption is also not as efficient in terms of CPU computations. Consequently, hybrid systems, such as those described in the section of this chapter titled "Public Key Infrastructure (PKI)," are more commonly used than pure asymmetric system.

Encryption Key Size

When using ciphers, one of the decisions that has to be made is the size of the cryptovariable or key. This will prove to be very important, because the strength of many encryption applications and cryptosystems is measured by key size. But does the size of the encryption key really matter? And how exactly does key size affect the strength of an algorithm? Typically, the length of the key increases the number of random selections that will have to be guessed in order to break the code. Creating a larger universe of possibilities that need to be checked increases the time required to make guesses, and thus a longer key will directly influence the strength of the encryption.

It may surprise you to learn that when it comes to cryptosystems, the security of encrypted data is *not* dependent on keeping the encrypting algorithm secret; in fact, algorithms should be (and often are) published, so that research to uncover their weaknesses can be done. Instead the security of any cryptosystem depends on keeping some or all of the elements of the cryptovariable(s) or key(s) secret, and effective security is maintained by manipulating the size (bit length) of the keys and by following proper procedures and policies for key management.

For a simple example of how key size is related to encryption strength, suppose you have an algorithm that uses a three-bit key. You may recall from earlier in the chapter that keyspace is the amount of space from which the key can be drawn. Also, you may recall that in binary notation, three bits can be used to represent values from 000 to 111, which correspond to the numbers 0 to 7 in decimal, and thus a keyspace of eight keys. This means that with an algorithm that uses a three-bit key you have eight possible keys to choose from (the numbers 0 to 7 in binary are 000, 001, 010, 011, 100, 101, 110, 111). If you know how many keys you have to choose from, you can program a computer simply to try all the keys and see if it can crack the encrypted message.

The preceding statement presumes a few things: 1) you know the algorithm, 2) you have the encrypted message, and 3) you have time on your hands. It is easy to satisfy the first criterion. The encryption tools that use the Data Encryption Standard (DES) can be purchased over the counter. Many of these tools are based on encryption algorithms that are standards, as is DES itself, therefore it is relatively easy to get a cryptosystem based on DES that would enable you to decrypt an encrypted message if you possess the key. The second criterion requires the interception of an encrypted message, which is illegal, but not impossible. As for the third criterion, the task required is a brute force attack, in which a computer randomly (or sequentially) selects possible keys of the known size and applies them to the encrypted text, or a piece of the encrypted text. If the result is plaintext—bingo! But as indicated earlier in this chapter, it can take quite a long time to exert brute force on the more advanced cryptosystems. In fact, the strength of an algorithm is determined by how long it takes to guess the key. Luckily, however, once set to a task, computers do not require much adult supervision, so you probably won't have to quit your day job.

But when it comes to keys, how big is big? From the example at the beginning of this section, you learned that a three-bit system has eight keys to guess. An eight-bit system has 256 keys to guess. Note, however, that if you use a 32-bit key, puny by modern standards, you have to guess almost 16.8 million keys. Even so, a modern PC, such as the one described in Table 8-7, could do this in mere seconds. But, as Table 8-7 shows, the amount of time needed to crack a cipher by guessing its key grows very quickly—that is, exponentially with each additional bit.

One thing to keep in mind here is that even though the estimated time to crack grows so rapidly with respect to the number of bits in the encryption key and the odds of cracking seem at first glance to be insurmountable, Table 8-7 doesn't account for the fact that computing power has increased (and continues to increase). Therefore, these days even the once-standard 56-bit encryption can't stand up to brute force attacks by personal computers, especially if multiple computers are used together to crack these keys. Each additional computer reduces the amount of time needed. Two computers can divide the possibilities and crack the key in approximately half the time and so on. Thus, two hundred and eighty five computers can crack a 56-bit key in one year, ten times as many would do it in a little over a month.

TABLE 8-7 Encryption Key Power

Number of Bits in Key	Odds of Cracking: 1 in	Estimated Time to Crack*
8	256	.000032 seconds
16	65,536	.008192 seconds
24	16,777,216	2.097 seconds
32	4,294,967,296	8 minutes 56.87 seconds
56	72,057,594,037,927,900	285 years 32 weeks 1 day
64	18,446,744,073,709,600,000	8,090,677,225 years
128	3.40282E+38	5,257,322,061,209,440,000,000 years
256	1.15792E+77	2,753,114,795,116,330,000,000,000,000,000,000,000,000,000,000 years
512	1.3408E+154	608,756,305,260,875,000,000,000,000,000,000,000,000,000,000,000,000,000,000,000,000,000,000,000,000,000,000,000,000,000,000,000 years

[NOTE] *Estimated Time to Crack is based on a general-purpose personal computer performing eight million guesses per second.

Conclusions Regarding the Principles of Cryptography

Why do encryption systems such as DES use different elements or operations? Consider the following: if you use the same operation (XOR, substitution, or transposition) multiple times in a row, you gain no additional benefit. For example, if you use a substitution cipher, and substitute B for A, and then R for B, and then Q for R, it is essentially the same as substituting Q for A. So no benefit is gained from the additional operations. Similarly, if you transpose a character in position 1, then position 4, then position 3, what's the difference between doing this and moving it from position 1 to position 3 in the first place? Since there is no net advantage for sequential operations, each subsequent operation must be different. Therefore, if you substitute, then transpose, then XOR, then substitute again, you will have dramatically scrambled, substituted, and recoded the original plaintext with ciphertext that is untraceable without the key.

Cryptography Tools

The capabilities to conceal the contents of sensitive messages and to verify the contents of messages and identities of their senders can be useful in all areas of business. To be actually useful, these cryptographic capabilities must be embodied in tools that allow IT and information security practitioners to apply the elements of cryptography in the everyday world of computing. A number of the more widely used tools that bring the functions of cryptography to the world of information systems are discussed in this section of the chapter.

Public Key Infrastructure (PKI)

Public Key Infrastructure (PKI) is an integrated system of software, encryption methodologies, protocols, legal agreements, and third-party services that enables users to communicate securely. PKI systems are based on public key cryptosystems and include digital certificates and certificate authorities (CAs).

Digital certificates are public key container files that allow computer programs to validate the key and identify to whom it belongs. (Please note that more information about digital certificates is provided in later sections of this chapter.) PKI and the digital certificate registries they contain enable the protection of information assets by making verifiable digital certificates readily available to business applications. This, in turn, allows the applications to implement several of the key characteristics of information security and to integrate these characteristics into business processes across an organization. These processes include the following:

- Authentication: Individuals, organizations, and Web servers can validate the identity of each of the parties in an Internet transaction.
- Integrity: Content signed by the certificate is known to be unaltered while being moved from host to host or server to client.
- Privacy: Information is protected from being intercepted during transmission.

- Authorization: The validated identity of users and programs can be used to enable authorization rules that remain in place for the duration of a transaction; this reduces some of the overhead required and allows for more control of access privileges for specific transactions.
- Nonrepudiation: Customers or partners can be held accountable for transactions, such as online purchases, which they cannot later deny.

A typical PKI solution protects the transmission and reception of secure information by integrating the following components:

- A **certificate authority (CA)**, which issues, manages, authenticates, signs, and revokes users' digital certificates, which typically contain the user's name, public key, and other identifying information.
- A **registration authority (RA)**, which operates under the trusted collaboration of the certificate authority and can be delegated day-to-day certification functions, such as verifying registration information about new registrants, generating end-user keys, revoking certificates, and validating that users possess a valid certificate.
- Certificate directories, which are central locations for certificate storage that provide a single access point for administration and distribution.
- Management protocols, which organize and manage the communications between CAs, RAs, and end users. This includes the functions and procedures for setting up new users, issuing keys, recovering keys, updating keys, revoking keys, and enabling the transfer of certificates and status information among the parties involved in the PKI's area of authority.
- Policies and procedures that assist an organization in the application and management of certificates, the formalization of legal liabilities and limitations, and actual business practice use.

Common implementations of PKI include: systems to issue digital certificates to users and servers; directory enrollment; key issuing systems; tools for managing the key issuance; and verification and return of certificates. These systems enable organizations to apply an enterprise-wide solution that provides users within the PKI's area of authority the means to implement authenticated and secure communications and transactions.

The CA performs many housekeeping details regarding the use of keys and certificates within the zone of authority for which it is established. Each user authenticates him or herself with the CA, and the CA can issue new or replacement keys, track keys issued, provide a directory of public key value for all known users, and perform other management activities. When a private key is compromised or when the user loses the privilege of using keys in the area of authority, the CA can revoke the keys used by that user. The CA will periodically distribute a **certificate revocation list (CRL)** to all users that identifies all revoked certificates. When important events occur, specific applications can make a real-time request to the CA to verify any user against the current CRL.

The issuance of certificates (and the keys inside of them) by the CA provides the applications that users employ to perform secure e-business transactions with the ability to take both encryption and nonrepudiation actions. Some applications allow users to generate their own certificates (and the keys inside of them), but a key pair generated by the end user can only provide nonrepudiation and cannot be used for reliable encryption. A central system operated by a CA or RA can generate cryptographically strong keys that will be considered by all users to be independently trustworthy and can provide services for users such as private key backup, key recovery, and key revocation.

The strength of a cryptosystem relies on both the raw strength of its key's complexity and overall quality of its key management security processes. PKI solutions can provide an organization with several mechanisms for limiting access and possible exposure of the private keys. These mechanisms include password protection, smart cards, hardware tokens, and other hardware-based key storage devices that are memory-capable (like flash memory or PC memory cards). PKI users should select the key security mechanisms that provide a level of key protection appropriate to their needs. Managing the security and integrity of the private keys used for nonrepudiation or the encryption of data files is a critical activity for all of the users of encryption and nonrepudiation services within the area of trust managed by the PKI application.[9]

Digital Signatures

Digital signatures were created in response to the rising need to verify information transferred using electronic systems. Currently, asymmetric encryption processes are used to create digital signatures. When an asymmetric cryptographic process uses the sender's private key to encrypt a message, the sender's public key must be used to decrypt the message—when the decryption happens successfully, it provides verification that the message was sent by the sender and cannot be refuted. This process is known as **nonrepudiation** and is the principle of cryptography that gives credence to the authentication mechanism collectively known as a digital signature. **Digital signatures** are, therefore, encrypted messages that can be mathematically proven to be authentic.

The management of digital signatures has been built into most Web browsers. As an example, the Internet Explorer digital signature management screen is shown in Figure 8-5. In general, digital signatures should be created using processes and products that are based on the Digital Signature Standard (DSS). When processes and products are certified as being compliant with DSS, they have been approved and endorsed by U.S. federal and state governments, as well as many foreign governments, as a means of authenticating the author of an electronic document. NIST has approved a number of algorithms to be used to generate and verify digital signatures. These algorithms can be used in conjunction with the sender's public and private keys, the receiver's public key, and the Secure Hash Standard (described later in this chapter) to quickly create messages that are both encrypted and cannot be repudiated. The process used to accomplish this first creates a message digest using the hash algorithm, which is then input into the digital signature algorithm along with a random number to be used for generating the digital signature. The digital signature function also depends upon the sender's private key and other information provided by the CA. The resulting encrypted message contains the digital signature and will then be verified by the recipient through the use of the sender's public key.

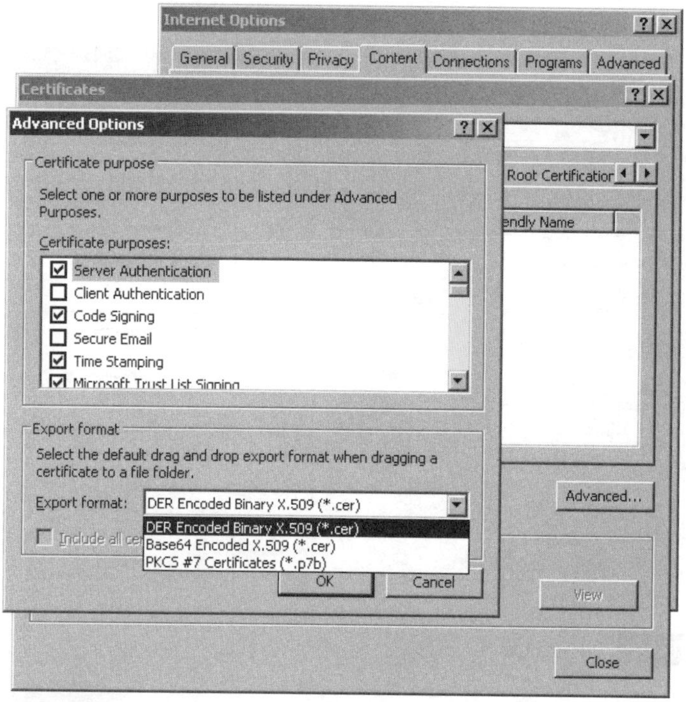

FIGURE 8-5 Managing Digital Signatures

Digital Certificates

As noted earlier in this chapter, a digital certificate is an electronic document or container file that contains a key value and identifying information about the entity that controls the key. The certificate is often issued by a third party that certifies the authenticity of the information it contains. A digital signature is attached to the certificate's container file to certify that this file is from the entity that it claims to be from and has not been modified from its original format. As was also noted earlier, a certificate authority is a software agent that manages the issuance of certificates and serves as the electronic notary public by verifying the certificates' worth and integrity. This process of verification can be seen by users when they download and update software on the Internet. The pop-up window in Figure 8-6 shows, for example, that the files downloaded did in fact come from the purported agency, Amazon.com, and thus can be trusted.

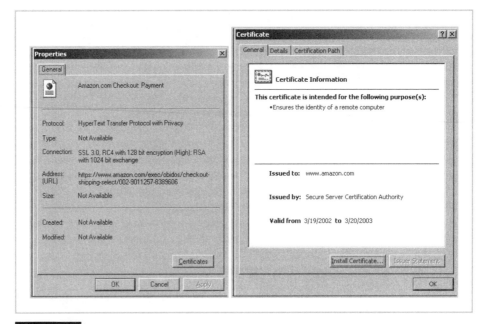

FIGURE 8-6 Digital Certificates

Digital certificates are electronic documents that can be part of a process of identification associated with the presentation of a public key. Unlike digital signatures, which help authenticate the origin of a message, digital certificates authenticate the cryptographic key that is embedded in the certificate. When used properly these certificates enable diligent users to verify the authenticity of any organization's certificates. This is much like what happens when the Federal Deposit Insurance Corporation issues its "FDIC" logo to banks to help assure bank customers that their bank is authentic. Different client-server applications use different types of digital certificates to accomplish their assigned functions:

- The CA application suite issues and uses certificates that identify and establish a trust relationship with a CA to determine what additional certificates can be authenticated.
- Mail applications use Secure/Multipurpose Internet Mail Extension (S/MIME) certificates for signing and encrypting e-mail as well as for signing forms.
- Development applications use object-signing certificates to identify signers of object-oriented code and scripts.
- Web servers and Web application servers use Secure Socket Layer (SSL) certificates to authenticate servers via the SSL protocol (which is described in an upcoming section) in order to establish an encrypted SSL session.
- Web clients use client SSL certificates to authenticate users, sign forms, and participate in single sign-on solutions via SSL.

Two popular certificate types in use today are those created using Pretty Good Privacy (PGP) and those created using applications that conform to International Telecommunication Union's (ITU-T) X.509 version 3. You should know that X.509 v3, whose structure is outlined in Table 8-8, is an ITU-T recommendation that essentially defines a directory service that maintains a database (also known as a repository) of information about a group of users holding X.509 v3 certificates. An X.509 v3 certificate binds a **distinguished name (DN)**, which uniquely identifies a certificate entity, to a user's public key. The certificate is signed and placed in the directory by the CA for retrieval and verification by the user's associated public key. X.509 v3 does not specify an encryption algorithm; however, RSA with its hashed digital signature is recommended.

TABLE 8-8   X.509 v3 Certificate Structure[10]

Version
Certificate Serial Number
Algorithm ID ■   Algorithm ID ■   Parameters
Issuer Name
Validity ■   Not Before ■   Not After
Subject Name
Subject Public Key Info ■   Public Key Algorithm ■   Parameters ■   Subject Public Key
Issuer Unique Identifier (Optional)
Subject Unique Identifier (Optional)
Extensions (Optional) `   ■   Type ■   Criticality ■   Value
Certificate Signature Algorithm
Certificate Signature

Hybrid Cryptography Systems

Except in the case of digital certificates, pure asymmetric key encryption is not widely used. Asymmetric key encryption is more often used in conjunction with symmetric key encryption—thus, as part of a hybrid encryption system. The most common hybrid system is based on the **Diffie-Hellman Key Exchange method**, which is a method for exchanging private keys using public key encryption. With Diffie-Hellman, asymmetric encryption is used to exchange **session keys**. These are limited-use symmetric keys for temporary communications; they allow two organizations to conduct quick, efficient, secure communications based on symmetric encryption. Diffie-Hellman provided the foundation for subsequent developments in public key encryption. Because symmetric encryption is more efficient than asymmetric for sending messages, and asymmetric encryption doesn't require out-of-band key exchange, asymmetric encryption can be used to transmit symmetric keys in a hybrid approach. Diffie-Hellman avoids the exposure of data to third parties that is sometimes associated with out-of-band key exchanges.

A hybrid encryption approach is illustrated in Figure 8-7, and it works as follows: Alex at XYZ Corp. wants to communicate with Rachel at ABC Corp., so Alex first creates a session key. Alex encrypts a message with this session key, and then gets Rachel's public key. Alex uses Rachel's public key to encrypt both the session key and the message, which is already encrypted. Alex transmits the entire package to Rachel, who uses her private key to decrypt the package containing the session key and the encrypted message, and then uses the session key to decrypt the message. Rachel can then continue to use only this session key for electronic communications until the session key expires. The asymmetric session key is used in the much more efficient asymmetric encryption and decryption processes. After the session key expires (usually in just a few minutes) a new session key will be chosen and shared using the same process.

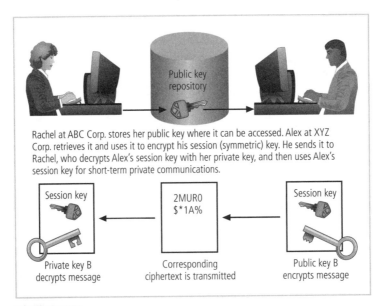

Rachel at ABC Corp. stores her public key where it can be accessed. Alex at XYZ Corp. retrieves it and uses it to encrypt his session (symmetric) key. He sends it to Rachel, who decrypts Alex's session key with her private key, and then uses Alex's session key for short-term private communications.

FIGURE 8-7 Example of Hybrid Encryption

Steganography

Steganography is a process of hiding information and has been in use for a long time. In fact the word "steganography" is derived from the Greek words *steganos* meaning "covered" and *graphein* meaning "to write." The Greek historian Herodotus reported on one of the first steganographers when he described a fellow Greek sending a message to warn of an imminent invasion by writing it on the wood beneath a wax writing tablet. If the tablet were intercepted, it would appear blank.[11] While steganography is technically not a form of cryptography, it is related to cryptography in that it is also a way of transmitting information so that the information is not revealed while it's in transit. The most popular modern version of steganography involves hiding information within files that appear to contain digital pictures or other images.

To understand how modern steganography works in this specific case, you must first understand a little about how images are stored. Most computer graphics standards use a combination of three color values (red, blue, and green (RGB)) to represent a picture element, or pixel. Each of the three color values usually requires an 8-bit code for that color's intensity (e.g., 00000000 for no red and 11111111 for maximum red). Each color pixel of an image requires 24 bits to represent the color mix and intensity. Some image encoding standards use more or fewer bits per pixel, but for the purposes of this discussion, 24-bit color will suffice. When a picture is created (by a digital camera or a computer program), the number of horizontal and vertical pixels captured and recorded is known as the image's *resolution*. Thus, for example, if 1024 horizontal pixels are recorded and 768 vertical pixels are captured, the image has a 1024×768 resolution and would commonly be said to have 786,432 pixels or three-quarters of a *megapixel*. Thus, an image that is 1024×768 pixels contains 786,432 groups of 24 bits to represent the red, green, and blue data. The raw image size can be calculated as 1024×768×24, or 5.66 megabytes. There are plenty of bits in this picture data file in which to hide a secret message.

To the naked eye, there is no discernable difference between a pixel with a red intensity of 00101001 and another slightly different pixel with a red intensity level of 00101000. In other words, the two different values will result in pixels that do have a discernable difference. This inability to perceive difference on part of humans provides the steganographer with one bit per color (or three bits per pixel) to use for encoding data into an image file. If a steganographic process uses three bits per pixel for all 786,432 pixels, it will be able to store 236 kilobytes of hidden data within the uncompressed image.

Some steganographic tools can calculate the maximum size image that can be stored before being detectable. In addition to digital photos, messages can be hidden in any computer file that does not utilize all of its available bits. Some applications are capable of hiding messages in .bmp, .wav, .mp3, and .au files, as well as in unused storage space on CDs and DVDs. One program can take a text or document file and hide a message in the unused whitespace.

After the attacks of September 11, 2001, U.S. federal agencies were worried that terrorist organizations were "hiding maps and photographs of terrorist targets and posting instructions for terrorist activities on sports chat rooms, pornographic bulletin boards, and other websites" through the use of steganographic methods. No documented proof of this activity was ever publicized.[12]

Protocols for Secure Communications

Many of the applications currently used on the Internet and within organizations to keep confidential information private are not true cryptosystems in and of themselves. Instead they are applications to which cryptography-based protocols have been added in order to provide a sufficient level of security. The same could be said for Internet protocols. In fact, some experts have gone further—noting that the Internet and its corresponding protocols were not designed with security in mind at all and that security was added later, as an afterthought. Regardless of whether or not this is true, it can be said that the lack of threats in the environment during the Internet's construction and infancy allowed it to grow rapidly but also enabled it to grow without the advanced security features that are required in the complex threat environment found on the Internet today. As the level of threats grew, so did the need for additional security measures. In other words, the growth of the Internet created the need for Internet security. The following sections overview some of the key protocols that add security to existing applications and protocols used in data communications over the Internet.

Securing Internet Communication with S-HTTP and SSL

S-HTTP (Secure Hypertext Transfer Protocol) and SSL (Secure Socket Layer) are two protocols designed to enable secure network communications across the Internet. S-HTTP and SSL ensure Internet security through different mechanisms and can be used independently or together.

Netscape developed the **Secure Socket Layer (SSL)** protocol to use public key encryption to secure a channel over the public Internet, thus enabling secure communications. Most popular browsers, including Internet Explorer, support the implementation of SSL. In addition to providing data encryption, integrity, and server authentication, SSL can, when properly configured, provide client authentication.

The SSL protocol works as follows: after a client and a server establish a normal HTTP session and the client requests access to a portion of the Web site that requires secure communications, the server sends a message to the client indicating that a secure connection needs to be established. The client responds by sending its public key and security parameters. This handshaking phase is completed when the server finds a public key match and responds by sending a digital certificate to the client in order to authenticate itself. The client must then verify that the received certificate is valid and trustworthy. Now the SSL session is established. As long as the session remains active, any amount of data can be transmitted securely until either the client or server severs the secure connection.

SSL provides two layers of protocol within the TCP framework: SSL Record Protocol and Standard HTTP. The **SSL Record Protocol** is responsible for the fragmentation, compression, encryption, and attachment of an SSL header to the cleartext prior to transmission. Received encrypted messages are decrypted and reassembled for presentation to the higher levels of the protocol. The SSL Record Protocol provides basic security and communication services to the top levels of the SSL protocol stack. **Standard HTTP** provides the Internet communication services between client and host without consideration for encryption of the data that is communicated over the connection between client and server.

Secure-HTTP (S-HTTP) is an extended version of the Hypertext Transfer Protocol that provides for the encryption of individual messages between a client and server across the Internet. S-HTTP is the application of SSL over HTTP, which allows the encryption of all information passing between two computers through a protected and secure virtual connection. Unlike SSL, in which a secure channel is established for the duration of a session, S-HTTP is designed for sending only individual messages across the Internet and therefore a session for each individual exchange of data must be established before the communication can occur. To establish a session, the client and server must have compatible cryptosystems and agree on the configuration. The S-HTTP client then must send the server its public key so that the server can generate a session key. The session key from the server is then encrypted with the client's public key and returned to the client. The client decrypts the key using its private key, and the client and server now possess identical session keys, which they can use to encrypt the messages sent between them.

S-HTTP can provide for confidentiality, authentication, and data integrity through a variety of trust models and cryptographic algorithms. In addition, this protocol is designed for easy integration with existing HTTP applications and for implementation in conjunction with HTTP.

Securing E-mail with S/MIME, PEM, and PGP

In an attempt to inject some degree of security into e-mail, a notoriously insecure communication medium, a number of cryptosystems have been adapted to work with today's dominant e-mail protocols. Some of the more popular adaptations included Secure Multipurpose Internet Mail Extensions, Privacy Enhanced Mail (PEM), and Pretty Good Privacy (PGP).

Secure Multipurpose Internet Mail Extensions (S/MIME) builds on the encoding format of the Multipurpose Internet Mail Extensions (MIME) protocol by adding encryption and authentication through the use of digital signatures based on public key cryptosystems. **Privacy Enhanced Mail (PEM)** was proposed by the Internet Engineering Task Force (IETF) as a standard to function with the public key cryptosystems. PEM uses 3DES symmetric key encryption and RSA for key exchanges and digital signatures. **Pretty Good Privacy (PGP)** was developed by Phil Zimmermann and uses the IDEA Cipher for message encoding. PGP also uses RSA for symmetric key exchange and digital signatures. PGP is discussed in more detail in a later section in this chapter.

The first Internet e-mail standard that gained common use was SMTP/RFC 822, also referred to as SMTP, but this standard had problems including a number of security-related shortcomings and limitations, such as the inability to transmit executable files or binary objects, and the inability to handle character sets other than 7-bit ASCII. These limitations made SMTP unwieldy for organizations that wanted to have robust e-mail that supported international character sets and could be used more securely. MIME, the Multipurpose Internet Mail Extension, whose message header fields are shown below in Table 8-9, was developed to address the problems associated with SMTP. From Table 8-9, you can see that MIME's message header fields were designed to identify and describe better the e-mail message and provide for flexibility in handling a variety of e-mail content. In addition to the message header fields, the MIME specification included predefined content types and conversion transfer encodings, such as 7-bit, 8-bit, binary, and radix-64, which it used to deliver e-mail messages reliably across a wide range of systems.

TABLE 8-9   MIME Message Header Fields[13]

Header Field	Function
MIME-version	States conformity to RFCs 2045 and 2046
Content-ID	Identifies MIME entities
Content-type	Describes data in body of message
Content-description	Describes body object
Content-transfer-encoding	Identifies type of conversion used in message body

S/MIME, which was created as an extension to improve on and interoperate with MIME, represents the second generation of enhancements to the SMTP standard. MIME and S/MIME share very similar message header fields, except for those added to support new functionality. Like MIME, S/MIME uses a canonical form format, which allows it to standardize message content type between systems, but it has the additional ability to sign, encrypt, and decrypt messages. Table 8-10 summarizes the functions and algorithms used by S/MIME. It should be mentioned that PGP is functionally similar to S/MIME, incorporates some of the same algorithms, and can, to some degree, interoperate with S/MIME.

TABLE 8-10 **S/MIME Functions and Algorithms**

Function	Algorithm
Hash code for digital signatures	Secure Hash Algorithm 1(SHA-1)
Digital signatures	DSS
Encryption session keys	ElGamal (variant of Diffie-Hellman)
Digital signatures and session keys	RSA
Message encryption	3DES, RC2

Securing Web Transactions with SET, SSL, and S-HTTP

Just as PGP, PEM, and S/MIME work to secure e-mail operations, a number of related protocols work to secure Web browsers, especially at electronic commerce sites. Among these are Secure Electronic Transactions (SET), Secure Socket Layer (SSL), Secure Hypertext Transfer Protocol (S-HTTP), Secure Shell (SSH-2), and IP Security (IPSec). SSL and S-HTTP were discussed earlier in this chapter.

Secure Electronic Transactions (**SET**) was developed by MasterCard and VISA in 1997 to provide protection from electronic payment fraud. SET uses DES to encrypt credit card information transfers and RSA for key exchange. SET provides the security for both Internet-based credit card transactions and credit card swipe systems in retail stores. As mentioned, Secure Socket Layer was developed by Netscape in 1994, also to provide security in online electronic commerce transactions. SSL uses a number of algorithms, but mainly relies on RSA for key transfer and IDEA, DES, or 3DES for encrypted symmetric key-based data transfer. Figure 8-6, which was presented earlier, shows the kind of certificate and SSL information that is displayed when you are checking out of an e-commerce site. If your Web connection does not automatically display such certificates, you can right-click in your browser's window and select *Properties* to view the connection encryption and certificate properties.

Securing TCP/IP with IPSec and PGP

Internet Protocol Security (**IPSec**) is an open source protocol to secure communications across any IP-based network such as LANs, WANs, and the Internet. The protocol is designed to protect data integrity, user confidentiality, and authenticity at the IP packet level. IPSec is the cryptographic authentication and encryption product of the IETF's IP Protocol Security Working Group. It is often described as being the security system from

IP version 6 (the future version of the TCP/IP protocol), retrofitted for use with IP version 4 (the current version). IP Security (IPSec) is defined in Request for Comments (RFC) 1825, 1826, and 1827 and is widely used to create Virtual Private Networks (VPNs), which were described in Chapter 6. IPSec itself is actually an open framework for security development within the TCP/IP family of protocol standards.

IPSec includes the IP Security Protocol itself, which defines the information to be added to an IP packet as well as how to encrypt packet data; and the Internet Key Exchange, which uses an asymmetric-based key exchange and negotiates the security associations. IPSec works in two modes of operation: transport and tunnel. In **transport mode** only the IP data is encrypted, not the IP headers. This allows intermediate nodes to read the source and destination addresses. In **tunnel mode** the entire IP packet is encrypted and is then placed as the content portion of another IP packet. This requires other systems at the beginning and end of the tunnel to act as proxies and to send and receive the encrypted packets. These systems then transmit the decrypted packets to their true destinations.

IPSec combines several different cryptosystems in its operations:

- Diffie-Hellman key exchange for deriving key material between peers on a public network
- Public key cryptography for signing the Diffie-Hellman exchanges to guarantee the identity of the two parties
- Bulk encryption algorithms, such as DES, for encrypting the data
- Digital certificates signed by a certificate authority to act as digital ID cards[14]

Within IPSec, IP layer security is obtained by the use of an application header protocol or an encapsulating security payload protocol. The **application header (AH) protocol** provides system to system authentication and data integrity verification, but does not provide secrecy for the content of a network communication. The **encapsulating security payload (ESP) protocol** provides secrecy for the contents of network communications as well as system to system authentication and data integrity verification. When two networked systems form an association that involves encryption and authentication keys, algorithms, and key lifetimes, they can implement either the AH or the ESP protocol, but not both. If the security functions of both the AH and ESP are required, multiple security associations must be bundled to provide the correct sequence through which the IP traffic must be processed to deliver the desired security features.

The AH protocol is designed to provide data integrity and authentication of IP packets. Although confidentiality protection is not provided by AH, IP packets are protected from replay attacks and address spoofing as well as other types of cyberattacks against open networks. Figure 8-8 provides insight into the packet format of the IPSec authentication header protocol. As shown in this diagram, the Security Parameter Index (SPI) references the session key and algorithm used to protect the data being transported. Sequence numbers allow packets to arrive out of sequence and be re-sequenced. The integrity check value (ICV) of the authentication data serves as a checksum to verify that the packet itself is uncorrupted or unaltered. Whether used in IPv4 or IPv6, authentication secures the entire packet, excluding mutable fields in the new IP header. In tunnel mode, however, the entire inner IP packet is secured by the authentication header protocol.

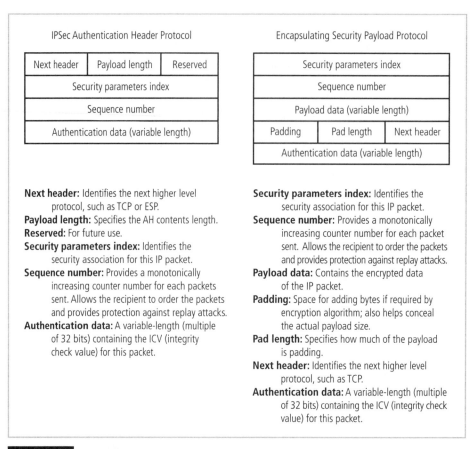

IPSec Authentication Header Protocol

Next header	Payload length	Reserved
Security parameters index		
Sequence number		
Authentication data (variable length)		

Encapsulating Security Payload Protocol

Security parameters index		
Sequence number		
Payload data (variable length)		
Padding	Pad length	Next header
Authentication data (variable length)		

Next header: Identifies the next higher level protocol, such as TCP or ESP.

Payload length: Specifies the AH contents length.

Reserved: For future use.

Security parameters index: Identifies the security association for this IP packet.

Sequence number: Provides a monotonically increasing counter number for each packets sent. Allows the recipient to order the packets and provides protection against replay attacks.

Authentication data: A variable-length (multiple of 32 bits) containing the ICV (integrity check value) for this packet.

Security parameters index: Identifies the security association for this IP packet.

Sequence number: Provides a monotonically increasing counter number for each packet sent. Allows the recipient to order the packets and provides protection against replay attacks.

Payload data: Contains the encrypted data of the IP packet.

Padding: Space for adding bytes if required by encryption algorithm; also helps conceal the actual payload size.

Pad length: Specifies how much of the payload is padding.

Next header: Identifies the next higher level protocol, such as TCP.

Authentication data: A variable-length (multiple of 32 bits) containing the ICV (integrity check value) for this packet.

FIGURE 8-8 IPSec Headers

The encapsulating security payload protocol provides confidentiality services for IP packets across insecure networks. ESP can also provide the authentication services of AH. Figure 8-8 shows information on the packet header for ESP. ESP in tunnel mode can be used to establish a virtual private network, assuring encryption and authentication between networks communicating across the Internet. In tunnel mode, the entire IP packet is encrypted with the attached ESP header. A new IP header is attached to the encrypted payload, providing the required routing information. In this manner the packet can be securely routed across the Internet.

An ESP header is inserted into the IP packet prior to the TCP header, with an ESP trailer placed after the IPv4 packet. Additionally, if authentication is desired, an ESP authentication data field is appended after the ESP trailer. The complete transport segment, in addition to the ESP trailer, is encrypted. For an IPv6 transmission, the ESP header is placed after the hop-by-hop and routing headers. Encryption under IPv6 covers the transport segment and the ESP trailer. Authentication in both IPv4 and IPv6 covers the ciphertext data plus the ESP header. IPSec ESP compliant systems must support the implementation of the DES algorithm utilizing the CBC (cipher block chaining) mode, which includes the following encryption algorithms: Triple DES, IDEA, RC5, CAST, and Blowfish.

Pretty Good Privacy (PGP) is a hybrid cryptosystem originally designed in 1991 by Phil Zimmermann. PGP combined some of the best available cryptographic algorithms to become the open source *de facto* standard for encryption and authentication of e-mail and file storage applications. Both freeware and low-cost commercial versions of PGP are available for a wide variety of platforms. Table 8-11 provides the functions for PGP.

TABLE 8-11   PGP Function[15]

Function	Algorithm	Application
Public key encryption	RSA/SHA-1 or DSS/SHA-1	Digital signatures
Conventional encryption	3DES, RSA, IDEA or CAST	Message encryption
File management	ZIP	Compression

PGP Suite of Security Solutions

The PGP security solution provides six services: authentication by digital signatures, message encryption, compression, e-mail compatibility, segmentation, and key management.

As you can see in Table 8-11, one of the algorithms used in the public key encryption in PGP is Secure Hashing Algorithm 1 (SHA-1), which is used to compute hash values for calculating a 160-bit hash code based on the plaintext message. The hash code is then encrypted with DSS or RSA and appended to the original message. The receiver uses the sender's public key to decrypt and recover the hash code. Using the same encryption algorithm, the receiver then generates a new hash code from the same message. If a comparison of the two hash codes is identical, then the message and the sender are authentic.

In addition to sending a digitally signed message, the sender may want the entire contents of the message protected from unauthorized view. 3DES, IDEA, or CAST, which are all standard algorithms, may be used to encrypt the message contents with a unique, randomly generated 128-bit session key. The session key is encrypted by RSA, using the recipient's public key, and then appended to the message. The receiver uses his private key with RSA to decrypt and recover the session key. The recovered session key can now be used to decrypt the message. Authentication and message encryption can be used together by first digitally signing the message with a private key, encrypting the message with a unique session key, and then encrypting the session key with the intended recipient's public key.

PGP uses the freeware ZIP algorithm to compress the message after it has been digitally signed but before it is encrypted. This saves space and generates a more secure encrypted document.

PGP also uses a process known as Radix-64, which encodes data conversion and assures that encrypted data can be transferred using e-mail systems by maintaining the required 8-bit blocks of ASCII text. The format maps three octets of binary data into four ASCII characters and appends a cyclic redundancy check (CRC) to detect transmission errors.

With many Internet facilities imposing restrictions on maximum message size, PGP can automatically subdivide messages into a manageable stream size. This segmentation is completed after all other encryption and conversion functions have been processed. At the recipient end, PGP reassembles the segment's message blocks prior to decompression and decryption.

While PGP does not impose a rigid structure for public key management, several approaches are suggested. PGP can assign a level of trust within the confines of PGP, but it does not manage the actual degree of trust the user should place in any specific key. Trust can be addressed and assured by using the public key ring structure. In a public key ring structure, each specific set of public key credentials is associated with a key legitimacy field, a signature trust field, and an owner trust field. These fields contain a trust-flag byte that identifies whether the credential is trusted in each of these three regards. In the event that the trust of a given credential has been broken, as when a key is compromised, the owner can issue a digitally signed key revocation certificate that updates the credential trust bytes when the credential is next verified.

Attacks on Cryptosystems

Historically, attempts to gain unauthorized access to secure communications have used brute force attacks in which the ciphertext is repeatedly searched for clues that can lead to the algorithm's structure. These attacks are known as ciphertext attacks, and involve a hacker searching for a common text structure, wording, or syntax in the encrypted message that can enable him or her to calculate the number of each type of letter used in the message. This process, known as frequency analysis, can be used along with published frequency of occurrence patterns of various languages and can allow an experienced attacker to crack almost any code quickly if the individual has a large enough sample of the encoded text. To protect against this, modern algorithms attempt to remove the repetitive and predictable sequences of characters from the ciphertext.

Occasionally, an attacker may obtain duplicate texts, one in ciphertext and one in plaintext, which enable the individual to reverse-engineer the encryption algorithm in a **known-plaintext attack** scheme. Alternatively, attackers may conduct a **selected-plaintext attack** by sending potential victims a specific text that they are sure the victims will forward on to others. When the victim does encrypt and forward the message, it can be used in the attack if the attacker can acquire the outgoing encrypted version. At the very least, reverse engineering can usually lead the attacker to discover the cryptosystem that is being employed.

Most publicly available encryption methods are generally released to the information and computer security communities for testing of the encryption algorithm's resistance to cracking. In addition, attackers are kept informed of which methods of attack have failed. Although the purpose of sharing this information is to develop a more secure algorithm, it has the danger of keeping attackers from wasting their time—that is, freeing them up to find new weaknesses in the cryptosystem or new, more challenging means of obtaining encryption keys.

In general, attacks on cryptosystems fall into four general categories: man-in-the-middle, correlation, dictionary, and timing. Although many of these attacks were discussed in Chapter 2, they are reiterated here in the context of cryptosystems and their impact on these systems.

Man-in-the-Middle Attack

A **man-in-the-middle attack**, as discussed in Chapter 2, is designed to intercept the transmission of a public key or even to insert a known key structure in place of the requested public key. Thus, attackers attempt to place themselves between the sender and receiver, and once they've intercepted the request for key exchanges, they send each participant a valid public key, which is known only to them. From the perspective of the victims of such attacks, their encrypted communication appears to be occurring normally, but in fact the attacker is receiving each encrypted message and decoding it (with the key given to the sending party), and then encrypting and sending it to the originally intended recipient. Establishment of public keys with digital signatures can prevent the traditional man-in-the-middle attack, as the attacker cannot duplicate the signatures.

Correlation Attacks

As the complexities of encryption methods have increased, so too have the tools and methods of cryptanalysts in their attempts to attack cryptosystems. **Correlation attacks** are a collection of brute-force methods that attempt to deduce statistical relationships between the structure of the unknown key and the ciphertext that is the output of the cryptosystem. Differential and linear cryptanalysis, both of which are advanced methods of breaking codes that are beyond the scope of this discussion, have been used to mount successful attacks on block cipher encryptions such as DES. If these advanced approaches can calculate the value of the public key, and if this can be achieved in a reasonable time, all messages written with that key can be decrypted. The only defense against this kind of attack is the selection of strong cryptosystems that have stood the test of time, thorough key management, and strict adherence to the best practices of cryptography in the frequency of changing keys.

Dictionary Attacks

In a **dictionary attack**, the attacker encrypts every word in a dictionary using the same cryptosystem as used by the target. The attacker does this in an attempt to locate a match between the target ciphertext and the list of encrypted words from the same cryptosystem. Dictionary attacks can be successful when the ciphertext consists of relatively few characters, as for example files which contain encrypted usernames and passwords. If an attacker acquires a system password file, the individual can run hundreds of thousands of potential passwords from the dictionary he or she has prepared against the stolen list. Most computer systems use a well-known one-way hash function to store passwords in such files, but this can almost always allow the attacker to find at least a few matches in any stolen password file. After a match is located, the attacker has essentially identified a potential valid password for the system under attack.

Timing Attacks

In a **timing attack**, the attacker eavesdrops during the victim's session and uses statistical analysis of the user's typing patterns and inter-keystroke timings to discern sensitive session information. While timing analysis may not directly result in the decryption of sensitive data, it can be used to gain information about the encryption key and perhaps the cryptosystem in use. It may also eliminate some algorithms as possible candidates, thus narrowing the attacker's search. In this narrower field of options, the attacker can increase the odds of eventual success. Once the attacker has successfully broken an encryption, he or she may launch a **replay attack**, which is an attempt to resubmit a recording of the deciphered authentication to gain entry into a secure source.

Defending From Attacks

Encryption is a very useful tool in protecting the confidentiality of information that is in storage and/or transmission. However, it is just that—another tool in the information security administrator's arsenal of weapons against threats to information security. Frequently, unenlightened individuals describe information security exclusively in terms of encryption (and possibly firewalls and antivirus software). But encryption is simply the process of hiding the true meaning of information. Over the millennia, mankind has developed dramatically more sophisticated means of hiding information from those who should not see it. No matter how sophisticated encryption and cryptosystems have become, however, they have retained the same flaw that the first systems contained thousands of years ago: If you discover the key, that is, the method used to perform the encryption, you can determine the message. Thus, key management is not so much the management of technology but rather the management of people.

Encryption can, however, protect information when it is most vulnerable—that is, when it is outside the organization's systems. Information in transit through public or leased networks is an example of information that is outside the organization's control. With loss of control can come loss of security. Encryption helps organizations secure information that must travel through public and leased networks by guarding the information against the efforts of those who sniff, spoof, and otherwise skulk around. As such, encryption is a vital piece of the security puzzle.

Chapter Summary

- Encryption is the process of converting a message into a form that is unreadable to unauthorized individuals.

- The science of encryption, known as cryptology, encompasses cryptography (making and using encryption codes) and cryptanalysis (breaking encryption codes).

- Cryptology both has a long history and continues to change and improve.

- Two basic processing methods are used to convert plaintext data into encrypted data—bit stream and block ciphering. The other major methods used for scrambling data include the substitution ciphers, transposition ciphers, XOR function, Vigenère cipher, and the Vernam cipher.

- The strength of many encryption applications and cryptosystems is described by key size. All other things held equal, the length of the key will directly influence the strength of the encryption.

- Hash functions are mathematical algorithms that generate a message summary or digest that can be used to confirm the identity of a specific message and to confirm that the message has not been altered.

- Most cryptographic algorithms can be grouped into two broad categories, symmetric and asymmetric. In practice, most popular cryptosystems use a hybrid combination of symmetric and asymmetric algorithms.

- Public Key Infrastructure is an integrated system of software, encryption methodologies, protocols, legal agreements, and third-party services that enables users to communicate securely. PKI includes digital certificates and certificate authorities.

- Digital Signatures are encrypted messages that are independently verified as authentic by a central facility and provide nonrepudiation. A digital certificate is an electronic document, similar to a digital signature, that is attached to a file to certify that the file is from the organization it claims to be from and has not been modified from its original format.

- Steganography is the process of hiding information, and while it is not properly a form of cryptography, it is related to cryptography in that both are ways of transmitting information without allowing it to be revealed in transit.

- S-HTTP (Secure Hypertext Transfer Protocol), Secure Electronic Transactions (SET), and SSL (Secure Socket Layer) are protocols designed to enable secure communications across the Internet. IPSec is the protocol used to secure communications across any IP-based network such as LANs, WANs, and the Internet. Secure Multipurpose Internet Mail Extensions (S/MIME), Privacy Enhanced Mail (PEM), and Pretty Good Privacy (PGP) are protocols that are used to secure electronic mail. PGP is a hybrid cryptosystem that combines some of the best available cryptographic algorithms and has become the open source de facto standard for encryption and authentication of e-mail and file storage applications.

- Unauthorized access to secure communications is often attempted by brute force attacks or cipher-text attacks using a frequency analysis of the encoded text. Therefore, modern algorithms attempt to remove the repetitive and predictable statistical bias from the ciphertext. Occasionally attackers may obtain duplicate texts, one in ciphertext and one in plaintext, which enable them to reverse-engineer the encryption algorithm. This is referred to as a known-plaintext attack or a selected-plaintext attack. Attacks used against cryptosystems include the man-in-the-middle attack, correlation attacks, dictionary attacks, and timing attacks.

- Most well-known encryption methods are released to the information and computer security communities for testing, which leads to the development of more secure algorithms.

Review Questions

1. What are cryptography and cryptanalysis?
2. What were some of the first uses of cryptography?
3. What is a key, and what is it used for?
4. What are the three basic operations in cryptography?
5. What is a hash function, and what can it be used for?
6. Why is it important to exchange keys "out of band" in symmetric encryption?
7. What is the fundamental difference between symmetric and asymmetric encryption?
8. How does Public Key Infrastructure protect information assets?
9. What are the six components of PKI?
10. What is the difference between digital signatures and digital certificates?
11. What drawbacks to symmetric and asymmetric encryption are resolved by using a hybrid method like Diffie-Hellman?
12. What is steganography, and what may it be used for?
13. What security protocols are predominantly used in Web-based electronic commerce?
14. What security protocols are used to protect e-mail?
15. IPSec can be used in two modes. What are they?
16. Which kind of attack on cryptosystems involves using a collection of pre-identified terms? Which kind of attack involves sequential guessing of all possible key combinations?
17. Using a modern Pentium 4 computer, how long would it take to crack a cryptosystem that is based on a 32-bit key? 56-bit key? 64-bit key?
18. What is the average key size of a "strong encryption" system in use today?
19. What is the standard for encryption currently recommended by NIST?
20. What is the most popular symmetric encryption system used over the Web? The most popular asymmetric system? Hybrid system?

Exercises

1. Go to a popular online electronic commerce site like Amazon.com. Select several items for your shopping cart. Go to check out. When you get to the screen that asks for your credit card number, right-click on the Web browser and select "Properties." What can you find out about the cryptosystems and protocols in use to protect this transaction?

2. Repeat Exercise 1 on a different Web site. Does this site use similar or different protocols? Describe them.

3. Go to the Web site for PGP, *http://www.pgp.com/products/freeware.html*. Download and install the freeware version of PGP. Using PGP and your favorite e-mail program, send a PGP-signed e-mail to your instructor. What appears different in this e-mail compared to your previous e-mails?

4. Visit the NIST Web site and view the document "Introducing the Advanced Encryption Standard," which can be found at *http://csrc.nist.gov/publications/fips/fips197/fips-197.pdf*. Review the FIPS-197 standard. Examine the document to determine an overview of the development and implementation of this cryptosystem.

5. Search the Web for steganography tools. What do you find? Download and install a trial version of one of the tools. Embed a text file within an image. In a side-by-side comparison of the two images, can you tell the difference between the original image and the image with the embedded file?

Case Exercises

Charlie was just getting ready to head home when the phone rang. Caller ID showed it was Peter.

"Hi, Peter," he said into the receiver. "Want me to start the file cracker on your spreadsheet?"

"No, thanks," Peter answered, taking the joke well. "I remembered my passphrase. But I want to get your advice on what we need to do to make the use of encryption more effective and to get it properly licensed for the whole company to use. I see the value in using it for certain kinds of information, and I think we need to plan for its use. I'm just worried about the next time I forget a passphrase, or even worse, what if someone gets hurt or leaves the company, how would we get their files back?"

"We'd use a feature called key recovery, which is usually part of PKI software," said Charlie. "Actually, if we invest in a PKI software, we could solve that problem as well as several others."

"OK," said Peter. "Can you see me tomorrow at 10 o'clock to talk about this PKI solution, and how we can make better use of encryption?"

Questions:

1. Was Charlie exaggerating when he gave Peter an estimate for the time that would be required to crack the encryption key using a brute force attack?

2. Are there any tools that an individual like Peter can use safely to avoid losing his or her passphrase without using key recovery?

Endnotes

1. Torbjorn Anderson. "Polyalphabetic Substitution." *Le Canard Volant Non Identifie Online.* 30 January 1999. [Cited 29 July 2002]. Available from the World Wide Web <*http://www.cvni.net/radio/nsnl/*>.

2. Ronald L. Krutz and Russell Dean Vines. *The CISSP Prep Guide: Mastering the Ten Domains of Computer Security.* (New York: John Wiley and Sons Inc., 2001), 131.

3. Savard, John (1999). "The Advanced Encryption Standard (Rijndael)." Viewed online 3/31/04 at *http://home.ecn.ab.ca/~jsavard/crypto/co040401.htm.*

4. National Institute of Standards and Technology. *Data Encryption Standards (DES).* FIPS PUB 46-3. (25 October 1999).

5. Steve Burnett and Stephen Paine. RSA Security's Official Guide to Cryptography. (New York: Osborne/McGraw-Hill, 2001).

6. Special thanks to our reviewer for this example: Robert Statica, Associate Director, Cryptography and Telecommunications Laboratory, New Jersey Institute of Technology.

7. Steve Burnett and Stephen Paine. *RSA Security's Official Guide to Cryptography.* (New York: Osborne/McGraw-Hill, 2001).

8. Steve Burnett and Stephen Paine. *RSA Security's Official Guide to Cryptography.* (New York: Osborne/McGraw-Hill, 2001).

9. Stefan Kelm. "The PKI Page." *Secorvo Security Consulting Online.* [Cited 29 July 2002]. Available from the World Wide Web <*http://www.pki-page.org/*>.

10. William Stallings. *Cryptography and Network Security, Principles and Practice.* (New Jersey: Prentice Hall, 1999).

11. Conway, Maura. "Code Wars: Steganography, Signals Intelligence, and Terrorism." Viewed online 4/01/04 at *http://www.cs.tcd.ie/Diana.Wilson/MSC%20MIS/Other%20articles/Completed%20Paper2.doc.*

12. Declan McCullagh. "Bin Laden: Steganography Master?" Available on the World Wide Web at <http://www.wired.com/news/politics/0,1283,41658,00.html>.

13. William Stallings. *Cryptography and Network Security, Principles and Practice.* (New Jersey: Prentice Hall, 1999).

14. Cisco Systems, Inc. "White Paper: IPSec." *Cisco Online.* (21 November 2000) [Cited 1 July 2002]. Available from the World Wide Web <*http://www.cisco.com/warp/public/cc/so/neso/sqso/eqso/ipsec_wp.htm.*>

15. The International PGP Home Page. *PGPI Online.* [Cited 29 July 2002]. Available from the World Wide Web <*http://www.pgpi.org/*>.

Physical Security

> If someone really wants to get at the information, it is not difficult if they can gain physical access to the computer or hard drive.
>
> **MICROSOFT WHITE PAPER, JULY 1999**

AMY WINDAHL WAS BACK EARLY from lunch. As she was walking toward the SLS building from the parking lot, she saw one of the accounting clerks go through the building's double glass doors. After him went in a person she didn't recognize, a tall, blond man in nondescript business casual clothes. The two of them walked past the security guard station in the lobby and headed for the elevator. Amy waited for the next elevator and pressed the button for her floor.

When the elevator doors opened, she saw the blond man again, this time standing in the second floor elevator lobby and looking at the company's phone list. She walked over to the doors to the hallway that led to that floor's offices and cocked her right hip, where her badge was clipped, toward the sensor for the locks. When she heard the magnetic lock release, Amy pulled the door open and went through. As the door began to shut, the stranger grabbed it and came through behind her.

Amy realized now that she had a "tailgater," a person who follows the people who manage to remember to bring their badges to work. She had seen the security bulletin just last week emphasizing that tailgaters should be reported. Everyone in the staff meeting had had a good laugh about turning each other in the next time any two of them came through the door together. But now she was beginning to understand the seriousness of the bulletin.

Amy turned around quickly, to head back into the lobby, and found herself face-to-face with the blond man. "Excuse me," she said. The stranger stepped back to let her pass and then continued down the hall. Amy picked up the lobby phone and dialed the number for building security.

"Security," a voice answered.

"Hi, Amy Windahl here. I work in the IT department on the second floor. I just had a stranger tailgate into the second floor offices. Do you guys want to check it out?"

"Yes, ma'am. We have someone on the floor already. I'll have him meet you in the lobby in two minutes," said the security dispatcher.

When the security officer appeared, Amy said, "He went down the hall, toward the programming offices. He's tall, heavy, has green slacks, a tan shirt, a leather jacket—oh, and he has blond hair."

The guard said, "Wait here. If he comes through here without me, call dispatch at extension 3333. I'll be right back."

Amy sat down on the chair by the phone. After three or four minutes, she saw the blond man walking briskly toward the doors. The guard was right behind him. As the stranger opened the door, the guard called out, "Sir, please stop. I need to speak with you. What's your name?" Before the blond man could answer, the elevator opened, and two more guards came into the lobby.

The stranger responded, "Alan Gaskin."

The guard asked, "What's your business here?"

"Just visiting a friend," said the stranger.

"And who would that be?" the guard asked.

The stranger looked a bit surprised, and then said, "Uh, William Walters, uh, in the accounting department, I think."

The guard reached for his wireless handheld terminal and punched a few buttons. Then he said, "Mr. Gaskin, there are no employees with that name working here, in accounting or any other department. Do you want to try another answer?"

The stranger looked a little confused and took a few steps toward the stairwell. But the other two guards moved up and cut him off. As the guards took the blond man by the upper arms to keep him from escaping, a brown paper bag dropped out from under his jacket, its contents spilling out on the carpet. Amy saw several office badges, a watch, two palmtop computers, and several cell phones.

The first guard immediately radioed dispatch. "Contact the city police and advise them we have a trespasser. We will press charges." The other guards led the man toward the elevators, while the first guard told Amy: "You need to call your supervisors and tell them you will be delayed. We must take a statement from you."

LEARNING OBJECTIVES:

Upon completion of this material, you should be able to:

- Understand the conceptual need for physical security
- Identify threats to information security that are unique to physical security
- Describe the key physical security considerations for selecting a facility site
- Identify physical security monitoring components
- Recognize the essential elements of physical access control within the scope of facilities management
- Understand the importance of fire safety programs to all physical security programs
- Describe the components of fire detection and response
- Understand the impact of service interruptions of supporting utilities
- Understand the technical details of uninterruptible power supplies and how they are used to increase availability of information assets
- Discuss critical physical environment considerations for computing facilities
- Discuss the countermeasures used against the physical theft of computing devices

Introduction

As discussed in Chapter 1, information security encompasses the protection of both data and physical information assets. So far, a wide variety of subjects that focus on protecting the technical aspects of data have been examined: firewalls, intrusion detection systems, and monitoring software. In addition, a number of management topics, such as risk assessments, risk analysis, and risk control, have been presented.

Physical security addresses the design, implementation, and maintenance of counter-measures that protect the physical resources of an organization. This means the physical protection of the people, the hardware, and the supporting system elements and resources associated with the control of information in all its states: transmission, storage, and processing. Most of the technology-based controls discussed up to this point can be circumvented if an attacker gains physical access to the devices being controlled. For example, when employees fail to secure the server console, the operating system running on that computer is vulnerable to attack. In other words, if it is easy to steal the hard drives from a computer system, then it is easy to steal the information contained on the hard drives. As a result, physical security should receive as much attention as logical security in the development of information security programs. This attention assures a solid foundation for the security program.

In earlier chapters, you encountered a number of threats to information security that could be classified as threats to physical security. For example, an employee accidentally spilling coffee on his or her laptop represents a threat to the physical security of the information in the computer—in this case, the threat takes the form of an act of human error or failure. A compromise to intellectual property can include an employee without an appropriate security clearance copying a classified marketing plan. A deliberate act of espionage or trespass could be exemplified by a competitor sneaking into a facility with a camera. Deliberate acts of sabotage or vandalism can be physical attacks on individuals or property, with deliberate acts of theft being perhaps the most common of these threats. Examples include employees stealing computer equipment, credentials, passwords, and laptops. Quality of service deviations from service providers, especially power and water, also represent physical security threats. In his book, *Fighting Computer Crime*, Donn B. Parker lists the "Seven Major Sources of Physical Loss" as follows:

1. Extreme temperature: heat, cold
2. Gases: war gases, commercial vapors, humid or dry air, suspended particles
3. Liquids: water, chemicals
4. Living organisms: viruses, bacteria, people, animals, insects
5. Projectiles: tangible objects in motion, powered objects
6. Movement: collapse, shearing, shaking, vibration, liquefaction, flow waves, separation, slide
7. Energy anomalies: electrical surge or failure, magnetism, static electricity, aging circuitry; radiation: sound, light, radio, microwave, electromagnetic, atomic[1]

Just as with all other areas of security, the implementation of physical security requires sound organizational policy. Policy guides the planning of physical security in the development life cycle and serves as a reference to organizational objectives through the ongoing maintenance and use phases. Physical security policies direct users of information assets in the appropriate use of computing resources and information assets, as well as in the protection of their own personal safety in day-to-day operations. Physical security is designed and implemented in several layers. Each community of interest in the organization is responsible for components within these layers.

- **General management:** Responsible for the security of the facility in which the organization is housed and the policies and standards for secure operation. This includes exterior security, fire protection, building access, as well as other controls such as guard dogs and door locks.

- **IT management and professionals:** Responsible for environmental and access security in technology equipment locations and for the policies and standards of secure equipment operation. This includes access to server rooms, power conditioning, server room temperature and humidity controls, as well as more specialized controls like static and dust contamination controls.

- **Information security management and professionals:** Responsible for performing risk assessments and implementation reviews for the physical security controls implemented by the other two groups.

Physical Access Controls

There are a number of physical access controls that are uniquely suited to governing the movement of people within an organization's facilities—that is, controlling their physical access to company resources. Until now, the topic of access control within the discussion of information security has often been with regard to logical access to systems. In this age of the Internet, logical access is a topic worthy of a significant amount of discussion, but the control of physical access to the assets of the organization is also of critical importance. Sometimes the technology used for physical security can overlap with that used for logical security. Some of these overlaps involve the use of biometrics, smart cards, or wireless enabled keycards, which are used for controlling access to locked doors, information assets, and information system resources.

Before examining access controls, you need to understand the concept of a secure facility and its design. An organization's general management oversees physical security. Commonly, access controls for a building are operated by a group called **facilities management**. Larger organizations may have an entire staff dedicated to facilities management, while smaller organizations often outsource these responsibilities.

From the point of view of facilities management, a **secure facility** is a physical location that has been engineered with controls designed to minimize the risk of attacks from physical threats. The notion of a secure facility usually brings to mind military bases, maximum-security prisons, and nuclear power plants. Although securing a facility to minimize risks from physical attacks requires some adherence to established rules and procedures, the environment does not necessarily have to be as severe and constraining as that of these examples. Although some compromises are often part of the process, it is also not always necessary to sacrifice appearance to minimize risk from physical attacks. In fact, a secure facility may be able to use its natural terrain, traffic flow, and degree of urban development to its advantage. A secure facility can complement these features with protection mechanisms, such as fences, gates, walls, guards, and alarms.

Controls for Protecting the Secure Facility

There are a number of physical security controls and issues that an organization's communities of interest should consider when implementing physical security inside and outside the facility. Some of the major controls are:

- Walls, Fencing, and Gates
- Guards
- Dogs
- ID Cards and Badges
- Locks and Keys
- Mantraps
- Electronic Monitoring
- Alarms and Alarm Systems
- Computer Rooms and Wiring Closets
- Interior Walls and Doors

Walls, Fencing, and Gates

One of the oldest and most reliable methods of providing physical security on the premises, controls in the form of walls, fencing, and gates deter unauthorized access to the facility. While not every organization will have a need to implement external perimeter controls such as these, walls and fences with suitably constructed gates are an essential starting point for organizations whose employees require access to the real estate the organization owns or controls. These types of controls vary widely in appearance and function, ranging from everyday chain link or privacy fences used to indicate subtly where people are supposed to park or walk, to imposing concrete or masonry barriers designed to withstand the blast of a terrorist car-bomb. Each application of exterior perimeter control will require the proper planning by an expert to assure that the control meets the security goals required, along with sensitivity to the fact that this type of control is usually an aspect of an organization's appearance that many people will see very often.

Guards

Guards have the ability to apply human reasoning. Other controls such as fences and walls with gates are static, and therefore unresponsive to actions, or they are programmed to respond with specific actions to specific stimuli, such as opening for someone who has the correct key. Guards can evaluate each situation as it arises and thus make reasoned responses. Most guards have clear **standard operating procedures (SOPs)** that help them to act decisively in unfamiliar situations. In the military, for example, guards are provided with general orders (see the Offline on guard duty) as well as special orders that are unique to their posts.

OFFLINE

Guard Duty

Adapted from "Guard Duty," *www.armystudyguide.com/guard_duty/studyguide.htm* and from "General Military Knowledge" *http://www.military-net.com/education/ mpdgeneral.html*

In the military, guard duty is a serious responsibility. A guard must memorize, understand, and comply with his general orders, and the orders particular to his or her assignment.
   "General Orders:
   1. I will guard everything within the limits of my post and quit my post only when properly relieved.
   2. I will obey my special orders and perform all of my duties in a military manner.
   3. I will report violations of my special orders, emergencies, and anything not covered in my instructions to the commander of the relief."[2]
   How do guards comply with the responsibilities of their assignments? They apply the force necessary to accomplish their missions, including deadly force in approved situations. Deadly force is the application of coercive control that may result in death or severe bodily harm. It is applied only to the minimum extent necessary to make an apprehension.
   "Deadly force can only be used for [the following situations]:
   1. Self-defense in the event of imminent danger of death or serious bodily harm;
   2. To prevent the actual theft or destruction of property designated for protection; and
   3. As directed by the Standard Operating Procedures of his individual guard post."[3]

Dogs

If an organization is protecting highly valuable resources, dogs can be a valuable part of physical security if they are integrated into the plan correctly and managed properly. Guard dogs are useful because their keen senses of smell and hearing can detect intrusions that human guards cannot, and they can be placed in harm's way when it's necessary to avoid risking the life of a human.

ID Cards and Badges

One area of access control that ties physical security with information access control is the use of identification cards and name badges. An **identification (ID) card** is typically worn concealed, whereas a **name badge** is visible. These devices can serve a number of purposes. First, they serve as simple forms of biometrics in that they use an individual's face to identify the person and authenticate his or her access to the facility. The cards may be coded in some visible way as to which buildings or areas may be accessed. Second, ID cards that have a magnetic strip or radio chip that can be read by automated control devices allow an organization to authorize which individuals can have access to restricted areas within the facility. ID cards and name badges are not foolproof, however; and even the cards designed to communicate with locks can be easily duplicated, stolen, and modified. Because of this inherent weakness, such devices should not be an organization's only means of controlling access to restricted areas.

Another inherent weakness of this type of physical access control technology is the human factor. As depicted in this chapter's opening vignette, **tailgating** occurs when an authorized individual presents a key to open a door, and other individuals, who may or may not be authorized, also enter through. Launching a campaign to make employees aware of tailgating is one way to combat this problem. There are also technology-based means of discouraging tailgating, such as mantraps (discussed in a following section) or turnstiles. These extra levels of control are usually expensive, in that they require floor space and/or construction, as well as inconvenient for those required to use them. Consequently, anti-tailgating controls are only used where there is an overriding concern for authorized entry.

Locks and Keys

There are two types of locks based on how the mechanism is activated: mechanical and electromechanical. The **mechanical lock** may rely on a key that is a carefully shaped piece of metal, which a person rotates to turn tumblers to release secured loops of steel, aluminum, or brass (as in, for example, brass padlocks). Alternatively, a mechanical lock may have a dial that causes the proper rotation of slotted discs until the slots on multiple disks are aligned, and permits the retraction of a securing bolt (as in combination and safe locks). Although mechanical locks are simple in concept, some of the technologies that go into the development of these physical security devices are quite complex. Some of these modern enhancements have led to the creation of the electromechanical lock. **Electromechanical locks** can accept a variety of inputs as keys, including magnetic strips on ID cards, radio signals from name badges, personal identification numbers (PINs) typed into a keypad, or some combination of these to activate an electrically powered servo to unlock the mechanism.

Locks can also be divided into four categories based on the triggering process: manual, programmable, electronic, and biometric. **Manual locks**, padlocks, and combination locks are commonplace and well understood. If you have the key (or combination) you can gain access to the resources secured behind the lock. These locks are often preset by the manufacturer and therefore unchangeable. In other words, once manual locks are installed into doors, they can only be changed by highly trained locksmiths. Thus, their use is often limited to controlling access to a single door. Programmable locks can be changed after they are put in service, allowing for combination or key changes without a locksmith and even allowing the owner to change to another access method (key or combination) to upgrade security. Many examples of these types of locks are presented in Figure 9-1. Mechanical push button locks, shown in the left-most photo in Figure 9-1, are popular for securing computer rooms and wiring closets, as they have a code that can be reset and they don't require electricity to operate.

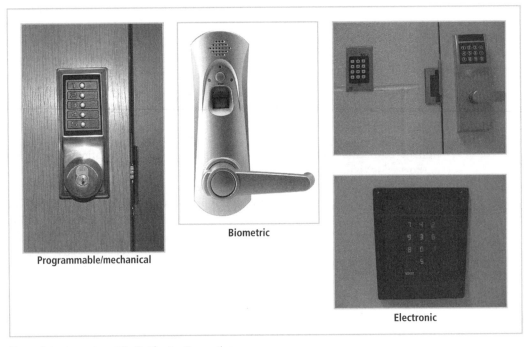

Programmable/mechanical

Biometric

Electronic

Biometric image courtesy of the BioThentica Corporation

FIGURE 9-1 Locks

Electronic locks can be integrated into alarm systems and combined with other building management systems. Also, these locks can be integrated with sensors to create a number of various combinations of locking behavior. One such combination would be a system that coordinates the use of fire alarms and locks to improve safety during alarm conditions (i.e., fires). Here, the system would change the degree of authorization required to access a location when that location is in an alarm condition. Another example of a combination system would be one in which a lock is fitted with a sensor that notifies guard stations when that lock has been activated. Another common form of electronic locks are *electric strike* locks, which are used when individuals announce themselves and are *buzzed* into a building. In general, electronic locks lend themselves to uses where they can be activated or deactivated by a switch controlled by an agent, usually a secretary or guard. Electronic push button locks, like their mechanical cousins, have a numerical keypad over the knob, requiring the individual user to enter a personal code and open the door. These locks usually use battery backups to power the keypad in case of a power failure.

As mentioned in the ID card section, some locks require smart cards—keys that contain computer chips. These smart cards can carry critical information, provide strong authentication, and offer a number of other features. Keycard readers based on smart cards are commonly used for securing computer rooms, communications closets, and other restricted areas. The card reader can track entry and provide accountability. In a locking system configured in this way, the access level of individuals can be adjusted according to their current status (i.e., current employee, recently resigned) and thus does not require replacement of the lock. A specialized type of keycard reader is the **proximity reader**, which—instead of requiring individuals to insert their cards—allows them simply to place their cards within the lock's range for recognition. With some of these readers, the lock can recognize the card even when it is inside a pocket.

The most sophisticated locks are **biometric locks**. Finger, palm, and hand readers, iris and retina scanners, and voice and signature readers fall into this category. The technology that underlies biometric devices was discussed in Chapter 7.

As part of general management's responsibility for an organization's physical environment, the management of keys and locks is a fundamental concern. As will be discussed in Chapter 11, when individuals are hired, fired, laid off, or transferred, their access controls, whether physical or logical, must be properly adjusted. Failure to do so can result in instances of employees cleaning out their offices by taking more than their personal effects. Also, when locksmiths are hired, they should be carefully screened and monitored, as there is a chance that these individuals could have complete access to the facility.

Sometimes locks fail, and thus facilities need to have alternative procedures in place for controlling access. These procedures must take into account that locks fail in one of two ways: when the lock of a door fails and the door becomes unlocked, that is a **fail-safe lock**; when the lock of a door fails and the door remains locked, this is a **fail-secure lock**. In practice, the most common reason why technically sophisticated locks fail is due to a loss of power and activation through fire control systems. A fail-safe lock is usually used to secure an exit, where it is essential for human safety that in the event of, for instance, a fire, the lock is open. In contrast, a fail-secure lock is used when human safety in the area being controlled is not the dominant factor. One example of this would be a situation in which the security of nuclear or biological weapons needs to be controlled; here, the reality is that preventing a loss of control of these weapons is more critical to security (meaning it is a security issue of greater magnitude) than protecting the lives of the personnel guarding the weapons.

Understanding lock mechanisms is important, because locks can be exploited by an intruder to gain access to the secured location. If an electronic lock is short circuited, it may become fail-safe and allow the intruder to bypass the control and enter the room.

Mantraps

A common enhancement for locks in high security areas is the mantrap. A **mantrap** is a small enclosure that has an entry point and a different exit point. The individual entering the facility, area, or room enters the mantrap, requests access through some form of electronic or biometric lock and key, and if his or her access is confirmed, exits the mantrap into the facility. The enclosure is called a mantrap because if the individual's access is denied, the mantrap does not allow him or her to exit until a security official overrides the automatic locks of the enclosure. Figure 9-2 provides an example of a typical mantrap layout.

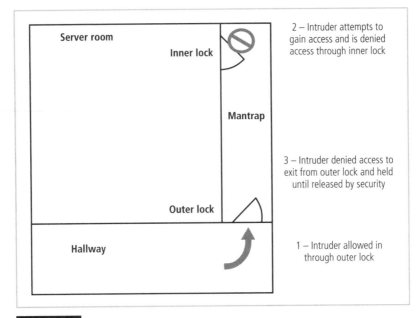

FIGURE 9-2   Mantraps

Electronic Monitoring

To record events within a specific area that guards and dogs might miss, or to record events in areas where other types of physical controls are not practical, monitoring equipment can be used. Although you may not know it, many of you are, thanks to the silver globes attached to the ceilings of many retail stores, already subject to cameras viewing you from odd corners—that is, video monitoring. On the other end of these cameras are video cassette recorders (VCRs) and related machinery that capture the video feed. Electronic monitoring includes **closed-circuit television (CCT)** systems. Some CCT systems collect constant video feeds, while others rotate input from a number of cameras, sampling each area in turn.

These video monitoring systems have drawbacks: for the most part they are reactive and do not prevent access or prohibited activity. Another drawback to these systems is that when they are monitored in real time people must be involved because science has not yet developed intelligent systems capable of reliably evaluating a video feed. This means that to determine if unauthorized activities have occurred a member of the security staff must constantly review the information in real time or review the information collected in video recordings. For this reason, CCT is most often used to collect data for areas that have already been broken into, and thus it becomes more of an evidence collection device than a detective instrument. In high security areas (such as banks, casinos, and shopping centers), however, security personnel monitor CCT systems constantly, looking for improprieties and suspicious activity.

Alarms and Alarm Systems

Closely related to monitoring are the alarm systems that notify the appropriate individual when a predetermined event or activity occurs. Similar to IDS systems (which, as discussed in Chapter 7, detect a logical intrusion event), alarms can be used to detect a *physical* intrusion or other untoward event. This could be a fire, a break-in or intrusion, an environmental disturbance, such as flooding, or an interruption in services, such as a loss of power. One example of alarm systems is the burglar alarm commonly found in residential and commercial environments. Burglar alarms detect intrusions into unauthorized areas and notify either a local or remote security agency to react. To detect intrusions, these systems rely on a number of different types of sensors: motion detectors, thermal detectors, glass breakage detectors, weight sensors, and contact sensors. **Motion detectors** detect movement within a confined space and are either active or passive. Some motion sensors emit energy beams, usually in the form of infrared or laser light, ultrasonic sound or sound waves, or some form of electromagnetic radiation. If the energy from the beam projected into the area being monitored is disrupted, the alarm is activated. Other types of motion sensors are passive in that they constantly measure the energy (infrared or ultrasonic) from the monitored space and detect rapid changes in this energy. The passive measurement of these energies can be blocked or disguised and is therefore fallible. **Thermal detectors** work by detecting rates of change in the ambient temperature in the room. They can, for example, detect when a human, with a temperature of 98.6 degrees Fahrenheit, enters a room of 65 degrees Fahrenheit, because the human's presence changes the room's ambient temperature. Thermal detectors are also used in fire detection (as will be described in later sections). **Contact and weight sensors** work when two contacts are connected as, for example, when a foot steps on a pressure-sensitive pad under a rug, or a window being opened triggers a pin and spring sensor. **Vibration sensors** also fall into this category, except that they detect movement of the sensor rather than movement in the environment.

Computer Rooms and Wiring Closets

Computer rooms and wiring and communications closets are facilities that require special attention to ensure the confidentiality, integrity, and availability of information. For an outline of the physical and environmental controls needed for computer rooms, read the Technical Details box entitled "Physical and Environmental Controls for Computer Rooms."

Logical access controls are easily defeated if an attacker gains physical access to the computing equipment. Custodial staff members are often the least scrutinized of employees (and nonemployees) who have access to an organization's offices. Yet custodians are given the greatest degree of unsupervised access. They are often handed the master keys to the entire building and then ignored, even though they collect paper from every office, dust many desks, and move large containers from every area. It is therefore not difficult for this type of worker to gather critical information and computer media or copy proprietary and classified information. All this is not to say that an organization's custodial staff should be held under constant suspicion of espionage, but to state that the wide-reaching access that custodians have can be a vulnerability that attackers exploit to gain unauthorized information. Factual accounts exist of technically trained agents being placed as custodians in the offices of their competition. Thus, custodial staffs should be carefully managed not only by the organization's general management, but also by IT management.

Interior Walls and Doors

The security of information assets can sometimes be compromised by the nature of the construction of the walls and doors of the facility. The walls in a facility are typically of two types: standard interior and firewall. Building codes require that each floor have a number of **firewalls**, or walls that will limit the spread of damage should a fire break out in an office. While the network firewalls discussed in an earlier chapter isolate the logical sub networks of the organization, physical firewalls isolate the physical spaces of the organization's offices. Between the firewalls, standard interior walls are erected to compartmentalize the individual offices. Unlike firewalls, these interior walls reach only part way to the next floor, which leaves a space above the ceiling of the offices but below the top of the storey. This space is called a **plenum** and is usually one to three feet high. This type of construction allows for ventilation systems that can inexpensively collect return air from all the offices on the floor. For security, however, this design is not ideal, because it means that an individual can climb over the wall from one office to the other. As a result, all high-security areas, such as computer rooms and wiring closets, must have firewall-grade walls surrounding them. This provides physical security not only from potential intruders, but also from fires.

The doors that allow access into high security rooms should also be evaluated. Standard office-grade doors provide little or no security. For example, one of the authors of this textbook once locked himself out of his office by accidentally breaking the key off in the lock. When the locksmith arrived, he carried a curious contraption. Instead of disassembling the lock or using other locksmith secrets, he carried a long piece of heavy-duty wire, bent into the shape of a bow, with a string tied to each end. He slid one end of this bow through the one-inch gap under the door, stood it on one end and yanked the string. The wire bow slid over the door handle and the string looped over it. When the locksmith yanked the string, the door swung open. This information is not meant to teach you how to access interior offices but to warn you that no office is completely secure. How can you avoid this problem? In most interior offices, you can't. Instead, IT security professionals must educate the organization's employees about how to secure the information and systems within their offices.

Returning to the issue of securing doors, it's recommended that push or crash bars be installed on computer rooms and closets. These bars are much more difficult to open from the outside than the standard door pull handles, and thus provide much higher levels of security, but they also still provide the needed levels of safety in the event of an emergency.

TECHNICAL DETAILS

Physical and Environmental Controls for Computer Rooms

Adapted from "Guide for Developing Security Plans for Information Technology Systems"[4] by M. Swanson, NIST Special Publication 800-18, December 1998.

The following list of physical and environmental controls for computer rooms is intended to be representative, not comprehensive.

- Card keys for building and entrances to work area
- Twenty-four-hour guards at all entrances and exits
- Cipher lock on computer room door
- Raised floor in computer room
- Dedicated cooling system
- Humidifier in tape library

continued

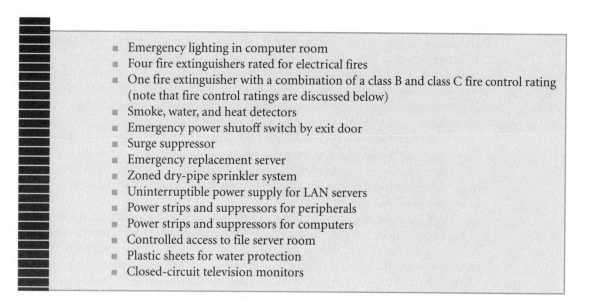

- Emergency lighting in computer room
- Four fire extinguishers rated for electrical fires
- One fire extinguisher with a combination of a class B and class C fire control rating (note that fire control ratings are discussed below)
- Smoke, water, and heat detectors
- Emergency power shutoff switch by exit door
- Surge suppressor
- Emergency replacement server
- Zoned dry-pipe sprinkler system
- Uninterruptible power supply for LAN servers
- Power strips and suppressors for peripherals
- Power strips and suppressors for computers
- Controlled access to file server room
- Plastic sheets for water protection
- Closed-circuit television monitors

Fire Security and Safety

The most important concern of physical security is the safety of the people who work in the organization. The most serious threat to that safety is the possibility of fire. Fires account for more property damage, personal injury, and death than any other threat to physical security. As a result, it is imperative that physical security plans examine and implement strong measures to detect and respond to fires and fire hazards.

Fire Detection and Response

Fire suppression systems are devices installed and maintained to detect and respond to a fire, potential fire, or combustion situation. These devices typically work to deny an environment of one of the three requirements for a fire to burn: temperature (ignition source), fuel, and oxygen.

While the temperature of ignition or **flame point** of a material may vary, it can be as low as a few hundred degrees. Paper, the most common combustible in the office, has a flame point of 451 degrees Fahrenheit (a fact that is used to dramatic effect in Ray Bradbury's novel *Fahrenheit 451*). Paper can reach that temperature when it is exposed to a carelessly dropped cigarette butt, malfunctioning electrical equipment, or other accidental or purposeful misadventures.

Water and water mist systems, which are described in detail in subsequent paragraphs, work both to reduce the temperature of the flame in order to extinguish it and to saturate some categories of fuels (such as paper) to prevent ignition. Carbon dioxide systems (CO_2) rob fire of its oxygen. Soda acid systems deny fire its fuel, preventing the fire from spreading. Gas-based systems, such as Halon and its Environmental Protection Agency-approved replacements, disrupt the fire's chemical reaction but leave enough oxygen for people to survive for a short time. Before a fire can be suppressed, however, it must be detected.

Fire Detection

Fire detection systems fall into two general categories: manual and automatic. **Manual fire detection systems** include human responses, such as calling the fire department, as well as manually activated alarms, such as sprinklers and gaseous systems. One consideration with manual fire detection systems is the fire alarm itself. Organizations must use care when manually triggered alarms are tied directly to suppression systems, as false alarms are not uncommon. Organizations should also ensure that proper security remains in place until all employees and visitors have been cleared from the building and their evacuation has been verified. During the chaos of a fire evacuation, an attacker can easily slip into offices and obtain sensitive information. To help prevent such intrusions, it is a common business practice among fire safety programs to designate an individual from each office area as a floor monitor.

There are three basic types of fire detection systems: thermal detection, smoke detection, and flame detection. The **thermal detection systems** contain a sophisticated heat sensor that operates in one of two ways. In the first, known as **fixed temperature**, the sensor detects when the ambient temperature in an area reaches a predetermined level, usually between 135 degrees Fahrenheit and 165 degrees Fahrenheit, or 57 degrees Centigrade to 74 degrees Centigrade.[5] In the second approach, known as **rate-of-rise**, the sensor detects an unusually rapid increase in the area temperature within a relatively short period of time. In either case, if the criteria are met, the alarm and suppression systems are activated. Thermal detection systems are inexpensive and easy to maintain. Unfortunately, thermal detectors usually don't catch a problem until it is already in progress, as in a full-blown fire. As a result, thermal detection systems are not sufficient means of fire protection in areas where human safety could be at risk. They are also not recommended for areas with high-value items, or items which could be easily damaged by high temperature.

Smoke detection systems are perhaps the most common means of detecting a potentially dangerous fire, and they are required by building codes in most residential dwellings and commercial buildings. Smoke detectors operate in one of three ways. In the first, **photoelectric sensors** project and detect an infrared beam across an area. If the beam is interrupted (presumably by smoke), the alarm or suppression system is activated. In the second, an **ionization sensor** contains a small amount of a harmless radioactive material within a detection chamber. When certain by-products of combustion enter the chamber, they change the level of electrical conductivity with the chamber and activate the detector. Ionization sensor systems are much more sophisticated than photoelectric sensors and can detect fires much earlier, as invisible by-products can be detected long before enough visible material enters a photoelectric sensor to trigger a reaction. The third category of smoke detectors is the air-aspirating detector. **Air-aspirating detectors** are very sophisticated systems and are used in high-sensitivity areas. They work by taking in air, filtering it, and moving it through a chamber containing a laser beam. If the laser beam is diverted or refracted by smoke particles, the system is activated. These types of systems are typically much more expensive than the less effective models; however, they are much better at early detection and more commonly used in areas where extremely valuable materials are stored.

The third major category of fire detection systems is the **flame detector**. The flame detector is a sensor that detects the infrared or ultraviolet light produced by an open flame. These systems require direct line of sight with the flame and compare the flame's light signature to a database of known flame light signatures to determine whether or not to activate the alarm and suppression systems. While highly sensitive, flame detection systems are expensive and must be installed where they can scan all areas of the protected area. They are not typically used in areas with human lives at stake; however, they are quite suitable for chemical storage areas where normal chemical emissions might activate smoke detectors.

Fire Suppression

Fire suppression systems can consist of portable, manual, or automatic apparatus. Portable extinguishers are used in a variety of situations where direct application of suppression is preferred, or fixed apparatus is impractical. Portable extinguishers are much more efficient for smaller fires, because they avoid the triggering of an entire building's sprinkler systems and the damage that can cause. As described below, portable extinguishers are rated by the type of fire they can combat:

- Class A Fires: Those fires that involve ordinary combustible fuels such as wood, paper, textiles, rubber, cloth, and trash. **Class A fires** are extinguished by agents that interrupt the ability of the fuel to be ignited. Water and multipurpose, dry chemical fire extinguishers are ideal for these types of fires.

- Class B Fires: Those fires fueled by combustible liquids or gases, such as solvents, gasoline, paint, lacquer, and oil. **Class B fires** are extinguished by agents that remove oxygen from the fire. Carbon dioxide, multipurpose dry chemical, and Halon fire extinguishers are ideal for these types of fires.

- Class C Fires: Those fires with energized electrical equipment or appliances. **Class C fires** are extinguished with agents that must be non-conducting. Carbon dioxide, multipurpose, dry chemical, and Halon fire extinguishers are ideal for these types of fires. Never use a water fire extinguisher on a Class C fire.

- Class D Fires: **Class D fires** are those fueled by combustible metals, such as magnesium, lithium, and sodium. Fires of this type require special extinguishing agents and techniques.

The Technical Details box on Halon and the EPA provides additional details on the ban on new installations of Halon-based systems and the approved replacements.

TECHNICAL DETAILS

Halon Q & A

Halon Substitutes under SNAP as of 26 April 2000[6]
From The Environmental Protection Agency, Online, July 10, 2002.

When was the production of Halons banned?

Under the Clean Air Act (CAA), the United States banned the production and import of virgin Halons 1211, 1301, and 2402 beginning January 1, 1994, in compliance with the Montreal Protocol on Substances that Deplete the Ozone Layer. Recycled Halon and inventories produced before January 1, 1994 are now the only sources of supply. EPA's final rule published March 5, 1998 (63 FR 11084) bans the formulation of any blend of two or more of these Halons with one exception. An exemption is provided for Halon blends formulated using recycled Halon solely for the purpose of aviation fire protection, provided that blends produced under this exemption are recycled to meet the relevant

continued

purity standards for each individual Halon. A fact sheet summarizing this rule is also available from the Stratospheric Ozone Protection Hotline.

Must I now dismantle my Halon fire protection system?

No. It is legal to continue to use your existing Halon system. It is even legal to purchase recycled Halon and Halon produced before the phase-out to recharge your system.

However, because Halons deplete the ozone layer, users are encouraged to consider replacing their system and making their Halon stock available for users with more critical needs.

Are there any federal laws on emissions of Halons?

EPA's final rule published March 5, 1998 (63 FR 11084) prohibits the intentional release of Halon 1211, Halon 1301, and Halon 2402 during the testing, repairing, maintaining, servicing, or disposal of Halon-containing equipment or during the use of such equipment for technician training. The rule also requires appropriate training of technicians regarding emissions reduction and proper disposal of Halon and Halon-containing equipment. The rule became effective April 6, 1998.

What are the acceptable substitutes for Halon?

There are a number of acceptable substitutes for Halon 1211 and 1301 (the two most common types of Halon-based systems).

The options discussed above are presented in Table 9-1.

Table 9-1 Acceptable Substitutes

Acceptable Substitutes for Halon 1211 Streaming Agents under the Significant New Alternatives Policy (SNAP) Program as of April 26, 2000[7]

Substitute	Trade Name	Comments
HCFC-123	FE-232	Nonresidential uses only
HCFC-124	FE-241	Nonresidential uses only
[HCFC Blend] B	Halotron 1	Nonresidential uses only
[HCFC Blend] C	NAF P-III	Nonresidential uses only
[HCFC Blend] D	Blitz III	Nonresidential uses only
Gelled Halocarbon / Dry chemical suspension	Envirogel	Allowable in the residential use market
[Surfactant Blend] A	Cold Fire, Flameout	
Water mist systems using potable or natural sea water		
Carbon dioxide		
Dry chemical		
Water		
Foam		

continued

Acceptable Substitutes for Halon 1301 Total Flooding Agents under the Significant New Alternatives Policy (SNAP) Program as of April 26, 2000		
Substitute	Trade Name	Comment
Powdered Aerosol C	PyroGen, Dynameco	For use in unoccupied areas only
Powdered Aerosol A	SFE	For use in unoccupied areas only
Carbon dioxide system		Design must adhere to OSHA 1910.162(b)(5) and NFPA Standard 12
Water		Water mist systems using potable or natural sea water
Foam A	Phirex+	This agent is not a clean agent, but is a low-density, short duration foam

Manual and automatic fire response can include installed systems designed to apply suppressive agents. These are usually either sprinkler or gaseous systems. All **sprinkler systems** are designed to apply liquid, usually water, to all areas in which a fire has been detected, but an organization can choose from one of three implementations: wet-pipe, dry-pipe, or pre-action systems. A **wet-pipe** system has pressurized water in all pipes and has some form of valve in each protected area. When the system is activated, the valves are opened, allowing water to sprinkle the area. This is best for areas where the fire represents a severe risk to people, but where damage to property is not a major concern. The most obvious drawback to this type of system is damage to office equipment and materials that results from these items being soaked in water. A wet-pipe system is not usually considered appropriate in computer rooms, wiring closets, or anywhere electrical equipment is used or stored. There is also the risk of accidental or unauthorized activation. Figure 9-3 shows a water sprinkler system that works this way: when the ambient temperature reaches 140 degrees Fahrenheit to 150 degrees Fahrenheit, the special liquid in the glass tube boils, causing the tube to shatter and allowing the valve to open, which permits the flow of water over the diffuser, which then disperses the water throughout the area.

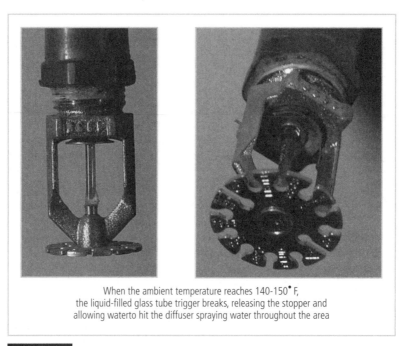

When the ambient temperature reaches 140-150° F,
the liquid-filled glass tube trigger breaks, releasing the stopper and
allowing waterto hit the diffuser spraying water throughout the area

FIGURE 9-3 Water Sprinkler System

A **dry-pipe system** is designed to work in areas where electrical equipment is used. Instead of containing water, the system contains pressurized air. The air holds valves closed, keeping the water away from the target areas. When a fire is detected, the sprinkler heads are activated, the pressurized air escapes, and water fills the pipes and exits through the sprinkler heads. This reduces the risk of leakage from the system when it is not activated. Some sprinkler systems are installed as a **deluge system**, in which all of the individual sprinkler heads are kept open, and as soon as the system is activated, water will be immediately applied to all areas. It is not, however, the optimal solution for computing environments, as there are other more sophisticated systems that can both suppress the fire and maintain the integrity of computing equipment.

A variation of the dry-pipe system is the **pre-action system**. This approach has a two-phase response to a fire. The system is normally maintained with nothing in the delivery pipes. When a fire has been detected, the first phase is initiated, and valves allow water to enter the system. At that point, the system is in a state identical to that found in a wet-pipe system. The pre-action system does not deliver water into the protected space until the individual sprinkler heads are triggered, at which time water is sprinkled into only the area of the activated sprinkler head.

Water mist sprinklers are the newest form of sprinkler systems and rely on ultra fine mists instead of traditional shower-type systems. The water mist systems work like traditional water system in reducing the ambient temperature around the flame, therefore minimizing its ability to sustain the necessary temperature needed to maintain combustion. Unlike traditional water sprinkler systems, however, these systems produce a fog-like mist that, because the droplets are much less susceptible to gravity, stays buoyant (airborne) much longer. As a result, a much smaller quantity of water is required; also the fire is extinguished more quickly, which causes less collateral damage. Relative to gaseous systems (to be discussed shortly), water-based systems are low cost, nontoxic, and require minimal retrofit for an existing sprinkler system.

Gaseous Emission Systems

Gaseous (or chemical gas) emission systems can be used in the suppression of fires. They are often found protecting chemical and electrical processing areas, as well as facilities that house computing systems. A typical configuration of such systems is shown in Figure 9-4.

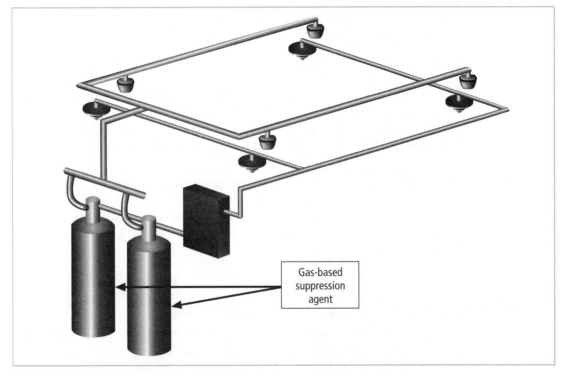

Gas-based suppression agent

Image is courtesy of Reliable Fire Equipment Company, Alsip, Illinois

FIGURE 9-4   Gaseous Fire Suppression System

Gaseous fire suppression systems are either self-pressurizing or must be pressurized with an additional agent. Until recently there were only two major types of gaseous systems: carbon dioxide and Halon. Carbon dioxide extinguishes a fire by removing its supply of oxygen. Unfortunately, any living organisms that also rely on oxygen are similarly extinguished. As a result, carbon dioxide systems are not commonly used in residential or office environments where people or animals are likely to be present. The alternative is Halon. Halon is one of a few chemicals designated as a **clean agent**, which means that it does not leave any residue after use, nor does it interfere with the operation of electrical or electronic equipment. As a result, Halon gas-based systems are the preferred solution for computer rooms and communications closets. Unlike carbon dioxide, Halon does not rob the fire of its oxygen but instead relies on a chemical reaction with the flame to extinguish it. As a result, Halon is much safer than carbon dioxide when people or animals are present and the system is activated. Although Halon can cause suffocation like a carbon dioxide system, the dosage levels required are much higher, and therefore Halon-based systems provide additional time for people to exit areas safely. As mentioned in the Offline on Halon, the EPA has classified Halon as an ozone-depleting substance, and therefore new installations of the controlled types of Halon are prohibited in commercial and residential locations. There are a number of alternatives, also presented in the Offline box, although, as in the case of the refrigerant Freon, the alternatives are reported to be less effective than Halon. These alternative clean agents are described below:

- FM-200 (very similar to Halon 1301) is safe in occupied areas.
- Inergen is a high-pressure agent composed of nitrogen, argon, and carbon dioxide.
- Carbon dioxide, although riskier than Halon, is an acceptable alternative.
- FE-13 (trifluromethane) is one of the newest and safest clean agents. It is similar to the most commonly used clean agents (Inergen and FM-200) and is safe for human exposure until concentrations reach 30%, and can therefore allow additional time for staff to make a safe exit from protected spaces. Unlike FM-200, FE-13 also can be installed with high ceiling nozzles and can be used in low-temperature situations.

A typical physical security plan requires that every building have clearly marked fire exits and maps posted throughout the facility. It is important to have drills to rehearse fire alarm responses and designate individuals to be in charge of escorting everyone from the location and ensuring that no one is left behind. It is also important to have fire suppression systems that are both manual and automatic, and that are inspected and tested regularly.

Failure of Supporting Utilities and Structural Collapse

Supporting utilities, such as heating, ventilation and air conditioning, power, water, and other utilities, have a significant impact on the continued safe operation of a facility. Extreme temperatures and humidity levels, electrical fluctuations and the interruption of water, sewage, and garbage services can create conditions that inject vulnerabilities in systems designed to protect information. Thus, each of these utilities must be properly managed in order to prevent potential damage to information and information systems.

Heating, Ventilation, and Air Conditioning

Although traditionally a facilities management responsibility, the operation of the heating, ventilation, and air conditioning (HVAC) system can have dramatic impact on information and information systems operations and protection. Specifically, the areas within the HVAC system that need to be adjusted to reduce risk to information-carrying systems are temperature, filtration, humidity, and static electricity.

Temperature and Filtration

Computer systems are electronic and as such are subject to damage from extreme temperature and particulate contamination. Temperatures as low as 100 degrees Fahrenheit can damage computer media, and at 175 degrees Fahrenheit, computer hardware can be damaged and destroyed. At the other end of the thermometer, when the temperature approaches 32 degrees Fahrenheit, media is susceptible to cracking, and computer components can actually freeze together. Rapid changes in temperature, from hot to cold or from cold to hot, can produce condensation, which can create short circuits or otherwise damage systems and components. The optimal temperature for a computing environment (and for people) is between 70 and 74 degrees Fahrenheit. Properly installed and maintained systems will keep the environment within the manufacturer-recommended temperature range and fully filter all particles from the air flow from the HVAC system. In the past, the degree of filtration perceived to be necessary for computing facilities was higher than it is today. Also, manufacturers of computing equipment have, over the years, designed computers to work in typical office environments better, and thus the need to provide extensive filtration for air conditioning is now limited to particularly sensitive environments such as chip fabrication and component assembly areas. In other words, filtration is no longer a significant factor for most commercial data processing facilities.

Humidity and Static Electricity

Humidity is the amount of moisture in the air. High humidity levels create condensation problems, and low humidity levels can increase the amount of static electricity in the environment. With condensation comes the short-circuiting of electrical equipment and the potential for mold and rot in paper-based information storage. **Static electricity** is caused by a process called **triboelectrification**, which occurs when two materials are rubbed or touched and electrons are exchanged, and results in one object becoming more positively charged and the other more negatively charged. When a third object with an opposite charge or ground is encountered, electrons flow again, and a spark is produced. One of the leading causes of damage to sensitive circuitry is **electrostatic discharge (ESD)**. Integrated circuits in a computer are designed to use between two and five volts of electricity, and any voltage level above this range introduces a risk of microchip damage. Static electricity is not even noticeable to humans until levels approach 1,500 volts, and the little blue spark can't be seen until the level approaches 4,000 volts. Moreover, a person can generate up to 12,000 volts of static current by merely walking across a carpet. Table 9-2 shows some static charge voltages and the damage they can cause to systems.

Table 9-2 Static Charge Damage in Computers [8]

Volts	Results
40	High probability of damage to sensitive circuits and transistors
1,000	Scrambles monitor display
1,500	Can cause disk drive data loss
2,000	High probability of system shutdown
4,000	May jam printers
17,000	Causes certain and permanent damage to almost all microcircuitry

In general, ESD damage to chips produces two types of failures. Immediate failures, also known as catastrophic failures, occur right away, are usually totally destructive, and require chip replacement. Latent failures or delayed failures can occur weeks or even months after the damage is done. The damage may not be noticeable, but the chip may suffer intermittent problems. (It has been observed, however, that with the overall poor quality of some of the current popular operating systems, this type of damage may be hard to notice.) As a result, it is imperative to maintain the optimal level of humidity, which is between 40% and 60%, in the computing environment. Humidity levels below this range create static, and levels above create condensation. Humidification or dehumidification systems can assist in the regulation of these conditions.

Ventilation Shafts

One last discussion point within the topic of HVAC is the security of the ventilation system air ductwork. While the ductwork in residential buildings is quite small, in large commercial buildings, it may be large enough for an individual to climb through. This is one of Hollywood's favorite methods for how villains or heroes should enter buildings. In practice, these ventilation shafts aren't quite as negotiable as Hollywood would have you believe. In fact, with moderate security precautions, these shafts can be completely eliminated as a security vulnerability. In most new buildings, the ducts to the individual rooms are no larger than 12 inches diameter and are flexible and insulated tubes. Note that the pressurized ducts are often found in the return-air plenum. The size and nature of the ducts precludes most people from using them, but access may be possible via the plenum. If the ducts are much larger, the security team can install wire mesh grids at various points to compartmentalize the runs. In any case, the ventilation system is one more area within the HVAC system that must be evaluated for security.

Power Management and Conditioning

Electrical power is another aspect of the organization's physical environment that is usually considered within the realm of physical security. As discussed in Chapter 2, not only is electrical quantity (the voltage level and the amperage rating) of concern, but the quality of the power (the frequency, noisiness and grounding) is of importance as well. The most critical factor for power systems used by information-processing equipment is that they be properly installed and correctly grounded. Interference with the normal pattern of the electrical current is also referred to as **noise** in the current. Computers may use the normal 60 Hertz cycle of the electricity in alternating current to synchronize their clocks. Any noise that interferes with this cycle can result in inaccurate time clocks or, even worse, unreliable internal clocks inside the CPU.

Grounding and Amperage

Grounding ensures that the returning flow of current is properly discharged to the ground. If the grounding elements of the electrical system are not properly installed, anyone touching a computer or other electrical device could act as a ground source, which would cause damage to equipment and injury or death to the person. Computing and other electrical equipment in areas where water can accumulate must be uniquely grounded, using ground fault circuit interruption (GFCI) equipment. GFCI is capable of quickly identifying and interrupting a ground fault, a situation in which an individual has come into contact with water and represents a better ground than the electrical circuit's current source.

Power should also be provided in sufficient amperage to support needed operations. Nothing is more frustrating than plugging in a series of computers, only to have the circuit breaker trip. Consult a qualified electrician when designing or remodeling computer rooms to make sure sufficiently high amperage circuits are available to provide the needed power. Overloading a circuit not only causes problems with the circuit tripping, but can also create a load on an electrical cable that is in excess of what the cable is rated to handle, and thus increase the risk of overheating and perhaps fire.

Uninterruptible Power Supply (UPS)

The primary power source for an organization's computing equipment is most often the electric utility that serves the area where the organization's buildings are located. This source of power can experience interruptions. Therefore, organizations should identify the computing systems that are vital to their operations (in other words, the systems that must continue to operate during interruptions) and make sure those systems are connected to a device that assures the delivery of electric power without interruption—that is, an **Uninterruptible Power Supply (UPS)**.

The capacity of UPS devices is measured using the volt-ampere (or VA) power output rating. UPS devices typically run up to 1,000 VA and can be engineered when needed to exceed 10,000 VA. A typical PC might use 200 VA, and a server in a computer room may need 2,000 to 5,000 VA, depending on how much running time is needed. Figure 9-5 shows a number of UPS types. Of those shown, this section describes the following basic configurations: the standby, ferroresonant standby, line-interactive, and true online (also known as double conversion online).

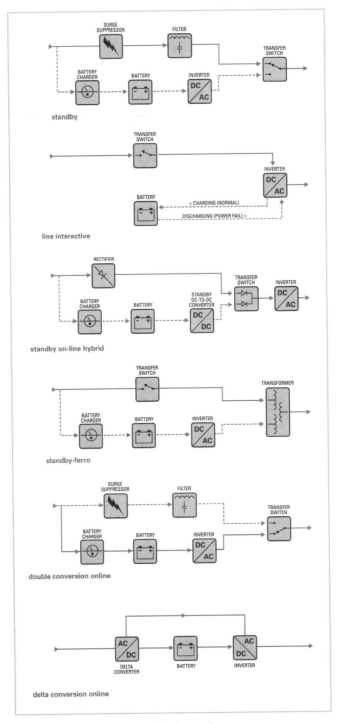

Courtesy of American Power Conversion Corporation

FIGURE 9-5 Types of Uninterruptible Power Supplies[9]

A **standby** or **offline UPS** is an offline battery backup that detects the interruption of power to the power equipment. When the power stops flowing to the equipment, the UPS activates a transfer switch that then provides power from batteries, through a DC to AC converter, until the power is restored or the computer is shut down. Because this type of UPS is not truly uninterruptible, it is often referred to as a standby power supply (SPS). The advantage of an SPS is that it is the most cost-effective type of UPS. However, the significant drawbacks, such as the limited run time and the amount of time it takes to switch from standby to active, may outweigh the cost savings. Switching time may also become an issue because very sensitive computing equipment may not be able to handle the delay in transfer once the power stops, and thus this equipment may reset and even suffer data loss or damage. SPS systems also provide no power conditioning, a feature of more sophisticated UPS (discussed below). As a result, an SPS is seldom used in critical computing applications and is best suited for home and light office use.

A **ferroresonant standby UPS** improves upon the standby UPS design. This UPS is still an offline UPS, with the electrical service still providing the primary source of power and the UPS serving as a battery backup. The primary difference is that a ferroresonant transformer replaces the UPS transfer switch. The transformer provides line filtering to the primary power source, reducing the effect of some power problems and reducing noise that may be present in the power as it is delivered. This transformer also stores energy in its coils, thereby providing a buffer to fill in the gap between the interruption of service and the activation of an alternate source of power (usually a battery backup). This greatly reduces the probability of system reset and data loss. Ferroresonant standby UPS systems are better suited to settings that require a large capacity of conditioned and reliable power, since they are available for uses up to 14,000 VA. With the improvement in other UPS designs, however, many manufacturers have abandoned this design in favor of other configurations.

The **line-interactive UPS** has a substantially different design than the previously mentioned UPS models. In the line-interactive UPS, the internal components of the standby models are replaced with a pair of inverters and converters. The primary power source, as in both the SPS and the ferroresonant UPS, remains the power utility company, with a battery serving as backup. However, the inverters and converters both charge the battery and provide power when needed. When utility power is interrupted, the converter begins supplying power to the systems. Because this device is always connected to the output as opposed to relying on a switch to become connected, this model has a much faster response time and also incorporates power conditioning and line filtering.

The **true online UPS** works in the opposite fashion to a standby UPS. In an online UPS, the primary power source is the battery, and the power feed from the utility is constantly recharging this battery. This model allows constant use of the system, while completely eliminating power fluctuation. True online UPS can deliver a constant, smooth, conditioned power stream to the computing systems. If the utility-provided power fails, the computer systems are unaffected, as long as the batteries hold out. The online UPS is considered the top-of-the-line option and as such is the most expensive. The only major drawback, other than cost, is that the process of constantly converting from the AC feed from the utility to the DC used by the battery storage and then converting back to AC for use by the systems creates high levels of heat. An improved model resolves this issue by incorporating a device known as a delta-conversion unit, which allows some of the incoming power to be fed directly to the destination computers, thus reducing the amount of energy wasted and heat generated. Should the power fail, the delta unit shuts off, and the batteries automatically compensate for the increased power draw.

Selecting the best UPS can be a lesson in electrical engineering, because you must calculate the load that the protected systems will require from the UPS. This can be quite complex and proves challenging in practice. Fortunately, many UPS vendors provide sample scenarios that aid in the selection of the optimal device. Because a high-quality UPS large enough for many applications may cost several thousand dollars, it is advisable to select the smallest UPS necessary to provide the desired effect. To calculate manually the rating needed in a UPS, you should begin by examining the computer systems and all connected support equipment to be protected. For example, the back panel of a monitor may indicate that the monitor is rated at 110 volts and 2 amps. Since volts times amps yields the power needs of a device, to calculate the power you need to run this device, you would multiply 110 by 2. This multiplication shows that the rating of the monitor is 220 VA. Now suppose the computer draws 3 amps at 110 volts, and therefore has a rating of 330 VA. Together the total is 550 VA. Once you have this information, you can then select a UPS capable of supporting this voltage level. Generally, UPS systems provide information on how long they would run at specific VA levels. Some smaller scale UPSs can run for approximately six minutes at 600 VA at full voltage. You should look for a UPS that provides enough time both for the computing equipment to ride out minor power fluctuations and for the user to shut down the computer safely if necessary.

Emergency Shutoff

One important aspect of power management in any environment is the need to be able to stop power immediately should the current represent a risk to human or machine safety. Most computer rooms and wiring closets are equipped with an emergency power shutoff, which is usually a large red button that is prominently placed to facilitate access, and has an accident-proof cover to prevent unintentional use. These devices are the last line of defense against personal injury and machine damage in the event of flooding or sprinkler activation. The last person out of the computer room hits the switch, preventing the water from short-circuiting the computers and destroying computers that are still energized. While it is never advisable to allow water to come into contact with a computer, there is a much higher probability of recovering the systems if they were not powered up when wet. At a minimum, hard drives and other sealed devices may be recoverable. In fact, some disaster recovery companies specialize in water damage recovery.

Water Problems

Another critical utility infrastructure element is water service. On the one hand, lack of water poses problems to systems, including the functionality of fire suppression systems, and the ability of water chillers to provide air-conditioning. On the other hand, a surplus of water, or water pressure, poses a real threat. Flooding, leaks, and the resulting presence of water in areas where it should not be is catastrophic to paper and electronic storage of information. Water damage can result in complete failure of computer systems and the structures that house them. It is therefore important to integrate water detection systems into the alarm systems that regulate overall facilities operations.

Structural Collapse

Unavoidable environmental factors or forces of nature can cause failures in the structures that house the organization. Structures are designed and constructed with specific load limits, and overloading these design limits, intentionally or unintentionally, inevitably results in structural failure. Personal injury and potential for loss of life are also high in these conditions. Scheduling periodic inspections by qualified civil engineers will enable managers to identify potentially dangerous structural conditions before the structure fails.

Maintenance of Facility Systems

Just as with any phase of the security process, the implementation of the physical security phase must be constantly documented, evaluated, and tested; also once the physical security of a facility is established, it must be diligently maintained. Ongoing maintenance of systems is required as part of the systems' operations. Documentation of the facilities configuration, operation, and function should be integrated into disaster recovery plans and standard operating procedures. Testing provides information necessary to improve the physical security in the facility and identifies weak points.

Interception of Data

The next major area of physical security is the physical interception of data. There are three methods of data interception: direct observation, interception of data transmission, and electromagnetic interception. The first method is *direct observation*, where an individual must be close enough to the information to breach confidentiality. The physical security mechanisms described in the previous sections restrict the possibility of an individual accessing unauthorized areas and therefore directly observing information. There is, however, a corresponding risk when the information is removed from a protected facility. If an employee is browsing documents over lunch in a restaurant or takes work home, the risk of direct observation rises substantially. If a competitor knows that an organization's employees frequently take classified information home, the competitor can more easily intercept vital information at the employee's home than at the office. Incidences of interception, such as shoulder surfing, can be avoided, if employees are either prohibited from removing sensitive information from the office or required to implement strong security at their homes.

The second method, *interception of data transmissions*, has become easier in the age of the Internet. If attackers can access the media carrying the transmission of data, they needn't be anywhere near the source of the information. In some cases, as with Internet usage, the attacker can use sniffer software, which has been described in previous chapters, to collect data. Other means of interception, such as tapping into a LAN, require some proximity to the organization's computers or networks. It is important for network administrators to conduct a physical inspection of all data ports periodically, to ensure that no unauthorized taps have occurred. If direct wiretaps are a concern, the organization should consider using fiber-optic cable, as the difficulty of splicing into this type of cable makes it much more resistant to tapping. If wireless LANs are used, the organization should be concerned about eavesdropping, since these LANs allow an attacker to snoop from a location that can, depending on the strength of the wireless access points (WAPs), be hundreds of feet outside the organization's building. Since wireless LANs are uniquely susceptible to eavesdropping, and current generation wireless sniffers are very potent tools, all wireless communications should be secured via encryption. Incidentally, it may interest you to know that the U.S. federal laws that deal with wiretapping do not cover wireless communications, except for commercial cellular phone calls, as courts have ruled that users have no expectation of privacy with radio-based communications media.

The third method of data interception, *electromagnetic interception*, sounds like it could be from a *Star Trek* episode. For decades, scientists have known that electricity moving through cables emits electromagnetic signals (EM). It is possible to eavesdrop on these signals, and therefore to determine the data carried on the cables without actually tapping into them. In 1985, scientists proved that computer monitors also emitted radio waves, and that the image on the screens could be reconstructed from these signals.[10] More recently, scientists have determined that certain devices with LED displays actually emit information encoded in the light that pulses in these LEDs.[11]

Whether devices that emit electromagnetic radiation (EMR) can actually be monitored in such a manner that the data being processed or displayed can be reconstructed is a matter that has been subject to debate (and rumor) for many years. James Atkinson, an electronics engineer certified by the National Security Agency (NSA), says that there is no such thing as practical monitoring of electronic emanations and claims that stories about such monitoring are just urban legends. He goes on to say that most modern computers are shielded to prevent interference with other household and office equipment—not to prevent eavesdropping. Atkinson does concede that receiving emanations from a computer monitor is theoretically possible, but notes that it would be an extremely difficult, expensive, and impractical undertaking.[12]

Legend or not, a good deal of money is being spent by the government and military to protect computers from electronic remote eavesdropping. In fact, the U.S. government has developed a program, named **TEMPEST**, to reduce the risk of EMR monitoring. (In keeping with the speculative fancy surrounding this topic, some believe that the acronym TEMPEST was originally a code word created by the U.S. government in the 1960s, but was later defined as Transient Electromagnetic Pulse Emanation Surveillance Technology or Telecommunications Electronics Material Protected from Emanating Spurious Transmissions.) In general, TEMPEST involves the following types of procedures: ensuring that computers are placed as far as possible from outside perimeters, installing special shielding inside the CPU case, and implementing a host of other restrictions, including maintaining distances from plumbing and other infrastructure components that carry radio waves. Additional information about this subject and the controls that have been developed can be found at *http://www.dss.mil/isec/chp11nis.htm*. Regardless of whether the threat from eavesdropping on electromagnetic emanations is real, many procedures that protect against emanations also protect against threats to physical security.

Mobile and Portable Systems

Although the physical security associated with mobile and portable computing systems substantially overlaps other security areas, these computers are important enough to warrant additional mention. With the increased threat to overall information security for laptops, handhelds, and PDAs, mobile computing requires even more security than the average in-house system. Most of these mobile computing systems have valuable corporate information stored within them, and some are configured to facilitate the user's access into the organization's secure computing facilities. Forms of access include VPN connections, dial-up configurations, and databases of passwords. In addition, many users keep the locations of files and clues about the storage of information in their portable computers. Many users like the convenience of allowing the underlying operating systems to remember their usernames and passwords because it simplifies their ability to access information and because they frequently have multiple accounts, with different usernames and passwords, to manage. While it is tempting to allow operating systems to assist in the accessing of frequently needed accounts, the downside of setting up these arrangements on a portable system is obvious: loss of the system means loss of the access control mechanisms.

A relatively new technology to support the location of lost or stolen laptops can provide additional security. One type of this technology is CompuTrace, computer software that is stored on a laptop's hardware, as illustrated in Figure 9-6. Periodically, when the computer is on the Internet, the software reports itself and the electronic serial number of the computer on which it is installed to a central monitoring center. If the laptop is reported to have been stolen, this software can trace the computer to its current location for possible recovery. The software is so versatile that it is undetectable on the system, even if the thief knows the software is installed. Moreover, CompuTrace remains installed even if the laptop's hard drive is formatted and the operating system is reinstalled.

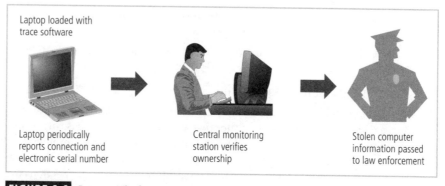

Laptop loaded with trace software

Laptop periodically reports connection and electronic serial number

Central monitoring station verifies ownership

Stolen computer information passed to law enforcement

FIGURE 9-6 Laptop Theft Deterrence

Also available for laptops are burglar alarms made up of a PC card or other device that contains a motion detector. If the device is armed, and the laptop is moved more than expected, the alarm triggers a very loud buzzer or horn. The security system may also disable the computer or use an encryption option to render the information stored in the system unusable.

For maximum security, laptops should be secured at all times. If you are traveling with a laptop, you should have it in your possession at all times. Special care should be exercised when flying, as laptop thefts are common in airports. The list below comes from the Metropolitan Police of the District of Columbia and outlines steps you can take to prevent your laptop from being stolen or carelessly damaged:

- Don't leave a laptop in an unlocked vehicle, even if the vehicle is in your driveway or garage, and never leave it in plain sight, even if the vehicle is locked—that's just inviting trouble. If you must leave your laptop in a vehicle, the best place is in a locked trunk. If you don't have a trunk, cover it up and lock the doors.
- Parking garages are likely areas for thefts from vehicles, as they provide numerous choices and cover for thieves. Again, never leave your laptop in plain sight; cover it or put it in the trunk.
- Do be aware of the damage extreme temperatures can cause to computers.
- Carry your laptop in a nondescript carrying case, briefcase, or bag when moving about. Placing it in a case designed for computers is an immediate alert to thieves that you have a laptop.
- Going to lunch, or taking a break? Don't leave a meeting or conference room without your laptop. Take it with you, or you run the risk that it won't be there when you return.
- Lock the laptop in your office during off-hours. Don't have your own office? Use a cable lock that wraps around a desk or chair leg. Or put the laptop in a locked closet or cabinet.
- Don't let unaccompanied strangers wander around in your workplace. Offer assistance and deliver the visitors to their destinations.
- Apply distinctive paint markings to make your laptop unique and easily identifiable. Liquid white-out is a good substance to apply.
- Consider purchasing one of the new theft alarm systems specially made for laptops.
- Be aware that if your computer is stolen, automatic logins can make it easy for a thief to send inappropriate messages with your account.
- Back up your information on disks today, and store the disks at home or the office.[13]

Remote Computing Security

Remote site computing is rapidly growing in popularity. Remote site computing involves a wide variety of computing sites that are distant from the base organizational facility and includes the entire spectrum of telecommuters (or telecomputers). **Telecommuting** involves computing that uses telecommunications facilities that encompass connections over the Internet, connections using dial-up connections, connections over leased point-to-point links between offices, and other connection mechanisms used by employees while traveling.

Individuals telecommuting from home deserve special attention. One of the appeals of telecommuting for both the employee and employer is that by avoiding traffic congestion, hazards of travel, expensive parking, and long commutes, telecommuting employees have more time to focus on the actual work they do rather than on the distractions related to work. But as more individuals consider telecommuting, the risk to organizational information traveling through the often unsecured connections that telecommuters use is substantial. The problem is that not enough organizations provide their employees with secure connections to their office networks, and even fewer provide secure systems, should the employee's home computer be compromised. To provide a secure extension of the organization's internal networks, all external connections must be secured. To secure the entire network, the organization must dedicate security resources to protecting these home connections. Although the installation of a VPN may go a long way toward protecting the data in transmission, telecommuters frequently store office data on their home systems, in home filing cabinets, and on off-site media. To assure a secure process, the computers that telecommuters use to access the network must be made *more* secure than the organization's systems, as they are outside the security perimeter. An attacker breaking into someone's home would probably find a much lower level of security than if the same attacker were to access an office system. Most office systems require users to log in, but the telecommuter's home computer is probably the employee's personal machine, and thus is likely to have a much less secure operating system and may not use a password. Telecommuters must use a securable operating system that requires password authentication, such as Windows NT/2000/XP. They must store all loose data in locking filing cabinets and loose media in locking fire safes. They must treat the home office more carefully than they would the on-site office, as the general level of security for the average home is lower than that of a commercial building.

The same goes for the mobile computer and the off-site office worker. Employees using notebooks in hotel rooms should presume that their unencrypted transmissions are being monitored, and that any unsecured notebook computer can be stolen. The off-site worker using leased facilities does not know who else is physically attached to the network and therefore who else might be listening to his or her data conversations. VPNs are a must in all off-site to on-site communications, and the use of associated advanced authentication systems is strongly recommended.

Although it is possible to secure remote sites, organizations cannot assume that employees will invest their own funds for security. Many organizations barely tolerate telecommuting for a number of reasons, including the expectation that the employee must be issued two sets of computing equipment, one for the office and one for the home. This extra expense is difficult to justify, especially when the employee is the only one gaining the benefit from telecommuting. In those rare cases in which allowing an employee or consultant to telecommute is the only way to gain extremely valuable skills, the organization is usually willing to do what is necessary to secure its systems. Only when additional research into telecommuting clearly displays a financial bottom-line advantage to telecommuting do organizations begin to invest sufficient resources into securing the equipment of their telecommuters. As a caveat, there are several quality organizations that openly embrace and support telecommuting. These organizations are typically one of three groups. The first is the mature and therefore fiscally sound organization with a sufficient budget to support telecommuting and the need to enhance its standing with employees and to improve its organizational image. In recent years, the availability of telecommuting has become a factor in the ranking contests undertaken by various magazines. Some organizations seek to improve employee work conditions and also gain a higher level in the best-places-to-work ranking by adding telecommuting as an option for employees. The second group is the new high-technology company, with a large number of geographically diverse employees who telecommute almost exclusively. These companies use technology extensively and are determined to make the adoption of technology and its use the cornerstone of their organizations. The third group overlaps with the second and is referred to as the virtual organization. A virtual organization is a group of individuals brought together for a specific task, usually from different organizations, divisions, or departments. These individuals form a virtual company, either in leased facilities or through 100% telecommuting arrangements. When the job is done, the organization is either redirected or dissolved. These organizations rely almost exclusively on remote computing and telecommuting to function, but they are extremely rare and therefore not well documented or studied.

Special Considerations for Physical Security Threats

Now that the field of physical security has been introduced, there are a number of special considerations for physical security threats that should be examined. The first of these is the decision to develop physical security in-house or to outsource it. As with any aspect of information security, the make-or-buy decision should not be made lightly. There are a number of qualified and professional agencies that provide consulting and services in the area of physical security. The benefits of outsourcing physical security include gaining the experience and knowledge of these agencies, many of which have been in the field for decades. Outsourcing unfamiliar operations always frees an organization to focus on its primary objectives, rather than being distracted by support operations. The downside includes high expense, the loss of control over the individual components of the physical security solution, and need to trust another company to perform an essential business function. An organization must not only trust the processes used by the contracted company but also its ability to hire and retain trustworthy employees who respect the privacy of the hiring organization even though they have no allegiance to it. This level of trust is often the most difficult aspect of the decision to outsource, because the reality of outsourcing physical security is that *nonemployees* will be providing a safeguard that the organization administers only marginally.

Another consideration that is related to physical security deals with social engineering. As discussed in previous chapters, social engineering involves using people skills to obtain information from employees that should not be released. While most social engineers prefer to use the telephone and computer to make their contacts and solicit information, there are those who attempt to access the information more directly. As the previously mentioned cases in which technically proficient agents are placed into janitorial positions at a competitor's office prove, there are a number of ways an outsider can gain access to an organization's resources. Most organizations do not, for example, have very thorough procedures for authenticating and controlling nonemployees who access their facility. When there is no procedure in place, no one gives the wandering repairman, service worker, or city official a second look. It is not difficult to dress like a telephone repairman, construction worker, or building inspector and move freely throughout a building. Some might even say that to go almost anywhere in any building, all one really needs is a clipboard and an attitude. If you look as if you have a mission and appear competent, most people will leave you alone. How can organizations combat this type of attack? By requiring that all individuals entering the facility display appropriate visitor badges and be escorted appropriately when they are in restricted areas.

Inventory Management

Like other organizational resources, computing equipment should be inventoried and inspected on a regular basis. The management of a computer inventory is an important part of physical security. How else would corporate security know if an employee has been pilfering computer supplies or took organizational equipment home when he or she quit? Similarly, classified information should also be inventoried and managed. In the military, whenever a classified document needs to be reproduced, a stamp is placed on the original before it is copied. This stamp states the document's classification level and the text imprint "___ of ___" so that the person making the copies can mark the sequence number for each copy as well as the total number of copies being made. If, for example, 25 copies are to be made, the person responsible for copying the document writes 26 in the right blank, makes copies, and then numbers them. Why 26 and not 25? The original is always document number 1. After the numbering, each classified copy is issued to the assigned person, who signs for the document. While this procedure may be overkill for most organizations, it does ensure that the inventory management of classified documents is secure at all times. Also, the formality of having to sign for a document cements its worth in the mind of the receiver.

The physical security of computing equipment, data storage media, and classified documents will vary for each organization. The common feature of all such control systems is the balance that must be achieved between the need for control and the costs (both economic and productivity-related) that are associated with the implementation of the control.

Chapter Summary

- Physical security addresses the design, implementation, and maintenance of countermeasures that protect the physical resources of an organization.

- Many threats to information security can also be classified as threats to physical security. An organization's policy should guide the planning of physical security in the development life cycle and serve as a reference to organizational objectives through the ongoing maintenance and use phases.

- In the context of facilities management, a secure facility is a physical location that has been engineered with controls designed to minimize the risk of attacks from physical threats. A secure facility can use the natural terrain, traffic flow, and urban development, and can complement them with protection mechanisms, such as fences, gates, walls, guards, and alarms, to protect information resources and people effectively.

- A part of general management's responsibility for the physical environment, the management of keys and locks is a fundamental concern.

- A fail-safe lock is usually used on an exit door where human safety in the event of, for example, a fire is the essential consideration. A fail-secure lock is used when human safety is not a factor.

- Monitoring equipment can record events that guards and dogs might miss and can be used in areas where other types of physical controls are not practical.

- Just as with any phase of the security process, the implementation of the physical security phase must be constantly documented, evaluated, and tested; also once the physical security of a facility is established, it must be diligently maintained.

- Fire detection systems are devices that detect and respond to a fire or potential fire. Fire suppression systems stop the progress of a fire once it's activated.

- There are three basic types of fire detection systems: thermal detection, smoke detection, and flame detection.

- There are four environmental variables controlled by HVAC systems that can cause damage to information-carrying systems: temperature, filtration, humidity, and static electricity.

- Computer systems depend on specific power needs to function; when power levels are too high, too low, or too erratic, computer circuitry can be damaged or destroyed. The power provided to computing and networking equipment should contain no unwanted fluctuations, and should have no embedded signaling.

- Water problems and the weakening and subsequent failure of a building's physical structure clearly represent potential threats to the integrity and availability of information assets.

- Data can be intercepted electronically and manually. There are three routes of data interception: direct observation, interception of data transmission, and interception of electromagnetic radiation.

- TEMPEST is a technology that prevents the loss of data that may result from the emissions of electromagnetic radiation (EMR).

- With the increased threat to overall information security for laptops, handhelds, and PDAs, organizations should be aware that mobile computing requires even more security than the average in-house system.

- Remote site computing should require a secure extension of the organization's internal networks and special attention to security for any connected home or off-site computing technology.

- Like computing equipment, classified information should also be inventoried and managed. If multiple copies of a classified document are made, they should be numbered and tracked.

Review Questions

1. What is physical security? What are the primary threats to physical security? How are they manifested in attacks against the organization?

2. How do the roles of IT, security, and general management differ with regard to physical security?

3. How does physical access control differ from logical access control as described in earlier chapters? How is it similar?

4. Define a secure facility. What is the primary objective of designing such a facility? What are some of the secondary objectives you might strive to achieve in designing a secure facility?

5. Why are guards considered the most effective form of control for situations that require decisive action in the face of unfamiliar stimuli? Why are they usually the most expensive controls to deploy? When should dogs be used for physical security?

6. List and describe the four categories of locks. In which situation is each type of lock preferred?

7. What are the two possible modes that locks use when they fail? What implications does this have for human safety? In which situation is each mode preferred?

8. What is a mantrap? When should it be used?

9. What is the most common form of alarm? What does it detect? What types of sensors are commonly used in this type of alarm system?

10. Describe a physical firewall that is used in buildings. List the reasons you can think of for why an organization might need a firewall for physical security controls.

11. What is considered the most serious threat within the realm of physical security? Why is it valid to consider this threat the most serious?

12. What are the three requirements for a fire to start and continue to burn? How do fire suppression systems manipulate the three requirements to interrupt fires?

13. List and describe the three fire detection technologies covered in the chapter. Which is the most commonly used in the world today?

14. List and describe the four classes of fire described in the text. Does the class of a fire dictate how to control the fire?

15. What is the problem with Halon?

16. What does HVAC stand for? Why is this a topic of concern for physical security? What four physical characteristics of the indoor environment are controlled by a properly designed HVAC system? What are the optimal temperature and humidity ranges for computing systems?

17. List and describe the four primary types of UPS systems. Which is the most effective and the most expensive, and why?

18. What two critical factors are impacted when water is not available in a facility? Why are these factors important to the operation of the organization's information assets?

19. List and describe the three fundamental ways that data can be intercepted. Why is data interception considered to be a part of physical security? How can you protect against each of the data interception methods?

20. What can you do to reduce the risk of laptop theft?

Exercises

1. Assume that your organization is planning to have a server room that functions without human beings—in other words, the functions of the room are automated (such a room is often called a lights-out server room). Describe the fire control system(s) you would include in that room.

2. Assume that you have converted part of an area of general office space into a server room. Describe the factors you would consider for each of the following areas of concern:
   a. Walls and doors
   b. Physical access control
   c. Fire detection
   d. Fire suppression
   e. Heating, ventilating, and air conditioning
   f. Power quality and distribution

3. Assume that you have been asked to review the power needs for a stand-alone computer system. It processes important but noncritical data and does not have to be online at all times. It does, however, store valuable data that could be corrupted if the power to the system were suddenly cut off. As you consider the needs of this system, which UPS features should concern you? Which type of UPS approach would you recommend for this situation?

4. Using the floor plan of a building you are familiar with, design an electronic monitoring plan that includes closed-circuit television, burglar alarms with appropriate sensors, fire detectors, and fire suppression and physical access controls for key entrances.

5. Define the required wattage for a UPS for the following systems:

    a. Monitor: 2 amps; CPU: 3 amps; printer: 3 amps

    b. Monitor: 3 amps; CPU: 4 amps; printer: 3 amps

    c. Monitor: 3 amps; CPU: 4 amps; printer: 4 amps

    Search the Web for a UPS that provides the wattage necessary to run the systems listed above for at least 15 minutes during a power outage.

Case Exercises

Amy walked into her office cubicle and sat down. The entire episode with the blond man had taken her over two hours. Plus, the police officers had told her the district attorney would also be calling to make an appointment to speak to her, which meant she would have to spend even more time dealing with this incident. She hoped her manager would understand.

Questions:

1. What security awareness and training documents and posters seem to have an impact in this event?

2. Do you think Amy should have done anything differently? What?

Endnotes

1. Donn B. Parker. *Fighting Computer Crime.* (New York: John Wiley and Sons Inc., 1998), 250–251.

2. Military-net.com. "General Military Knowledge." *Military-net.com Online.* [Cited 10 July 2002]. Available from the World Wide Web <*http://www.military-net.com/education/mpdgeneral.html*>.

3. Army Study Guide.com. Online [Cited 23 September 2002]. Available from the World Wide Web <*http://armystudyguide.com/guard_duty/studyguide.htm*>.

4. Marianne Swanson. *Guide for Developing Security Plans for Information Technology Systems (December 1998).* National Institute of Standards and Technology SP 800-18, 30 [Cited 10 July 2002]. Available from the World Wide Web <*http://csrc.nist.gov/publications/nistpubs/800-18/Planguide.PDF*>.

5. Nick Artim. *An Introduction to Fire Detection, Alarm, and Automatic Fire Sprinklers.* Emergency Management, Technical Leaflet 2, sec. 3. Middlebury: Fire Safety Network).

6. Environmental Protection Agency. "Halon Substitutes Under SNAP as of 26 April 2000." *EPA Online* [Cited 10 July 2002]. Available from the World Wide Web <*http://www.epa.gov/ozone/snap/fire/halo.pdf*>.

7. Environmental Protection Agency. "Halon Substitutes Under SNAP as of 26 April 2000." *EPA Online* [Cited 10 July 2002]. Available from the World Wide Web <*http://www.epa.gov/ozone/snap/fire/halo.pdf*>.

8. Webopedia. "Static Electricity and Computers." *Webopedia Online* (March 2002). [Cited 10 July 2002]. Available from the World Wide Web <*http://www.webopedia.com/DidYouKnow/Computer_Science/2002/static.html*>.

9. Charles M. Kozierok. "Uninterruptible Power Supply Types." *PC Guide Online.* (17 April 2001) [Cited 10 July 2002]. Available from the World Wide Web <*http://www.pcguide.com/ref/power/ext/ups/types.htm*>.

10. Wim Van Eck. "Electromagnetic Radiation from Video Display Units: An Eavesdropping Risk?" *Computers & Security* 4 (1985): 269–286.

11. Joe Loughry and David A. Umphress. "Information Leakage from Optical Emanations." *ACM Transactions on Information and System Security* 7, no. 7, accepted March 2002.

12. PC Privacy. "Is Tempest a Threat or Hoax?" *PC Privacy* 8, no. 4 (April 2000).

13. Metropolitan Police of the District of Columbia. "Tips for Preventing Laptop Computer Theft." *Government of The District of Columbia Online* [Cited 10 July 2002]. Available from the World Wide Web <*http://mpdc.dc.gov/info/consumer/laptop_theft.shtm*>.

Implementing Information Security

> Change is good. You go first!
>
> **DILBERT (BY SCOTT ADAMS)**

KELVIN URICH ARRIVED EARLY FOR the change control meeting. Sitting in the large conference room, he reviewed his notes and then flipped through the handouts one final time. After the meeting last week, during which the technical review committee members had approved his ideas, he was confident that the project plan he'd come up with was tight and well-ordered.

He knew that the series of change requests this project would generate would keep the technical analysts in the company busy for months to come, but he hoped the scope and scale of the project, and the vast improvements it was sure to bring to the SLS information security program, would inspire his colleagues. To make sure the project would proceed smoothly, he had loaded his handouts with columns of tasks, subtasks, and action items, and had assigned dates to every action step. He had also already assigned which people would implement each required task. He checked that that handouts were stapled properly, and that he had plenty of copies. Everything was under control, he thought with relief.

Naomi Jackson, the change control supervisor, also arrived a few minutes early. She saw Kelvin and gave him a nod as she placed a stack of revised agendas in the middle of the conference table. Everyone attending had received the detailed report of planned changes the previous day. Charlie Moody came in, also nodding to Kelvin, and took his usual seat.

Once the room filled, Naomi said, "Time to get started." She picked up her copy of the planned change report and announced the first change control item for discussion, Item 742.

One of the members of the UNIX support team responded, "As planned." This short statement meant to all of the regular attendees that this item was a routine maintenance check that was going to happen in the upcoming planned maintenance window—that is, next Sunday afternoon.

Since no one else said anything, Naomi continued down the list in numeric order. Most items received the response "As planned" from the sponsoring team member. Once in a while, someone answered "Cancelled" or "Will be rescheduled," but for the most part, the review of the change items proceeded as usual until they came to Kelvin's group of change requests for information security.

Naomi said, "Items 761 through 767. Kelvin Urich from the security team is here to discuss these items all at once with the change control group."

Kelvin started by sending his handouts around the table. He waited, a little nervously, until everyone had a copy, and then began speaking: "I'm sure most of you are already aware of the information security upgrades we have been working on for the past few months. We've created an overall strategy based on the revised policies that were published last year and a detailed analysis of the threats we face with the systems we have. Since becoming project manager, I have created what I think is a very workable plan. First, the seven change requests on the list today are all network changes and are all top priority. I have more changes planned for coming weeks, and I will be sending each department head a complete list of all planned changes and the expected dates. Of course, detailed change requests will be filed in advance for these change control meetings, but each department can know when it is coming up by checking the master list. As I said, there are more changes coming, and I hope we can all work together to make this a success." He looked at Naomi to indicate he was finished.

"Uh, comments or questions?" asked Naomi.

Instantly six hands shot into the air. All of them belonged to senior technical analysts. Kelvin realized belatedly that none of these analysts were on the technical review committee that had approved his plan last week. He also noticed that half the people in the room, like Amy Windahl from the user group and training committee, were busy pulling calendars and PDAs out of briefcases and bags, and that Davey Martinez from Accounting was engaged in a private but heated discussion with Charlie Moody, Kelvin's boss—and that Charlie did not look pleased.

Above the noise, Kelvin heard someone ask, "Who does he think he is to dump this much work on us all at once?" Someone else was heard to say, "This isn't going to happen on this schedule."

In the midst of the sudden state of chaos that had broken out during an otherwise orderly meeting, it occurred to Kelvin that his plan might not be as simple as he'd thought. He braced himself—it was going to be a very long afternoon.

LEARNING OBJECTIVES:

Upon completion of this material, you should be able to:

- Understand how an organization's information security blueprint becomes a project plan
- Understand the numerous organizational considerations that must be addressed by a project plan
- Appreciate the significance of the project manager's role in the success of an information security project
- Understand the need for professional project management for complex projects
- Follow technical strategies and models for implementing the project plan
- Identify the nontechnical problems that organizations face in times of rapid change

Introduction

Kelvin got off to a bad start with some of his coworkers. As the project manager, he should have considered a number of issues when developing his draft of the project plan. At the very least, he should have realized that implementing an information security project takes time, effort, and a great amount of communication and coordination within an organization. This chapter and the next discuss the two stages of the SecSDLC implementation phase and describe how the information security blueprint can be executed successfully. In general, the implementation phase is accomplished by changing the configuration and operation of the organization's information systems to make them more secure. It includes changes to:

- Procedures (for example, through policy)
- People (for example, through training)
- Hardware (for example, through firewalls)
- Software (for example, through encryption)
- Data (for example, through classification)

As you may recall from earlier chapters, the security systems development life cycle (SecSDLC) is a process for collecting information about an organization's objectives, its technical architecture, and its information security environment. These elements form the information security blueprint, from which the protection of the confidentiality, integrity, and availability of the organization's information is built. Regardless of whether this information is in storage, being transmitted, or being processed, it is to be secured through the application of controls that include policy, education and training, and technology.

During the implementation phase, the organization translates its blueprint for information security into a concrete **project plan**. The project plan delivers instructions to the individuals who are executing the implementation phase. These instructions focus on the security control changes that are needed to improve the security of the hardware, software, procedures, data, and people that make up the organization's information systems. The project plan as a whole must describe how to acquire and implement the needed security controls and create a setting in which those controls achieve the desired outcomes.

Before a project plan can be developed, however, management should articulate and coordinate the organization's information security vision and objectives with the communities of interest involved in the execution of the plan. This type of coordination ensures that only the controls that add value to the organization's information security program are incorporated into the project plan. If a statement of the vision and objectives for the organization's security program does not already exist, one must be developed and incorporated into the project plan. The vision statement should be concise. It should state the mission of the information security program and its objectives. In other words, the project plan is built upon the vision statement, which serves as a compass for guiding the changes necessary for the implementation phase. The components of the project plan should never conflict with the organization's statement of vision and objectives.

Project Management for Information Security

Once the organization's vision and objectives are documented and understood, the processes for translating the blueprint into a project plan can be defined. As the opening vignette of this chapter illustrates, organizational change is not easily accomplished. The following sections discuss the issues a project plan must address, including project leadership; managerial, technical, and budgetary considerations; and organizational resistance to the change.

The major steps in executing the project plan are:

- Planning the project
- Supervising tasks and action steps
- Wrapping up

The project plan can be developed in any number of ways. Each organization has to determine its own project management methodology for IT and information security projects. Whenever possible, information security projects should follow the organization's project management practices. If your organization does not have clearly defined project management practices, you can apply the following general guidelines on project management, the details of which are presented in the upcoming sections:

- Developing the Project Plan
- Project Planning Considerations
- Scope Considerations
- The Need for Project Management

Developing the Project Plan

Planning for the implementation phase involves the creation of a detailed project plan. The task of creating a project plan to implement the information security blueprint is often assigned to either a project manager or the project champion. This individual manages the project and delegates parts of it to other decision makers. Often the project manager is an individual from the IT community of interest, because most other employees lack the information security background and the appropriate management authority and/or technical knowledge within the organization to accomplish the goals of an information security project.

The creation of the project plan itself can be accomplished using a simple planning tool, such as the **work breakdown structure (WBS)**, an example of which is shown later in Tables 10-1 and 10-2. With a WBS approach, the project plan is first broken down into several major tasks. Each of these major project tasks (along with their necessary attributes) are placed into the WBS:

- Work to be accomplished (activities and deliverables)
- Individuals (or skill set) assigned to perform the task
- Start and end dates for the task (when known)
- Amount of effort required for completion in hours or work days
- Estimated capital expenses for the task
- Estimated noncapital expenses for the task
- Identification of dependencies between and among tasks

Each major task on the WBS is then further divided into either smaller tasks (subtasks) or specific action steps. For the sake of simplicity, the sample project plan to be described in this chapter (and summarized in Tables 10-1 and 10-2) divides each major task only into action steps. Be aware that in an actual project plan, major tasks are often much more complex and must be divided into subtasks before action steps can be determined and assigned to the individual or skill set. Given the variety of projects possible, there are few formal guidelines for deciding which level of detail—that is, at which level a task or subtask should become an action step—is appropriate for a given project. There is, however, one hard-and-fast rule you can use to make this determination: a task or subtask becomes an action step when it can be completed by one individual or skill set and when it includes a single deliverable.

The WBS can be prepared with a simple desktop PC spreadsheet program. More complex project management software tools may be used, but their use—you should be warned—often leads to a common pitfall of project management known as projectitis. **Projectitis** is a phenomenon in which the project manager spends more time documenting project tasks, collecting performance measurements, recording project task information, and updating project completion forecasts than in accomplishing meaningful project work. Recall Kelvin's handouts from the opening vignette, which were loaded with dates and details. Kelvin fell into the trap of projectitis by developing an elegant, detailed plan before gaining consensus for the changes that it required. As he is new, Kelvin did not realize that using simple software tools helps the project manager focus on organizing and coordinating with the individuals assigned to the project team.

Work to Be Accomplished

The first step in the WBS approach is to identify the work to be accomplished. This encompasses both activities and deliverables. A **deliverable** is a completed document or program module that can either serve as the beginning point for a later task or become an element in the finished project. Ideally, the project planner provides a label for the task followed by a thorough description. The description should be complete enough to avoid ambiguity during the later tracking process, yet not so detailed as to make the WBS unwieldy. For instance, if the task is to write firewall specifications for the preparation of a request for proposal (RFP), the planner would note that the deliverable is a specification document suitable for distribution to vendors.

Assignees

The project planner should describe the skill set or type of individual person, often called a **resource**, needed to accomplish the task. But the actual naming of individuals should be avoided in the early planning efforts, a rule Kelvin ignored when he named individuals for every task in the first draft of his project plan. Instead of assigning individuals, the project plan should focus on roles or known skill sets as they are used in the organization. For example, if any of the engineers in the networks group can write the specifications for a router, the assigned resource would be noted as "network engineer" on the WBS. As planning progresses, however, the specific tasks and action steps can and should be assigned to individuals. For example, when *only* the manager of the networks group can evaluate the responses to the RFP and make an award for a contract, the project planner should identify the network manager as the resource assigned to this task.

Start and End Dates

In the early stages of planning, the project planner should focus on determining only completion dates for major milestones within the project. A **milestone** is a specific point in the project plan when a task (and its action steps) that has a noticeable impact on the progress of the project plan as a whole is complete. For example, the date for sending the final RFP to vendors is considered a milestone, because it signals that all RFP preparation work is complete. Assigning too many dates to too many tasks early in the planning process causes projectitis to increase. This is another mistake Kelvin made in his meeting, and a significant cause of the resistance he faced from his coworkers. Planners can avoid this pitfall by assigning only key or milestone start and end dates early in the process. Later in the planning process, planners may add additional start and end dates as needed.

Amount of Effort

Planners need to estimate the effort required to complete each task, subtask, or action step. Estimating effort hours for technical work is a complex process. Even when an organization has formal governance, technical review processes, and change control procedures, it is always good practice to ask the individuals who are most familiar with the work or familiar with similar types of work to make these estimates. After these estimates are made, all individuals assigned to action steps should review the estimated effort hours, understand the tasks, and agree with the estimates. Had Kelvin collaborated with his peers more effectively and adopted a more flexible planning approach, much of the resistance he encountered in the meeting would not have emerged.

Estimated Capital Expenses

Planners need to estimate the expected capital expenses for the completion of each task, subtask, or action item. While each organization budgets and expends capital according to its own established procedures, most differentiate between capital outlays for durable assets and expenses for other purposes. Be sure to determine the practices in place at the organization where the plan is to be used. For example, a firewall device costing $5,000 may be a capital outlay for a given organization, but the same organization might not consider a $5,000 software package to be a capital outlay because it may have accounting rules that classify all software as expense items, regardless of cost.

Estimated Noncapital Expenses

Planners need to estimate the expected noncapital expenses for the completion of each task, subtask, or action item. Some organizations require that this cost include a recovery charge for staff time, while others exclude employee time and only plan contract or consulting time as a noncapital expense. Organizations follow their own established procedures in classifying different kinds of expenses as being capital or noncapital. As mentioned earlier, it is important to determine the practices in place at the organization where the plan is to be used. For example, at some companies a project to implement a firewall may charge only the costs of the firewall hardware as capital and consider all costs for labor and software as expense, with the idea that the hardware element is a durable good that has a life that will span many years. Another organization might use the aggregate of all cash outflows associated with the implementation as the capital charge and make no charges to the expense category. The justification behind using this aggregate, which might include charges for items like hardware, labor, and freight, is that the usefulness of the newly implemented capability is expected to last for many years and is considered an improvement to the organization's infrastructure. At the other extreme, a third company may charge the whole project as expense if the aggregate amount falls below a certain threshold, under the theory that small projects are considered to be a cost of ongoing operations.

Task Dependencies

Planners should note wherever possible the dependencies of other tasks or action steps on the task or action step at hand. The tasks or action steps that come before the specific task at hand are called **predecessors**. Tasks or action steps that come after the task at hand are called **successors**. There can, however, be more than one type of dependency, but such details are typically covered in courses on project management and are beyond the scope of this text.

An example project plan is provided below to help you better understand the process of creating one. In this example, a small information security project has been assigned to Jane Smith for planning. The project is to design and implement a firewall for a single small office. The hardware is a standard organizational product and will be installed at a location that already has a network connection.

Jane's first step is to list the major tasks:

1. Contact field office and confirm network assumptions.
2. Purchase standard firewall hardware.
3. Configure firewall.
4. Package and ship firewall to field office.
5. Work with local technical resource to install and test.
6. Coordinate vulnerability assessment by penetration test team.
7. Get remote office sign-off and update all network drawings and documentation.

The first draft of Jane's WBS-based project plan is shown in Table 10-1.

Table 10-1   Example Project Plan Work Breakdown Structure – Early Draft

	Task or subtask	Resources	Start and end dates	Estimated effort in hours	Estimated capital expense	Estimated non-capital expense	Dependencies
1	Contact field office and confirm network assumptions	Network architect	S:9/22 E:	2	0	200	
2	Purchase standard firewall hardware	Network architect and purchasing group	S: E:	4	4,500	250	1
3	Configure firewall	Network architect	S: E:	8	0	800	2
4	Package and ship to field office	Student intern	S: E:10/15	2	0	85	3
5	Work with local technical resource to install and test	Network architect	S: E:	6	0	600	4
6	Complete vulnerability assessment by penetration test team	Network architect and penetration test team	S: E:	12	0	1,200	5
7	Get remote office sign-off and update all network drawings and documentation	Network architect	S: E:11/ 30	8	0	800	6

After all the individuals involved reviewed and refined Jane's plan, she revised it to add more dates to the tasks listed. This more detailed version is shown in Table 10-2. Note that this version of the project plan has been further developed and illustrates the breakdown of tasks 2 and 6 into action steps.

Table 10-2   Example Project Plan Work Breakdown Structure – Later Draft

	Task or SubTask	Resources	Start and End Dates	Estimated Effort in Hours	Estimated Capital Expense	Estimated Non-capital Expense	Dependencies
1	Contact field office and confirm network assumptions	Network architect	S:9/22 E:9/22	2	0	200	
2	Purchase standard firewall hardware						
2.1	Order firewall through purchasing group	Network architect	S:9/23 E:9/23	1		100	1
2.2	Order firewall from manufacturer	Purchasing group	S:9/24 E:9/24	2	4,500	100	2.1
2.3	Firewall delivered	Purchasing group	E:10/3	1		50	2.2
3	Configure firewall	Network architect	S:10/3 E:10/5	8	0	800	2.3
4	Package and ship to field office	Student intern	S:10/6 E:10/15	2	0	85	3
5	Work with local technical resource to install and test	Network architect	S:10/22 E:10/31	6	0	600	4
6	Penetration test						
6.1	Request Penetration test	Network architect	S:11/1 E:11/1	1	0	100	5
6.2	Perform Penetration test	Penetration test team	S:11/2 E:11/12	9	0	900	6.1
6.3	Verify that results of penetration test were passing	Network architect	S:11/13 E:11/15	2	0	200	6.2
7	Get remote office sign-off and update all network drawings and documentation	Network architect	S:11/16 E:11/30	8	0	800	6.2

Project Planning Considerations

As the project plan is developed, adding detail is not always straightforward. The section below discusses considerations that are important to project planners as they decide what should be included in the work plan, how to break tasks into subtasks and action steps, and how to accomplish the objectives of the project. The considerations and constraints that should be factored in when creating a project plan fall under several major categories, each of which is also described below.

Financial Considerations

No matter what information security needs exist in the organization, the amount of effort that can be expended depends on the funds available. A cost benefit analysis (CBA), typically prepared in the Analysis Phase of the SecSDLC, must be reviewed and verified prior to the development of the project plan. The CBA identifies the impact that a specific technology or approach can have on the organization's information assets and what it may cost.

Each organization has its own approach to the creation and management of budgets and expenses. In many organizations, the information security budget is a subsection of the overall IT budget. In other cases, information security is a separate budget category that may have the same degree of visibility and priority as the IT budget. Regardless of where in the budget information security items are located, monetary constraints determine what can (and cannot) be accomplished.

It should also be noted that the budgeting practices used by public and private organizations are often different. Public organizations are often more predictable in their budget processes than private organizations. Because the budgets of public organizations are usually based on the results of legislation or public meetings, the amount of the future budgets is often known well in advance. The downside is that if additional funding is needed during a fiscal year for operations such as information security, the funds must come from a different spending category. In addition, some public organizations rely on temporary or renewable grants for their budgets, and thus their expenses must be determined when the grant applications are written. If new expenses arise, funds must be requested in new grant applications. Also, grant expenditures are usually audited and cannot be misspent. There is one unique twist to the budgets at many public institutions: all budgeted funds must be spent in one fiscal year. If not, the budget is reduced by the unspent amount the next fiscal year. The result is that public organizations have "end-of-fiscal-year-spend-a-thons," to spend all their remaining funds before the end of the fiscal year. If you are employed by a public organization, you should know that this is often the best time to acquire, for example, that remaining piece of technology needed for the information security architecture.

Private (for-profit) organizations have different budgetary constraints. The marketplace, not a legislature, usually determines these constraints. Thus, if a for-profit organization does not generate revenue, there can be no funding for any information security expenditure.

When a for-profit organization needs to fund a project to improve security, the funding comes from the company's capital and expense budgets. Each for-profit organization determines its capital budget and the rules for managing capital spending and expenses differently. In almost all cases, however, budgetary constraints impact the planning and actual expenditures for information security. For example, a preferred technology or solution may be sacrificed for a less desirable but more affordable solution. The budget ultimately guides the information security implementation.

To justify the amount budgeted for a security project at either a public or for-profit organization, it may be useful to benchmark expenses of similar organizations. Most for-profit organizations publish the components of their expense reports. Similarly, public organizations must document how funds were spent. A savvy information security project manager might find a number of similarly sized organizations with larger expenditures for security and use these as justification for his planned expenditures. While such tactics may not improve this year's budget, they could improve the budget in future years. Ironically, attackers can also help information security project planners justify the information security budget. If, during the year, attacks have successfully compromised secured information systems, management may be more willing to support the information security budget.

Priority Considerations

In general, the most important information security controls in the project plan should be scheduled first. When budgetary constraints are considered, they may also have an effect on the assignment of a project's priorities. As discussed in Chapter 4, the implementation of controls is guided by the prioritization of threats and the value of the information assets that are threatened. A control that is not considered as important as other choices may be moved ahead of more important options if it addresses a group of specific vulnerabilities and will cumulatively improve the security posture of the organization to a greater degree than other individual controls, even if they have a higher individual priority.

Time and Scheduling Considerations

Time is another constraint that has a broad impact on the development of the project plan. Time can impact a project plan at dozens of points in its development, including the following: time to order and receive a security control, which is subject to backlogs at the vendor or manufacturer; time to install and configure the control; time to train the users; and time to realize the return on investment of the control. The one universal rule is that time waits for no one. If a control must be in place before a new electronic commerce product can be implemented, the selection of a particular type or model of technology may be influenced by the speed of acquisition and implementation of the various alternatives.

Staffing Considerations

The lack of enough qualified, trained, and available personnel also constrains the project plan. An experienced staff is often needed to implement available technologies and to develop and implement policies and training programs. If no staff members are trained to configure a firewall that is being purchased, someone must be trained, or someone who is experienced with that particular technology must be hired.

Procurement Considerations

All IT and information security planners must consider the acquisition of goods and services. There are a number of constraints on the selection process for equipment and services in most organizations, specifically in the selection of certain service vendors or products from manufacturers and suppliers. These constraints may change the specifics of a particular technology or even eliminate the technology as a viable choice. For example, in a recent budget cycle, the authors' lab administrator was considering selecting an automated risk analysis software package. The leading candidate promised to integrate everything, including vulnerability scanning, risk weighting, and control selection. Upon receipt of the RFP, the vendor issued a bid to accomplish the desired requirements for a heart-stopping $75,000, plus a 10% annual maintenance fee. If an organization has an annual information security capital budget of $30,000, it would have to eliminate a package like this from consideration—despite how promising the software's features were.

Organizational Feasibility Considerations

Another consideration that must be assessed when creating a project plan is the ability of the organization to adapt to change. To put it another way, the feasibility of the organization successfully assimilating the proposed change is a factor that must be evaluated when determining if a project will be successful. Policies require time to develop, and new technologies require time to be installed, configured, and tested. In addition, employees need training on both the new policies and new technology components. Employees also need to understand how the new information security program impacts their working lives. The goal of the project plan is to avoid new security components from directly impacting the day-to-day operations of the individual employees. This means that changes should be transparent to systems users, unless the new technology is actually intended to change to procedures, by, for example, requiring additional authentication or verification. The organization must therefore develop and conduct training sessions that minimize the impact of the changes before new technologies come online. Waiting to schedule training until after the new processes are in place (that is, after the users have had to deal with the changes without preparation) can create tension and resistance, and possibly undermine security operations altogether. Unless properly trained, users may develop ways to work around difficult or unfamiliar security procedures, and their bypassing of controls may creating additional vulnerabilities. Conversely, users should not be prepared so far in advance that they forget the new training techniques and requirements. The optimal time to schedule training is usually one to three weeks before the new policies and technologies come online.

Training and Indoctrination Considerations

The size of the organization and the normal conduct of business may preclude a single large training program on new security procedures or technologies. In this case, the organization should conduct a phased-in or pilot approach to implementation, such as roll-out training for one department at a time (see the section titled "Conversion Strategies," to be found later in the chapter, for details about various types of implementation approaches). When the project involves a change in policies, it may be sufficient to brief all supervisors on the new policy and assign them the task of updating end users in regularly scheduled meetings. Project planners must ensure that compliance documents are also distributed and that all employees are required to read, understand, and agree to the new policies.

Scope Considerations

It is unrealistic for an organization to install all information security components at once. A concept known as **project scope** concerns the boundaries (i.e., maximum and minimum levels) of time and effort-hours needed to deliver the planned features and quality level of the project deliverables. The scope of any given project plan should be carefully reviewed and kept to the smallest level consistent with the project's objectives. In the case of information security, project plans should not attempt to implement the entire security system at one time. (Some guidance about how to decide which elements of a security program to deploy in order to keep a project's scope to a reasonable size can be found in the discussion of the bull's-eye approach, which appears later in the chapter in the section titled "Technical Topics of Implementation".) There are several reasons why the scope of information security projects must be evaluated and adjusted with care. First, in addition to the constraints of handling so many complex tasks at one time, information security implementations experience the problems of having interrelated conflicts between the installation of information security controls and the daily operations of the organization. In addition, the installation of new information security controls may conflict with existing controls. For example, suppose installing a new packet filtering router and a new application proxy firewall at the same time caused a conflict between the controls, and as a result, the organization's users were blocked from accessing the Web. Which technology caused the conflict? Was it the router, firewall, or an interaction between the two? As this example shows, it is best to limit the scope of implementation to manageable tasks. This does not mean that the project should only allow change to one component at a time; but it does mean the appropriate plan will carefully consider the number of tasks that are planned for the same time in a single department.

Recall from the opening vignette that all of Kelvin's change requests were in the area of networking. In general, as the number of items included in any given change cycle increases, it becomes increasingly difficult to anticipate all of the interactions and complexities that will inevitably arise. One of the main problems with Kelvin's plan was that if his changes were not deployed exactly as planned, or if unanticipated complexities arose, there would have been extensive disruption to Sequential Label and Supply's ability to function. This is especially likely because Kelvin's changes were focused on the area of networking, where the dependencies are particularly complex. Initiating many changes at the same time in the network area of responsibility can, for example, lead to an error in the deployment of the primary firewall rules and thus result in the interruption of all Internet connectivity, which might, in turn, make the early detection of (and recovery from) the original error more difficult. In other words, a project with a large scope can cause many business disruptions that might otherwise have been avoided if only one change were being implemented at that time.

The Need for Project Management

Project management requires a unique set of skills and a thorough understanding of a broad body of specialized knowledge. In the opening vignette, Kelvin's inexperience as a project manager makes this all too clear. In the following section, you will read about the basic elements of project management. Note that the cursory overview of project management provided here does not prepare an individual to assume the role of project manager for a project of any significant size. Realistically, most information security projects require a trained project manager—a CISO, or a skilled IT manager who is versed in project management techniques and can oversee the project. In addition, even experienced project managers are advised to seek expert assistance when engaging in a formal bidding process to select advanced or integrated technologies or outsourced services.

Supervising Implementation

Although it is not an optimal solution, some organizations choose to designate a champion from the general management community of interest to supervise the implementation of an information security project plan. In this case, groups of tasks are delegated to individuals or teams from the IT and information security communities of interest. An alternative is to designate a senior IT manager or the CIO of the organization to lead the implementation. In this case, the detailed work is delegated to cross-functional teams.

The optimal solution is to designate a suitable person from the information security community of interest, because the inherent focus of the project is on the information security needs of the organization. In the final analysis, each organization must find the leadership for project implementation that best suits its specific needs and the personalities and politics of the organizational culture.

Executing the Plan

Once a project is underway, it is managed to completion using a process known as a **negative feedback loop** or cybernetic loop, which ensures that progress is measured periodically. In the negative feedback loop process, measured results are compared to expected results. When significant deviation occurs, corrective action is taken to bring the task that is deviating from the plan back into compliance with the projection, or else the projection is revised in light of new information. See Figure 10-1 for an overview of this process.

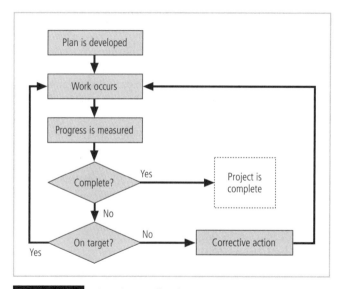

FIGURE 10-1 Negative Feedback Loop

Corrective action is required because of two basic situations: either the estimate was flawed or performance has lagged. When an estimate is flawed, as when the number of effort-hours required is underestimated, the plan should be corrected and downstream tasks updated to reflect the change. When performance has lagged, due, for example, to high turnover of skilled employees, corrective action may take the form of adding resources, making longer schedules, or reducing the quality or quantity of the deliverable. Corrective action decisions are usually expressed in terms of trade-offs. Often a project manager can adjust one of the three following planning parameters for the task being corrected:

- Effort and money allocated
- Elapsed time or scheduling impact
- Quality or quantity of the deliverable

When a task is lagging behind expectations, it is failing in one or more of these parameters. When too much effort and money is being spent, you may decide to slow the rate of completion of the project tasks and take longer, or to lower the deliverable quality or quantity. If the task is taking too long to complete, you should probably add more resources in staff time or money, or else lower deliverable quality or quantity. If the quality of the deliverable is too low, you must usually add more resources in staff time or money, or take longer to complete the task. Of course, there are complex dynamics between these variables, and these simplistic solutions do not serve in all cases, but this simple trade-off model can assist the project manager in analyzing the options available.

Project Wrap-up

Project wrap-up is usually handled as a procedural task and assigned to a mid-level IT or information security manager. These managers collect documentation, finalize status reports, and deliver a final report and a presentation at a wrap-up meeting. The goal of the wrap-up is to resolve any pending issues, critique the overall effort of the project, and draw conclusions about how to improve the process for the future.

Technical Topics of Implementation

Some parts of the implementation process are technical in nature and deal with the application of technology, while others are not and deal instead with the human interface to technical systems. In the following section, the more technical topics of conversion strategies, prioritization among multiple components, outsourcing, and technology governance are discussed. The major section that follows will deal with the less technical topics.

Conversion Strategies

As the components of the new security system are planned, provisions must be made for the changeover from the previous method of performing a task to the new method. Just like IT systems, information security projects that must be developed and deployed require careful conversion planning. In both cases, the four basic approaches used for changing from an old system or process to a new one are explained next:

- Direct changeover: Also known as going "cold turkey," a **direct changeover** involves stopping the old method and beginning the new. This could be as simple as having employees follow the existing procedure one week, and then use a new procedure the next. Some cases of direct changeover are simple, such as a change that involves requiring employees to use a new password (which uses a stronger degree of authentication) beginning on an announced date; some may be more complex, such as requiring the entire company to change procedures when the network team disables an old firewall and activates a new one. The primary drawback to the direct changeover approach is that if the new system fails or needs modification, users may be without services while the system's bugs are worked out. Complete testing of the new system in advance of the direct changeover helps to reduce the probability of these problems.
- Phased implementation: A **phased implementation** is the most common conversion strategy and involves rolling out a piece of the system across the entire organization. This could mean that the security group implements only a small portion of the new security profile, giving users a chance to get used to it and resolving small issues as they arise. This is usually the best approach to security project implementation. For

example, if a new VPN solution that employees can use to connect to the organization's network while they're traveling is to be introduced, then each week one department might be added to the group allowed to use the new VPN, and this process would continue until all departments are using the new approach.

■ Pilot implementation: The **pilot implementation** involves implementing all security improvements in a single office, department, or division, and resolving issues within that group before expanding to the rest of the organization. The pilot implementation works well when an isolated group can serve as the "guinea pig," which keeps the implementation from dramatically impacting the performance of the organization as a whole. The operation of a research and development group, for example, may not impact the real-time operations of the organization and could assist security in resolving issues that emerge.

■ Parallel operations: The **parallel operations** strategy involves running the new methods alongside the old methods. In general, this means running two systems concurrently, and in terms of information systems, it might involve, for example, running two firewalls concurrently. Although this approach is usually a complex operation, it can be one that reinforces an organization's information security by allowing the old system(s) to serve as backup for the new systems if they fail or are compromised. Drawbacks usually include the need to deal with both systems and maintain both sets of procedures.

The Bull's-Eye Model for Information Security Project Planning

A proven method for prioritizing a program of complex change is the **bull's-eye method**. This model has been used by many organizations and called many different things. The fundamental concept is that issues are addressed from the general to the specific and that the focus is on systematic solutions instead of individual problems. The increased capabilities—that is increased expenditures—are used to improve the information security program in a systematic and measured way. As presented here and illustrated in Figure 10-2, the approach relies on a process of evaluating project plans in a progression through four layers: policies, networks, systems, and applications. Each layer is defined below:

1. Policies: The layer that needs attention first is shown as the outer ring in the bull's-eye diagram. The centrality of policies has been noted extensively in this textbook and is fully detailed in Chapter 5. Thus, as you may recall, the foundation of all effective information security programs is sound information security and information technology policy. Since policy establishes the ground rules for the use of all systems and describes what is appropriate and what is inappropriate, it enables all other information security components to function correctly and have the desired effects in improving the organization's information security program. Therefore, when deciding how to implement complex changes and choose from conflicting options, it is often useful to have or create policy to clarify what the organization is trying to accomplish with its efforts.

2. Networks: In the past, most information security efforts focused on this layer, and so until recently information security was often considered synonymous with network security. In today's computing environment, implementing information security is more complex because an organization's networking infrastructure often comes into contact with threats originating from the public network. Those organizations new to the Internet find (as soon as their organization policy environment defines how their networks should be defended) that designing and implementing an effective

DMZ is the primary way to secure an organization's networks. Secondary efforts in this layer include providing the authentication and authorization that are necessary when allowing users to connect over public networks to the organization's systems.

3. Systems: Many organizations find that the problems of configuring and operating information systems in a secure fashion become more difficult as the number and complexity of these systems grow. This layer includes computers used as servers, desktop computers, and systems used for process control and manufacturing systems.

4. Applications: The layer that receives attention last is the one that deals with the application software systems used by the organization to accomplish its work. This includes packaged applications, such as office automation and e-mail programs, as well as high-end enterprise resource planning (ERP) packages than span the organization. Custom application software developed by the organization for its own needs is also included.

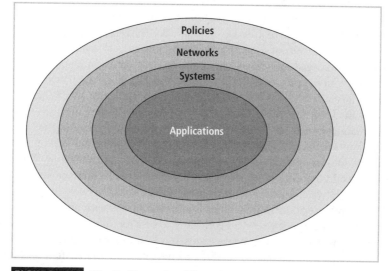

FIGURE 10-2 The Bull's-eye Model

By reviewing the information security blueprint and the current state of the organization's information security efforts in terms of the four layers of this model, project planners can find guidance about where to lobby for expanded information security capabilities. The bull's-eye model can also be used to evaluate the sequence of steps taken to integrate parts of the information security blueprint into a project plan. As suggested by its bull's eye shape, this model dictates the following reasoning:

- Until sound and useable IT and information security policies are developed, communicated, and enforced, no additional resources should be spent on other controls.
- Until effective network controls are designed and deployed, all resources should be spent to achieve this goal (unless, of course, resources are needed to revisit the policy needs of the organization).
- After policies and network controls are implemented, implementation should focus on the information, process, and manufacturing systems of the organization. Until there is well-informed assurance that all critical systems are being configured and operated in a secure fashion, all resources should be spent on reaching that goal.

- Once there is assurance that policies are in place, networks are secure, and systems are safe, attention should move to the assessment and remediation of the security of the organization's applications. This is a complicated and vast area of concern for many organizations. Most organizations neglect to analyze the impact of information security on existing purchased and self-developed systems. As in all planning efforts, attention should be paid to the most critical applications first.

It is important to remember that the implementation of the bull's-eye model or any other model must be tempered with judgment and experience.

To Outsource or Not

Not every organization needs to develop an information security department or program of its own. Just as some organizations outsource part of or all of their IT operations, so too can organizations outsource part of or all of their information security programs. The expense and time required to develop an effective information security program may be beyond the means of some organizations, and therefore it may be in their best interest to hire professional services to help their IT departments implement such a program.

When an organization has outsourced most or all IT services, information security should be part of the contract arrangement with the outsourcer. When an organization retains the IT department, it may choose to outsource some of the more specialized information security functions. Small and medium-sized organizations often hire outside consultants for penetration testing and information security program audits. Organizations of all sizes frequently choose to outsource network monitoring functions both to make certain that their systems are secured by acceptable levels of service and to gain assistance in watching for attempted or successful attacks.

The subject of outsourcing for IT, information security, and other common infrastructure and corporate services continues to be a focus for many organizations. Because of the complex nature of these decisions, it is best to hire the finest outsourcing specialists possible, and then retain the best attorneys possible to negotiate and verify the legal and technical intricacies of the outsourcing contract.

Technology Governance and Change Control

Other factors that determine the success of an organization's IT and information security are technology governance and change control processes.

Technology governance is a complex process that an organization uses to manage the impacts and costs that result from technology implementation, innovation, and obsolescence. This matter deals with how frequently technical systems are updated, and how technical updates are approved and funded. Technology governance also facilitates the communication about technical advances and issues across the organization.

Medium and large organizations deal with the impact of technical change on the operation of the organization through a **change control** process. By managing the process of change, the organization can:

- Improve communication about change across the organization
- Enhance coordination between groups within the organization as change is scheduled and completed

- Reduce unintended consequences by having a process to resolve potential conflict and disruption that uncoordinated change can introduce
- Improve quality of service as potential failures are eliminated and groups work together
- Assure management that all groups are complying with the organization's policies regarding technology governance, procurement, accounting, and information security

Effective change control is an essential part of the IT operation in all but the smallest organizations. The information security group can also use the change control process to ensure that the essential process steps that assure confidentiality, integrity, and availability are followed when systems are upgraded across the organization.

Nontechnical Aspects of Implementation

There are aspects of the information security implementation process that are not technical in nature and deal instead with the human interface to technical systems. In the section that follows, the topic of creating a culture of change management and the considerations for organizations facing change are discussed.

The Culture of Change Management

In any major project, the prospect of change, the familiar shifting to the unfamiliar, can cause employees to build up, either unconsciously or consciously, a resistance to that change. Regardless of whether the changes are perceived as good (as in the case of information security implementations) or perceived as bad (such as a downsizing or massive restructuring), employees often tend to prefer the old way of doing things. Even when employees embrace changes, the stress of actually making the changes and adjusting to the new procedures can increase the probability of mistakes or create vulnerabilities in systems. By understanding and applying some of the basic tenets of change management, project managers can lower employee resistance to change, and can even build resilience for changes, thereby making ongoing change more palatable to the entire organization.

The basic foundations of change management require that those making the changes understand that organizations typically have cultures that represent their mood and philosophy for conducting business. Disruptions to this culture that are caused by change must be properly addressed and their effects minimized. One of the oldest models of change is the Lewin change model[1], which consists of:

- Unfreezing
- Moving
- Refreezing

Unfreezing involves thawing out hard-and-fast habits and established procedures. Moving is the transition between the old way and the new. Refreezing is the integration of the new methods into the organizational culture, which is accomplished by creating an atmosphere in which the changes are accepted as the preferred way of accomplishing the necessary tasks.

Considerations for Organizational Change

Steps can be taken to make an organization more amenable to change. These steps reduce resistance to change at the beginning of the planning process and encourage members of the organization to be more flexible as changes occur during project implementation.

Reducing Resistance to Change from the Start

The level of resistance to change impacts the ease with which an organization is able to implement the procedural and managerial changes that it needs. The more ingrained the existing methods and behaviors are within the organization, the more difficult making the change is likely to be. It's best, therefore, to improve the interaction between the affected members of the organization and the project planners in the early phases of an information security improvement project. The interaction between these groups can be improved through a three-step process in which project managers must communicate, educate, and involve.

Communication is the first step and the most crucial. As a project manager, you must communicate with the employees, notifying them that a new security process is being considered, and that their feedback is essential to making it work. You must also constantly update the employees on the progress of the SecSDLC and provide information on the expected completion dates. This ongoing series of updates keeps the process from being a surprise at the last minute, and primes individuals to accept the change more readily when it finally arrives.

At the same time, you must also use updates to educate employees about exactly how the proposed changes will affect them both personally and within the organization. While detailed information may not be available in earlier stages of a project plan, details that can be shared with employees may emerge as the SecSDLC progresses. Education also involves teaching employees to use the new systems once they are in place. This, as discussed earlier, means delivering a high-quality training program at the appropriate times.

Finally, project managers can reduce resistance to change by involving employees in the project plan. This means getting key representatives from user groups to serve as members of the SecSDLC development process. In systems development, this is referred to as joint application development or JAD. An approach that creates a liaison between IT and information security implementers and the general population of the organization can serve the project team well in early planning stages, when unforeseen problems with acceptance of the project may rise and need to be addressed.

Developing a Culture that Supports Change

An ideal organization fosters resilience to change. This means the organization has come to expect that change is a necessary part of the culture, and that embracing change is more productive than fighting it. To develop such a culture, the organization must successfully accomplish many projects that require change. A resilient culture can be either cultivated or undermined by management's approach. Strong management support for change, with a clear executive-level champion, enables the organization to recognize the necessity and strategic importance of the change. Weak management support, with over-delegated responsibility and no champion, sentences the project to almost-certain failure. In this case, employees sense the low priority that has been given to the project and do not communicate with representatives from the development team because the effort seems useless.

Chapter Summary

- The implementation phase of the security systems development life cycle involves making changes to the configuration and operation of the organization's information systems in order to make them more secure. These changes include changes to procedures, people, hardware, software, and data.

- During the implementation phase, the organization translates its blueprint for information security into a concrete project plan that instructs individuals on the execution of the implementation phase.

- Before developing a project plan, management should articulate and coordinate the organization's information security vision and objectives with the involved communities of interest.

- The major steps in executing the project plan are planning the project, supervising tasks and action steps within the project plan, and wrapping up the project plan.

- Each organization determines its own project management methodology for IT and information security projects. Whenever possible, an organization's information security projects should be in line with the organization's project management practices.

- Planning for the implementation phase involves the creation of a detailed project plan.

- The project plan can be created by using a simple planning tool such as the approach known as the work breakdown structure (WBS). The plan can be prepared with a simple desktop PC spreadsheet program or with more complex project management software tools. The WBS involves addressing major project tasks (and their related attributes) such as the following:
  - work to be accomplished (activities and deliverables)
  - individuals (or skills set) assigned to perform the task
  - start and end dates for the task (when known)
  - amount of effort required for completion (in hours or days)
  - estimated capital expenses for the task
  - estimated noncapital expenses for the task
  - identification of task interdependencies

- Constraints and considerations should be addressed when developing the project plan, including financial, procurement, priority, time and scheduling, staffing, scope, organizational feasibility, training and indoctrination, change control, and technology governance considerations.

- Organizations usually designate a professional project manager to lead a security information project. Alternatively, some organizations designate a champion from a senior level of general management or a senior IT manager such as the CIO of the organization.

- Once a project is underway, it can be managed to completion using a process known as a negative feedback loop or cybernetic loop. This process involves measuring variances from the project plan and then taking corrective action when needed.

- As the components of the new security system are planned, provisions must be made for the changeover from the previous method of performing a task (or, in some cases, not performing the task) to the new method(s). The four common conversion strategies for performing this changeover are:
  - direct changeover
  - phased implementation
  - pilot implementation
  - parallel operations

- The bull's-eye model is a proven method for prioritizing a program of complex change. Using this method, the project manager can address issues from the general to the specific and focus on systematic solutions instead of individual problems.

- When the expense and time required to develop an effective information security program is beyond the reach of an organization, it is best for the organization to outsource to competent professional services.

- Technology governance is a complex process that an organization uses to manage the impacts and costs resulting from technology implementation, innovation, and obsolescence.

- The change control process is a method that medium and large organizations use to deal with the impact of technical change on the operation of the organization.

- As with any project, there are certain aspects of change that must be addressed. In any major project, the prospect of moving from the familiar to the unfamiliar can cause employees to resist change consciously or unconsciously.

Review Questions

1. What is a project plan? List what a project plan can accomplish.
2. What is the value of a statement of vision and objectives? Why is it needed before a project plan is developed?
3. What categories of constraints to project plan implementation are noted in the chapter? Explain each of them.
4. List and describe the three major steps in executing the project plan.
5. What is a work breakdown structure (WBS)? Is it the only way to organize a project plan?
6. What is projectitis? How is it cured or its impact reduced?
7. List and define the common attributes of the tasks of a WBS.
8. How does a planner know when a task has been subdivided to an adequate degree and can be classified as an action step?
9. What is a deliverable? Name two uses for deliverables.
10. What is a resource? What are the two types?
11. Why is it a good practice to delay naming specific individuals as resources early in the planning process?
12. What is a milestone, and why is it significant to project planning?
13. Why is it good practice to assign start and end dates sparingly in the early stages of project planning?
14. Who is the best judge of effort estimates for project tasks and action steps? Why?
15. Within project management, what is a dependency? What is a predecessor? What is a successor?
16. What is a negative feedback loop? How is it used to keep a project in control?
17. When a task is not being completed according to the plan, what two circumstances are likely to be involved?
18. List and describe the four basic conversion strategies (as described in the chapter) that are used when converting to a new system. Under which circumstances is each of these the best approach?
19. Describe the bull's-eye model for information security project planning by listing and describing its four layers.
20. What is technology governance? What is change control? How are they related?

Exercises

1. Create a first draft of a WBS from the scenario below. Make assumptions as needed based on the section about project planning considerations and constraints in the chapter. In your WBS, describe the skill sets required for the tasks you have planned.

   Scenario
   > Sequential Label and Supply is having a problem with employees surfing the Web to access material the company has deemed inappropriate for use in a professional environment. The technology exists to insert a filtering device in the company Internet connection that blocks certain Web locations and certain Web content. The vendor has provided the company with some initial information about the filter. The filter is a hardware appliance that costs $18,000 and requires a total of 150 effort-hours to install and configure. Technical support on the filter costs 18% of the purchase price and includes a training allowance for the year. A software component that runs on the administrator's desktop computer is needed for administering the filter, and it costs $550. A monthly subscription provides the list of sites to be blocked and costs $250 per month. The administrator must spend an estimated four hours per week for ongoing administrative functions.

   Items you should consider:

   - Your plan requires two parts, one for deployment and another for ongoing operation after implementation.
   - The vendor offers a contracting service for installation at $140 per hour.
   - Your change control process requires a 17-day lead time for change requests.
   - The manufacturer has a 14-day order time and a 7-day delivery time for this device.

2. If you have access to a commercial project management software package (Microsoft Project, for example), use it to complete a project plan based on the data shown in Table 10-2. Prepare a simple WBS report (or Gantt chart) showing your work.

3. Write a job description for Kelvin Urich, the project manager described in the opening vignette of this chapter. Be sure to identify key characteristics of the ideal candidate, as well as his or her work experience and educational background. Also, justify why your job description is suitable for potential candidates of this position.

4. Search the World Wide Web for job descriptions of project managers. You can use any number of Web sites, including *www.careerjournal.com* or *www.dice.com*, to find at least 10 IT-related job descriptions. What common elements do you find among the job descriptions? What is the most unusual characteristic among them?

Case Exercises

Charlie looked across his desk at Kelvin, who was absorbed in the sheaf of handwritten notes from the meeting. Charlie had asked Kelvin to come his office to discuss the change control meeting that had occurred earlier that day.

"So what do you think?" he asked.

"I think I was blindsided by a bus!" Kelvin replied sheepishly. "I thought I had thought through the project plan and managed all the possible effects of the change. I tried to explain this, but everyone acted as if I had threatened their jobs."

"In a way you did," Charlie stated. "Some people believe that change is the enemy."

"But these changes are important."

"I agree," Charlie said, nodding. "But successful change usually occurs in small steps. What's your top priority?"

"All the items on this list are top priorities," Kelvin stressed. "I haven't even gotten to the second tier."

"So what should you do to accomplish these top priorities?" Charlie asked.

"I guess I should reprioritize within my top tier, but what then?"

"The next step is to build support before the meeting, not during it." Charlie smiled. "Never go into a meeting where you haven't done your homework, especially when other people in the meeting can reduce your chance of success."

1. What project management tasks should Kelvin perform before his next meeting?

2. What change management tasks should Kelvin perform before his next meeting, and how do these tasks fit within the project management process?

3. Had you been in Kelvin's place, what would you have done differently to prepare for this meeting?

Endnotes

1. Edgar H. Schein. "Kurt Lewin's Change Theory in the Field and in the Classroom: Notes Toward a Model of Managed Learning." Working paper, MIT Sloan School of Management. [Cited 20 July 2002]. Available from the World Wide Web <http://www/sol-ne.org/res/wp/10006.html#one>.

Security and Personnel

11

> I think we need to be paranoid optimists.
>
> **ROBERT J. EATON, CHAIRMAN OF THE BOARD OF MANAGEMENT OF DAIMLERCHRYSLER AG (RETIRED)**

WHILE DRINKING HER COFFEE, Iris Majwubu browsed through her e-mail inbox. Mixed in among the newsletters and unsolicited offers for travel deals and mortgage loans was a message from Charlie Moody. The subject line of the message was "I need to see you." As she opened the message, Iris wondered why on earth the Senior Manager of IT needed to see her. The e-mail read:

From: Charles Moody [cmoody@slsco.com]

To: Iris Majwubu [imajwubu@slsco.com]

Subject: I need to see you

    Iris,

    Since you were a material witness in the investigation, I wanted to advise you of the status of the Magruder case. We completed all of the personnel actions on this matter yesterday, and it is now behind us.

    You might like to know that the best guess from the Corporate Security Department is that you helped us resolve this security matter in its early stages, and so no company assets were compromised.

    Please set up an appointment with me in the next few days to discuss a few things.

--Charlie

451

A week later, Iris entered Charlie Moody's office. He was sitting behind his desk and stood as she entered.

"Come in," Charlie said. "Have a seat."

Iris still didn't know why Charlie had wanted to see her. Nervously, she choose a chair closest to the door, not anticipating that Charlie would come around his desk and sit down next to her. As he took his seat, Iris noticed that the folder in his hand looked like her personnel file, and she took a deep breath.

"I'm sure you're wondering why I asked you here," said Charlie smiling. "The company really appreciated your efforts in the Magruder case. Because you followed policy and acted so quickly, we avoided a significant loss. You were right to bring that issue to your manager's attention and avoid confronting Magruder directly. You not only made the right choice, but you acted quickly and showed a positive attitude throughout the whole situation—basically, I think you demonstrated an information security mindset. And that's why I'd like to offer you a transfer to Kelvin Urich's information security group. I think Urich's team would really benefit from having someone like you on board."

"I'm glad I was able to help," Iris began, "but I'm not sure what to say. I've been a DBA for three years here. I really don't know much about information security other than what I learned from the company training and awareness sessions."

"That's not a problem," Charlie said. "What you don't know you can learn." He smiled again. "So how about it, are you interested in the job?"

Iris said, "It sounds interesting, but to be honest I hadn't been considering a career change just now." She paused for a moment, then added: "I am willing to think about it, though. But I have a few questions…."

LEARNING OBJECTIVES:

Upon completion of this material, you should be able to:

- Understand where and how the information security function is positioned within organizations
- Understand the issues and concerns related to staffing the information security function
- Identify the credentials that professionals in the information security field may acquire to gain recognition in the field
- Appreciate how an organization's employment policies and practices can support the information security effort
- Understand the special security precautions that must be taken when contracting nonemployees
- Recognize the need for the separation of duties
- Understand the special requirements needed for the privacy of personnel data

Introduction

Iris is correct in asking questions before taking the position offered by Charlie. Just as each potential employee and potential employer look for the best fit, each organization should examine the options possible for staffing the information security function. When implementing information security in an organization, there are many human resource issues that must be addressed. First, the entire organization must decide how to position and name the security function within the organization. Second, the information security community of interest must plan for the proper staffing (or adjustments to the staffing plan) for the information security function. Third, the IT community of interest must understand the impact of information security across every role in the IT function and adjust job descriptions and documented practices accordingly. Finally, the general management community of interest must work with the information security professionals to integrate solid information security concepts into the personnel management practices of the organization.

Understanding the impact of change on the personnel management practices of the organization is another important step in achieving a successful implementation phase of the security system development life cycle (SecSDLC). To gauge the impact of such change, the organization should conduct a behavioral feasibility study *before* the implementation phase—that is, in the analysis phase. As part of establishing behavioral feasibility, the study should address the impact of the changes that will be necessary for implementation. Thus, it should include an investigation of the levels of employee acceptance of—and resistance to—change. In the case of information security systems, experience has shown that employees often feel threatened when an organization is creating or enhancing an overall information security program. Employees may perceive such a program to be a manifestation of a Big Brother attitude, in which case they might have questions such as:

- Why is management monitoring my work or my e-mail?
- Will information security staff go through my hard drive looking for evidence to fire me?
- How can I do my job well now that I have to deal with the added delays of the information security technology?

As indicated in Chapter 10, resolving these sorts of doubts and reassuring employees about the role of information security programs are fundamental objectives of the implementation process. Thus, it is important to gather employee feedback early and respond to it quickly. This chapter will explore the issues involved in positioning the information security unit within the organization as well as those pertaining to staffing the information function. It will also discuss how to manage the many personnel challenges that arise across the organization–and demonstrate why these challenges can (and should) be considered part of the organization's overall information security program.

Positioning & Staffing the Security Function

Although there are several valid models for how the information security department should be placed within an organization, the model used often in large organizations places the information security department within the information technology department and usually designates that it is to be headed by the CISO (or CSO, Chief Security Officer), who reports directly to the company's top computing executive, or CIO. Such a structure implies that the goals and objectives of the CISO and CIO are aligned. This is not always the case, however. By its very nature, an information security program can, at times, be at odds with the goals and objectives of the information technology department as a whole. The CIO, as the executive in charge of the organization's technology, strives to create efficiency in the processing and accessing of the organization's information, and thus, anything that limits access or slows information processing can compete with the CIO's mission for the entire organization. In contrast, the CISO's function is more like that of an internal auditor in that this individual must direct the information security department to examine existing systems in order to discover information security faults and flaws in technology, software, and employees' activities and processes. These examinations can disrupt the processing and accessing of an organization's information. As it's been discovered that the goals and objectives of CIOs and CISOs tend to contradict each other (in other words, that the mission statements of the two functions conflict), the trend among many organizations has been to separate their information security function from their IT division.

As a result, the vision of having separate IT and information security functions is currently shared by many executives. An article titled "Where the Chief Security Officer Belongs" published by the IT-industry magazine *InformationWeek* summarizes the reasoning behind this vision, perhaps as succinctly as possible: "the people who do and the people who watch shouldn't report to a common manager."[1] A 2002 survey conducted by the consulting firm Meta Group found that while only 3% of its clients actually position the information security department outside IT, these clients regarded this positioning as the mark of a forward-thinking organization. Another group, Forrester Research, feels that the traditional structure of having the CISO/CSO report to the CIO structure will be prevalent for years to come, but that this structure will begin to involve numerous variations in which various IT sections report information to the CSO, and thereby provide IS departments the critical input and control they need to protect the organization's IT assets.[2] In general, the research data seems to suggest that while many organizations feel that it is important that the CISO/CSO function as an independent, executive-level decision maker, the relationship between information security and IT is currently too closely aligned for the organizations to take on the challenge of separating the two departments.

Actually, there are many ways to position the information security program within an organization. In his book *Information Security Roles and Responsibilities Made Easy*, Charles Cresson Wood has compiled many of the best practices regarding the positioning of information security programs from many industry groups. According to Wood, the information security function can be placed within any of the following organizational functions:

- IT function, as a peer of other sub-functions such as networks, applications development, and the help desk
- Physical security function, as a peer of physical security or protective services
- Administrative services function, as a peer of human resources or purchasing
- Insurance and risk management function
- Legal department

Once an information security function's organizational position has been settled, the challenge for the entire organization then is to design a reporting structure for the information security function that balances the competing needs of each of the communities of interest. In many organizations, the placement of the information security unit in the reporting structure is a function of the fact that no one actually wants to manage it; in such cases, the unit winds up being moved from place to place within the organization without regard to the impact such changes may have on its effectiveness. Organizations should find a rational compromise by placing the information security function where it can best balance its duty to enforce organizational policy (that is, monitor compliance) with its ability to provide the education, training, awareness, and customer service needed to make information security an integral part of the organizational culture.

Regardless of where the information security function is placed, building the information security team is both an art and a science. As the next section shows, staffing the information security function should be based on both the science of measuring technical, educational, and work experience and the art of assessing the skills needed for success.

Staffing the Information Security Function

The selection of information security personnel is based on a number of criteria. Some of these factors are within the control of the organization and others are not. Consider the fundamental concept of supply and demand. When the demand for any commodity—in this case, a critical technical skill needed for many information security roles—increases too quickly, supply initially fails to meet the demand. Many future IS professionals seek to enter the security market by gaining the skills, experience, and credentials they need to qualify as a new supply. In other words, they enter high-demand markets by changing jobs, going to school, or becoming trained. Until the new supply reaches the demand level, organizations must pay the higher costs associated with limited supply. Once the supply meets or exceeds the demand, the organizations that are hiring people with these skills become selective, and the amount they are willing to pay drops. Hiring trends swing back and forth like a clock pendulum, from one end (high demand, low supply) to the other (low demand, high supply), because the real economy, unlike an econometric model, is seldom in a state of equilibrium. The year 2002 saw the information security industry experience a period of high demand, with few qualified and experienced individuals available for organizations seeking their services. The economic realities of 2003 and 2004—namely, a climate of lower demand for all IT professionals—have produced more limited job growth for information security practitioners. But the latest forecasts for hiring in IT in general and information security in particular project more openings than qualified candidates over the next five to seven years.[3]

Qualifications and Requirements

There are a number of factors that influence an organization's hiring decisions. Because information security has only recently emerged as a separate discipline, the hiring decisions in this field have been further complicated by a lack of understanding among organizations about what qualifications a potential information security hire should exhibit in order to be deemed competent. Currently in many organizations, the staff of information security teams lacks established roles and responsibilities. For the information security discipline to move forward, the following factors must be addressed:

- The general management community of interest should learn more about the skills and qualifications for both information security positions and those IT positions that impact information security.

- Upper management should also learn more about the budgetary needs of the information security function and the positions within it. This will enable management to make sound fiscal decisions for both the information security function and the IT functions that carry out many of the information security initiatives.
- The IT community of interest as well as the general management community need to learn more about the level of influence and prestige the information security function should be given in order to be effective. This is especially true for the role of chief information security officer.

The following sections address the job requirements for information security professionals, methods for entering the field, descriptions of positions, professional certifications, and finally, recommendations to those who are seeking to enter the field or who are already working in the field.

In most cases, organizations look for a technically qualified information security generalist who has a solid understanding of how an organization operates. In many other career fields, the more specialized professionals become, the more marketable they are. In the information security discipline, however, overspecialization is often a risk. It is important, therefore, to balance one's technical skills with general information security knowledge.

When hiring information security professionals, organizations frequently look for individuals who understand:

- How an organization operates at all levels
- That information security is usually a management problem and is seldom an exclusively technical problem
- How to work with people and collaborate with end-users, and have strong communications and writing skills
- The role of policy in guiding security efforts, and the role of education and training in making employees and other authorized users part of the solution, rather than part of the problem
- Most mainstream IT technologies (not necessarily as experts, but as generalists)
- The terminology of IT and information security; this is the basis for subsequent knowledge and skills needed for the specific positions
- The threats facing an organization and how these threats can become attacks
- How to protect the organization's assets from information security attacks
- How business solutions (including technology-based solutions) can be applied to solve specific information security problems

Entry into the Information Security Profession

Many information security professionals enter the field through one of two career paths: first, ex-law enforcement and military personnel are often involved in national security and cyber-security tasks and move from those environments into the more business-oriented world of information security; and second, technical professionals find themselves working on information security applications and processes more often than on traditional IT assignments. Networking experts, programmers, database administrators, and systems administrators are individuals who may find themselves in the latter circumstance. In recent years, a third (perhaps in some sense more traditional) career path has developed. It involves college students who are selecting and tailoring their degree programs to prepare for work in the field of information security. Figure 11-1 illustrates these career paths.

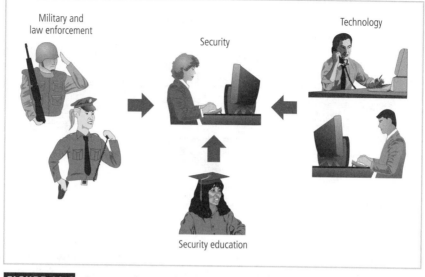

FIGURE 11-1 Career Paths to Information Security Positions

Many hiring managers in the information security field prefer to recruit a security professional who has already proven IT skills and professionalism in another field of IT. IT professionals who move into information security, however, tend to focus on technology—sometimes in place of general information security issues. Organizations can foster greater professionalism in the information security discipline by expanding beyond the hiring of proven IT professionals and instead filling positions by matching qualified candidates to clearly defined information security expectations and position descriptions.

Information Security Positions

The use of standard job descriptions can increase the degree of professionalism in the information security field as well as improve the consistency of roles and responsibilities among organizations. Organizations anticipating a revision of these roles and responsibilities can consult Charles Cresson Wood's book *Information Security Roles and Responsibilities Made Easy*, which offers a set of model job descriptions for information security positions. The book also identifies the responsibilities and duties of the members of the IT staff whose work involves information security.[4] Figure 11-2 illustrates a standard reporting structure for information security positions.

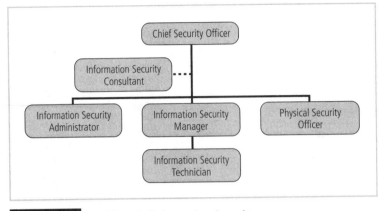

FIGURE 11-2 Positions in Information Security

Another study of information security positions, done by Schwartz, Erwin, Weafer, and Briney, found that positions can be classified into one of three areas: those that *define* information security programs, those that *build* the systems and create the programs to implement the information security controls within the defined programs, and those that *administer* the information security control systems and programs that have been created.

> Definers provide the policies, guidelines and standards...They're the people who do the consulting and the risk assessment, who develop the product and technical architectures. These are senior people with a lot of broad knowledge, but often not a lot of depth...[Builders are] the real techies, who create and install security solutions...[Administrators] operate and administrate the security tools [and] the security monitoring function and...continuously improve the processes, performing all the day-to-day...work...We often try to use the same people for all of these roles. We use builders all the time... If you break your infosec professionals into these three groups, you can recruit them more efficiently, with the policy people being the more senior people, the builders being more technical and the operating people being those you can train to do a specific task.[5]

Examples of some of the job titles that appear in Figure 11-2 are discussed in the following sections.

Chief Information Security Officer (CISO or CSO). This position is typically considered the top information security officer in the organization. As indicated earlier in the chapter, the CISO is usually not an executive-level position and frequently the person in this role will report to the chief information officer. Though CISOs are business managers first and technologists second, they must also be conversant in all areas of information security, including the technical, planning, and policy areas. In many cases, the CISO is the major definer or architect of the information security program of the organization. The CISO performs the following functions:

- Manages the overall information security program for the organization
- Drafts or approves information security policies
- Works with the CIO on strategic plans, develops tactical plans, and works with security managers on operational plans

- Develops information security budgets based on available funding
- Sets priorities for the purchase and implementation of information security projects and technology
- Makes decisions or recommendations on the recruiting, hiring, and firing of security staff
- Acts as the spokesperson for the information security team

Qualifications and Position Requirements: The most common qualification for this type of position is the Certified Information Systems Security Professional (CISSP) accreditation, which is described later in this chapter. A graduate degree is also often required, although it may be from a number of possible disciplines, including information systems, computer science, another information technology field, criminal justice, military science, business, or other fields related to the broader topic of security. To qualify for this level position, the candidate must demonstrate experience as a security manager (see the description of this position in the next section), and present experience with planning, policy, and budgets. As mentioned earlier, some organizations prefer to hire individuals with law enforcement experience. The following is an example of a typical job description for a CISO:

Position: Director of Security

Responsibilities: Reporting to the Senior Vice President of Administration, the Director of Corporate Security will be responsible for all issues related to the security and protection of the company's employees, executives, facilities, proprietary data and information. Accountable for the planning and design of the company's security programs and procedures, this individual will facilitate protection from and resolution of theft, threats, and other situations that may endanger the well-being of the organization. Working through a small staff, the Director will be responsible for executive protection, travel advisories, employee background checks, and a myriad of other activities throughout the corporation on a case-by-case basis. The Director will serve as the company's chief liaison with law enforcement agencies and, most importantly, will serve as a security consultant to all of the company's autonomously run divisions. Travel requirements will be extensive.

Qualifications: The ideal candidate will have a successful background with a federal law enforcement agency, or other applicable experience, that will afford this individual an established network of contacts throughout the country. Additional private industry experience with a sizeable corporation—or as a consultant to same—is preferable. A proactive attitude with regard to security and protection is a must. The successful candidate must be capable of strategically assessing [...] client security needs and have a track record in areas such as crisis management, investigation, facility security, and executive protection. Finally, the candidate should have a basic understanding of the access and use of electronic information services as they apply to security issues. We seek candidates who are flexible enough to deal with varied business cultures and who possess the superior interpersonal skills to perform well in a consulting role where recommendations and advice are sought and valued, but perhaps not always acted upon. A college degree is required.[6]

Security Manager. Security managers are accountable for the day-to-day operation of the information security program. They accomplish objectives identified by the CISO and resolve issues identified by technicians. Management of technology requires an understanding of the technology administered, but does not necessarily require proficiency in the technology's configuration, operation, and fault resolution. (Note that there are a number of positions with titles that contain the word *manager* or other language that suggests management responsibilities, but only those people who are responsible for management functions, such as scheduling, setting relative priorities, or administering budgetary control, should be considered true managers.)

Qualifications and Position Requirements: It is not uncommon for a candidate for this position to have a CISSP. Traditionally, managers earn the CISSP or CISM, and technical professionals earn the Global Information Assurance Certification (GIAC). (A number of certifications that are common in the information security files such as CISSP, CISM, and GIAC, are discussed later in the chapter.) Security managers must have the ability to draft middle- and lower-level policies as well as standards and guidelines. They must have experience in traditional business matters: budgeting, project management, hiring, and firing. They must also be able to manage technicians, both in the assignment of tasks and the monitoring of activities. Experience with business continuity planning is usually a plus. The following is an example of a typical security manager job description. You should note, however, that there are several different types of security managers, as the security manager position is much more specialized than that of CISO. Thus, when applying for a particular job, you should read that job's description carefully, as this is the best way to determine exactly what the employer is looking for.

Position: Information Security Manager

Job description: This management position reports to the Chef Information Security Officer. The successful candidate will manage the development of the information security programs and control systems in conformance with organizational policy and standards across the organization. This is a high-visibility role that involves the day-to-day management of IT Security staff and their career development. The principal accountabilities for this role are as follows:

- Develop and manage information security programs and control systems under the supervision of the CISO in conjunction with the evolving information security architecture of the organization.
- Monitor performance of information security programs and control systems to maintain alignment with organizational policy and common industry practices for emerging threats and technologies.
- Prepare and communicate risk assessments for business risk in software developments as well as ongoing systems events (to include merger, acquisition, and divestiture) and ensure effective risk management across the organization's IT Systems.
- Represent the information security organization in the organization's change management process.
- Perform assigned duties in the area of incident response management and disaster recovery response.
- Supervise assigned staff and perform other general management tasks as assigned including budgeting, staffing, and employee performance reviews.

Compare the general job description above with this more specific job description found in a recent advertisement:

Position: IT Security Compliance Manager

Job description: A job has arisen for an IT Security Compliance Manager reporting to the IT Security Manager. In this role you will manage the development of the client's IT Security standards and operate a compliance program to ensure conformance at all stages of the systems lifecycle. This is a key, hands-on role with the job holder taking an active part in the delivery of the compliance program. The role will also involve the day-to-day management of IT Security staff and their career development. The principal accountabilities for this role are as follows:

- Develop and manage an IT security compliance program.
- Develop the client's security standards in line with industry standards and emerging threats and technologies.
- Identify IT-related business risk in new software and game developments and ensure that effective risk management solutions are identified and complied with.
- Manage and conduct IT security compliance reviews in conjunction with Operational and IT Audit staff.
- Conduct investigations into security breaches or vulnerabilities.

Candidate profile: The ideal candidate should have five years experience of managing the implementation of technical security controls and related operational procedures and must have sound business risk management skills. You must have a flexible approach to working and must be able and willing to work unsociable hours to meet the demands of the role.[7]

The second example illustrates the confusion that currently exists in the information security field regarding job titles and reporting relationships among information security professionals. Where the first job description identifies responsibilities for the position and describes points where information security interacts with other business functions, the second commingles responsibilities among several business functions and does not seem to reflect a clearly defined role for the position or the information security unit within the organization. Until some similarity in job titles and expected roles and responsibilities emerges, information security job candidates should carefully research roles and responsibilities for each position they apply to instead of relying solely on the implications of the job's title.

Security Technician.   Security technicians are the technically qualified individuals tasked to configure firewalls, deploy IDSs, implement security software, diagnose and troubleshoot problems, and coordinate with systems and network administrators to ensure that an organization's security technology is properly implemented. The position of security technician is often offered as an entry-level position, but to be hired in this role, candidates must possess some technical skills. This often poses a dilemma for applicants since many seeking to enter a new field find it is difficult to get a job without experience, and experience comes only when they have been hired for a job. Just as in the networking arena, security technicians tend to be specialized, focusing on one major security technology group (firewalls, IDSs, servers, routers, or software) and further specializing in one particular software or hardware package, such as Check Point firewalls, Nokia firewalls, or Trip Wire IDSs. These areas are sufficiently complex to warrant a high level of specialization. But if individuals hired for one of these positions want to move up in the corporate hierarchy, they must expand their knowledge horizontally—that is, gain an understanding of the general organizational issues related to information security, as well as its technical areas.

Qualifications and Position Requirements: The technical qualifications and position requirements for a security technician are varied. Organizations prefer the expert, certified, proficient technician. Regardless of the area, the particular job description covers some level of experience with a particular hardware and software package. Sometimes familiarity with a technology secures an applicant an interview; however, actual experience in using the technology is usually required. The following is a typical job announcement for a security technician:

Position: Firewall Engineering Consultant

Job Description: Working for an exciting customer-focused security group within one of the largest managed network providers in Europe. You will have the opportunity to expand your experience and gain all the technical and professional support to achieve within the group. Must have experience to third line technical support of firewall technologies. Check Point certified. Experienced in Nokia systems.

Package: Possible company car, discretionary bonus, private health care, on-call pay, and overtime pay.[8]

Because overtime and on-call pay are listed, this is probably an hourly position rather than a salaried one, which is commonly the case for security technician positions. The move to a salaried position is typically a move from technician to manager.

Credentials of Information Security Professionals

As mentioned earlier, many organizations seek industry-recognized certifications when reviewing the credentials of applicants. This is often done to screen candidates for the level of technical proficiency required for the various security positions. Unfortunately, however, most of the existing certifications are relatively new and not fully understood by hiring organizations. As such, the certifying bodies are working hard to educate employers and potential professionals on the value and qualifications of their certificate programs. In the meantime, employers are trying to understand the match between certifications and the position requirements, and hopeful professionals are trying to gain meaningful employment based on their newly received certifications. This section presents information on the current and planned certifications that have achieved some degree of recognition. You may recall that Chapter 3 briefly touched on some of this material in the discussion of professional associations and their codes of ethics. In this chapter, the description of each certification contains the qualifications of recipients, the knowledge tested, and the means of testing.

Certified Information Systems Security Professional (CISSP) and Systems Security Certified Practitioner (SSCP)

Considered the most prestigious certification for security managers and CISOs, the Certified Information Systems Security Professional or CISSP is one of two certifications offered by the International Information Systems Security Certification Consortium (ISC)^2 (see *www.isc2.org*). In order to sit for the CISSP exam, the candidate must possess at least three years of direct full-time security professional work experience in one or more of the 10 domains of information security knowledge listed below. The CISSP exam itself, which covers all 10 domains, consists of 250 multiple-choice questions and must be completed within six hours.

- Access control systems and methodology
- Applications and systems development
- Business continuity planning
- Cryptography
- Law, investigation, and ethics
- Operations security
- Physical security
- Security architecture and models
- Security management practices
- Telecommunications, network, and Internet security

The CISSP certification requires both the successful completion of the examination and an endorsement by a qualified third party, typically another CISSP-certified professional, the candidate's employer, or a licensed, certified, or commissioned professional. Ostensibly, this is to guarantee that the individual meets the qualifications and requirements of the overall process. The breadth and depth covered in each of the 10 domains makes the CISSP one of the most challenging certifications on the market to achieve. Once a candidate receives the CISSP, he or she must earn a specific number of continuing education credits every three years to retain this certification.

In recent years, the CISSP certification program has added a set of concentration exams. These additional designations are the ISSEP: Information Systems Security Engineering Professional; the ISSAP: Information Systems Security Architecture Professional; and the ISSMP: Information Systems Security Management Professional. These certification extensions are designed to work in tandem with the CISSP credential. As such, to sit for any of these concentration examinations, one must be a CISSP professional in good standing. A CISSP may demonstrate more in-depth knowledge in information security architecture by obtaining the ISSAP credential, much like an English major at a university might demonstrate knowledge in Shakespeare by concentrating in British Literature.[9]

The development of the ISSEP concentration exam and its topical content are described by (ISC)^2 as follows:

> ISSEP stands for Information Systems Security Engineering Professional. ISSEP was developed under a joint agreement between (ISC)^2 and the United States National Security Agency, Information Assurance Directorate (NSA/IAD). The motivation and justification for NSA's involvement in this project is found in NSD 42 and the Federal Technology Transfer Act of 1986 (15 U.S.C. Section 3710A) [...] The ISSEP provides the means for (ISC)^2 to offer CISSPs a mechanism to demonstrate specific competence in the concentrated area of information security engineering. [...] The

major domains of the ISSEP examination are: Systems Security Engineering, Certification and Accreditation, Technical Management, and U.S. Government Information Assurance Regulations.[10]

The development of the ISSAP concentration exam and its topical content are described by (ISC)[2] as follows:

> ISSAP stands for Information Systems Security Architecture Professional. The development of concentration examinations is a direct response to (ISC)[2] research indicating that these needs of information security professionals were not being met. This examination is designed to provide CISSPs with a mechanism to demonstrate competence in the more in-depth and concentrated requirements of information security architecture, within the broader scope of information security knowledge identified in the CBK and required for CISSP certification. The major domains for this examination are: Access Control, Systems and Methodologies, Telecommunications and Network Security, Cryptography, Requirements Analysis & Security Standards, Guidelines, Criteria, and Technology Related BCP and DRP.[11]

The development of the ISSMP concentration exam and its topical content are described by (ISC)[2] as follows:

> ISSMP stands for Information Systems Security Management Professional. The development of concentration examinations is a direct response to (ISC)[2] research indicating that these needs of information security professionals were not being met. This examination is designed to provide CISSPs with a mechanism to demonstrate competence in the more in-depth and concentrated requirements of information security management [...] The major domains for this examination are: Enterprise Security Management Practices, Enterprise-Wide System Development Security, Overseeing Compliance of Operations Security, Understanding BCP, DRP, and COOP, and Law, Investigations, Forensics, and Ethics.[12]

Each CISSP concentration exam consists of 125 to 150 questions, depending on the subject matter, and has an allowed testing time of three hours. When a candidate passes the concentration exam, the credential obtained then runs concurrently with the underlying CISSP credential. During subsequent certification periods, 20 of the 120 Continuing Professional Education (CPE) hours already required for the underlying CISSP certificate must be in the specific area of concentration. For example, if a CISSP-certified professional took the ISSMP concentration exam and passed, he/she would be required to document that at least 20 of the total 120 CPE hours required for the CISSP certificate were in the specific area of information security management.[13]

Given the difficulty involved in mastering all 10 domains, many information security professionals seek other, less rigorous, certifications. In response, (ISC)[2] has developed its second certification: the Systems Security Certified Practitioner or SSCP. SSCP was designed to recognize mastery of an international standard for information security and understanding of a common body of knowledge (sometimes called the CBK). The SSCP certification is oriented toward the security administrator. Like the CISSP, the SSCP certification is more applicable to the information security manager than the technician, because most questions focus on the operational nature of information security. In other words, the SSCP focuses "on practices, roles, and responsibilities as defined by experts from major IS industries."[14] Even so, an information security technician seeking advancement can benefit from acquiring this certification.

The SSCP exam consists of 125 multiple-choice questions, and must be completed within three hours. Instead of the ten domains of the CISSP, the SSCP covers seven domains:

- Access controls
- Administration
- Audit and monitoring
- Risk, response, and recovery
- Cryptography
- Data communications
- Malicious code and malware

The SSCP is considered by many to be the little brother of the CISSP. It is a widely recognized certification and is easier to obtain than the CISSP. The seven domains are not a subset of the CISSP domains, but are an independent organization of similar content. The CBK defined for the SSCP contains slightly more technical content than the CBK for the CISSP. Just as with the CISSP, an SSCP recipient must earn continuing education credits to retain the certification, or else retake the exam.

Certified Information Systems Auditor (CISA) and Certified Information Security Manager (CISM)

Although it does not primarily focus on information security certification, the Certified Information Systems Auditor or CISA certification contains many information security components. The Information Systems Audit and Control Association (ISACA) offers the CISA certification for auditing, networking, and security professionals and the CISM certification for information security management professionals. All ISACA certifications have the following common requirements:

- Successful completion of the requisite examination
- Experience as an information systems auditor, with a minimum of five years' professional experience in an area of direct interest to the certification
- Agreement to the ISACA Code of Professional Ethics
- Continuing education policy that requires maintenance fees and a minimum of 20 contact hours of continuing education each year and a minimum of 120 contact hours over the three-year certification period

The CISA certification is open to those who have passed the CISA exam. The exam is offered once a year and covers the following areas of information systems auditing:

- The IS audit process (10%)
- Management, planning, and organization of IS (11%)
- Technical infrastructure and operational practices (13%)
- Protection of information assets (25%)
- Disaster recovery and business continuity (10%)
- Business application systems development, acquisition, implementation, and maintenance (16%)
- Business process evaluation and risk management (15%)

An alternative to the CISA certificate program is the CISM. This certificate is open to those who have passed the CISM exam, also offered once a year. This exam covers the following areas of information security practices:

- Information security governance (21%)
- Risk management (21%)
- Information security program management (21%)
- Information security management (24%)
- Response management (13%)

Both the CISA and CISM are well-regarded certifications for prospective CISO and information security managers to acquire.

Global Information Assurance Certification (GIAC)

The System Administration, Networking, and Security Organization, better known as SANS (*www.sans.org*), developed a series of technical security certifications in 1999 that are known as the Global Information Assurance Certification or GIAC family of certifications (see *www.giac.org*). At the time the GIAC was established, there were no technical certifications available elsewhere. Before the GIAC was available, anyone who wished to be certified to work in the technical security field could obtain only vendor-specific networking or computing certifications, such as the MCSE (Microsoft Certified Systems Engineer) or CNE (Certified Novell Engineer). Now, an individual can choose to attain the various GIAC certifications separately or pursue a comprehensive certification known as the GIAC Security Engineer (GSE). GIAC also has a managerial certification, the GIAC Information Security Officer (GISO). Like the SSCP, the GISO is an overview certification that combines basic technical knowledge with an understanding of threats, risks, and best practices.

The various individual GIAC certifications include:

- GIAC Security Essentials Certification (GSEC)
- GIAC Certified Firewall Analyst (GCFW)
- GIAC Certified Intrusion Analyst (GCIA)
- GIAC Certified Incident Handler (GCIH)
- GIAC Certified Windows Security Administrator (GCWN)
- GIAC Certified UNIX Security Administrator (GCUX)
- GIAC Information Security Officer - Basic (GISO - Basic)
- GIAC Systems and Network Auditor (GSNA)
- GIAC Certified Forensic Analyst (GCFA)
- GIAC Security Leadership Certificate (GSLC)

Unlike other certifications, the GIAC certifications require the applicant first to complete a written practical assignment. This assignment is intended to require the applicant to demonstrate his or her abilities and skills by putting them into practice. These assignments are submitted to the SANS Information Security Reading Room for evaluation by security practitioners. Only when the practical assignment is complete is the candidate allowed to take the online exam.

SANS provides the following instructions for individuals interested in GIAC certification:

- Complete a practical/research paper and one or two exams (depending on your certification track).
- Your practical must receive a passing grade before you will be authorized to take the exams.
- Complete the online exams for that particular subject via the GIAC Web site. Most exams are 75 questions (multiple choice), and must be completed within two hours. A few of the exams are 90 questions and must be completed within three hours.
- If you submit an acceptable practical and pass your exams, you will be GIAC certified.[15]

Before candidates are even allowed to sit for the final certification for obtaining the GIAC Security Engineer designation, which is considered the pinnacle of GIAC certifications, they must earn *all* of the various GIAC certifications *and* receive honors recognition in at least one. GIAC is designed not only to test an individual's knowledge of a field, but also requires application of that knowledge through a practicum. While there are a growing number of entry-level certifications such as the Security+ and SCP certificates (both of which are described in forthcoming sections), GIAC is currently the only certification for advanced technical knowledge.

Security Certified Professional (SCP)

One of the newest certifications in the information security discipline is the Security Certified Professional or SCP certification (see *www.securitycertified.net*). The SCP certification provides two tracks: the SCNP (Security Certified Network Professional) and the SCNA (Security Certified Network Architect). Both tracks are designed for the security technician and have dominant technical components, although SCNA also emphasizes authentication principles. Also, even though both SCNP and SCNA have a networking focus, they concentrate on network security rather than on true networking (which, for example, is covered by MSCE and CNE).

The SCNP track focuses on firewalls and intrusion detection, and requires two exams:[16]

- Network Security Fundamentals (NSF)
- Network Defense and Countermeasures (NDC)

The SCNA program focuses more on authentication, including biometrics and PKI. The two exams in the SCNA certification are:

- PKI and Biometrics Concepts and Planning (PBC)
- PKI and Biometrics Implementation (PBI)

Although not as detailed as the GIAC certifications, SCP programs provide those new to the career field of information security a useful mechanism to getting started and are a vendor-neutral means by which a practitioner can document professional and technical skills.

TruSecure ICSA Certified Security Associate (TICSA)

The TICSA certifications are among the first certifications to be offered by service vendors. TruSecure Corporation is a well-known service vendor and is promoting the ICSA security practitioner tracks. The ICSA (Internet Certified Security Associate) approach is put forward as a vendor-neutral approach to hardware/software that focuses on providing "certifications that are skills- and knowledge-based, technology specific, and pragmatic." As with other certifications, a candidate must demonstrate appropriate experience and training before being allowed to sit for the ISCA examinations. The promoters of these certificates describe them as follows: "Complementary to CISSP, in as much as it is designed for the IT practitioner responsible for ensuring security principles are applied in the context of their daily job scope; and it represents a stepping stone toward higher-level security management."[17] In fact, the managing director of (ISC)[2] has endorsed these certifications as more technical than the SSCP. The TICSA certification is highly technical and is targeted towards network and systems administrators. According to TruSecure, to attain the TICSA, a candidate must (1) have two years experience in an area of information security in one of the TruSecure areas of risk (see the bulleted list in the next paragraph), (2) have at least 48 hours of training or coursework in security, (3) complete the written exam, and (4) subscribe to the TruSecure ICSA Security Practitioner Code of Ethics.

Because these examinations are based largely on the TruSecure methodology, they cannot be considered vendor-neutral. The examination is also based on the following six categories of risk, as defined by TruSecure:

- Electronic
  - External and internal
  - Hacking and sniffing
  - Spoofing
- Malicious code
  - Viruses and worms
  - Java and ActiveX
  - Trojans
- Physical
  - Theft and terminal hijack
- Human social engineering
- Privacy
- Downtime
  - DoS attacks
  - Bugs
  - Power
  - Civil unrest
  - Natural disasters[18]

The exam consists of approximately 70 multiple-choice questions and must be completed within 90 minutes.

Security+

CompTIA (*www.comptia.com*) introduced the first truly vendor-neutral technical professional IT certifications—the A+ series. Offered as part of the A+ program, the Security+ certification focuses on the key skills that are necessary to perform security, but is not tied to a particular software or hardware vendor package. According to the CompTIA Web site, "the CompTIA Security+ certification tests for security knowledge mastery of an individual with two years on-the-job networking experience, with emphasis on security. The exam covers industry-wide topics, including communication security, infrastructure security, cryptography, access control, authentication, external attack and operational and organization security."[19] In order to obtain the Security+ certification, applicants only have to take a single, 100-question exam within 90 minutes, offered through most online testing centers. Successful applicants will score at least 764 on a scale of 100 – 900. The exam objectives focus on "General Security Concepts (30% of the exam); Communication Security (20%); Infrastructure Security (20%); Basics of Cryptography (15%); and Operational/Organizational Security (15%)."[20]

Certified Information Forensics Investigator

There is a new certification under development by the International Information Systems Forensics Association (*www.infoforensics.org*). Called the Certified Information Forensics Investigator (CIFI), this certification "is specifically developed for experienced information forensics investigators who have practical experience in performing investigation for law enforcement or as part of a corporate investigations team. The CIFI certification is designed to demonstrate expertise in all aspects of the information investigative process and is dedicated to bringing a level of consistency to the profession than can be recognized outside the field."[21] The common body of knowledge (CBK) for the CIFI includes the following domains:

- Auditing
- Incident response teams
- Law and investigation
- Tools and techniques
- Traceback
- Countermeasures

The CIFI exam contains 200 questions covering the six CBKs. Applicants must score 75% or better to pass. Additional information on the certification and the CBKs is available on the International Information Systems Forensics Association's Web site.

Related Certifications

There are a number of certifications that are related to the field of information security or contain information security components. Such certifications have been developed by the following companies and associations:

- Brainbench
- Check Point Software Technologies Ltd.
- Cisco Systems
- Entrust
- Information Systems Audit and Control Association
- International Webmasters Association
- Learning Tree International
- Novell Corporation
- Microsoft Corporate
- Sun Corporation
- Pine Mountain Group
- Prosoft Training
- RSA Security Inc.

- Symantec
- Tivoli Systems[22]

The details of these certifications are too varied to cover here. Additional information on these and other certifications can be found on these companies' Web sites.

Cost of Being Certified

Certifications cost money, and the better certifications can be quite expensive to attain. Some certification exams can run as much as $500 per examination, and their entire educational track can cost several thousand dollars. The cost of the formal training required to prepare the candidate for the certification can also be significant. While these courses should not serve as the candidate's only means of preparations for the certification exam, they can help candidates round out their knowledge and fill in gaps. As mentioned earlier, some of the exams, such as the CISSP, are very broad and others very technical. Even an experienced professional would find it difficult to sit for one of these exams without some preparation. Many candidates teach themselves through trade press books. Others prefer the structure of classroom training, because it includes practicing the technical components on equipment the candidate may not be able to access on his or her own. At any rate, certifications are designed to recognize experts in their respective fields, and the cost of certification is meant to limit the number of candidates who take exams just to see if they can pass. Most examinations admit only candidates with two and three years of expertise in the skills being tested. Before attempting a certification exam, the successful candidate does all the required homework. Candidates for certification should look into the exam criteria, purpose, and requirements in order to ensure that the time and energy devoted to pursuing the certification are well spent. Figure 11-3 shows several approaches to preparing for security certification.

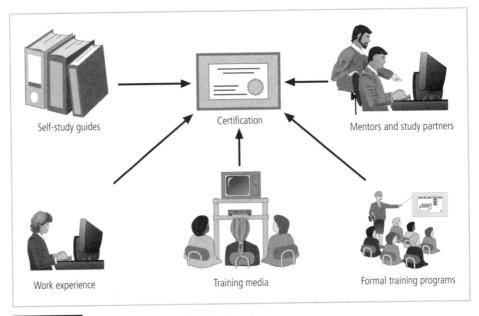

FIGURE 11-3 Preparing for Security Certification

Advice for Information Security Professionals

As a future information security professional, you may benefit from keeping the following suggestions in mind when you enter the information security job market:

- Always remember: Business before technology. Technology solutions are tools for solving business problems. Information security professionals are sometimes guilty of looking for ways to apply the newest technology to problems that do not require technology-based solutions.

- When evaluating a problem, look at the source of the problem first, determine what factors impact the problem, and see where organizational policy can lead you in the design of a solution that is independent of technology; then use technology to deploy the controls necessary for the implementation of the solution. Technology can provide elegant solutions for some problems, but for others, it only adds to the difficulties.

- Your job is to protect the organization's information and information systems resources. Never lose sight of the goal: protection.

- Be heard and not seen. Information security should be transparent to the users. With minor exceptions, the actions taken to protect the information should not interfere with the users' actions. Information security supports the work of end users, not the other way around. The only routine communications that should be conducted from the security team to the users should be the periodic awareness messages, training announcements, newsletters, and e-mails.

- Know more than you say, and be more skillful than you let on. Don't try to impress users, managers, and other nontechnical people with your level of knowledge and experience. One day you just might run into a Jedi master of information security who puts you in your place.

- Speak *to* users, not *at* them. While you are talking to users, use their language, not yours. Users aren't impressed with techno-babble and jargon. They may not comprehend the TLAs (three letter acronyms), technical components, software, and hardware necessary to protect their systems, but they do know how to short-circuit your next budget request or pick out the flaws in your business report.

- Your education is never complete. As sensitive as you are to the idea that information technology is ever evolving, you must be equally sensitive to the idea that information security education is never complete. Just when you think you have mastered the latest skills, you will encounter changes in threats, protection technology, your business environment, or the regulatory environment. As a security professional, you must expect to continue with the learning process throughout your entire career. This is best accomplished through periodic seminars, training programs, and formal education. Even if the organization (or your pocketbook) cannot afford the more extensive and expensive training programs and conferences, you can keep abreast of the market by reading trade literature (magazines), textbooks, and news articles on security. You can also subscribe to the many mailing lists for information security professionals. Several are listed in the Offline entitled "What's in a Name?" Join at least one professional information security association, such as the Information Systems Security Association (*www.issa.org*). Whatever approach you take, keep on top of the reading, never stop learning, and make yourself the best-informed security professional possible. It can only enhance your worth to the organization and your career.

OFFLINE

What's in a Name?

Here are some of the job titles listed in the job search databases that were reviewed to prepare this section. See if you can guess the position level based on the title.

- Senior security analyst
- SAP security analyst
- Security supervisor
- Direct loss prevention manager
- Security officer (not a guard job)
- Loss prevention consultant
- Site supervisor—security
- Safeguards and security specialist

To perform your own job title search or to search for an actual job in the field of information security, you can begin by reviewing the job search databases at the following Web sites:

- *http://justsecurityjobs.com*
- *http://www.salary.com/careers/layouthtmls/crel_searchjob_IT10000225.html*
- *http://securityjobs.net*
- *http://jobsearch.usajobs.opm.gov/a9dhs.asp*
- *http://www.itsecurityjobs.com*
- *http://www.usajobs.opm.gov/homeland.asp*
- *http://www.csoonline.com/jobs/index.cfm*
- *http://seclists.org/lists/security-jobs/2004/Jul/0067.html*

Employment Policies and Practices

To create an environment in which information security is taken seriously, an organization should make information security a documented part of every employee's job description. In other words, the general management community of interest should integrate solid information security concepts into the organization's employment policies and practices. The section that follows examines the important information security-related issues associated with recruiting, hiring, firing, and managing human resources in an organization.

From an information security perspective, the hiring of employees is a responsibility laden with potential security pitfalls. Therefore, the CISO and information security manager should establish a dialogue with the human resources department to provide information security input to the guidelines used for hiring all personnel. Figure 11-4 highlights some of the hiring issues.

Certifications

Policies

Background checks

Covenants and
agreements

Contracts

FIGURE 11-4 Hiring Issues

Job Descriptions

The process of integrating information security perspectives into the hiring process begins with reviewing and updating all job descriptions. To prevent people from applying for positions based solely on access to sensitive information, the organization should avoid revealing access privileges to prospective employees when it advertises open positions.

Interviews

The next point of contact with a potential employee is the job interview. Some interviews are conducted with members of the human resources staff, and others include members of the department for which the new position is being offered. An opening within the information security department creates a unique opportunity for the security manager to educate HR on the various certifications and the specific experience each certification requires, as well as the qualifications of a good candidate. For all other areas of the organization, information security should, for the same reason mentioned during the discussion of job descriptions, advise HR to limit the information provided to the candidate about the responsibilities and access rights that the new hire would have. For those organizations that include on-site visits as part of their initial or follow-up interviews, it is important to exercise caution when showing a candidate around the facility. Avoid tours through secure and restricted sites. Candidates who are shown around may be able to retain enough information about the operations or information security functions to become a threat.

Background Checks

A background check should be conducted before the organization extends an offer to a candidate. A background check is an investigation into the candidate's past that specifically looks for criminal or other types of behavior that could indicate potential for future misconduct. There are a number of government regulations that govern what the organization can investigate, and how much of the information uncovered can be allowed to influence the hiring decision. The security manager and HR manager should discuss these matters with competent legal counsel to determine what state and federal (and perhaps international) regulations impact the hiring process.

Background checks differ in the level of detail and depth with which they examine a candidate. In the military, background checks determine the individual's level of security classification, a requirement for many positions. In the business world, a background check can determine the level of trust the business places in the individual. Individuals being considered for security positions should expect to be subjected to a moderately high level of background check. Those considering careers in law enforcement or high-security positions may even be required to submit to polygraph tests. The following is a list of various types of background checks with the type of information each looks into:

- Identity checks: Validation of personal identity and Social Security number
- Education and credential checks: Validation of institutions attended, degrees and certifications earned, and certification status
- Previous employment verification: Validation of where candidates worked, why they left, what they did, and for how long
- Reference checks: Validation of references and integrity of reference sources
- Worker's compensation history: Investigation of claims from worker's compensation
- Motor vehicle records: Investigation of driving records, suspensions, and DUIs
- Drug history: Screening for drugs and drug usage, past and present
- Credit history: Investigation of credit problems, financial problems, and bankruptcy
- Civil court history: Investigation of involvement as the plaintiff or defendant in civil suits
- Criminal court history: Investigation of criminal background, arrests, convictions, and time served

As mentioned, there are federal regulations regarding the use of personal information in employment practices, including the Fair Credit Reporting Act (FCRA), which governs the activities of consumer credit reporting agencies and the uses of the information procured from these agencies.[23] These credit reports generally contain information on a job candidate's credit history, employment history, and other personal data.

Among other things, the FCRA prohibits employers from obtaining these reports unless the candidate is informed in writing that such a report will be requested as part of the employment process. FCRA also allows the candidate to request information on the nature and type of reporting used in the making of the employment decision and subsequently enables the candidate to learn the content of these reports. The FCRA also restricts the periods of time these reports can address. Unless the candidate earns more than $75,000 per year, the report can contain only seven years' worth of negative credit information. If the candidate earns $75,000 or more per year, there is no time limitation. Note that "any person who knowingly and willfully obtains information on a consumer from a consumer reporting agency under false pretenses shall be fined under title 18, United States Code, imprisoned for not more than two years, or both."[24]

Employment Contracts

Once a candidate has accepted a job offer, the employment contract becomes an important security instrument. Many of the policies discussed in Chapter 5, specifically the fair and responsible use policies, require an employee to agree in writing to monitoring and nondisclosure agreements. If an existing employee refuses to sign these contracts, the security personnel are placed in a difficult situation. They may not be able to force the employee to sign, nor to deny the employee access to the systems necessary to perform his or her duties. With new employees, however, security personnel are in a different situation since the procedural step of policy acknowledgment can be made a requirement of employment. Policies that govern employee behavior and are applied to all employees may be classified as "employment contingent upon agreement." This classification means the employee is not actually employed until he or she agrees in a written affidavit to conform with these binding organizational policies. Some organizations choose to execute the remainder of the employment contract *after* the candidate has signed the security agreements. Although this may seem harsh, it is a necessary component of the security process. Employment contracts may also contain restrictive clauses regarding the creation and ownership of intellectual property while the candidate is employed by the organization. These provisions may require the employee to protect the information assets of the organization actively— especially those assets that are critical to security.

New Hire Orientation

As new employees are introduced into the organization's culture and workflow, they should receive as part of their new employee orientation an extensive information security briefing. All major policies should be explained, along with the procedures for performing necessary security operations and the new position's other information security requirements. In addition, the levels of authorized access should be outlined for the new employees, and training should be provided to them regarding the secure use of information systems. By the time new employees are ready to report to their positions, they should be thoroughly briefed on the security component of their particular jobs, as well as the rights and responsibilities of all personnel in the organization.

On-the-Job Security Training

The organization should integrate the security awareness education described in Chapter 5 into a new hire's ongoing job orientation, and make it a part of every employee's on-the-job security training. Keeping security at the forefront of employees' minds helps minimize employee mistakes and is, therefore, an important part of the information security team's mission. Formal external and informal internal seminars should also be used to increase the security awareness level of employees, especially that of security employees. An example of the importance of proper and ongoing security training awareness of employees can be found in the *9/11 Commission Report*, which is a congressional examination (published in 2004) of the events leading up to the terrorist attacks of September 11, 2001. As the following excerpt shows, upon reviewing the videotapes made at the security checkpoints in airports when the terrorists were passing through, security investigators found the security process inadequate, not from a technological standpoint, but from a human one:

> When the local civil aviation security office of the Federal Aviation Administration (FAA) later investigated these security screening operations, the screeners recalled nothing out of the ordinary. They could not recall that any of the passengers they screened were CAPPS selectees. We asked a screening expert to review the videotape of the hand-wanding, and he found the quality of the screener's work to have been "marginal at best." The screener should have "resolved" what set off the alarm; and in the case of both Moqed and Hazmi, it was clear that he did not.[25]

This excerpt illustrates how physical security is dependent on the human element. As with physical security, the maintaining of information security also depends heavily on the consistent vigilance of people. In many information security breaches, the hardware and software usually accomplished what they were designed to do, but people failed to make the correct decisions and follow-up choices. To conclude, education and regular training of employees and authorized users are important elements of information security—and therefore cannot be ignored.

Performance Evaluation

To heighten information security awareness and minimize workplace behavior that poses risks to information security, organizations should incorporate information security components into employee performance evaluations. For example, if employees have been observed writing system passwords on sticky notes stuck to their monitor, they should be warned, and if such behavior continues, they should be reminded of their failure to comply with the organization's information security regulations during their annual performance review. In general, employees pay close attention to job performance evaluations, and are more likely to be motivated to take information security seriously if their performance with respect to information security tasks and responsibilities is documented in these evaluations.

Termination

Leaving the organization may or may not be a decision made by the employee. Organizations may downsize, be bought out or taken over, shut down, run out of business, or simply be forced to lay off, fire, or relocate their work force. In any event, when an employee leaves an organization, there are a number of security-related issues that arise. Key among these is the continuity of protection of all information to which the employee had access. Therefore, when an employee prepares to leave an organization, the following tasks must be performed:

- Access to the organization's systems must be disabled.
- Removable media must be returned.
- Hard drives must be secured.
- File cabinet locks must be changed.
- Office door lock must be changed.
- Keycard access must be revoked.
- Personal effects must be removed from the organization's premises.

After the employee has delivered keys, keycards, and other business property, he or she should be escorted from the premises.

In addition to the tasks listed above, many organizations use an **exit interview** to remind the employee of contractual obligations, such as nondisclosure agreements, and to obtain feedback on the employee's tenure in the organization. At this time, the employee should be reminded that should he or she fail to comply with contractual obligations, civil or criminal action may be initiated.

In reality, most employees are allowed to clean out their own offices and collect their personal belongings, and simply asked to return their keys. From a security standpoint, these procedures are/would be considered risky and lax, for they expose the organization's information to disclosure and theft. To minimize such risks, an organization should ideally have security-minded termination procedures that are followed consistently—in other words, they are followed regardless of what level of trust the organization had placed in the employee and what the level of cordiality is generally maintained in the office environment. But this kind of universally consistent approach is a difficult and awkward practice to implement (which is why it's not often applied). Given the realities of workplaces, the simplest and best method for handling the out-processing of an employee may be to select, based on the employee's reasons for leaving, one of the scenarios that follows.

Hostile departures include termination for cause, permanent downsizing, temporary lay-off, or some instances of quitting. Before the employee knows that he or she is leaving, or as soon as the hostile resignation is tendered, the security staff should terminate all logical and keycard access. In the case of involuntary terminations, the employee should be escorted into the supervisor's office for the bad news. Upon receiving the termination notice, or tendering a hostile resignation, the employee should be escorted to his or her office, cubicle, or personal area and allowed to collect personal effects. No organizational property should be allowed to be taken from the premises, including diskettes, pens, papers, and books. Regardless of the claim the employee has on organizational property, he or she should not be allowed to take it from the premises. If there is property that the employee strongly wishes to retain, the employee should be informed that he or she can submit, in writing, a list of the particular items and the reasons why he or she should be allowed to retain it. After the employee's personal property has been gathered, the employee should be asked to surrender all company property such as but not limited to keys, keycards, organizational identification, physical access devices, PDAs, pagers, cell phones, and portable computers. The employee should then be escorted out of the building.

Friendly departures include resignation, retirement, promotion, or relocation. In this case, the employee may have tendered notice well in advance of the actual departure date. This scenario actually makes it much more difficult for the security team to maintain positive control over the employee's access and information usage. Employee accounts are usually allowed to continue to exist, though an expiration date can be set for the employee's declared date of departure. Another complication associated with friendly departures is that until their departure date employees can come and go at will, which means they are usually collecting their own belongings and leaving under their own cognizance. As with hostile departures, employees should be asked to drop off all organizational property on their final way out.

In either circumstance (hostile or friendly), the offices and information used by the employee must be inventoried, files must be stored or destroyed, and all property must be returned to organizational stores. It is possible in either situation that the employees foresee their departure well in advance and, perhaps thinking that such items may be valuable in their future employment, start taking home organizational information such as files, reports, and data from databases. This may be impossible to prevent. Only by scrutinizing systems logs after the employee has departed and sorting out authorized actions from systems misuse or information theft can the organization determine if there has been a breach of policy or a loss of information. In the event that information is illegally copied or stolen, the action should be declared an incident and the appropriate policy followed. Figure 11-5 overviews some termination activities.

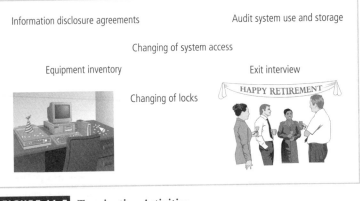

Information disclosure agreements

Audit system use and storage

Changing of system access

Equipment inventory

Exit interview

Changing of locks

HAPPY RETIREMENT

FIGURE 11-5 Termination Activities

Security Considerations for Nonemployees

A number of individuals who are not subject to rigorous screening, contractual obligations, and eventual secured termination often have access to sensitive organizational information. As outlined in the sections that follow, relationships with individuals in this category should be carefully managed to prevent a possible information leak or theft.

Temporary Employees

Temporary employees are hired by the organization to serve in a temporary position or to supplement the existing workforce. These employees may not actually work for the organization where they are performing their duties, but may instead be the paid employees of a "temp agency" or organization that provides specifically qualified individuals at the paid request of another company. Temps typically perform secretarial or administrative support, and thus may be exposed to a wide range of information. As they are not employed by the host organization, they are often not subject to the contractual obligations or general policies of other employees. If these individuals violate a policy or cause a problem, the strongest action the host organization can take is to terminate the relationships with the individuals and request that they be censured. The employing agency is under no contractual obligation to do this, however, though it may censure the employee to appease a powerful or lucrative client.

From a security standpoint, temporary employees' access to information should be limited to that which is necessary for them to perform their duties. The organization can attempt to have temporary employees sign nondisclosure agreements and fair use policies, but the temp agency may refuse, forcing the host organization to choose between arranging for a new temp agency, going without the assistance of a temp worker, or allowing the temp to work without the agreement. This can create a situation that is awkward and potentially dangerous, as temporary workers may inadvertently gain access to information that does not directly relate to their responsibilities. The only way to combat this threat is to ensure that the temp's supervisor restricts the information to which the temp has access and makes sure all employees follow good security practices, especially those practices relating to clean desk policies and the security of classified data. Temps can provide great benefits to the host organization, but should not be employed at the cost of sacrificing information security.

Contract Employees

Contract employees are typically hired to perform specific services for the organization. In such cases, the host company often makes a contract with a parent organization rather than with an individual for a particular task. Typical contract employees include groundskeepers, maintenance service people, electrical contractors, mechanical service contractors, and other service repair people. Although some individuals may require access to virtually all areas of the organization to do their jobs, they seldom need access to information or information resources, except in the case where the organization has leased computing equipment or has contracted with a disaster recovery service. Contract employees may also need access to various facilities, but this does not mean they should be allowed to wander freely in and out of buildings. To maintain a secure facility, all contract employees should be escorted from room to room, as well as into and out of the facility. When these employees report for maintenance or repair services, the first step security personnel should take is to verify that these services are actually scheduled or called for. As indicated in earlier chapters, it is not unheard of for an attacker to dress up as a telephone repairman, maintenance technician, or janitor to gain physical access to a building, and therefore, direct supervision of contract employees is a necessity.

Another necessary aspect of hiring contract employees is making certain that restrictions or requirements are negotiated into the contract agreements when they are activated. The following regulations should be negotiated well in advance: the facility requires 24 to 48 hours notice of a maintenance visit; the facility requires all on-site personnel to undergo background checks; and the facility requires advance notice for cancellation or rescheduling of a maintenance visit.

Consultants

Sometimes on-site contracted employees are self-employed or they are employees of an organization hired for a specific, one-time purpose. These people are typically referred to as consultants, and they have their own security requirements and contractual obligations. Consultants should have all specific requirements for information or facility access integrated into their contracts before these individuals are allowed into the workplace. Security and technology consultants especially must be prescreened, escorted, and subjected to nondisclosure agreements to protect the organization from possible intentional or accidental breaches of confidentiality. It is human nature (and a trait often found among consultants) to brag about the complexity of a particular job or an outstanding service provided to another client. If the organization does not want the consultant to mention its relationship with the consultant, or to disclose the least detail about its particular system configuration, the organization must write these restrictions into the contractual agreement. It should be noted that consultants typically request permission to present their work to other companies as part of their resumes, but a client organization is not obligated to grant this permission and can even explicitly deny permission in writing. Organizations should also remember that just because they are paying an information security consultant, this doesn't mean the protection of their information is the consultant's number one priority.

Business Partners

On occasion, businesses find themselves in strategic alliances with other organizations desiring to exchange information, integrate systems, or simply discuss operations for mutual advantage. In these situations, there must be a prior business agreement that specifies the level of exposure both organizations are willing to endure. Sometimes, one division of a company enters a strategic partnership with an organization that directly competes with another one of the company's own divisions. If the strategic partnership evolves into an integration of the systems of both companies, there is a chance that competing groups may exchange information that neither parent organization expected to share. As a result, there must be a meticulous, deliberate process of determining what information is to be exchanged, in what format, and to whom. Nondisclosure agreements must be in place. And as discussed in Chapter 2, the level of security of both systems must be examined before any physical integration takes place, because when systems are connected, the vulnerability of any one system becomes the vulnerability of all.

Separation of Duties and Collusion

Separation of duties is a cornerstone in the protection of information assets and in the prevention of financial loss. **Separation of duties** is a control used to reduce the chance of an individual violating information security and breaching the confidentiality, integrity, or availability of information. The control stipulates that the completion of a significant task that involves sensitive information should require at least two people. The idea behind this separation is that if only one person had the authorization to access a particular set of information, there may be nothing the organization could do to prevent this individual from copying the information and removing it from the premises. Separation of duties is especially important, and thus commonly implemented, when the information in question is of a financial nature. Consider, for example, how in a bank two people are required to issue a cashier's check. The first is authorized to prepare the check, acquire the numbered financial document, and ready the check for signature. The process then requires a second person, usually a supervisor, to sign the check. Only then can the check be issued. If one person had the authority to perform both functions, that person could write a number of checks, sign them, and steal large sums from the bank. The same level of control should be applied to critical data. One programmer updates the system, and a supervisor or coworker accesses the file location in which the updates are stored. Or, one employee can be authorized to run backups to the system, and another to install and remove the physical media. This method of checks and balances requires two or more people to work together to complete a task and is designed to reduce the risk of **collusion**—that is, of unscrupulous workers conspiring to commit an unauthorized task. The assumption behind such controls is that the odds of two people being willing and able to misuse or abuse the system are much lower than that of one. Related to the concept of separation of duties is that of **two-man control**, the requirement that two individuals review and approve each other's work before the task is categorized as finished. This is distinct from separation of duties, in which the two people work in sequence. In two-man control, each person completely finishes the necessary work, and then submits it to the other coworker. Each coworker then examines the work performed, double-checking the actions performed, and making sure no errors or inconsistencies exist. Figure 11-6 illustrates these operations.

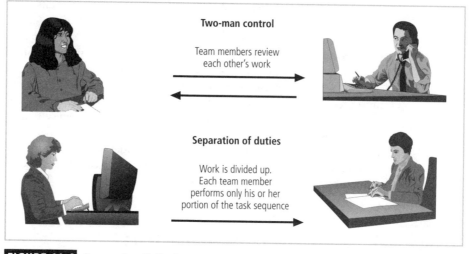

FIGURE 11-6   Preventing Collusion

Another control used to prevent personnel from misusing information assets is job rotation. **Job rotation** or **task rotation** is the requirement that every employee be able to perform the work of another employee. If it is not feasible that one employee learn the entire job of another, then the organization should at least try to ensure that for each critical task it has multiple individuals on staff who are capable of performing the task. Job or task rotations such as these can greatly increase the chance that an employee's misuse of the system or abuse of the information will be detected by another. They also ensure that no one employee is performing actions that cannot be physically audited by another employee. In general, this method makes good business sense. One threat to information is the inability of an organization to perform the tasks of one employee in the event that the employee is unable or unwilling to perform his or her duties. If everyone knows at least part of the job of another person (thus serves, in effect, as part of a human RAID system), the organization can survive the loss of any one employee.

This leads to a control measure that may seem surprising: mandatory vacations. Why should a company *require* its employees to take vacations? A mandatory vacation, of at least one week, provides the organization with the ability to audit the work of an individual. Individuals who are stealing from the organization or otherwise misusing information or systems are, in general, reluctant to take vacations, for fear that their actions will be detected. Therefore, all employees should be required to take at least one one-week vacation, so that their jobs can be audited. All this is not meant to imply that employees are untrustworthy, but rather to show how organizations must be creative—even consider the security situation as a potential attacker would—with the control measures they apply. In this case, the practice of mandatory vacations is effective because it ensures that employees who want to abuse the system know that there is a strong probability of being caught. On a final note, information security professionals who think this practice impugns the character of their coworkers and thus is probably rarely implemented should note that in some industries bonding authorities, auditing agencies, or oversight boards not only require mandatory vacations, but apply this requirement universally (i.e., to all employees).

One last topic to be covered was mentioned earlier, but warrants repeating. Employees should be provided access to the minimal amount of information for the minimal amount of time necessary for them to perform their duties. In other words, there is no need for everyone in the organization to have access to all information. This is referred to as the principle of **least privilege**. Similar to the concept of need-to-know, least privilege ensures that no unnecessary access to data exists, and that only those individuals who must access the data do so. The whole purpose of information security is to allow those people with a need to use the information contained in a given system to do so without being concerned about the system's ability to maintain the confidentiality, integrity, and availability of the information. Organizations should keep in mind that everyone who can access data probably will, and that such a situation could have devastating consequences on the organization's information security.

Privacy and the Security of Personnel Data

Another topic related to personnel and security is the security of personnel and personal data. Organizations are required by law to protect employee information that is sensitive or personal, as was discussed in Chapter 3. This includes employee addresses, phone numbers, Social Security numbers, medical conditions, and even names and addresses of family and relatives. While personnel data is, in principle, no different from other data that an organization's information security group must protect, there is a great deal more regulation covering its protection. As a result, information security groups should ensure that this data receives at least the same level of protection that the other important data in the organization—such as intellectual property, strategic planning, and other business-critical data—does.

Chapter Summary

- The placement of the information security function within the organization is a key decision facing the entire organization. The most popular options involve placing the information security function within the IT function or within the physical security function. Organizations searching for a rational compromise should place the information security function where it can balance its need to enforce organizational policy with its need to deliver service to the entire organization.

- The selection of information security personnel is based on a number of criteria. Some of these factors are within the control of the organization and others are not.

- In most cases, organizations look for a technically qualified information security generalist, with a solid understanding of how an organization operates in addition to the following attributes:

    - An attitude that information security is usually a management problem, not an exclusively technical problem

    - Good people skills, communications skills, and writing skills, and a tolerance for users

- An understanding of the role of policy in guiding security efforts
- An understanding of the role of education and training in making the user part of the solution
- An understanding of the threats facing an organization and how these threats can become attacks, as well as an understanding of how to protect the organization from information security attacks
- A working knowledge of many of the most common technologies, and a general familiarity with most mainstream IT technologies

- Many information security professionals enter the field through one of two career paths: via law enforcement or military personnel, or from other technical information systems professions. In recent years, college students have been able to take courses that prepare them to enter the information security workforce directly.

- During the hiring process for an information security position, an organization should use standard job descriptions to increase the degree of professionalism among applicants and also to make sure the position's roles and responsibilities are consistent with those of similar information security positions in other organizations. Studies of information security positions have found that they can be classified into one of three areas: those that define, those that build, and those that administer. Some of the most common job titles found in the information security discipline are:
  - Chief information security officer
  - Security manager
  - Security technician

- When filling various information security positions, many organizations indicate the level of proficiency required for the job by specifying that the candidate have recognizable certifications. Some of the more popular certifications are:
  - Certified Information Systems Security Professional (CISSP) and Systems Security Certified Practitioner (SSCP)
  - Global Information Assurance Certification (GIAC) family of certifications
  - Security Certified Professional (SCP)
  - TruSecure ICSA Certified Security Associate (TICSA)
  - Security+
  - Certified Information Systems Auditor (CISA)
  - Certified Information Forensics Investigator

- The general management community of interest should integrate solid concepts regarding information security into the organization's employment policies and practices. Areas where information security should be a consideration include:
  - Hiring: Job descriptions, interviews, and background checks
  - Employment contracts
  - New hire orientation
  - On-the-job security training
  - Performance evaluation
  - Termination

- Organizations may need the special services of nonemployees, but the resulting relationships should be carefully managed to prevent information leaks or theft. The categories of nonemployees are:
    - Temporary employees
    - Contract employees
    - Consultants
    - Business partners
- Separation of duties is a control used to reduce the chance of any one individual violating information security and breaching the confidentiality, integrity, or availability of information. The principle behind this control is that any major task that involves sensitive information should require two people to complete.
- Privacy and security of personnel and personal data have government-mandated requirements for special security considerations and must be covered in the organization's information security program.

Review Questions

1. Who in an organization should decide where in the organizational structure the information security function should be located? Why?

2. List and describe the options available for the location of the information security functions within the organization. Discuss the advantages and disadvantages of each option.

3. For each of the major types of information security job titles covered in the chapter, list and describe the criteria used for selection.

4. What are some of the factors that influence an organization's information security hiring decisions?

5. What general attributes do organizations seek in candidates when hiring information security professionals across all positions? Prioritize the list and justify your ranking.

6. What are the critical considerations when dismissing an employee? Do these change according to whether the departure is "friendly" or "hostile," or according to which position the employee is departing from?

7. How do the security considerations for temporary or contract employees differ from those for regular full-time employees?

8. What two career paths do most experienced professionals take when moving into the information security discipline? Are there other pathways available? If so, describe them.

9. Why is it important to use specific and clearly defined job descriptions for hiring information security professionals?

10. What functions does the CISO perform, and what are the key qualifications and requirements for the position?

11. What functions does the security manager perform, and what are the key qualifications and requirements for the position?

12. What functions does the security technician perform, and what are the key qualifications and requirements for the position?

13. What rationale should an aspiring information security professional use in acquiring professional credentials?

14. List and describe the credentials of the various information security certifications listed in this chapter.

15. Who should pay for the expenses of certification? Why?

16. List and describe the standard personnel practices that are part of the information security function. What happens to these practices when they are integrated with information security concepts?

17. Why shouldn't an organization give an employee candidate a tour of secure areas during the candidate's interview?

18. List and describe the typical relationships that organizations have with nonemployees. What are the special security precautions that an organization must consider for workers involved in these associations, and why are they significant?

19. What is separation of duties? How can it be used to improve an organization's information security practices?

20. What is collusion? How does the separation of duties impact collusion?

Exercises

1. Search your library's database and the Web for an article related to individuals violating their organization's policy and being terminated. Did you find many? Why or why not?

2. Go to the (ISC)² Web site at *www.isc2.org*. Research the knowledge areas included in the tests for both the CISSP and the SSCP. What areas must you study that are *not* included in this text?

3. Using the Web, identify some certifications with an information security component that were not discussed in this chapter.

4. Search the Web for at least five job postings for a security administrator. What qualifications do the listings have in common?

5. Search the Web for three different employee hiring and termination policies. Review each and look carefully for inconsistencies. Do each of the policies have sections addressing information security requirements? What clauses should a termination policy contain to prevent disclosure of an organization's information? Create your own version of either a hiring or termination policy.

Case Exercises

After her meeting with Charlie, Iris returned to her office. When she had completed her daily assignments, she pulled out a blank notepad and began to make some notes about the information security position Charlie had offered her.

Questions:

1. What questions should Iris ask Charlie about the new job, about Kelvin's team, and about the future of the company?

2. What questions should Iris ask Kelvin about the new job?

Endnotes

1. Hayes, M. "Where the Chief Security Officer belongs." InformationWeek. Feb 25, 2002. Viewed online 5/4/03. Available from the World Wide Web <*http://www.informationweek. com/story/showArticle.jhtml?articleID=6500913*>.

2. Steve Hunt. "The CISO in 2010 still touches technology." 26 May 2004. [Cited 13 August 2004]. Available from the World Wide Web <*http://www.csoonline.com/analyst/report2566.html*>.

3. Paul Kaihla. "The Coming Job Boom." *Business 2.0*, September 2003.

4. Charles Cresson Wood. *Information Security Roles and Responsibilities Made Easy.* (Houston, Tex.: PentaSafe Corporation, 2002), 55–94.

5. Eddie Schwartz, Dan Erwin, Vincent Weafer, and Andy Briney. "Roundtable: Infosec Staffing Help Wanted!" *Information Security Magazine Online.* (April 2001) [Cited 22 July 2002]. Available from the World Wide Web <*http://www.infosecuritymag.com/ articles/april01/features_roundtable.shtml*>.

6. Security Jobs Network, Inc. "Sample Job Descriptions: Director of Security." *Security Jobs Network, Inc. Online.* [Cited 21 July 2002]. Available from the World Wide Web <*http://securityjobs.net/documents/Director%20of%20Security%20Position,%20Cox. html*>.

7. IT Security Jobs. "IT Vacancies." *SSR Personnel Online.* (22 July 2002) [Cited 22 July 2002]. Available from the World Wide Web <*http://www.ssr-personnel.com/vacancies/ IT.HTM#t1525l*>.

8. IT Security Jobs. "623873—Firewall Engineering Consultant." *SSR Personnel Online.* (16 July 2002) [Cited 22 July 2002]. Available from the World Wide Web <*http://www.itsecurityjobs.com/ vacancies.htm*>.

9. International Information Systems Security Certification Consortium (23 June 2004) [Cited 23 June 2004]. Available from the World Wide Web <*https://www.isc2.org/*>.

10. International Information Systems Security Certification Consortium (23 June 2004) [Cited 23 June 2004]. Available from the World Wide Web <*https://www.isc2.org/*>.

11. International Information Systems Security Certification Consortium (23 June 2004) [Cited 23 June 2004]. Available from the World Wide Web <*https://www.isc2.org/*>.

12. International Information Systems Security Certification Consortium (23 June 2004) [Cited 23 June 2004]. Available from the World Wide Web <*https://www.isc2.org/*>

13. International Information Systems Security Certification Consortium (23 June 2004) [Cited 23 June 2004]. Available from the World Wide Web <*https://www.isc2.org/*>.

14. International Information Systems Security Certification Consortium, Inc. *"About SSCP Certification."* ISC² Online [Cited 22 July 2002]. Available from the World Wide Web <*http://www.isc2.org/cgi/content.cgi?category=20*>.

15. Global Information Assurance Certification. "GIAC: Steps to Certification General Instructions." *SANS Institute Online.* [Cited 22 July 2002]. Available from the World Wide Web <*http://www.giac.org/steps.php#instructions*>.

16. Security Certified Programs. "Certifications." *Ascendant Learning, LLC Online.* [Cited 22 July 2002]. Available from the World Wide Web <*http://www.securitycertified.net/ certifications.htm*>.

17. Trusecure. "TICSA Certification." *Trusecure Online.* [Cited 22 July 2002]. Available from the World Wide Web <*http://www.truesecure.com/solutions/certifications/ticsa/*>.

18. Trusecure. "TICSA Certification." *Trusecure Online.* [Cited 22 July 2002]. Available from the World Wide Web <*http://www.truesecure.com/solutions/certifications/ticsa/*>.

19. CompTIA. "CompTIA Security+ Certification." [Cited 13 August 2004]. Available from the World Wide Web <*http:// http://www.comptia.com/certification/security/default.aspx*>.

20. CompTIA. "Security+ Exam Objectives, v. 1.0." [Cited 13 August 2004]. Available from the World Wide Web <*http://www.comptia.com/certification/Security/Security_Objectives.pdf*>.

21. IISFA. "About the CIFI Certification." [Cited 13 August 2004]. Available from the World Wide Web <*http://www.infoforensics.org/certification/certification.asp*>.

22. GoCertify. "Security Certifications." *Anventure Online.* [Cited 21 July 2002]. Available from the World Wide Web <*http://gocertify.com/security*>.

23. Background Check International, LLC. "BCI," *BCI Online.* [Cited 22 July 2002]. Available from the World Wide Web <*http://www.bcint.com/legal.html*>.

24. Federal Trade Commission. *Fair Credit Reporting Act,* 2002. 15 U.S.C., S. 1681 et seq.

25. September 11th Commission Final Report, July 2004.

12

Information Security Maintenance

> The only thing we can predict with certainty is change.
>
> **JAYNE SPAIN, DEPARTMENT OF CHILDREN AND FAMILY LEARNING, STATE OF MINNESOTA**

CHARLIE MOODY LEANED BACK IN his chair. It was Monday morning, the first workday after the biggest conversion weekend in the implementation of Sequential Label and Supply's information security project. Charlie had just completed his review of the results of the implementation steps. So far, everything had gone according to plan. The initial penetration tests run on Sunday afternoon were clean, and every change request processed in the past 3 months had gone through without any issues. Charlie was eager for the routine to return to normal, that is, to the way things had been before the attack on the company's network had triggered the changes of the past few months.

Kelvin Urich tapped on the open door of Charlie's office. "Hey, Charlie," he said, "have you seen the e-mail I just sent? There's an urgent vulnerability report on BUGTRAQ about the version of UNIX we use. The vendor just released a critical patch to be applied right away. Should I get the system programming team started on working on the patch?"

"Oh yes. Get them to pull the download from the vendor's FTP site as soon as they can," said Charlie. "But before they install it on the production systems, be sure they try it out on the test lab servers. If that looks okay, have them patch the development servers for the HQ development team. Oh, and could you get these change orders into change control ASAP, and add the production server change request to the paperwork for the overnight change window tonight?"

"I'll get right on it," Kelvin said.

After Kelvin left, Charlie pulled up BUGTRAQ on his PC. He was reading about the new vulnerability when there was another knock on his door. It was Iris Majwubu.

"Hi, Charlie," Iris said. "Got a second?"

"Sure, Iris. How have you been? Settling in with Kelvin's team, okay?"

She smiled and nodded. "Yeah, they are a good group. They have me studying the documentation trail from the time before the security program was implemented. I came to see you about the reassessment of the information asset inventory and the threat-vulnerability update that you had asked for."

Charlie was confused for a second, but then he remembered what Iris was referring to. "Oh, right," he said, with a slight grimace. "Sorry—I had put the quarterly asset and threat review out of my mind while we were busy with the implementation of the blueprint. I suppose it's time to start planning for the regular reviews, isn't it?"

Iris handed him a folder and said, "Here's the first draft of the plan for the review project. Kelvin has already seen it, and he suggested I review it with you. Could you take a look and let me know when you would like to go over it?"

LEARNING OBJECTIVES:

Upon completion of this material, you should be able to:

- Understand why maintenance of the information security program is needed on an ongoing basis.
- Recognize recommended security management models.
- Define a model for a full maintenance program.
- Identify the key factors involved in monitoring the external and internal environment.
- Understand how planning and risk assessment tie into information security maintenance.
- Understand how vulnerability assessment and remediation tie into information security maintenance.
- Understand how to build readiness and review procedures into information security maintenance.

Introduction

Upon successfully implementing and testing a new and improved information security profile, an organization may begin feeling more confident about the level of protection it is providing for its information assets. But it shouldn't, really. In all likelihood, a good deal of time has passed since the organization began implementing the changes mandated by an upgraded information security program. In that time, the dynamic aspects of the organization's environment have, by definition, changed. Which of the aspects of a company's environment may be dynamic? Virtually all of them. The threats that were originally assessed in the early stages of the project's SecSDLC have probably changed, and new priorities have emerged. New types of attacks, such as new viruses, worms, and denial-of-service attacks, along with new variants of existing attacks, have also probably emerged; in addition, a host of other variables outside and inside the organization have most likely shifted.

Developing a comprehensive list of all the possible dynamic factors in an organization's environment is beyond the scope of this text, but here is a sample of some changes that may occur in an organization and have a bearing on its information security environment:

- New assets are acquired.
- New vulnerabilities associated with the new or existing assets emerge.
- Business priorities shift.
- New partnerships are formed.
- Old partnerships dissolve.
- Organizational divestiture and acquisition occur.
- Employees who are trained, educated, and made aware of the new policies, procedures, and technologies leave.
- New personnel are hired, thus possibly creating new vulnerabilities.

As the preceding list shows, by the time a cycle of the SecSDLC is completed, there's a high probability that the environment of an organization will have changed considerably. Working under such circumstances, an information security team will no doubt be required to assure management periodically that the information security program is accommodating these types of changes. If the program is not adjusting adequately to change, it may be necessary to begin the cycle again. If an organization deals successfully with change and has created procedures and systems that can be adjusted to the environment, the existing security improvement program will probably continue to work well. The decision to continue with the current information security improvement program or to revisit the investigation, analysis, and design phases anew depends on how much change has occurred and how well the organization and its program for information security maintenance have done in accommodating the inevitable changes. The way an information security team continues to adapt to the changes as they occur is by using an information security maintenance model as a guide.

As part of a preliminary step in the maintenance process, the CISO determines whether the information security group can adapt adequately and maintain the information security profile of the organization or whether the macroscopic process of the SecSDLC must start anew and involve developing a fundamentally new information security profile. It is less expensive and more effective to deal with change when an information security program is being designed and implemented. It is more expensive to reengineer the information security profile again and again. Note that even when an information security program is adapting and growing, the processes of maintenance and change management generally mirror the overall process of the SecSDLC, differing only in scope. In other words, as deficiencies are found and vulnerabilities pinpointed, the projects to maintain, extend, or enhance the information security program to address these weaknesses follow the familiar SecSDLC steps of investigation, analysis, design, and implementation.

Before learning about the maintenance model recommended by the text and the components of that model, you will need some background on the management and operation of an information security program. The first part of this chapter outlines an approach to security management so that you become familiar with the process and the challenges it poses for the organization.

Once an organization has improved its information security posture, its security group must turn its attention to the maintenance of security readiness. As has been described earlier in this textbook, the information security community of interest, led by the CISO, must constantly monitor the three components of the **security triple:** threats, assets, and vulnerabilities. This means that while the organization continues on with its operations, the security team constantly monitors the organization's systems and the environments in which the systems operate. The team also reviews security publications, notification lists, and e-mails to stay on top of the latest general and specific threats to its information security. As threats evolve or new vulnerabilities in the systems emerge, the information security team must determine if a shift in the priorities of the organization's security posture is required. If so, the team must reevaluate the entire matrix of threat priorities and the corresponding matrix of controls. If no change in the security posture is required, monitoring continues. The same procedure should be followed when the organization acquires new information assets. When this happens, the security team should reevaluate the asset prioritization list and adapt it to shifts in the equations for information asset value. Only by creating an aggressive external and internal monitoring program can the information security team hope to stay abreast of changes in the environment.

Security Management Models

To manage and operate the ongoing security program, the information security community must adopt a management model. In general, management models are frameworks that structure the tasks of managing a particular set of activities or business functions. The example presented in the upcoming section is a modified variant of the ISO network management model.

The ISO Network Management Model

The ISO network management model is a five-layer approach that provides structure to the administration and management of networks and systems. The core ISO model addresses management and operation through five areas:

- Fault management
- Configuration and name management
- Accounting management
- Performance management
- Security management

Although the original form of the ISO model is not directly applicable to the management of an information security program, the model can be modified to support the various administrative tasks found in most information security programs. Thus, for the purposes of information security management, the five areas of the ISO model can be transformed as follows:

- Fault management
- Configuration and change management
- Accounting and auditing management
- Performance management
- Security program management

Each of these five key areas is examined in detail in the sections that follow.

Fault Management

In the original ISO model, fault management is the process of identifying, tracking, diagnosing, and resolving faults in the system. Because information security involves systems based both on people and technology, the model must be transformed so that fault management of information security programs applies to both people and technology. In essence, fault management in an information security management model involves identifying faults in the applied information security profile and then addressing them through remediation.

Remediation is often perceived as a process of fault detection and correction. One method of finding faults involves the vulnerability assessment processes used to find the physical and logical vulnerabilities present in both information security and related nonsecurity systems. This assessment is most often accomplished with penetration testing. *Penetration testing* involves security personnel simulating or performing specific and controlled attacks to compromise or disrupt their own systems by exploiting documented vulnerabilities. Penetration testing is commonly performed on network connections from outside the organization, as security personnel attempt to exploit vulnerabilities in the system from the attacker's viewpoint. The information security personnel who perform penetration testing are often consultants or outsourced contractors, and are commonly referred to as **whitehat hackers**, **ethical hackers**, **tiger teams**, or **red teams**. What these people are called is less important than what they do. Unfortunately, some information security administrators focus too much on such labels and hesitate to hire outside consultants to conduct penetration tests. Information security administrators who have not looked at their systems through the eyes of an attacker are failing to maintain readiness. They should realize that the best procedures and tools to use in penetration testing and other vulnerability assessments are the procedures and tools of the hacker community. An additional important part of this process is documenting the intelligence gathered during the penetration test and then using it to make sure the vulnerabilities that allowed the penetration to succeed are repaired promptly.

Another aspect of fault management is the monitoring and resolution of user complaints. As discussed in earlier chapters, the first clue that an attack is underway often comes from reports by observant users. Similarly, the first clue that a security system has a fault or error may also come from user feedback. In many organizations, help desks handle these user reports as well as other systems problems. If an organization does not have a help desk in place, it should probably consider establishing one or, at the very least, make other provisions to allow users to report suspicious systems problems. The Offline titled "The Help Desk" discusses the function and organization of help desks.

In addition to providing the services described in this Offline, help desk personnel must be trained to distinguish a security problem from other system problems. As the help desk personnel screen problems, they must also track the activities involved in resolving each complaint in a help desk information system (you may recall that a fictional help desk information system, the Information Status and Issues System, or ISIS, was described in Chapter 1's opening vignette). The tracking process is commonly implemented using a **trouble ticket**, which is a means of documenting the outstanding issue. A trouble ticket is opened when a user calls about an issue, and is closed when help desk (or technical support) personnel resolve the issue. One key advantage to having formal help desk software is the ability to create and develop a knowledge base of common problems and solutions. This knowledge base can be searched when a user problem comes up; and if the problem is similar to one that was already reported and resolved, the process of resolving complaints can be speeded up. This knowledge base can also generate statistics on the frequency of problems by type, by user, or by application, and thus can detect trends and patterns in the data. Incidentally, some user problems may actually be created or influenced by a security program since modifications to firewalls, implementations of IDS rules, or new systems policies in the network can directly impact how users interact with the systems. A significant number of help desk trouble tickets are, therefore, related to user access issues such as passwords and other authentication, authorization, and accountability issues. Proper user training and ongoing awareness campaigns can reduce these problems, but never completely eliminate them.

As mentioned earlier, the tracking of trouble tickets includes tracking problem resolution. This may require that a technical support technician visit the user's office to examine equipment or observe the user's procedures. Or it may require that the technical support technician interact with other departments or workgroups. It is not uncommon for the help desk team to include a security technician specifically for this purpose. In any case, the person working to resolve the trouble ticket must document not only the diagnosis, but also the resolution, as both are invaluable components of the knowledge base and will be useful for resolving similar trouble tickets. Once the problem has been resolved and the results documented, the ticket is closed.

OFFLINE

The Help Desk

With a relatively small investment in an IT help desk, an organization can improve the quality of its IT support and information security functions. A small help desk with only a few call agents can provide good—perhaps excellent—service for an organization of several hundred users. Large organizations can also achieve strong improvements in customer service through the use of a help desk; but as more than one help desk is usually required to meet their needs, these organizations must be sure to provide their help desks with adequate funding and professional management.

Although it may function differently in different organizations, a help desk commonly provides the following services:

- A single point of contact for service requests from users
- Initial screening of requests, answering of most common questions, solving of most common problems, and dispatching of other types of calls to other units
- Data entry of all calls into a tracking system
- Dispatch of service providers to respond to calls
- Reporting and analysis of call volumes, patterns, and process improvement

Other services that may be integrated into the help desk often include:

- Deskside support for common IT applications such as Windows, end-user computing tools, and common applications
- New-user management
- User removal processes
- Password management
- Smart card management
- Knowledge management for service requests and optimum resolutions

- Server configuration
- Network monitoring
- Server capacity monitoring
- Virus activity monitoring and virus pattern management

While each organization has its own approach to creating and growing a help desk solution, many help desk organizations evolve through discernable phases and alter the mix of services they offer over time.[1] The smooth operation of a help desk, when integrated with the IT and information security functions, can greatly increase the quality of the services offered by both of these functions.

Configuration and Change Management

The information security management model continues with **configuration management** and **change management**. Configuration management is the administration of the configuration of the components of the security program. Change management is the administration of changes in the strategy, operation, or components of the information security program. Both configuration and change management administration involve nontechnical as well as technical changes.

Interestingly, many of the most significant changes are nontechnical. Nontechnical changes are those that do not affect the technology deployed for information systems in the hardware, software, and data system elements, but instead affect two other system components—people and procedures. The IT managers and professionals of an organization are responsible for the organization's information-processing systems. The information security community, however, should ensure that the technical systems of information security are managed independently from traditional IT equipment, except when there is overlap. In cases of overlap (as there would be, for example, with a filtering router), joint management is necessary. The ultimate goal is to ensure that all information technology is properly managed with a focus on those systems directly affecting the success of the information security program.

Nontechnical Change Management. When implementing changes to the information security program, the organization will also probably need to implement a number of new policies and procedures. Consequently, the implementation effort will produce documents that will need to be changed when they are insufficient, outdated, or inaccurate. To support this process, a document manager should be assigned to maintain a master copy of each document, record and archive the revisions made, and keep copies of the revisions, along with editorial comments on what was added, removed, or modified. A library of these sorts of documents can become unwieldy. Thus, the organization may wish to implement online archives to maintain the documents and revisions. It is important to be able to track changes to these documents, and to determine why and by whom the changes were made. It is also important that the record include insight into the environment that caused the change. Without this type of record keeping, organizations may fall into situations in which some of their members are working from older versions of critical policy or procedural documents, while management is expecting adherence to the newer version.

As mentioned in earlier chapters, policies are not considered to be implemented and enforceable until they have been disseminated, read, understood, and agreed to. Thus, as these policies are revised, the updated versions must be disseminated to all involved personnel, and user agreement must be gathered and documented. The management of the agreement documentation constitutes an administrative challenge, as many security policies and procedures contain sensitive information that the organization may not wish to disclose. The most effective way to manage changes to documents is to include the revision version number in the header, along with the file name, and revision date, and to physically distribute the documents to all parties affected. As the new documents are distributed, all older versions should be collected and destroyed, to prevent the end users from throwing them out carelessly or continuing to use them. To support the distribution and control of the documents, each copy should, as was discussed in previous chapters, be labeled "Copy ____ of ____," where the first blank represents the sequence number of this specific copy, and the second is the total number of copies that now exist, including the original. Also, when employees receive new versions of a policy (and return old versions), they should sign for the new revision. Employees should also be given a confirmation form that states that they have read the policies and that they agree to them, and they must be required to return the confirmation form by a specified date.

The organization can make the management of these documents easier for its employees by issuing each of them a special binder for storing the most current version of all plans, policies, and procedures. This binder should be uniquely colored, labeled, and stored to prevent binder camouflage—that is, the loss of a binder on a shelf of similar binders. One must be careful not to overdo the unique coloring and labeling of binders, however, as over-labeling can cause as much confusion as the use of the bland, white, unlabeled alternative. Lastly, the storage of these binders should reflect the level of sensitivity of the documents they contain.

Modern, Web-based software is available to make the creation of policy content, modification of policy content, and dissemination of policy, as well as the processes used for record keeping of agreement documentation, more manageable. One example product, noted also in Chapter 5, is NetIQ Policy Center. NetIQ Policy Center incorporates policy content from information security policy expert Charles Cresson Wood, and enables organizations to require that its users be tested on policy knowledge. This product can also record agreement from users that they have read and understood a specific policy or procedure.

Technical Configuration and Change Management. Just as documents should have version numbers, revision dates, and other features designated to monitor and administer the changes made to them, so should the technical components of systems, such as software, hardware, and firmware. There are several terms associated with the management of configuration and change in technical components. Each of these is presented here:

- Configuration item: A hardware or software item that is to be modified and revised throughout its life cycle.
- Version: The recorded state of a particular revision of a software or hardware configuration item. The version number is often noted in a specific format: M.N.b. In this notation, "M" is the major release number, and "N.b" can represent various minor releases or builds within that major release.
  - Major release: A significant revision of the version from its previous state.
  - Minor release (update or patch): A minor revision of the version from its previous state.
  - Build: A snapshot of a particular version of software assembled (or linked) from its various component modules.

- Build list: A list of the versions of components that make up a build is called a build list.
- Configuration: A configuration is a collection of components that make up a configuration item.
- Revision date: The date associated with a particular version or build.
- Software library: A collection of configuration items that is usually controlled and that developers use to construct revisions and to issue new configuration items.

To make these definitions more concrete, consider the following hypothetical example: XYZ Security Solutions Corporation develops a new software application—Panacea, the Ultimate Security Solution. Panacea is the configuration item. Panacea's configuration consists of three major software components: See-all, Know-all, and Cure-all. Thus, Panacea is Version 1.0, and it is built from its three components. The build list is See-all 1.0, Know-all 1.0, and Cure-all 1.0, as this is the first major release of the overall application and its components. For now, the revision date is the date associated with the first build. To create Panacea, the programmers at XYZ Security Solutions Corporation had pulled information from their software library. Suppose now that while the application is being used in the field, the programmers discover a minor flaw in a subroutine. When they correct this flaw, they would issue the minor release, Panacea 1.1. If at some point they need to make a major revision to the software to meet changing market needs or to fix more substantial problems with the subcomponents, they would issue a major release, Panacea 2.0.

Actually, both product developers and users participate in configuration management. The developers focus on managing the build list and keeping up with the development of major and minor releases, while the users monitor the implementation of versions and track the latest releases as well as which computers in their organizations are running each of the released versions.

There are four steps associated with configuration management.[2]

1. Configuration identification: The identification and documentation of the various components, implementations, and states of configuration items
2. Configuration control: The administration of changes to the configuration items and the issuance of versions
3. Configuration status accounting: The tracking and recording of the implementation of changes to configuration items
4. Configuration audit: Auditing and controlling the overall configuration management program

While the other three steps/procedures can be performed by any organization that uses technology to solve problems, configuration control is usually only performed by an entity that actually develops its own versions.

In general, configuration and change management should be undertaken so that it does not interfere with the use of the technology. One individual on the security team should be appointed as the configuration manager or change manager and made responsible for maintaining the appropriate data elements in the organization's cataloging mechanism, such as the specific version, revision date, and build associated with each piece of hardware and software implemented. In some cases, it may be better to have someone outside the implementation process document the process, as this person will not be distracted by the installation, configuration, and troubleshooting of the new implementation. In the case of minor revisions, it may be simpler to have a procedure in place that involves documenting the machines on which a revision was installed, the date and time of the installation, and the name of the installer. While the documentation procedures required for the configuration and change management processes may seem onerous, they will enable security teams to quickly and accurately determine exactly which systems are impacted when a new vulnerability arises. When stored in a comprehensive database along with risk, threat, and attack information, configuration information enables organizations to respond quickly to new and rapidly changing threats and attacks.

Accounting and Auditing Management

The next category in the information security management model involves chargeback accounting and systems monitoring. **Chargeback accounting** enables organizations to charge their internal departments for system use. For example, when the human resources department uses 30 seconds of CPU time on a mainframe, the IT department, which bought and maintains the mainframe, will charge HR for that amount of use. While chargebacks for CPU cycle time are seldom used today, the use of certain kinds of resources, such as the resources on a computing system (like a server or a desktop computer), are commonly tracked, as are charges for hours of time spent by various specialists like network architects or software engineers. These fees allow the recovery of IT expenses from non-IT units.

A byproduct of the process of charging for the use of resources is that the organization is able to measure when it may require additional resources. Accounting management involves the monitoring of the use of a particular component of a system. It also seeks to determine when systems are ready for upgrade or replacement.

Auditing is the process of reviewing the use of a system, not to check performance, but rather to determine if misuse or malfeasance has occurred. Most of the computer-based systems used in information security can create logs of their activity. These logs are a vital part of the detective functions associated with identifying what happened, when it happened, and how it happened. The management of systems logs in large organizations is a complex process and is sometimes considered to be an art in itself. Unless the security (or systems) administrators are vigilant in the review of these logs, the logs can pile up quickly because systems are constantly writing the activity that occurs on them. Fortunately, automated tools known as log analyzers can consolidate various systems logs, perform comparative analysis, and detect common occurrences or behavior that is of interest. The behavior of interest may include anomalous network activity (such as port scanning), malware signatures, hacking attempts, and illicit use of controlled network resources or computer systems. Log analyzers, a component of some IDSs, can detect activities in real time. Each type of IDS (host-, network-, and application-based) also create logs. These logs are invaluable records of events and should be archived and stored for future review as needed. It is not unheard of for systems intruders to attempt to cover their tracks by erasing entries in logs. To prepare for this, wise administrators configure their systems to create duplicate copies of the logs and to store these copies on sources that cannot be easily modified, like optical disk technologies such as CD-R and DVD-R.

Many vendors offer log consolidation and analysis features. One multiple-vendor approach to log centralization and analysis is offered by the NetIQ Corporation in their VigilEnt Intrusion Manager product. This software product, like offerings from other vendors, allows for the analysis of its own IDS components. NetIQ is similar to other leading software companies in the field of information security management in that it allows for the integration of log files from the products, such as firewalls and network equipments, of other vendors.

Performance Management

Because many information security technical controls are implemented on common IT processors, they are affected by the same factors as most computer-based technologies. It is therefore important to monitor the performance of security systems and their underlying IT infrastructure to determine if they are working effectively. This type of performance monitoring is especially important for network appliances, such as firewalls and content filters, that look for inappropriate use of Internet resources and operate as pass-by devices. When these types of appliances are not sized correctly or are not properly tuned for sufficient performance, the actions they are designed to block are not stopped.

Some common system and network metrics used in performance management are also applicable in security, especially when the components being managed involve the ebb and flow of network traffic. The following list offers a few rules of thumb that security personnel can use when exploring the issues of system and network performance.[3]

- When the memory usage associated with a particular CPU-based system averages 50–60% or more over prolonged periods, consider adding more memory.
- When the CPU usage associated with a particular CPU-based system averages 50–60% or more over prolonged periods, consider an upgrade for the CPU.
- When the network traffic on a particular link averages 50–60% or more for prolonged periods, consider an upgrade to the link, which can be accomplished by either increasing the bandwidth available or segmenting the traffic.
- When the amount of data stored on a particular hard drive averages 50–60% or more of available capacity for a prolonged period, consider an upgrade for the hard drive, which can be accomplished by either replacing the hard drive with a larger drive or adding additional drives.

To evaluate the performance of a security system, administrators must establish performance baselines within the system. Previous chapters of this text covered the procedures for establishing baselines across industries (see Chapter 4) and within organizations (also known as benchmarking, which was also discussed in Chapter 4). In this context, a **performance baseline** is an expected level of performance against which all subsequent levels of performance are compared. For example, network traffic levels are deemed to be high when traffic reaches or surpasses the level of the performance baseline. To put it another way, the planning of capacity upgrades should begin before users complain about slow-loading Web pages.

Organizations must establish baselines for a number of different criteria and for various periods of time, such as days of the week, weeks of the year, months of the year, and times of day (AM and PM), among others. To accomplish this effectively, the organization must monitor all possible variables, collecting and archiving performance baseline data and then analyzing it. After the performance baseline matrix is established, continued monitoring and data collection will allow the administrators to compare current performance against the performance baseline and therefore to determine if an abnormal level of activity is occurring. Performance baselines are established for network traffic and also for firewall performance and IDS performance. In fact, many security-related technologies rely on some form of performance baseline to interpret various levels of computer activity. Also, for many systems, such as behavior-based (statistical anomaly) IDSs, establishing their own baselines is already integral to their mode of operation. These systems compare activity against their baselines to determine if an attack or intrusion is occurring.

Security Program Management

Once an information security program is functional, it must be operated and managed. While the ISO five-area-based framework is designed to support the structuring of a management model, it focuses more on ensuring that various areas are addressed, rather than guiding the actual conduct of management. In order to assist in the actual management of information security programs, organizations should adopt a formal management standard that can provide some insight about what processes and procedures are needed. Two standards that were previously discussed in Chapter 5 are designed to assist in this effort. The first of these standards is the ISO 17799 Code of Practice for Information Security Management. The second is British Standard (BS) 7799 (Part 2), which specifies requirements for establishing, implementing, and documenting an information security management system (ISMS). BS 7799 (Part 2) introduces a process model with a set of steps called Plan-Do-Check-Act. These steps are part of a management system approach to developing, implementing, and improving the effectiveness of an organization's information security management with regard to the management of risk. The Plan-Do-Check-Act process involves the following steps:[4]

1. Plan: Perform a risk analysis of the vulnerabilities faced by the organization.
2. Do: Apply internal controls to manage risk.
3. Check: Undertake periodic and frequent review to verify effectiveness.
4. Act: Develop incident response plans as necessary.

As the two standards noted above are not truly open standards (you have to pay to get them), dissemination is limited to those who are willing to pay their purchase price. It should be noted, however, that these ISO and BS series standards may be worth the cost to many organizations—not only because they are widely recognized, but also because they can fill in any gaps in the management of information security that an organization's CISO might discover.

In summary, while there are other management approaches that organizations may adopt to manage their ongoing information security programs, this modified version of the ISO model that was presented here is a solid approach that can serve as a useful starting point. Even though this model does not offer a lot of detail, it does provide a comprehensive overview of the overall management needed for a security program. Within such management frameworks, the maintenance of the security program requires specific management efforts, many of which will be discussed in the next section.

The Maintenance Model

While a management model such as the ISO model deals with methods to *manage* and *operate* systems, a maintenance model is designed (in ways that complement the chosen management model) to focus organizational effort on *maintaining* systems. An approach that is recommended by this text for dealing with change caused by information security maintenance is presented in Figure 12-1. This figure diagrams a full maintenance program and will serve as a framework for the discussion of maintenance that follows.

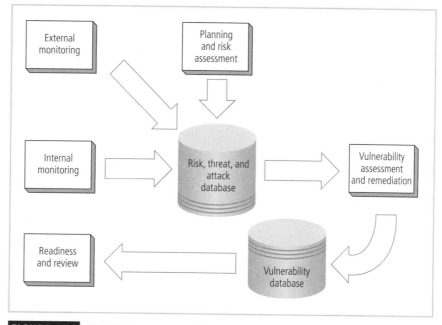

FIGURE 12-1 The Maintenance Model

The recommended maintenance model is based on five subject areas or domains:

- External monitoring
- Internal monitoring
- Planning and risk assessment
- Vulnerability assessment and remediation
- Readiness and review

In the sections that follow, each of these domains is explored and their interaction discussed.

Monitoring the External Environment

During the Cold War of the twentieth century, the western alliance, led by the United States and Britain, confronted the Soviet Union and its allies. A key component of the western alliance's defense was maintaining the ability to detect early warnings of attacks. Interestingly, one could say that the image of the ever-vigilant team of radar operators scanning the sky for incoming attacks using a global network of sensors also represents the current world of information security, where teams of information security personnel must guard their respective organizations against an environment full of dangerous and debilitating threats. While the stakes for modern-day organizations are not equivalent (that is, they do not typically involve the possibility of nuclear Armageddon), they are nevertheless very high—especially as organizations become more and more information-dependent.

The objective of the **external monitoring domain** within the maintenance model is to provide the early awareness of new and emerging threats, threat agents, vulnerabilities, and attacks that the organization needs in order to mount an effective and timely defense. Figure 12-2 shows the primary components of the external monitoring process.

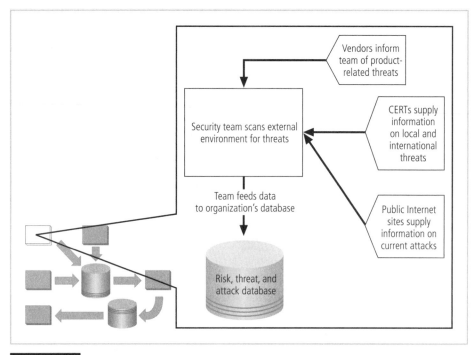

FIGURE 12-2 External Monitoring

External monitoring entails collecting intelligence from various data sources, and then giving that intelligence context and meaning for use by decision makers within the organization.

Data Sources

Acquiring data about threats, threat agents, vulnerabilities, and attacks is not difficult. There are many sources of raw intelligence and relatively few costs associated with gathering the intelligence. What is challenging (and can be expensive) is turning this flood of good and timely data into information that decision makers can use. For this reason, some organizations outsource this component of the maintenance model. Companies like TruSecure can provide a complete tailored supply of processed intelligence to organizations that can afford their subscription fees. Other providers supply varying levels of analysis and timeliness for their clients.

As shown in Figure 12-2, external intelligence can come from three classes of sources:

- Vendors: When an organization uses specific software products as part of its information security program, the vendor often provides either direct support or indirect tools that allow user communities to support each other. This support often includes intelligence on emerging threats.
- CERT organizations: Computer emergency response teams (CERTs) exist in varying forms around the world. Often, US-CERT (*www.us-cert.gov*) is viewed as the definitive authority. Many states have CERT agencies, and many countries have CERT organizations to deal with specific national issues and threats. Your local, state, or national government may have a CERT outreach program to provide the notification services to you at no direct cost. The U.S. Department of Homeland Security works with the CERT/CC

program at Carnegie Mellon to provide the services at US-CERT. More information about this joint program is available at *www.cert.org/about/US-CERT.html*.

- Public network sources: Many publicly accessible information sources, both mailing lists and Web sites, are freely available to those organizations and individuals who have the time and expertise to make use of them. Table 12-1 lists some of these information security intelligence sources.

TABLE 12-1   External Intelligence Sources

Source Name	Type	Comments
Bugtraq	Mailing list	Bugtraq is a set of moderated mailing lists full of detailed, full-disclosure discussions and announcements about computer security vulnerabilities (see descriptions of the individual mailing lists in the table entries that follow). The primary mailing list, called simply Bugtraq, provides time-sensitive coverage of emerging vulnerabilities, documenting how they are exploited, and reporting on how to remediate them. Individuals can register for the flagship mailing list or any one of the entire family of Bugtraq mailing lists at *http://online.securityfocus.com/cgi-bin/sfonline/subscribe.pl*.
Bugtraq focus-ids	Mailing list	This mailing list contains information about intrusion detection systems vulnerabilities, and discusses both how to exploit them and how to use them in defending networks.
Bugtraq focus-ms	Mailing list	This mailing list discusses the inner workings and underlying software weaknesses of Microsoft software products. It includes detailed discussions on the various security mechanisms available to help assess, secure, and remediate Microsoft software products.
Bugtraq forensics	Mailing list	This mailing list is a discussion of technical and process methodologies for the application of computer forensics. The discussion is centered around technical methodology, audit trail analysis (technical procedures), general post-mortem analysis (technical procedures), products and tools for use in this field (technical discussion), process methodology for evidence-handling (technical discussion), search and seizure (nontechnical procedures and discussion), and evidence-handling policies (nontechnical procedures and discussion).
Bugtraq incidents	Mailing list	This is a lightly moderated mailing list that facilitates the quick exchange of security incident information. Topics include: information about root kits and back-doors, new Trojan horses, viruses and worms, sources of attacks, and telltale signs of intrusions.

TABLE 12.1 External Intelligence Sources (continued)

Source Name	Type	Comments
Bugtraq pen-test	Mailing list	The penetration-testing mailing list is designed to allow people to converse about professional penetration testing. The list is not OS-specific and has discussions on many varieties of networks and devices.
Bugtraq vuln-dev	Mailing list	This mailing list contains reports of potential or undeveloped vulnerabilities. This is a full-disclosure list and can include exploit code.
Bugtraq focus-virus	Mailing list	This mailing list discusses the inner workings and underlying issues of the various products, tools, and techniques available that may help secure systems from virus threats.
CERT/CC and US-CERT	Web site	The CERT Coordination Center (CERT/CC) is a center of Internet security expertise and is located at the Software Engineering Institute, a federally funded research and development center operated by Carnegie Mellon University. CERT/CC and the U.S. Department of Homeland Security support the Web site, which is usually considered the definitive authority to be consulted when emerging threats become demonstrated vulnerabilities. See CERT/CC's home page at *www.cert.org*.
US-CERT Advisory Mailing List	Mailing list	The CERT/CC in conjunction with the U.S. Department of Homeland Security provides the National Cyber Alert System, which can send e-mail advisory and supporting information to registered organizations and individuals. You can select the type of notifications you need and register for the desired advisory list at *www.us-cert.gov/cas/index.html*.
Internet Security Systems (ISS)	Web site	This is a commercial site with a focus on the vendor's own commercial IDS and other security products. The site also provides breaking news about emerging threats, and allows individuals to subscribe to alerts. See *www.iss.net*.
Insecure Mailing List Archive	Web site	Insecure.org (at *www.insecure.org*) is the creation of the well-known hacker Fyodor. He and his associates operate insecure.org and provide the Internet community with software (Nmap is the best known of the insecure.org tools) and information about vulnerabilities. Many topics are covered in the available lists at *www.seclists.org/*.
NESSUS-DEVEL	Mailing list	This is a noncommercial Web site dedicated to the Nessus vulnerability scanner. The Nessus Web site has information about emerging threats and how to test for them. It can be found at *www.nessus.org*.

TABLE 12.1   External Intelligence Sources (continued)

Source Name	Type	Comments
Nmap-hackers	Mailing list	This list is intended to facilitate the development of Nmap, a free network exploration tool. Read the file at *http://lists.insecure.org/about/nmap-hackers.txt* to learn how to subscribe.
Packet Storm	Web site	This commercial site focuses on current security tool resources. *http://packetstorm.org.*
Security Focus Online	Web site	This commercial site provides general coverage and commentary on information security. *http://online.securityfocus.com.*
Snort-sigs	Mailing list	This mailing list includes announcements and discussion of Snort, an open source IDS. The list includes discussions and information about the program and its rule sets and signatures. It can be a useful source for information about detecting emerging threats. Individuals can register for this mailing list at *http://lists.sourceforge.net/lists/listinfo/snort-sigs.*

Regardless of where or how external monitoring data is collected, in order to be useful it must be analyzed in the context of the organization's security environment. To perform this evaluation, and take appropriate actions in a timely fashion, the CISO must:

- Staff the function with people that have the correct depth and breadth of technical information security knowledge, as well as a comprehensive understanding of the organization's complete IT infrastructure and a thorough grounding in the business operations of the organization;
- Provide documented and repeatable procedures;
- Train the primary and backup staff assigned to perform the monitoring tasks;
- Equip assigned staff with proper access and tools to perform the monitoring function;
- Cultivate the expertise among the monitoring analysts, so they can perform analytic steps to cull meaningful summaries and actionable alerts from the vast flow of raw intelligence;
- Develop suitable communications methods for moving processed intelligence to designated internal decision makers in all three communities of interest—that is, in IT, information security, and general management; and
- Integrate the incident response plan (IRP) with the results of the external monitoring process to produce appropriate, timely responses.

Monitoring, Escalation, and Incident Response

The basic function of the external monitoring process is to monitor activity, report results, and escalate warnings. The optimum approach for escalation is based on a thorough integration of the monitoring process into the IRP (discussed in Chapter 5). The monitoring process has three primary deliverables:

- Specific warning bulletins issued when developing threats and specific attacks pose a measurable risk to the organization. The bulletins should assign a meaningful risk-level to the threat to help decision makers in the organization formulate the appropriate response.
- Periodic summaries of external information. The summaries present either statistical results (for example, the number of new or revised CERT advisories per month) or itemized lists of significant new vulnerabilities.
- Detailed intelligence on the highest risk warnings. This information prepares the way for the detection and remediation of vulnerabilities in the later steps of vulnerability assessment. This intelligence can include identifying which vendor updates apply to which vulnerabilities as well as which types of defenses have been found to work against the specific vulnerabilities reported.

Data Collection and Management

Over time, the external monitoring processes should capture knowledge about the external environment in a format that can be referenced both across the organization as threats emerge and for historical use. This can be accomplished using e-mail, Web pages, databases, or even paper-and-pencil recording methods, so long as the essential facts are communicated, stored, and can be used to make queries when needed. In the final analysis, external monitoring collects raw intelligence, filters it for relevance to the organization, assigns it a relative risk impact, and communicates these findings to the decision makers in time to make a difference. As an alternative view of the way data flows into the monitoring process, a data flow diagram (DFD) approach may prove useful. On the left-hand side of Figure 12-3, a level 0 data flow diagram for the entire maintenance process shows how data flows in the overall process. On the right-hand side, a level 1 diagram for the external data collection process shows the sources of external monitoring data in more detail.

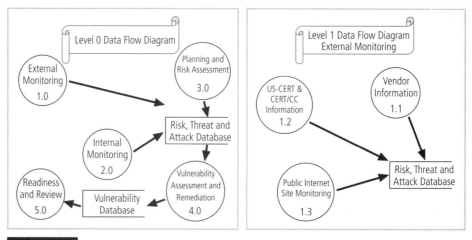

FIGURE 12-3 Data Flow Diagrams for External Data Collection

Monitoring the Internal Environment

It is just as important to monitor the internal computing environment of an organization as it is the external environment. The primary goal of the **internal monitoring domain** is to maintain an informed awareness of the state of all of the organization's networks, information systems, and information security defenses. This awareness must be communicated and documented, especially for components that are exposed to the external network. Internal monitoring is accomplished by:

- Building and maintaining an inventory of network devices and channels, IT infrastructure and applications, and information security infrastructure elements;
- Leading the IT governance process within the organization to integrate the inevitable changes found in all network, IT, and information security programs;
- Monitoring IT activity in real-time using intrusion detection systems (IDS) to detect and initiate responses to specific actions or trends of events that introduce risk to the organization's information assets; and
- Monitoring the internal state of the organization's networks and systems. This recursive review of the network and system devices that are online at any given moment and of any changes to the services offered on the network is needed to maintain awareness of new and emerging threats. This can be accomplished through automated difference-detection methods that identify variances introduced to the network or system hardware and software.

The value of internal monitoring is high when the resulting knowledge of the network and systems configuration is fed into the vulnerability assessment and remediation maintenance domain. But this knowledge becomes invaluable when incident response processes are fully integrated with the monitoring processes.

Figure 12-4 shows the component processes of the internal monitoring domain, which are discussed in the sections that follow.

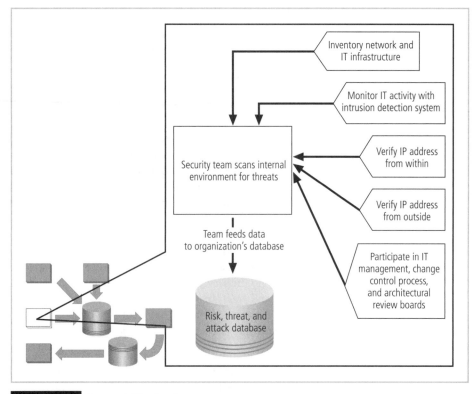

FIGURE 12-4 Internal Monitoring

Network Characterization and Inventory

Organizations should have a carefully planned and fully populated inventory of all their network devices, communication channels, and computing devices. This inventory should certainly include servers, and it is advisable that it also include desktop applications and partner interconnections. These *partner interconnections* are network devices, communications channels, and applications that may not be owned by the organization but are essential to the continued operation of the organization's partnership with another company. The process of collecting this information is often referred to as *characterization*, as it is the systematic collection of the characteristics of the network and computer devices present in the environment.

Once the characteristics of the network environment have been identified and collected as data, they must be carefully organized and stored using a manual or automated mechanism that allows for timely retrieval and rapid integration of disparate facts. For all but the smallest network environments, this demands a relational database. The attributes of the network devices (systems, switches, gateways, and the like) to be stored have been discussed in earlier chapters (namely, in the discussion on information asset identification in Chapter 4). In contrast to the attributes collected for risk management, which are concerned with economic and business value, the characteristics collected here (concerned with manufacturer and software versions) are about technical functionality—and they should be kept highly accurate and up-to-date. Also, the technology underpinning the storage of this data should be stand-alone and portable, for there is a good chance that when this data is called into action, to support incident responses and disaster recovery, server or network access may be unavailable.

The Role of IT Governance

The topic of IT governance has been discussed in several earlier chapters. The primary value of active engagement in an organization-wide IT governance process is the increased awareness of the impact of change. The process of building awareness of change requires a leadership and educational role for the CISO and his or her team. This awareness must be translated into a description of the risk that is created by the change. Such a description of risk, often called a risk assessment, is then revealed and promoted in the organization during the IT governance process. The awareness of change that flows from IT governance is based on two primary activities within the IT governance process:

- Architecture review boards: Many organizations have a group designated to plan, review, and approve managed technology. This group also coordinates the acquisition and adoption of new technologies. The group can go by a number of different names, from *technical architecture team* to *network review board*. Whatever the name, the group directs the orderly introduction of change in information technology across the organization. In addition to alerting the information security team of changes to come, this group has a second valuable outcome: by being present on the governance committee, the group's information security participant(s) can educate the IT community about the impact of a given change on information security. The participants can also educate the IT community on correct processes, so that the information security risk becomes part of the decision to adopt and deploy new information technology.
- IT change control process: Most organizations of appreciable size have implemented one or more mechanisms to control change in their networks, IT infrastructures, and IT applications. Often this governance function is assigned to a committee of department heads and technical experts. This change control committee serves the multiple purposes of:
  - Making the information security group aware of planned changes in IT systems
  - Making the IT community aware of changes planned in the information security infrastructure
  - Allowing the information security participant(s) to educate the change control community about information security risk and how this risk should be managed in the organization

Making Intrusion Detection Systems Work

Chapter 7 examined the technology of intrusion detection systems. To be put to the most effective use, the information that comes from the IDS must be integrated into the maintenance process. An IDS will generate a seemingly endless flow of alert messages that often make little difference to the immediate operational effectiveness of the information security program. Except for an occasional real-time alert that is evaluated as being real (and not a false positive), the IDS is reporting events that have already occurred. Given this, the most important value of the raw intelligence provided by the IDS is that it can be used to prevent future attacks by providing indicators of current or imminent vulnerabilities. Whether the organization outsources IDS monitoring, staffs IDS monitoring 24/7, staffs IDS monitoring during business hours, or merely ignores the real-time alerts from IDS, the log files from the

IDS engines can be mined for information that can be added to the internal monitoring knowledge base.

Another element of IDS monitoring is traffic analysis. Analyzing the traffic that flows through a system and its associated devices can often be a critically important process, as it identifies the most frequently used devices. Also, the analyzing of attack signatures from unsuccessful system attacks can help identify weaknesses in various security efforts. An example of the type of vulnerability exposed via traffic analysis can be observed when an organization is trying to determine if all its device signatures have been adequately masked. In general, the default configuration setting of many network devices allows the device to respond to any request with a device signature message that identifies the device's make and model and perhaps even its software level. In the interest of greater security, many organizations require that all devices be reconfigured to conceal their device signatures. Now suppose one such organization performs an analysis of unsuccessful attacks, and the analysis reveals that lesser-known UNIX attacks are being launched against one of its servers. This discovery might inform the organization that the server under attack is responding to requests for OS type with its device signature.

Detecting Differences

One approach that can improve the situational awareness of the information security function uses a process known as difference analysis to quickly identify changes to the internal environment. A **difference analysis** is a procedure that compares the current state of a network segment (the systems and services it offers) against a known previous state of that same network segment (the baseline of systems and services). Any differences between the current state and the baseline state that are unexpected could be a sign of trouble and will need to be investigated. Table 12-2 shows how several kinds of difference analyses can be used.

TABLE 12-2   Types of Difference Analysis

Suggested Frequency	Method of Analysis	Data Source	Purpose
Quarterly	Manual	Firewall rules	To verify that new rules follow all risk assessment and procedural approvals; identify illicit rules; ensure removal of expired rules; and detect tampering
Quarterly	Manual	Edge router rules	To verify that new rules follow all risk assessment and procedural approvals; identify illicit rules; ensure removal of expired rules; and detect tampering
Quarterly	Manual	Internet footprint	To verify that public Internet presence (addresses registered to the organization) is accurate and complete

TABLE 12-2	Types of Difference Analysis (continued)		
Suggested Frequency	Method of Analysis	Data Source	Purpose
Monthly	Automated	Fingerprint all IP addresses	To verify that only known authorized devices offering critical services can be reached from the internal network
Weekly	Automated	Fingerprint services on critical servers on the internal network	To verify that only known and approved services are offered from critical servers in the internal network
Daily	Automated	Fingerprint all IP addresses from the outside	To verify that only known and approved servers (and other devices) can be reached from the public network
Hourly	Automated	Fingerprint services on critical servers exposed to the Internet	To enable the e-mail notification of administrators if unexpected services become available on critical servers exposed to the Internet

Be sure to note that Table 12-2 lists suggestions for *possible* difference analyses. Each organization should identify what differences it wants to measure and its criteria for action. The value of difference analysis depends on the quality of the baseline, which is the initial snapshot portion of the difference comparison. It also depends on the degree to which the notification of discovered differences can induce action.

Planning and Risk Assessment

The primary objective of the **planning and risk assessment domain** is to keep a lookout over the entire information security program. This is done in part by identifying and planning ongoing information security activities that further reduce risk. Also, the risk assessment group identifies and documents risks introduced by both IT projects and information security projects. It also identifies and documents risks that may be latent in the present environment. The primary objectives of this domain are:

- Establishing a formal information security program review process that complements and supports both the IT planning process and strategic planning processes
- Instituting formal project identification, selection, planning, and management processes for information security follow-up activities that augment the current information security program
- Coordinating with IT project teams to introduce risk assessment and review for all IT projects, so that risks introduced by the launching of IT projects are identified, documented, and factored into decisions about the projects
- Integrating a mindset of risk assessment across the organization to encourage other departments to perform risk assessment activities when any technology system is implemented or modified

Figure 12-5 illustrates the relationships between the components of this maintenance domain. Note that there are two pivotal processes: the planning needed for the information security programs and evaluation of current risks using operational risk assessment. A discussion of both of these topics plus their relationship to both IT and information security projects follows.

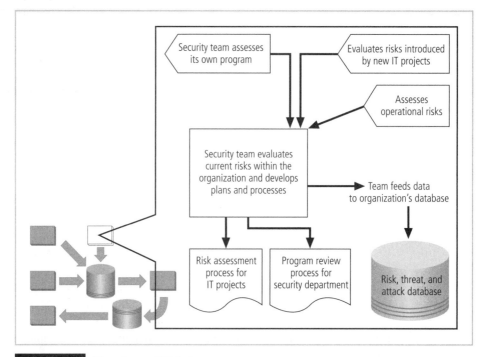

FIGURE 12-5   Planning and Risk Assessment

Information Security Program Planning and Review

Periodic review of an ongoing information security program coupled with planning for enhancements and extensions is a recommended practice for any organization. The strategic planning process should examine the future IT needs of the organization and the impact those needs have on information security.

An approach recommended by this textbook is to take advantage of the fact that most organizations have annual capital budget planning cycles. In this approach, the IT organization has an annual project planning process that closely follows the annual operational planning processes of other organizational units. The IT organization develops an annual list of project ideas for project planning. Each of the projects on the list then has an estimate prepared for the effort needed to complete it and the capital it might require; also a preliminary assessment of the risks associated with each project is prepared. These assessments become part of the organization's project-planning document. When capital and expense budgets are made final, the projects to be funded are chosen using the planning information already prepared. This allows executives to make informed decisions about which projects to fund. The organization then follows up with quarterly reviews of progress, which include an updated project risk assessment. As each project nears completion, an operational risk assessment group reviews the impact of the project on the risk profile of the organization. The sponsors of the project, and perhaps other organization executives, then determine if the risk level is acceptable, if the project requires additional risk remediation, or if the project must be aborted.

Projects that organizations might fund to maintain, extend, or enhance the information security program will arise in almost every planning cycle. Larger information security projects should be broken into smaller, incremental projects. Doing this is important for several reasons:

- Smaller projects tend to have more manageable impacts on the networks and users.
- Larger projects tend to complicate the change control process in the implementation phase.
- Shorter planning, development, and implementation schedules reduce uncertainty for IT planners and financial sponsors.
- Most large projects can easily be broken down into smaller projects, giving the security team more opportunities to change direction and gain flexibility as events occur and circumstances change.

Security Risk Assessments

A key component in the engine that drives change in the information security program is a relatively straightforward process called an **information security operational risk assessment** (RA for short). The RA is a method of identifying and documenting the risk that a project, process, or action introduces to the organization and may also involve offering suggestions for controls that can reduce that risk. The information security group is in the business of coordinating the preparation of many different types of RA documents, including:

- Network connectivity RA: Used to respond to network change requests and network architectural design proposals. May be part of or support a business partner's RA.
- Dialed modem RA: Used when a dial-up connection is requested for a system.
- Business partner RA: Used when a proposal for connectivity with business partners is being evaluated.
- Application RA: Used at various stages in the life cycle of a business application. Content depends on the project's position in the life cycle when the RA is prepared. Usually, multiple RA documents are prepared at different stages. The definitive version is prepared as the application is readied for conversion to production.
- Vulnerability RA: Used to assist in communicating the background, details, and proposed remediation as vulnerabilities emerge or change over time.
- Privacy RA: Used to document applications or systems that contain protected personal information that needs to be evaluated for compliance with privacy policies of the organization and relevant laws.
- Acquisition or divesture RA: Used when planning for reorganization as units of the organization are acquired, divested, or moved.
- Other RA: Used when a statement about risk is needed for any project, proposal, or fault that is not contained in the preceding list.

The RA process identifies risks and proposes controls. Most RA documents are structured to include the components shown in Table 12-3. Most training programs on information security include training sessions for the preparation of RA documents.

TABLE 12-3 Risk Assessment Documentation Components

Component	Description	When and How Used
Introduction	A standard opening description to explain the RA to readers who are unfamiliar with the format. The exact text varies for each RA template.	Found in all RA document templates
	Here is an example: "The primary purpose of the security risk assessment is to identify computer and network security risks to information assets that may be introduced to the organization by the issue described in this risk assessment document. This security risk assessment is also used to help identify security controls planned or proposed. Further, the sections below may identify risks that are not adequately controlled by the planned controls."	
Scope	A statement of the boundaries of the RA.	Found in all RA document templates
	Here is an example: "To define the security and control requirements associated with project X running application Y with access via Internet and the migration of that application into the organization's environment."	
Disclaimer	A statement that includes language that identifies limits in the risk assessment based on where in the project life cycle the report was developed. The information available at different times in the life of the project will affect how comprehensive and accurate the report is. Often, risk assessments are the most imprecise at the earliest stages of a project, and it is important that decision-makers are made aware of the lack of precision in the risk assessment when it is based on incomplete information. This statement is sometimes removed in the final RA when all information about the project is available, but it may be left in order to provide awareness that some imprecision in the assessment of risk is inherent in the process.	Found in all draft RA document templates; some issues may remain in the disclaimer in some final RA templates
	Here is an example: "The issues documented in this report should not be considered all inclusive. A number of strategic and tactical decisions will be made during the development and implementation stages of the project, and therefore the security	

TABLE 12-3 Risk Assessment Documentation Components (continued)

Component	Description	When and How Used
	control deliverables may change based on actual implementation. Any changes should be reassessed to ensure that proper controls will still be enacted."	
Information security resources	A list of the names of the information security team members who collected information, analyzed risk, and documented the findings.	Found in all RA document templates
Other resources	A list of the names of the other organization members who provided information, assisted in analyzing risk, and documented the findings.	Found in all RA document templates
Background	A documenting of the proposed project, including network changes, application changes, and other issues or faults.	Found in all RA document templates
Planned controls	A documenting of all controls that are planned in the proposed project, including network changes, application changes, and other issues or faults.	Found in all RA document templates
IRP and DRP planning elements	A documenting of the incident response and disaster planning elements that have been or will be prepared for this proposed project, including network changes, application changes, and other issues or faults.	Recommended in all document templates
Opinion of risk	A summary statement of the risk to the organization introduced by the proposed project, network change, application, or other issue or fault. Here is an example: "This application as it currently exists is considered high risk. IMPORTANT NOTE: Because of the high risk of the current implementation and the potential for high impact on the organization if system or data is compromised in any way, this notification needs to be escalated to the director or manager who would be held responsible for the added expense or loss of revenue associated with such a compromise. In addition, an acknowledgement of and signing off on the understanding of the nature of the risk and the urgency of correcting it must be returned to the CISO of the organization."	Found in all RA document templates

TABLE 12-3 Risk Assessment Documentation Components (continued)

Component	Description	When and How Used
Recommendations	A statement of what needs to be done to implement controls within the project to limit risk from the proposed project.	Found in all RA document templates
	Here is an example: "A project team should be formed to assist the operating unit and technical support team to create a comprehensive plan to address the security issues within application X. Specific areas of concern are: authentication and authorization. The corrections of configuration errors found in the platform security validation process must continue. All user accounts need to be reviewed and scrubbed to determine whether the user or service account requires access. All user accounts need to be reviewed and assigned the appropriate privileges. Integrity: The Web server function of the application needs to be separated from the application and database server."	
Information security controls recommendations summary	A summary of the controls that are planned or needed, using the security architecture elements of the system as an organizing method. The following categories of information are recommended to be documented in tabular form: ■ Security architecture elements and what they provide: 　■ Authentication: The user is verified as authentic. 　■ Authorization: The user is allowed to use the facility or service. 　■ Confidentiality: Content must be kept secret from unintended recipients. 　■ Integrity: Data storage must be secure, accurate and precise. 　■ Accountability: Actions and data usage can be attributed to specific individuals. 　■ Availability and reliability: Systems work when needed. 　■ Privacy: System complies with organizational privacy policy. ■ Security requirement written for a general audience in terms of the organization's information security policies using the following core principles of information security: 　■ Authentication: Must conform to organizational authentication policies. 　■ Authorization: Must conform to organization authorization and usage policies.	Recommended in all document templates

TABLE 12-3 Risk Assessment Documentation Components (continued)

Component	Description	When and How Used
	▪ Confidentiality: Must comply with the requirement to protect data in transit from interception and misuse by using hard encryption.	
	▪ Integrity: Must process data with procedures that ensure freedom from corruption.	
	▪ Accountability: Must track usage to allow actions to be audited at a later time for policy compliance.	
	▪ Availability and reliability: Must be implemented to assure an availability that measures up to current organizational expectations.	
	▪ Privacy: Must process, store, and transmit data using procedures sufficient to meet legal privacy requirements.	
	▪ Security controls planned or in place: Identify controls for each architectural element.	
	▪ Planned completion date when the control will be fully operational.	
	▪ Who is responsible: Which group or individuals are accountable for implementing the control?	
	▪ Status: What is the status of the control implementation?	

A risk assessment's identification of the systemic or latent vulnerabilities that introduce risk to the organization can provide the opportunity to create a proposal for an information security project. When used as part of a complete risk management maintenance process, the RA can support the information security program as a powerful and flexible tool that helps identify and document risk and remediate the underlying vulnerabilities that expose the organization to risks of loss.

Vulnerability Assessment and Remediation

The primary goal of the **vulnerability assessment and remediation domain** is to identify specific, documented vulnerabilities and remediate them in a timely fashion. This is accomplished by:

- Using vulnerability assessment procedures that are documented to collect intelligence about networks (internal and public-facing), platforms (servers, desktops, and process control), dial-in modems, and wireless network systems safely
- Documenting background information and providing tested remediation procedures for the reported vulnerabilities
- Tracking vulnerabilities from when they are identified until they are remediated or the risk of loss has been accepted by an authorized member of management
- Communicating vulnerability information including an estimate of the risk and detailed remediation plans to the owners of the vulnerable systems

- Reporting on the status of vulnerabilities that have been identified
- Escalating unrepaired vulnerabilities to higher levels of management to make sure the proper level of management is involved in the decision to accept the risk of loss associated with them

Figure 12-6 illustrates the process flow of the vulnerability assessment and remediation domain. Using the inventory of environment characteristics stored in the risk, threat, and attack database, the vulnerability assessment processes identify and document vulnerabilities. These vulnerabilities are stored, tracked, and reported within the vulnerability database until they are remediated.

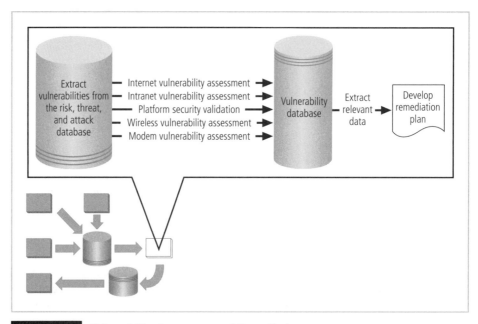

FIGURE 12-6   Vulnerability Assessment and Remediation

The process of identifying and documenting specific and provable flaws in the organization's information asset environment is called **vulnerability assessment (VA)**. As shown in Figure 12-6, there are five common vulnerability assessment processes: Internet VA, intranet VA, platform security validation, wireless VA, and modem VA. While the exact procedures associated with each can vary, these five vulnerability assessment processes can serve many organizations as they attempt to balance the intrusiveness of vulnerability assessment with the need for a stable and effective production environment. Some organizations pursue a strategy of monthly vulnerability assessments that involves all five processes. Others perform an Internet vulnerability assessment weekly and choose from the other four processes on a rotating monthly or quarterly basis. These choices depend on the quantity and quality of the resources dedicated to vulnerability assessments.

Internet Vulnerability Assessment

The **Internet vulnerability assessment** process is designed to find and document the vulnerabilities that may be present in the public-facing network of the organization. Because attackers from this direction can take advantage of any loophole or flaw, this assessment is usually performed against all public-facing addresses, using every possible penetration testing approach. The steps in the process are:

- Planning, scheduling, and notification of the penetration testing: To perform the data collection phase of this assessment, large organizations often need an entire month, using nights and weekends but avoiding change control blackout windows. (The latter are periods when changes are not allowed on the organization's systems or networks.) This degree of scanning results in vast quantities of test results and many hours of analysis effort (as explained in the section that follows). A rule of thumb is that every hour of scanning results in two to three hours of analysis. Therefore, planning should accommodate spreading out the scanning times so that analysis is being performed on fresh scanning results over the course of the assessment period. Also, the various technical support communities should be given the detailed plan so that they know when each device is scheduled for testing and what tests are used. This makes disruptions caused by invasive penetration testing easier to diagnose and recover from.

- Target selection: Working from the network characterization database elements that are stored in the risk, threat, and attack database, the penetration targets are selected. As previously noted, most organizations choose to test every device that is exposed to public access of the Internet.

- Test selection: This step involves using the external monitoring intelligence to configure a test engine (such as Nessus) for the tests to be performed. The selection of the test library to be employed usually evolves over time, and matches the evolution of the threat environment. After the ground rules are established, there is usually little debate about the risk level of the tests used. After all, if a device is placed in a public-facing role, it must be able to take everything the Internet can send its way, including the most aggressive penetration test scripts.

- Scanning: The penetration test engine is unleashed at the scheduled time using the planned target list and test selection. The results of the entire test run are logged to text log files for analysis. This should be a monitored process, so that if an invasive penetration test causes a disruption to a targeted system, the outage can be reported immediately and recovery activities can be initiated. You should note that the log files generated by this scanning, along with all of the data generated in the rest of this maintenance domain, must be treated as highly confidential.

- Analysis: A knowledgeable and experienced vulnerability analyst screens the test results for the **candidate vulnerabilities** logged during scanning. During this step, the analyst must perform three tasks:

  - Classify the risk level of the candidate vulnerability as needing attention or as an acceptable risk.

  - Validate the existence of the vulnerability when it is deemed to be a significant risk— that is, the risk is higher than the risk appetite of the organization. This validation is important because it establishes the *reality* of the risk; the analyst must therefore use manual testing, human judgment, and a large dose of discretion. The goal of this step is to tread lightly and cause as little disruption and damage as possible while removing false positive candidates from further investigation. These proven cases of real vulnerabilities can now be considered **vulnerability instances**.

- Document the results of the verification by saving a **trophy** (usually a screenshot) that can be used to convince skeptical systems administrators that the vulnerability is real.
- Record keeping: In this phase, the organization must record the details of the documented vulnerability in the vulnerability database, identifying the logical and physical characteristics and assigning a response risk level to the vulnerability to differentiate the truly urgent from the merely critical. When coupled with the criticality level from the characteristics in the risk, threat, and attack database, these records can help the systems administrators discern which items they need to remediate first.

As the list of documented vulnerabilities is identified for the Internet information assets, these confirmed items are moved to the remediation stage.

Intranet Vulnerability Assessment

The **intranet vulnerability assessment** process is designed to find and document selected vulnerabilities that are likely to be present on the internal network of the organization. The attackers of intranets are often internal members of the organization, affiliates of business partners, or automated attack vectors (such as viruses and worms). This assessment is therefore usually performed against selected critical internal devices with a known, high value, and thus requires the use of selective penetration testing. The steps in the process are almost identical to the steps in the Internet vulnerability assessment, except as noted below:

- Planning, scheduling, and notification of the penetration testing: Most organizations are amazed at how many devices exist inside even a moderately sized network. Bigger networks contain staggering numbers of networked devices. In order to plan a meaningful assessment process, the planner should be aware that any significant degree of scanning will result in vast quantities of test results and many hours of analysis effort (see the description that follows). The same rule of thumb noted previously for Internet vulnerability assessment applies: every hour of scanning results in two to three hours of analysis. So organizations must plan accordingly. Just as in Internet scanning, the various technical support communities should be notified, but it should be noted that these are probably different individuals than those notified for Internet scanning. Like the Internet support teams, the intranet support teams use this information to make any disruptions caused by invasive penetration testing easier to diagnose and recover from. In contrast to Internet systems administrators who prefer the penetration testing to be performed at low-demand periods (such as nights and weekends for commercial operations), intranet administrators often prefer penetration testing (both scanning and analysis) be performed during working hours. The best process takes the systems administrator's planning needs into account when the schedule is built.

- Target selection: Like the Internet vulnerability assessment process, the intranet scan starts with the network characterization database elements stored in the risk, threat, and attack database. Intranet testing has so many target possibilities, however, that a more selective approach is required. At first, the penetration test scanning and analysis should focus on testing only the highest value, most critical systems. As the configuration of these systems is improved, and fewer candidate vulnerabilities are found in the scanning step, the target list can be expanded. The list of targeted intranet systems should eventually reach equilibrium so that it targets as many systems as can be scanned and analyzed with the resources dedicated to the process.
- Test selection: The testing for intranet vulnerability assessment usually uses different criteria from Internet scanning. The selection of the tests to be performed usually evolves over time, and matches the evolution of the threat environment. Most organizations focus their intranet scanning efforts on a few, very critical vulnerabilities at first, and then expand the test pool to include more test scripts. The degree to which an organization is willing to accept risk while scanning and analyzing also affects the selection of test scripts. If the organization is unwilling to risk disruptions to critical internal systems, test scripts that pose such risks should be avoided and alternate means to confirm safety from those vulnerabilities should be pursued.
- Scanning: Intranet scanning is the same process as used for Internet scanning. Just as in Internet scanning, the scanning process should be monitored so that if an invasive penetration test causes disruption, it can be reported for repair.
- Analysis: Despite the differences in targets and tested vulnerabilities, the intranet scan analysis is essentially identical to the Internet analysis. It follows the same three steps: classify, validate, and document.
- Record keeping: Once again, this process step is identical to the one followed in Internet vulnerability analysis. Organizations should use the similarities between the processes to their advantage by sharing the database, the reports, and the procedures used for record keeping, reporting, and follow-up.

By both leveraging the common assessment processes and using difference analysis on the data collected during the vulnerability assessment, an organization can identify a list of documented internal vulnerabilities, which are the essential pieces of information needed for the remediation stage.

Platform Security Validation

The **platform security validation (PSV)** process is designed to find and document the vulnerabilities that may be present because there are misconfigured systems in use within the organization. These misconfigured systems fail to comply with company policy or standards as adopted by the IT governance groups and communicated in the information security and awareness program. Fortunately, automated measurement systems are available to help with the intensive process of validating the compliance of platform configuration with policy. Two products known to provide this function are Symantec Enterprise Security Manager and NetIQ VigilEnt Security Manager. Other products are also available that can perform this function, but the approach and terminology presented here are based on the NetIQ product.

- Product selection: Typically an organization implements a PSV solution in the information security program deployment. That solution serves for ongoing PSV compliance as well. If a product has not yet been selected, a separate information security project is required to select and deploy a PSV solution.

- Policy configuration: As organizational policy and standards evolve, the policy templates of the PSV tool must be changed to match. After all, the goal for any approach selected is to be able to measure how well the systems comply with policy.
- Deployment: All systems that are mission critical should be enrolled in PSV measurement. If the organization can afford the associated licensing and support costs and can dedicate sufficient resources to the PSV program, it should enroll all of its devices. Security personnel should remember that attackers often come into a network using the weakest link, which may not be a critical system itself, but could be connected to critical systems.
- Measurement: Using the PSV tools, the organization should measure the compliance of each enrolled system against the policy templates. Deficiencies should be reported as vulnerabilities.
- Exclusion handling: Some provision should be made for the exclusion of specific policy or standard exceptions. For instance, one metric is to determine the user accounts that never expire. Some organizations have adopted practices that assume the risk of having service accounts that do not expire or that have change intervals that are longer than standard user accounts. If the proper organizational decision makers have made an informed decision to assume that risk, the automated PSV tool should be able to exclude the assumed risk factor from the compliance report.
- Reporting: Using the standard reporting components in the PSV tool, most organizations can inform the systems administrators of deficiencies that need remediation.
- Remediation: Systems out of compliance need to be updated with configurations that comply with policy. When the PSV process shows an outstanding configuration fault that has not been promptly remedied, the information about the vulnerable system should flow to the vulnerability database to assure remediation.

The ability of PSV software products to integrate with a custom vulnerability database is not a standard feature, but most PSV products on the market have the ability to provide data extracts that can be imported to the organization's vulnerability database for integrated use in the remediation phase. If this degree of integration is not needed or cannot be justified, the stand-alone reporting capabilities of the products can generate sufficient reports for the remediation functions of this maintenance domain.

Wireless Vulnerability Assessment

The **wireless vulnerability assessment** process is designed to find and document the vulnerabilities that may be present in the wireless local area networks of the organization. Because attackers from this direction are likely to take advantage of any loophole or flaw, this assessment is usually performed against all publicly accessible areas using every possible wireless penetration testing approach. The steps in the process are:

- Planning, scheduling, and notification of the wireless penetration testing: This is a noninvasive scanning process, and can be done almost anytime without notifying systems administrators. Even if company culture requires that administrators be notified, the organization should still consider scheduling some unannounced scans as administrators have been known to turn off their wireless access points on scheduled test days to avoid detection and the resulting remediation effort. Times and days should be rotated over time to detect wireless devices that are used for intermittent projects.

- Target selection: All areas of the organization's premises should be scanned with a portable wireless network scanner, with special attention to the following: all areas that are publicly accessible; all areas in range of commonly available products (such as 802.11b); and areas where visitors might linger without attracting attention. Because the radio emissions of wireless network equipment can act in surprising ways, all locations should be tested periodically.
- Test selection: Wireless scanning tools should look for all wireless signals that do not meet the organization's minimum level of encryption strength.
- Scanning: The walking scan should survey the entire target area and identify all wireless local area network (WLAN) access points that are not cryptographically secure.
- Analysis: A knowledgeable and experienced vulnerability analyst should screen the test results for the WLANs that have been logged as previously described. During this step, the analyst should perform these steps:
  - Remove false positive candidates from further consideration as vulnerabilities while causing as little disruption or damage as possible.
  - Document the results of the verification by saving a screenshot or other documentary evidence (often called a trophy). This serves a double purpose. It can convince skeptical systems administrators that the vulnerability is real. It also documents those wireless access points that are transient devices and thus may be off the air at a later time.
- Record keeping: Good reporting makes the effort to communicate and follow-up much easier. Just as in earlier vulnerability assessment phases, effective reporting maximizes results.

At this stage in the process, the wireless vulnerabilities are documented and ready for remediation.

Modem Vulnerability Assessment

The **modem vulnerability assessment** process is designed to find and document any vulnerability that is present on dial-up modems connected to the organization's networks. Because attackers from this direction take advantage of any loophole or flaw, this assessment is usually performed against all telephone numbers owned by the organization, using every possible penetration testing approach. One of the elements of this process involves using scripted dialing attacks against a pool of phone numbers; this is often called **war dialing**. The steps in the modem vulnerability assessment process are:

- Planning, scheduling, and notification of the dial-up modem testing: Most organizations find that they need to run the dial-up modem-testing appliance (dedicated system and software, such as PhoneSweep) continuously. Because this is a 24/7 operation, planning of schedules and notification is not required.
- Target selection: All telephone numbers controlled by the organization should be in the test pool, unless the configuration of the phone equipment on premises can assure that no number can be dialed from the worldwide telephone system.
- Test selection: The entire set of tests in the testing product should be used, including tests for dial-in modems, callback modems, and facsimile machines.

- Scanning: This is a 24/7 process. The raw vulnerability reports should be prepared daily or weekly for the analysis steps that follow.
- Analysis: A knowledgeable and experienced modem vulnerability analyst should screen the test results to eliminate false positives and document the vulnerabilities using the process steps common to the Internet, intranet, and wireless vulnerability assessments already noted. The end result is a list of documented modem vulnerabilities ready for remediation.

Now that each group of vulnerability assessments has been described, a discussion of the record keeping process is in order.

Documenting Vulnerabilities

The vulnerability database, like the risk, threat, and attack database, both stores and tracks information. It should provide details about the vulnerability being reported as well as a link to the information assets characterized in the risk, threat, and attack database. While this can be done through manual data storage, the low cost and ease of use associated with relational databases makes them a more realistic choice.

The data stored in the vulnerability database should include:

- A unique vulnerability ID number for reporting and tracking remediation actions
- Linkage to the risk, threat, and attack database based on the physical information asset underlying the vulnerability; the IP address is a good choice for this linkage
- Vulnerability details usually based on the test script used for the scanning step of the process; if the Nessus scanner is used, each test script has an assigned code (NASL or Nessus attack scripting language) that can identify the vulnerability effectively
- Dates and times of notification and remediation activities
- Current status of the vulnerability instance, such as found, reported, or repaired
- Comments are always useful to add to the vulnerability instance since they give the analyst the chance to provide the systems administrators with detailed and specific information about how to fix the vulnerability
- Other fields as needed to manage the reporting and tracking processes in the remediation phase

The vulnerability database is an essential part of effective remediation as it helps organizations avoid losing track of specific vulnerability instances as they are reported and remediated.

Remediating Vulnerabilities

The final process in the vulnerability assessment and remediation domain is the remediation phase. The objective of remediation is to repair the flaw causing a vulnerability instance or remove the risk associated with the vulnerability. Alternatively, informed decision makers with the proper authority may, as a last resort, decide to accept this risk.

When approaching the remediation process, it is important to recognize that building relationships with those who control the information assets is the key to success. In other words, success depends on the organization adopting a team approach to remediation, in place of cross-organizational push and pull.

Remediation of vulnerabilities can be accomplished by accepting or transferring the risk, removing the threat, or repairing the vulnerability.

Acceptance or Transference of Risk. In some instances, risk must either simply be acknowledged as being part of an organization's business process, or else the organization should buy insurance to transfer the risk to another organization. The information security professional must assure the general management community that the decision to accept the risk or buy insurance for the organization was made by properly informed decision makers. Further, these decision makers must have the proper level of authority within the organization to assume the risk. In reality, however, many situations where risk is assumed violate these conditions, as described below:

- Decisions are made at the wrong level of the organization. Thus, for example, it is problematic when systems administrators decide to skip using passwords on a critical application server because it creates more work for them.
- Decisions are made by uninformed decision makers. Thus, for example, it is problematic when a project manager convinces an application sponsor that database-level security is not needed in an application and that all users need unlimited access to all data because the sponsor may not realize all of the implications of this decision.

In the final analysis, the information security group must make sure the right people make risk assumption decisions and that these people are aware of both the potential impact of their decision and the cost the possible security controls.

Threat Removal. In some circumstances, threats can be removed without requiring a repair of the vulnerability. For example, if an application can only run on an older desktop system that cannot support passwords, the older desktop system can be removed from the network and stored in a locked room or equipment rack to be used only as a stand-alone device. With this, the vulnerability can no longer be exploited, and the risk has been removed. Other vulnerabilities may be amenable to controls that do not require an expensive repair, but do allow the risk associated with the vulnerability to be successfully removed from the situation. An example of such a control would be disabling the Web services on a server that provides other important services instead of taking the time to update the Web software on the server.

Vulnerability Repair. The optimum solution in most cases is to repair the vulnerability. Applying patch software or implementing a workaround to the vulnerability often accomplishes this. Many recent vulnerabilities have exploited Web servers on Windows operating systems. In this case, simply updating the version of the installed Web server removes the vulnerability. Simple repairs are possible in other cases, too. For instance, if an account is flagged as a vulnerability because it has a password that has not been changed for longer than the specified interval, changing the password removes the vulnerability. Of course, the most common repair is the application of a software patch; this usually makes the system function in the expected fashion and removes the vulnerability.

Readiness and Review

The primary goal of the **readiness and review domain** is to keep the information security program functioning as designed and to keep it continuously improving over time. This is accomplished by:

- Policy review: Policy needs to be reviewed and refreshed from time to time to ensure that it's sound—in other words, that it provides a current foundation for the information security program.

- Program review: Major planning components should be reviewed on a periodic basis to ensure that they are current, accurate, and appropriate.
- Rehearsals: When possible, major plan elements should be rehearsed.

The relationships among the sectors of the readiness and review domain are shown in Figure 12-7. As the diagram indicates, policy review is the primary initiator of the readiness and review domain. As policy is revised or current policy is confirmed, the various planning elements are reviewed for compliance, the information security program is reviewed, and rehearsals are held to make sure all participants are capable of responding as needed.

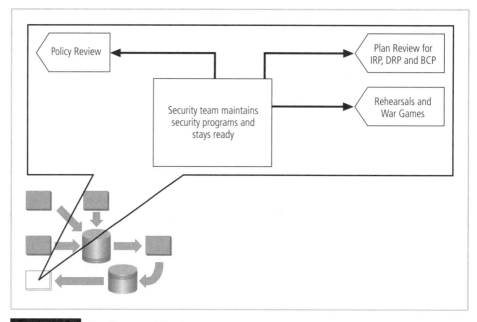

FIGURE 12-7 Readiness and Review

Policy Review and Planning Review
Policy needs to be reviewed periodically. The topic of policy management and policy review was covered in Chapter 5. The planning and review process for IRP, DRP, and BCP was also covered in Chapter 5.

Program Review
As policy needs shift, a thorough and independent review of the entire information security program should be undertaken. While an exact timetable for review is not proposed here, many organizations find that the CISO should conduct a formal review annually. Earlier in this chapter, the role of the CISO in the maintenance process was discussed. The CISO uses the results of maintenance activities and the review of the information security program to determine if the *status quo* can adequately meet the threats at hand.

If the current information security program is not up to the challenges, the CISO must determine if incremental improvements are possible, or if it is time to launch a new initiative to restructure the information security function within the organization.

Rehearsals and War Games

Where possible, major planning elements should be rehearsed. Rehearsal adds value by exercising the procedures, identifying shortcomings, and providing security personnel the opportunity to improve the security plan before it is needed. In addition, rehearsals make people more effective when an actual event occurs.

Rehearsals that closely match reality are called **war games**. A war game or simulation puts a subset of plans in place to create a realistic test environment. This adds to the value of the rehearsal and can enhance training.

What is the issue that most often keeps CISOs awake at night? CISOs typically find themselves counting sheep because of the maintenance issues covered in this chapter. A solid maintenance program can complement every information security program, and over time can even strengthen a weak program.

Chapter Summary

- Change is a reality for most organizations, which is why organizations should have procedures to deal with changes in the operation and maintenance of the information security program.

- The CISO decides whether the information security program can adapt to change as it is implemented or whether the macroscopic process of the SecSDLC must be started anew to develop a fundamentally new information security profile.

- The maintenance model recommended in this chapter is made up of five subject areas or domains. They are:
    - External monitoring
    - Internal monitoring
    - Planning and risk assessment
    - Vulnerability assessment and remediation
    - Readiness and review

- To stay current, the information security community of interest, led by the CISO, must constantly monitor the three components of the security triple—that is, threats, assets, and vulnerabilities.

- To assist the information security community in managing and operating the ongoing security program, the organization should adopt a management model. Management models are frameworks that are structured along the tasks of managing a particular set of activities or business functions.

- In this chapter, it was shown how the ISO network management model could be modified to serve as an information security management model. This information security management model contains the following elements:
    - Fault management
    - Configuration and change management
    - Accounting and auditing management
    - Performance management
    - Security program management

- The objective of the external monitoring domain of the maintenance model is to provide an early awareness of new and emerging threats, threat agents, vulnerabilities, and attacks so that an effective and timely defense can be mounted.

- The objective of the internal monitoring domain is to maintain an informed awareness of the state of all the organization's networks, information systems, and information security defenses. The security team documents and communicates this awareness, particularly when it concerns system components that face the external network.

- The primary objective of the planning and risk assessment domain is to keep an eye on the entire information security program.

- The primary objectives of the vulnerability assessment and remediation domain are to identify specific, documented vulnerabilities and to remediate them in a timely fashion.

- The primary objectives of the readiness and review domain are to keep the information security program functioning as designed and to keep it improving over time.

Review Questions

1. List and define the factors that are likely to shift in an organization's information security environment.
2. Who decides if the information security program can adapt to change adequately?
3. List and briefly describe the five domains of the maintenance model.
4. What is the security triple? Why is it important?
5. In general, what is a management model? What does it accomplish?
6. What changes needed to be made to the standard ISO model to adapt it for use in security management?
7. What is fault management? What steps does it involve?
8. What is vulnerability assessment?
9. What is penetration testing?
10. What is the difference between configuration management and change management?
11. What is a performance baseline?
12. Describe the Plan-Do-Check-Act process. What does it accomplish?
13. What are the objectives of the external monitoring domain of the maintenance model?
14. List and describe four vulnerability intelligence sources. Of those that you listed, which seems the most effective? Why?
15. What does CERT stand for? Is there more than one CERT?
16. What are the primary objectives of the internal monitoring domain?
17. What is network characterization? When is it done?
18. What is the objective of the planning and risk assessment domain of the maintenance model? Why is this important?
19. What is the primary goal of the vulnerability assessment and remediation domain of the maintenance model? Is this important to an organization with an Internet presence? Why?
20. List and describe the five vulnerability assessment processes described in the text. Can you think of some other assessment processes that might exist?

Exercises

1. Search the World Wide Web for the Forum of Incident Response and Security Teams (FIRST). In your own words, what is the forum's mission?

2. Search the World Wide Web for two or more sites that discuss the ISO management model. What other components of network management, as outlined by this model, can be adapted for use in the security management model?

3. This chapter lists five tools that can be used by security administrators, network administrators, and hackers alike. Search the World Wide Web for three to five other tools that fit this same description. Who do the sites promoting these tools claim to support?

4. Using the names of the tools you found in Exercise 3, and a browser on the World Wide Web, find a site that claims to be dedicated to supporting hackers. Do you find any references to any other hacker tools? If you do, create a list of the tools with their names and a short description of what they do and how they work.

5. Using the risk assessment documentation components presented in the chapter, draft a tentative risk assessment of one area (a lab, department, or office) of your university. Outline the critical risks you found, and discuss these with your class.

Case Exercises

Remember from the beginning of this book how Amy's day started? Now imagine how it could have been:

It started out like any other day for Amy at the Sequential Label and Supply Company. She liked her technical support job at the help desk. Taking calls and helping the office workers with PC problems was not glamorous, but it was challenging and paid pretty well.

The phone rang. That was not a big deal for Amy. She answered her phone about 35 times an hour, 315 times a day, nine days every two weeks. The first call of the day started out the same as usual, with a worried user hoping Amy could help him out of a jam. The call display on her screen gave her all the facts: the user's name, his phone number, the department in which he worked, where his office was on the company campus, and a list of all the calls he'd made in the past.

"Hi, Bob," Amy said. "Did you get that document formatting problem squared away after our last call?"

"Sure did, Amy. Hope we can figure out what's going on today."

"We'll try, Bob. Tell me about it."

"Well, I need help setting a page break in this new spreadsheet template I'm working on," Bob said.

Amy smiled to herself. She knew spreadsheets well, so she would probably be able to close this call on the first contact. That would help her call statistics, which was one of the ways her job performance was measured.

Little did Amy know that roughly four minutes before Bob's phone call, a specially pro-grammed computer out at the edge of the SLS network had made a programmed decision. This computer was generally known as postoffice.seqlbl.com, but it was called the "e-mail gateway" by the networking, messaging, and information security teams at SLS. The decision it had made was just like many thousands of other decisions it made in a typical day. In this case, the decision was to block the transmission of a file that had been attached to an e-mail addressed to Bob.Hulme@seqlbl.com. The gateway had determined that Bob didn't need an executable program that had been attached to that e-mail message, which (the gateway also determined) originated from somewhere on the Internet but contained a forged reply-to address from Davey Martinez at SLS. In other words, the gateway had delivered the e-mail to Bob Hulme, but not the attachment.

When Bob had gotten the e-mail, all he saw was that another unsolicited commercial e-mail with an unwanted executable had been blocked. He had deleted the nuisance message without a second thought.

While she was talking to Bob, Amy looked up to see Charles Moody walking calmly down the hall. Charlie, as he liked to be called, was the senior manager of the server administration team and also the company's chief information security officer. Kelvin Urich and Iris Majwubu were trailing behind Charlie as he headed from his office to the door of the conference room. Amy thought, "It must be time for the weekly security status meeting."

She was the user representative on the company information security oversight committee, so she was due to attend this meeting. Amy continued talking Bob through the procedure for setting up a page break and decided she would join the information security team for coffee and bagels as soon as she finished her call.

Questions:

1. What area of the ISO-based security management model addresses the actions of the content filter described here?
2. What recommendations would you give Sequential Label and Supply Company for how it might select a security management model?

Endnotes

1. Jeanne Cuff. "Grow Up: How Mature Is Your Help Desk?" *Compass America, Inc.* [Cited August 15, 2002]. Available from the World Wide Web *<http://www.compassamerica.com/white_papers/GrowUpWP.pdf>*.
2. R. L Krutz and R.D.Vines. *The CISSP Prep Guide.* (New York: Wiley 2001), p. 253.
3. Varun Singh. "Intelligent Networking." *Network Computing.* [Cited September 10, 2001]. Available from the World Wide Web *<http://www.nc-india.com/coverstories/stories/31284.html>*.
4. Gamma. "BS7799: How it works." [Cited August 15, 2002]. Available from the World Wide Web *<http://www.gammassl.co.uk/bs7799/works.html>*.

Glossary

A

access The ability to use, manipulate, modify, or affect an object.

access control A security measure such as a badge reader that admits or prohibits users from entering sensitive areas.

access control list (ACL) A list of people or other entities permitted to access a computer resource.

accident One of three general categories of unethical and illegal behavior in which the individuals with authorization and privileges to manage information within the organization cause harm or damage inadvertently—that is, without intent to do harm.

accuracy An attribute of information in which the data is free of errors and has the value that the user expects.

acquired value The value an asset has gained over time within an organization.

Active vulnerability scanners Devices that scan networks for highly detailed information. An "active" scanner is one that initiates traffic on the network in order to determine security holes.

address restrictions Rules designed to prohibit data packets with certain addresses or partial addresses from passing through devices.

Advanced Encryption Standard (AES) A Federal Information Processing Standard (FIPS) that specifies a cryptographic algorithm for use within the U.S. government to protect unclassified information.

after-action review A detailed examination of the events that occur from the first detection of a security breach to the final recovery.

aggregate information Information created by combining pieces of data that are not considered private in themselves, but raise privacy concerns when taken together.

air-aspirating detectors Sophisticated systems that are used in high-sensitivity areas. They filter air by moving it through a chamber containing a detector.

alarm An indication, which may take the form of audible signals, e-mail messages, pager notifications, pop-up windows, or log entries, that a system has just been attacked and/or continues to be under attack. Synonymous with Alert.

alarm clustering A consolidation of almost identical alarms into a single higher-level alarm to reduce the total number of alarms generated, thereby reducing administrative overhead, and also to indicate a relationship between the individual alarm elements.

alarm compaction A form of alarm clustering that is based on frequency, similarity in attack signature, similarity in attack target, or other similarities; it is also designed to reduce the total number of alarms generated, thereby reducing administrative overhead, and also to indicate a relationship between the individual alarm elements when they have specific similar attributes.

alarm filtering The process of classifying the attack alerts that an Intrusion Detection System produces in order to distinguish/sort false positives from actual attacks more efficiently.

alert An indication, which may take the form of audible signals, e-mail messages, pager notifications, pop-up windows, or log entries, that a system has just been attacked and/or continues to be under attack. Synonymous with Alarm.

alert message A scripted description of a security breach that points the recipient to a specific section of a response plan for immediate action.

alert roster A document containing contact information on the individuals to be notified in the event of a security breach.

algorithm A set of steps or mathematical calculations used in solving a problem.

annualized cost of the safeguard (ACS) The total cost of owning and operating the specific control for each year of its expected operational life.

annualized loss expectancy (ALE) The overall loss an organization could incur from the specified threat over the course of an entire year.

annualized rate of occurrence (ARO) The anticipated rate of occurrence of a loss from the specified threat over one year.

application firewall *See* application-level firewall.

application gateway *See* application-level firewall.

application header (AH) protocol A feature of the IPSec protocol that can enhance protection from address spoofing and other modes of attack on open networks.

application protocol verification A process in which higher-order protocols (e.g., HTTP, FTP, Telnet) are examined for unexpected packet behavior, or improper use.

application-based IDS (AppIDS) A refinement of the host-based IDS in which the intrusion detection system examines an application for abnormal events, such as users exceeding their authorization, invalid file executions, or other activities that would indicate that there is a problem in the normal interaction between the users, the application, and the data.

application-level firewall Synonymous with application firewall. A device, typically a computer, that provides a defense between a network inside the firewall and a network outside the firewall (the Internet) that could pose a threat to the inside network. All traffic to and from the network must pass through the firewall, so that unauthorized traffic can be blocked.

asset The organizational resource that is being protected. An asset can be logical, such as a Web site or information owned or controlled by the organization; or an asset can be physical, such as a computer system, or other tangible object.

asset valuation The process of assigning financial value or worth to each information asset.

Association of Computing Machinery (ACM) An organization that focuses on the ethics of security professionals.

asymmetric encryption Synonymous with public key encryption. A method of communicating on a network using two different but related keys, one to encrypt and the other to decrypt messages.

asynchronous tokens Devices that use a challenge-response method, in which a server challenges a user during login with a numerical sequence. The user places the sequence into a token, which generates a response that is entered to gain access.

attack An act that is an intentional or unintentional attempt to compromise the information and/or the systems that support it.

attack profile A detailed description of the activities that occur during an attack.

attack protocol A series of steps or processes used by an attacker, in a logical sequence, to launch an attack against a target system or network.

attack scenario end case The summary that describes the attack, and the most likely outcome from the attack and associated costs from that outcome when assessing the impact to information assets from a specific attack profile.

auditing A process of reviewing the use of a system, not to check performance but rather to determine if misuse or malfeasance has occurred.

authenticity A quality or state of information characterized by being genuine or original rather than reproduced or fabricated.

availability A quality or state of information characterized by being accessible and correctly formatted for use without interference or obstruction.

availability disruption A situation in which a product or service is not delivered to the organization as expected.

avoidance The risk control strategy that attempts to prevent the exploitation of the vulnerability.

B

back door Synonymous with trap door. An electronic hole in software that is left open by accident or intention. Can be installed by a virus or worm.

back-hack Hacking into a hacker's system to find out as much as possible about the hacker.

baseline A value or profile of a performance metric against which changes in the performance metric can be usefully compared.

baselining The analysis of measures against established standards. In information security, baselining is the comparison of security activities and events against the organization's future performance.

bastion host   A dedicated server that receives screened network traffic. Usually prepared with extra attention to detail and hardened for use in an unsecured or limited security zone. Sometimes referred to as a sacrificial host.

behavior-based IDS   Synonymous with statistical anomaly-based IDS. A device that collects data from normal traffic to establish a baseline. The IDS compares periodic data samples with the baseline to highlight irregularities.

behavioral feasibility   Synonymous with operational feasibility. The examination of user acceptance of proposed security measures.

benchmarking   The process of seeking out and studying the practices used in organizations that produce desired results in your organization.

benefit   The value that an organization recognizes by using controls to prevent losses associated with a specific vulnerability.

best business practices   Synonymous with best practices and recommended practices. Procedures that provide a superior level of security for an organization's information.

best practices   Security efforts that seek to provide a superior level of performance in the protection of information.

biometric locks   Access-control devices that use a biometric detection device as a release mechanism.

blackout   A lengthy loss of power.

boot virus   A program that infects the key operating system files located in a computer's boot sector.

bottom-up approach   A method of establishing security policies that begins as a grassroots effort in which systems administrators attempt to improve the security of their systems.

brownout   A prolonged drop in voltage.

brute force attack   The application of computing and network resources to try every possible combination of options of a password.

buffer overflow   An application error that occurs when more data is sent to a buffer than it can handle.

bull's-eye method   A proven method for prioritizing a program of complex change whose fundamental concept is that issues are addressed from the general to the specific and that the focus is on systematic solutions instead of individual problems.

business continuity plan (BCP)   A plan for the continuation of business activities if a catastrophic event occurs, such as the unrecoverable loss of an entire database, building, or operations center.

business impact analysis   The first phase in the development of the continuity planning process. It extends the risk assessment process to determine the priority for risks in the area of information security.

C

C.I.A. triangle   The industry standard for computer security since the development of the mainframe. It is based on three characteristics that describe the utility of information: confidentiality, integrity, and availability.

cache servers   Servers used by proxy servers to temporarily store frequently accessed pages.

candidate vulnerabilities   A possible vulnerability detected by an automated tool. Will be screened by an analyst to ascertain if it is an actual vulnerability.

capability table   Synonymous with capabilities table. A list that specifies data items or physical devices (for example, printers) that users are authorized to access.

centralized IDS control strategy   A control strategy for intrusion detection systems (IDSs) in which all IDS control functions are implemented and managed in a central location.

CERT Coordination Center   Center of Internet security expertise located at the Software Engineering Institute. A federally funded research and development center operated by Carnegie Mellon University.

certificate authority (CA)   An agency that manages the issuance of digital certificates and serves as the electronic notary public to verify their worth and integrity.

certificate revocation list (CRL)   A list distributed by the certificate authority that identifies all revoked certificates.

champion   An executive who manages a security project.

change control   A process to assure an organization that changes to systems are managed and all parties that need to be informed are aware of the planned changes.

change management   The administration of changes in strategy, operations, or components of the information security program.

chargeback accounting   A method for organizations to internally charge their departments for system use.

chief information officer (CIO)   An executive-level position in which the person is in charge of the organization's computing technology, and strives to create efficiency in the processing and accessing of the organization's information.

chief information security officer (CISO)   This position is typically considered the top information security officer in an organization. The CISO is usually not an executive-level position, and frequently the person in this role will report to the chief information officer (CIO).

cipher   Synonymous with cryptographic algorithm. A mathematical function that is used to encrypt and decrypt an original message (plaintext).

ciphertext   A message that is formed when plaintext data is encrypted.

civil law   A wide variety of laws that are recorded in volumes of legal code available for review by the average citizen.

Class A fires   Those fires that involve ordinary combustible fuels such as wood, paper, textiles, rubber, cloth, and trash. They are extinguished by agents that interrupt the ability of the fuel to be ignited. Water and multipurpose dry chemical fire extinguishers are ideal for these types of fires.

Class B fires   Those fires fueled by combustible liquids or gases, such as solvents, gasoline, paint, lacquer, and oil. They are extinguished by agents that remove oxygen from the fire. Carbon dioxide, multipurpose dry chemical, and Halon fire extinguishers are ideal for these types of fires.

Class C fires   Those fires with energized electrical equipment or appliances. They are extinguished with agents that must be nonconducting. Carbon dioxide, multipurpose dry chemical, and Halon fire extinguishers are ideal for these types of fires. A water fire extinguisher must never be used on a Class C fire.

Class D fires   Those fires fueled by combustible metals, such as magnesium, lithium, and sodium. Fires of this type require special extinguishing agents and techniques.

clean agent   A fire suppression system active ingredient that leaves no residue after application, nor does it interfere with the operation of electrical or electronic equipment.

clean desk policy   Rules that require each employee to secure all information in its appropriate storage container at the end of each day.

cleartext   Synonymous with plaintext. The unencrypted message that will be encrypted into ciphertext for transmission over an unsecured channel.

clipping level   As detected by an intrusion detection system, a level of network activity that is higher than an established baseline and therefore suspect.

closed-circuit television (CCT)   An electronic monitoring system. Some of these systems can be made to collect constant video feeds, whereas others rotate input from a number of cameras, sampling each area in turn.

code   Synonymous with code words. The distinct words or phrases that replace other words or phrases within the original plaintext syntax before encryption.

cold site   An alternate site that can be used by an organization if a disaster occurs at the home site. Contains rudimentary services and facilities.

collusion   The act of conspiring together to commit a security breach.

Communication Act of 1934   An act that regulates interstate and foreign telecommunications.

Communications Decency Act of 1996 (CDA)   An act that attempted to define indecency and was immediately ensnarled in legal debate.

communications security   Securing information in transit using tools such as cryptographic systems.

community of interest   A group of individuals united by shared interests or values within an organization.

competitive advantage   The leverage gained by an organization that supplies superior products or services. Establishing a competitive business model, method, or technique allows an organization to provide a product or service that is superior to others in the marketplace.

competitive disadvantage   The leverage lost by an organization that supplies products or services perceived to be inferior to other organizations.

competitive intelligence   Information gained legally that gives an organization an advantage over its competition.

computer forensics   The process of collecting, analyzing, and preserving computer-related evidence related to a breach of security.

Computer Fraud and Abuse Act of 1986 (CFA Act)   The cornerstone of many computer-related federal laws and enforcement efforts. Defines and formalizes laws to counter threats from computer-related acts and offenses.

Computer Professionals for Social Responsibility (CPSR)   A public organization for technologists concerned with the impact of computer technology on society.

computer security   A term that in the early days of computers specified the need to secure the physical location of hardware from outside threats. This term later came to stand for all actions taken to preserve computer systems from losses. It has evolved into the current concept of information security as the scope of protecting information in the organization has expanded.

Computer Security Act of 1987   An act that requires all federal computer systems that contain classified information to contain surety plans, and requires periodic security training for all individuals who operate, design, or manage such systems.

Computer Security Division (CSD)   An organization that raises the awareness of issues on information security, especially on new and emerging technologies.

Computer Security Institute (CSI)   An organization that focuses on information protection, especially policy development, risk analysis, and security awareness.

confidence value   A value associated with an intrusion detection system's ability to detect and identify an attack correctly.

confidentiality   The quality or state of information that prevents disclosure or exposure to unauthorized individuals or systems.

configuration management   The administration of the configuration of the components of a system.

configuration rules   The specific configuration codes entered into security systems to guide the execution of the system when information is passing through it.

content filter   A software device that allows administrators to work within a network to restrict accessibility to information.

contingency plan (CP)   The program developed to prepare for, react to, and recover from events that threaten the security of the information assets of an organization.

contract employees   Individuals who are hired to perform specific services for the organization.

control   Synonymous with safeguard and countermeasure. A security mechanism, policy, or procedure that can counter system attack, reduce risks, and resolve vulnerabilities.

correlation attacks   Attempts to deduce the statistical relationships of the structure of the key and the output of the cryptosystem.

cost avoidance   The money saved by using a control to avoid the financial impact of an incident.

cost benefit analysis   Synonymous with economic feasibility study. The comparison of the cost of protecting an asset with the worth of the asset or the costs of the compromise of an asset.

cracker   An individual who removes an application's software protection that is designed to prevent unauthorized duplication, or a criminal hacker.

cracking   Attempting to reverse-calculate a password.

criminal law   Laws that address violations harmful to society and that are actively enforced through prosecution by the state.

crisis management   The actions taken during and after a disaster.

crossover error rate (CER)   Evaluation criteria for biometric technologies, the crossover rate is the point at which the number of false rejections (denial of access to authorized users) equals the number of the false acceptances (granting of access to unauthorized users).

cryptogram   The unintelligible encrypted or encoded message resulting from an encryption. Synonymous with ciphertext.

cryptography   From the Greek work *kryptos*, meaning hidden, and *graphein*, meaning to write. The enciphering and deciphering of coded messages.

cryptology   The science of encryption. A field of study that encompasses cryptography and cryptanalysis.

cryptosystem   The manual or computer-based systems that are used to code or transform data for secure transmission and storage.

cryptovariable   Also known as the key, the information used in conjunction with an algorithm to create the ciphertext from the plaintext or derive the plaintext from the ciphertext. This can be a series of bits used by a computer program, or it can be a passphrase used by humans.

cultural mores   Fixed moral attitudes or customs of a particular group.

cyberactivist   Synonymous with hacktivist. An individual who uses technology as a tool for civil disobedience.

cyberterrorism   The act of hacking to conduct terrorist activities through network or Internet pathways.

D

data classification scheme   A method of categorizing the levels of confidentiality of an organization's data.

data custodians   Individuals who are responsible for the storage, maintenance, and protection of information.

Data Encryption Standard (DES) An algorithm that is federally approved for encryption. The algorithm is based on the Data Encryption Algorithm (DEA), which uses a 64-bit block size and a 56-bit key.

data owners Individuals who determine the level of classification associated with data.

data users Synonymous with end users. Individuals who use computer applications for their daily work.

Database Right A United Kingdom version of the Directive 95/46/EC.

database shadowing A process that duplicates data in real-time using databases at a remote site or to multiple servers.

de facto standards Informal norms. Early Internet connections were based on de facto standards.

de jure standards Formally recognized norms. As the Internet developed, de jure standards were established for its connections.

decipher The act of using an algorithm and the correct key to reverse the process of encryption.

decryption The decoding of data to reveal a secret message.

defense in depth The multiple levels of security controls and safeguards that an intruder faces.

deliverable A completed document or program module that can serve either as the beginning point for a later task or as an element in the finished project.

Delphi technique Named for the oracle at Delphi, a process in which a group rates or ranks asset values or threats to assets.

deluge system A sprinkler system that contains valves that are kept open, so that when the first phase of sprinkler heads are activated, the water is immediately applied to various areas without waiting for a second phase to trigger the individual sprinkler heads.

demilitarized zone (DMZ) An intermediate area between a trusted network and an untrusted network.

denial-of-service (DoS) An attack in which the abuser sends a large number of connection or information requests to overwhelm and cripple a target.

Department of Homeland Security (DHS) U.S. federal agencies created in 2003 through the Homeland Security Act of 2002, which was passed in response to the events of September 11, 2001. DHS is made up of five directorates, or divisions, through which it carries out its mission of protecting the people as well as the physical and informational assets of the United States.

detective controls Control functions that warn organizations of violations of security principles, or organizational policies, or attempts to exploit vulnerabilities.

dictionary attack A form of brute force attack on passwords that uses a list of commonly used passwords instead of random combinations.

difference analysis A procedure that compares the current state of a network segment (the systems and services it offers) against a known previous state of that same network segment (the baseline of systems and services).

differential backup The storage of all files that have been changed or added since the last full backup.

Diffie-Hellman Key Exchange method A method for exchanging private keys using public key encryption.

digital certificates Electronic documents attached to a file that certify that the file is from the organization it claims to be from and has not been modified from the original format.

Digital Millennium Copyright Act (DMCA) An American version of an international effort to reduce the impact of copyright, trademark, and privacy infringement, especially through the removal of technological copyright protection measures.

digital signatures Encrypted messages that are independently verified as authentic by a central facility (registry).

direct attacks Attacks on a computer system that are initiated from the computer of an abuser.

direct changeover A modification to work practices that involves stopping the old method and beginning the new.

Directive 95/46/EC A European Union act that regulated the processing of personal data and the transmittal of such data to protect individual rights.

disaster recovery plan (DRP) A program to limit losses during a disaster and resume business afterwards.

discretionary access controls A type of data access control in which data users are allowed to grant access to their peers.

disk duplexing For backup purposes, the use of twin drives, each with its own drive controller. A variation of disk mirroring.

disk mirroring A backup and recovery technique that uses twin drives in a computer system. Also known as RAID Level 1.

disk striping   For backup purposes, the creation of one large logical volume across several hard disk drives and the storage of data in segments, called stripes, across all the disk drives in an array.

distinguished name (DN)   Used with digital certificates, a series of name-value pairs that uniquely identify a certificate entity to a user's public key.

distributed denial-of-service (DDoS)   An attack in which a coordinated stream of connection requests is launched against a target from many locations at the same time.

dry-pipe system   A sprinkler system that is designed to work in areas where electrical equipment is used by spraying pressurized air rather than water.

due care   The actions that demonstrate that an organization makes sure that every employee knows what is acceptable or not acceptable behavior, and knows the consequences of illegal or unethical actions.

due diligence   The actions that demonstrate that an organization has made a valid effort to protect others.

dumb cards   ID cards or ATM cards with magnetic stripes containing the digital (and often encrypted) user personal identification number (PIN) against which a user input is compared.

dumpster diving   The retrieval of information from refuse that could prove embarrassing to the company or could compromise the security of information.

dust contamination   A threat to the hardware components of information systems that falls in the forces of nature or acts of God category because it is unexpected or can occur with very little warning. Dust contamination can shorten the life of information systems or disrupt normal operations, causing unplanned downtime.

dynamic packet filtering firewall   A firewall that allows only a particular packet with a particular source, destination, and port address to enter through the firewall.

E

E-mail spoofing   The process of sending an e-mail with a modified field. The modified field is often the address of the originator.

earthquake   A threat to the hardware components of information systems that falls in the forces of nature or acts of God category because it is unexpected or can occur with very little warning. As a sudden movement of the earth's crust caused by the release of stress accumulated along geologic faults, or by volcanic activity, earthquakes can cause direct damage to all or part of the information system or, more often, to the building that houses it.

Economic Espionage Act (EEA)   An act designed to prevent abuse of information gained by an individual working in one company and employed by another.

economic feasibility study   Synonymous with cost benefit analysis. The comparison of the cost of protecting an asset with the worth of the asset or the costs if the asset is compromised.

EISP   *See* enterprise information security policy.

electromechanical locks   Locking devices that can accept a variety of inputs as keys, including magnetic strips on ID cards, radio signals from name badges, personal identification numbers (PINs) typed into a keypad, or some combination of these to activate an electrically powered servo to unlock the mechanism.

Electronic Communications Privacy Act of 1986   Synonymous with the Federal Wiretapping Act. A collection of statutes that regulate the interception of wire, electronic, and oral communication. These statutes work in conjunction with the Fourth Amendment of the U.S. Constitution, which provides protections from unlawful search and seizure.

electronic locks   Locks that can be integrated into alarm systems and combined with other building management systems—specifically, these locks can be integrated with sensors to create a number of various combinations of locking behavior.

electronic vaulting   The transfer of large batches of data to an off-site facility.

electrostatic discharge (ESD)   A spark produced from a buildup of static electricity.

elite hacker   An expert hacker who develops software scripts and program exploits that are used by those in the second category, that of the novice, or unskilled hacker.

encapsulating security payload (ESP) protocol   A component of the IPSec protocol that provides confidentiality to the data packets being transmitted.

encipher   To encrypt or convert plaintext into the equivalent ciphertext.

encryption   The process of converting an original message into a form that is unreadable by unauthorized individuals.

end users   Synonymous with data user. An individual who uses computer applications for his daily work.

enterprise information security policy (EISP)   Also known as a general security policy, IT security policy, or information security policy, this policy is based on and directly supports the mission, vision, and direction of the organization and sets the strategic direction, scope, and tone for all security efforts.

enticement The process of attracting attention to a system by placing tantalizing bits of information in key locations.

entrapment The act of luring an individual into committing a crime to get a conviction.

ethical hackers Information security personnel who perform penetration testing are often consultants or outsourced contractors; they are commonly referred to as whitehat hackers, tiger teams, or red teams.

ethics Behaviors that are socially acceptable.

European Council Cyber-Crime Convention An organization designed to create an international task force to oversee a range of security functions associated with Internet activities and to standardize technology laws across international borders.

evidence The proof of an action or intent.

exclusive OR operation (XOR) A function of Boolean algebra in which two bits are compared, and if the two bits are identical, the result is a binary 0. If the two bits are not the same, the result is a binary 1.

exit interview A discussion at the end of employment that reminds an employee of contractual obligations, such as nondisclosure agreements and obtains feedback on the employee's tenure in the organization.

expert hacker A master of several programming languages, networking protocols, and operating systems, who also exhibits a mastery of the technical environment of the targeted system.

exploit A technique used to compromise a system.

exposure A single instance of a system being open to damage.

exposure factor (EF) An element of a formula for calculating the value associated with the most likely loss from an attack, or single loss expectancy (SLE). In SLE = asset value x exposure factor (EF), exposure factor equals the percentage loss that would occur from a given vulnerability being exploited.

external monitoring domain The sector of a maintenance model that provides early awareness of new and emerging threats.

F

facilities management The operation of an organization's physical security commonly including access controls for a building.

fail-safe lock A lock that ensures ability to exit. When the lock of a door fails, the door becomes unlocked.

fail-secure lock A lock that ensures entrance is prohibited. When the lock of a door fails the door remains locked.

false accept rate The percentage or value associated with the rate at which fraudulent users or nonusers are allowed access to systems or areas as a result of a failure in the biometric device.

false attack stimulus An event that triggers alarms and causes a false positive when no actual attacks are in progress.

false negative The failure of an intrusion detection system (IDS) to react to an actual attack event. Of all failures, this is the most grievous, because the very purpose of an IDS is to detect attacks.

false positive An alarm or alert that indicates that an attack is in progress or that an attack has successfully occurred when in fact there was no such attack.

false reject rate The percentage or value associated with the rate at which authentic users are denied or prevented access to authorized areas as a result of a failure in the biometric device.

fault The complete loss of power for a moment.

Federal Privacy Act of 1974 U.S. law that regulates the government in the protection of individual privacy. It was created to ensure that government agencies protect the privacy of individuals' and businesses' information and to hold those agencies responsible if any portion of this information is released without permission.

ferroresonant standby (UPS) A device that replaces a UPS transfer switch. The transformer provides power conditioning and line filtering to the primary power source, reducing the effect of power outages.

field change order (FCO) An authorization issued by an organization for the repair, modification, or update of a piece of equipment.

file hashing Method for ensuring information validity. Involves a file being read by a special algorithm that uses the value of the bits in the file to compute a single large number called a hash value.

Financial Services Modernization Act Synonymous with the Gramm-Leach-Bliley Act of 1999. This act contains provisions on facilitating affiliation among banks, securities firms, and insurance companies. The act has significant impact on the privacy of personal information used by these industries.

fingerprinting   A data-gathering process that discovers the assets that can be accessed from a network. Usually performed in advance of a planned attack. This is the systematic examination of the entire set of Internet addresses of the organization.

fire   A threat to the hardware components of information systems that falls in the forces of nature or acts of God category because it is unexpected or can occur with very little warning. In this context, this threat is usually a structural fire that damages the building housing the computing equipment that comprises all or part of the information system. Also encompasses smoke damage from a fire and/or water damage from sprinkler systems or firefighters.

fire suppression systems   Systems designed to stop the progress of a fire once it's activated.

firewall   Synonymous with application firewall and application-level firewall. A computer that provides a defense between a network inside the firewall and a network outside the firewall (the Internet) that could pose a threat to the inside network. All traffic to and from the network must pass through the firewall, so that unauthorized data can be blocked.

firewall subnet   Multiple firewalls that create a buffer between networks inside and outside an organization.

fixed temperature   A fire detection system that contains a sensor that detects when the ambient temperature in an area reaches a predetermined level.

flame detector   A sensor that detects the infrared or ultraviolet light produced by an open flame.

flame point   The temperature of ignition.

flood   A threat to the hardware components of information systems that falls in the forces of nature or acts of God category because it is unexpected or can occur with very little warning. A flood usually involves an overflowing of water onto land that is normally dry, causing direct damage to all or part of the information system or to the building that houses all or part of the information system.

footprinting   The identification of the Internet addresses that are owned or controlled by an organization.

Fourth Amendment of the U.S. Constitution   U.S. law that protects from unlawful search and seizure, cited in various other laws such as Electronic Communications Privacy Act of 1986.

Freedom of Information Act (FOIA)   An act that provides every person the right to request access to federal agency records or information that are not matters of national security.

full backup   A full and complete backup of the entire system, including all applications, operating systems components, and data.

fully distributed IDS control strategy   An intrusion detection system (IDS) control strategy in which all control functions and sensors are applied at the physical location of each IDS component. Thus, each sensor/agent is best configured to deal with its own environment.

G

gateway router   A device that is designed primarily to connect the organization's systems to the outside world.

Georgia Computer Systems Protection Act   State regulation passed by the state of Georgia in 1991 that seeks to protect information and establishes penalties for the use of information technology to attack or exploit information systems.

gold standard   A subcategory within best practices consisting of practices that are typically viewed as "the best of the best."

Gramm-Leach-Bliley Act of 1999   U.S. law that contains a number of provisions focusing on facilitating affiliation among banks, securities firms, and insurance companies.

grounding   A process that ensures that the returning flow of current is properly discharged to the ground.

H

hackers   People who use and create computer software for enjoyment or to gain access to information illegally.

hacking   Writing computer programs for enjoyment or gaining access to a computer illegally.

hacktivist   Synonymous with cyberactivist. An individual who uses technology as a tool for civil disobedience.

hash algorithms   Security utilities that mathematically combine every character in a message to create a fixed-length number (usually 128 bits in length) that is a condensation, or fingerprint, of the original message.

hash functions   Mathematical algorithms that generate a message summary or message digest that allows a hash algorithm to confirm that the content of a specific message has not been altered.

hash value   Synonymous with message digest. A single large number created when a file is read by a special algorithm that uses the value of the bits in the file to compute the number. The hash value ensures information validity.

Health Insurance Portability and Accountability Act of 1996 (HIPPA)   Synonymous with the Kennedy-Kassebaum Act. This act protects the confidentiality and security of health care data by establishing and enforcing standards for the storage and transmission of sensitive personal information.

hierarchical roster   A list of names of people who are called in the case of an emergency. Each person in turn calls the next person.

honey net   A network or system subnet that is configured to misdirect hackers by resembling networks or system subsystems that are rich with information.

honey pots   Computer servers configured to misdirect hackers by resembling production systems that contain substantial information.

host-based IDS (HIDs)   Devices that are installed on a computer system to monitor the status of files stored on that system and protect them from security breaches.

hot site   Synonymous with business recovery site. A remote location with systems identical or similar to a home site for use after a disaster.

human firewall   The concept that automated systems by themselves are not able to provide the most effective defense against electronic attackers and that human judgment is an essential part of any planned defense of information assets.

humidity   The amount of moisture in the air.

hurricane or typhoon   A threat to the hardware components of information systems that falls in the forces of nature or acts of God category because it is unexpected or can occur with very little warning. In this context, these tropical cyclones, which typically originate in the equatorial regions of the Atlantic Ocean or Caribbean Sea or eastern regions of the Pacific Ocean and usually involve heavy rains, can directly damage all or part of the information system or, more likely, the building that houses it.

hybrid VPN   A type of virtual private network (VPN) that combines trusted VPNs with secure VPNs, providing encrypted transmissions (as in secure VPN) over some or all of a trusted VPN network

I

identification (ID)   Security tools, usually in the form of badges or cards, that verify the identify of individuals

ignorance   One of three general categories of unethical and illegal behavior in which the individuals with authorization and privileges to manage information within the organization cause harm or damage because they do not know the policy and procedures of an organization.

incident   An attack on an organization's information assets.

incident candidate   A potential incident or ambiguously identified attack that could be an actual attack.

incident classification   The process of determining whether an actual security breach occurred.

incident damage assessment   The determination of the scope of a breach of the confidentiality, integrity, and availability of information immediately following an incident.

incident reaction   Actions outlined in an incident response plan for security information that guide an organization in attempting to stop an incident, mitigate the impact of an incident, and provide information for recovery.

incident response (IR)   Activities taken to plan for, detect, and correct the impact of an incident on information assets.

incident response plan (IRP)   A program to establish procedures an organization's staff would follow if it were attacked.

incremental backup   The archives of files that have been modified on a particular day.

indirect attacks   Attacks on a computer system that are initiated from a system or resource that itself has been attacked.

industrial espionage   Information gained illegally that gives an organization an advantage over its competition.

information security   The protection of information and the systems and hardware that use, store, and transmit that information.

information security operational risk assessment   A method to identify and document the risk that a project, process, or action introduces to the organization.

information security policy   An organization's rules for the protection of the information assets of the organization.

information system (IS)   The entire set of software, hardware, data, people, and procedures necessary to use information as a resource in the organization.

Information Systems Audit and Control Association (ISACA)   A professional association focused on auditing, control, and security.

Information Systems Security Association (ISSA) A nonprofit society of information security professionals.

Information Warfare (IW) An offensive organized and lawful operation conducted by a sovereign state that involve the use of information technology.

integrity The quality or state of being whole, complete, and uncorrupted.

intent One of three general categories of unethical and illegal behavior in which the individuals with authorization and privileges to manage information within the organization cause harm or damage because they intend to do so. Criminal or unethical intent goes to the state of mind of the individual performing the act.

internal monitoring domain The sector of a maintenance model whose primary goal is to maintain an informed awareness of the state of all of the organization's networks, information systems, and information security defenses.

International Information Systems Security Certification Consortium, Inc. (ISC)² An international consortium dedicated to improving the quality of security professionals.

Internet Engineering Task Force (IETF) A group of professionals in the fields of computing, networking, and telecommunications who develop the Internet's technical foundations.

Internet Protocol Security (IPSec) An open source protocol for securing communications across any IP-based network such as LANs, WANs, and the Internet.

Internet Society (ISOC) A nonprofit, nongovernmental, international organization for professionals that supports the development and implementation of education, standards, policy, and education and training to promote the Internet.

intranet vulnerability assessment The process of finding and documenting vulnerabilities that are likely to be present on the internal network of an organization.

intrinsic value The essential worth of an asset.

intrusion A type of attack on information assets in which the instigator attempts to gain entry into a system or disrupt the normal operations of a system with, almost always, the intent to do malicious harm

intrusion detection systems (IDSs) Devices that inspect data communication flows to identify patterns that may indicate that hacking is underway.

ionization sensor A smoke detection device that contains a small amount of a harmless radioactive material within a detection chamber. When certain by-products of combustion enter the chamber, they change the level of electrical conductivity with the chamber and activate the detector.

ISSP *See* issue-specific policy.

issue-specific security policy (ISSP) A program that addresses specific areas of technology and contains a statement on the organization's position on each specific issue.

J

job rotation Synonymous with task rotation. A security check that requires that every employee is trained to perform the work of another employee.

jurisdiction A court's right to hear a case because a wrong was committed in its territory or involving its citizenry.

K

Kennedy-Kassebaum Act Also known as Health Insurance Portability and Accountability Act of 1996 (HIPAA), this law is an attempt to protect the confidentiality and security of health-care data by establishing and enforcing standards and by standardizing electronic data interchange.

Kerberos A cryptosystem that uses symmetric key encryption to validate an individual user to various network resources.

kernel proxy The fifth and final form of a firewall.

key A random and secret value that is placed within an algorithm to code information.

keyspace The entire range of values that can possibly be used to construct an individual key.

knowledge-based IDS Synonymous with signature-based IDS. A device that examines data traffic for signature matches with predefined, preconfigured attack patterns.

known-plaintext attack A method of attacking a cryptosystem that relies on knowledge of some or all of the plaintext that was used to generate a ciphertext.

L

landslide or mudslide A threat to the hardware components of information systems that falls in the forces of nature or acts of God category because it is unexpected or can occur with very little warning. Specifically, this is the downward sliding of a mass of earth and rock that may directly damage all or part of an information system or, more likely, the building that houses it.

lattice-based access control   A matrix of authorizations that control access to data.

laws   Rules adopted for determining expected behavior in modern society and drawn from ethics.

least privilege   A security measure by which employees are provided access to a minimal amount of information for a minimal amount of time necessary for them to perform their duties.

liability   The legal obligation of an entity that includes responsibility for a wrongful act and the legal obligation to make restitution.

lightning   A threat to the hardware components of information systems that falls in the forces of nature or acts of God category because it is unexpected or can occur with very little warning. An abrupt, discontinuous natural electric discharge in the atmosphere, lightning usually directly damages all or part of an information system an/or its power distribution components.

likelihood   The overall rating of the probability that a specific vulnerability within an organization will be successfully attacked.

line-interative UPS   A type of uninterruptible power supply (UPS) in which the internal components of the standby models are replaced with a pair of inverters and converters.

link encryption   A series of encryptions and decryptions between a number of systems, wherein each system in a network decrypts the message sent to it and then reencrypts it using different keys and sends it to the next neighbor. This process continues until the message reaches the final destination.

log file monitor (LFM)   An approach to intrusion detection systems that is similar to the one used for network-based intrusion detection systems (NIDSs). Using LFM, the system reviews the log files generated by servers, network devices, and even other IDSs.

long arm jurisdiction   A law that reaches across the country or around the world to pull an accused individual into its court systems.

M

macro virus   A virus that is contained in a downloaded file attachment such as word processing documents, spread sheets, and database applications.

mail bomb   Synonymous with denial-of-service attack. An attack in which the abuser sends a large number of connection or information requests to overwhelm and cripple a target.

malicious code   Synonymous with malware. Software designed to damage, destroy, or deny service to the target system.

malware   Synonymous with malicious code. Software designed to damage, destroy, or deny service to the target system.

man-in-the-middle   Synonymous with TCP hijacking. An attack in which the abuser records data packets from the network, modifies them, and inserts them back into the network.

man-in-the-middle attack   An attack designed to intercept the transmission of a public key or even to insert a known key structure in place of the requested public key.

managerial controls   Security processes that are designed by strategic planners and implemented by the security administration of an organization.

mandatory access controls   The regulations that control access to information resources.

mantrap   A small physical enclosure that is used in secure facilities that has an entry point and a different exit point.

manual fire detection systems   Manually activated alarms, such as sprinklers and gaseous systems.

manual locks   Locks that are often preset by the manufacturer and therefore unchangeable, thus once they are installed into doors, they can be changed only by highly trained locksmiths.

mechanical lock   Locks that rely on a key that is a carefully shaped piece of metal that a person rotates or a dial that causes the proper rotation of slotted discs to release secured loops of steel, aluminum, or brass.

message authentication code (MAC)   A sequence of bits calculated from data (either plaintext or ciphertext) and a secret key. It is included in a message with the data in order to allow data authentication. Note: The function used to generate this code must be a one-way function.

message digest   Synonymous with hash value. A single large number created when a file is read by a special algorithm that uses the value of the bits in the file to compute the number. The hash value ensures information validity.

methodology   A formal approach to solving a problem based on a structured sequence of procedures.

metrics-based measures   Benchmarking comparisons based on numerical standards such as numbers of successful attacks; staff-hours spent on systems protection; dollars spent on protection; numbers of security personnel; estimated value in dollars of the information lost in successful attacks and loss in productivity hours associated with successful attacks.

milestone   A specific point in the project plan when a task and its action steps are complete and have a noticeable impact on the progress of the project plan as a whole.

minutiae   Used in biometrics, unique points of reference that are digitized and stored in an encrypted format for comparison with scanned human characteristics.

mission   A written statement of an organization's purpose.

mitigation   A control approach that attempts to reduce the impact caused by the exploitation of vulnerability through planning and preparation.

modem vulnerability assessment   The process of finding and documenting any vulnerability that is present on dial-up modems connected to an organization's networks.

monitoring port   A specially configured connection on a network device that is capable of viewing all of the traffic that moves through the entire device. Also known as a switched port analysis (SPAN) port or mirror port.

monoalphabetic substitution   In encryption, the substitution of one value for another using a single alphabet.

motion detectors   Alarm systems that detect movement within a confined space.

mutual agreement   A contract between two or more organizations that specifies how each assists the other in the event of a disaster.

N

name badge   A form of identification that, unlike an ID card, is typically visible.

National Information Infrastructure Protection Act of 1996   An act that modified several sections of the Computer Fraud and Abuse Act and increased penalties for selected crimes

National InfraGard Program   A cooperative effort between the FBI's Cleveland Field Office and local technology professionals to protect critical national information.

National Infrastructure Protection Center (NIPC)   An organization that serves as the U.S. government's center for threat assessment, warning, investigation, and response to threats or attacks against critical U.S. infrastructures.

National Security Agency (NSA)   The organization responsible for signal intelligence and information system security.

need-to-know   A category within a data classification structure that grants access to individuals based on the fact that they require the information to perform their jobs.

negative feedback loop   Synonymous with cybernetic loop. A process to manage a project that ensures that progress is measured periodically and that measured results are compared to expected results.

network security   The protection of the networks (systems and hardware) that use, store, and transmit an organization's information.

network-based IDS (NIDs)   Devices that are installed on networks to monitor patterns of network traffic to detect unusual and therefore threatening activity.

noise   Interference with the normal pattern of the electrical current.

nondiscretionary controls   Controls that are managed by a central authority in the organization and can be based on an individual's role—role-based controls—or a specified set of tasks the individual is assigned—task-based controls.

nonrepudiation   The principle of cryptography that gives credence to the authentication mechanism collectively known as a digital signature. In this asymmetric cryptographic process, the sender's private key is used to encrypt a message, and the sender's public key must be used to decrypt the message—when the decryption happens successfully, it provides verification that the message was sent by the sender and cannot be refuted.

O

object   A passive entity in an information system that receives or contains information.

object of an attack   The object or entity being attacked.

offline UPS   Synonymous with standby uninterruptible power supplies (UPS). An offline battery backup that detects the interruption of power to equipment.

operational controls   Measures that deal with the operational functionality of security in an organization.

operational feasibility   Synonymous with behavioral feasibility. The examination of user acceptance of proposed security measures.

operations security   A process used by an organization to deny an adversary information (generally not confidential information) about its intentions and capabilities by identifying, controlling, and protecting the organization's planning processes or operations. OPSEC does not replace other security disciplines—it supplements them.

organizational culture   The specific social and political atmosphere within a given organization that determines the organization's procedures and policies and willingness to adapt to changes.

organizational feasibility   A comparison of how proposed information security alternatives contribute to the efficiency, effectiveness, and overall operation of an organization.

P

packet filtering firewall   Networking devices that filter data packets based on their headers as they travel in and out of an organization's network.

packet monkeys   Hackers of limited skill (known as script kiddies) who use automated exploits to engage in distributed denial-of-service attacks.

packet sniffer   A network tool that collects copies of packets from the network and analyzes them.

padded cell   A honey pot that has been protected so that that it cannot be easily compromised.

parallel operations   A method of modifying work practices that involves using the new methods alongside the old methods.

partially distributed IDS control strategy   An intrusion detection system (IDS) control strategy in which individual agents can still analyze and respond to local threats, but they are required to report to a hierarchical central facility—which creates a blended approach that enables the organization to detect widespread attacks and also intelligent attackers who probe an organization through multiple points of entry before they launch a concerted attack.

passive vulnerability scanner   A vulnerability scanner that listens in on the network and determines vulnerable versions of both server and client software.

passphrase   A series of characters, typically longer than a password, from which a virtual password is derived.

password   A private word or combination of characters that only the user knows.

password attack   An attempt to repeatedly guess passwords to commonly used accounts.

performance baseline   An expected level of system performance against which all subsequent levels of performance are compared.

performance gap   The difference between the measure of an organization's success and that of others.

permutation cipher   Synonymous with transposition cipher. The rearranging of values within a block to create coded information.

personal security   A process of assuring the personal safety of individuals or groups of people associated with the organization.

phased implementation   An approach to implementing new security systems that involves rolling out a piece of a new system across the entire organization.

photoelectric sensors   A type of smoke detector that projects and detects an infrared beam across an area. If the beam is interrupted (presumably by smoke), the alarm or suppression system is activated.

phreaker   A person who hacks the public telephone network to make free calls and disrupt services.

physical security   An aspect of information security that addresses the design, implementation, and maintenance of countermeasures that protect the physical resources of an organization.

pilot implementation   The changing of work practices that involves implementing all security improvements in a single office, department, or division, and resolving issues within that group before expanding to the rest of the organization.

plaintext   Synonymous with cleartext. The unencrypted message that will be encrypted into ciphertext for transmission over an unsecured channel.

planning and risk assessment domain   The domain of the security maintenance model concerned with keeping a "weather eye" on the entire information security program by identifying and planning organization information security activities that further reduce risk.

platform security validation (PSV)   A process designed to find and document the vulnerabilities that may be present because of misconfigured systems that are in use within an organization.

plenum   In an office building the space above the ceiling, below the floor above.

policy   A body of expectations that describes acceptable and unacceptable behaviors of employees in the workplace.

policy administrator   The champion and manager of an information security policy.

political feasibility   An analysis that defines what changes can and cannot occur within an organization based on the consensus and relationships between the communities of interest.

polyalphabetic substitutions   In encryption, the substitution of one value for another, using two or more alphabets.

polymorphic threat   A threat that changes its apparent shape over time, to become a new threat not detectable by techniques looking for a preconfigured signature.

port scanners   The tools used to identify (or finger-print) computers that are active on a network.

possession   The quality or state of having ownership or control of some object or item.

pre-action system   A sprinkler system that has a two-phase response to a fire.

predecessors   In a project plan, the tasks or action steps that come before the specific task at hand.

pretty good privacy (PGP)   A hybrid cryptosystem that combines some of the best available cryptographic algorithms. PGP is the open source *de facto* standard for encryption and authentication of e-mail and file storage applications.

preventive controls   The implementation of an organizational policy or a security principle, such as authentication or confidentiality to protect a vulnerability.

privacy   The state of being free from unauthorized observation.

Privacy Enhanced Mail (PEM)   Standard proposed by the Internet Engineering Task Force (IETF) to function with the public key cryptosystems.

Privacy of Customer Information Section   Part of the common carrier regulation that specifies that any proprietary information shall be used explicitly for providing service, and not for any marketing purposes.

private key encryption   Synonymous with symmetric encryption. Private key encryption is a method of communicating on a network using a single key to both encrypt and decrypt a message.

private law   Laws that regulate the relationship between the individual and the organization, and that encompass family law, commercial law, and labor law.

process-based measures   Benchmarking comparisons that are generally less focused on numbers and more strategic than metrics-based measures.

profile   An organization's apparent security program as visible to those inside or outside of the organization.

project plan   A program that delivers instructions to individuals for carrying out the implementation stage of the security systems development life cycle.

project team   For information security, a group of individuals with experience in the requirements of both technical and nontechnical fields.

projectitis   The phenomenon of becoming so engrossed in project administration that the project itself suffers.

protocol stack verification   A process in which a network-based intrusion detection system (NIDS) looks for invalid data packets—i.e., packets that are malformed under the rules of the TCP/IP protocol.

proximity reader   A type of access control device that does not require keycard insertion.

proxy firewall   Synonymous with proxy server.

proxy server   Synonymous with proxy firewall. A server that is configured to look like a Web server and performs actions on behalf of that server to protect it from hacking.

public key encryption   Synonymous with asymmetric encryption. A method of communicating on a network using two different keys, one to encrypt and the other to decrypt a message.

Public Key Infrastructure (PKI)   An integrated system of software, encryption methodologies, protocols, legal agreements, and third-party services that enables users to communicate securely

public law   A law that regulates the structure and administration of government agencies and their relationships with citizens, employees, and other governments.

Q

qualitative assessment   An evaluation process that is based on characteristics that do not use numerical measures.

quantitative assessment   The evaluation of an organization's assets, estimated values, and formulas.

R

RADIUS (Remote Authentication Dial-In User Service)   A system that authenticates the credentials of users who are trying to access an organization's network through a dial-up connection.

rate-of-rise   A fire detection system in which a sensor detects an unusually rapid increase in the area temperature, within a relatively short period of time.

readiness and review domain   The domain of the security maintenance model concerned with keeping the information security program functioning as designed and keeping it continuously improving over time.

recommended practices   Synonymous with best practices and best business practices. Procedures that provide a superior level of security for an organization's information.

red team   Synonymous with ethical hacker, tiger team, and white-hat hacker. Consultants or outsourced contractors who are hired to perform controlled attacks to compromise or disrupt systems by using documented vulnerabilities.

redundancy   The implementation of multiple types of technology that prevent the failure of one system from compromising the security of information.

Redundant Array of Inexpensive Drives (RAID)
A form of data backup for online usage that uses a number of hard drives to store information across multiple drive units, so as to minimize the impact of a single drive failure.

registration authority (RA)   A component of a Public Key Infrastructure system that operates under the trusted collaboration of the certificate authority and can be delegated day-to-day certification functions, such as verifying registration information about new registrants, generating end-user keys, revoking certificates, and validating that users possess a valid certificate.

remote journaling   The transfer of live transactions to an off-site facility.

replay attack   An attack in which an abuser has successfully broken an encryption and attempts to resubmit the deciphered authentication to gain entry to a secure source.

residual risk   The risk that remains to an information asset after an existing control has been applied.

resource   An individual or skill set whose function is detailed in a project plan.

restitution   The compensation for a misdeed.

reverse firewalls   Content filters whose primary function is to restrict internal access to external material.

risk   The probability that something can happen.

risk appetite   The quantity and nature of risk that organizations are willing to accept.

risk assessment   The analysis of a danger to assign a risk rating or score to an information asset.

risk assessment specialist   An individual who understands financial risk assessment techniques, the value of organizational assets, and security methods.

risk control   The process of applying controls to reduce the risks to an organization's data and information systems.

risk identification   The formal process of examining and documenting the security of an organization's information technology.

risk management   The process of identifying vulnerabilities in an organization's information system and taking steps to assure its confidentiality, integrity, and availability.

role-based controls   A type of access control in which individuals are allowed to use data based on their positions in an organization.

RSA algorithm   The *de facto* standard for public use encryption applications. The security of the algorithm is based on the computational difficulty of factoring large composite numbers and computing the *eth roots modulo*, a composite number for a specified odd integer *e*.

S

sacrificial host   Synonymous with bastion host. A dedicated firewall that enables a router to prescreen data packets to minimize the network traffic and load on a proxy server.

sag   A momentary incidence of low voltage.

salami theft   Aggregation of information used with criminal intent.

Sarbanes-Oxley Act of 2002   A critical piece of legislation that affects the executive management of publicly traded corporations and public accounting firms.

script kiddies   Hackers of limited skill who use expertly written software to exploit a system but do not fully understand or appreciate the systems they hack.

Secure Electronic Transactions (SET)   A means of securing Web transactions that was developed by MasterCard and VISA in 1997 to provide protection from electronic payment fraud.

secure facility   A physical location that has been engineered with controls designed to minimize the risk of attacks from physical threats.

Secure Hash Standard (SHS)   An encryption norm that specifies SHA-1 (Secure Hash Algorithm 1) as a secure algorithm for computing a condensed representation of a message or data file.

Secure Multipurpose Internet Mail Extensions (S/MIME)   A specification developed to increase the security of e-mail that adds encryption and user authentication.

Secure Socket Layer (SSL)   A protocol for transmitting private information securely over the Internet.

Secure VPNs   A type of private and secure network connection, or VPN, that uses security protocols and encrypts traffic transmitted across unsecured public networks like the Internet.

Secure-HTTP (S-HTTP)   A protocol designed to enable secure communications across the Internet. S-HTTP is the application of SSL over HTTP, which allows the encryption of all information passing between two computers through a protected and secure virtual connection.

security   To be protected from adversaries—from those who would do harm, intentionally or otherwise.

Security And Freedom Through Encryption Act of 1999   An attempt by Congress to provide guidance on the use of encryption. Provided measures for public protection from government intervention.

security blueprint   A plan for the implementation of new security measures in an organization.

security clearance   A level of authorization to classified material that an individual is granted after a formal evaluation process.

security domains   Aread within a computer system in which users can safely communicate.

security education, training, and awareness (SETA)   An education program designed to reduce the number of security breaches that occur through the lack of employee security awareness.

security framework   An outline of the overall information security strategy for the organization and a roadmap for planned changes to the information security environment of the organization.

Security Manager   An individual role within an organization. Sometimes equivalent to the CISO or CSO, but in some cases reporting to the CISO. Will supervise others involved in the information security function and provide planning, direction, supervision, and control to those employees.

security model   A collection of security rules that represents the implementation of a security policy.

security perimeter   The edge between the outer limit of an organization's security and the beginning of the outside world.

security policy   Synonymous with security program policy (SPP), a general security polity, IT security policy, and information security policy. A set of rules developed to protect an organization's assets.

Security policy developers   An individual who understands the organizational culture, existing policies, and requirements for developing and implementing security policies.

security posture   Synonymous with security profile and information security program. The implementation of an organization's security policies, procedures, and programs.

Security professionals   A specialist in the technical and nontechnical aspects of security information.

security profile   Synonymous with security posture and information security program. The implementation of an organization's security policies, procedures, and programs.

Security Technician   An individual role within the information security function assigned to perform configuration, operation, or monitoring actions on a technical information technology system used to implement information security controls.

selected-plaintext attack   A crypto system attack in which the attackers send a target a section of plaintext they want encrypted and returned in order to reveal information about the target's encryption systems.

Separation of duties   A control used to reduce the chance of an individual violating information security and breaching the confidentiality, integrity, or availability of the information.

sequential roster   A list of people who are called by a single person in the case of an emergency.

server fault tolerance   Technologies and techniques used to make a server computing system more resistant to failure. Will include designing server systems using redundant components (power supplies, disk drives, processors, and others) configured in ways that allow the system to continue operating even when one or more components fail.

service bureau   A service agency that provides a service for a fee.

service level agreement (SLA)   The contract of a Web host provider covering responsibility for Internet services as well as for hardware and software used to operate the Web site.

session keys   Limited-use symmetric keys for encrypting electronic communication.

shoulder surfing   The act of observing information without authorization by looking over a shoulder or spotting information from a distance.

signature-based IDS   Synonymous with knowledge-based IDS. A device that examines data traffic for signature matches with predefined, preconfigured attack patterns.

signatures   Preconfigured, predetermined attack patterns.

single loss expectancy (SLE)   The calculation of the cost incurred in a single instance when a specific asset within an organization is attacked.

Site Policy   The rules and configuration guidelines governing the implementation and operation of IDSs within the organization.

Site Policy Awareness   The ability of intrusion detection system to dynamically modify its site policies in reaction or response to environmental activity.

smart card   A device that contains a computer chip that can verify and validate a number of pieces of information about an individual above and beyond a PIN.

smoke detection   Systems that detect a potentially dangerous fire and are required by building codes in most residential dwellings and commercial buildings.

sniffer   A program or device that can monitor data traveling over a network.

social engineering   The process of using social skills to convince people to reveal access credentials or other valuable information to the attacker.

software piracy   The unlawful use or duplication of software-based intellectual property.

Spam   Unsolicited commercial e-mail.

spike   A momentary increase in voltage.

spoofing   A technique used to gain unauthorized access to computers, whereby the intruder sends messages to a computer with an IP address indicating that the message is coming from a trusted host.

sprinkler systems   Devices that are designed to apply liquid, usually water, to all areas in which a fire has been detected.

SSL Record Protocol   A protocol responsible for the fragmentation, compression, encryption, and attachment of an SSL header to the cleartext prior to transmission.

Standard HTTP   A protocol that provides the Internet communication services between client and host without consideration for encryption of the data that is communicated over the connection between client and server.

standard of due care   A legal term that becomes relevant when organizations adopt levels of security for a legal defense and therefore might be required to show that they have done what any *prudent* organization would do in similar circumstances.

standard operating procedures (SOPs)   Documentation provided to members of the organization that describes the actions to be taken in compliance with policy when certain conditions prevail.

standards   Detailed statements of actions that comply with policy.

standby UPS   Synonymous with offline uninterruptible power supplies (UPS). An offline battery backup that detects the interruption of power to equipment.

state table   A feature of stateful inspection firewalls that tracks the state and context of each packet in the conversation by recording which station sent what packet and when.

stateful inspection firewall   Devices that track network connections that are established between internal and external systems.

static electricity   The spark that occurs when two materials are rubbed or touched and electrons are exchanged, resulting in one object becoming more positively charged and the other more negatively charged.

statistical anomaly-based IDS (stat IDS)   Synonymous with behavior-based IDS. A device that collects data from normal traffic to establish a baseline. The IDS compares periodic data samples with the baseline to highlight irregularities.

steganography   A method of hiding the existence of a secret message.

strategic planning   The process of moving an organization towards its vision by accomplishing its mission.

strong authentication   In access control, security systems that use two or more authentication mechanisms.

subject   An *active* entity that interacts with an information system and causes information to move through the system for a specific purpose. Examples include individuals, technical components, and computer processes.

subject of an attack   A computer or other system that is used as an active tool to conduct an attack.

substitution cipher   In encryption, the substitution of one value for another.

successors   In a project plan, the tasks or action steps that come after the task at hand.

sunset clause   Prevents a temporary policy from becoming a permanent mistake by specifying a discontinuation date.

supplicant   A prospective user who, in the context of access control, seeks to use a protected system, logically access a protected service, or physically enter a protected space.

surge   A prolonged increase in voltage.

symmetric encryption   Synonymous with private key encryption. Symmetric encryption is a method of communicating on a network using a single key to both encrypt and decrypt a message.

synchronous tokens   Authentication devices that are synchronized with a server, so that each device (server and token) uses the time or a time-based database to generate a number that is entered during the user login phase.

System Administration, Networking, and Security Institute (SANS)   A professional organization dedicated to the protection of information and systems.

system integrity verifiers   Synonymous with host-based IDSs (HIDSs).

systems administrators   An individual responsible for administering information systems.

systems development life cycle (SDLC)   A methodology for the design and implementation of an information system.

systems specific security policies (SysSPs)   A program that addresses the particular use of certain systems. This could include firewall configuration policies, systems access policies, and other technical configuration areas.

T

tailgating   A security breach that occurs when an authorized individual gains admission to a secure area by presenting a badge or key and is directly followed into the area by an unauthorized individual.

task rotation   Synonymous with job rotation. A security check that requires that every employee is trained to perform the work of another employee.

task-based controls   A type of data access control in which individuals are allowed to use data, based on their job responsibilities.

TCP hijacking   Synonymous with man-in-the-middle. An attack in which the abuser records data packets from the network, modifies them, and inserts them back into the network.

team leader   For information security, a project manager who understands project management, personnel management, and technical requirements.

technical controls   Measures that address the tactical and technical issues related to designing and implementing security in an organization, as well as issues related to examining and selecting the technologies appropriate to protecting information.

technical feasibility   Evaluation performed by a project team to determine whether the design, implementation, and management of controls of a given project are technically viable.

technology governance   A complex process that an organization uses to manage the impacts and costs caused by technology implementation, innovation, and obsolescence.

Telecommunications Deregulation and Competition Act of 1996   An act that attempted to modernize the archaic terminology of the 1934 act.

telecommuting   The act of working at a site that is distant from the base organizational facility.

TEMPEST   A technology that involves the monitoring of devices that emit electromagnetic radiation (EMR) in such a manner that the data can be reconstructed.

Terminal Access Controller Access Control System (TACACS)   A remote access system that validates a user's credentials.

The Federal Privacy Act of 1974   An act that regulates the government in the protection of individual privacy. Created to insure that government agencies protect the privacy of individual and business information and to hold those agencies responsible if any portion of this information is released without permission.

theft   The act of stealing.

thermal detection systems   Fire detection systems that contain a sophisticated heat sensor.

thermal detectors   A type of alarm sensor for detecting intrusions that works by detecting rates of change in the ambient temperature in the room.

threat   An object, person, or other entity that represents a danger to an asset.

threat agent   A specific instance or component that represents a danger to an organization's assets. Threats can be accidental or purposeful, for example lightning strikes or hackers.

threat assessment   The examination of a danger to assess its potential to impact an organization.

ticket   In a client/server environment, an identification card for a particular client that verifies to a server that the client is requesting services and that the client is a valid member of a system and therefore authorized to receive services.

tiger team   Synonymous with ethical hacker, white-hat hacker, and red team. Consultants or outsourced contractors who are hired to perform controlled attacks to compromise or disrupt systems by using documented vulnerabilities.

time-share   A site that is leased by an organization in conjunction with a business partner for use if a disaster occurs at the home site.

timing attack An attack in which an abuser explores the contents of a Web browser's cache. These attacks allow a Web designer to create a malicious form of cookie to store on the client's system.

top-down approach A methodology of establishing security policies that is initiated by upper management.

tornado or severe windstorm A threat to the hardware components of information systems that falls in the forces of nature or acts of God category because it is unexpected or can occur with very little warning. Because these storms are typically rotating columns of air whirling at destructively high speeds, they can directly damage all or part of an information system or, more likely, the building that houses it.

tort law Laws that allow individuals to seek recourse against others in the event of personal, physical, or financial injury.

transference The control approach used by an organization to shift the risks from one asset to another.

transport mode One of the two modes of operation of the IP Security Protocol. In transport mode, only the IP data is encrypted, not the IP headers.

transposition cipher Synonymous with permutation cipher. The rearranging of values within a block to create coded information.

trap and trace A combination of resources that detect an intrusion and trace it back to its source.

trap door Synonymous with back door. An electronic hole in software that is left open by accident or intention. Can be installed by a virus or worm.

trespass The act of entering a premises or system without authorization.

triboelectrification A process that causes static electricity and occurs when two materials are rubbed together causing electrons to be exchanged and one object to become more positively charged and the other more negatively charged. When a third object with an opposite charge or ground is encountered, electrons flow again and a spark is produced.

triple DES (3DES) Synonymous with 3DES. An enhancement to the Data Encryption Standard (DES). An algorithm that uses up to three keys to perform three different encryption operations.

Trojan horses Software programs that hide their true nature (usually destructive), and reveal their designed behavior only when activated.

trophy A piece of evidence (usually a screenshot) that can be used to convince skeptical system administrators that the vulnerability is real.

trouble ticket A process for tracking problems reported to an information technology help desk.

True Attack Stimulus An event that triggers alarms and causes an intrusion detection system (IDS) to react as if a real attack is in progress.

true online UPS An top-of-the-line, expensive type of uniterruptible power supply (UPS) that is capable of delivering a constant, smooth, conditioned power stream to computing systems.

trusted network A network such as an intranet that is inside an organization's firewall and is therefore protected from security breaches.

trusted VPN A type of private and secure network connection that uses leased circuits from a service provider and conducts packet switching over these leased circuits. Also known as a legacy VPN.

tsunami A threat to the hardware components of information systems that falls in the forces of nature or acts of God category because it is unexpected or can occur with very little warning. Specifically, this is a very large ocean wave caused by an underwater earthquake or volcanic eruption that can directly damage all or part of an information system or, more likely, the building that houses it.

tunnel mode One of the two modes of operation of the IP Security Protocol. In tunnel mode, the entire IP packet is encrypted and placed as payload into another IP packet.

two-man control A security check that requires that two individuals review and approve each other's work before a task is categorized as finished.

U

U.S. Secret Service A department within the Department of the Treasury. Provides protective services for key members of the U.S. government and detects and arrests any person committing a United States federal offense relating to computer fraud.

U.S.A. Patriot Act of 2001 This act modified a wide range of existing laws to provide law enforcement agencies with a broader latitude of actions to combat terrorism-related activities.

Uninterruptible Power Supply (UPS) A backup power source for major computer systems.

United Nations Charter   The mission statement of the U.N., which includes provisions for information security during information warfare.

unskilled hacker   An individual who depends on the expertise of others to abuse systems.

untrusted network   A network outside an organization's firewall, such as the Internet.

utility   The quality or state of having value for an end purpose. Information has utility if it serves a purpose.

V

Vernam cipher   An element of cryptosystems that was developed at AT&T and uses a set of characters only one time for each encryption process. Also known as the one-time pad.

vibration sensors   A type of alarm sensor for detecting intrusions that works by detecting movement of the sensor rather than movement in the environment.

Vigenère cipher   An advanced type of substitution cipher that uses a simple polyalphabetic code and involves using the Vigenère Square. which is made up of 26 distinct cipher alphabets.

virtual organization   A group of individuals brought together through electronic communication for a specific task, usually from different organizations, divisions, or departments.

virtual password   A password calculated or extracted from a passphrase that meets system storage requirements.

Virtual Private Network (VPN)   A network within a network that typically allows a user to use the Internet as a private network.

virus   Software that attaches itself to another program and can cause damage when the host program is activated.

virus hoaxes   E-mails sent warning of the latest and most dangerous viruses that are fictitious.

vision   A written statement of the organization's goals.

vulnerability   Weakness or fault in a system or protection mechanism that exposes information to attack or damage.

vulnerability assessment (VA)   The process of identifying and documenting specific and provable flaws in the organization's information asset environment.

vulnerability assessment and remediation domain   The identification of specific, documented vulnerabilities and their timely remediation.

vulnerability instances   The existence of a vulnerability that is deemed a significant risk.

W

war dialer   An automatic phone-dialing program that dials every number in a configured range (e.g., 555-1000 to 555-2000), and checks to see if a person, answering machine, or modem picks up.

war dialing   An attack that uses scripted dialing against a pool of phone numbers.

war game   A simulation of an attack on an organization's information assets.

warm site   An alternate site that can be used by an organization if a disaster occurs at the home site. Frequently includes computing equipment and peripherals with servers but not client workstations.

water mist sprinklers   A new form of sprinkler systems that produce ultra fine mists instead of the showers characteristic of traditional systems.

waterfall model   A methodology of the system development life cycle in which each phase of the process begins with the information gained in the previous phase.

well-known vulnerabilities   System weaknesses that have been examined, documented, and published.

wet-pipe   A type of sprinkler system that contains pressurized water in pipes and has a valve in each protected area.

white-hat hacker   Synonymous with ethical hacker, tiger team, red team. Consultants or outsourced contractors who are hired to perform controlled attacks to compromise or disrupt systems by using documented vulnerabilities.

wireless vulnerability assessment   The process designed to find and document the vulnerabilities that may be present in wireless local area network.

work breakdown structure (WBS)   A planning approach that breaks a project plan into specific action steps.

work factor   The amount of effort (usually in hours) required to perform cryptanalysis on an encoded message so that it may be decrypted when the key or algorithm (or both) are unknown.

Worm   A virus that replicate itself on other machines.

Z

zombies   Machines that have been compromised and directed towards a target. They are executed remotely (usually by a transmitted command) by the attacker.

Index

A

AAR (after-action review), 222
Abu Wahshiyyaan-Nabati, 344
access
  balancing, 17–18
  defined, 30
access control list (ACL), 136
  ACL policies, 179–180
access control(s). *See also* controls;
  physical security
  defined, 135
  devices, 332–336
    authentication, 332
    supplicant, 332
  discretionary controls, 136
  in general, 135
  non-discretionary controls
    role-based controls, 136
    task-based controls, 136
  physical access controls, 392–400
  types of, 135–136
    lattice-based access control,
      135–136
    mandatory access controls
      (MACs), 135
accessibility. *See also* availability
  compared to availability, 10
  vs. security, 17
accident, 95
account, as incident, 217
accountability, risk control, 149
accounting and auditing
  management, 498
accuracy, 10. *See also* integrity
ACL. *See* access control list (ACL)
ACLU (American Civil Liberties
  Union), 11
ACM, Inc., 130
ACM (Association for Computing
  Machinery), 89, 96, 97
acquired value, 150
ACR (Armored Cavalry Regiment), 213

ACS (annualized cost of the
  safeguard), 154
active intrusion prevention, 317
active vulnerability scanners, 323–327
acts of God. *See also* physical security;
  threat
  threat
    forces of nature, 56–57
      dust, 57
      earthquake, 56
      electrostatic discharge, 57
      fire, 56
      flood, 56
      hurricane, 57
      landslide/mudslide, 56
      lightning, 56
      tornado, 56–57
      tsunami, 57
Adams, Scott, 427
address restrictions, 243–244
Adleman, Leonard, 345
administration. *See also* management;
  security professionals
  responsible individual, 183–184
  systems, 26
Advanced Encryption Standard (AES),
  360. *See also* encryption
Advanced Research Project Agency
  (ARPANET), 5, 6
Advance Free Fraud (AFF), 66
AES (Advanced Encryption
  Standard), 360
AFF (Advance Free Fraud), 66
after-action review (AAR), 222
aggregate information, 79
Agnitum Outpost Firewall, 255
AH protocol (application header (AH)
  protocol), 379
air-aspirating detectors, 402
air conditioning, physical security
  and, 408
AirSnare, 330, 331

alarm(s). *See also* access control(s)
  and alarm systems, 398–399
  audible, 297
  burglar, 417
  clustering, 286
  compaction, 286
  defined, 284–285
  filtering, 286
  visual, 297
Alberti, Leon Battista, 344
ALE (annualized loss expectancy), 154
alert, in intrusion detection systems,
  284–285
alert message, 219
alert roster, 218
algorithm
  cryptographic, 357–366
  defined, 346
  hash, 356
  RSA, 362–365
Altavista.com, 319
Amazon.com, 51, 119
American Civil Liberties Union
  (ACLU), 11
amperage, 410–411
analysis
  SDLC, 21
  SecSDLC, 23
analysis phase, SDLC, 21
Anderson, James, 3, 17, 162
annualized cost of the safeguard
  (ACS), 154
annualized loss expectancy (ALE), 154
annualized rate of occurrence
  (ARO), 154
application-based IDS (AppIDS)
  advantages of, 295
  disadvantages of, 295
  in general, 294–295
application firewall, 245–246, 247
application gateway, 245–246, 247
application header (AH) protocol, 379

application-level firewall, 245–246, 247

application protocol verification, 290

applications, for safe operations, 37–38

architectural layer, 148

Armored Cavalry Regiment (ACR), 213

ARO (annualized rate of occurrence), 154

ARPANET (Advanced Research Project Agency), 5, 6

art, security as, 29

Arthur Andersen LLP., 173

Art of War (Sun Tzu Wu), 38

assessment

    damage, 211

    incident damage, 221

    Internet vulnerability assessment, 519–520

    Intranet vulnerability assessment, 520–521

    modem vulnerability assessment, 523–524

    qualitative, 164

    risk, 137–138, 146

    security risk assessment, 513–517

    vulnerability, 131, 517–518

    wireless vulnerability assessment, 522–523

asset

    defined, 30, 112

    information asset

        classification, 118–119

        prioritizing assets, 121

        valuation, 119–121, 133–134, 150–154

    intrinsic value, 150

    technology, safeguarding, 38

asset identification and valuation

    cost benefit analysis (CBA), 150–153

    in general, 115–116

    hardware, software, and network assets, 116–117

    attributes, 117–118

    people, procedures, and data assets, 116

asset inventory, 113

    partner interconnections, 508

asset valuation

    components of, 150–153

    defined, 150

Association for Computing Machinery (ACM), 89, 96, 97

asymmetric encryption, 361–362, 366

asynchronous tokens, 333

Asynchronous Transfer Method (ATM), 258

ATM (Asynchronous Transfer Method), 258

Attack. *See also* incident; threat

    attack profile, 210

    attack scenario end case, 211

    backdoor, 61–62

    brute force attack, 62

        password attack, 62

    buffer overflow, 67–68

    computers as the subject and object of, 17

    cryptosystem

        correlation attack, 383

        defending from attacks, 384

        dictionary attack, 62, 383

        known-plaintext attack, 382

        man-in-the-middle attack, 64, 383

        selected-plaintext attack, 382

        timing attack, 384

    defined, 30, 60

    denial-of-service attack, 51, 62–63

    distributed denial-of-service (DDoS) attack, 62–63

    in general

        threat agent, 60

        vulnerability, 60

    hoaxes, 61

    mail bombing, 65

    malicious code, 60–61

    password crack, 62

    protocol, 318

    recovery from, 127

    sniffer, 66

    software attack, 51–56

    spam, 65

    spoofing, 63

    terminology

        direct attack, 16

        indirect attack, 16

        object of an attack, 16

        subject of an attack, 16

    timing attack, 68

Attrition.org, 49

audible alarm, intrusion detection system and, 297

auditing management, 498

audit trail, 147

Australia, computer ethics in, 90

authentication

    defined, 332

    digital certificates, 368

    risk control, 148

    securing with Kerberos, 271–273

    strong authentication, 332

authenticity, 10

authorization

    digital certificate, 369

    risk control, 148–149

automated policy management, 185

automated response, 225

automated tools, risk management, 118

availability

    C.I.A triangle, 8

    defined, 10

    discussed, 10

    risk control, 148

availability disruption, 58

avoidance

    cost, 149

    defined, 138–139

    strategies for risk control, 138–139

B

Babbage, Charles, 344

Bace, Rebecca, 284

backdoor, 51, 61–62. *See also* attack

back door/trap door, 55

background checks, for potential information security employees, 473–474

back-hack, 316

Back Orifice, 61

backups

    backup media, 223

    data storage and management, 222–223

    differential backup, 222

    full backup, 222

    incremental backup, 223

    RAID, 222

    strategies

        grandfather, father, son, 223–224

        Tower of Hanoi, 224

Bacon, Francis, 3344

Bacon, Roger, 344

badges, 394–395

Barricade Demilitarized Zone Configuration screen, 254

Barricade Intrusion Detection Configuration screen, 252–253
baseline. *See also* benchmark
    applying best practices, 158–159
    benchmarking and, 159
    performance, 499
    VISA security model, 195–196
bastion host, 256
Battista, Giovanni, 344
BCP. *See* business continuity plan (BCP)
behavior-based IDS. *See* statistical anomaly-based IDS (stat IDS)
Bell Labs, 7
Bellsouth, 115
benchmark
    baseline (*See* baseline)
    in general, 155
    metrics-based measures, 155
        gold-based measures, 155
        performance gap, 155
        process-based measures, 155
    problems with, 158–159
Beruk, Peter, 42
best business practices
    applying best practices, 157–158
    baseline and, 159
    defined, 156
    problems with, 158–159
    VISA security model, 195–196
BIA. *See* business impact analysis (BIA)
Biometric locks, 397
biometrics
    acceptability of, 336
    authentication and, 333
    effectiveness of, 335
        crossover error rate (CER), 334
        false accept rate, 335
        false reject rate, 335
        ranking effectiveness and acceptance, 336
Bisbey, Hollingworth, 6
bit stream methods, 347
black boxes, 48
blackbox scanners (fuzzers), 324–325
Black Ice Defender from Network ICE, 255
blackmail, 49
blackout, 58
block cipher methods, 347
blow-by screens, 42
Blowfish, 380

blue boxes, 47
blueprint
    hybrid, 196
    information security blueprint, 186
    security blueprint, 31, 186
book/running key cipher, 356
boot virus, 52
"Bootlegged Software Could Cost Community College" (Patton), 42
bottom-up approach, 18
Bradbury, Ray, 401
British Standard (BS) 7799, 500
brownout, 58
Brunner, John, 52
brute force, 62. *See also* attack
BS7799, 187
BSA (Business Software Alliance), 41
bsd-airtools, 330
BSP. *See* best business practices
buffer overflow, 67–68. *See also* attack
bugs, 60. *See also* software; threat
Bugtraq, 60, 503–504
bull's-eye model, 442–444
burglar alarms, 417
business continuity plan (BCP)
    continuity strategies
        cold site, 229
        hot site, 143, 229
        mutual agreement, 230
        off-site data storage, 230
        service bureau, 229–230
        time-shares, 229
        warm site, 229
    defined, 207, 228
    developing, 228
    discussed, 142, 144
business impact analysis (BIA)
    attack scenario, 211
    business unit analysis, 211
    damage assessment, 211
    discussed, 209–210
    subordinate plan classification, 211–212
    threat identification, 210
business partners, 480
business recovery site, hot site, 143
Business Software Alliance (BSA), 41
business unit analysis, 211

C

CA. *See* certificate authority (CA)
CAA (Clean Air Act), 403
cache servers, 202
Caesar, Julius, 343, 349, 353
Caesar block cipher, 353
Canaday, Rudd, 7
candidate vulnerabilities, 519–520
capability table(s), 136, 179, 180
capital expenses estimate, in project plan, 432–433
Carnegie Mellon University, 195
CAST, 380
CBA. *See* cost benefit analysis (CBA)
CBC (cipher block chaining), 380
CCT (closed-circuit television), 398
CDA (Communications Decency Act of 1996), 78
CDA (Telecommunications Deregulation and Competition Decency Act of 1996), 78, 80
CD Universe, 48
Central Intelligence agency (CIA), specialty classification scheme, 123–124
CER (crossover error rate), 335
CERT/CC. *See* CERT Coordination Center (CERT/CC)
CERT (Computer Emergency Response Team), 195–196, 502
CERT Coordination Center (CERT/CC)
    discussed, 99
    as intelligence source, 504
    Web site, 56, 157
Certificate Authority (CA), 119, 369, 371. *See also* certifications; digital certificate
certificate revocation list (CRL), 369
certifications
    Association for Computing Machinery (ACM), 89, 96, 97
    Certification for Information Systems Security Consortium (ISC)², 98
    Certified Information Forensics Investigator, 469
    Certified Information Security Manager (CISM), 465–466
    Certified Information Systems Auditor (CISA), 465–466
    Certified Information Systems Security Professional (CISSP), 459, 463–465

Computer Security Institute (CSI), 96, 98, 205
  cost of, 470
  digital certificates, 368–369, 371–373
  Global Information Assurance Certification (GIAC), 98
  Information Systems Audit and Control Association (ISACA), 96, 98
  International Information Systems Security Certification Consortium, Inc. (ISC)², 97, 98
  other organizations
    CERT Coordination Center, 56
    Computer Professionals for Social Responsibility (CPSR), 99
    Computer Security Division (CSD), 99
    Internet Engineering Task Force (IETF), 99
    Internet Society (ISOC), 97, 99
  public key infrastructure certificate authority, 119
  related certifications, 469–470
  Security+, 468–469
  Security Certified Professional (SCP), 467
  System Administration, Networking, and Security Institute (SANS), 98
  TruSecure ICSA Certified Security Associate (TICSA), 467–468
Certified Information Forensics Investigator, 469
Certified Information Security Manager (CISM), 465–466
Certified Information Systems Auditor (CISA), 465–466
Certified Information Systems Security Professional (CISSP), 459, 463–465
CERTs (computer emergency response teams), 66
CFA Act. See Computer Fraud and Abuse Act of 1986 (CFA Act)
CGI (Common Gateway Interface), 318
champion
  for contingency planning, 208
  role of, 26 (See also management)
change control, 444
change management. See also management
  configuration and, 495–498
  culture of, 445
  defined, 495
  non-technical, 495–496
  technical configuration and, 496–498

characterization, 508
chargeback accounting, 498
chief information officer (CIO). See also chief information security officer (CISO or CSO); security professionals
  as champion, 19, 26
  responsibilities, 26
chief information security officer (CISO or CSO), 26, 458–459. See also security professionals
Chin, Fred, 35, 36
CIA. See Central Intelligence agency (CIA)
CIO. See chief information officer (CIO)
cipher, 346. See also cryptography; encryption
  book/running key cipher, 356
cipher block chaining (CBC), 380
ciphertext, 343, 346
  attacks, 382–383
circuit gateway, 246
CISA (Certified Information Systems Auditor), 465–466
CISCO security kernel, 248
CISM (Certified Information Security Manager), 465–466
CISO or CSO. See chief information security officer (CISO or CSO)
CISSP (Certified Information Systems Security Professional), 459, 463–465
civil law, 77
class (A/B/C/D) fires, 403
classification, information, 122–123
clean agent, 407
Clean Air Act (CAA), 403
clean desk copy, 125
clean desk policy, 125, 185
cleartext, 347
Clipper Chip, 78
clipping level, 296
closed-circuit television (CCT), 398
Cloudnine, 51
CNN.com, 51
code, 346
  malicious, 51, 60–61
Code of Practice for Information Security Management ISO 17799, 500
Code Red, 52, 61
cold site, 229
"cold turkey," 441
Cold War, 4–5, 501

Collin, Barry, 50
collusion, 480
commercial-grade firewall appliances, 248–249
commercial-grade firewall systems, 249
Common Gateway Interface (CGI), 318
communications, quality of service and, 58
Communications Act of 1934, 78, 80
Communications Decency Act of 1996 (CDA), 78
communications security (COMSEC), 8, 123
community of interest, 27–28
competitive advantage, 111
competitive disadvantage, 111
competitive intelligence, 43
comprehensive, in information asset classification, 119
CompTIA, 468
computer. See also laptop computer
  personal computer, 7
  remote security, 418–420
  static charge damage in, 409
  zombies, 62
Computer Emergency Response Team, Coordination Center (CERT/CC). See CERT Coordination Center (CERT/CC)
Computer Emergency Response Team (CERT), 195–196, 502
computer ethics, 90
computer forensics, 221
Computer Fraud and Abuse Act of 1986 (CFA Act), 77, 80
Computer Intrusion Squad, 233
Computer Professionals for Social Responsibility (CPSR), 99
computer rooms
  physical and environmental controls for, 400–401
  and wiring closets, 399
computers
  personal computer, 7
  as subject and object of an attack, 16, 17
  threat to, 80
computer security. See also information security (IS)
  history
    in general, 3–4
    MULTICS, 7
    present, 8
    1960s, 4–5

1990s, 7–8
1970s and 1980s, 5–7
Computer Security Act of 1987, 78, 80
Computer Security Division (CSD), 99
Computer security industry (C.I.A)
   triangle, 8–9, 112
Computer Security Institute (CSI), 96,
   98, 205
Computer Security Resource Center
   (CSRC), 99
Computerworld, 142
CompuTrace, 417
COMSEC (communications security),
   8, 123
confidence value, 285
confidential data, 122
confidentiality, 10–12
   C.I.A. triangle, 8
   discussed, 10–13
   privacy and, 11–12
   risk control, 148
   security clearances and, 124
configuration, and change
   management, 485–498
configuration monitoring, 147
configuration rules, 179
Consensus Roadmap, 63
consultants, 479
contact and weight sensors, 399
content filter, 268–269
contingency planning
   business impact analysis (BIA)
      attack scenario, 211
      business unit analysis, 211
      damage assessment, 211
      subordinate plan classification,
         211–212
   components of, 207
   in general, 206
   incident response planning, 212
   major steps in, 209
   model for, 230—231
      planning document, 231–232
   timeline, 208
continuity planning, 23. *See also* continuity strategy
continuity strategy. *See also* continuity
   planning
   discussed, 206–234
contract employees, 479
contracts, for potential information
   security employees, 474–475
control function, 147

controls. *See also* access control(s)
   categories of, 135
   defined, 30
   management, 198–199
   operational, 199
   risk reduction, 134–135
   technical, 199
control strategy, IDS
   centralized, 306, 307
   fully distributed, 307, 308
   in general, 305–306
   partially distributed, 308–309
copyright law. *See also* law; legal issues
   enforcement, 42
   Freedom of Information Act of 1966
      (FOIA), 85
   U.S., 83–84
   in the U.S., 83–84
correlation attack, 383
cost
   of certifications, 470
   cost benefit analysis (CBA), 150
   of project plan security
      implementation, 432
cost avoidance, 149
cost benefit analysis (CBA), 436
   annualized loss expectancy
      (ALE), 154
   annualized rate of occurrence, 154
   asset valuation, 150–153
   benchmark
      in general, 155
      metrics-based measures, 155–156
   benefit, 150
   best business practices, 156
   cost, 150
   due diligence, 156
   formula, 154
   in general, 149
   single loss expectancy (SLE), 153
Covey, Stephen, 171
CPSR. *See* Computer Professionals for
   Social Responsibility (CPSR)
cracker, 47. *See also* hacker
   phreaker, 47–48
cracking, password, 62
crash, as incident, 216
CRC (cyclic redundancy check), 381
credit card
   Secure Electronic Transaction, 378
   theft, 48
criminal law, 77
crisis management, 227–228

CRL (certificate revocation list), 369
"Cross-National Differences in
   Computer-Use Ethics" (Whitman,
   Townsend, Hendrickson), 92–94
crossover error rate (CER), 335
cryptogram, 346, 349
cryptographic algorithms, 357–366
   Advanced Encryption Standard
      (AES), 360–361
   asymmetric encryption, 361–366
   cipher block chaining (CBC), 380
   Data Encryption Standard
      (DES), 359
   symmetric encryption, 357
   Triple DES (3DES), 359
cryptographic notation, 358
cryptography. *See also* cipher; cryptosystem; encryption
   cipher methods, 347
   cryptosystems elements, 347
      book or running key cipher, 356
      cryptographic algorithms, 357–366
      hash functions, 356–357
      monoalphabetic substitution, 348
      polyalphabetic substitution, 348
      single polyalphabetic, 348
         Vignère cipher, 350
      substitution cipher, 347–348
      transposition cipher, 352–353
      Vernam cipher, 355–356
   defined, 342–343
   encryption definitions, 346–347
   encryption key size, 366–367
   principles of, 346
   tools
      digital certificates, 368–369,
         371–373
      digital signatures, 370
      hybrid cryptography systems,
         373–374
      public key infrastructure (PKI),
         368–370
      stenography, 374–375
cryptology
   defined, 342
   history of, 343–346
cryptosystem
   attacks, 382–384
      correlation attack, 383
      defending from, 384
      dictionary attack, 62, 383
      man-in-the middle attack, 383
      timing attack, 384

defined, 346
elements of, 347–366
hybrid, 373–374
one-time pad, 355–356
cryptovariable, 346
CSD (Computer Security Division), 99
CSI (Computer Security Institute), 96, 98, 205
CSI/FBI (Computer Security Institute/Federal Bureau of Investigation), 39
CSRC (Computer Security Resource Center), 99
cultural mores, 77
customer, privacy of information, 78–79
customer information section, privacy of, 78–79
cyberactivist, 49–50. *See also* hacker
Cyber Crime Convention, 87
cyberterrorism, 50–51
cyclic redundancy check (CRC), 381

D

DAC (discretionary access controls), 136
Dachb0den labs, 330
damage assessment, incident, 221
data. *See also* data ownership; information
   classification and management, 122–124
      data classification scheme, 123
      military data classification scheme, 123–124
   collection and management, 506
   custodians, 27
   health-care, 79–80
   information
      information system component, 15
      protecting, 38
   interception of data transmissions, 415–416
   risk identification, 115, 116
   sources, 502–505
      external intelligence sources, 503–505
   storage and management, 222–223
database right, 88
database shadowing, 230
data classification scheme, 122
data custodians, 27

Data Encryption Standard (DES), 359
data flow diagram (DFD), 506
data interception, 415–416
data ownership, 27
data storage, off-site, 230
data users, 27
DDoS attack (distributed denial-of-service (DDoS) attack), 62–63
Deception toolkit, 314, 315
decipher, 346
decryption, 343
Deerfield Personal Firewall, 255
de facto standards, 7, 174
de jure standards, 174
deliverable, in project plan, 431
Dell.com, 51
Delphi technique, 165
deluge system, 406
Demarc Pure Secure, total intrusion detection, 290
demilitarized zone (DMZ)
   discussed, 200, 201, 246
   screened subnet firewall with DMZ, 259
denial-of-service (DoS) attack, 51, 62–63, 68
Department of Defense (DoD), 123
   ARPANET, 5, 6
Department of Homeland Security (DHS), 99, 100
DES (Data Encryption Standard), 359
3DES (Triple DES), 359
detective control, 147
detectors, 399
   air-aspirating detector, 402
   flame detector, 402
   motion detectors, 399
   thermal detectors, 399
deterrence, 95
DFD (data flow diagram), 506
DHCP (dynamic host control protocol), 117
DHS (Department of Homeland Security), 99, 100
dial-up, VPN *vs.*, 276
dial-up protection
   in general, 270
      war dialer, 270
   RADIUS and TACACS, 270–271
dictionary attack, 62, 383
difference analysis
   defined, 510

types, 510–511
differential backup, 222
Diffie, Whitefield, 345
Diffie-Hellman Key Exchange method, 373–374
digital certificate, 368–369, 371–373. *See also* certifications; digital signature
Digital Millennium Copyright Act (DMCA), 87—88
digital signature, 370
Digital Signature Standard (DSS), 370
digital subscriber line (DSL), 249
Dilbert (Scott Adams), 427
direct attack, 16
direct changeover, 441
direct observation, interception of data and, 415
disaster recovery, 23
disaster recovery plan (DRP). *See also* continuity planning
   crisis management, 227–228
   defined, 207
   discussed, 143, 144, 226
   recovery operations, 228
discretionary access controls (DAC), 136
disk duplexing, 225
disk mirroring, 224
disk stripping, 224
distinguished name (DN), 373
distributed denial-of-service (DDoS) attack, 62–63. *See also* denial-of-service (DoS) attack
DMCA (Digital Millennium Copyright Act), 87–88
DMZ. *See* demilitarized zone (DMZ)
DN (distinguished name), 373
DNS (Domain Name Service), 261, 263
documentation
   incident reaction, 219
   risk assessment, 137–138, 514–517
   risk management, 163
   vulnerability, 524
DoD. *See* Department of Defense (DoD)
dogs, 394
Domain Name Service (DNS), 261, 263
doorknob rattling, 287
DoS (denial-of-service (DoS) attack), 51, 62–63, 68
DRP. *See* disaster recovery plan (DRP)
dry-pipe system, 406

DSL (digital subscriber line), 249
DSS (Digital Signature Standard), 370
dstumber, 330
dual-homed host firewall, 257–258
due care, 103–104
due diligence, 104, 156
dumb cards, 333
dumpster diving, 125
Duncan, David B., 173
dust, 57. *See also* threat
dynamic filtering, 244–245
dynamic host control protocol (DHCP), 117
dynamic packet filtering firewall, 245, 248
dynamic port, 263

E

earthquake, 56. *See also* threat
Eaton, Robert J., 451
ebay.com, 51
echo (TCP service), 63
ECMA (European Computer Manufacturers Association), 273
Economic Espionage (EEA) Act of 1996, 81, 82–83
economic feasibility study. *See* cost benefit analysis (CBA)
EDT (Electronic Disturbance Theater), 49
education. *See also* training
   and ethics, 94–95
   implementation, 139
EF (exposure factor), 153
effort estimate, in project plan, 432
EISP (enterprise information security policy), 23, 175
electric strike locks, 396
electromagnetic interception, 416
electromagnetic radiation (EMR), 416
electromagnetic signals (EM), 416
electromechanical locks, 395
Electronic Communications Privacy Act of 1986, 81
Electronic Disturbance Theater (EDT), 49
Electronic Freedom Frontier, 78
Electronic Frontier Foundation, 359
electronic lock, 396–397
electronic monitoring, 398

electronic serial numbers. *See* media access control (MAC) address
electronic vaulting, 330
electrostatic discharge (ESD), 57, 409
Eli Lilly and Co., privacy violations, 11
elite hacker, 44
e-mail
   attack
      mail bombing, 65
      spoofing, 10, 63
   intrusion detection system and, 298
   securing with S/MIME, PEM, and PGP, 377–378
   Trojan horse program, 51, 54–55, 60
   virus transmission, 52
EM (electromagnetic signals), 416
emergency shutoff, power management and, 414
employees. *See also* people; security professionals
   business partners, 480
   consultants, 479
   contract employees, 479
   emergency information cards, 227
   information security program and, 438
   job rotation, 481
   notification of key personnel, 218–219
   organization's information security and, 40
   privacy and security of, 482
   staffing considerations, 437
   temporary employees, 478–488
   verifying head count, 227
Employment, policies and practices, 472–477
EMR (electromagnetic radiation), 416
encapsulating payload (ESP) protocol, 379–380
encipher, 346
encryption. *See also* cryptography
   asymmetric, 361–362
   link, 346
   pvblic key, 361, 381
   symmetric, 357, 358
encryption key size, 366–367
end user, 27
"Enemy at the Gates: Threats to Information Security" (Whitman), 128–129
England, computer ethics, 91

Enigma, 4
Enron Corp., 173
enterprise information security policy (EISP), 23, 175
enterprise resource planning (ERP), 443
enticement, 317
entity, controlling, 118
entrapment, 317
environment, intrusion detection system (IDS) and, 300
Environmental Protection Agency, 403
ephemeral ports, 321
equal error rate, 335
ERP (enterprise resource planning), 443
escalation, 506
ESD (electrostatic discharge), 57, 409
espionage
   deliberate acts of, 43–48
   Economic Espionage (EEA) Act of 1996, 81, 82–83
   industrial, 43
   legal issues, 82–83
   Security and Freedom Through Encryption Act of 1999, 82
   shoulder surfing, 43
ESP protocol (encapsulating payload (ESP) protocol), 379–380
E911 system, 115
Ethereal, 329, 330
Ethernet, 5, 258
ethical hacker, 493
ethics. *See also* law; legal issues
   certifications
      Association of Computing Machinery (ACM), 89, 96, 97
      Computer Security Institute (CSI), 96, 98, 205
      Information Systems Audit and Control Association (ISACA), 96, 98
      International Information Systems Security Certification Consortium, Inc. (ISC)², 97, 98
      System Administration, Networking, and Security Institute (SANS), 98
   "Cross-National Differences in Computer Use Ethics," 92–95
   cultural differences, 89–95
   deterrence to unethical behavior, 95
   distinguished from law, 77
   education and, 94–95

illicit use, 91
    misuse of corporate resources, 91–92
    professional organizations and codes
        of, 96–102
    software license infringement, 90
    Ten Commandments of Computer
        Ethics, 90
E*TRADE, 51
European Computer Manufacturers
    Association (ECMA), 273
European Council Cyber-Crime
    Convention, 86–87
European Union Law Portal, 87
event, as disaster, 218
evidence, defined, 221
eWeek, 46
Excite.com, 51
exclusive OR operation (XOR)
    bit stream methods, 347
    defined, 353
    encryption, 354–355
    truth table, 354
execution, of project plan, 440–441
exit interview, 476
expert hacker, 44
exploit, defined, 30
Export Administration Act of 1979, 82
export laws, 82–83
exposure, defined, 30
exposure factor (EF), 153
external data, 122–123
external monitoring domain, 501
extortion, 39, 48–49. See also threat

F

facilities management, 393
Fahrenheit 451 (Bradbury), 401
fail-safe lock, 397
fail-secure lock, 397
false accept rate, 335
false attack stimulus, 285
false negative, 285
false positive, 285
false reject rate, 335
Farahidi, Abu 'Abd al-Rhaman, 344
FASP (Federal Agency Security
    Practices), 195
FASP(Federal Agency Security
    Project), 156
fault, 58
fault management, 493–495
    trouble ticket, 493

FBI National Infrastructure protection
    Center (NIC), 101
FCO (field change order), 118
FDDI (Fiber Distributed Data
    Interface), 258
FDIV (Pentium floating-point division
    bug), 59
federal agencies, U.S., 99–102, 233
Federal Agency Information
    Security, 80
Federal Agency Security Practices
    (FASP), 195
Federal Agency Security Project
    (FASP), 156
Federal Bureau of Investigation (FBI)
    computer crimes and, 233
    National Infrastructure protection
        Center (NIC), 101
    specialty classification scheme,
        123–124
    2000Computer Security
        Institute/Federal Bureau of
        Investigation (CSI/FBI), 39
Federal Information Processing
    Standard (FIPS), 6, 360
Federal Privacy Act of 1974, 79, 81
feedback, negative feedback loop, 440
Feistel, Dr. Horst, 345
fencing, physical security and, 393
ferroresonant standby UPS, 413
Fiber Distributed Data Interface
    (FDDI), 258
field change order (FCO), 118
Fighting Computer Crime (Parker), 392
file, as incident, 216
file hashing, 12
File Security and the UNIX system
    Crypt Command" (Reeds/
    Weinberger), 6
file transfer protocol (FTP), 258, 263
filtering
    alarm, 286
    content filter, 268–269
    defined, 268–269
    external filtering firewall rule set, 267
    firewall, 242–245
    internal filtering firewall rule set, 268
    packet filtering firewall, 242–245
    packet filtering router, 244, 256
    physical security and, 408–409
Financial considerations, in project
    plan, 436–437

Financial Services Modernization Act,
    80, 81
fingerprinting, 287, 320, 356. See also
    hacking
fingerprint recognition, 334, 336
FIPS (Federal Information Processing
    Standard), 6, 360
fire, 56. See also threat
fire detection, 402–403
    and response, 401–408
fire safety, detection and response, 401
fire security and safety, 401–408
fire suppression
    gaseous emission systems, 407–408
    "Halon Substitutes," 403–405
    sprinkler systems, 405–407
    systems, 401
Firewalk tool, 322
firewall
    architectures
        dual-homed host firewall,
            257–258
        in general, 256
        packet filtering routers, 256
        screened host firewall, 256
        screened subnet firewall (with
            DMZ), 258–259
        SOCKS server, 259–260
    configuration and management
        best practices for firewall, 261–262
        configuration and management,
            260–261
    defined, 201
    development
        fifth generation, 248
        first generation, 247
        fourth generation, 248
        in general, 247
        second generation, 247
        third generation, 248
    discussed, 241
    human firewall, defined, 140, 198
    processing mode
        address restrictions, 243
        application gateway, 245–246
        circuit gateway, 246
        hybrid firewall, 247
        MAC layer firewall, 246
        packet filtering, 242–245
    rules, 244, 262–268
    selecting, 260
    structure

commercial-grade firewall
appliances, 248–249
commercial-grade firewall
systems, 249
in general, 248
residential-grade firewall software,
254–255
small office/homeoffice (SOHO)
firewall appliances, 249–254
software *vs.* hardware, SOHO
firewall, 255–256
subnet, 201
types of
firewall subnet, 201
and OSI model, 247
firewall analysis tools
Firewalk, 322
in general, 321
HPING, 322
Nmap, 322
fixed temperature, 402
flame detector, 402
flame point, 401
flood, 56. *See also* threat
Floriciz, Boris, 51
Fluffi Bunni, 49
FM. *See* log file monitors (LFM)
FOIA. *See* Freedom of Information Act
of 1966 (FOIA)
footprinting, 287, 318
forensics investigator, 469
Forrester Research, 454
Fourth Amendment of the
U.S. Constitution, 79
Freedom of Information Act of 1966
(FOIA), 85
Friedman, William Frederick, 345
friendly departures, employees, 477
FTP. *See* file transfer protocol (FTP)
full backup, 222
fully distributed IDS control strategy,
307, 308
fuzzers (blackbox scanners), 324–325

G

Gartner Group, 140
gaseous emission systems, 407–408
gates, physical security and, 393

gateway
application, 245–246
circuit, 246
router, 201
General Electric (GE), 7
General Motors, 141
general security policy, 135
Georgia Computer Systems Protection
Act, 85
Georgia Pacific Corporation (G-P), 122
GFCI (ground fault circuit
interruption), 410
GFI LANguard Network Security
Scanner (NSS), 323
GIAC (Global Information Assurance
Certification), 98
Global Grid Forum, 196
Global Information Assurance
Certification (GIAC), 98
gold-based measures, 155
gold standard, benchmark, 155
government
data classification scheme, 123
Federal Agency Security Project
(FASP), 156
G-P (Georgia Pacific
Corporation), 122
Gramm-Leach-Bliley (GLB) Act of
1999, 80, 81
Grampp and Morris, 6
Greenpeace, 50
ground fault circuit interruption
(GFCI), 410
grounding, 410–411
Guard Duty, 394
guards, 394
"Guide for Developing Security Plans
for Information Technology Systems"
(Swanson), 400–401

H

hacker. *See also* hacking
defined, 44
cracker, 47
cyberactivist, 49–50
cyberterrorist, 49–50
expert hacker, 44
hacktivist, 49
phreaker, 47–48
script kiddies, 44–45
unskilled hacker, 44

elite hacker, 44
ethical hacker, 493
incident detection, 215–218
information theft, 12
notification by, 217
packet monkeys, 44
script kiddies, 44–45
unskilled hacker, 44
war dialer, 270
Web site, 318
whitehat hacker, 493
hacker tools, 217
hacking
defined, 30
fingerprinting, 287, 320, 356
footprinting, 287, 318
packet sniffer, 66, 329
port scanners, 320–321
vulnerability scanning, 323–329
Hack PCWeek, 44, 45–47, 45- 47
"Gibraltar Hack," 46–47
hackpcweek, 46
hacktivist, 49
Halon-based systems, 403–405
handprint recognition, 334, 336
hardware
information system component,
14–15
risk identification, 115, 116–117
hardware addresses. *See* media access
control (MAC) address
hardware failure, 59. *See also* threat
Harrison, Miller, 239, 281
hash algorithms, 356
hash functions, 356–357. *See also* secure
hash standard (SHS)
hash algorithms, 356
message authentication code
(MAC), 356
message digest, 356
secure hash standard (SHS), 357
hashing, file hashing, 12
hash value, 12
Hayes, Peter, 341
health-care data, 79–80
Health insurance Portability and
Accountability Act of 1996 (HIPAA),
79–80, 81
heating, physical security and, 408
Hellman, Martin, 345
Hendrickson, Anthony, R., 92–94

HIDS. *See* host-based IDS (HIDS)

hierarchical roster, 218

Hill, Napoleon, 281

HIPAA (Health insurance Portability and Accountability Act of 1996), 79–80, 81

Hoax Busters, 56

hoaxes, 61

Homeland Security Act of 2002, 100

honey net, 314

honey pot
   advantages and disadvantages of, 315–316
   defined, 314

Hong Kong, computer ethics in, 91

Horowitz, Alan S., 142

host-based IDS (HIDS), 202
   advantages of, 294
   deploying, 312
   disadvantages of, 294
   discussed, 291–294
   Tripwire HIDS, 293–294

hostile departures, employees, 477

hot site, 143, 229

hot swapped, 225

HPING, 322

HTTP. *See* Hypertext Transfer Protocol (HTTP)

human factor, in physical access control, 395

human firewall, 140, 198

Human Firewall Council, 140–141, 239

Human Firewall Project, 140–141, 196

humidity, physical security and, 409–410

Huns, 15

hurricane, 57. *See also* threat

hybrid cryptography systems, 373–374

hybrid firewall, 247

hybrid VPN, 274

Hypertext Transfer Protocol (HTTP)
   port number, 263
   secure (S-HTTP), 376–377
   standard, 376

I

IAD (Information Assurance Directorate), 101

IBM, 359

ICMP (Internet Control Message Protocol), 261

ICV (integrity check value), 379

IDEA, 380

identification (ID) card, 394–395

IDS. *See* intrusion detection system (IDS)

IEC (International Electrotechnical Commission), 187

IESG (Internet Engineering Steering Group), 99

IETF (Internet Engineering Task Force), 99, 194

ignorance, 95

IM (instant messaging), 37

implementation
   non-technical aspects of project plan, 445–446
   SDLC, 22, 429
   SecSDLC, 24
   supervising, of project plan, 439–440
   technical aspects of project plan, 441–445

inadvertent acts. *See also* threat
   acts of human error
      discussed, 40
      examples, 39

incident. *See also* attack
   defined, 207, 212
   documentation, 219

incident candidate, 216

incident classification, 216

incident containment strategies, 219–220

incident damage assessment, 221

incident detection, 215–218. *See also* incident reaction; incident response plan (IRP); intrusion detection system (IDS)
   incident indicators, 216–218

incident planning, 213–214

incident reaction. *See also* incident reaction plan (IRP)
   defined, 218
   documenting and incident, 219
   incident containment strategies, 219–220
   notification of key personnel, 218–219

incident recovery
   after-action review, 222
   backup media, 223–225
   damage assessment, 221
   in general, 220, 221–222
   prioritizing of effort, 221
   recovery, 221–222

incident response (IR). *See also* incident response plan (IRP)
   automated, 225
   defined, 212
   monitoring, escalation, and incident response, 506
   phases, 212–213

incident response plan (IRP). *See also* continuity planning
   description, example, timeframe, and deployment, 144
   defined, 207, 214
   discussed, 142–143, 212, 214
   in general
      format and content, 214
      storage, 214
      testing, 214–215

incremental backup, 223

indirect attack, 16

industrial espionage, 43

information. *See also* data; information asset
   aggregate, 79
   classification, 122–123
   competitive intelligence, 43
   extortion, 39, 48–49

information architecture, layers in, 148–149

information asset. *See also* asset; information characteristics
   classification, 118–119
   prioritizing assets, 121
   separation of duties and collusion, 480–482
   valuation, 119–121, 133–134

Information Assurance Directorate (IAD), 101

information characteristics. *See also* information classification
   accuracy, 10
   authenticity, 10
   availability, 10
   confidentiality, 10–12
   integrity, 12
   possession, 12–13
   utility, 12

information classification
   defined, 185
   discussed, 185–186
      clean desk policy, 185

information security blueprint, 186–203

Information Security Forum, 196
information security function
   positioning and staffing
      entry into information security
         profession, 456–457
      in general, 453–455
      information security positions,
         457–462
      qualifications and requirements,
         455–456
information security (INFOSEC), 123
information security (IS). *See also*
   information security policy
   as art, 29
   balancing, 17–18
   components of, 9
   discussed, 8–9
      C.I.A. triangle, 8–9
      NSTISSC model, 8
   duties
      data protection, 38
      enabling safe operation, 37–38
      protecting organization, 37
      protecting technology, 38
   employment policies and practices,
      472–477
   ethics and, 89–95
   history
      in general, 3–4
      MULTICS, 7
      present, 8
      1960s, 4–5
      1990s, 7–8
      1970s and 1980s, 5–7
   implementation, 18–19
   ISO 17799/BS7799, 187–189
   management and professionals, 28
   NIST models, 189–203
   physical design, 241
   program planning and review,
      512–513
   project management for, 430–441
   project team, 26–27
   as science, 29
   as social science, 29
   terminology, 30–31
   threats to, 39, 126
   VISA security model
      baselining and best business
         practices, 195–196
      in general, 195

information security management
   system (ISMS), 187, 500
information security managers,
   responsibilities of, 112
information security operational risk
   assessment (RA), 513–517
information security policy. *See also*
   information security (IS); policy
   definitions, 174–175
   enterprise, 23, 175
   in general, 172–174
   mission, 174
   policy, 174
   security policy, 175
   standards, 174
   strategic planning, 174
   systems-specific policy (SysSP)
      ACL policies, 179–180
      in general, 179
      rule policies, 181–183
   vision, 174
information security project team
   champion, 26
   end users, 27
   in general, 26
   risk assessment specialists, 27
   role in risk management, 111
   security policy developers, 27
   security professionals, 27
   systems administrators, 27
   team leader, 26
Information Security Roles and
   Responsibilities Made Easy (Wood),
   454, 457
information system (IS)
   components, 14–16, 115–118
      data, 15
      hardware, 14–15
      networks, 16
      people, 15–16
      procedures, 16
      securing, 16–17
      software, 14
   security *vs.* access, 17–18
Information Systems Audit and Control
   Association (ISACA), 96, 98, 465–466
Information Systems Audit and Control
   Association of Professional Security
   Consultants, 196
Information Systems Security
   Association (ISSA), 89, 97, 98, 205

Information Systems Security
   Engineering Professional (ISSEP),
   463–465
Information Technology - Code of
   Practice for Information Security
   Management, 187
information technology (IT)
   governance, 509
   management and professionals,
      28, 392
   professional organizations for, 97–98
   risk management and responsibilities
      of, 113–114
Information Warfare (IW), 88
INFOSEC (information security), 123
Inovant, 3, 162
In search of Excellence (Peters and
   Waterman), 141
Insecure Mailing List Archive, 504
instances, vulnerability, 520
Instant messaging (IM), 37
integrity
   C.I.A. triangle, 8
   digital certificate, 368
   discussed
      file hashing, 12
      hash value, 12
   protecting with technology, 12
   risk control, 148
integrity, discussed, 12
integrity check value (ICV), 379
Intel
   Pentium II chip, 59
   Xeon chip, 59
intellectual property (IP). *See*
   also threat
   compromise, 41–42
   defined, 41
   value of, 151–152
intent, 95
interception of data transmissions,
   415–416
interior walls and doors, 399–400
internal data, 122
International Electrotechnical
   Commission (IEC), 187
International Information Systems
   Security Certification Consortium,
   Inc. (ISC)[2], 97, 98, 205
International Organization for
   Standardization/International
   Telecommunications Union
   (ISO/ITU-T), 273

International Organization for
Standardization (ISO)
    ISO 17799, 500
    ISO 17799/BS7799, 187–189
    ISO/IEC 17799, 187–189
    model
        accounting and auditing
            management, 498
        configuration and change
            management, 495–498
        fault management, 493–495
        in general, 492
        performance management, 499
        security program
            management, 500
International Telecommunication
    Union (ITU-T) X.509 v.3, 372–373
Internet, 7, 58
Internet Blue Ribbon Campaign, 78
Internet Control Message Protocol
    (ICMP), 261
Internet Engineering Steering Group
    (IESG), 99
Internet Engineering Task Force
    (IETF), 99, 194
Internet Engineering Task force
    (IETF), 377
Internet protocol security (IPSec),
    378–381
Internet Security and Acceleration
    (ISA), 276
Internet Security Systems (ISS), 504
Internet Security Task Force, 195
Internet Service Provider (ISP), 58
    communications, 57
    Internet service, 57
    power irregularities, 58
Internet service provider (ISP), 249
Internet Society (ISOC), 97, 99, 194
Internet vulnerability assessment,
    519–520
interviews, for potential information
    security employees, 473
Intranet vulnerability assessment,
    520–521
intrinsic value, 150
intrusion, defined, 283
intrusion detection, 147
intrusion detection system (IDS). See
    also incident detection
    deployment and implementation,
        305–312
    in general, 284, 507

limitations of, 305
making it work, 509–510
measuring effectiveness, 312–313
network-based IDS (NIDS), 202,
    288–291
reasons for using, 286–288
response behavior, 297–299
selecting approaches and products,
    300–304
strengths of, 304–305
terminology, 284–286
types and detection methods,
    288–296
Intrusion Detection Systems (Bace and
    Mell), 284
inventory
    management, 421
    network characterization and,
        508–509
investigation
    SDLC, 21
    SecSDLC, 23
ionization sensor, 402
IP. *See* intellectual property (IP)
IP address, risk identification, 117
IP packet structure, 242
IPSec (Internet protocol security),
    378–381
IP spoofing, 63
IR. *See* incident response (IR)
IRP. *See* incident response plan (IRP)
IS. *See* information system (IS)
ISACA (Information Systems Audit and
    Control Association), 96, 98, 465–466
ISA (Internet Security and
    Acceleration), 276
ISC² (International Information
    Systems Security Certification
    Consortium, Inc.), 87, 98, 205
ISMS (information security manage-
    ment system), 187, 500
ISO. *See* International Organization for
    Standardization (ISO)
ISOC (Internet Society), 97, 99, 194
ISO/ITU-T. *See* International
    Organization for Standardization/
    International Telecommunications
    Union (ISO/ITU-T)
ISO network management model,
    492–500
    fault management, 493–495
ISP. *See* Internet service provider (ISP)

ISSEP (Information Systems Security
    Engineering Professional), 463–465
ISS (Information Systems Security
    Association), 89, 97, 98, 205
ISS (Internet Security Systems), 504
issue-specific policy, 135
issue-specific security policy (ISSP). *See
    also* information security policy
    in general, 176–177
        creation and management, 176
        sample, 177–178
IT. *See* information technology (IT)
ITU-T (International Telecommunica-
    tion Union) X.509 v.3, 372–373
IW (Information Warfare), 88

J

JAD (joint application development
    team), 19
Jefferson, Thomas, 344
Jerome Stevens Pharmaceuticals, 11
Jfs, 46
job descriptions, for information secu-
    rity employees, 473
job rotation/task rotation, 481
joint application development team
    (JAD), 19
jurisdiction, 104

K

Kehoe, Brendan P., 54
Kennedy-Kassebaum Act, 79–80
Kennesaw State's Center for Informa-
    tion Security Education, 205
Kerberos
    discussed, 271–273
    securing authentication with,
        271–273
    ticket, 272
kernel proxy, 248
key, 346
key registration, 92
keys and locks, 395
key size, encryption, 366–367
keyspace, 346
keystroke pattern recognition, 334, 336
Klez, 52, 53
knowledge-based IDS. *See* signature-
    based IDS
known-plaintext attack, 382

Koch, Hugo Alexander, 345
Kodak, 141
Kublai Khan, 15

L

LaBrea, 317
landslide, 56. *See also* threat
LAN (Local Area Network), 7, 16
laptop computer. *See also* computer;
  physical security
  security, 418
  theft, 15
  theft deterrence, 417
lattice-based access control, 135–136
law
  civil law, 77
  computer crime laws, 77–78
    Communication Act of 1934, 78
    Computer Fraud and Abuse Act of
      1986 (CFA Act), 77, 80
    Computer Security Act of 1987,
      78, 80
    National Information
      Infrastructure Protection Act of
      1996, 77, 81
    Telecommunications
      Deregulation and Competition
      Decency Act of 1996 (CDA),
      78, 80
    U.S.A. Patriot Act of 2001, 78
  copyright law, 83–84
  criminal law, 77
  defined, 77
  export and espionage law, 82–83
    Economic Espionage (EEA) Act of
      1996, 81, 82–83
    Security and Freedom Through
      Encryption Act of 1999, 82
  financial reporting
    Sarbanes-Oxley Act of 2002,
      84–85
  international law
    Digital Millennium Copyright Act
      (DMCA), 87—88
    European Council Cyber-Crime
      Convention, 86–87
    in general, 85
    United Nations Charter, 88
  local regulations, 85
  policy *vs.*, 89
  private law, 77
  public law, 77

state regulations, 85
  Georgia Computer Systems
    protection Act, 85
tort, 77
U.S. federal agencies, 99–102
  Department of Homeland
    Security (DHS), 100
  FBI National Infrastructure
    protection Center (NIC), 101
  National InfraGard Program, 101
  National Security Agency (NSA),
    78, 101, 416
  U.S. Secret Service, 67, 102
law enforcement involvement
  benefits of, 234
  drawbacks of, 234
  federal authorities, 233
  in general, 232–233
  local law enforcement, 233
  state investigative services, 233
Layer 2 Tunneling Protocol (L2TP),
  274, 276
least privilege, 482
legacy VPN, 274
legal issues, privacy concerns, 78–79
Lewin change model, 445
liability
  defined, 103
  limitations of, 179
  organizational liability, 103–104
licenses, software, 42
Lichtenberg, G. C., 109
lightning, 56. *See also* threat
line-interactive UPS, 413
link encryption, 346
Local Area Network (LAN), 7, 16
locks and keys, 395. *See also* access
  control(s)
log file monitors (LFM), 296
logical design phase
  SDLC, 21–22
  SecSDLC, 23–24
logical location, 118
logic bombs, 51
long arm jurisdiction, 104
L2TP. *See* Layer 2 Tunneling
  Protocol (L2TP)

M

MAC address (media access control
  (MAC) address), 117

MAC layer firewall, 246–247
MAC (message authentication
  code), 356
macro virus, 52
MACs (mandatory access controls), 135
Mafiaboy, 47, 51- 52
Magruder, Henry, 75
mail bombing, 65
maintenance
  and change
    SDLC, 22
    SecSDLC, 24
  of facility systems, physical security
    and, 415
  in general, 490–492
  model
    in general, 500–501
    monitoring external environment,
      501–506
    monitoring internal environment,
      507511
    planning and risk assessment,
      511–527
Majwubu, Iris, 75, 451
malicious code, 51, 60–61. *See also*
  attack
malware, 51. *See also* software
managed controls, 198–199
management. *See also* champion;
  change management; management
  failures; organization; security
  professionals
  of classified data, 124–125
  crisis, 227–228
  data collection and manage-
    ment, 506
  data storage and, 222–223
  of firewall, 260–261
  information security and
    professionals, 28
  information technology (IT) and
    professionals, 28
  performance, 499
  risk management and
    responsibilities of, 113
  role in physical security, 392
  security program management, 500
management controls, 198–199. *See also*
  controls
management failures. *See also* threat
  technological obsolescence, 60
mandatory access controls (MACs), 135

ManHunt, 316
man-in-the-middle attack, 64, 383. *See also* attack
mantrap, 397, 398
manual fire detection systems, 402
manual locks, 395
manufacturer
    model number/part number, 117–118
    name, 117
Marcinko, Richard, 215
MARS, 360
Massachusetts Institute of Technology (MIT), 7
mass mail, 61
Master Card, 378
Maxus, 49
McAfee VirusScan, 52
McDonald's Corporation, 139
McIIro, Doug, 7
mechanical lock, 395
media access control (MAC) address, 117
Mell, Peter, 284
message authentication code (MAC), 356
message digest, 356
message of the day, 4
Meta Group, 454
Metasploit Framework, 327
Metcalfe, Robert M. "Bob," 5
methodology, SDLC, 20
metrics-based measures, 155
Metropolitan Police of the District of Columbia, 418
microprocessor, 7
Microsoft
    best security practices, 157
    buffer overflow, 68
    TCSEC C–2 certificate, 17
    White Paper (1999), 389
milestone, in project plan, 432
minutiae, 334
mission, defined, 174
Missouri State Information Infrastructure Protection Agency, 295
mitigation
    business continuity plan, 143, 144
    defined, 142
    disaster recovery plan, 143, 144
    incident response plan (IRP) (*See* incident response plan (IRP))

MIT (Massachusetts Institute of Technology), 273
Mitnick, Kevin, 48, 67
mobile and portable systems, 417–420
modem vulnerability assessment, 523–524
monitoring
    electronic, 398
    external environment, 501–506
        data collection and management, 506
        data sources, 502–505
        monitoring, escalation, and incident response, 506
    internal environment
        difference analysis, 510–511
        in general, 507
        intrusion detection, 509–510
        IT governance, 509
        network characterization and inventory, 508–509
        planning and risk assessment, 511–517
    port, 289
monoalphabetic substitution, 348
Mora, Luis, 46
Morris, Robert, 52, 54
Morris, Thompson, 6
MOTD. *See* message of the day
motion detectors, 399
moving, in Lewin change model, 445
MS-Blaster, 52
mudslide, 56. *See also* threat
Multiplexed Information and Computing Service, 7
multivector attack, 60
Murphy's Law, 59
mutual agreement, defined, 230
mutually exclusive, 119
MyDoom worm attack, 52, 63

N

name badge, 394
Named Projects, 124
names. *See also* password
    default, 62
    risk identification, 117
National Bureau of Standards, 78
National Information Infrastructure Protection Act of 1996, 77, 81
National InfraGard Program, 101

National Infrastructure Protection Center (NIPC), 101
National Institute for Standards and Technology (NIST)
    Computer Security Division, 96
    security models, 189–193
    SP 800-12, 189, 204
    SP-800-14, 189–192
    SP 800-18, 192–193
    SP 800-26, 159
    SP 800-27, 159
    SP 800-30, 121, 133
    SP 800-31, 299, 305
National Security Agency (NSA), 78, 101, 416
National Security Telecommunications and Information Systems Security Committee (NTSISSC), 8
    security model, 13
National Training Standard for Information Security Professionals (NTSISSI), 13
NAT (Network Address Translation), 248
Need-to-know, 123–124
negative feedback loop, 440
Nessus, 323, 324
NESSUS-DEVEL, 504
NetGuard and Esafe Desktop from Aladdin, 255
Netherlands, computer ethics, 90, 91
NetIQ Corporation, 185
NetNanny software, 269
Netscape, 376, 378
Netsky, 52
NetStumbler, 330, 331
network
    configuration, 262
    information system component, 16
    security, 8
    trusted network, 241
    untrusted network, 241
Network Address Translation (NAT), 248
network asset. *See also* asset
    risk identification, 115, 116–117
network-based IDS (NIDS), 202, 288–291
    advantages of, 291
    deploying, 310–311
    disadvantages of, 291

host-based IDS (HIDS) advantage over, 292

signature matching, 290

network characterization and inventory, 508–509

network protocol analyzer, 329

network review board, 509

NeVO product, 327, 328

new hire orientation, for information security employees, 475

Nguyen, Laverne, 239–240, 281

NIDS. *See* network-based IDS (NIDS)

Nigerian National Petroleum Company, 66

Nimda, 52, 61

NIPC (National Infrastructure Protection Center), 101

NIST. *See* National Institute for Standards and Technology (NIST)

Nmap, 321, 322

Nmap-hackers, 505

noise, 285, 410

noncapital expenses estimate, in project plan, 433

Nondiscretionary controls, 136

nonrepudiation, 370

digital certificate, 369

non-technical change management, 495–496

Norton Personal Firewall, 255

Novell, 180

Novell Border Manager, 269

NSA (National Security Agency), 78, 101, 416

NSS (GFI LANguard Network Security Scanner), 323

NSTISSI (National Training Standard for Information Security Professionals), 13

NTSISSC (National Security Telecommunications and Information Systems Security Committee), 8

O

object, defined, 31

object of an attack, 16

offline UPS (standby), 413

offsite-site disaster data storage, 230

one-time pad, 355–356

on-the-job security training, for information security employees, 475–476

"On the Security of UNIX" (Ritchie), 6

OpenView, 148

operating system detection tools, 322–323

operating system (OS), 118

operational controls, 199. *See also* controls

operational feasibility, 160

operations security (OPSEC), 8, 123

OPSEC. *See* operations security (OPSEC)

Organization. *See also* management; communities of interest

communities of interest

in general, 27

IS management and professionals, 28

IT management and professionals, 28

organizational management and professionals, 28

role of, 113–114

data ownership, 27

environment in, 111

information security in, 37–38

security professionals and, 26–27

organizational change, considerations for, 446

organizational culture, 27

organizational feasibility

in project plan, 438

risk management and, 159–160

organizational liability, 103–104

OS. *See* operating system (OS)

OSI, firewall types and, 246–247

outsourcing, 142, 444

P

Packet Factory, 322

packet filtering firewall, 242–245

packet filtering router, 244, 256

packet monkeys, 44

packet sniffer, 66, 329

Packet Storm, 505

PAC (privilege attribute certificate), 273

padded cell

advantages and disadvantages of, 315–316

defined, 315

padlocks, 395

Page message, intrusion detection system and, 298

Panacea, 497

Paradice, David, 92

parallel operations, 442

Parker, Donn B., 392

partially distributed IDS control strategy, 308–309

partner interconnections, 508

passive vulnerability scanner, 327–328

passphrase, 333

password, 332

cracking, 62

virtual, 333

password attack, 62. *See also* attack

Password Security: A Case History (Morris and Thompson) 6

Patton, Natalie, 42

PCWeek, 45

PEM (privacy enhanced mail), 377

penalty, 95

penetration tester, 326

penetration testing, 493

Pentium floating-point division bug (FDIV), 59

people

information system component, 15–16

risk identification, 115, 116

as weakest link, 15

performance baseline, 499

performance evaluation, for information security employees, 476

performance gap, 155

performance management, 499

permutation cipher, 352

personal security, 8

personnel data, privacy and security of, 482

Peters, Tom, 151

PGP. *See* Pretty Good Privacy (PGP)

phased implementation, 441

Phone message, intrusion detection system and, 298

photoelectric sensors, 402

phreaker, 47–48. *See also* hacker

physical design, of information security program, 241

physical design phase

SDLC, 22

SecSDLC, 24

physical failure

in general, 408

humidity and static electricity, 409–410

structural collapse, 415
temperature and filtration, 408–409
ventilation shafts, 410
physical location, 118
physical security, 8. *See also* access
control(s); acts of God; fire security
and safety; security
data interception, 415–416
design and implementation, 392
fire security and safety, 401–408
fire detection response, 401–408
"Guide for Developing Security
Plans for Information Technology
Systems" (Swanson), 400–401
introduction to, 391–392
inventory management, 421
maintenance of facility systems, 415
mobile and portable systems,
417–420
physical access controls
controls for protecting the secure
facility, 393–400
alarms and alarm systems,
398–399
computer rooms and wiring
closets, 399
dogs, 393
electronic locks, 396–397
electronic monitoring, 398
fencing, 393
gates, 393
guards, 394
ID guards and badges, 394–395
interior walls and doors,
399–400
locks and keys, 395
mantraps, 397
walls, 393
in general, 392–393
physical failure
in general, 408
heating, ventilation, and air
conditioning, 408–410
power management and
conditioning, 410–415
structural collapse, 415
water problems, 414
threats, 420–421
pilot implementation, 442
piracy
combating, 42
in United States, 90

PKI. *See* public key infrastructure (PKI)
plaintext, 343, 347, 348. *See also*
encryption
planning
contingency (*See* contingency
planning)
continuity, 23
information security program
planning, 512–513
project plan, 429
review, 526
risk assessment
domain, 511
IS program planning and review,
512–513
platform security validation (PSV),
521–522
plenum, 400
Poe, Edgar Allan, 341
Point to Point Tunneling Protocol
(PPTP), 276
PoizonBox, 61
policy. *See also* information security
policy; policy management
defined, 89, 135, 174
general security policy, 135
issue-specific policy, 135
program security policy, 135
review and modification, 178
system-specific policy, 135
violations of, 178
vs. law, 89
policy management. *See also*
information security policy
automated, 185
in general, 183
policy administrator, 183–184
policy and revision date, 184
sunset clause, 184
procedures and practices, 184
review schedule, 184
policy review, 526
political feasibility, 161
Pollitt, Mark, 50
polyalphabetic substitution, 348
polymorphic threat, 55, 60
polymorphism, 55
POP3 (Post Office Protocol
version 3), 263
port
dynamic or private, 263
monitoring, 289

numbers, 263
user or registered, 262
port numbers, 321. *See also* hacking
port scanners, 320–321
port scanning utilities, 320–321
possession, information, 12–13
Post Office Protocol version 3
(POP3), 263
power irregularities, 58
power management and conditioning,
physical security and, 410
PPTP (Point to Point Tunneling
Protocol), 276
pre-action system, 406
predecessors tasks, 433
"Preliminary Notes on the Design of
Secure Military Computer Systems"
(Schel/Downey/Popek), 6
Pretty Good Privacy (PGP), 372.
See also privacy
origins of, 377, 381
security solutions, 381–382
preventive controls, 147
priority considerations, in project
plan, 437
privacy. *See also* confidentiality
ACLU Knocks Eli Lilly denounced
breach of, 11
confidentiality concern, 12
customer information, 78–81
aggregate information, 79
Federal Privacy Act of 1974, 79
Financial Services Modernization
Act, 80
Fourth Amendment of the U.S.
Constitution, 79
Health Insurance Portability and
Accountability Act of 1966
(HIPAA), 79
defined, 78
digital certificate, 368
in general, 78
Clipper Chip, 78
risk control, 149
and security of personnel data, 482
privacy enhanced mail (PEM), 377
private (for-profit) organizations,
financial considerations for, 436
private key encryption, 357
private law, 77
private port, 263
privilege attribute certificate (PAC), 273

procedures
    information system component, 16
    policy managers and, 184
    risk identification, 115, 116
process-based measures, 155
procurement considerations, in project
    plan, 437–438
productivity
    loss of, 152
    performance gap, 155
professional organizations
professional organizations, code of
    ethics, 96–102
professionals
    information security management
        and, 28
    information technology
        management and, 28
    organizational management and, 28
profile
    attack, 210
    security, 31
    user, 180
programs, defined, 135
program security policy, 135
projectitis, 431
project management, 429. See also
    management
    considerations in
        financial, 436–437
        organizational feasibility, 438
        priority, 437
        procurement, 437–438
        scope, 438–439
        staffing, 437
        time and scheduling, 437
        training and indoctrination
            considerations, 438
    developing, 430–435
        activities and deliverables, 431
        capital expenses estimate in,
            432–433
        effort estimate in, 432
        milestone, 432
        noncapital expenses estimate
            in, 433
        projectitis, 431
        resource, 432
        task dependencies, 433–434
        work breakdown structure
            (example), 434, 435
        work breakdown structure
            (WBS), 431

first draft example of, 434
implementation
    bull's-eye model, 442–443
    change management culture, 445
    conversion strategies, 441–442
    organizational change steps, 446
    outsourcing, 444
    technology governance and
        change control, 444–445
later draft example of, 435
need for, 439–441
need for project management
    executing the plan, 440–441
    in general, 439
    project wrap-up, 441
    supervising implementation,
        439–440
non-technical aspects of
    implementation, 445–446
security implementation, 427–477
technical aspects of implementation,
    441–445
project manager, for contingency
    planning, 208
project scope, 438
project team, 26
"Protection Analysis: Final Report"
    (Bisbey/Hollingworth), 5, 6
protocol analyzers, 317
protocols
    in general, 375–376
    IPSec (Internet protocol security),
        378–381
    PGP security solutions, 381–382
    pretty good privacy (PGP), 377
    privacy enhanced mail (PEM), 377
    secure electronic transactions
        (SET), 378
    secure-HTTP (S-HTTP), 376
    secure socket layer (SSL), 376
    S/MIME, 377–378
protocol stack verification, 290–291
proximity reader, 397
proxy firewall, 200, 201
proxy server, 200, 201, 245–246
PSV (platform security validation),
    521–522
public key encryption, 361, 381
public key infrastructure certificate
    authority, 119
public key infrastructure (PKI)
    certificate authority (CA), 369
    certificate revocation list (CRL), 369

defined, 368
digital certificates, 368–369
organizational growth and, 38
registration authority (RA), 369
public law, 77

Q

qualitative assessment, risk control
    and, 164
quantitative assessment, risk control
    and, 164

R

Radio Orphan Annie decoder pin,
    349, 350
RADIUS (Remote Authentication
    Dial-In User), 139, 270
Radix–64, 381
RAID. See redundant array of inexpen-
    sive drives (RAID)
RA (information security operational
    risk assessment), 513–517
Rand Report R–609, 6–7
RA (registration authority), 369
RAS (remote access server), 270, 276
RAS (Remote Authentication
    Service), 269
rate-of-rise, 402
RC5, 380
RC6, 360
readiness and review domain, 525–526
recommended practices. See best busi-
    ness practices
Recourse Technologies, 316
recovery, 221
red boxes, 48
red teams/tiger teams, 493
redundancy checks, 12
redundant array of inexpensive
    drives (RAID)
    data Storage and Management,
        222–223
    disk duplexing, 225
    disk mirroring, 224
    disk stripping, 224
    hot swapping, 225
    server fault tolerance, 225
    system backups and recovery,
        223–224
Reeds and Weinberger, 6
refreezing, in Lewin change model, 445

registered port, 262

registration authority (RA), 369

rehearsals, 527

remediating vulnerabilities
  accepting or transference of risk, 525
  introduction to, 524–525
  threat removal, 525
  vulnerability repair, 525

remediation domain, 517–518

remote access server (RAS), 270, 276

Remote Authentication Dial-In User Service (RADIUS), 139, 270

Remote Authentication Service (RAS), 269

remote computing security, 418–420

remote connection, protecting, 269–277

remote journaling, 230

remote procedure calls (RPC), 245

replay attack, 384

request for proposal (RFP), 431, 432

requests for comments (RFCs), 99

residential-grade firewall software, 254–255

residual risk, 134, 162–163

resistance, reducing, 446

resource, in project plan, 432

response options for an IDS, 297–299

restitution, 99

retina pattern recognition, 334, 336

revenue
  loss of, 152
  profit and, 120

reverse firewall, 268

RFCs (requests for comments), 99

RFP (request for proposal), 431, 432

Rijndael, 360–361

risk
  defined, 31
  residual risk, 134, 162–163

risk appetite, risk management and, 161–162

risk assessment. *See also* risk identification
  controls identification, 134–135
  defined, 132
  documentation, 137–138
  documentation components, 514–517
  introduction, 132
  likelihood, 133
  planning and, 511–517
  risk determination, 134

security risk assessment, 513

specialists, 27

valuation of information assets, 133–134

risk control. *See also* risk management
  architectural layer, 148
  best practices
    Delphi technique, 165
    in general, 164
    qualitative measures, 164
    quantitative assessment, 164
  categories
    control function, 147
    detective controls, 147
    in general, 147
    preventive controls, 147
  cycle, 147
  defined, 110
  evaluation, assessment, and maintenance of, 146–147
  information security principles
    accountability, 149
    authentication, 148
    authorization, 148–149
    availability, 148
    confidentiality, 148
    integrity, 148
    privacy, 149
  strategies
    avoidance, 138–139
    in general, 138
    selecting, 145–161
  strategy layer, 148

risk identification. *See also* risk management; threat
  and assessment deliverables, 138
  asset identification and valuation
    in general, 115–116
    hardware, software, network asset identification, 116–118
    people, procedures, data asset identification, 116
    prioritizing assets, 121–122
  components of, 114
  data classification and management, 122–124
  defined, 110
  information asset
    classification, 118–119
    prioritizing assets, 121
    valuation, 119–121, 150–154
  risk management tools, 118

risk management. *See also* risk control
  acceptance, 144–145
  automated tools, 118
  avoidance, 138–139
  components of, 111–112
  data management, 124–125
  defined, 23, 110, 112
  documenting results, 163
  feasibility studies
    cost benefit analysis (CBA), 149–159
    in general, 149
      cost avoidance, 149
    organizational feasibility, 159–160
    political feasibility, 161
    technical feasibility, 160–161
  in general, 112
  information security professional role in, 111
  IS responsibilities, 113
  IT responsibilities, 113–114
  management and users responsibilities, 113
  mitigation, 142–144
  residual risk and, 134, 162–163
  risk appetite, 161–162
  security clearances, 124
  strategy
    evaluation, assessment, maintenance of, 146
  transference, 141

Risk Management for Information Technology Systems (NIST), 121

Ritchie, Dennis, 6, 7

Rivest, Ronald, 345

Roberts, Larry, 5

role-based controls, 136

roster
  alert roster, 218
  hierarchical roster, 218
  sequential roster, 218

Rousseau, Jean-Jacques, 76

router
  gateway, 201
  packet filtering router, 244, 256

RPC (remote procedure calls), 245

RSA algorithm, 362–365

S

sabotage, 39, 49–51. *See also* threat

sacrificial host, 256

safeguard. *See also* controls
  defined, 30
  implementing, 0
sag, 58
salami theft, 12
SAM (Security Account Manager), 62
Sam Spade, 319
SANS Institutes Global Information
  Assurance Certification, 97
SANS (SysAdmin, Network, Security
  Institute), 98, 205
SANS (System Administration,
  Networking, and Security Institute),
  98, 205
Sarbanes-Oxley Act of 2002, 81, 84–85
Savard, John, 360
SBU data (sensitive but unclassified
  (SBU) data), 123
scanners
  port, 320–321
  vulnerability, 323–328
scanning and analysis tools. *See also*
  encryption
  firewall analysis tools, 321–322
  in general, 317–320
    attack protocol, 318
    finger printing, 320
    foot printing, 318
    operating system detection tools,
      322–323
    packet sniffers, 329
    port scanners, 320–321
    trap and trace, 316–317
    vulnerability scanners, 323–328
    wireless security tools, 330–331
Schell, Downey, and Popek, 6
Schiffman, Mike, 322
science, security as, 29
SCO Group, 63
scope considerations, in project plan,
  438–439
SCP (Security Certified
  Professional), 467
screened host firewall, 256
screened subnet firewall (with DMZ),
  258–259
script kiddies, 44–45. *See also* hacker
SDLC. *See* systems development life
  cycle (SDLC)
SearchSecurity.com, 196
secret data, 123
secret key, 357

Secret Service, 67, 102, 233
SecSDLC. *See* security systems
  development life cycle (SecSDLC)
SecSDLC risk management system
  components, 115
secure communications
  protocols
    securing e-mail with S/MIME,
      PEM, and PGP, 377–378
    securing Internet communication
      with S-HTTP and SSL,
      376–377
    securing TCP/IP with IPSec and
      PGP, 378–382
    securing web transactions with
      SET, SSL, and S-HTTP,
      378–382
  protocols for, 375–382
secure electronic transactions
  (SET), 378
Secure European System for Applications in a Multivendor Environment
  (SESAME), 273
secure facility, 393
Secure Hashing Algorithm 1
  (SHA–1), 381
secure hash standard (SHS), 357
secure-HTTP (S-HTTP), 376–377
secure multipurpose Internet mail
  extensions (S/MIME), 377–378
secure shell (SSH–2), 378
secure socket layer (SSL), 276, 376, 378
secure VPN, 274
SecurID, 148
securing Internet communication with
  S-HTTP and SSL, 376–377
securing TCP/IP with IPSec and PGP,
  378–382
Securities and Exchange Commission, 233
security. *See also* information security
  (IS); physical security; security implementation; security systems development life cycle (SecSDLC)
  defined, 8
  intrusion detection system and, 301
  law enforcement involvement, in
    general, 232–233
  layers
    communications security, 8
    information security, 8
    network security, 8
    operations security, 8

    personal security, 8
    physical security, 8
Security+, 468–469
Security Account Manager (SAM), 62
Security and Freedom Through
  Encryption Act of 1999, 82
security architecture
  components
    DMZ, 200, 201
    firewalls, 200
    proxy server, 200, 201
  defense in depth, 199–200
    redundancy, 199–200
  in general, 199
  intrusion detection, 200
  security domain, 200
  security perimeter, 200
security artesan, 28
security blueprint, 31, 186
Security Certified Professional
  (SCP), 467
security clearances
  discussed, 124
    need-to-know, 124
security education, training, and
  awareness program (SETA)
  discussed, 203–204
  security awareness, 205
  security education, 204–205
  security training, 2–5
Security Focus Online, 505
security framework, 186
security function. *See* information
  security function
security implementation
  bottom-up approach, 18
  change control, 444
  change management
    culture, 445
  conversion strategies
    direct changeover, 441
    outsourcing, 444
    parallel operations, 442
    phased implementation, 441
    pilot implementation, 442
  moving, 445
  organizational change
    culture, 446
    resistance reduction, 446
  project plan
    bull's-eye model, 442–444
    costs and effort, 432

deliverable, 431
developing, 430–435
execution, 440–441
milestone, 432
predecessors, 433
successors, 433
supervising, 439–440
wrap-up, 441
project plan considerations
feasibility considerations, 438
financial considerations, 436–437
priority considerations, 437
procurement considerations, 437–438
scope considerations, 438–439
staffing considerations, 437
time and scheduling considerations, 437
training considerations, 438
refreezing, 445
supervising, 439–440
technology governance, 444–445
top-down approach, 19
unfreezing, 445
security management models, ISO network management model, 492–500
security manager, 459–461. See also security professionals
security model, defined, 31
security organizations, 99
security parameter index (SPI), 379
security policy. See also information security policy
defined, 175
information, 172–174
types of, 135
security policy developer, 27
security posture/profile, 31
security professionals, 27, 28. See also employees; management
advice for, 471
credentials of, 462–471
in general, 26
hiring and termination
background checks, 473–474
employment contracts, 474–475
interviews, 473
jobs description, 473
orientation, 475
performance evaluation, 476
termination, 476
training, 475–476

key U.S. laws, 80–82
professional organizations of interest to, 96–97
role in risk management, 111
security profile/posture, 31
security program management, 500
security project team. See information security project team
security systems development life cycle (SecSDLC)
compared to SDLC, 25
defined, 429
in general, 23
phases of, 23–24
security technician, 461–462
security technologies, defined, 135
security tools, wireless, 330–331
security training. See security education, training, and awareness program (SETA)
security triple, 492
selected-plain text attack, 382
senior management
CIO, 26
CISO, 26
sensitive but unclassified (SBU) data, 123
sensors
contact and weight sensors, 399
ionization sensor, 402
photoelectric sensors, 402
vibration sensors, 399
separation of duties, 480
September 11, 2001, 15, 100
Sequential Label and Supply, 35, 341
sequential roster, 218
serial numbers, 117
Serpent, 360
server fault tolerance, 225
service bureau, 229–230
Service Level Agreement (SLA), 58
SESAME. See Secure European System for Applications in a Multivendor Environment (SESAME)
session keys, 373
SETA (security education, training, and awareness program), 203–204
SET (secure electronic transactions), 378
Seven Habits of Highly Effective People (Covey), 171
Shakespeare, William, 35
Shamir, Adi, 345
Shannon, Claude, 345

SHA–1 (Secure Hashing Algorithm 1), 381
The Shockwave Rider (Brunner), 52
shoulder surfing, 43
SHS (secure hash standard), 357
S-HTTP (secure-HTTP), 376, 378
signature-based IDS, 295–296
signature recognition, 334, 336
signatures, 295
Significant New Alternatives Policy (SNAP) program, 404–405
SIIA (Software & Information Industry Association), 41
Silverman, Robert, 42
Simple Mail Transport Protocol (SMTP), 65, 261, 263
Simple network Management Protocol (SNMP), 61, 220, 263, 264, 298
simulation, incident response plan, 215
Singapore, computer ethics in, 91
single loss expectancy (SLE), 153
single polyalphabetic, 348
Sircam, 52
site policy, 286
site policy awareness, 285
SLA (Service Level Agreement), 58
SLE (single loss expectancy), 153
small office/homeoffice (SOHO) firewall appliances, 249–254
smart card, 333, 396
Smart IDS, 285
S/MIME (secure multipurpose Internet mail extensions), 377–378
smoke detection, 402. See also fire safety
SMTP/RFC 822, 377
SMTP (Simple Mail Transport Protocol), 65, 261, 263
sniffer, 66, 317. See also packet sniffer
SNMP (Simple Network Management Protocol), 61, 263, 264, 298
Snort sigs, 505
The Social Contract Or Principles of Political Right (Rousseau), 76
social engineering, 66–67. See also attack; people
social science, security as, 29
SOCKS server, 259–260
software
bugs, 60
information system component, 14
residential-grade firewall software, 254–255
risk identification, 115, 116–117

software attacks
  back door/trap door, 55
  hoaxes, 55–56
  malicious code, 51
  malware, 51
  polymorphism, 55
  Trojan horses, 54–55, 60
  virus, 52, 60
  worms, 52–53, 60
software firewalls, 255
technical failures, 60
violating licenses, 42
vs. hardware: SOHO firewall,
  255–256
software failure, 60. *See also* threat
Software & Information Industry
  Association (SIIA), 41
software license, 41–42
  blow-by screens, 42
  "Bootlegged Software Could Cost
    Community College" (Patton), 42
  infringement, 90–91
software piracy, 41
Software Publishers Association
  (SPA), 42
SOHO firewall devices, 250
SOPs (standard operating
  procedures), 394
Sourcefire, 327
Spain, Jayne, 489
spam, 64
SPAN (switched port analysis), 289
SPA (Software Publishers
  Association), 42
SPIKE, 324, 325, 326
spike, 58
SPI (security parameter index), 379
spoofing, 63
  e-mail, 10
sprinkler systems, 405
SPS (standby power supply), 413
SSH–2 (secure shell), 378
SSL record protocol, 376
SSL (secure socket layer), 276, 376, 378
staffing
  chief information security officer
    (CISO or CSO), 26, 458–459
  consultant, 479
  entry into security profession,
    456–457
  information security function,
    455–462

manager, 459–460
in project plan, 437
qualifications and requirements,
  455–456
technician, 461–462
standard HTTP, 376
standard of due care, 155
standard operating procedures
  (SOPs), 394
standards
  de facto standards, 7, 174
  defined, 174
  de jure standards, 174
standby (offline UPS), 413
standby power supply (SPS), 413
stateful inspection firewall, 245, 248
state investigative services, 233
state table, 245
static electricity, 409
static electricity, physical security and,
  409–410
static filtering, 244–245, 247
statistical anomaly-based IDS (stat IDS)
  advantage of, 296
  in general, 296
steganography, 347
stenography, 374–375
strategic planning, defined, 174
strategy layer, 148
strong authentication, 332
structural collapse, physical security
  and, 415
subject, defined, 31
subject of an attack, 16
substitution cipher, 347–348, 353
successors tasks, 433
Sun Tzu, 112, 113
supplicant
  authentication addresses, 333
  characteristics of, 333–334
  knowledge of, 332
  technology produced, 334–335
SurfControl, 269
SurfControl software, 269
surge, 58
Swanson, M, 400–401
Sweden, computer ethics, 90, 91
switched port analysis (SPAN), 289
Sygate Personal Firewall, 255
Symantec Norton Anti-Virus, 52, 60
symmetric encryption, 357, 358
synchronous tokens, 333

SysAdmin, Audit, Network, Security
  Institute (SANS), 49
SysSP. *See* systems-specific policy (SysSP)
System Administration, Networking,
  and Security Institute (SANS), 98, 205
system integrity verifiers. *See* host-
  based IDS (HIDS)
systems administrators, 27
systems development life cycle (SDLC),
  20–22. *See also* security systems
  development life cycle (SecSDLC)
  in general, 20
    compared to SecSDLC, 25
  methodology, 20
  phases, 20–21
    analysis, 21
    implementation, 22
    investigation, 21
    logical design, 21–22
    maintenance and change, 22
    physical design, 22
systems environment, intrusion
  detection system and, 300
systems management, 178
Systems Security Certified Practitioner
  (SSCP), 463–465
systems-specific policy (SysSP), 135
  in general, 179
    access control lists (ACLs), 179
    rule policies, 181–183

T

TACACS (Terminal Access Controller
  Access), 270–271
tailgating, 395
task-based controls, 136
task dependencies, in project plan,
  433–434
TCP (Transmission Control Protocol),
  64, 243
TCSEC–2, 17
team leader, 26
technical architecture team, 509
technical configuration, change
  management and, 496–498
technical controls, 199. *See also* controls
technical failures. *See also* threat
  hardware failure, 59
  software failure, 60
technical feasibility, 160–161
technical specifications, intrusion
  detection systems (IDSs) and, 300

technology
  application, 139
  defined, 135
  safeguarding assets, 38
  technological obsolescence, 60
technology governance, 444–445
Technology Manager's Forum, 196
Telecommunications Deregulation and
  Competition Decency Act of 1996
  (CDA), 78, 80
Telecommunications Electronics
  Material Protected from Emanating
  Spurious Transmissions, 416
telecommuting, 418
telnet, 263
TELNET application server, 246
temperature, physical security and,
  408–409
TEMPEST program, 416
temporary employees, 478–479
Tenable Network Security, 327
"Ten Top Commandments of
  Computer Ethics," 90
Terminal Access Controller Access
  (TACACS), 270–271
termination, for information security
  employees, 476–477
terminology, intrusion detection
  system, 284–286
testing
  contingency plan, 232
  incident response plan, 214
  penetration, 493
  physical security, 415
theft. See also threat
  deliberate, 51
  laptop, 15
  salami, 12
"The Help desk," 493–495
thermal detection systems, 402
thermal detectors, 399
Thompson, Ken, 7
threat. See also attack; risk identification
  acts of God
    forces of nature, 39, 56–57
  defined, 31, 39
  deliberate acts
    blackmail, 39
    espionage or trespass, 39, 43–48
    extortion, 39, 48–49
    intellectual property (IP) compro-
      mise, 39, 41–42

sabotage or vandalism, 39, 49–51
    software attacks, 39
    theft, 39, 51
deviation in quality of service
    availability disruption, 58
    communications issues, 58
    discussed, 57–58
    Internet service, 58
    power irregularities, 58
deviations in quality of service, 39
"Enemy at the Gates: Threats to
    Information Security," 128–129
in general, 38–39
identification, 126
inadvertent acts
    acts of human error, 39, 40
to information security, 39
management failures
    technological obsolescence, 39
physical security, 420–421
removal, 525
technical failures
    in general, 59
    hardware failure, 39, 59
    software failure, 39
    software failures, 60
understanding, 113
threat agent
    defined, 31, 60
    identifying and prioritizing, 126–128
threat assessment, 126–128
threat identification. See also risk
    identification
    discussed, 126
    time-shares, 229
3DES (Triple DES), 359, 380
ticket, 272
TICSA (TruSecure ICSA Certified
    Security Associate), 467–468
tiger teams/red teams, 493
time and scheduling, in project
    plan, 437
Time sharing Computer Systems
    (Wilkes), 6
Time-To-Live (TTL) packets, 322
timing attack, 68, 384. See also attack
Tiny Personal Firewall, 255
Tivoli, 148
token
    asynchronous, 333
    synchronous, 333

Token Ring, 258
top-down approach, 19
top secret data, 123
"Top Ten Security Mistakes"
    (Horowitz), 142
tornado, 56. See also threat
tort law, 77
Townsend, Anthony, M., 92–94
training. See also education
    implementation, 139
    on-the-job, 475–476
    security education, training, and
      awareness program (SETA),
      203–204
training and indoctrination
    considerations, in project plan, 438
transference, 141. See also risk
    management
Transient Electromagnetic Pulse
    Emanation Surveillance
    Technology, 416
Transmission Control Protocol (TCP),
    64, 243
transport mode, 379
transport mode VPN, 275
transposition cipher, 352–353
trap and trace systems, 316–317. See
    also incident response (IR); scanning
    and analysis tools
trap door, 62, 362
trespass, 43–48. See also threat
triboelectrification, 409
Triple DES (3DES), 359, 380
Tripwire, 165, 181, 292–293
Trithemius, Johannes, 344
Trojan horses, 51, 54–55, 60. See
    also threat
trophy, 520
trouble ticket, 493
true attack stimulus, 285
true online UPS, 413–414
TrueSecure Corporation, 61
TruSecure ICSA Certified Security
    Associate (TICSA), 467–468
trusted network, 241
trusted VPN, 274
tsunami, 57. See also threat
TTL (Time-To-Live) packets, 322
tunnel mode, 379
tunnel mode VPN, 276–277
Twofish, 360
two-man control, 480

2000Computer Security Institute/ Federal Bureau of Investigation (CSI/FBI), 39
Type II error, 335
typhoon, 57. *See also* threat

U

UDP (user datagram protocol), 243, 244
unclassified data, 123
unfreezing, in Lewin change model, 445
uninterruptible power supply (UPS), 58, 411
    types of, 412, 413–415
United Nations Charter, 88
United States
    computer ethics in, 90–91
    federal agencies, 99–102
    laws, 77–85
    military classification scheme, 123
UNIX, 7
"UNIX Operating System Security" (Grampp and Morris), 6
unprotected shares, vulnerabilities, 61
unskilled hacker, 44
untrusted network, 241
UPS. *See* uninterruptible power supply (UPS)
Urban Legend Reference Pages, 56
Urich, Kelvin, 239–240
U.S.A. Patriot Act of 2001, 78, 82
US-CERT, 502, 504
user
    data, 27
    end, 27
    risk management and responsibilities of, 113
User datagram protocol (UDP), 243, 244
user data protocol (UDP), 10
user policies, 180
user port, 262
user profiles, 180
utility, discussed, 12

V

VA. *See* vulnerability assessment (VA)
vandalism, 39, 49–51. *See also* threat
VCR (video cassette recorder), 398
vendors, data sources and, 502–505

ventilation, physical security and, 408, 410
ventilation shafts, 410
Vernam, Gilbert S., 345
Vernam cipher, 355–356. *See also* cipher; encryption
vibration sensors, 399
vice president of information. *See* chief information officer (CIO)
vice president of information technology (VP-IT), 19
video cassette recorder (VCR), 398
VigilEnt Policy, 185
Vignère cipher, 350
Vignère square, 350, 351, 352
virtual password, 333
Virtual Private Network Consortium (VPNC), 274
Virtual Private Network (VPN)
    hybrid VPN, 274
    secure VPN, 274
    transport mode, 275
    trusted, 274
    tunnel mode, 276–277
    vs. dial-up, 276
virus. *See also* threat
    description of, 60, 61
    detection, 12
    discussed, 52
        boot virus, 52
        macro virus, 52
    hoaxes, 55–56
VISA, 378
VISA security model
    baselining and best business practices, 195–196
    in general, 195
vision, defined, 174
visual alarm, intrusion detection system and, 297
voice pattern recognition, 334, 336
VP-IT (vice president of information technology), 19
VPN. *See* Virtual Private Network (VPN)
VPNC (Virtual Private Network Consortium), 274
VPN *vs.* dial up, 276
VP of information technology. *See* chief information officer (CIO)
VP of systems. *See* chief information officer (CIO)

vulnerability. *See also* vulnerability assessment (VA); vulnerability identification
    candidate, 519–520
    defined, 31, 60
    documenting, 524
    remediating vulnerability, 524–525
    well-known, 31
    worksheet, 137
vulnerability assessment (VA). *See also* risk assessment
    defined, 518
    of hypothetical DMZ router, 131
    Internet vulnerability assessment, 519–520
    modem vulnerability assessment, 523–524
    platform security validation (PSV), 521–522
    and remediation, 517–518
    wireless vulnerability assessment, 522–523
vulnerability identification, 130–132. *See also* risk identification
vulnerability instances, 520
vulnerability scanners. *See also* hacking
    active vulnerability scanners, 323–327
    passive vulnerability scanner, 327–328
    products and Web pages, 328

W

Wales, computer ethics in, 91
walls, physical security and, 393
WAPs (wireless access points), 249, 416
war dialer, 270
war dialing, 523
war games, 527
warm site, 229
Warren, Earl, 75
wasp trap syndrome, 317
water, physical security and, 414
waterfall model SDLC, 20
Waterman, Robert, 141
water mist sprinklers, 406
WBS (work breakdown structure), 431
web browsing, vulnerabilities, 61
Web pages, of vulnerability scanners and products, 328
web scripts, attacks, 60

Web site
    defacement, 49, 51
        denial-of-service attack, 51–52
        sabotage or vandalism, 49–51
well-known vulnerabilities, 31
WEP (Wired Equivalent protocol), 330
wet-pipe system, 405
"Wget," 319
whitehat hacker, 493
Whitman, Michael, 90, 92
Wilkes, Maurice, 6
Williams, Gladys, 35, 36
windstorm, 56. *See also* threat
Wired Equivalent protocol (WEP), 330
wireless access points (WAPs), 249, 416
wireless local area network
    (WLAN), 523
wireless security tools, 330–331

wireless vulnerability assessment,
    522–523
WLAN (wireless local area
    network), 523
Wood, Charles Cresson, 37, 454, 457
work breakdown structure (WBS), 431
work factor, 347
worksheet
    inventory, 120
    vulnerability risk, 137
    of weighted factor analysis, 122
World War II, 3
worm
    detection, 12
    discussed, 51, 52–53, 60
    hoaxes, 55–56
Wu, Sun Tzu, 38
www.phrack.com, 46

X

XOR (exclusive OP operation), 347
XProbe, 322

Y

Yahoo.com, 51

Z

"Zen and the Art of the Internet"
    (Kehoe), 54
Ziff Davis Media, Inc, 47
Zimmermann, Phil, 346, 377, 381
zombies, 62
Zone Lans ZoneAlarm, 255